Parts of a Flying Bird

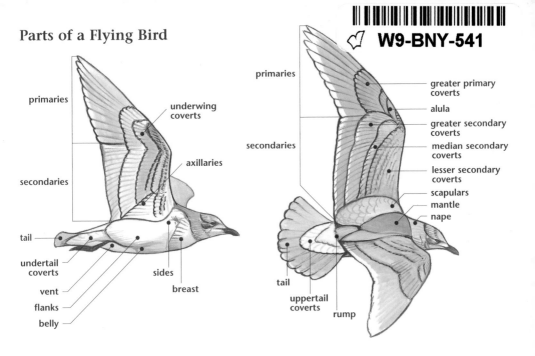

primaries

underwing coverts

secondaries

axillaries

tail

undertail coverts

sides

vent

breast

flanks

belly

primaries

secondaries

greater primary coverts

alula

greater secondary coverts

median secondary coverts

lesser secondary coverts

scapulars

mantle

nape

tail

uppertail coverts

rump

Bare Parts of a Bird's Head

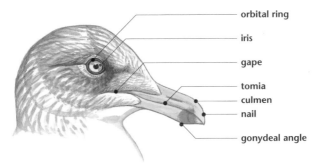

orbital ring

iris

gape

tomia

culmen

nail

gonydeal angle

Egg Shapes

The four basic egg shapes as described throughout this book are shown here, from left to right: elliptical (Snowy Egret), subelliptical (Virginia Rail), oval (American Robin), and pyriform (Pectoral Sandpiper). Each of these basic shapes can occur in an elongated ("long") or shortened ("short") form; the term "rounded" is used for short elliptical eggs. Eggs are not painted to scale, in order to emphasize differences in shape, rather than size. References to egg shape are based on *A Guide to the Nests, Eggs, and Nestlings of North American Birds* (second edition), by Paul Baicich and Colin Harrison.

NATIONAL AUDUBON SOCIETY

The SIBLEY GUIDE

to Bird Life & Behavior

A Chanticleer Press Edition

NATIONAL AUDUBON SOCIETY

The SIBLEY GUIDE
to Bird Life
& Behavior

Illustrated by
DAVID ALLEN SIBLEY

Edited by
CHRIS ELPHICK
JOHN B. DUNNING, JR.
DAVID ALLEN SIBLEY

 Alfred A. Knopf, New York

To our parents

John and Claire Dunning

Marilyn and Dennis Elphick

Fred and Peggy Sibley

*for, among other things, instilling in us
an appreciation of the natural world*

This is a Borzoi Book.
Published by Alfred A. Knopf, Inc.

Copyright © 2001 by Chanticleer Press, Inc.
All rights reserved under International and Pan-American Copyright Conventions.
Published in the United States by Alfred A. Knopf, Inc., New York, and simultaneously
in Canada by Random House of Canada Limited, Toronto. Distributed by Random House,
Inc., New York.

www.randomhouse.com

Knopf, Borzoi Books, and the colophon are registered trademarks of Random House, Inc.

Prepared and produced by Chanticleer Press, Inc., New York.

Printed and bound by Dai Nippon Printing Co., Ltd., Hong Kong.

First Edition
Published October 2001
Second Printing, August 2002

Library of Congress Cataloging-in-Publication Data available.

National Audubon Society® is a registered trademark of National Audubon Society, Inc.,
all rights reserved.

National Audubon Society

The mission of NATIONAL AUDUBON SOCIETY *is to conserve and restore natural ecosystems,
focusing on birds, other wildlife, and their habitats, for the benefit of humanity and the earth's
biological diversity.*

One of the largest environmental organizations, Audubon has 550,000 members, 100
sanctuaries and nature centers, and 508 chapters in the Americas, plus a professional staff
of scientists, educators, and policy analysts.

The award-winning *Audubon* magazine, sent to all members, carries outstanding articles
and color photography on wildlife, the environment, and conservation. Audubon also
publishes *Audubon Adventures,* a children's newspaper reaching 450,000 students. Audubon
offers nature education for teachers, families, and children through camps and workshops, plus unique, traveling degree programs through Audubon Expedition Institute.

Audubon sponsors books, on-line nature activities, and travel programs to exotic places
like Antarctica, Africa, Baja California, and the Galápagos Islands. For information about
Audubon, please contact: NATIONAL AUDUBON SOCIETY Membership Dept., 700 Broadway, New York, NY 10003-9562; (800) 274-4201 or (212) 979-3000; www.audubon.org.

Contents

Part II Bird Families of North America

Appendices

Introduction

The popularity of bird-watching has increased tremendously over the past few decades, and it is now estimated that about 60 million North Americans watch birds at least occasionally. This increase has occurred for many reasons: Birding is a hobby that can be enjoyed by anyone, anywhere, and at any time, and it requires no specialized skills and very little equipment. Moreover, finding and identifying birds offers physical and intellectual challenges for people at any level of expertise and gives observers an entry into the world of nature.

Watching and identifying birds quickly leads to curiosity about how and why birds do the things they do. How does a tiny chickadee survive subzero temperatures? How does an albatross cross miles of ocean without flapping? Why do male wood-warblers have two distinct song types?

The answers, or proposed answers, exist in technical papers and in textbooks, but such resources are often inaccessible to birders, and the information of most interest to amateurs is frequently embedded in a wealth of technical detail. Our aim in this book is to provide an introduction to the great variety and complexity of bird life—a book written by and for birders that will help readers interpret and understand the things they see in the field.

Throughout the book we have tried to combine scientific accuracy and detail with understandable and readable prose, condensing and organizing the huge body of ornithological knowledge into a series of relatively short chapters. The book focuses on North American birds and is intended as a companion to *The Sibley Guide to Birds*, a field guide that describes the identification of North American birds. That first book enables people to distinguish the birds they see; this book describes how those birds live their lives.

We hope that this book will serve two functions. First, it can act as a general reference on the biology of North American birds. Whether you are a backyard birder wondering why some House Finches at your feeders are yellow rather than red, an advanced birder interested in Fox Sparrow taxonomy, or someone looking for an introduction to the science of ornithology, we hope this book will answer your questions.

Second, it was our intention to produce a book that a birder could simply pick up and read, just to learn about a group of birds. For this reason, we have planned the bulk of the book as a series of chapters, each synthesizing current knowledge about a particular family of North American birds. This volume gives readers an overview of what is known about the biology of North American birds, plus, for those who wish to delve further, an accessible introduction to the more detailed literature.

How the Book Is Organized

The book is divided into two parts. Part I: The World of Birds provides a basic overview of bird biology, with chapters covering the way birds' bodies work, bird evolution, behavior, habitats, and conservation. Part II: Bird Families of North America includes chapters on the families of birds that occur in North America, written by expert birders and ornithologists familiar with the family described.

The family chapters all have a similar structure, although authors were encouraged to depart from the general outline in order to highlight topics particularly relevant to each family. These chapters all provide an overview of the taxonomy, foraging and breeding biology, and conservation status of the family. Each family chapter also includes a Worldwide Family Features box that summarizes key information for the family worldwide and, where appropriate, a short section on the occurrence of "accidentals," species that have occurred in North America but that are too rare to have been included in *The Sibley Guide to Birds*.

The book contains a glossary of terms and a checklist of North American birds. The index includes the names of species discussed throughout the book and topics covered in Part I. The front endpaper presents annotated illustrations of the parts of a bird and of egg shapes; the back endpaper provides a map of the region covered by the book.

Bird Names and Classification

The names and classification of bird species sometimes change as new information about their biology becomes available. In addition, some birds have different common names in different parts of the world, and different authorities use different classification schemes. In order to minimize confusion when referring to species, we have followed the American Ornithologists' Union's (AOU) *Check-list of North American Birds* (the seventh edition, published in 1998, and the 42nd supplement, published in 2000), as our standard for naming birds and describing their taxonomic relationships. Where there is disagreement over classification, or potential for name or taxonomic changes in the future, these topics are usually discussed in the Taxonomy sections of the family chapters.

For the names of species that are not included in the AOU Check-list (which only covers birds found in the Americas from Panama north), we have used *A World Checklist of Birds*, by Burt L. Monroe, Jr., and Charles G. Sibley (Yale University Press, New Haven, Conn., 1993). This checklist differs substantially from the AOU Check-list in its arrangement of birds. Although many of these classification differences are discussed in the family chapters, we have followed the AOU system as the primary classification for this book. In cases where classification changes have occurred since the publication of Monroe and Sib-

ley's checklist, and for the scientific names of subspecies (which are not covered in the AOU or Monroe and Sibley checklists), we also consulted James Clements' *Birds of the World: A Checklist* (Ibis Publishing Co., Vista, Calif., 2000).

Sources of Information

In addition to the dozens of people who have contributed directly to this book, literally thousands of ornithologists and birders, professionals and amateurs alike, have produced the massive body of information upon which the book is based.

Due to the constraints of space, and because we wanted to make the book as readable as possible, we have chosen not to follow the common practice in the scientific literature of inserting citations into the text. However, some sources were so fundamentally important to the production of this book that they must be mentioned. Readers who want to learn more about the topics covered are directed to these sources, which are described below. In addition, a list of key references for each chapter will be posted on the Internet at *www.sibleyart.com* to direct interested readers to the original sources and more detailed information.

For more on the subjects covered in Part I, readers might consult several general texts that were key to preparing the chapters. Frank B. Gill's *Ornithology* (second edition, W. H. Freeman and Company, New York, 1995), a very readable and highly recommended textbook used in college courses throughout the world, provides much more detail on the topics described in the first three chapters. Another excellent textbook, with a focus on avian anatomical structure, is the *Manual of Ornithology*, by Noble S. Proctor and Patrick J. Lynch (Yale University Press, New Haven, Conn., 1993). For a discussion of behavioral terms and concepts we suggest John Alcock's *Animal Behavior: An Evolutionary Approach* (sixth edition, Sinauer Associates, Sunderland, Mass., 1998), another leading college textbook. For information on North

American plant communities and distributions, we used *North American Terrestrial Vegetation*, edited by Michael G. Barbour and William Dwight Billings (second edition, Cambridge University Press, Cambridge, 1999).

Key sources for the family chapters were two ongoing series: *Handbook of the Birds of the World*, edited by Josep del Hoyo, Andrew Elliott, and Jordi Sargatal (Lynx Edicions, Barcelona, 1992–present) and the *Birds of North America* series, edited by Alan F. Poole, Peter Stettenheim, and Frank B. Gill (The Birds of North America, Philadelphia, 1992–present). The handbook is a monumental work that is rapidly becoming the primary source for general information on the world's birds. To date, six of a projected 12 volumes have been produced, covering most nonpasserine families. These books, which collectively number several thousand pages, contain detailed accounts of the biology of each bird family, along with summary information on each species of bird found in the world.

Equally impressive is the *Birds of North America* series, another ongoing project that comprises detailed monographs summarizing all that is known about the biology of each species found in North America and Hawaii. For detailed information on bird families, we direct readers to the handbook; for specific information on North American species we suggest *Birds of North America*.

Other major references for species that occur widely in Europe were *The Birds of the Western Palearctic*, edited by Stanley Cramp, K.E.L. Simmons, and C.M. Perrins (Oxford University Press, Oxford, 1977–1994) and its updated *Concise Edition*, edited by David Snow and C.M. Perrins (Oxford University Press, Oxford, 1998). For the latest developments in ornithological research, readers can peruse the major ornithological journals, which include *The Auk, The Condor, Ibis, Journal of Avian Biology, Journal of Field Ornithology*, and *The Wilson Bulletin*. Many other journals focus on specific groups of birds or geographic regions.

Worldwide Family Features

In general, the text of each family chapter refers specifically to the family in North America. (In this book we use "North America" to refer to the continental United States and Canada—that is, North America north of Mexico but excluding Greenland.) In addition to the main text, each family chapter contains a Worldwide Family Features box that provides a brief overview of the family's characteristics worldwide.

These boxes first give the range of body lengths, from the smallest species to the largest, along with a brief description of the type of bird found in the family (waterbird, songbird, etc.)

Next the box notes the number of species and genera included in the family, and the family's geographic distribution, both worldwide and in North America. Worldwide species and genus counts are based on Monroe and Sibley's *World Checklist of Birds*, updated in some cases by recent changes presented in the Clements checklist. In families where the taxonomic treatment differs between the AOU Check-list and the other checklists, we adjusted species and genus counts to conform with the AOU Check-list. For example, if the AOU Check-list splits a species that is given as a single species in Monroe and Sibley, we added one species to the global species count taken from Monroe and Sibley; likewise, we adjusted counts when family assignment differed among checklists.

North American counts are based on the AOU Check-list as it stands at the beginning of 2001. For North American counts, the boxes give first the number of regularly occurring species and then the number of additional "accidentals." Any distinction between "regulars" and "accidentals" is necessarily somewhat arbitrary because of changing distribution patterns and knowledge about the occurrence of birds. For our purposes when categorizing species we followed the decisions used to determine whether a species should be included in *The Sibley*

Guide to Birds. In the field guide, species were generally included if they had occurred at least 10 times within the previous 25 years. As space allowed, a few other species were added based on guesses that the rate of sightings would increase. In addition, species that have occurred more often than this guideline would suggest, but only on remote Bering Sea islands, were omitted from the field guide because most birders in North America are extremely unlikely to encounter these birds. The Accidental Species sections in the family chapters of our book are intended to provide an overview of the occurrence of species not covered in the field guide; hence, throughout this book we define accidentals as those species that did not meet the criteria for inclusion in the field guide.

Where appropriate the boxes also give information on species that have been introduced to the continent or that have become extinct.

Next the box provides a summary of diet and foraging techniques, general lifestyle (sociality, breeding system, propensity to make long-distance movements, etc.), the age at which members of the family begin to breed, and characteristics of the nest and nest site, eggs, and young. In these descriptions, ranges of numbers refer to the family as a whole; thus the clutch size range for the family Rallidae is 1–18, which means that some species lay as few as one egg, while others lay up to 18.

Finally, the box describes what is known about how long members of the family live. For each family we give ages for the oldest birds recorded and what is known about adult annual survival rates (that is, the percentage of adult birds that survive from one year to the next). For most birds, survival is not well studied, and these estimates may be low for many species or may be based on information from only a small proportion of the species in a family. For information on the maximum ages of North America birds, readers can visit the U.S. Geological Survey's Bird Banding Laboratory website *(www.pwrc.usgs.gov/bbl/)*.

For detailed information about the biology of individual species readers can consult *Handbook of the Birds of the World* and *Birds of North America* accounts. Summary information for each species is also given in *The Birder's Handbook*, by Paul R. Ehrlich, David S. Dobkin, and Darryl Wheye (Simon and Schuster, New York, 1988), *Lives of North American Birds*, by Kenn Kaufman (Houghton-Mifflin, New York, 1996), and *A Guide to the Nests, Eggs, and Nestlings of North American Birds*, by Paul J. Baicich and Colin J.O. Harrison (second edition, Academic Press, London, 1997).

Conservation

A recurrent theme throughout this book is that the continent's birds face a multitude of conservation problems. Probably the greatest challenge facing ornithologists today is determining how we can reverse population declines and prevent once-familiar species from becoming extinct. Each family chapter in this book provides an overview of the conservation status of the family. Some of these sections are very short; unfortunately, most are quite long.

In addition to providing a general overview, the Conservation sections often refer to specific information on the conservation of certain species. In particular, chapters identify species currently listed as threatened or endangered under the U.S. Endangered Species Act and, in some cases, by equivalent state and provincial legislation. The text also notes species included on the WatchList, a list of species that are considered especially vulnerable and potential future candidates for endangered species listing, sponsored by the National Audubon Society and Partners in Flight. The information in this book is based on the lists available in early 2001, but the composition of such lists will change as the status of individual species changes. Updated lists can be found on the Internet at *www.audubon.org/bird/watch* (WatchList) and *http://ecos.fws.gov/webpage/* (U.S. threatened and endangered species list).

The chapter Populations and Conservation gives a general overview of bird conservation in North America.

We strongly urge anyone interested in birds to learn more about their conservation, lest they disappear from our lives. For an account of many of the conservation issues facing North American birds, we recommend Robert A. Askins' exceptional book *Restoring North America's Birds* (Yale University Press, New Haven, Conn., 2000). For the latest on population trends continent-wide and locally, readers can visit the U.S. Geological Survey's Breeding Bird Survey website *(www.mp2-pwrc.usgs.gov/bbs/)*. To find out more—and to help—readers can contact the following organizations:

National Audubon Society
700 Broadway
New York, NY 10003-9562
www.audubon.org

The Nature Conservancy
4245 N. Fairfax Drive
Arlington, VA 22203-1606
www.nature.org

Birdlife International
Wellbrook Court
Girton Road
Cambridge, CB3 0NA, UK
www.wing-wbsj.or.jp/birdlife/

Acknowledgments

This book would not have happened were it not for a great deal of help from a huge number of people. First and foremost, we thank the authors who contributed chapters, and who endured the many changes in style and organization that occurred as the book evolved.

For their detailed and insightful reviews of chapters in Part I, we thank Noble Proctor and Michael Reed (Flight, Form, and Function), Chris Thompson (molt terminology box), Carla Cicero and Joel Cracraft (Origins, Evolution, and Classification), Ian Jones and Dave Delehanty (Behavior), Wayne Petersen (Habitats and Distributions), and Bob Askins (Populations and Conservation). Thanks also to Ned Brinkley, who provided information used for the Oceans section of the chapter on Habitats and Distributions, and to John Cameron Yrizarry for his careful review of the artwork throughout the book.

While fact-checking the book, we relied on numerous colleagues to answer questions outside our areas of expertise. We thank them all for answering our apparently arcane and usually completely out-of-context queries. In particular, Beth Misner did considerable research for us, and Margaret Rubega fielded an inordinate number of questions on just about everything.

We have been extremely fortunate to work with an excellent editorial and design team at Chanticleer Press: publisher Andrew Stewart; associate publisher Alicia Mills; editor-in-chief George Scott; editors Anne O'Connor, Pamela Nelson, John Tarkov, Amy Hughes, Lisa Leventer, James Waller, Lisa Lester, Michelle Bredeson, and Elizabeth Wright; art director Drew Stevens; design and production: Brian Boyce, Bernadette Vibar, Katherine Thomason, Jennifer Dahl, Michiyo Uno, Sui Ping Cheung, and Arthur Riscen; indexer Catherine Dorsey; and Gary Antonetti and the mapmakers at Ortelius Design. In particular, we thank project editor Patricia Fogarty for her tremendous patience and good humor in dealing with the three of us, and in making sure that we didn't miss too many deadlines . . . at least not too frequently.

Most importantly, we thank our families—Joan, Margaret, Beth, Evan, Joel, Owen, Nathaniel, and Bobby—for their support throughout, and especially for their enormous patience during the last few months of this project.

Finally, we thank all the birders who have encouraged us to learn more about birds over the years. No doubt there is still much for us to learn. We encourage readers to let us know of any errors that we have made by contacting us at *www.sibleyart.com*, where updates will be posted. Thanks.

*David Allen Sibley, Chris Elphick,
and John B. Dunning, Jr.*

PART I

THE WORLD OF BIRDS

Flight, Form, and Function

Throughout history, birds have been the subjects of poetry and myth, celebrated as stirring creatures whose ability to soar in midair symbolizes freedom, power, and wonder. They provide exceptional examples of the adaptations that organisms have evolved to take advantage of their environment, and because they are active during the day and not particularly secretive, birds are highly visible. For all these reasons, they are among our most studied groups of organisms.

Birds form a highly distinct class of vertebrates, the class Aves. All birds have features that distinguish them from other living organisms—in particular, their feathers, bills, and vocal apparatuses. The most successful flying vertebrates, they have occupied an enormous diversity of habitats; they have unique hard-shelled eggs that provide protection not available to other egg-laying animals; and their respiratory systems are the most efficient found among vertebrates. However, an accurate sense of what a bird is can best be acquired not by looking at isolated traits but rather by exploring the unique manner in which a bird's biological elements function together. This chapter discusses many of the basic features of birds, and the ways in which they are adapted to their environments.

The Implications of Flight

The central theme of bird evolution is flight. Most avian features can be related back to this fundamental adaptation. The avian forelimbs are dedicated almost entirely to aerial flight, for instance. To meet the diverse demands of survival without hands, birds have been subject to a fascinating evolutionary makeover.

Flight Anatomy and Weight Limitations

Flight requires a body light enough to be lifted without excessive expenditure of energy yet strong enough to withstand the many stresses of aerial life. To maintain efficiency in the air, birds must minimize their weight as much as possible. In some cases this constraint has limited the characteristics birds can evolve; in others it has resulted in weight-reducing adaptations.

For example, birds are the only vertebrate group in which all species reproduce using external eggs; that is, unlike some reptiles, fish, and mammals, no bird gives birth to fully developed young. Reproduction using external eggs minimizes the time during which females must carry developing young in their bodies, thus minimizing the time during which the added weight of the eggs makes flying difficult.

Hollow bones, a highly efficient digestive system, and the lack of a heavy, toothed jaw are all examples of avian adaptations that help to lighten a bird's mass. These adaptations are discussed further below.

Coordination, Balance, and Orientation

Birds have evolved compact, centralized bodies, without heavy appendages that would complicate maneuverability in flight. Most birds also have a low center of gravity and legs that are jointed so as to center the body's weight over the feet. This enables birds to walk and perch without losing balance. On some birds, such as loons and grebes, the legs are located farther back on the body to achieve greater efficiency in the water. As a consequence, these birds have poor balance and are awkward on land; some species have such difficulty on land that they can take flight only from the water.

Birds have particularly efficient sensory, nervous, and muscular systems for the coordination of flight activity. Shorebirds, for instance, can respond almost instantly to movements of their flock-mates so that the entire flock sweeps across the landscape as a seemingly coordinated unit.

Life Without Forelegs

The fact that the forelimbs of birds are dedicated to flight has had many consequences. For example, birds have a greater number of neck vertebrae than mammals, allowing them to reach objects, including their own bodies, with their bills instead of their forelimbs. Tremendous variation in the bills and feet of different species allows birds to accomplish a number of different feeding and maintenance tasks that many other vertebrates perform with their forelimbs.

The highly ritualized social interactions among birds may also be a consequence of their lack of effective forelimbs: Because they cannot grapple or paw to solve problems, in many cases birds instead employ display rituals or vocal communications.

For all the trade-offs involved, the survival value conferred by an ability to fly—for example, in evading predators, reaching patchily distributed food resources, or following changes in the seasons—must be very high. Virtually all of the world's birds do fly. The exceptions include very large birds and species that live in special environments without mammalian predators, such as oceanic islands and Antarctica. Flightless birds have fared poorly in a modern world where humans can reach remote islands, bringing with them predators such as rats and cats.

Feathers

Of all the organisms living on Earth, only birds have feathers. The adaptive significance of feathers is at least three-fold: They are instrumental in flying; they play a critical role in temperature regulation; and their color patterns are essential in both display and camouflage.

The number of feathers on a bird's body can vary from around 1,000 on hummingbirds to more than 25,000 on swans. Waterfowl tend to have a comparatively large number of feathers, and birds living at high latitudes may have a greater number in winter. Although the feather is a symbol of lightness, feathers still account for between 15 and 20 percent of a bird's total weight. A bird's skeleton, by contrast, is often less than half the weight of the feathers.

Like reptilian scales and human fingernails, feathers at maturity are dead structures made of an insoluble protein called keratin. Most feathers include a stiff central *shaft*. The largely hollow portion of the shaft that attaches to the skin is called the *calamus;* the remainder of the shaft is called the *rachis*. Two *vanes* extend laterally from the rachis, each one composed of many separate branches called *barbs*. Adjoining barbs are usually interlocked by a series of projections *(barbules)* and tiny hooks *(barbicels)*. This interlocking system allows a feather vane

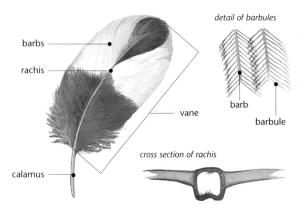

barbs

rachis

vane

calamus

detail of barbules

barb

barbule

cross section of rachis

Structure of a feather. *Each feather is composed of several structural parts. The central shaft, made up of the calamus and the rachis, is not round in cross section but is grooved on the underside for greater rigidity. A series of parallel barbs, which together form a flat vane (or web) on each side of the shaft, branch away from the shaft. From each of these barbs many tiny barbules branch off, with a system of hooks and ridges that holds the barbs together.*

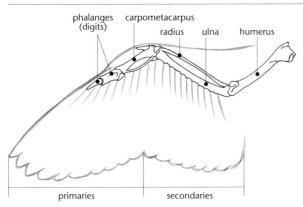

phalanges carpometacarpus
(digits)
            radius   ulna   humerus

primaries   secondaries

Wing bones with attached flight feathers. The two groups of flight feathers are distinguished by the bone to which they attach. The primaries attach to the bones of the outer wing (the phalanges and the carpometacarpus), which form the manus and mostly correspond to the human hand. The secondaries (including the tertials, the flight feathers closest to the body) form the inner wing and attach to the ulna, which corresponds to the human forearm.

to act as one unit as air flows over it. The feathers of some flightless birds, such as the Ostrich *(Struthio camelus)* of Africa, have lost the interlocking system, giving them a fluffy look. Though durable, feathers require daily maintenance to keep them clean, properly aligned, and free of parasites.

Feather Types

Birds have a number of different types of feathers, each with a specific set of functions. The long feathers of the wing *(remiges)* and tail *(rectrices)* are collectively called the *flight feathers*. The shape of these feathers determines the movement of air over the wings, which creates the aerodynamic forces that enable flight (see Aerodynamics, below).

Flight feathers of the wing include the long *primaries*, located near the wingtip, and the shorter *secondaries*, which line the trailing edge of the inner wing. The primaries are anchored to the *manus*, the avian equivalent of mammalian hand bones, while the secondaries are attached to the *ulna* in the "lower arm." In many large birds that fly great distances, the tips of the primaries are blackened by melanin, a pigment whose durability lessens wear on the wingtips.

The number of primaries varies among species, from as few as three or four to as many as 16; however, 10 primaries is typical. The number of secondaries varies with body size; hummingbirds have only six or seven, while albatrosses can have as many as 40.

Contour feathers, which line the body and cover the base of the major wing and tail feathers, provide birds with waterproofing, insulation, and streamlining. Many contour feathers have a prominent downy *after-shaft* (or *after-feather*) that extends from the base of the rachis, contributing to insulation. The contour feathers that cover the bases of the flight feathers, called *coverts,* are found along both the upper and lower surfaces of the remiges and rectrices.

Tail feathers are connected to the *pygostyle,* a bone at the base of the spine composed of fused vertebrae. In general, tail feathers play an important function in controlling flight, especially in enabling a bird to change direction or to reduce flight speed quickly. In particular species, the rectrices can have additional specialized uses. Woodpeckers prop their short, stiff rectrices against tree trunks to support themselves while they hammer at the bark. A number of birds—among them peacocks, birds-of-paradise, and lyrebirds—have developed elaborate displays that involve modified rectrices or uppertail coverts.

There are several additional feather types. Beneath the contour feathers lie *semiplumes* and *down feathers,* both fluffier than flight or contour feathers because they lack the interlocking system of barbules and barbicels. These feathers trap air and insulate against heat loss, improving the bird's ability to stay warm. The extent and insulation ability of down plumage varies with climate.

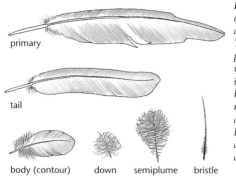

primary

tail

body (contour)   down   semiplume   bristle

Feather types. Feathers come in a great variety of sizes and shapes, but most of the variation can be categorized into a few main feather types. The long, rigid flight feathers include the primaries and secondaries (not shown) of the wing, and the long feathers of the tail. The body is covered by an outer shell of contour feathers. Underneath the contour feathers of the body many species grow short, fluffy feathers called down and semiplumes that provide insulation. Bristles are modified feathers with no barbs, only a bare, hair-like shaft; many species have bristles around the eyes, nostrils, and mouth.

For example, Arctic-nesting eiders produce down feathers whose insulation quality exceeds that of domestic geese, chickens, and temperate-breeding ducks.

Bristles are long, stiff feathers with mostly naked shafts, usually located near the mouth and eyes. Bristles near the mouth, referred to as *rictal bristles,* are prominent in some bird groups (see the Tyrant Flycatchers and the Nighthawks and Nightjars chapters) but not others. The purpose of these bristles remains uncertain. They are most developed on species that catch active, flying insects. Some researchers have suggested that rictal bristles help funnel moving prey into the bird's mouth. Experimental removal of the bristles does not seem to affect the bird's ability to catch prey, however, apparently refuting the idea that the bristles act as "bug nets." These same experiments do suggest that the bristles may help prevent particles from entering the bird's eyes during prey capture.

Molts and Plumages

Although feathers have many advantages, they are not perfect as a permanent body covering. The rigors of life can damage and batter feathers. Worn feathers have a reduced capacity to insulate and support birds in flight. Consequently, birds periodically replace their feathers though the process called *molt.*

A knowledge of molts and plumages is very useful for bird identification—even critical with some bird groups. Separating adult and juvenile plumages is particularly important, for example, in shorebird identification (see the Sandpipers, Phalaropes, and Allies chapter). Another classic identification problem that is helped by an understanding of molts and plumages is the separation of Hammond's *(Empidonax hammondii)* and Dusky *(E. oberholseri)* Flycatchers. These two species are extremely similar when in the same plumage. As a further complication, migrating individuals in the fall rarely give species-specific call notes. However, adult Hammond's Flycatchers molt their worn feathers on the breeding grounds, while adult Duskys wait until they reach the winter range. The birder who learns that a bird with dull, worn feathers in fall is most likely an adult Dusky Flycatcher has a way to distinguish this species during migration.

In most birds, contour feathers are not attached uniformly all over the skin surface; instead, they are attached to specific patches of skin called feather tracts, or *pterylae.* Some birds, including Ostriches, penguins, and kiwis, are unusual in that their contour feathers are not restricted to pterylae and are attached evenly over their skin.

During a single molt, birds usually replace all the feathers in a given tract, but they may not molt all the tracts at the same time. If a bird molts all the tracts within a short time, it is said to undergo a *complete molt.* If the feathers in only a few tracts or parts of tracts are replaced, the molt is referred to as a *partial molt.* Molts can be prolonged events, taking weeks or months to complete in some cases.

Basic and Alternate Plumages

Most North American birds replace all their feathers during a complete molt in late summer or early fall. At this time food is still plentiful, breeding is finished, and migration has not yet begun. Birds thus have the resources to undertake the energetically demanding process of feather replacement. The new covering of feathers birds grow in late summer is the plumage they will have throughout fall and winter. Virtually all birds undergo this molt, and the resulting feathers are collectively called the *basic plumage*. This late-summer molt is referred to as the *prebasic molt,* because it produces the basic plumage.

Many birds also undergo a second molt, usually in the spring prior to breeding. This molt is called the *prealternate molt* and results in the *alternate plumage*. This molt provides many species with an opportunity to alter their appearance for the breeding season. In these species the drab basic plumage is replaced with a brighter alternate plumage, especially bright in males, that is important in breeding displays. North American birders are familiar, for example, with the bright spring colors of buntings, grosbeaks, and wood-warblers.

In other species the prealternate molt results in a garb more suitable for the summer habitat. Ptarmigan molt from a white basic plumage, suitable for life in the snow, to a mottled brown and reddish alternate plumage that provides more effective camouflage in tundra vegetation during the summer months.

Partial and Complete Molts, and Feather Wear

Prealternate molts are often partial molts, replacing only certain feathers or groups of feathers. Birds may molt only the feather tracts on the head, or they may molt all the contour feathers but not the wing and tail feathers. Individuals in the process of molting can have a strange combination of basic and alternate plumage, and might look different from anything pictured in most field guides.

Some species deviate from the typical pattern of a complete prebasic molt followed by a partial prealternate molt. In some birds that live in very abrasive environments, such as the dense marshes filled with stiff vegetation used by the Marsh Wren *(Cistothorus palustris),* both the prebasic molt and the prealternate molt are complete. The feathers of these birds suffer more wear than is normal for birds in other habitats and so need more frequent replacement.

Some birds have no prealternate molt at all, undergoing only a single, complete prebasic molt each year. Obviously these birds do not change their appearance for the breeding season by growing a new set of feathers. However, their appearance can change due to feather wear. Freshly molted European Starlings *(Sturnus vulgaris),* for example, are brightly speckled with colors and dots in the fall, but by spring the speckled feather edges have worn away, leaving solid black feathers on the breeding birds. The Snow Bunting *(Plectrophenax nivalis)* develops a brighter appearance through wear as it enters the breeding season; males can sometimes be seen rubbing against the snow to accelerate feather wear.

Plumage and Age

Most songbirds develop their adult appearance when they are a year old. After this time, individuals of all ages look alike. The adult plumages that these older birds share are called the *definitive basic plumage* and the *definitive alternate plumage*. Some species, especially gulls and eagles, can take three or four years or more to reach their definitive plumages. These birds pass through a series of plumages that allows the ages of individuals to be determined. In specialized identification guides devoted to these groups, the different plumages are referred to as *first basic, second alternate,* and so on.

Molt Terminology

Molt can be a fascinating, confusing, or just downright annoying topic, depending on your perspective. Much of the confusion derives from the multitude of names used for different molts and plumages. Those naming schemes most familiar to birders identify a bird's appearance based on the season or on events in the bird's annual cycle. People often refer to a bird as being in "summer," "breeding," or even "nuptial" plumage.

Although intuitively simple, these schemes have a number of drawbacks. Naming molts after the season, for example, is problematic because many birds migrate between hemispheres. A North American birder might refer to an Arctic Tern *(Sterna paradisaea)* with a white forehead as being in "winter plumage"; however, for most of the time Arctic Terns look like this they are actually experiencing summer, albeit in the Southern Hemisphere. Equally, in the tropics, where there is no distinct summer and winter, the system breaks down.

Using the bird's breeding status also can create difficulties—for example, in tropical and subtropical birds that breed throughout the year, or in species with unusual molt patterns, such as male ducks, which may acquire their so-called "breeding plumage" in late fall or winter, months before they actually reproduce.

Another problem is that some birds can change their appearance without actually molting into new plumage; feather wear alone can produce new colors. So a bird's appearance can change because of molt, feather wear, or some combination of these two things.

Yet a further complication arises for scientists trying to understand the evolution of molting patterns. To do this, they need to know how the molts of different species relate to one another—for example, to determine which molt has been added or lost in a species that has an unusual number of molts.

For all these reasons many scientists, and increasing numbers of birders, have switched to using the *Humphrey-Parkes system* (named after ornithologists Philip Humphrey and Kenneth Parkes, who devised it in 1959) for naming molts. This system, which uses neutral names such as "basic" and "alternate" for different plumages, attempts to standardize molt terminology in a manner that can be unambiguously applied to all birds.

Unlike other systems, which name molts in terms of the feathers that are lost (for example, a "postbreeding" molt replacing the "breeding" plumage), the Humphrey-Parkes system relates a plumage's name directly to the molt at which the feathers were grown. For instance, in the Humphrey-Parkes system the alternate plumage is the group of feathers grown during the prealternate molt.

Humphrey and Parkes also pointed out that in traditional usage the word "plumage" can mean three different things—the set of feathers that are grown during a specific molt, the bird's overall appearance, or the entire coat of feathers that cover the bird's body at one time. In their scheme, they restricted use of the term to the first of these meanings and suggested the terms "aspect" to refer to a bird's overall appearance at a given time and "feather coat" for its body covering.

Since birds do not always replace all of their feathers during a single molt, a bird's coat of feathers often includes feathers from more than one molt. As a consequence, many birds referred to as being in "alternate plumage" during the breeding season in fact have a mixture of alternate and basic plumages.

Because of such fundamental differences between the various naming systems, it is not always possible to simply equate one set of terms with another; hence the terms "basic" and "alternate" plumage are not simply replacements for "winter" and "breeding" plumage.

Young birds in plumages that identify them as immatures are often tolerated by territorial adults that chase off intruding birds in adult plumage. The young birds therefore benefit from the plumage that identifies their age. Age-specific plumage may also serve in the formation of dominance hierarchies and mate selection.

Juvenile birds are often on a somewhat different molt schedule than are older birds. Altricial young (those born naked) first develop a downy covering, then molt a set of body and flight feathers while still in the nest. Birds in this *juvenal plumage* are often quite different in appearance from adults. The young birds leave the nest with juvenal plumage; then in late summer, when their parents are molting into the basic plumage, the young birds molt most of their feathers. Unlike their parents, which undergo a complete molt at this time, juveniles often retain their flight feathers.

The first basic plumage of juveniles can be very similar to the definitive basic plumage of adults; however, with a close look the juveniles often can be distinguished from adults by their worn wing and tail feathers.

Unusual Molt Patterns

There are some unusual patterns of molt involving changes in timing or extra molts. One of the best known of these results in the *eclipse plumage* of male ducks: In late summer, many male ducks molt into a drabber, more female-like set of feathers. There is a short period during this prebasic molt when the birds are flightless because they molt their flight feathers simultaneously. In late fall or early winter, soon after this molt is complete, the males begin their prealternate molt back into the colorful alternate plumage associated with breeding. Thus male ducks complete their prealternate molt long before most birds start it.

Why do these birds molt twice in such quick succession? Like basic plumages in many other species, the drab eclipse plumage is presumably more cryptic and helps the males avoid predation during their flightless period. But because ducks form pair bonds during the winter, the males cannot afford to wait until spring to molt back into their breeding colors, so they wear the eclipse plumage for only a short period.

Another unusual molt pattern is *delayed plumage maturation,* in which birds reach sexual maturity before they attain their definitive plumages. In most bird species that exhibit delayed plumage maturation—such as the Black-headed Grosbeak *(Pheucticus melanocephalus)* and the Orchard Oriole *(Icterus spurius)*—females attain their definitive breeding colors from the prealternate molt that precedes the first breeding season after hatching. Young males, however, still look like immatures or even like females after this molt. These males must wait a full year or longer before their prealternate molt yields the definitive plumage of fully adult breeding males.

Aerodynamics

Unlike earthbound animals, birds are exquisitely attuned to the demands imposed by getting off the ground and staying in the air. Collectively these demands are referred to as *aerodynamics.*

Lift and Drag

There are two essential elements of aerodynamics: lift and drag. *Lift* is the force that gets a bird off the ground and keeps it in the air. Lift, whether in animals or machines, is produced by air moving around and past an *airfoil,* such as a wing. Airfoils produce lift as a byproduct of their shape.

Physical laws ordain that the air flowing over the top of the wing must reach the back of the wing (the trailing edge) at the same time as air flowing under the wing. The curvature of the wing forces air to travel farther across the top surface than across the bottom. In order to travel the longer distance in the same amount of time, the air passing over the top of the wing must flow faster than the air flowing underneath the wing. This faster-moving air results in lower air

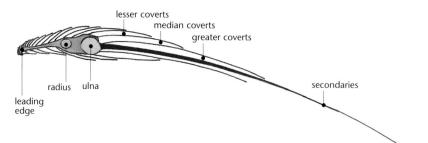

Airfoil shape of a wing in flight. The feathers of a bird's wing are arranged to create an airfoil shape that is incredibly streamlined. In this cross section of the inner wing, the bones and tendons form the bulky front part of the airfoil. The marginal coverts cover the leading edge of the wing. The long secondaries trail back and curve slightly downward, while the rows of secondary coverts streamline and enhance the airfoil shape.

pressure above the wing than below. The net result is lift, an upwardly directed force that, if strong enough, causes the bird to rise off the ground.

In birds, uniquely among flying vertebrates, feathers are used to transform the forelimbs into an airfoil. The shape of the flight feathers is aerodynamic; every feather is an airfoil. Flight feathers, especially those of the wing, are asymmetrical: The outer vane (located on the feather's leading edge) is relatively narrow, and the inner vane is wide. This arrangement creates a feather that is curved in cross section, with the peak of the curve very near the leading edge. This shape sets up the situation described above: Air travels faster over the top of the feather than across the bottom. In turn, the wing feathers overlap to give the whole wing an aerodynamic shape (blunt in front, tapered to the back) that also functions as an airfoil. The shape of a bird's wing in cross section is similar to that of some airplane wings.

The second aerodynamic force affecting flight is *drag*, which reduces lift by slowing the air moving over the wing. Turbulence, one important cause of drag, results when airflow over the wing is disturbed. Drag slows down a flying object. Structural features of the flight feathers, as well as their alignment during flight, help reduce drag. To land, birds adjust their wings so as to create more drag, slowing themselves down.

The flight feathers also help control flight at slow speeds and assist in landing by modifying airflow to prevent a premature "stall," which occurs when drag catastrophically exceeds lift and the object in flight falls from the air. This control is attained by allowing air to pass through open slots between feathers.

Control in flight is also gained through lift generated by the *alula*, a group of small feathers on the forward edge of the wing near the base of the primaries. Raising the alula feathers into the air flowing over the wing generates additional lift.

Forms of Flight
Birds generate lift by getting air moving past their outstretched wings. They can accomplish this by merely holding their wings out and facing into a strong wind. This approach is exemplified by a gull remaining on a perch in a storm until it opens its wings and rises straight up and backward into the air.

Birds can also move air past their wings by falling, such as when a hawk jumps from a tree with outstretched wings to glide away. The hawk falls very slowly until it encounters an updraft of air. If not for drag, the hawk would be able to glide horizontally indefinitely.

Birds can also make air move over their wings by flapping them. The way that wing-flapping generates lift is complex; basically, flapping generates *thrust,* a force that drives the bird forward and

How feathers move in flight. *The feathers of a bird's wing are arranged so that they develop thrust primarily on the downstroke but also on the upstroke. On the downstroke the primary feathers form a solid airfoil that pushes the bird forward. On the upstroke the feathers separate to allow air to pass easily between them, but each feather flexes to create a mini fan-blade shape that generates some forward thrust. Small birds generate thrust on the downstroke only. The Orchard Oriole is shown.*

opposes the slowing effects of drag. (Planes create thrust with propellers or jet engines.) The energetic cost of flapping flight is lowest at intermediate speeds and higher at both slow and fast speeds, much like an automobile engine that is most efficient at moderate speeds.

Hovering is the most energetically expensive form of flying. A bird using flapping or gliding flight benefits from the lift generated when moving air flows over the wings. When hovering in still air, however, a bird must generate all of its lift by the movement of its wings alone, expending a great deal of energy.

Hummingbirds can hover because of their small size and a particular arrangement of the joints in their wings, which allows the wings to be moved in a figure-eight pattern. This generates lift on both the upstroke and the downstroke of the wingbeat. Other species, such as the Belted Kingfisher *(Ceryle alcyon)* and the American Kestrel *(Falco sparverius),* can hover for short periods, but none is as efficient at hovering as the hummers.

Wing Shape, Wing-loading, and Aspect Ratio

Lift is produced as a wing deflects air downward and the amount of air that is deflected, and thus the amount of lift produced, depends on both the wing's area and shape. Long, broad wings have a large wing area, which allows birds to deflect more air downward than with short or narrow wings. Thus gliding birds that move long distances often have large wing areas and can create lift from even a minor movement of air.

Variation in wing size and shape is expressed by two terms: wing-loading and

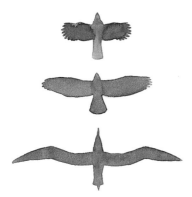

Variation in wing shape. *The Ruffed Grouse (*Bonasa umbellus, *top silhouette) has small wings for its weight (high wing-loading) and short, broad wings (low aspect ratio) so it must flap quickly and maintain a high airspeed to remain airborne, and it glides poorly. Swainson's Hawk (*Buteo swainsoni, *center) has relatively larger wings (lower wing-loading) and longer, narrower wings (higher aspect ratio) and can fly more slowly with infrequent flapping. The Laysan Albatross (*Phoebastria immutabilis, *bottom) has a relatively small wing area (high wing-loading) but very long, narrow wings (high aspect ratio) so it requires a high airspeed to stay airborne but can glide very efficiently in windy environments, such as the open ocean.*

aspect ratio. *Wing-loading* describes total body weight per unit of wing area. Birds with high (heavy) wing-loading have to support a lot of weight on a relatively small wing surface. Consequently they need to maintain high airspeeds as a way of generating lift. Wing-loading is a relative measure; large birds do not necessarily have heavy wing-loadings. Any bird with wings that are small relative to the bird's body mass will have a heavy wing-loading.

Grouse are heavily wing-loaded and must flap their wings rapidly and fly fast in order to fly at all. This is energetically taxing, and grouse tend not to fly far. Broad-winged Hawks *(Buteo platypterus)*, which are about the same overall size as grouse, have light wing-loading because of the wing dimension for which they were named. Broad-winged Hawks can fly slowly for a long time, flapping slowly and infrequently.

High wing-loading is a cost that some birds have been unable to avoid. Very large birds such as swans and eagles cannot "afford" wings large enough to reduce their wing-loading, as very large wings are difficult to flap and can be very heavy.

The second term that describes variation in wing shape is *aspect ratio,* the ratio of the wing's length to its width. A high ratio indicates a long, narrow wing, and a low ratio describes a wing with more similar length and width. Increasing aspect ratio, for a particular wing area, reduces drag because it lessens the influence of the turbulence that is generated at the wing tips. A high aspect ratio enables a bird to glide at a shallow angle to the horizontal and travel farther before having to flap.

Albatrosses and many of their relatives have heavy wing-loadings offset by a high aspect ratio. These birds have very long, narrow wings for their body size. Even though they have to move fast to stay aloft, they can glide for long distances under most conditions.

Wing length and shape also influence *wingbeat frequency.* Birds that flap frequently have heavy wing-loadings, low aspect ratios, or both. These birds cannot maintain shallow glides and are able to travel only short distances between bouts of flapping. Birds that flap infrequently have light wing-loadings, high aspect ratios, or both.

In addition to variation in wing shape and size, birds use a variety of behaviors to enhance their flight capabilities. Many of these behaviors are discussed in the family chapters of this book.

Feet, Bills, and Digestion

Because their forelimbs are dedicated to flight, birds perform many routine functions of feeding with their feet and bills. In addition, birds' digestive tracts do much of the work accomplished by teeth in other animals. Thus it makes sense to discuss feet, bills, and digestion together.

Feet
Many people think that a bird's knees bend backward. Birds actually walk on their toes, however, and the backward-oriented joints that seem to be their knees are their ankles. The true knees are

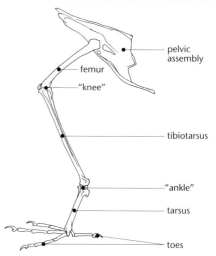

Leg and foot bones. Birds essentially spend their lives standing on tip-toe. A comparison of the avian leg and foot bones to human bones reveals that a bird's bare tarsus ("lower leg") corresponds to the human foot, while what we call a bird's foot is really just the toes. The Rock Dove (Columba livia) is shown.

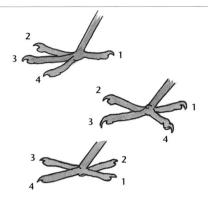

Toe arrangements. The usual arrangement of three toes in front and one in back is termed anisodactyly (top). The toes are numbered 1 to 4; toe number 1 is the hind toe, and 2 to 4 are the front toes from inner to outer. In some families, toe number 4 has shifted to the back (zygodactyly, center). In trogons alone, toe number 2 has shifted to the back (heterodactyly, bottom).

in most cases hidden close to the bird's body. The extended projections that we call bird feet are made up of greatly extended toe bones. Starting at the toe tips and working upward, one sees that avian joints bend the same way human joints do—birds' joints are just in unexpected places.

Birds' feet have a wide variety of uses, including locomotion (running, walking, hopping), clinging, climbing, carrying, perching, killing prey, preening, holding food, cradling eggs, aerial courtship, swimming, steering underwater, and absorbing the impact of water landings, to name just a few.

Most birds have toes arranged in an *anisodactyl* manner, with three toes pointing forward and one toe pointing to the rear. The hind toe, called the *hallux*, is the structural equivalent of the big toe on a human foot. Other birds, such as owls, cuckoos, woodpeckers, and parrots, have a *zygodactyl* arrangement, with two toes forward and two toes back.

Lobes and palmations (webbing between the toes) assist in swimming or walking on loose surfaces. Some species have special adaptations in their foot structure; for instance, Ospreys *(Pandion haliaetus)* have spiked scales on the bottoms of their feet that enable them to grab slippery fish, and Great Blue Herons *(Ardea herodias)* have a serrated talon used in preening.

Bills

A bird's bill consists of a bony interior covered with an outer plate of keratin (the *rhamphotheca*). It is structurally reinforced by internal bony "struts," called *trabeculae*. Although bills may seem rigid, they possess some flexibility, allowing birds a degree of dexterity with their bills. The connection between the upper jaw and the skull is jointed, and some species have flexible joints along their bills. For example, when watching a flock of dowitchers it is often possible to see a bird opening just the very tip of its bill; this dexterity allows these birds to grab hold of prey deep in the mud.

In shorebirds that probe for food below the soil surface, such as curlews and the American Woodcock *(Scolopax minor)*, the bill tip contains concentrations of tactile sensors used in locating prey.

The bill is highly modified for a variety of activities. In the realm of feeding alone, different bill types have evolved for cutting and crushing seeds, catching and holding fish, probing tree crevices, probing mud, chiseling wood, stabbing and seizing prey, filtering water, tearing flesh, transporting food, and so on. Birds also use their bills to straighten mussed feathers, gather nest material, and grapple with rivals. As birds of different ages or sexes can have bills that differ in shape or color, bills can help both birds and birders identify the age or sex of individuals.

Bill shape is sometimes well matched to specific foods, but many birds' diets change seasonally, and their bills must be capable of managing all dietary extremes. Many songbirds change their diet during the year—from insects in the breeding season to seeds, berries, and other vegetable matter in winter.

Bill specialization can be a mixed blessing. For example, crossbills with different beak sizes differ in their efficiency when feeding on different conifer seeds. Red Crossbills *(Loxia curvirostra),* with their big bills, can husk the large seeds of pine trees in less than a third of the time required by White-winged Crossbills *(L. leucoptera).* White-wingeds, however, with their smaller, finer bills, are much more adept when it comes to tiny spruce seeds and take half as much time as Reds.

Apart from the work done by their bills, birds' mouths perform only limited functions for processing food. Birds' tongues are well supplied with tactile sensors, allowing birds to identify food items and position them in the mouth for crushing and swallowing. The tongues of some birds are highly specialized. The Northern Shoveler *(Anas clypeata),* for example, has extensive fringing on the sides of its tongue, which helps filter food from the water. Many woodpeckers' tongues are very long and barbed, and the saliva of some is sticky—features that help them capture insect prey.

Digestion

Avian digestion is highly efficient—as it must be to provide energy rapidly for birds' prodigious metabolic needs. The digestive system works quickly, minimizing the time that heavy, undigested food remains in the body. Berry-eating birds such as the Phainopepla *(Phainopepla nitens)* can process food in as little as half an hour, and ducks can pass shellfish in less than 45 minutes.

The *digestive tract* is relatively short in birds that eat fruit, meat, and insects, and longer in those that eat seeds, other plant matter, and fish. The basic *esophagus* is a simple, narrow tube, which often widens into a sack-like *crop,* where food can be stored temporarily. The esophagus can stretch considerably to accommodate large prey, such as when an egret swallows a large fish whole.

A bird's stomach has two chambers: the *proventriculus,* where the breakdown of food particles into nutrients is initiated with digestive enzymes, and the *gizzard,* where food is ground up. The proventriculus is the smaller of the two chambers, and sometimes may appear to be just an enlargement of the esophagus. The gizzard is a muscular chamber lined with rough keratin and sandy grit (which the bird ingests); both of these are used to pulverize hard food substances.

In the avian digestive system, the gizzard performs the function filled by molars in toothed animals. Gizzard development is greatest in birds that eat seeds, which often require considerable grinding.

In species whose diets change during the year, the gizzard may also change, "toughening up" to handle seeds in winter, for example, and then softening in summer, when insects are the staple food. The longer intestines in birds that eat plant material give their digestive system more time to extract nutrients from

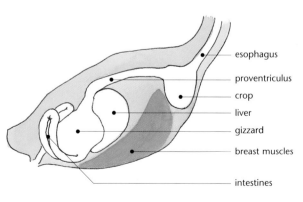

Digestive system. *Birds have a relatively simple but highly efficient digestive system and pass food quickly. Food is swallowed and passes through the esophagus to the crop, where it can be stored, if necessary. Next, food continues to the proventriculus and the gizzard, which together are equivalent to the human stomach. In these organs food is broken down by enzymes and acids and is ground up by muscular action. Finally, the food passes through the relatively short intestines.*

esophagus

proventriculus

crop

liver

gizzard

breast muscles

intestines

Cormorant swallowing large prey. *Birds have a remarkable ability to expand the mouth and stretch the esophagus to swallow large prey. The large fish that this Double-crested Cormorant* (Phalacrocorax auritus) *is swallowing can be seen as a prominent bulge in the neck as it slides down.*

these relatively indigestible foods. In some species that switch from an insect diet in summer to seeds in winter, such as towhees, the total gut length increases in winter.

Small side pockets on the large intestines aid in the digestion of plant material. These pockets, called *caeca*, are most prominent in gallinaceous birds (quail, chickens, and relatives) and may act as reservoirs of digestive bacteria for fermenting partially digested material.

Bones and Muscle

The avian skeleton is phenomenally well adapted for flight. The major bones of aerial birds are not solid but filled with air spaces, often with internal "struts" that provide structural integrity. In three regions of the avian skeleton—the thorax, pelvis, and outer wing—a number of bones that occur separately in most other vertebrates are fused together, conferring enhanced structural rigidity that helps birds endure the enormous mechanical stresses of flying. This fusion is greatest in birds that dive from heights into the water, as the mechanical stresses are most demanding during this activity.

The bones of the thorax include the uniquely avian *furcula*, or "wishbone," which is composed of the two clavicles (collarbones) fused where their ends

meet. During flight the ends that are not fused spread apart and then spring back to their relaxed position in synchrony with the wingbeats. The function of this movement is not well understood, but scientists believe it helps respiration in flight, much as the movement of the diaphragm aids breathing in mammals.

The *sternum* (breastbone) of flying birds has a projection called the *keel,* to which the flight muscles have their primary attachment. In fossilized birds, the presence or absence of the keel is a clue to whether an extinct species could fly. Each rib has a bony brace that overlaps the adjoining rib to provide structural reinforcement to the entire rib cage; these braces are collectively called the *uncinate processes.*

The avian pelvis is highly fused and forms a lightweight but secure point of attachment for the leg, tail, and abdominal muscles. The three lowest lumbar vertebrae of the back and the six upper vertebrae in the tail are fused with the back portion of the pelvis to form a strong lower spinal bone called the *synsacrum,* which is in turn fused with the other bones of the pelvis to form a connected pelvic girdle. In addition, the most posterior tail vertebrae are fused into a flat bone called the *pygostyle* to which the tail feathers attach.

Many of the avian bones that are equivalent to the mammalian hand and wrist bones have been greatly reduced, fused, or modified. For example, the

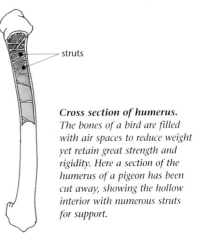

struts

Cross section of humerus. *The bones of a bird are filled with air spaces to reduce weight yet retain great strength and rigidity. Here a section of the humerus of a pigeon has been cut away, showing the hollow interior with numerous struts for support.*

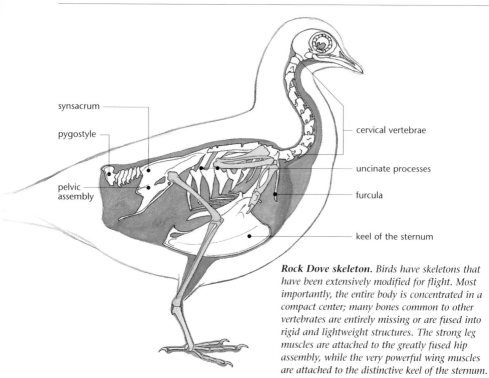

synsacrum

pygostyle

pelvic
assembly

cervical vertebrae

uncinate processes

furcula

keel of the sternum

Rock Dove skeleton. Birds have skeletons that have been extensively modified for flight. Most importantly, the entire body is concentrated in a compact center; many bones common to other vertebrates are entirely missing or are fused into rigid and lightweight structures. The strong leg muscles are attached to the greatly fused hip assembly, while the very powerful wing muscles are attached to the distinctive keel of the sternum.

carpometacarpus of the avian wing is equivalent to the various bones that make up a human wrist. Other wing bones are connected by well-articulated joints, which give birds considerable flexibility in the way they hold their wings both when resting and in flight.

Birds' locomotive muscles are made up of two basic tissue types: Red-muscle fibers (the familiar dark meat of poultry) support endurance-oriented, aerobic metab-olism, while white-muscle fibers are in-volved in explosive, anaerobic move-ments of relatively short duration. Muscles used mostly for sustained flight or walking tend to contain a large con-centration of red-muscle fibers, whereas muscles used mainly in brief activity, such as the explosive flights that grouse and pheasants use to escape predators, contain a greater concentration of white-muscle fibers.

Flight muscles: Front view of the body in cross section. The furcula ("wishbone") is visible in the center, connected at each end to the coracoid bones and then to the humeri. The cross section of the sternum shows the deep keel of the breastbone and the powerful muscles that attach to it. Note that the supracoracoideus muscles, which are used to raise the wings, are attached to the sternum and the top of the humerus; the latter attachment runs through a "pulley" system, which gives added power. The attachment of these muscles to the sternum keeps the center of gravity below the wings, allowing more stable flight. The larger pectoralis muscles, which are used to lower the wings, are partially cut away in this view to expose the bones and the supracoracoideus muscles.

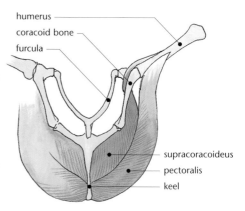

humerus

coracoid bone

furcula

supracoracoideus

pectoralis

keel

Neck flexibility. *The folklore that owls can turn their heads in a complete circle is not true, but they can turn their heads nearly 180 degrees to look directly behind them. A juvenile Ferruginous Pygmy-Owl (Glaucidium brasilianum) is shown.*

Birds that fly allocate an enormous percentage of their body resources to the flight muscles, which can account for 20 to 25 percent of their total body mass. Both of the major flight muscles—the *pectoralis*, which lowers the wing for its downstroke, and the *supracoracoideus*, which raises the wing on its recovery stroke—are attached to the sternum. In most birds, the downstroke of the wing is the "power stroke," and the pectoralis is substantially larger than the supracoracoideus. But in hummingbirds, which hover, and penguins, which use their wings to propel themselves underwater, both upstroke and downstroke generate considerable thrust. In these species, the two major flight muscles are of similar size.

In full flight, a bird's wings can beat very rapidly (27 strokes per second in chickadees, more than 50 strokes per second in hummingbirds). When a bird is flying at its normal pace, the flight muscles develop oscillatory rhythms that are self-sustaining for brief periods, so that nerve stimulation to the muscles need not occur on each stroke. The effect is like a spinning bicycle wheel, which once in motion needs only an occasional boost to sustain a constant speed.

Some of birds' most complicated skeletal features and muscle processes occur in the neck, which has between 13 and 25 vertebrae, compared to seven neck vertebrae in mammals. The added agility that results allows the neck to play several subtle but important roles. Most important, since birds lack hands with which to preen themselves and remove parasites, they must use their bills for this purpose, except for preening the head, which birds normally accomplish by scratching with the foot.

Reaching all points on the body to maintain the feathers requires great neck flexibility and extension. Even birds that appear short-necked at rest may actually be holding their necks in an S-shaped position, thus concealing the actual length. Birds' flexible necks also enable them to turn their heads in many directions, allowing them to keep a careful watch on their surroundings. Owls are especially renowned for their ability to swivel their heads to look behind them.

Another area where bones have been reduced or fused in comparison with

Parts of a bill. *A bird's bill consists of a horny sheath, called the rhamphotheca, supported by several internal bones. The keratin that forms the rhamphotheca is constantly growing and constantly worn away with use. Shown is a Herring Gull* (Larus argentatus) *skull with the horny rhamphotheca covering the bony parts of the bill.*

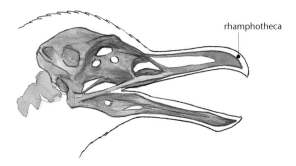

rhamphotheca

other vertebrates is the avian skull. The most obvious example of this reduction and fusion is the lightweight bill. With no teeth to support, the heavy jaws seen in mammals and reptiles are replaced in birds with the light *maxilla* (the upper part of the bill) and *mandible* (the lower part). The mandible is composed of five bones, four of which are so fused together that the original bones are difficult to distinguish. Although not strictly correct, birders often refer to the parts of the bill as the upper and lower mandible.

When a bird first hatches, the skull has relatively little calcium, layers of which are added throughout the first year of life. Bird banders often can identify very young birds by looking between the feathers and through the translucent skin on the birds' heads for the dark pink color that indicates unossified skull layers. In adult birds, the fully calcified skull looks whitish and stippled with small dots; the stippling is caused by the development of tiny columns of bone between the layers of bone in the adult skull. The process of *skull ossification,* as the development of the mature skull is called, takes about six months; therefore the age of many young birds in their first fall or early winter can be determined by their dark-colored skulls.

Respiration and Metabolism

Birds maintain their core body temperatures at levels higher than those found in mammals of similar size. Avian temperatures typically range from about 104° to 111° F (40°–44° C). With increased body temperature, nerve impulses travel more rapidly and muscle strength increases. This allows birds to extend the scope of their activities greatly, engaging in highly aerobic behaviors such as long-distance migration.

The downside of high body temperatures is that they require a high level of sustained energy expenditure. Given these demands, there is considerable survival value in generating metabolic energy quickly and efficiently, especially at times of peak activity. This is where birds' exceptional respiratory and circulatory systems come into play.

Respiration
The avian respiratory system has many specialized and unique features. The spongy tissue that forms the lungs is denser than in mammals and takes up about half the space. Despite their smaller size, however, bird lungs weigh as much as those of mammals of similar size, and they function much more efficiently. Each time a bird breathes, it replaces nearly all the air from the prior breath, whereas in mammals a significant amount of air remains in the lungs.

Unlike mammals, birds are equipped with a series of internal *air sacs* connected to the lungs. These air sacs can occupy up to 20 percent of the body cavity, including some of the space within large, hollow bones.

When a bird inhales, it draws air through the nares (nostrils), air sacs, and lungs, creating a one-way airflow that is highly efficient in exchanging oxygen and waste gases. The air is exhaled from the final set of air sacs into the bronchi and then out from the nares.

As the bird breathes, air passes through a folded region called the *conchae,* located in the nasal septum just behind the nares. On the intake, the conchae warm and cleanse air entering from the outside; during exhalation, they collect moisture condensing from the warm, humid air leaving the bird's body, thereby helping to limit water loss during respiration.

Circulation
In comparison to animals of similar size, birds have hearts that are larger than all other vertebrates and that can be double the size of mammalian hearts. The largest-hearted birds—those with the greatest need to get oxygen and nutrients to the organs and muscles throughout their bodies—include the strongest fliers, the deepest divers, and species that live at high altitudes or in cold climates.

Respiratory system. Unlike the simple in-out breathing cycle of mammals, the complex avian respiratory system is a continuously moving stream of air. It takes two complete inhale-exhale cycles for air to pass through the whole system. With each inhalation (blue arrows), fresh air is drawn into the posterior air sacs; with subsequent exhalations (orange arrows) and inhalations, this air next passes to the lungs, then the anterior air sacs, and then out of the body. A number of smaller air sacs are not shown here, including air sacs inside the larger bones.

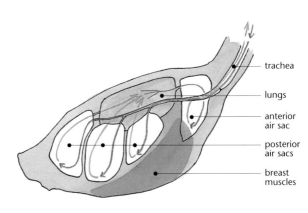

trachea

lungs

anterior air sac

posterior air sacs

breast muscles

Birds have four-chambered hearts that are similar to those of mammals except that birds can more fully drain their ventricles, thus increasing blood flow. A drawback of such high-performance features of the avian circulatory system is the extraordinarily high blood pressures that result, making birds susceptible to heart failure at times of high stress.

Metabolism

Prolonged and flexible flight activity requires a high level of physiological support. Birds are endothermic ("warm-blooded")—that is, they generate heat through their body metabolism in order to maintain a stable body temperature. High body temperatures allow them to forage early and late in the day, times when ectothermic ("cold-blooded") prey are less able to evade pursuit. Birds can sustain activity over long time periods, which gives them another advantage over prey species and potential competitors with less robust metabolisms.

Passerine birds (songbirds) have the highest basal metabolic rates (BMRs)—metabolic rates when at rest—of all vertebrates; nonpasserines have BMRs that are 50 to 60 percent lower than those of passerines.

During typical daily activities, the metabolic rate of birds is two and a half to four times greater than the BMR, but during flight it can increase to at least 10 times the BMR and occasionally much more. When measured in terms of the energy spent per distance traveled, however, avian flight is highly economical. It has been estimated, for example, that a songbird flying a distance of 1 kilometer expends less than 1 percent of the energy that a mouse would use to run the same distance.

Heat Management

An important by-product of metabolism is heat, and birds have evolved a large number of mechanisms to reduce the excess heat produced by their high metabolism.

Although birds lack sweat glands, they can perspire through the skin and thus reduce body heat. Birds can also get rid of excess body heat by panting, which allows water to evaporate from the surface of the air sacs. In order to increase the cooling effects of panting, many birds engage in *gular fluttering,* in which they rapidly vibrate the throat. This behavior is especially common in cormorants and pelicans, which have quite large throat pouches.

To avoid overheating, birds may become less active during the heat of the day, or they may bathe, seek shady resting spots, or soar at high altitudes where the air is cool.

Thermoregulation. A male Northern Cardinal (Cardinalis cardinalis) *is shown here with the feathers fluffed up (left) for retaining heat during cold weather, and feathers compressed (right) to avoid capturing additional heat during hot weather.*

Cold Management

When birds are not managing excess heat production, they are often coping with the cold. As with heat management, birds deal with extreme cold in various ways. Many feathers (down, semiplumes, and after-shafts) have significant insulating properties. In fact, feathers provide better insulation than mammalian hair. By fluffing out its contour feathers, a bird creates air pockets between the feathers and the skin that help retain heat. When resting, a bird can tuck its head or other body parts with exposed skin into its feathers to conserve heat.

Below a certain temperature, birds begin to shiver the pectoralis (and sometimes the leg) muscles to increase metabolism and generate extra heat. Some birds (for example, Inca Doves, *Columbina inca*) cluster together in cold weather or even rest in pyramid-shaped piles in order to conserve heat en masse. Grouse bury themselves in snow, and other birds roost in tree cavities or in dense foliage or brush piles to minimize heat loss.

In cold weather, birds' bodies can reduce heat loss by constricting the flow of warm blood through the leg arteries into exposed feet and legs, where the blood would be cooled. This is accomplished in two different ways: by reducing the diameter of the arteries or by transferring heat from the arterial blood to the cooler blood in the adjacent veins before the venous blood reenters the body. Birds can reduce heat loss in their extremities by up to 90 percent through these two techniques, which allow a gull to stand on ice in winter without losing too much body heat. Small releases of warm blood into the leg arteries prevent the skin and tissues of the feet from freezing. The same heat exchange system is used to cool birds' brains when they overheat.

Another strategy for coping with cold conditions is to simply stop maintaining body temperature at its normal high level. By allowing its core body temperature to drop, a small bird can conserve a considerable amount of energy, which may help it survive cold nights or periods of low food availability. While in this state, called *torpor,* birds are inactive and do not respond to most things going on around them. Unlike humans, for whom extreme hypothermia is generally lethal, these birds are able to raise their temperatures back to a normal level when conditions improve.

This use of torpor has been observed most often in hummingbirds and nighthawks and nightjars, but torpor also occurs in a number of other species. Unlike hibernating mammals, birds do not generally stay in a state of torpor for long periods, although some researchers have suggested that Common Poorwills *(Phalaenoptilus nuttallii)* may undergo true long-term hibernation.

Excretion

All vertebrates must dispose of the nitrogenous waste that is produced as a by-product of metabolism. In birds and reptiles, nitrogen is excreted as uric acid in semi-solid droppings. In contrast, mammals produce urea, which is toxic unless diluted in water and excreted as urine. For egg-laying organisms, in which wastes from the embryo must be retained inside the egg during early development, uric acid has considerable advantages over urea because it does not require dilution and is insoluble in water. Consequently a lot of nitrogen waste can be stored in the little space that is available within the egg. Another advantage for birds is that they do not need to drink copious amounts of water simply to flush nitrogen from their bodies. The whitish uric acid is mixed with undigested, darker feces to produce the familiar white-and-dark pattern of bird droppings.

Many predatory birds regurgitate pellets of hair, bones, shells, and other parts of their prey that are not easily digested. Owls are perhaps best known for this behavior, but it is also employed by various other species, including hawks, cormorants, gulls, and shrikes. These pellets do not contain feces or uric acid, because the pellets are produced in the stomach and expelled through the mouth, rather than continuing through the intestinal system.

Senses and Vocal Apparatus

Birds possess a number of well-developed sensory capabilities. Most people are aware of the keen vision and hearing possessed by most birds, and the tactile sensors in the bills of some birds are noted above. Other senses also can be important. For example, scientists are beginning to understand that smell can be a significant sense for at least some species.

Vision

In birds the dominant sense, by far, is vision. Birds' eyes are so large relative to their skulls that there is no room left to rotate them, as mammals can; birds must turn their heads frequently to align their field of view.

The acuity of avian eyesight is unparalleled among vertebrates: On average, birds can see two to three times more sharply than humans, and some raptors can sight small prey more than a mile away. The eye shape in certain raptors, notably eagles, is elongated, which may increase the sharpness of the images they see. This visual acuity arises from a suite of specialized anatomical traits.

Diurnal birds' retinas are densely packed with the color receptor cells called *cones;* a bird's eye can have two to five times more cones per square millimeter than are typically found in a human eye. The back of a bird's eye is flatter than a mammal's, and the cones are more uniformly distributed across the retina, giving birds a wider in-focus viewing area.

Color vision in the cones of diurnal birds is enhanced by pigmented oil droplets, a physiological system that is entirely different from—and probably superior to—the color reception mechanism in humans. The function of the oil droplets is not fully understood, but in addition to sharpening the perception of color, particular kinds of droplets appear to reduce glare.

As in mammals that are active at night, nocturnal birds' retinas have relatively

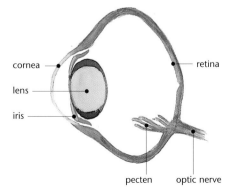

cornea

lens

iris

pecten   optic nerve

retina

Parts of a bird's eye. The eyes of birds are similar to human eyes, with a cornea, lens, iris, and retina, but they are much larger in relation to the size of the head; in fact, some large birds of prey have larger eyes than humans. The pecten is an eye structure found only in birds (although a related structure is found in reptiles). Its function is unclear, but it may help in circulating blood into the eye for nutrition and waste exchange. The eye of the Red-tailed Hawk (Buteo jamaicensis) is shown.

few cones. Instead, their retinas possess a comparatively large number of *rods,* which do not support color vision but are sensitive to dim light. Diurnal birds have a relatively small number of rod cells, most of which are located along the periphery of the retina.

The *fovea,* a concentrated mass of cones with only a few rods, is located in a retinal depression near the optic nerve and is highly developed in sharp-eyed birds. Many aerial specialists that need critical distance information—including raptors, terns, hummingbirds, swallows, and kingfishers—have a second fovea, called the *temporal fovea* (or *lateral fovea*), located toward the side of the eye, which is thought to improve binocular vision.

Birds can generally see into the near-ultraviolet and ultraviolet (UV) range, which human eyes cannot detect. Some species, such as the Budgerigar *(Melopsittacus undulatus),* have areas of their plumage that appear brightly patterned under UV light, suggesting that these birds look different to one another than they do to humans. Studies in the 1990s determined that Eurasian Kestrels *(Falco tinnunculus)* can use UV light to hunt for mice. Mice use urine to mark their trails, and urine absorbs UV light, so that areas of concentrated urine (that is, the mouse trails) appear as black lines to an organism that can see in the UV spectrum. Thus falcons can see the mouse trails directly and concentrate their watching on the most likely places where mice will move.

Another capability found in some birds but not humans is the ability to discern polarized light. Homing pigeons, among other birds, can see the polarization of sunlight, which may assist them in navigation.

Hearing

Birds lack conspicuous external ears. In their place, specialized feathers known as *auriculars,* or *ear coverts,* help protect the ear opening while offering little resistance to sound. The shape of the outer ear passage—and, in some species, of the facial feathering itself—helps to funnel sound into the inner ear, where the sound-receptive organ (the *cochlea*) is located. The degree of funneling is especially extensive in owls, which hunt mammalian prey by night and thus rely heavily on sound.

The internal structure of the avian ear is simpler than that of mammals. Birds have only one bone, the *columella,* for transmitting sounds, versus three in mammals, but acuity does not appear to suffer.

Avian hearing is best developed in nocturnal birds, which use hearing for hunting as well as communicating. A Barn Owl *(Tyto alba)* can capture a mouse in total darkness based on sound alone, but humans are nearly as adept at tracking horizontal movements in the dark. The Barn Owl excels as a mouser because it can also track movement in the vertical dimension—a capacity that guides the owl's descent as it swoops in for a kill. Nocturnal owls have a large number of hearing receptors in their brains (more than 47,000, by one count), whereas diurnal owls, such as the Little Owl *(Athene noctua)* of Eurasia, have far fewer (11,000).

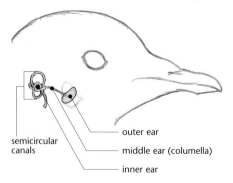

Ear canal of a pigeon. The ears of birds resemble those of humans in that they are composed of three sections. The outer ear canal channels sound to the eardrum. The middle ear transfers sound vibrations from the eardrum through a bone, the columella, to another membrane. In the inner ear the vibrations from the columella are transferred to a fluid-filled chamber where hair-like cilia convert the vibrations to nerve impulses. Also in the inner ear are the semicircular canals—three loops, each in a different plane—that provide information on balance.

semicircular canals

outer ear

middle ear (columella)

inner ear

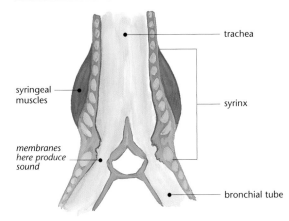

The syrinx. *The vocal organ of a bird, called the syrinx, lies at the end of the trachea, where the trachea forks into the two bronchial tubes. A set of muscles control membranes that restrict the air flow through the tubes and thus produce sound. The exact position and the structure of the syrinx varies greatly among species, and some birds lack it altogether. The syrinx of a generalized passerine is shown.*

As a group, birds can hear a wider range of sounds than can humans. Individual species tend, however, to have fairly specialized hearing ranges, so in one-on-one, species-to-species comparisons humans often have a broader range of sound perception. While birds appear to be no better at hearing soft sounds than are humans, woodpeckers can hear grubs moving below the bark of trees and pigeons are able to detect the extremely low-frequency (infrasound) rumbling that often precedes earthquakes.

Sound Production

In many cases, the most important auditory stimuli for birds are the sounds of other birds, including territorial rivals and family or flock members. Underlying all avian vocal activity is the *syrinx*, an organ unique to birds. The syrinx is located at the first major branching of the windpipe (trachea), where the two largest bronchial tubes converge.

There are general parallels between the syrinx in birds and the larynx in mammals. Both, for example, produce sound when air is forced through the trachea, causing thin membranes to vibrate. But the syrinx is a far more elaborate sound-generating mechanism. It is highly efficient, creating sound from nearly all the air that passes through it. The human larynx, by comparison, uses only about 2 percent of exhaled air.

Because the syrinx straddles two separate tracheal tubes, each equipped with separate sound-producing membranes and neural connections, birds are capable of producing two separate sounds at once—as evidenced by the eerie "duetting" songs of thrushes. Songbirds can even sing out of one side of their syrinx while sneaking small, quick breaths through the other during song pauses.

The unparalleled modulation and variety of birds' songs have been linked to the complex musculature of the syrinx. Storks, New World vultures, and other species that are unable to use their syringeal muscles are extremely limited in the range of vocalizations they can make. The complexity of the syringeal muscles is an important feature that distinguishes the two main suborders—the *oscines* and *suboscines*—within the order Passeriformes, the passerines or songbirds. (The word "oscine" derives from the Latin *canere*, "to sing.") The suboscines are similar to nonpasserines in having less complex syringeal musculature than do the oscine songbirds.

Song complexity of different species, however, is not entirely related to the complexity of the syrinx. Some oscine families, such as the Corvidae (crows and jays), are not known as great singers, despite their complex syrinx. The corvids, however, can produce an impressive variety of sounds, although many are not musical to the human ear.

Suboscines and oscines differ in other ways; for instance, the oscines generally need to learn their songs, while in the suboscines songs are innate. In North America the suboscines are represented only by the tyrant flycatchers; all other passerines are in the oscine group.

Taste, Smell, and Other Senses

Compared with vision and hearing, birds' other senses are decidedly secondary. Taste, in particular, appears poorly developed. While birds do have taste buds, their number is tiny—the few species examined have between 25 and 70, whereas humans have about 10,000. Birds' few taste buds are located toward the rear of the mouth, where they may assist in the final decision whether or not to swallow a food item.

For many years, it was believed that the sense of smell in most birds was as poorly developed as the sense of taste. In part this was because the *olfactory bulb,* the part of the avian brain that receives input from the smell receptors, is generally quite small. It was even suggested that some birds (especially songbirds) might not be able to smell at all. Increasingly, scientists are finding that smell can be very well developed in birds. Some bird groups have more elaborate olfactory bulbs (for example, vultures, tubenoses, and nocturnal birds), and there is evidence that olfaction plays a significant role in their lives.

The Turkey Vulture *(Cathartes aura),* which has an exceptionally large olfactory bulb, locates carrion by detecting the odor of a chemical (ethyl mercaptan) that is emitted by rotting meat. Many tubenoses likewise use olfaction to locate food at sea, and if their nostrils are plugged some cannot find their nest burrows in the dark.

A final sense that has been studied in birds is the ability to detect Earth's magnetic field and to use this information for navigation. Experiments have not clearly determined the exact mechanism involved, nor have they revealed exactly how birds process magnetic information. Some evidence suggests that tiny crystals of magnetite embedded near the olfactory nerves or photosensitive pigments in the eye may play a role.

Bird Intelligence

Expressions such as "bird brain" and "dumb as a dodo" imply that birds are not intelligent, and some avian behaviors appear to support this impression. Species that evolved on remote islands with no significant predators can seem absurdly oblivious to humans, even those who threaten the birds' lives. Two extinct island species, the Great Auk *(Pinguinus impennis)* of the North Atlantic and the Dodo *(Raphus cucullatus)* of Mauritius, were both killed off by sailors seeking fresh meat. In both species, individual birds seemed unable to respond to the harm that humans intended them, even as they observed the slaughter of their comrades.

In a similar if less lethal vein, geese can be duped into accepting doorknobs as eggs; some oystercatchers will incubate artificial eggs much larger than the adult bird; and goslings can be imprinted to accept humans as their mothers.

The existence of these stereotypic behaviors should not obscure the highly refined and adaptive behaviors that birds exhibit in other situations. Many birds will not accept cowbird eggs in their nests (much less doorknobs) and will remove them or cover them over when discovered. Others are capable of remarkable feats of recognition, as when male songbirds learn to recognize a nearby competitor by voice, even when the competitor sings a previously unheard song. Gulls can recognize the face of an individual human even after a long absence.

Some avian behaviors, awe-inspiring to observe in nature, make us wonder how intelligent birds must be to perform them. Flocks of shorebirds will race along the edges of beaches, turning and changing directions in the blink of an eye, without an obvious leader coordinating movements among the birds. Is such intricate behavior a sign of intelligence?

Researchers using computer models have been able to simulate this type of flocking behavior by assigning each simulated flock member a simple set of decision rules (for example, if the bird to my left turns right, then I turn right, and so on); such rules allow the computer flock to behave in a highly synchronized manner without following the directions of a single leader. This is analogous to fans in a stadium rising in a "wave," each taking cues from the person in the next seat. Thus dramatic behaviors such as coordinated flock movements are a sign of rapid response to complex stimuli, but not necessarily a mark of intelligence.

Bird Brains

Birds have larger brains relative to their body size than all other vertebrates except mammals. Their higher-brain structure differs subtly but significantly from that of mammals. All vertebrates are similar in lower-brain organization, which controls basic bodily functions such as temperature regulation. The role of the cerebral cortex (higher brain) in mammals, however, is largely replaced in birds by a layer of brain tissue called the *hyperstriatum*. In birds, learning abilities seem to increase with the size of the hyperstriatum, and the experimental removal of tissue from this region hampers learning; loss of a region called the *Wulst* is particularly devastating.

In birds, a brain structure called the *hippocampus* is important for consolidating short-term memories. In birds that engage in caching (hiding seeds or nuts in particular locations and returning later to retrieve them), the hippocampus is disproportionately large. When the hippocampus is removed in caching species such as the Black-capped Chickadee *(Poecile atricapilla)*, the birds can still cache seeds but are no longer able to relocate them from memory. Mammals that cache food, such as foxes and squirrels, also find their caches using spatial memory, but it is not known if the same brain centers are involved.

The motor-control areas of a bird's brain are large and well developed, presumably to assist in such highly complex behaviors as flight. Optical centers of the brain are likewise accentuated, reflecting birds' strong reliance on vision.

Possibly the most interesting aspect of the avian central nervous system, however, is its role in the control of song. While almost all birds are capable of vocalization, song is a complex activity that often must be learned by young birds, especially in oscine passerines. Forms of learned vocalization also occur in parrots and hummingbirds.

Learning implies that higher-brain activity must be complex in the control of song. This control is associated with two *song-control centers* in the avian brain. If the links between these centers and the syrinx are interrupted, a bird is unable to produce normal song.

Problem-solving Ability

So are birds intelligent or do they simply follow their instincts? To answer this question, we first must decide what is meant by "intelligence." In traditional experimental psychology, intelligence is the ability to "learn how to learn"—that is, to solve problems of a given class correctly when first confronted, then to solve problems of a similar nature with increasing speed when they are encountered again.

Some birds—most notably crows, ravens, and other corvids—have demonstrated an ability to solve problems. We cannot expect all birds to demonstrate an equivalent degree of intelligent behavior, however, any more than we would expect the same quality of mental performance from a shrew and a chimpanzee. Underscoring the principle that intelligence is one adaptive trait among many, we can see that it has evolved selectively among different bird families.

How do birds compare with other creatures in problem-solving ability? In various laboratory experiments, it has been shown that both birds and mammals vary considerably in their ability to solve problems. Crows and parrots often perform as well as dogs in tests that involve reasoning or learning, whereas chickens, doves, cats, and rabbits are less successful. Blue Jays *(Cyanocitta cristata)* are able to master food-locating tasks that cats and Squirrel Monkeys cannot perform well.

Birds exhibit some of their most distinctive intellectual skills in problems involving abstract numbers and shapes. Birds can learn to "count" sounds—for example, they can distinguish between one tone and two—to obtain a reward. Many birds have been able to master this problem, but a number of mammals find the task exceedingly difficult.

Birds can solve practical problems of many types. One study showed that Black-capped Chickadees and Red-breasted Nuthatches *(Sitta canadensis)* can distinguish an empty sunflower seed husk from one containing food solely by weight. In another study, when presented with a chunk of meat hanging below it on a string, a Common Raven *(Corvus corax)* was able to retrieve the meat by lifting the string with its bill, stepping on the string to hold it, then repeating the process.

Pigeons have demonstrated the ability to form "cognitive classes," distinguishing photos containing people from photos without people, identifying water in diverse forms (droplets, puddles, lakes), and distinguishing oak leaves from the leaves of other trees.

A final area in which birds show evidence of intelligence is their ability to learn by imitation. In an oft-cited example, a group of Great Tits *(Parus major,* close relatives of North American chickadees) in Great Britain learned to pry the cardboard lids off milk containers in order to pilfer the contents (these glass milk bottles were capped with lids that were rather easily removed). When dairy farmers began to use lids made of metal foil, the birds learned to open them, too. Several generations of Great Tits and several other species, including Blue Tits *(Cyanistes caeruleus)*, European Starlings,

Insightful learning. *Many species of birds have shown the ability to learn in captivity, but proving that such learning exists in the wild is extremely difficult. One of the few cases known involves Green Herons* (Butorides virescens) *that learned to drop bread crumbs into the water, then capture the fish that rose to the bait.*

and Great Spotted Woodpeckers *(Dendrocopos major)*, learned the behavior by imitation.

In another classic example, caged Blue Jays learned to avoid eating Monarch butterflies—which are distasteful because of the alkaloids they ingest as caterpillars—by watching other Blue Jays in adjoining cages. House Sparrows *(Passer domesticus)* have even learned to open automatic doors to grocery stores, cafés, and other sources of food by hovering in front of the electric eye sensors.

Studies have defined many other kinds of avian learning and intelligence, such as behaviors involving navigation (especially the ability to form internal "maps" of geographic territories), limited tool use, and sophisticated social interaction, including purported language ability in species such as the African Gray Parrot *(Psittacus erithacus)*. Obtaining a fuller appreciation of birds' intelligent behavior is among the most fascinating frontiers of ornithological study.

Rick Cech, John B. Dunning, Jr.,
Chris Elphick, and Margaret Rubega

Origins, Evolution, and Classification

Some of the most controversial issues in ornithology concern the evolution of birds. Whether it is a question of which organisms the birds evolved from or which methods should be used to define and classify different bird species, there seems to be constant, and often acrimonious, debate. In part the problem is that scientists are trying to understand events that happened millions of years ago, and we may never know exactly what happened. Nonetheless, the development of new techniques and the discovery of new information are constantly refining our understanding of these events even if they do not completely resolve the discussion.

The Origin of Birds

Debate over avian origins was spurred in 1861, when a fossil of a bird-like creature was unearthed in a lithographic limestone quarry in Bavaria, Germany. Called *Archaeopteryx lithographica* (*archae* is Latin for "ancient," *pteryx* is Greek for "wing"), this crow-size animal lived about 150 million years ago. *Archaeopteryx* is anatomically intermediate between birds and reptiles: Feathers that are almost indistinguishable in form from modern flight feathers are clearly visible on its wings and tail, yet it also has many reptilian features, including teeth. Although *Archaeopteryx* seems to have been capable of some sort of aerial activity, its flight anatomy differed from that of modern birds, and there is debate over whether it was capable of flapping flight.

Birds Are Reptiles

Before the discovery of *Archaeopteryx*, taxonomists had already suggested a close relationship between birds and reptiles because of the large number of anatomical features shared by the two classes of animals. The significance of *Archaeopteryx* therefore lay mostly in its apparently intermediate status: Here was a "missing link" between two major groups of animals of just the sort proposed in Charles Darwin's new theory, which had been fully laid out in his book *On the Origin of Species by Means of Natural Selection* only two years earlier.

What was still unclear was which group of reptiles gave rise to birds. For more than a hundred years after *Archaeopteryx* was first discovered, it was one of only a handful of known avian fossils. During this time, varying opinions held sway as to the exact sequence of evolutionary events that linked birds and reptiles.

The idea that birds may have evolved from dinosaurs was voiced first in the 1860s by English biologist Thomas Huxley. In 1926 the Danish paleontologist

Archaeopteryx lithographica. *Fossil discoveries have provided concrete evidence that birds evolved from reptiles.* Archaeopteryx, *shown at left, next to an American Crow for scale, had characteristics of modern birds but retained features that were clearly reptilian.*

Gerhard Heilman rejected this idea, reasoning that birds must have originated separately from a predinosaur reptilian ancestor on the basis that bird-like dinosaurs lacked a furcula (the fused collarbones, or "wishbone").

In 1973, Yale paleontologist John Ostrom again proposed a bird–dinosaur link and suggested that birds were descended from small bipedal dinosaurs of the theropod group called coelurosaurs. *Archaeopteryx* was so similar to a coelurosaur that a specimen of *Archaeopteryx* discovered in 1951 was misidentified until 1973 as a theropod dinosaur because it lacked obvious impressions of feathers.

On the basis of numerous similarities, most paleontologists currently consider a theropod origin of birds to be the best-supported view of avian evolution. Yet ardent opposition from a minority of paleontologists persists, fueled by various disagreements over issues such as differences in tooth and finger structure between theropods and *Archaeopteryx*.

Recent Discoveries New non-avian dinosaur fossils emerging from an excavation begun in China in 1994 have stoked the debate. One of these fossils (*Sinosauropteryx,* or "Chinese dragon feather") is covered with filamentous structures that some scientists believe are "protofeathers." Two others *(Caudipteryx* and *Protoarchaeopteryx)* clearly had feathers, but feathers too primitive to have supported flight. These fossils lend support to the idea that birds are descended from dinosaurs.

Other interesting finds included *Sinornis santensis,* a sparrow-size, toothed bird that lived in China 120 million years ago and that had skeletal features similar to both theropod dinosaurs and *Archaeopteryx. Sinornis* also had many skeletal features, especially of the flight apparatus, that were intermediate in character between those of *Archaeopteryx* and modern birds.

Hundreds of fossils of a toothless bird nearly as old as *Archaeopteryx,* dubbed *Confuciusornis,* have also been found; some (thought to be males) sported elongated tail feathers rather like those of a Scissor-tailed Flycatcher *(Tyrannus forficatus).*

Modern Birds The Cretaceous period ended 65 million years ago in a wave of mass extinctions. Apparently none of the known toothed early birds survived this bottleneck. Representatives of at least one lineage of early birds, however, presumably survived to become the ancestors of modern birds.

After the end of the Cretaceous period, "modern" toothless bird species proliferated. During the early Cenozoic era (about 50 to 60 million years ago) huge, flightless, carnivorous birds made a relatively brief appearance; some were more than 6 feet (1.8 m) tall and had heads as large as those of horses. Most modern bird orders were present by the end of the Eocene epoch, 37 million years ago, and most modern bird genera existed by the end of the Miocene epoch, 5 million years ago.

Origins of Flight, Feathers, and Warm Body Temperatures

Questions regarding the ancestry of modern birds are closely linked to questions about how birds developed the ability to fly. Birds are not the only animals to have evolved this ability, but they are the only ones to use feathers for the necessary airfoil. Thus, the evolution of flight in birds depended on feathers. But since feathers serve other functions (such as display and insulation), it is not necessarily true that the evolution of feathers depended on flight. Feathers also could have developed initially to provide insulation to help maintain high body temperature. (Warm bodies are required to sustain the kind of activity needed for flapping flight because the chemical reactions required to support rapid repetitive muscle contractions proceed most efficiently at higher temperatures.)

Thus feathers and the ability to maintain warm body temperatures metabolically (endothermy) were prerequisites for flapping flight in birds. But did birds start flying by flapping? There are two major lines of thought about how, and when, birds evolved the feathers and high internal body temperatures that allowed them to engage in flapping flight.

The "Trees-down" Theory For much of the 20th century, the conventional theory held that early birds were arboreal and that flight developed from primitive gliding activities similar to those of flying squirrels, which leap from tree to tree. According to this arboreal theory, feathers developed from early reptilian scales.

The earliest "protofeathers" in this scenario were envisioned as arising from a genetic mutation that elongated or enlarged scales. Individuals with longer scales benefited because these scales would have increased the surface area of the outstretched forearms, which would have slowed the rate of fall—and thus increased the distance of horizontal travel—when leaping from tree to tree. These advantages, in turn, it is proposed, would have had survival benefits by reducing the risk of death from falling, or from accidentally landing on the ground, where predators waited.

Further scale elaboration would have increased these advantages, and longer, more aerodynamically shaped scales would have been selected for. Over the generations, as scales became more feather-like, short glides gave way to long ones, and gliding flight became possible. Simple gliders could have evolved into intermediate forms like *Archaeopteryx*, which may have supplemented gliding with weak flapping, and thence to modern birds with flapping flight. Endothermy need not have arisen until birds were well differentiated from other reptiles and feathers were sufficiently elaborate to provide some insulating advantage.

This theory was generated largely from the observation that *Archaeopteryx* had feet that could have grasped a branch. These grasping feet are taken as evidence that *Archaeopteryx* lived in trees, which makes the trees-down theory plausible.

The "Ground-up" Theory In contrast, the cursorial, or terrestrial, theory posits that early birds were ground-dwelling, bipedal predators that chased down prey on foot and captured victims with clawed forelimbs. This sort of behavior, like flapping flight, is best (though not exclusively) supported by a high body temperature. Warm-bodied predators can sustain the rapid, repetitive muscle contractions used for running after prey for longer stretches of time than cold-bodied predators. Feathers may have developed for insulation, which would have improved the retention of body heat. Later, feathers might also have improved prey capture or balance while running by increasing the surface area of the extended forelimbs. As feathers enlarged, an airfoil (see the chapter Flight, Form, and Function) developed, flight became possible, and the advantages of flight drove further elaboration of feather structure.

The ground-up idea arose from John Ostrom's proposal linking *Archaeopteryx* to theropod dinosaurs, which were apparently all active, terrestrial, bipedal predators, and which increasingly are thought of as likely to have been able to maintain high body temperatures.

The Current State of the Debate Where does this leave the discussion? Not surprisingly, those who believe that birds are descended from dinosaurs tend to support the terrestrial theory of the origin of flight, while those who do not believe birds are dinosaurs tend to find the arboreal theory convincing.

The discovery of *Caudipteryx* and *Proto-archaeopteryx* in China has added to the debate by demonstrating that some clearly non-avian dinosaurs had feathers. Since these two animals were terrestrial predators, they lend support to the ground-up theory and suggest that a life in the trees was not a prerequisite for the evolution of feathers.

Nonetheless, neither scenario has gained complete acceptance within the scientific community, and the polarization of the two sides seems to promote extremes of opinion. It is possible that both theories are at least partially correct. For instance, early birds may have lived both on the ground and in the trees.

How Bird Species Originate

A number of processes are thought to contribute to speciation (the process by which new species arise), but the primary force producing diversity in birds appears to be breeding isolation. The isolation of a population of birds from other birds with which they might interbreed can be achieved in several ways. The most obvious is through separation by physical barriers that cannot easily be breached; scientists refer to this as *geographic isolation.*

How does physical isolation contribute to speciation? Locking two canaries in separate cages doesn't make them two different species. The answer is reproduction and time. In sexually reproducing animals such as birds, the production of eggs and sperm requires replication of parental genes. A very small percentage of all gene copies have "mistakes," random changes in the code contained in the original gene. These changes in the genetic code are called *mutations,* and they cause new heritable characteristics (or new variations of existing characteristics) to arise in the embryo that receives them.

Some of these new characteristics are harmful and will disappear from the population because the birds that receive them have lower reproduction rates than other birds in the population. Some mutations are advantageous and will become widespread because they enhance the reproductive success of the birds that have them. Many mutations are neutral and confer no advantage or disadvantage; these can also spread through a population.

In a population of birds where individuals freely interbreed new mutations can spread throughout the whole population, maintaining a high degree of similarity among individuals. In contrast, when a population of similar birds is "split" by a physical barrier that prevents interbreeding, different groups of mutations accumulate in the birds on either side of the barrier.

Some genetic mutations may accumulate in only one population because they are advantageous under the conditions present on only one side of the barrier. Other mutations may accumulate in only one population because the barrier prevents transmission of mutations that arose on only one side of the barrier. Moreover, since neutral mutations arise in a random manner, those that accumulate on each side of the barrier may differ.

Over very long periods of time, these processes can result in sufficient genetic differences between the two groups of birds that they are no longer capable of interbreeding. This occurs either because the two populations are physically incapable of reproducing successfully, or because accumulated changes in characteristics such as song, breeding behavior, and appearance prevent them from recognizing each other as potential mates. In either case, they are said to be *reproductively isolated* and the features that prevent them from interbreeding are called *isolating mechanisms* (see Species Concepts, below).

Thus, on the basis of their restricted ranges, we can guess that the Island *(Aphelocoma insularis)* and Florida *(A. coerulescens)* Scrub-Jays differentiated from the more widely distributed Western Scrub-Jay *(A. californica)* when small populations of their shared ancestor became isolated. Over time, different mutations accumulated in the three populations, resulting in the differences we see today.

Geographic isolation is not the only isolating mechanism. For example, time can also isolate an ancestral population from its descendants. As mutations accumulate over long stretches of time, the original population is transformed into a group that is very different from its ancestors.

Species Diversification

If isolation produces most species of birds, why is it that the ranges of so many closely related species meet or overlap? The diversity we now see in modern birds is thought to be largely the product of repeated isolation events resulting from past climate swings and geographical changes. For instance, the advance of continental ice sheets during past cycles of glaciation is thought to have split some populations of birds, which evolved into new species during their isolation. During warming periods, the glaciers retreated and these isolated populations were reunited.

In some cases, the reunited populations may have changed enough that they could no longer reproduce with each other. If they were also different enough that they did not compete directly with each other for resources, they could coexist, and the end result was similar species with overlapping ranges and habitats. In cases where reunited populations did compete with each other, the competition may have provided a selective force driving further differentiation.

With sufficient time, this process of splitting populations followed by differentiation and subsequent reuniting can repeat many times and produce numerous species. For example, it has long

been proposed that prototypical wood-warblers evolved in the broadleaf forests of northern Central America by the late Miocene, about 9 million years ago. From Central America, these early wood-warblers are believed to have spread into North America, where their populations were repeatedly subdivided as glaciers advanced and retreated across the continent. Over the millennia, as populations were split and then re-split with each glacial advance, dozens of wood-warbler species arose; today there are more than 20 species in the genus *Dendroica* alone.

Exactly when particular bird species arose can be hard to determine. Ornithologists have long believed that many present-day bird species emerged over the last 2 million years, during the Pleistocene epoch, as a result of glacial isolation events. In 1997, ornithologists John Klicka and Robert Zink challenged this time line on the basis of a review of studies of songbird genetic information. They suggested that many species began to separate from each other much longer ago: In some cases, the divergence was initiated 2 to 5 million years ago.

In 1998, ornithologists John Avise and DeEtte Walker performed their own review and disputed Klicka and Zink's assertion that Pleistocene events did not play an important role in avian speciation. The use of genetic differences to

Geographic isolation. *The three species of scrub-jay are extremely similar to each other. The Island Scrub-Jay (bottom left, found only on Santa Cruz Island off the coast of southern California) and Florida Scrub-Jay (right, range shown in green) both have small ranges isolated from the widespread Western Scrub-Jay (top left, range shown in blue). This isolation is caused by an expanse of ocean in the case of the Island Scrub-Jay and by hundreds of miles of unsuitable forest and prairie habitat for the Florida Scrub-Jay.*

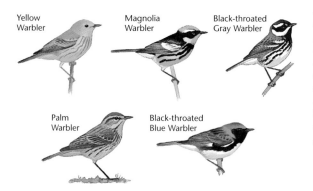

Yellow Warbler

Magnolia Warbler

Black-throated Gray Warbler

Palm Warbler

Black-throated Blue Warbler

Species diversification. The diversity of the wood-warbler genus Dendroica *is presumed to have arisen from repeated subdivision and differentiation of populations as glaciers advanced and retreated across North America over the last few millennia. Shown are five species representative of the genus.*

assign dates to the appearance of new species is clearly still subject to debate, but these new analyses signal the beginning of a reconsideration of conventional theory.

Classification

Since speciation occurs over very long time spans, we need to be able to tell when speciation is complete in order to determine how many species of birds there are. Every life list springs from the conviction that there are many species of birds and that it is possible to distinguish among them. Any novice can see that a chickadee and a crow are different, but the distinction between an American Crow *(Corvus brachyrhynchos)* and a Northwestern Crow *(C. caurinus)* is much less obvious. Are they different enough to be separate species? How do we tell? What is a species, anyway?

The bewildered birder will have noticed that even the experts cannot seem to agree on an answer to these questions. Robert Zink recently compiled a list of 28 different proposed definitions for the term "species," each distinct in some way. Why can't the experts agree on a simple definition?

Classification Schemes

In order to define a species, the basic unit of biological classification, it is important to agree on what it is that we want a classification to accomplish. At its simplest, a classification is merely a way to assign names to recognizable entities:

pencils, pens, pelicans, pigeons. This kind of classification neither requires nor provides any information other than that about similarity. Unavoidably, subjective decisions about which aspects of similarity are most important are brought to bear. The presence of lead in a writing implement makes it a pencil and not a pen, regardless of the nature of its casing. Similarly, a huge bill with a distensible pouch makes a bird a pelican and not a pigeon.

Traditionally, biological classification schemes have largely grouped and named birds on the basis of anatomical similarity. Degrees of similarity were eventually acknowledged by hierarchical groupings devised in the 18th century by Swedish naturalist Carolus Linnaeus. Species were defined as those groups of animals and plants that were more similar to each other than to any other organisms; they were designated by two-part (binomial) scientific names derived from Latin and Greek. The scientific name identifies an organism's *genus* (the name's first part) and *species* (the second part). A genus is a group of similar species, a *family* is a group of similar genera, an *order* is a group of similar families, a *class* is a group of similar orders, a *phylum* is a group of similar classes, and a *kingdom* is a group of similar phyla.

This system is still in use. Thus a Red Phalarope *(Phalaropus fulicaria)* belongs to the species *fulicaria,* the genus *Phalaropus* (phalaropes), the family Scolopacidae (sandpipers, phalaropes, and allies), the order Charadriiformes (shorebirds, gulls,

*Convergent evolution. Historically, classification schemes have been based on the degree of similarity among organisms. But this approach can be misleading when it comes to understanding evolutionary relationships. For example, the Magellanic Penguin (*Spheniscus magellanicus, *left) and the Thick-billed Murre (*Uria lomvia, *right) have converged on a similar body form because they are both seabirds that swim underwater in search of food, yet they are not at all closely related.*

auks, and allies), the class Aves (all birds), the phylum Chordata (all animals with a hollow nerve-cord along the back, including birds), and the kingdom Animalia (all animals, including vertebrates).

Additional levels of classification are also sometimes recognized. For example, species are sometimes subdivided into groups that breed in different geographic areas and that differ in slight, though consistent, ways from each other, but that are not considered sufficiently distinct to warrant status as separate species. These groups are referred to as subspecies, or races, and are named using a trinomial: *Passerculus sandwichensis beldingi* is the scientific name for "Belding's" Savannah Sparrow, a subspecies of the Savannah Sparrow *(Passerculus sandwichensis)* found in southern California saltmarshes.

Separating species. Since evolution is an ongoing process, determining when two groups of organisms are sufficiently distinct to be considered separate species is not always easy. For example, the Northwestern Crow (top) and the American Crow (bottom) are largely identical, yet they are currently classified as separate species based on slight differences in size and voice.

After Darwin proposed that new species arose by differentiation from old ones, the shortcomings of the earliest classification systems became apparent. Aside from their inherent subjectivity, classifications based on similarity alone do not necessarily convey information about the relationships among groups. Although similarity is a clue to relatedness (and indeed, all methods of classifying animals use similarity in some way), it can also be misleading. For example, the auks are superficially similar to penguins in many important ways, but these two groups are not at all closely related. Instead, their similarities result from *convergent evolution,* whereby similar features evolve independently in different groups that have similar lifestyles.

Most modern biologists believe that a classification of organisms should explicitly address degrees of relatedness among them and thus indicate, by its structure, the pattern of evolutionary history—the *phylogeny*—that gave rise to the groups we recognize today.

Methods of Classification
At present there are two fundamental approaches to building a classification.

Phenetic methods of classification simply group species into clusters based on some measure of their overall similarity. For example, a practitioner may take measurements of 30 bones in each bird's body, combine the measurements for each bird into an index that represents the bird's size and shape, and then group the birds according to the similarity of their index scores. These methods do not directly consider evolutionary relationships, but it is usually assumed that the most similar species are the most closely related. Because of convergent evolution, however, this assumption may not be true in some cases.

Cladistic (or *phylogenetic*) methods of classification are quite different. First, practitioners attempt to identify a group of characteristics (for example, bone features, behaviors, or genetic traits) that vary within a group of species. They then classify variations in those characteristics for each species. For example, if nest-building behavior was one of the characteristics, then each species could be coded according to whether or not its members build a cup nest or a nest with a roof. Once all the species have been classified according to each characteristic, an algorithm is used to determine the simplest way in which the observed pattern of variation in each characteristic could have arisen, assuming that all the species arose from a common ancestor. Cladistic methods do not combine the information on all the characteristics into a single index of similarity. Instead they create a "family tree" out of the patterns of variation in the characteristics.

Both of these methods can use many different types of information. Linnaeus's scheme was essentially phenetic in that he grouped birds on the basis of how similar their structure and plumage appeared to be to him. More recent phenetic methods are more sophisticated but use the same general approach. For example, ornithologists Charles Sibley and Jon Ahlquist's 1990 classification of the birds of the world uses phenetic information. In their scheme, the relationships among birds were determined using DNA–DNA hybridization. This method provides a single measure of the overall similarity of the DNA strands of pairs of bird species (see box). Many other recent systematic studies that use genetic information use cladistic methods.

In both phenetic and cladistic studies, the choice of characteristics and the

exact methods used to build the classification can influence the outcome. Different sets of characteristics, when used to examine relationships among the same group of birds, can result in (sometimes very) different phylogenies.

How are we to know which is the correct phylogeny? The sparseness of the fossil record means that we can never know the evolutionary history of any group for certain; therefore all phylogenies are hypotheses about a group's evolutionary history. As with any hypothesis, a phylogeny can be refuted by new or conflicting data; thus ornithological classifications are not static edifices, but works in progress.

In practice, avian systematists weigh the evidence for and against phylogenies, and look for the best-supported phylogeny given the available data. When many kinds of data tend to produce the same phylogeny (that is, show congruence), more confidence is placed in the phylogeny as an explanation of the relationships among organisms.

What Information Is Used to Build Classifications?

Many kinds of characteristics can be, and are, used to build classifications. *Morphological data* are those that arise from measurement of characteristics of a bird's form or appearance. Examples include the color of the plumage or bare parts of the skin and the presence, absence, or shape of skeletal or other anatomical structures. Morphological data have the longest history of use for building avian classifications because the earliest taxonomists lacked the means to observe and measure anything other than the bodies of birds.

With the advent of portable optics, it became easier to observe, characterize, and quantify the behavior typical of a species, and *behavioral data* are now often used to build phylogenies. Among the behavioral data used for classifications of birds have been sounds (including, but not limited to, vocalizations), stereotyped display movements, nest structure, and

DNA–DNA Hybridization

DNA–DNA hybridization measures the genetic similarity of two kinds of birds by determining how strongly their strands of DNA can be "mated." All DNA consists of two nucleotide chains (or strands) bonded to each other in the form of a double helix. All DNA strands are made up of only four kinds of nucleotides, each with a unique base: adenine (A), guanine (G), thymine (T), and cytosine (C). The order in which these appear on the strands differs among species. The two strands are linked by hydrogen bonds between As and Ts and between Gs and Cs.

In any individual of a given species, the DNA strands are strongly bonded to one another because all the nucleotide bases in each strand "line up" with their complementary base on the other strand, and all bond so that the two strands form a double helix. These bonds can be broken, and the strands separated, by heating the DNA.

If, after separation by heating, single strands of DNA from two kinds of birds are mixed together, some of them will "hybridize"—bond with a strand of DNA from the other kind of bird, forming a "hybrid" double helix containing one strand of DNA from each bird.

DNA–DNA hybridization analysis depends on the idea that if the birds are closely related, the hybrid double helix will be strong and stable because most of the bases on the two strands line up. If the birds are distantly related, fewer bases will be opposite their complementary base, and the double helix formed will be weak and easily broken.

The temperature at which the hybrid DNA separates can be used to infer how similar the two types of DNA are, since a better match requires a higher temperature to separate. This temperature can be used as a measure of how genetically similar the two kinds of birds are.

Charles Sibley and Jon Ahlquist used this approach to create a phylogeny (pattern of evolutionary history) of birds that differs in many ways from traditional classifications. Some of their conclusions about relationships among birds have been accepted—for example, that the storks and New World vultures are very closely related. Others have not.

Although Sibley and Ahlquist's classification scheme is now frequently cited by some in the birding and ornithological communities, it is by no means wholly or even largely accepted by all professional systematists or by the AOU's Committee on Classification and Nomenclature.

Avian systematists have criticized Sibley and Ahlquist's work on several counts, including their corrections of the error associated with their measurements, the assumptions they made about the way the genome evolves, and the fact that they only did a small percentage of all the possible DNA–DNA hybridizations among the species included in their classification. (To hybridize the DNA of every species of bird with every other species would require an impractically large number of experiments—Sibley and Ahlquist did about 1,700 crosses.) Despite these criticisms, the Sibley and Ahlquist classification is a monumental body of work and has revolutionized avian systematics by generating new ideas about avian evolution and relationships, and by stimulating further research.

*Changing classification. Although New World vultures were long classified as close relatives of the hawks, DNA–DNA hybridization and other studies have consistently supported the idea that New World vultures are in fact most closely related to storks. Shown are a Wood Stork (*Mycteria americana, left*) and a Turkey Vulture (*Cathartes aura, right*).*

Classification using behavioral data. For a long time the Willow (left) and Alder (right) Flycatchers were considered to be a single species, "Traill's Flycatcher." Among the criteria that scientists used to recognize them as different species were their distinctive vocalizations.

breeding systems. Behavioral data sometimes are particularly useful in revealing species that are morphologically extremely similar. For example, the Alder Flycatcher *(Empidonax alnorum)* and the Willow Flycatcher *(E. traillii)* were once considered a single species but are now recognized as separate species, in part because of differences in their vocalizations.

Biochemical data are of relatively recent origin (the means to acquire them became available only toward the end of the 20th century) and arise from techniques that allow observation and measurement of biologically active chemical compounds, especially DNA. The data produced by biochemical techniques are frequently referred to collectively as "genetic," although some biochemical techniques produce characterizations of gene products (such as proteins) or indirect measures of characteristics of the genome (for example, DNA–DNA hybridization; see box), while others directly describe the genetic code itself.

For example, before their DNA–DNA hybridization studies, Charles Sibley and his associates spent some years characterizing the differences among birds by using the molecular structure of the proteins in their egg whites, based on the assumption that closely related birds should have similar proteins. Similarly, for much of the 1980s many systematists used *gel electrophoresis,* a process that sorts (and thus makes it possible to identify) variants of common enzymes *(allozymes)* from bird body tissues by their molecular weights.

These gene products appear to evolve relatively slowly in birds and so they may not distinguish populations of birds that have been isolated for fairly short periods of time. For the most part, egg protein and allozyme data have been supplanted by data directly characterizing the genetic material itself. These kinds of data are differentiated by, among other things, which part of the cell the DNA being examined came from.

Mitochondrial DNA data characterize the composition of the circular DNA molecules found only in the mitochondria, the cell structures where energy storage and use takes place. Mitochondrial DNA evolves rapidly and is maternally inherited; an individual always gets all of its mitochondrial DNA from its mother.

Most recently, systematists have begun to use *nuclear DNA* data. Nuclear DNA data arise from analysis of the composition of the DNA drawn from the nucleus, the cell structure that controls all aspects of a cell's biology. Nuclear DNA is inherited in equal proportions from both mother and father in sexually reproducing animals like birds; thus the variation among birds in nuclear DNA tends to be high and reflects evolution in the entire population, rather than just the maternal lineages.

The increasing use of biochemical data to classify birds has given researchers a wealth of new information with which to examine the relationships among birds, but morphological and behavioral data continue to be widely used and can be extremely important when evaluating relationships. Sometimes several different types of information are combined into a single analysis, and information from a variety of sources is frequently used when considering changes to major classification schemes. Even with all this new information, however, there remain many uncertainties about avian relationships and there is clearly still much work to be done.

Species Concepts

Any attempt to build a phylogeny reflecting the relationships among species eventually culminates in the original problem: How do we recognize and define a species, the basic unit of systematic analysis? At present, the two most hotly argued species definitions in ornithology are the Biological Species Concept and the Phylogenetic Species Concept.

Biological Species Concept The Biological Species Concept (BSC), which was proposed by Ernst Mayr in 1942, defines a species as a group of "interbreeding natural populations that are reproductively isolated from other such groups." Two birds are reproductively isolated from each other if they cannot successfully produce offspring that can themselves reproduce.

Reproductive isolation takes several forms, some that prevent mating and some that prevent the development of healthy, fertile offspring even when mating occurs. For instance, where they occur together Clark's *(Aechmophorus clarkii)* and Western *(A. occidentalis)* Grebes are reproductively isolated from one another by their advertising calls—birds typically do not respond to advertising calls that do not match their own, and this prevents mating. The inability of the hybrid offspring of Eastern *(Sturnella magna)* and Western *(S. neglecta)* Meadowlarks to produce fertile eggs is another example of reproductive isolation.

The BSC has great intuitive appeal and has had an enormous influence on avian taxonomy and systematics. However, this and competing species concepts are currently under intense debate. On the broadest scale, one of the most important criticisms of the BSC, both theoretically and practically, is that it is not relevant for the many organisms that do not reproduce sexually, such as aphids and algae. Another is that the concept cannot be used to classify extinct organisms, because we can never know whether or not they could have interbred. Even if the BSC is restricted only to sexually reproducing animals such as birds, practical problems remain.

Critics point out that if populations of similar birds remain geographically isolated, we can only guess whether they would interbreed if they met. Proponents of the BSC counter that genetic and behavioral data exist that make it possible to infer whether geographically isolated birds could interbreed.

Another criticism is that strict adherence to the BSC would prescribe combining ("lumping") distinctly different birds—such as the Blue-winged *(Vermivora pinus)* and Golden-winged *(V. chrysoptera)* Warblers—into a single species because they interbreed widely and produce fertile offspring.

Most troublesome are cases that involve species that are not even each other's closest relatives. For instance, Bullock's Oriole *(Icterus bullockii)* and the Baltimore Oriole *(I. galbula)* were originally described as separate species but then were lumped into a single species (the "Northern Oriole") because their hybrid offspring are fertile. Subsequently they have been re-split, at least in part because genetic data indicate that Bullock's Oriole is more closely related to the Streak-backed Oriole *(I. pustulatus)* than to the Baltimore Oriole.

Proponents of the BSC suggest that these problems can be overcome by a careful analysis of whether two groups of birds can freely interbreed.

Phylogenetic Species Concept The Phylogenetic Species Concept (PSC) was first suggested in 1980 by evolutionary biologists Niles Eldredge and Joel Cracraft (and subsequently more explicitly formulated by Cracraft) as an alternative to the BSC. Its adoption has since been championed by several ornithologists, including Mary McKitrick and Robert Zink.

Squabbling over the details of the definition has resulted in several PSCs that differ subtly. One representative version defines a species as "the smallest aggregation of populations or lineages diagnosable by a unique combination of character states." In other words, a species is a group of birds related by evolutionary descent, all members of which are recognizably different, and in the same way, from all other birds. Under this definition, whether they can interbreed with another group of birds is less important than whether they are, and remain, differentiated from other groups.

Again, there is some intuitive appeal to this species definition—if it looks different, it is different—but the PSC is also not without problems. Critics of the PSC question how the distinctiveness of a population is maintained if not through reproductive isolation. Another problem is the one we started with: How distinct does a group of organisms have to be for us to call it a species?

As the technology of genetic analysis improves, it becomes possible to differentiate populations at smaller and smaller scales. This increase in resolution is desirable from a theoretical point of view—since it provides much more information about evolutionary history and pattern—but its practical implications are daunting to some. For example, an immediate application of the PSC to ornithological classification would result in extensive subdivision ("splitting") of currently recognized species, and many

"Lumping" and "splitting." Although once "lumped" as a single species because they hybridize and produce fertile young, Bullock's Oriole (top) and the Baltimore Oriole (bottom) are now not even thought to be each other's closest relatives.

subspecies recognized under the BSC would be considered full species. Proponents of the PSC have estimated that widespread use of this concept could double the number of bird species that are recognized around the world.

Critics also hold that the PSC suffers from the lack of a biological foundation—that is, the system can be applied to inanimate objects as well as to biological organisms.

The AOU Check-list The standard classification used by most North American ornithologists (and which has been followed in this book) is the American Ornithologists' Union's (AOU) *Check-list of North American Birds*. In the most recent (seventh) edition of the Check-list, the AOU's Committee on Classification and Nomenclature states that it "strongly and unanimously continues to endorse the biological species concept."

In practice, the committee incorporates a number of practical considerations when deciding whether populations of birds are "essentially" reproductively isolated; thus Herring *(Larus argentatus)*, Glaucous *(L. hyperboreus)*, Glaucous-winged *(L. glaucescens)*, and Western *(L. occidentalis)* Gulls are not lumped, despite the hybridization that occurs where their ranges meet. Moreover, the committee is undeniably influenced by information other than the inability to interbreed in its decisions about whether to lump populations into a single species or split them into two or more species.

The AOU Check-list, like any classification of biological organisms, is constantly being revised and refined. It will never be "completed." As differing views on species concepts are hammered out and new (and new kinds of) data are collected, the consensus on how to classify the diversity we see in birds will continue to change. The only certainty about the list, and about our understanding of the evolution of avian diversity, is that it is dynamic.

Rick Cech and Margaret Rubega

Behavior

A tightly packed flock of Dunlins *(Calidris alpina)* flashes along the edge of a beach, the whole flock turning as one, as if each bird is listening to the commands of a single leader. A group of Common Ravens *(Corvus corax)* boldly enters a campground, opening packages and stealing food from inside lunch boxes. A Green Heron *(Butorides virescens)* uses a feather as a fishing lure, placing the feather at various spots on the surface of a pond to try to attract small fish to within its reach. The behavior of birds such as these has fascinated naturalists, ornithologists, and amateur birders for centuries.

The Study of Bird Behavior

The modern scientific study of bird behavior began with the seminal work of Charles Darwin, a keen bird-watcher as well as a prominent scientist, on the mating displays, sexual selection, and evolution of island birds. The fascination with bird behavior began to find a firm scientific footing in the 1920s, when a group of mostly European researchers pioneered the science of ethology, the study of specific types of animal behavior through observation of free-ranging organisms. Because they were familiar and easily observed, birds were a popular study group for early ethologists.

Early studies concentrated on *stereotyped behaviors:* those performed with little variation in response to specific situations or stimuli. A gull chick pecks at the red spot on its parents' bill to encourage the adult to regurgitate food. The chick will peck at any red dot on a long, slender shape; the pecking is a stereotyped response to the stimulus. Such behaviors are instinctual; that is, they do not need to be learned, although they can be modified with experience. For example, gull chicks will peck at the

Instinctual responses. Newborn goslings will cower if this model passes overhead with the stubby end forward in imitation of a hawk but will ignore the model if it passes over with the opposite end forward, creating a less threatening silhouette.

first red spot on a bill they see, but the chicks will get more accurate and hit the right spot more frequently as they age.

A classic example of traditional ethology is Konrad Lorenz's demonstration that goslings kept in his presence during a critical imprinting period shortly after hatching would thereafter follow him around as though he were their mother. Another early, imaginative series of experiments showed that young geese would ignore a cross-shaped model passing overhead with its long end pointed forward (to resemble a long-necked goose in flight) but would cower or flee if the same shape passed by with its short end pointed forward (to resemble a long-tailed hawk). Classic books in this tradition, such as Niko Tinbergen's *The Herring Gull's World* (1953), remain fascinating to read.

The study of animal behavior has expanded dramatically since the days when ethologists probed the significance of individual behavioral traits, and there now exist a variety of scientific approaches. Behavioral ecologists seek to understand how organisms use behavior to meet social and environmental challenges. These studies often involve quantifying the costs and benefits of various behaviors to individuals that perform them. Behavioral psychologists study the role of learning and experience in the development of behavior. Physiologists examine behavior by studying physiological systems, such as the sensory organs, the nervous system, and hormones. Other behaviorists look at the external cues—including weather, seasonal changes, and the behavior of other organisms—that trigger certain behaviors.

One key approach to understanding avian behavior is time- and energy-budgeting, and how these are managed by an individual bird to maximize its reproductive success. Ornithologists have paid increasing attention in recent years to the strategies birds employ in energy-budgeting as a means of unraveling the mysteries of their behavior. The life tasks a North American bird must accomplish in the course of a year impose huge metabolic burdens. For instance, ecologists calculate that a White-crowned Sparrow (Zonotrichia leucophrys) must find a seed every four to five seconds during the winter day if it is to survive. Because of the extreme energetic pressures many birds face, they seldom attempt major life activities (such as molt, reproduction, and migration) simultaneously, instead performing each at a different time of the year.

To understand bird behavior, it is necessary to pursue several fundamentally different lines of inquiry: First, researchers take a descriptive approach and quantify the form and rate of performance of a behavior. At the next level, they investigate the environmental stimuli that are associated with the behavior or affect how it is performed. Finally, and perhaps most important, researchers use experiments to investigate how birds' skills and behavioral abilities relate to hypothesized benefits. Behavior is the most direct tool a bird has available to respond to its environment, and it ultimately determines whether it survives and breeds.

The Function of Behaviors

For birds, a useful distinction can be drawn between *self-maintenance behavior* that is aimed at accomplishing some specific task to maintain the physical condition of the individual, and *social behavior* that is intended to communicate information to another individual. Classic examples of maintenance behaviors include feeding, preening of feathers, and bathing, while vocalizations and courtship behaviors are social in nature. Sometimes this dichotomy is blurred because many behaviors function partially for maintenance and partially socially. Some maintenance behaviors have a social dimension. For example, feeding is a maintenance behavior, but many species feed while in flocks, and their foraging behavior is influenced by their social interactions.

Although social behavior is highly developed in birds, ornithologists still study maintenance because it accounts for a very significant portion of a bird's overall time and energy budget. In addition, many social behaviors appear to be derived from maintenance activities; that is, many displays are composed of fragments of maintenance behavior, performed in a ritualized fashion (see Displays Using Physical Movements and Posture, below).

Foraging. *Most birds spend much of their time foraging just to support their high energy needs. Here a Wilson's Phalarope (Phalaropus tricolor) is shown searching for small invertebrate prey.*

Daily and Seasonal Rhythms

Although many behaviors can be performed at any time, some occur in very predictable patterns that track the time of day or the seasons. These biological rhythms set the stage for all of a bird's other activities.

Daily Activity Patterns

A *circadian rhythm* is a regular, biological activity cycle with a duration of approximately 24 hours. Even when an animal is kept in total darkness, its sleep-and-wakefulness cycle maintains itself, revealing the existence of an internal biological clock that drives daily levels of wakefulness, body temperature, and other aspects of physiology. This biological clock is partially controlled by the pineal gland, a light-sensitive organ housed within the brain. Removal of this gland causes the circadian cycle in birds to disappear.

Even when the pineal gland is not manipulated, researchers have discovered that the circadian rhythm does not quite maintain itself without input from the environment. If an animal is kept in total darkness for a long period, its biological rhythms begin to atrophy. A natural day-night cycle is needed to tie the biological clock to a 24-hour day. If a researcher moves an animal used to one time zone to another time zone and exposes it to sunlight conditions there, the animal's biological clock will reset itself gradually, over a number of days, to the new conditions.

Seasonal Activity Patterns

Not all behaviors need to be performed on a daily basis. Some activities, such as territorial defense, breeding, and migration, occur only at specific times of the year. These seasonally appropriate behaviors, called *circannual behaviors*, together with necessary annual events such as molt, create a seasonal pattern of behavior called the annual cycle. Some circannual behaviors require a lot of time and energy and must be integrated into a daily routine already crowded with challenging maintenance demands.

Migratory activity is exceptionally strenuous, involving peak energy demands as much as seven to 15 times greater than the bird would use when resting. These higher energy demands may be expended over periods of continuous flight lasting between two and six days without rest. Scientists estimate that an equivalent feat of physical endurance for a human would be to run 4-minute miles for 80 hours straight.

Another energy-intensive activity is reproduction, which includes display and territorial behavior, courtship and mate selection, copulation, nest-building, egg development, incubation, care of the young, and pair-bond maintenance. At its peak, reproductive activity may increase a bird's total daily energy requirements by 50 percent, and its daytime energy needs by more than 100 percent. In males, displays and territorial defense account for a significant share of the extra activity, while in females, the production of eggs may double energy use.

Nest-building requires a variable amount of time and energy, depending on the type of nest and the availability of suitable materials. In some species it is a significant undertaking: Orioles weave fine "bag nests" of plant fibers lined with mosses and hair. Belted Kingfishers *(Ceryle alcyon)* spend up to a week digging their tunnel nests (2"/5 cm in diameter, up to 10'/3 m long) in riverside banks. Other species, such as terns and auks, may lay their eggs on bare sand or bedrock without any attempt at nest-building.

The daily energetic demands of reproduction can be substantial enough that they may not be met by daily food intake alone and therefore must be satisfied in part from accumulated fat reserves. The lengthy aerial display flights of male Sprague's Pipits *(Anthus spragueii)*, for example, performed repeatedly in the morning for as long as three hours, place great demands on the bird's accumulated bodily stores. Sometimes the process of building reserves for the reproductive cycle involves the accumulation of specific nutrients. Female Red-cockaded Woodpeckers *(Picoides borealis)* will store away bone fragments prior to the breeding season, apparently to use as a source of calcium during egg formation.

Although not a behavior per se, molt (the regular replacement of feathers; see

Migration. *Migration can be an extremely costly behavior for birds, which must expend a huge amount of energy during the long flights between winter and summer habitats. The White-winged Scoter* (Melanitta fusca) *migrates from central Canada and Alaska to winter along the Pacific and Atlantic coasts of North America. Shown here are a female (left) and two males.*

the chapter Flight, Form, and Function) requires many behavioral adjustments by birds. Molt is quite expensive metabolically, as birds require a substantial quantity of protein and minerals for feather synthesis. Experiments have found that daily energy needs during "peak molt" increase some 10 to 15 percent in warm surroundings and as much as 25 percent in colder weather. Further, while molt is in progress, the birds' feathers function less effectively in providing insulation and in sustaining flight. Some species (such as ducks) even become flightless when molting, which increases their vulnerability to predation.

Because the energetic costs of each of these activities are great, it makes sense that birds rarely attempt more than one of them at a time. Obviously, no birds migrate and breed at the same time. Few birds molt while they are breeding or while they are migrating. Some North American species, such as Cassin's Sparrow *(Aimophila cassinii),* may be molting when conditions become favorable for breeding; in cases such as these, the birds suspend their molt and then resume growing new feathers when breeding is over.

A combination of molt and migration has been documented in some North American birds. Some Greater Yellowlegs *(Tringa melanoleuca)* start molting before fall migration, suspend their molt while moving south, and then finish molting on their wintering grounds. In species

such as the Painted Bunting *(Passerina ciris)* and Bullock's Oriole *(Icterus bullockii),* birds migrate in the fall to areas south of their breeding range, molt into their basic plumage for the winter, and then continue their migration. Even these species with a *molt-migration,* however, do not undergo both of these energetically expensive stages of the life cycle simultaneously.

Control and Coordination of Seasonal Activity

While various physical and environmental factors act as cues for the control of seasonal activities, for most birds that nest in the temperate zone the most important external cue is change in day length. Increasing daylight periods in the spring set into motion a series of events that carry well into the following autumn.

Birds have light receptors in the brain that are sensitive to the extremely low light intensities that penetrate into the brain itself. Birds sense the length of day and night with these receptors rather than with their eyes. Stimulation of the brain receptors in the spring initiates a series of hormonal changes that results in the production of testosterone in the male and estrogen and other hormones in the female. These physiological changes in turn orchestrate a complex suite of seasonal behaviors that determines the timing of reproductive activities, migration, and molt.

In late summer birds enter what is called the *photorefractory period*, when their hormonal system ceases to respond to long daylight periods with a renewed production of sex hormones. Even if days are artificially lengthened in the laboratory, no response occurs. The effect in migrant species is to terminate reproductive behavior (especially extra breeding attempts) while there is still enough mild weather left to prepare for migration. Tropical birds have a weakly developed photorefractory period, or none at all, consistent with their reduced need to prepare for migration late in the summer and the reduced seasonal change in photoperiod in the tropics.

Suspended molt and migration. Although most birds molt either before or after they migrate south in the fall, some species, including this Greater Yellowlegs, may begin their molt on the breeding grounds, suspend the molt during fall migration, and then finish the molt on the winter range. During migration these birds may lack some flight feathers in their wings, as shown here.

Daily Maintenance Behaviors

Many of the avian behaviors that birders can observe throughout the year are life-sustaining activities collectively referred to as maintenance behaviors.

Feeding

The vast array of behaviors that birds have evolved in connection with feeding can be grouped into a number of broad categories: searching for food; identifying food; acquiring food; manipulating food; transporting food to a nest or cache; and recovering cached food for later consumption.

The exact behaviors involved in these tasks vary greatly in character and extent, depending mainly on the nature of

each species' diet. For example, albatrosses, which specialize in feeding on large but widely dispersed prey items such as squids, adopt a flight style that allows them to efficiently cover large areas with minimal energy expenditure. The primary adaptation for this style of flight is a wing shape that allows albatrosses to glide on minimal air currents (see the Aerodynamics section in the chapter Flight, Form, and Function, and the Shearwaters and Petrels chapter). Many raptors likewise spend considerable time soaring in search of a prey item (such as a mouse or a snake) that ventures into the open, a behavior assisted by their keen eyesight and broad, rounded wings.

Searching for Food Some types of food, such as brightly colored fruits, are readily found and eaten, but most birds must search for food items that are hidden in their environment. Food items can be unpredictable in their seasonal availability and across space. One explanation for site fidelity is that birds that get to know a site will be able to learn where to find food in their home range and therefore can search efficiently. Flocking is also partially a response to the problem of searching for food, as many eyes can search a large region more effectively than a single pair of eyes.

Seasonal activity. In most North American songbirds the initiation of breeding activities is cued by the spring's increasing periods of daylight. This American Robin (Turdus migratorius) *is carrying material to build its nest in preparation for breeding.*

Foraging of herons and egrets. Large members of the heron family, such as the Great Egret (Ardea alba, top left) and the Great Blue Heron (Ardea herodias, bottom left), often stalk their prey by quietly moving through shallow marshes and waiting for fish and other aquatic animals to swim close enough to be grabbed. The Snowy Egret (Egretta thula, right) will vary this technique by lightly stirring the surface of the water with its yellow toes; such action may either attract or scare fish into moving out of their hiding places.

Identifying Food Identification of food items is often a complex process; birds must select items that provide the necessary energy and nutrients, and avoid items that are unpalatable. Parrots, for instance, must distinguish among different kinds of fruit and determine which ones are ripe. It has been suggested that parrots' relatively high degree of intelligence may have evolved in connection with the complex food distinctions they need to make. In certain cases, rather than selecting foods, birds must avoid particular items when foraging.

Because birds benefit from efficient foraging, a bird needs to balance several factors in food selection, including ease of foraging and nutritional value. Some seeds eaten by birds are hard-shelled but nutritious, while others are easier to open yet less nourishing. Seed-eating bird species with relatively thick bills may be more efficient at opening hard seeds but may also be less adept at opening smaller or softer seeds than their thinner-billed relatives.

Acquiring Food Acquiring food items offers behavioral challenges for predatory birds whose prey can evade capture by fleeing. Some species of herons and egrets stalk quietly in marshes, moving slowly enough not to set off the built-in "motion detectors" that protect many of their prey species. Once a heron gets close, it spears or seizes its victim with a quick strike of its bill.

Many raptors capture their prey while it is on the ground or perched in a tree, administering the kill by piercing the prey with talons and sometimes also biting the back of its neck. Peregrine Falcons *(Falco peregrinus)* are noted for their aerial pursuit of prey and dramatic "kills" in which they capture or strike their prey in mid-flight. Stooping Peregrines sometimes flip over and grab a bird in flight from underneath, literally plucking the victim from the air. The most elaborate hunting technique among raptors is that of Harris's Hawk *(Parabuteo unicinctus)*, renowned for its complex team hunting (see the Hawks and Allies chapter).

Manipulating Food When a bird acquires a food item, it must often manipulate it in order to swallow or carry it. Songbirds will commonly remove inedible parts of large insects, such as the legs, before carrying the insect to the hungry young in the nest. Cardinals and grosbeaks use their heavy, conical bills to remove the thick husks of seeds before swallowing. A large, spiny fish will not go down a heron's gullet any old way; such a prey item often must be flipped many times in the bill before it is positioned properly for ingestion.

Transporting Food Once a bird obtains food, it may either eat it on the spot or transport it to a remote nest or cache site. Manipulating food items for easy transport is at times a formidable task, especially when a bird must carry a large quantity of small items over a considerable distance. In addition to holding food in the crop, birds have evolved a number of other means of carrying food. For example, puffins can align small fish sideways in their bills, allowing many fish to be carried to the young in a single flight. Other seabirds carry masses of small prey in pouches under the tongue or in the throat.

Recovering Cached Food A few species make great efforts to store food for later use, a behavior called caching. Acorn Woodpeckers *(Melanerpes formicivorus)* are known for their elaborate caching methods: They store acorns in holes chiseled with their bills, usually in the bark of live oaks or sycamores, but also sometimes in telephone poles or other wooden structures. As many as 50,000 acorns have been cached in a single tree.

Caching birds such as Clark's Nutcrackers *(Nucifraga columbiana)* are able to remember the occasionally far-flung locations of their cache sites with con-siderable accuracy by using prominent landscape features as cues. Species vary in the length of time they leave food cached and evidently in how long they can remember cache locations.

Feather Care

Well-preened feathers are necessary for insulation, waterproofing, aerodynamic efficiency, and effective social communication (via plumage displays). Loss of feather integrity due to parasites, fungi, bacteria, and wear can reduce the insulating and aerodynamic properties of the feathers and render display plumage less attractive to potential mates. Birds spend a large portion of their time preening; the exact amount depends on climate, weather conditions, feather function, and other factors.

A bird preens by fluffing its feathers and then combing them with its bill. This is done to ensure that all of the feather substructures are properly aligned and correctly interlocked (see the Feathers section in the chapter Flight, Form, and Function). A preening bird also squeezes a waxy oil onto its bill from the uropygial (or preen) gland—located at the base of the tail in most birds—and spreads the preen oil over its feathers. Ornithologists once believed that the primary function of preen oil was to provide waterproofing; the prevailing view is that preen oil is more important in keeping feathers from drying out and

Spatial memory. *Birds that cache food for later use, such as this Clark's Nutcracker, use distinctive rocks, logs, and other habitat features as cues to the locations of their buried food. Memory of these cues allows the bird to return and dig up most of the caches.*

Preening. *Feathers need daily care and maintenance; here a Bullock's Oriole uses its bill to smooth the vanes of its tail feathers.*

becoming brittle. Chemicals in the preen oil deter the growth of feather parasites, such as fungi and bacteria, and may deter feather mites and lice as well.

Areas that a bird cannot reach with the bill, such as parts of the head and neck, are usually preened by scratching with the foot. Some birds engage in mutual grooming (or *allopreening*) of hard-to-reach parts of the body.

Overall feather care is a complicated and time-consuming process. In addition to the time and energy devoted to normal preening, considerable energy is required for maintenance of emerging feathers during molt. The emergence of fresh *pinfeathers* from the skin in rigid shafts seems to be a highly uncomfort-

Allopreening Bushtits. *A Bushtit* (Psaltriparus minimus) *straightens its neighbor's feathers in hard-to-reach places. Such sharing of maintenance duties also can be a social behavior because it can help strengthen pair bonds or flock membership.*

able process. The bird must carefully remove the sheath around each new feather by biting or scratching as the feather emerges.

Locomotion

Birds have highly developed and well-diversified means of locomotion. The most common method is flight, but many birds also hop, walk, run, dive, and swim underwater; some even slide from place to place. Whether a given songbird walks or hops can be a useful identification tool, as members of different species often move in consistently different ways.

Most waterbirds use their feet to propel themselves through or under the water, but some aquatic species also use their wings to "fly" underwater. Penguins' wings are particularly adapted to this form of underwater locomotion, as they are reduced to the avian equivalent of flippers. The auks, the Northern Hemisphere's ecological equivalent of penguins, also use their small wings to propel themselves underwater. Unlike penguins, however, auks have retained the ability to fly.

The importance of diving and swimming for a particular species is reflected in the placement of its feet. Birds that spend a great deal of time in the water have a design conflict that they must overcome. The best placement for the feet of a swimming bird is toward the rear of the body, where paddling best moves

Maintaining a center of balance. Waterbirds that frequently walk on land, such as the American Wigeon (Anas americana, *left), have legs placed close to their center of gravity for better balance. This allows them to walk easily, but makes their swimming relatively inefficient. The legs of Common Loons (Gavia immer, *right) and other diving birds are placed more toward the rear of the body, making them efficient swimmers but poor walkers.*

the bird through water. To stand and walk easily on land, however, feet need to be placed near a bird's center of gravity, under the middle of the body. Loons, grebes, and cormorants have feet placed so far back on the body that they swim efficiently but are very awkward on land. Geese and dabbling ducks such as Mallards *(Anas platyrhynchos)* have feet more toward the center of the body and thus can walk on land much more easily but are poorer swimmers compared to the diving species.

Concealment

Concealment and seeking shelter are essential skills for birds in order to lessen the risks of predation and exposure to the elements. Anyone who has attempted to locate a furtive songbird in a dense thicket is familiar with the way a bird can conceal itself behind foliage and watch the observer through a small opening, with only a portion of its head visible. Concealment is also critical for avian predators attempting to sneak up on their prey.

Some marsh birds, such as rails and bitterns, instinctively remain motionless when alarmed, which hides them in the dense vegetation that is their normal habitat. When out in the open, however, they behave as if they are invisible and can sometimes be found standing motionless in plain view, making no effort to find a more effective hiding place.

Migration

One of the most dramatic forms of seasonal behavior exhibited by North American birds is migration, the regular movement of individuals between their breeding and wintering areas. The number of birds taking part in this semiannual event is so enormous, and the geographic territory they cover so vast, that it is difficult to gain a clear perspective on the process from any one vantage point. Perhaps this is why the pervasive role that migration plays in avian life was not fully grasped until the 19th century. The ancients knew that some large birds occupied different territories in summer and winter, but they also believed that small birds hibernated. Swallows, for instance, were thought to spend the winter under the mud of ponds or high in the mountains.

Migration is distinct from other kinds of avian movements in that it is seasonal, predictable, and repeated each year. Species such as albatrosses may fly huge distances to forage when not attending their nests during the breeding season, but these movements are not seasonal, and they do not result in the shift of populations from breeding to wintering habitat. Similarly, the movement of an individual from the area where it was hatched to another site where it will attempt to breed is called *dispersal* and does not fit the definition of migration.

Species such as Snowy Owls *(Nyctea scandiaca)* and many finches leave their breeding grounds only in harsh winters when food supplies are low. These movements are called *irruptions* or *invasions.* They differ from migration in that irruptions are not repeated annually and may be quite unpredictable.

Why Do Birds Migrate?

Migration was a central area of ornithological study during most of the 20th century. A fundamental question that researchers still seek to answer concerns the evolutionary costs and benefits that migrants experience. Why should a territory owner leave its hard-won piece of land and fly to parts unknown?

Migration can be understood to occur when its costs (which may be very high in terms of both energy and mortality risk) are lower than the benefits of using well-separated breeding and wintering grounds. Some species must migrate south in the winter because conditions are too harsh to support them on their breeding grounds. This is clearly true for insect-eating birds in Canada and the northern United States, where the numbers of available insects drop to almost zero along with the temperature. Unless an insectivorous bird can shift its diet in winter to fruit, insect eggs, or other more readily available food, it will not survive. Thus, despite the risks of migration, many birds may still fare better if they leave than if they brave the harsh northern winter.

It is less clear, however, why a bird would not remain as a resident on wintering grounds that may have a favorable climate year-round. A biological rationale may be found in differing rates of reproductive success between the tropical and temperate zones. If a northward migration in the spring results in higher reproductive success, it should benefit some birds to risk the journey. Temperate-zone nesters typically have larger clutches (four to six eggs or more) than do tropical breeders (two or three eggs). In addition, the interval between successive nestings for tropical birds is longer than for temperate species. Some tropical birds also suffer exceptionally high rates of nest predation.

These facts are consistent with the view that migrants fly north to breed in order to avail themselves of seasonally abundant food supplies, to avoid the high density of nest predators and parasites found in the tropics, and to take advantage of longer days for extended foraging.

Modes of Migration

Some migrants make long, nonstop flights over inhospitable habitats such as oceans, deserts, and mountains. Others make a series of "hops," of perhaps 150 to 200 miles (250–300 km) or shorter distances, pausing in between for a few days to refuel. In bad weather, birds that normally make long-distance flights may end up grounded for hours or days somewhere along the way. Such *fallouts* tend to delight local birders, but they are not a positive development from the standpoint of the migrant; for every bird that makes it to a safe resting spot when its migration is interrupted, many others might have perished.

Many migrants make the bulk of their movements at specific times of the day or night. *Diurnal migrants* often depend on thermal winds or updrafts (for example, hawks) or food resources that are available only during the day (swallows). Diurnal migrants fall into two groups, the *soarers* and the *non-soarers* (or *powered migrants*). Soaring consists of two components: rising by circling within rising air pockets and then gliding between the rising air pockets with few movements of the wings. The activity of soaring migrants (especially hawks) is concentrated in the midday hours when thermals occur. Some non-soaring diurnal migrants, such as blackbirds and swallows, are often *crepuscular,* typically beginning their flight shortly before dawn and flying most actively in the early morning, sometimes with a secondary activity peak in late afternoon.

Long-distance migration.
Among the champions of
migration, American Golden-
Plovers fly from eastern
Canada to South America
nonstop in the fall, passing
over open ocean for up to
several thousand miles without
making landfall. In spring,
these birds head north through
central North America to their
Arctic breeding grounds.

For other non-soarers, night provides the best conditions for migration because powered flight generates a large amount of body heat, and cooler nighttime temperatures allow this heat to be dissipated. Nighttime air tends to be less turbulent than daytime air, thus allowing the birds to maintain a steadier course while exerting less energy.

Nocturnal migrants, including wood-warblers, vireos, and thrushes, tend to commence their migratory flight about a half-hour after sunset. Visible on radar, this sometimes creates the impression of a great cloud rising from the landscape. It may be significant that the moment of departure for a nocturnal migrant coincides with the appearance of the first stars, yet also when it is still possible to make out the location of the setting sun below the horizon. Both cues may assist birds in orienting their flight (see Orientation and Navigation, below).

Long-distance migrants are species that move great distances, usually between continents, and include most birds that breed in North America and winter in the Caribbean or Central and South America. Species that move shorter distances, usually within continents, are called *short-distance migrants.* In mountainous regions, *elevational migrants* breed at the tops of mountains and move downslope to winter in the lowlands.

A final distinction can be made between *complete migrants,* species whose entire population leaves the breeding range, and *partial migrants,* species in which some individuals remain to overwinter on the breeding grounds. Some species show a range of migratory strategies, making it difficult to place them into such categories.

Migratory Behavior

Of the slightly more than 650 bird species that nest in North America, 75 percent engage in some form of migratory behavior. While wood-warblers account for a large percentage of migrant songbirds in terms of number of individuals, members of nearly every family of North American birds winter at least in part south of the United States.

During the last 50 years, scientists have accumulated a wealth of field data on the geography of migration, using a variety of techniques—including bird banding, seasonal censuses, tracking using radar, radio transmitters and satellites, and observation of migrants as they pass in front of the moon.

Many of today's birders were originally taught that migration occurs in rather well-defined channels, or *flyways,* that follow coastlines and major mountain and river systems. Field observations have confirmed that many individual species do follow historical migration routes quite faithfully, and that geographic features may funnel migrants into broadly defined corridors. But the high degree of dispersion and variability in migratory patterns suggests that migration does not occur in as neat a pattern as the flyways concept implies (see the Ducks, Geese, and Swans chapter).

One major theater of migratory activity that has been studied recently is the western Atlantic–Gulf of Mexico circuit.

Ornithologists have long known that American Golden-Plovers *(Pluvialis dominica)* make extended transoceanic flights each fall, traveling from eastern Canada or the northeastern United States to the northeastern coast of South America, an average flying distance of some 2,500 miles (4,000 km). Originally these plovers were thought to be the only birds to make such cross-Atlantic flights, but it is now known that tiny Blackpoll Warblers *(Dendroica striata)* and other species engage in similar migrations.

Studies of Dark-eyed Juncos *(Junco hyemalis)* from the early 1980s showed subtle migratory differences along age and sex lines. Specifically, adult female juncos migrate farthest south each winter, to the southern tier of the United States; young males migrate the shortest distance, often remaining in Canada; and adult males and young females winter at intermediate latitudes. Investigators explain these patterns by reasoning that young males may wish to remain nearest to the breeding grounds in order to have the best chance of obtaining a territory the following spring, before the socially dominant adult males arrive. Adult females may travel farthest south because they don't have to compete for territories and because winter survival increases as birds move farther south.

The Role of Fat
Fat is an ideal fuel for migratory birds. The amount of energy released per gram of metabolized fat is more than twice the amount released by burning carbohydrates or protein. Fat can be stored conveniently beneath the skin and in various cavities and organs around the body for efficient dispersion of weight. In addition, metabolized fat yields water (so-called *metabolic water*), again at a rate about twice that of carbohydrates or protein. Water production is particularly important since dehydration is as serious a threat to long-distance migrants as running out of fuel.

In nonmigrating birds, fat deposits generally account for 5 percent or less of the total body weight. Short-distance migrants carry between 15 and 25 percent fat (sometimes more). Long-distance migrants may build their fat reserves to 50 percent or more of their total body weight. Because of the thick subcutaneous fat layers they developed in the fall, Eskimo Curlews *(Numenius borealis)* were referred to as "dough-birds" by market hunters. Even very small birds sequester large amounts of fat relative to their size. A Ruby-throated Hummingbird *(Archilochus colubris)* adds 2 grams (0.07 oz) of fat to its 3-gram (0.11-oz) frame before setting out to fly nonstop across the Gulf of Mexico.

Ornithologists have developed mathematical models to predict how far a bird should be able to fly with a certain percentage of body weight as fat. It is estimated that a bird with 10 percent body fat has an effective migration range (assuming ideal flight conditions) of 300 to 500 miles (500–750 km), based on 10 to 20 hours of flying time. A bird with 50 percent body fat, by comparison, should be able to stay aloft for three to four days and achieve a total distance of about 1,800 to 2,500 miles (3,000–4,000 km).

Flight During Migration
Migrant birds have a greater degree of *primary projection* than nonmigrants; that is, the wings of long-distance migrants tend to be longer and more pointed than those of "short hop" migrants or sedentary relatives, and they produce less air resistance in flight without sacrificing lift. Migratory thrushes are a good example. The Hermit Thrush *(Catharus guttatus)*, a short-distance migrant, has a shorter primary projection than Swainson's *(C. ustulatus)* and Gray-cheeked *(C. minimus)* Thrushes, both of which fly to northern South America.

Of all the factors that determine migratory efficiency, the single most important variable may be the strength and direction of winds aloft. A strong headwind can decrease flight speed relative to a spot on the ground by 50 percent, and crosswinds also require additional energy expenditures. A strong tailwind, on the other hand, can increase flight efficiency dramatically. Radar studies indicate that migrants actively choose to migrate at times with appropriate wind direction, and they select their flight altitude in order to minimize headwinds and capitalize on tailwinds.

Birds obtain aerodynamic advantages by traveling in flocks. As a bird flies, the air moving around its wings and body deflects downward in some areas, such as just above or below the wing, while rising in other places; for example, circular air currents (called *vortices*) arise a few inches from each wingtip. Birds that travel alongside each other in linear or V-shaped flock formations capitalize on lift generated by their flockmates' vortices to assist flight. Theoretical energy gains may be as high as 40 percent, at least for large birds that stand to benefit most from extra lift because of their weight.

The soaring flight of some diurnal migrants involves specialized flight behavior and physical adaptations. The atmospheric phenomena behind this migratory style are *thermals,* upwellings of warm air caused by sunlight as it heats the ground layer. Thermals are often depicted as huge columns of warm air spiraling up from the ground, but in the temperate zone a better visual analogy would be the bubbles that boil up in a lava lamp. Soaring migrants hitch a ride on these ascending warm air masses to gain altitude.

When riding a thermal, soaring migrants spiral upward, wings extended fully with little or no flapping. Once the thermal has topped out, the migrant glides on to the next one, hopscotching its way along its migration route. Efficiency in both phases—soaring in the thermals and gliding between them—is important in determining the overall effectiveness of daytime migration.

Some soaring birds flap their wings occasionally as they glide between thermals to extend their travel distance and maintain airspeed. Soaring migrants often fly close to the bases of cumulus clouds formed by condensing thermals, but they seldom fly into the clouds for long, probably because of the lack of visibility and potentially dangerous air turbulence and precipitation.

Orientation and Navigation

Scientists have long wondered how migrating birds find their way, frequently at night, across vast geographical spaces to their ultimate destinations. The mystery is deepened by the uncanny accuracy with which many species are able to relocate specific breeding or wintering sites, year after year. Ornithologists know from more than 50 years of study and experimentation that migrating birds rely on various senses and behaviors to guide them. It appears that no single process or mechanism can account for all of the behaviors we see. Rather, the migratory guidance system of birds is built from a complex array of subsystems.

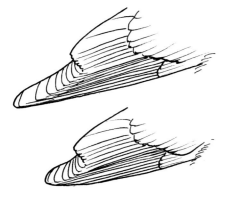

Primary projection. The wings of long-distance migrants have long primaries that project farther out from the secondaries, giving the wing a pointed shape for more aerodynamic flight. The folded wing of a long-distance migrant, such as the Connecticut Warbler (Oporornis agilis, *top), shows greater primary projection than that of the Common Yellowthroat* (Geothlypis trichas, *bottom), which migrates shorter distances.*

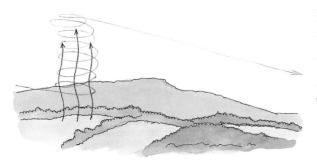

Riding thermals. Hawks and other large soaring migrants find columns of warm air (thermals) and ride the rising air currents in a spiral that takes the bird high into the sky. From these heights, the migrant glides slowly downward in its intended direction, searching for another thermal to help it continue its journey.

A basic distinction is drawn between orientation and navigation. Simply put, *orientation* is the ability of a bird to use an internal compass to accurately align itself in an appropriate direction when released into unfamiliar surroundings. *Navigation,* by comparison, is the ability to find a specific geographical location, from a known starting point. Navigation is usually thought to require some form of internal map, plus the ability to orient.

For hundreds of years, people keeping migratory birds in captivity have known about *migratory restlessness,* or *Zugunruhe.* During the migration season, caged birds of migratory species begin to thrash and flutter frenetically around their enclosures. This behavior begins shortly after dark and usually continues until midnight or later. Migratory restlessness is an innate behavior, controlled by hormones activated by changing day lengths. Using patterns of movements exhibited during migratory restlessness by captive birds of many different species, studies have shown that birds can orient properly when exposed to the sun, the night sky, or other orientation cues.

Many environmental stimuli have been investigated as possible cues for orientation and navigation. In general, these stimuli can be divided into two groups: compasses, which allow birds to orient themselves, and navigation aids, which allow birds to locate their position on an internal map. Some individual guidance mechanisms may incorporate both map and compass functions, making them especially difficult to study.

Orientation The *sun compass,* first verified experimentally around 1950, gives most—or maybe all—birds the ability to tell direction from the sun's position, at least in clear weather. Birds apparently are aware of where the sun should be at any time of the day because the sun compass works in conjunction with their internal circadian clock. For example, at 7:00 A.M. a bird "knows" that the sun should be in the east, a few degrees above the horizon, and that to head north the bird should keep the sun to its right.

Some birds use the *polarization pattern* of light as an orientation cue. Sunlight in most of the sky is scattered in all directions, which is to say it is not polarized (uni-directional). In one region of the sky, however, sunlight is oriented (polarized) in a direction perpendicular to the sun's location. This area of polarized light occurs in an arc about 90° away from the sun itself. Birds that can detect polarized light can determine the sun's position if they can see any part of this area of maximum polarization. This may be the principal means by which birds sense the position of the sun.

Since the region of polarized light is larger than the sun itself, birds can navigate using polarized light even on days with significant cloud cover, as long as there are some visible patches of clear sky in the correct region. The plane of the sun's polarized light in the evening sky can be determined for up to 45 minutes after the sun sets, so polarized light at sunset can be a principal cue for night-migrating birds in verifying their locations and calibrating other guidance mechanisms before departure.

Another environmental clue for orientation is the *star compass*. This guidance mechanism was also verified during the 1950s, but it wasn't until more than a decade later that ornithologist Stephen Emlen performed the key experiments with Indigo Buntings *(Passerina cyanea)* that defined the ultimate characteristics of the star compass. Unlike the sun, whose position overhead is useful for orientation only if the time of day is known, the stars provide an absolute point of reference. In the Northern Hemisphere, the main point of reference is the North Star, whose position overhead is constant, while the other stars seem to revolve around it.

The *magnetic compass* was the last of the three major compasses to be verified experimentally, but it is now viewed by many as the basic avian compass, particularly for long-distance migrants. The idea that magnetism might play a role in avian orientation was first suggested in 1947, but the concept initially faced broad skepticism in the scientific community. It was not until the late 1960s and early 1970s that investigators such as Wolfgang and Roswitha Wiltschko in Germany demonstrated conclusively that birds can orient to Earth's magnetic field.

Navigation Once a bird is airborne in migratory flight—its direction fixed by internal compass readings—it must continue to find its way along the desired migratory route; that is, a bird must navigate to its desired destination. Compared to the internal compasses used for orientation, the avian ability to navigate has not been well studied and is less well understood.

The most basic environmental cue that could be used as a *navigational landmark* is the outline of large geographic features, such as the coastlines of continents, mountain ranges, and major river systems, which birds may view from their elevated perspective in flight. There is little specific evidence to indicate

whether birds actually remember geographic landmarks in this way from year to year. Even if they do, nocturnal migrants might have difficulty seeing geographic features, thus limiting the value of purely visual orientation.

Anomalies in Earth's magnetic field create a magnetic "terrain" that birds may incorporate into an internal map they use for long-range navigation. Some researchers believe that Earth's magnetic field may provide a basis for avian navigation, as well as its role in orientation.

As a bird nears its destination, it may change from long-range navigation techniques to other methods, basing its final approach on local information sources, such as physical landmarks and even local smells. It has been demonstrated that homing pigeons—a domesticated form of the Rock Dove *(Columba livia)* that is specifically bred for homing—use local landmarks such as distinctive buildings to return to their home coops. There is little reason to suppose that migratory birds cannot use similar information as an aid for navigation.

A more controversial possibility is that birds use odors to close in on local destinations. The experimental literature on this question is equivocal, although it is known that some birds—such as Leach's Storm-Petrel *(Oceanodroma leucorhoa)*—have a strong olfactory sense that allows them to locate nest burrows.

Dispersal

While not all birds migrate, almost all individuals must leave the areas where they were raised and seek out a site of their own for breeding. After attempting to breed in one area, some individuals will give up on that spot and move to another. Both of these movements are called dispersal, and they differ from migration in that they are usually one-way trips with no regular return to the original location after a season.

Dispersal is a crucial component of the life history of most organisms, but such movements are usually difficult to quantify. Ornithologists have banded many thousands of nestlings with small leg rings, hoping to find out where the birds move to and where they attempt to breed, but most of these young birds are never seen again after they leave the nest. Mortality is often high in the first few months of a young bird's independence. This greatly lowers the likelihood of recovering a bird banded as a nestling. Furthermore, relocating dispersing birds is logistically difficult since one must search a greater and greater area as one moves away from the banding site.

The development of radio transmitters, which emit a signal researchers can use to locate a bird and which are light enough to attach to small birds, is revealing many secrets of dispersal. For example, in most species females disperse farther than males, while in a few species (including many ducks) the opposite is true. It appears to be important that the sexes travel different distances before settling on a new territory. If all young from a single family dispersed the same distances, young birds might find themselves searching for mates among close relatives. This would hamper successful breeding, since most species appear to avoid inbreeding.

Natal dispersal is the first movement of a young bird from the territory where it was raised to a potential breeding location, while *breeding dispersal* is the movement of adults between different breeding locations. In general, natal dispersal movements cover longer distances than breeding dispersal movements. In a few species, however, available areas without established breeders may be so rare that the young tend to stay on their natal territories for many years, waiting for a breeding opportunity to present itself nearby. In such cases, young may be recruited as helpers for their parents, resulting in a breeding system called cooperative breeding (see Reproductive Behavior, below).

Dispersing birds' exact paths and behavior in finding new locations are very poorly known. Several juvenile Eastern Screech-Owls *(Otus asio)* fitted with radio transmitters dispersed in a series of straight-line flights, each several kilometers in length, over a period of several nights. Presumably the owls searched the sites where they stopped at the end of each dispersal flight until they found an acceptable location.

In most species, dispersal is the least understood component of the life cycle. Ornithologists often do not even know during which season the young of a given species will disperse. Some open-country species such as the Field Sparrow *(Spizella pusilla)* seem to disperse in late summer or early fall, and young males can be heard singing in the territories that they will claim the following spring. In Black-capped Chickadees *(Poecile atricapilla)*, the critical dispersal time is in the fall, as young birds search for a chickadee flock with which they will overwinter; these chickadees will breed the next year with a mate from their winter flock. In other species, young stay with their parents throughout the winter in family flocks, presumably dispersing in early spring.

Communication

Birds engage in many behaviors that are predominantly undertaken for the purpose of communication or signaling. In fact, vocal communication ranks among the most complex of all avian traits.

Behavioral ecologists define a communication *signal* as a behavior that has evolved to alter the behavior of the receiver in a way that benefits the sender. A *display* is a ritualized signal intended to convey a specific message.

Communication may be directed at a variety of intended recipients. Males and females signal their relative status and value as mates. Individuals may signal dominance or territory ownership. Pursued birds may signal to predators that they are inedible or that they have spotted the predator and most likely would escape an attack. Flockmates signal where they are going or that they have detected a dangerous situation.

Clearly, these different contexts require a variety of signals. An individual trying to attract a mate may use a signal that allows its location to be easily determined, but the same individual sending a message about a predator may use a signal that does not reveal its position. Birders usually find that it is more difficult to find a bird giving alarm calls than one that is singing territorial songs.

Passive Communication: Plumage Patterns

A bird's plumage pattern is a form of communication. In the Northern Cardinal *(Cardinalis cardinalis)*, bright red feathers show that a bird is a male, while dull brown feathers during the breeding season signal a female. A young cardinal has a blackish bill, while adults have bright orange or red bills. Thus at certain seasons the combination of bill and plumage color indicates an individual cardinal's age and sex.

Plumage patterns are most effective for signaling when they have a conspicuous shape or color. Examples include strong geometric patterns (for example, the head markings of male Hooded Mergansers, *Lophodytes cucullatus*), isolated color patches (the crown patch of Ruby-crowned Kinglets, *Regulus calendula*), head stripes (White-crowned Sparrows), or repeated patterns (the tail markings of Elegant Trogons, *Trogon elegans*). Subtle differences in plumage pattern from bird

Distraction displays. *The function of the white tail tips of Eastern Towhees* (Pipilo erythrophthalmus) *is not known for certain, but one explanation is that they help distract predators and misdirect attacks to a part of the bird that can be lost, allowing the bird to escape.*

to bird can also assist in recognition of individuals.

Visual displays are often associated with specific plumage patterns that may have originally evolved to augment the display. The appearance of the plumage and the way it is presented together often form the signal. For instance, simple visual displays—a sudden flashing of bright colors—are effective in startling the observer with previously unseen aspects of the bird's appearance. If placed on a dispensable body part, such as the tip of a tail, this "flash" also may direct the predator away from the bird's body.

At certain times of the year, plumage patterns become more important for signaling other members of the same species than for deterring predators. Many male songbirds have alternate plumages with bold patterns that make displaying birds visually conspicuous. In contrast, a bird's drabber basic plumage provides camouflage at a time of year when there is little need for conspicuous display.

Displays Using Physical Movements and Posture

A key element of many display behaviors is movement or posture. Seabirds, grebes, and waterfowl are particularly well known for the highly ritualized displays they employ in courtship and during aggressive rivalry among males. These displays include a broad assortment of head-bobbing and head-throwing, bowing, sky-pointing, and wing displays. Most display movements are innate and highly stereotyped; indeed, they are so distinctive within some families that ornithologists have used them to map out relationships among species, hypothesizing that species with similar displays are closely related.

It has long been observed that many display movements appear to be derived from maintenance behaviors that have been reduced to simple repetitive motions. Examples include the movements a bird makes before taking off for flight (often a "pumping" motion) and the movements it makes before pecking.

Some display behaviors have their origins in conflict resolution. When facing a territorial rival, a bird may experience competing urges to flee and to fight; it cannot do both, and yet the combination of these urges causes a state of high agitation. The result is often *displacement behavior,* such as pecking the ground or wiping the bill obsessively against the feathers. Displacement behavior may appear completely inappropriate and useless, but it may allow the bird to avoid selecting either of two undesirable options: engaging in a potentially dangerous physical altercation, or fleeing and thus losing territorial advantage or social status.

Terns, boobies, and other colonial species aggressively defend their nest sites and a small area around the nest from all intruders. These species often have highly ritualized greeting and courtship displays to curb this aggressiveness when the mate approaches. Adult birds interacting with chicks may face similar conflicts, especially among raptors whose prey might be the size of their own young.

Much of avian display behavior seems designed to create a desired reaction by the target recipient, not necessarily to convey accurate information. In other words, territorial combatants or other signalers are often bluffing. In the avian world, relatively few territorial skirmishes actually lead to physical combat. Even the most threatening attack displays are followed by an actual physical assault only about half the time. A territorial competitor's best strategy may be to strike an aggressive and threatening pose, then gauge its final response based on how loudly its rival says, "Oh, yeah?"

The extent to which territorial displays are directed at repelling rival males, rather than attracting females, has been frequently addressed. In Red-winged Blackbirds *(Agelaius phoeniceus),* display of the red epaulets (shoulder patches) is intended to deter other males, since experimentally blackening them causes a displaying male to lose its territory but not its ability to attract females. Other experiments have shown that female Red-winged Blackbirds are more attracted to high-quality nesting territories than to bright shoulder markings.

Displays Using Sound

Birds are well known for using sound when displaying. Although these sounds mostly involve voice, some species also use nonvocal sounds to communicate.

Songs and Calls Vocal display has its roots in stereotyped chips and call notes, but among the oscine passerines (songbirds) it has reached an extraordinary level of development. Calls are usually defined as short, stereotyped vocalizations that are innate, while songs are more complex and often must be learned. Birds can have a dozen or more distinct calls, which they may use in specific ecological circumstances: Alarm calls signal danger, contact calls locate

Grouse displays. *Male grouse have very complex breeding displays that often simultaneously incorporate plumage, posture, movement, and sound. These displays are used to attract mates at leks and may help the birds recognize other members of their species. The displays of the closely related Gunnison Sage-Grouse (*Centrocercus minimus, *top) and Greater Sage-Grouse (*C. urophasianus, *bottom) have several differences, including the length and shape of the plumes on the back of the neck, the way these feathers and the rest of the body move, and the sounds the birds make.*

Territorial displays. The song-spread or ruff-out display of the Red-winged Blackbird is a familiar sight in spring over much of North America. This display is used in territorial defense rather than to attract females.

other individuals, flight calls keep the flock together, and so forth.

As with other forms of communication, specific avian vocalizations may sometimes appear in more than one context or be intended for more than one audience. Territorial song, for example, may convey one message to territorial rivals and another to potential mates. Male Marsh Wrens *(Cistothorus palustris)* competing for territories in small wetlands in western North America have developed a fantastic song repertoire, with individual birds using as many as 100 variations to hold their territory or attract females. Songbirds routinely learn to recognize the individual vocalizations of territorial neighbors.

Birds use different cues to recognize the songs of other members of their species. For example, White-throated Sparrows *(Zonotrichia albicollis)* rely on pitch and pattern; the result is the distinctive song that birders commit to memory as "Old Sam Peabody." Brown Thrashers *(Toxostoma rufum),* on the other hand, appear to discern thrasher songs from those of Gray Catbirds *(Dumetella carolinensis)* by the number of repeated syllables in a song sequence rather than a specific pattern.

Not all members of a species sound alike. Northern Cardinals in the southwestern United States sound different from those in the East. The subspecies groups of the Fox Sparrow *(Passerella iliaca)* sound different from one another throughout that species' range. This variability might be especially common in species with substantial geographic variations in other traits.

Song variation also occurs on a much smaller geographic scale. In several species, males that have territories close to one another adopt their neighbors' songs so that they have a similar set of vocalizations. If this set of songs lasts for a long time in an area (longer than the life of any given male), the birds are said to have a distinct *dialect* and a particular *song neighborhood.* This phenomenon is particularly well studied in the White-crowned Sparrow (see the New World Sparrows chapter).

A number of factors may affect the sound of a bird's territorial song. First, the song must carry well in its acoustic surroundings. Loud, low-frequency vocalizations such as those given by Bell's Vireo *(Vireo bellii)* carry well in low, dense thickets, while species such as the American Dipper *(Cinclus mexicanus)* and the Northern Waterthrush *(Seiurus noveboracensis)* have loud, ringing songs that can be heard over the low-frequency background noise of streams and waterfalls. The buzzy and complex songs of the Grasshopper Sparrow *(Ammodramus savannarum)* and the Bobolink *(Dolichonyx oryzivorus)* are more typical of birds of open country, where simple sustained vocalizations tend to be distorted by the wind and changes in air temperature common in grasslands.

Some songs may be tailored to meet the requirements of specific recipients. A male Chestnut-sided Warbler *(Dendroica pensylvanica)* gives a sharp, accented version of its territorial song when in the middle of its territory, and a different, unaccented form at the edge. Researchers have found that the accented version of

Territorial singing. The territorial songs of the Grasshopper Sparrow, like those of many open-country birds, are high-pitched and buzzy, which allows the songs to be heard for long distances in windy environments. Forest birds tend to use low-pitched sounds that carry better through vegetation.

the song is used to attract females, whereas the unaccented version works to deter rival males.

A central question in the study of avian song has been why males of some species sing so many songs. The number of different songs sung by an individual male is called the *song repertoire* and may vary from as few as one song per male (as in the Chipping Sparrow, *Spizella passerina*) to thousands (Brown Thrasher). While one might suspect that a bird with a repertoire of two or three songs delivers a distinctly different message with each song type, it strains credulity that thrashers have so many things to say that they need thousands of songs, each with a different message. More likely it is the actual variation that is the message: Males singing a large number of songs are communicating their status and quality through the number of songs they can sing, or perhaps through the variation among the songs within a bout of singing.

One way that large song repertoires signal the quality of a male is if songs are difficult to learn. A male with a large repertoire could be advertising that he is a better male than individuals who are unable to learn so many songs. A variation on this theme would be that more songs could be learned only with age; if females prefer older males (who have proved their superiority simply by surviving longer in a difficult world), they could use song repertoires in choosing quality mates.

Several other hypotheses try to explain the phenomenon of large song repertoires. One of these ideas cites as its conceptual basis the book and movie *Beau Geste,* in which a single French Foreign Legionnaire defends a desert fort after all his comrades have been killed. He props the bodies of his fellow soldiers along the fort's walls and fires their guns, thereby fooling the attackers into believing the fort is heavily defended. The "Beau Geste" hypothesis explains large song repertoires by proposing that a single bird sings many songs to fool newly arriving males into believing that the area is densely occupied with many birds. This might encourage the new arrivals to search elsewhere for a territory with less competition.

One problem with many hypotheses explaining male song repertoires is that the systems proposed would be subject to cheating; that is, a male that doesn't "play by the rules" would benefit substantially. For instance, a young male that learns songs faster than most would sound like an older male, which under at least one hypothesis would make him more attractive to females. A complete theory must account for these cheaters, too. This is an active area of song research.

Mimicry is well developed in starlings, mockingbirds and thrashers (the "mimic thrushes"), parrots, and several other groups. In some of these species, mimicry may be a way individual males can quickly add new sounds to their repertoire. This could be especially important if the variety of sounds in a repertoire is an important part of the signal. Thus we end up with Northern Mockingbirds *(Mimus polyglottos)* imitating squeaking fence gates or automobile backfires, sounds that could not be important messages in their own right. Perhaps for mimicking species, males with large repertoires are advertising themselves as fast learners, rather than as individuals with some other trait such as old age.

Nonvocal Sounds Many birds communicate primarily through simple sounds, including some they make mechanically without using their voice. A number of species generally thought to be mute make simple noises. For instance, storks use bill-clattering noises as part of their courtship, and in spite of its name, the Mute Swan *(Cygnus olor)* can hiss and grunt.

Many species depend on nonvocal sounds to communicate. Woodpeckers drum against hollow parts of trees to advertise their territoriality and to attract mates. If hollow trees are not available, a variety of other objects will suffice, including air vents, metal chimneys, and other parts of buildings. Male Ruffed Grouse *(Bonasa umbellus)* try to attract

Nonvocal sounds. Male Broad-tailed Hummingbirds have a modified primary feather that emits a high-pitched trill when the wings are moved rapidly through the air. These males audibly advertise their presence just by flying around in their territory, unlike many other hummingbird species whose males must perform special displays to announce their status.

females by rapidly beating their wings while standing on a display site, often a prominent log. The thumping sound carries well in the dense forests in which grouse are found; human observers often remark that they "feel" the low-frequency thumping more than they hear it.

Another example of nonvocal sounds is the high-pitched trill emitted by flying male Broad-tailed Hummingbirds *(Selasphorus platycercus)*. The trill, caused by air vibrating a tapered tip of one primary of each wing while the bird is moving at high speed, communicates the male's presence without additional expense— he gives the signal just by flying in his territory.

Reproductive Behavior

The most complex and important social interactions among birds usually take place in connection with reproductive behavior. The study of bird partnerships and mating styles has attracted tremendous attention in the last decade or so, as a number of the avian world's family secrets have come into scientific view.

Monogamy
Until recently, avian monogamy was considered a fairly simple and straightforward lifestyle. Ornithologists kept track of how pair bonds of different species formed and how long they lasted. But the simple idea of monogamous pair bonds was complicated in the early 1990s by the discovery that many apparently monogamous birds regularly engage in *extra-pair copulations,* in effect "cheating" on their mates. It was discovered, in short, that raising young together does not imply sexual fidelity.

Ornithologists now recognize that birds that appear to be partners raising young together can be *socially monogamous* (cooperating in raising young), *genetically monogamous* (in which the male and female together are the sole genetic parents of all the young), or both—or neither. More than 90 percent of all bird species are socially monogamous, but some level

Nesting. *Like their cousins the swans, many species of geese mate for life. Mated pairs like these* Canada Geese *(Branta canadensis)* will usually stay together until one of the birds dies, although divorce in unsuccessful pairs occurs occasionally.*

of cheating resulting in genetically diverse offspring appears to be common.

To be considered socially monogamous, a male and a female must partner for the duration of one or more breeding cycles. In some avian families, mated pairs remain together more or less continuously throughout adult life, and some of these species are genetically monogamous as well. Monogamy (both social and genetic) is well known among swans and geese but also occurs in eagles, albatrosses, and other groups. In some monogamous species, partners may remain together for only part of the year, typically during the breeding season. In either case, "divorce" can occur.

The value of monogamy presumably lies in the increased breeding success a bird can achieve with a known, stable partner. One key characteristic of many socially monogamous species is that two parents must provide care in order to raise the young successfully. When both the male and the female are necessary to provide adequate care, social monogamy is common and extra-pair copulations are not.

Extra-pair Copulations Scientists have observed extra-pair copulations even among birds with stable relationships that do not divorce. It is not yet known how many species engage in extra-pair copulations, since many species remain to be studied. However, it appears that

genetic monogamy may be the exception rather than the rule among birds.

The prevalence of extra-pair copulations has been brought to light by genetic studies of family relationships. Researchers take a small tissue sample (often blood or a growing feather) from parents and offspring, and compare the genetic compositions of the individuals. If the young in a nest have versions of their genes that do not match up with the DNA of their putative father, then these offspring must be the result of an extra-pair copulation between the female that laid the egg and some other male. Similarly, if offspring do not share their maternally derived mitochondrial DNA with the female attending the nest, it can be assumed that *nest parasitism* (sometimes called *egg-dumping*), the laying of eggs by another female into the nest, has occurred.

Assuming that a bird is socially monogamous, what would induce the female to accept or even solicit extra-pair copulations? Forced copulation is known in birds but is frequent in only a few groups such as waterfowl. Most extra-pair copulations observed in other species seem to involve the willing participation of the female, who is often the one that seeks them out. Extra-pair copulation may be a hedge against infertility in the female's primary partner, or it may be a means of increasing the genetic diversity of her young. Mating with additional males may allow a female to overcome the fact that her choice of mates was limited during pair formation and to produce some young fathered by a higher-quality male than her social mate.

In males, certain traits have been linked with the likelihood of successfully obtaining extra-pair copulations. These include bright plumage, variable or complex songs, and relatively large testes. If male participation is not essential in caring for the young, and if it is to the female's advantage to diversify the genetic composition of her brood, then males need to advertise themselves actively to females if they are to be chosen by females and pass along their genes. This would explain the bright plumage and alluring songs. In addition, a male in this situation should seek extra-pair copulations whenever possible in order to enhance his own breeding success, and large testes will help ensure an adequate supply of sperm.

Territorial Breeding

Monogamous birds may nest in a wide variety of social conditions, from isolated pairs to huge colonies sometimes numbering in the millions. Most birds nest within individually defended *territories*, which come in many shapes and sizes. Some birds also establish territories in nonbreeding habitats, sometimes to protect food resources.

"Full-function," or multi-purpose, breeding territories contain both food and nesting sites and are defended against intruders. Such territories are surprisingly dynamic; their sizes depend on the nutritional needs of the species and on the amount of available food within the territory. A territory with abundant food is normally smaller than a poor-quality territory, all other factors being equal. The boundaries of a territory may move during the breeding season, as the focus of activity shifts from courtship to feeding young. In some species, defended areas contain only a nest site or a reliable food source, but not both kinds of resources.

Colonial Breeding

About 13 percent of all bird species nest colonially. Examples of colonial nesting include the coastal breeding colonies of many seabird species. A primary inducement for colonial breeding is the scarcity of nest sites in a particular region that are both safe from predators and the elements, and near enough to abundant food supplies to support young.

The colonial lifestyle also permits cooperative protection from predators, as anyone who has been dive-bombed upon venturing into a tern colony will appreciate. Another advantage of colonial living is that individuals may learn from each other the locations of food resources, especially ephemeral foods with unpredictable distributions.

On the downside, the concentration of breeding pairs and chicks at a colony may actually attract predators the birds might not otherwise encounter, increase the spread of nest parasites such as mites

Great Blue Heron colony. *Many members of the heron, stork, and ibis families nest in noisy, messy colonies. These colonies are often found where tall trees are located in standing water, a combination that seems to reduce access to the nest for predators such as raccoons. In the Southeast, alligators in the water can reinforce the relative safety of the nest trees.*

Cooperative breeding. In species such as the Florida Scrub-Jay, birds called helpers or auxiliaries will help nesting members of their group perform parental-care duties. These helpers, often young from previous seasons, will defend the nest, feed the young, and bring food to the incubating females.

and lice, and heighten competition for food in the vicinity of the nest site. Colonial nesting is a trade-off, the value of which depends on subtle cost–benefit considerations.

Cooperative Breeding

Superficially similar to coloniality—but actually quite different—is cooperative breeding, which occurs in about 250 bird species worldwide. The best-known North American example of a cooperative breeder is probably the Florida Scrub-Jay *(Aphelocoma coerulescens)*. Cooperative breeders typically defend group territories against intruders. While the exact breeding arrangement within groups can vary significantly, classic cooperative breeding involves the enlistment of *nest helpers,* usually young birds that assist in both feeding and protecting the nestlings.

Helpers are often related to the nesting pair (they may come from previous broods), but in some instances they are young birds that have dispersed from their natal territory to join another group. Helpers usually increase the reproductive success of the breeding adults whose broods they are attending, and they also reduce breeding stress on the parent birds, which may reduce parental mortality.

The origins and ecology of helping behavior have been a topic of considerable debate. While cooperative breeding oc-curs in a wide variety of bird families and ecological conditions, a common theme is limited suitable habitat for new breeders, so that many birds are left with no opportunity to gain a breeding territory of their own. Young birds in this situation may choose to help a mated pair that has a territory. If the mated pair is closely related to the young birds, the helpers will share many genes with the offspring they are assisting; helping to raise close relatives indirectly accomplishes the primary goal of reproduction: to get one's genes into the next generation. Helpers may also benefit directly by learning how to raise young.

In Florida Scrub-Jays, whose breeding habitat is extremely limited, a helper can get an even more tangible benefit: acquiring a breeding territory of its own. The easiest way for a helper to gain its own territory is often to partition off part of the territory on which it is living. This is most easily accomplished on large territories, and larger territories can be defended by large flocks. By helping to raise other birds' offspring, the scrub-jay helper is aiding in the production of additional flock members, leading to a larger territory and possibly a piece it can call its own in the near future.

Other North American birds whose cooperative breeding systems have been well studied are the Acorn Woodpecker, the Red-cockaded Woodpecker, and the Mexican Jay *(Aphelocoma ultramarina)*.

Polygyny

A small percentage of the world's bird species are not socially monogamous. In these species some individuals mate and form pair bonds with multiple partners.

Promiscuity is the total absence of a stable social relationship among breeding adults, and therefore a lack of pattern with regard to who mates with whom. Promiscuity is actually very rare among birds. Some hummingbirds may mate promiscuously, but in most other species, nonmonogamous matings involve specific mating patterns.

Polygyny, in which a male bird forms breeding partnerships simultaneously with more than one female, has been documented in about 2 percent of all bird species. Most of the polygynous birds found in North America live in marshes or grassland habitats, including such common species as the Red-winged and Yellow-headed *(Xanthocephalus xanthocephalus)* Blackbirds. Polygyny also occurs in many grouse, some shorebirds, and the Marsh Wren, among other species. In some other common species, such as the Indigo Bunting, a small number of males (5 percent or less in most populations) are successful in attracting more than one female.

Males in polygynous arrangements are hard pressed to provide parental care to all of their offspring. In many polygynous systems, males provide no parental care at all. The strategy therefore works most successfully when the young are capable of a high degree of independent activity from birth or are raised in habitats where the female can find enough food without assistance.

Most polygyny occurs in habitats with uneven resource distributions, where a single successful male can claim a rich territory capable of supporting multiple broods. In these cases many females can be attracted to the rich territory, and the male gets many mates. The advantage of polygyny to the male is apparent, since he can increase his reproductive success by producing young with many females. Many males fail to attract even a single female, however, so mating success varies dramatically among males in most polygynous species.

The advantage to the female is less clear, but it may be that she is better off in a polygynous arrangement on a rich territory than she would be as the single mate of a male on a poor-quality territory.

Lekking In one extreme form of polygyny, called lekking, males collect in a group to engage in courtship displays. Lekking is found in 14 families of birds worldwide. The word *lek* can refer to either the group of displaying males or the location at which the males gather. In some species, the physical site of the displays is also called an *arena* or *booming ground.* Females visit the lek solely for the purpose of mating; they get no help from the males in rearing young, no access to food resources, nothing but the male's genetic contribution to their offspring.

Mating displays on a lek tend to be highly distinctive—for example, the booming and "dancing" of the grouse and the prairie-chickens, or the intricate display movements of shorebirds such as the Buff-breasted Sandpiper *(Tryngites subruficollis).* Males also frequently sport elaborate plumage that is displayed to male competitors and visiting females. In addition to the grouse and shorebirds, lekking occurs in some hummingbirds and in a number of tropical families.

The lekking arena is often a very small piece of ground where the males defend tiny territories within which they perform their displays. In other species, males form an *exploded lek,* where male display sites are dispersed over a larger area. Dominant males get the best positions in the arena and usually a large majority of the matings. Final courtship often takes place off the lek, however, so subordinate males get a chance to display to females while the dominant male is otherwise occupied.

Male reproductive success is extremely variable among members of a lek: High-status birds can attract a large number of females, whereas many low-status males may experience no success at all. So why do the low-status males participate? Researchers theorize that lekking behavior tends to persist in areas where males can monopolize neither food resources nor females and thus have just their genetic qualities to advertise to females. For males that reach the top position in a lek, the genetic payoff is substantial, and this tends to reinforce the system.

Females also receive some benefits from leks—assuming that they can raise their young without male assistance. Females can select among males more quickly and easily than they could in isolation, and young females can learn from older ones how to select males on the basis of traits that suggest a healthy individual. Females may visit several arenas and observe many males before consenting to courtship. Lekking males show little selectivity, by comparison. Researchers have noted that an unusually large number of hybrids occur in birds with this mating system, even among species that are fairly distant relatives.

Polyandry

In polyandry, a single female forms pair bonds with multiple males. Only about 1 percent of bird species in the world practice polyandry, and these are limited to just a few taxonomic groups, mainly relatives of the rails and shorebirds. In North America polyandry is found in shorebirds such as the Northern Jacana (*Jacana spinosa*), all three phalaropes, and the Spotted Sandpiper (*Actitis macularia*).

Polyandry can take several forms. In *classic polyandry*, the female lays eggs in separate nests, and different males take responsibility for the incubation and rearing of each brood, leaving the female free to seek out additional mates. For species such as the Northern Jacana and Spotted Sandpiper, abundant food on a successful female's territory helps her to attract many males and lay extra clutches.

In *cooperative polyandry*, the female lays eggs in only one nest but mates with several males to generate her clutch and shares incubation and parental care duties with the males. No North American breeding species show cooperative polyandry, but it is found in Antarctic skuas and several species of Australian birds.

In polyandrous species the sexual roles are often reversed. Females defend territories, actively court males, and compete with other females for male partners. In most bird species, males are somewhat bigger than females, but in the Spotted Sandpiper, females are some 25 percent larger than males. Female phalaropes develop bright breeding colors, while the males are comparatively drab. The fact that females are more colorful and larger in polyandrous species is an example of *reversed sexual dimorphism*.

The evolutionary reason polyandry has developed several times among birds is similar to that underlying polygyny: The biology of the species allows one sex to abandon its mate after initiating a reproductive attempt, in order to attract more mates. In polyandrous species it is the female that has this opportunity. Polyandry is probably rarer than polygyny because females invest more energy and nutrients in their eggs than males invest in their sperm; therefore, females normally experience a greater cost associated with abandoning a clutch of eggs than do males.

Polygynandry

In a very few species, individual females may end up paired with more than one male, and males may pair with more than one female. This complex breeding system, called polygynandry, has been best studied in a European songbird called the Hedge Accentor (*Prunella modularis*). In North America, Smith's Longspur (*Calcarius pictus*) and perhaps a few other species are polygynandrous.

One very well studied species has been described as "opportunistically polygynandrous." The Acorn Woodpecker has a complex mating strategy in which birds live in groups (primarily to defend stored acorns) and several females lay eggs in a single nest. These females compete with each other with regard to the number of eggs each lays in the nest, even to the point of throwing their rivals' eggs out of the nest. Males compete with each other for access to the females, and if a dominant male is removed from the group during egg-laying, he may throw all the eggs out of the nest upon his return and force everyone to start over again. Once the clutch is finally laid, all group members help raise the young.

Brood Parasitism

One other important breeding system is brood parasitism, in which females lay their eggs in nests built by other birds, the *hosts,* who become entirely responsible for care of the eggs and young. The parasites are therefore relieved of all parental duties. The most famous brood parasites are the European species of cuckoos and the North American cowbirds. (North American cuckoos rarely parasitize other birds' nests.) A number of other birds, especially pheasants and ducks, will also parasitize nests of their own or different species.

Brood parasitism is particularly interesting to evolutionary biologists because it pits various tactics by the parasites (including laying mimetic eggs and destroying host eggs and young) against those of the hosts (including rejecting parasitic eggs and abandoning parasitized nests).

Brood parasitism within a species *(intraspecific parasitism)* is fairly widespread. A laying female who loses her own nest will search for a place to lay the egg that is still developing in her reproductive tract. She may opt to "dump" the egg in a neighboring nest. Some birds regularly practice *egg-dumping,* perhaps to avoid losing all their reproductive effort if their own nest is destroyed. Egg-dumping is apparent if two new eggs appear in a nest during one day, as few birds lay more than one egg per day.

More extreme are the obligate brood parasites. Females of these species never build their own nest but depend solely

Brood parasitism. *Cowbird eggs are often identifiable in the nests of smaller host species: The parasitic eggs may be larger and marked differently from the eggs laid by the nest owner. Many host species seem to be unable to detect the unfamiliar object; such hosts are called "acceptor" species. Shown is a Brown-headed Cowbird egg in a Swamp Sparrow* (Melospiza georgiana) *nest.*

on hosts to raise their young. All of these females therefore practice *interspecific parasitism,* as they have no nests of their own species to parasitize. North American cowbird species are in this category.

Brown-headed *(Molothrus ater)* and Shiny *(M. bonariensis)* Cowbirds each have been reported to parasitize more than 200 species, while the Bronzed Cowbird *(M. aeneus)* uses fewer hosts. Female cowbirds systematically search for host nests and most often lay eggs in nests of hosts smaller than themselves. They can parasitize a single nest many times and may totally disrupt the hosts' breeding success (see the Blackbirds, Orioles, and Allies, and the Populations and Conservation chapters).

Parental Care

Researchers believe that most birds are socially monogamous because both parents are needed to raise chicks. The young of most songbirds, hawks, herons, and many other groups are *altricial* at hatching, meaning that they are weak, blind, naked, and unable to move long distances independently or maintain their own body temperatures. In short,

Precocial and altricial chicks. The newborn chicks of many waterbirds, such as the Sora (Porzana carolina, *left), are precocial in that they have open eyes, downy feathers, and are capable of independent movement within a few hours of hatching. Altricial chicks, which include most songbirds, such as the Gray Catbird (right), hatch blind, naked, and virtually helpless.*

the chicks are utterly helpless. Such young require intensive care from both parents.

Chicks of galliforms (grouse, quail, and their relatives), most waterbirds, and shorebirds are *precocial,* meaning that they are down-covered and capable of running and feeding themselves shortly after hatching. Precocial offspring need less care, and a single parent can often provide for them alone.

Parental care involves many responsibilities, the most obvious task being to feed the young. Parents often share feeding duties equally while the young are still in the nest. In some species the parents split the brood after fledging, with the male parent assuming all care of some fledglings and the female caring for the rest. In other birds, the male takes over care of all the young while the female prepares to lay a second clutch.

Altricial young cannot maintain their body temperatures, so the parents must keep them warm by brooding them. A brooding adult will sit on the nest (and young) as if he or she were still incubating and warm the young in that manner. Many precocial young also are not completely capable of maintaining their body temperatures in the first few days and need to be brooded at times by a parent, especially during poor weather.

Parents must also clean the nest by picking up the chicks' feces, which are wrapped in a mucous membrane called a *fecal sac.* Some adults eat the fecal sacs, while others carry them far from the nest and drop them. In finches and some other species, the young deposit their feces along the edge of the nest, where the waste accumulates over time, giving the nest a fouled appearance.

Parents also try to protect their eggs and young from predators. This protection may take several forms. Shorebirds such as the Killdeer *(Charadrius vociferus)* perform a *distraction display* when a predator (or birder) comes too close to the nest. A common distraction display consists of an adult moving away from the nest while dragging a wing as if it were injured; when the predator has been led far enough away from the nest, the adult flies off. Sparrows with camouflaged nests, such as Grasshopper and Bachman's *(Aimophila aestivalis)* Sparrows, rustle through the grass like a mouse as they leave their nest; again, the purpose seems to be to distract a potential predator from the nest and young.

Some species that live in flocks or nest in colonies will physically attack predators to drive them away from nests. Beachgoers who inadvertently enter a tern colony or people wandering too close to a Red-winged Blackbird nest are likely to get their heads hit by a defensive bird. When several birds join together in their efforts to rid their territory of an offending individual, the frenzied attacks are called *mobbing.* Mobbing can occur at any time of the year when directed at potential predators such as hawks and owls, but it is likely to be most deliberate during the breeding season. Single birds will also attack people or other animals that irritate them.

Other Breeding Behaviors

Most birds have species-specific courtship and mating rituals that can be almost as exhilarating to see as they must be to perform. Eagles and falcons are famous for aerial displays that demonstrate their spectacular mastery of flight. The territorial and courtship displays of humming-birds are no less dramatic. Many bird species have intricate nest-building behaviors. The weaving ability of orioles and the carpentry of woodpeckers are commonly cited examples. Many other examples are described in the individual family chapters in this book.

It should be noted, however, that birds are easily disturbed during their breeding attempts. It is common for some species such as meadowlarks to abandon nests disturbed during the nest-building or egg-laying stages. Repeated visits to a nest or to a courtship arena may cause increased predation on nests and breeding birds by dogs, Coyotes, and other predators that follow human scent. While it probably does no harm to pause for a short time during a morning's birding to observe breeding behavior, in many instances long-term observation of breeding can be conducted safely only from a hidden location such as a well-placed blind.

Understanding Behavior: The Outer Frontier

It is difficult to watch avian behavior for any length of time without being curious about its meaning. Why does a bird make particular choices and not others? A book that illustrates the rewards (and ardors) of careful behavioral research is Bernd Heinrich's *Ravens in Winter* (1989), a narrative account of a research program conducted in the 1980s. Heinrich logged more than 1,000 hours of painstaking field observation, much of it in an unheated cabin in the Maine woods during winter, exploring why Common Ravens engage in apparently altruistic group feeding.

Heinrich's study sought to explain the following observations. Common Ravens

Ravens tumbling. *Like raptors that nest in similar cliff habitats, Common Raven pairs perform spectacular aerial displays that involve intricate dives and gymnastics. These displays presumably help reinforce the pair bonds between mated birds.*

were in fact uncommon in the Maine woods during winter in the 1980s. Yet most of the carcasses at which ravens fed during the winter were consumed by crowds of ravens (ranging from 15 to almost 300 birds), rather than by individuals or pairs. Ravens patrolling the woods were generally seen in groups of one or two, and bait carcasses were typically first discovered by single birds or pairs. Heinrich found that upon discovering a carcass in the winter, ravens actually recruited other ravens to join in the feeding. This left two major questions that needed to be resolved: How do ravens accomplish this recruitment, and why do they choose to share their food?

In the course of his investigations, Heinrich adopted a number of working hypotheses—each of which his avian subjects refuted through their actions. Only after surmounting a daunting series of physical and intellectual challenges did Heinrich arrive at a successful explanation for his observations: Juvenile raven gangs use recruitment to gain access to carcasses being defended by territorial adults.

Heinrich raised and rejected many ideas during his research. At times the ravens appeared to act in contrary ways just to prove to Heinrich that he did not understand what was going on. *Ravens in Winter* is an excellent example of how field research on avian behavior is both frustrating and complex, and ultimately rewarding.

Rick Cech, John B. Dunning, Jr.,
and Chris Elphick

Habitats and Distributions

 Few creatures are as mobile as birds. This mobility gives them access to a wide variety of environments, and birds are found throughout North America. At the same time, no single species of bird can be found everywhere on the continent. Each species typically occurs within a limited range, and often only in specific habitats or at specific times of year. Even beginning birders recognize these predictable patterns of occurrence, and with study and experience such patterns can become a useful aid for finding and identifying birds.

Range and Habitat

A species' *range* is the geographic area or region in which it is found. Ranges can be described in different ways and at different levels of detail. Usually the range of a species can be described simply in terms of political boundaries or major geographic features. For example, the Black-throated Sparrow *(Amphispiza bilineata)* can be said to occur throughout much of the western United States, particularly within the region that lies between the Sierra Nevada–Cascade ranges and the Rocky Mountains. Many species undertake seasonal movements, and some species have entirely separate breeding and nonbreeding ranges, as well as specific migratory routes and stopover sites, so range descriptions often include details of seasonal occurrence.

A bird's *habitat* is the specific environment or ecological conditions in which that species lives. For example, while both rails and nuthatches range throughout much of North America, rails are found in marshy habitat, and nuthatches are found in woodland habitat. Habitat can be described at many scales, from the very general to the very specific: The breeding habitat of the Mourning Warbler *(Oporornis philadelphia)* can be described simply as "brushy areas" or in detail as "dense tangles of brambles among shrubs or small trees in damp areas without standing water and with scattered mature trees nearby."

Most habitat descriptions are based on vegetation, which reflects the climate, soil type, and other features of the local environment, and which supports the animal life in a given location. Efforts to measure habitat variables often focus on vegetation structure and attempt to quantify the presence and abundance of different plant species in the habitat.

The term *microhabitat* is used to refer to the subtle subdivisions within broad habitat types. While at first the birds in a particular location may appear to be a random mixture of species, closer observation reveals that they organize themselves into different microhabitats.

When species use different microhabitats within a broad habitat type, they are using the habitat in different ways. For example, the Ovenbird *(Seiurus aurocapillus)* and the Hairy Woodpecker *(Picoides villosus)* are both typical species of mature hardwood forest in eastern North America, and both are frequently found together in that habitat. However, each uses strikingly different microhabitats within the hardwood forest. Ovenbirds primarily use the shaded ground and understory beneath mature trees, while the woodpecker uses the tree trunks and branches but is not particular about the understory vegetation.

Variation in Habitat Use

Although microhabitat information can be a useful guide for finding and identifying species, it cannot always be relied upon, especially because habitat associations may vary regionally. For example, where the breeding areas of the very similar Louisiana *(Seiurus motacilla)* and Northern *(S. noveboracensis)* Waterthrushes overlap, Louisianas usually occur in thickly wooded ravines with fast-flowing streams, whereas Northerns frequent wooded swamps with standing water. However, both species may occur in both habitat types in areas where the two species do not overlap.

In other cases, habitat selection can even reverse between regions. In Arizona, where the ranges of Eastern *(Sturnella magna)* and Western *(S. neglecta)* Meadowlarks overlap, Easterns are found mainly in arid desert grasslands, while Westerns frequent irrigated agricultural lands and grassy lawns. Farther east in the Great Plains, where the ranges of different subspecies of the two meadowlark species overlap, Easterns are found in moist grasslands and Westerns in slightly drier areas.

Many species of birds use different habitats at different times of year. These habitat differences are due, at least in part, to the fact that nonbreeding habitats need not provide for nesting activities. Migratory species, especially, may be forced to use different habitats in different regions simply because limited choices are available. For example, Palm Warblers *(Dendroica palmarum)* nest in Canada in open, shrubby habitat with stunted trees around spruce bogs and winter mainly south of the United States where spruce bogs do not exist. Nevertheless, migratory birds use similar habitats throughout the year: Woodland birds tend to stay in woodland habitats, grassland birds in grasslands, and so on.

Many species have different habitat requirements for different life activities. For species such as the Hairy Woodpecker, all needs are met within the boundaries of their relatively small and self-contained territories, making their microhabitat associations fairly easy to describe. In other species, the habitat conditions required for nesting may be very different from those needed for foraging or roosting. For instance, the Turkey Vulture *(Cathartes aura)* has quite specific nesting needs—an undisturbed cave, rock crevice, or hollow tree trunk—but wanders widely over many different habitats in search of carrion to eat. Seabirds, swifts, hummingbirds, and swallows are other highly mobile birds that select very specific locations for nest sites but that travel widely in search of food.

Elevation. *Mountain ranges affect climate, which in turn influences the distribution of habitats and thus birds. Rainfall patterns, for example, are affected by mountain ranges; in addition, the colder temperatures of mountain ridges allow northern species to extend their ranges southward into otherwise warmer latitudes.*

ELEVATIONS		
feet		meters
5,000		1,500
2,000		600
1,500		450
0		0

Habitat Selection

The choices that birds make about where to spend their time are influenced by the birds' needs for survival and breeding and by the availability of habitats. Although people frequently talk about habitat "preferences" or "optimal habitat," these terms can be very misleading. Preferences are extremely difficult to ascertain because it is not always clear what options are available to a particular species, and individual birds may be unable to express their preferences fully. For example, many of Hawaii's native birds are found now only in deep forests at the tops of mountains. This does not mean that such forest habitats are preferred; instead, it reflects the fact that lowland forests have been largely destroyed and are no longer available.

Similarly, there are so many factors that affect habitat selection that it may be quite rare for any single habitat to be truly optimal—and even rarer that such optimal conditions can be identified. The topic of habitat quality is discussed further in the Populations and Conservation chapter.

Changing Distributions

All habitats change over time, and bird distributions change in response to these habitat shifts. Over short periods, a tidal area can transform from a vast, open mudflat suitable for shorebirds and egrets to a deepwater lagoon where diving ducks and grebes can feed, all in a matter of hours. Habitats also change seasonally and over a period of years as successional change proceeds in a plant community (see Succession, below). Over millennia, even the geographic location of different habitats shifts as the climate changes.

As habitat distributions change over long time spans, the barriers constraining bird species' distributions may be bridged, allowing species to increase their ranges. Conversely, as habitats disappear from an area, so do the birds that associate with those habitats. As a result of all this change, both the local distributions and large-scale ranges of birds are in constant flux.

Many of the most dramatic examples of recent changes in bird distributions involve human influence. As suburbs

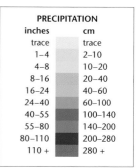

Average annual precipitation in North America. Precipitation has a profound impact on plant communities and thus has an indirect effect on birds. In general, rainfall declines from east to west, rising again sharply along the Pacific coast.

PRECIPITATION	
inches	cm
trace	trace
1–4	2–10
4–8	10–20
8–16	20–40
16–24	40–60
24–40	60–100
40–55	100–140
55–80	140–200
80–110	200–280
110 +	280 +

Habitat changes with elevation. As one climbs in elevation, changes in climate and resulting vegetation mirror the effects of traveling far to the north. In this example, a mountain in the southwestern United States rises in the space of a few miles from desert to tundra habitat. As the habitat changes, so do the associated birds; shown to the right are species representative of each habitat type.

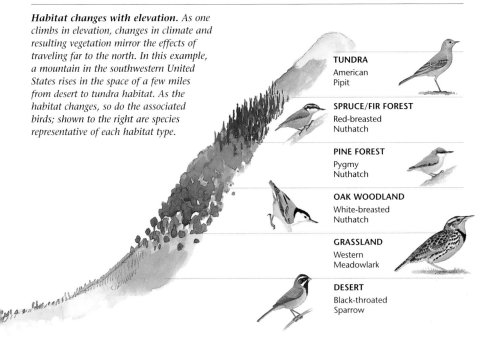

TUNDRA
American Pipit

SPRUCE/FIR FOREST
Red-breasted Nuthatch

PINE FOREST
Pygmy Nuthatch

OAK WOODLAND
White-breasted Nuthatch

GRASSLAND
Western Meadowlark

DESERT
Black-throated Sparrow

have expanded in northeastern North America, with increases in winter bird-feeding and berry-producing shrubs, species such as the Northern Mockingbird *(Mimus polyglottos)*, Tufted Titmouse *(Baeolophus bicolor)*, and Northern Cardinal *(Cardinalis cardinalis)* have expanded their ranges north. Similarly, in the Pacific states, as large numbers of fan palms have been planted in the expanding suburbs, the nesting range of the Hooded Oriole *(Icterus cucullatus)* has spread northward.

Habitat Distribution Patterns

Many factors determine which habitats and, in turn, which birds will be found in a particular place. Among the most important are geography and climate.

Geography

On a large scale, mountain ranges and oceans shape the climate of the continent. Oceans provide water vapor and moderate temperatures. Weather systems carry the moist, mild ocean air over the land, bringing water in the form of rain, snow, or other precipitation. Mountains force the air to rise, cooling it to the point where water vapor condenses and precipitates, leaving little moisture for regions on the downwind side of the mountains. The dry conditions in this *rain shadow* often help create and maintain desert and prairie habitats.

Air temperature decreases with elevation. In mountainous regions, the resulting climatic gradients mimic the effects of traveling toward the North or South Poles, and the vegetation changes accordingly. From the equator, one can reach tundra by traveling 4,350 miles (7,000 km) north or south, or by traveling 2.5 miles (4 km) vertically. The same effect can be seen dramatically in the southwestern United States, where one can travel from hot desert habitat to tundra in just a few miles. Northern vegetation types such as tundra extend into more southerly regions along mountain ranges.

Various other geographical features also influence the distribution of different plant communities. For example, geology and soil type determine the availability of different nutrients and the ease with which the soil retains water.

Climate

Climate has a profound, but often indirect, effect on bird distributions. Temperature and rainfall greatly influence the composition of plant communities, which, in turn, determines the availability of food, nest sites, and protective cover for birds to use.

Measurements of air temperature match well with many bird distributions. In particular, winter distributions are often influenced by the minimum temperatures of different regions. Most species are limited primarily by the availability of food rather than by the temperature per se. For example, the winter distribution of many species of waterbirds is determined by the presence of ice, which limits access to aquatic food. Similarly, cold temperatures reduce insect populations, preventing insectivorous birds from wintering in the north.

Precipitation patterns also influence the distributions of many bird species because precipitation directly affects plant communities. For instance, the transition from eastern deciduous forests to prairie in the Midwest is determined,

at least in part, by the decline in rainfall from east to west. This change in plant communities in turn determines the range boundaries for forest and grassland birds.

Habitat Boundaries

Because changes in geographic features and climate vary gradually as one moves from one place to another, habitats also change in a gradual way. While the concept of distinct habitats is intuitively quite simple, in reality the world is not neatly subdivided into discrete units, and it is often hard to draw exact boundaries between habitats.

For example, the distinction between a patch of forest and the farmland that surrounds it may be sharp and dramatic, but most natural boundaries are less clear-cut. A forest may gradually thin to become open woodland, then shrubland, and eventually grassland over a distance of many miles. In some cases, the edge between two broad habitat types may represent a separate habitat itself. These "edge habitats" (or *ecotones*, as they are often called) may harbor species

Average annual minimum temperatures. The winter distribution of many bird species is influenced by temperature. Frozen water and reduced insect populations are two results of cold temperatures that clearly affect bird populations.

AVERAGE ANNUAL MINIMUM TEMPERATURES	
Fahrenheit	Celsius
30° to 40°	0° to 5°
20° to 30°	−5° to −0°
10° to 20°	−10° to −5°
0° to 10°	−20° to −10°
−10° to 0°	−25° to −20°
−20° to −10°	−30° to −25°
−30° to −20°	−35° to −30°
−40° to −30°	−40° to −35°
−50° to −40°	−45° to −40°
below −50°	below −45°

Transitions between habitats. *Plant communities, and their associated bird communities, change gradually over time and space. This hypothetical example shows a gradual transition from grassland to mature forest and the species of grouse associated with each habitat type. Such a transition is found as one moves from the prairies to deciduous woodland to boreal forest. Greater Prairie-Chickens are gradually replaced by Sharp-tailed Grouse* (Tympanuchus phasianellus), *then Ruffed Grouse* (Bonasa umbellus), *and eventually by Spruce Grouse, as shown above from left to right. Given sufficient time, a similar transition could occur in one place, through plant succession.*

that typify both abutting habitats as well as species that are edge specialists. In a similar way, habitats may change over time—often following the same sequence of stages—as a plant community changes following a disturbance; this process is referred to as *succession.*

Succession

Plant succession is the natural process that takes place when a patch of disturbed habitat gradually changes into a mature plant community. Different species of plants replace (succeed) each other through a series of somewhat predictable stages that create distinct, but temporary, habitats over a period of decades. As the plant community changes, the associated bird community also changes.

In the most extreme cases, succession begins on a sterile surface such as bare rock. More commonly, successional change follows some disturbance that alters the vegetation on a patch of ground. Such disturbance can occur naturally, as a result of windstorms, lightning-sparked fires, mud deposited by floods, or the

draining of large abandoned beaver ponds. Alternatively, disturbance can be caused by humans, when clearing land for agriculture, mining, or building. In the past, Native Americans also cleared forests by burning, for game management and agriculture.

Even when land is completely cleared of vegetation, large numbers of weedy plants soon sprout, and within a year or two a successional grassland will form. After a few more years, the gradual growth of woody plants overwhelms the grasses, creating a successional shrubland. Trees eventually overtake the woody shrubs to form "second-growth" woodland, and finally the transition to forest replaces the first tree species with those characteristic of a mature forest. Even then, the forest continues to change gradually over centuries as conditions alter and favor new species.

Successional Habitats In the East, especially, grassland is often an ephemeral habitat, existing only as an early successional stage following disturbance. Because of both natural and human disturbances, grassland birds have been able to take advantage of a shifting mosaic of grassland patches interspersed within the eastern forests for thousands of years.

Successional grassland in the East is occupied by species also found in the midwestern prairies, such as the Eastern Meadowlark, Grasshopper Sparrow *(Ammodramus savannarum)*, and Bobolink *(Dolichonyx oryzivorus)*, although in several cases the eastern birds represent distinct subspecies.

Shrubland appears in the aftermath of a forest disturbance, such as a fire or windstorm, or else follows grassland as the next stage of succession. In many areas, shrubland occurs as a successional stage where humans have cleared trees for forestry, power lines, and the like, or in areas previously cleared for agriculture but that are now abandoned. As plant succession proceeds from grassland to forest, there is typically a period of several years when dense bushes and thickets dominate the land.

Early on in the process, when woody vegetation is just beginning to take hold, a few grassland bird species may remain in these areas, but eventually shrubland specialists replace them, and a few years later, woodland birds take over. The Brown Thrasher *(Toxostoma rufum)* and Yellow-breasted Chat *(Icteria virens)* are typical species of successional shrubland in the East. In western forests, shrubby clearings are often good places to find species such as MacGillivray's Warbler *(Oporornis tolmiei)*, the Spotted Towhee *(Pipilo maculatus)*, and the Green-tailed Towhee *(P. chlorurus)*.

The ephemeral nature of these successional habitats means that without disturbances they will disappear. Increasingly, this is happening as natural disturbance patterns are altered by humans and as forests regenerate. In many areas, nature reserves are now managed by mowing, burning, or other techniques in an effort to maintain certain early successional habitats and the birds associated with them.

Habitat Types

Described below are some of the major plant communities in North America, along with wetland, ocean, and human-created habitats. Each summary provides a brief overview of the broad habitat types and some of the typical birds that are associated with each habitat. These descriptions, however, are not exhaustive and do not attempt to describe all of the complexity and diversity within each category.

Forests and Woodlands

Forests are, simply put, habitats dominated by trees. Approximately 680 species of native trees grow in North America, and forests occupy nearly two-fifths of the continent's total land area. Forests are frequently the dominant habitat in areas where average summer temperatures are higher than 50° F (10° C) and where rainfall is both distributed throughout the growing season and sufficient to support trees.

There is much variation among North American forests. Some naturalists make a distinction between *true forest,* which has a closed canopy at least 30 feet (9 m) high, and *open forest* or *woodland,* in which trees are smaller or more widely spaced. Open forest often occurs in areas where the climate is too dry to support denser forest, where disturbances such as fire maintain a sparse distribution of trees, and in transitional zones between true forest and grassland. Fire plays a role in maintaining some forest ecosystems, especially southern pine woods that would revert to deciduous forest if not for periodic burns.

Forests are structurally the most complex terrestrial habitats, and they support much biological specialization. Across the continent, hundreds of bird species occur in forested habitats. Because forests provide many opportunities for concealment, forest birds can be difficult to locate. To observe these species, birders must mimic the skills of forest raptors

and learn to locate birds by ear or by spotting inconspicuous movements amid the foliage.

North American forests show considerable variation from west to east, except in the far north where the boreal forest spans the continent in a more or less continuous east–west belt. South of the boreal forest, mountain chains break up forest systems into distinctive western and eastern types, with much regional and local variation. Subtropical forest types occur in extreme southern Texas and at the tip of the Florida peninsula.

In more northerly regions, where the growing season is short, evergreen conifers have an advantage because they hold their needles year-round and can begin to photosynthesize as soon as spring returns. Conifers also grow well in dry climates and on sandy, well-drained soil because their needles are efficient in conserving water and nutrients. The ability to conserve water provides an additional advantage during long periods of very cold temperatures when water is frozen and unavailable to plants.

Deciduous trees, which must grow new leaves each year, need a longer growing season than conifers. Once their broad leaves are fully formed, however, they are particularly effective in capturing sunlight for photosynthesis, which gives them a competitive edge in areas with a sufficiently long growing season.

Boreal Forests

The boreal forest extends across the continent from Alaska to the Canadian Maritime Provinces. It consists mostly of firs, spruces, pines, and larches, with intermittent pockets of such cold-tolerant deciduous trees as poplars and birches. The boreal forest receives moderate amounts of precipitation and experiences long, cold winters, with snow for up to two-thirds of the year.

Most birds of the boreal forest are migratory and leave during the winter. In addition, intermittent failures of seed crops periodically force nominally resident species, such as the Pine Grosbeak *(Pinicola enucleator)*, to move southward in so-called irruption years. Similarly, cyclical infestations of the Spruce Budworm *(Choristoneura fumiferana)* caterpillar create "boom and bust" cycles for boreal insectivores such as the Bay-breasted Warbler *(Dendroica castanea)*.

Permanent residents of the boreal forest include the Northern Hawk Owl *(Surnia ulula)*, Spruce Grouse *(Falcipennis canadensis)*, Boreal Chickadee *(Poecile hudsonica)*, and many finches. In summer these species are joined by many thrushes, wood-warblers, and sparrows.

Scattered within the boreal forest are many small wetlands that, in the northern climate, take the form of open bogs. A small group of bird species breed in the stunted spruce surrounding these openings, including the Yellow-bellied Flycatcher *(Empidonax flaviventris)*, Palm Warbler, Lincoln's Sparrow *(Melospiza lincolnii)*, and Rusty Blackbird *(Euphagus carolinus)*.

Riparian Woodlands

Throughout the continent, access to water has a profound effect on vegetation, and low-lying areas support very different vegetation from hilltops. The associated bird species also differ, and rivers and streams with their adjacent riparian woodlands are always excellent places to watch birds.

These woods are significant habitats and support many bird species in all parts of the country. In grasslands and deserts that are otherwise too dry to support trees, riparian woods can be especially important bird habitats. In much of the West, riparian woodlands are dominated by cottonwoods and willows, with characteristic birds including Bullock's Oriole *(Icterus bullockii)*, the Yellow Warbler *(Dendroica petechia)*, and many other species. These linear strips of woodland provide both homes for resident species and conduits for migrating forest birds traveling over otherwise inhospitable land.

Riparian habitats in the arid Southwest are especially threatened by water diversion and grazing. These areas provide habitat for a number of uncommon or declining birds, including the "Southwestern" Willow Flycatcher *(Empidonax traillii extimus)*, Bell's Vireo *(Vireo bellii)*, and Abert's Towhee *(Pipilo aberti)*. Because the vegetation along rivers is often an extension of more southerly habitat types, several bird species reach their northern limit in riparian woodlands. These include the Rose-throated Becard *(Pachyramphus aglaiae)* and Thick-billed Kingbird *(Tyrannus crassirostris)* in Arizona and the Green Jay *(Cyanocorax yncas)* and Altamira Oriole *(Icterus gularis)* in Texas.

Western Forests

The wide variation in elevation, slope, soil type, and precipitation found in western North America results in a great variety of forest types, which are often distributed in a mosaic fashion within a small area. Although there is much local variation, these forests are typically dominated by conifers and oaks.

Northwestern Coastal Forests Along the northwestern coast of North America, the warm, moist air of the North Pacific bathes coastal forests in luxuriant rainfall and makes for comparatively mild winters. Under such conditions, a temperate rain forest of extraordinary grandeur has evolved. The northwestern coastal forests are among the few moist, temperate forest systems dominated by conifers, and they are home to some of the oldest and largest trees in the world, with some individuals reaching 500 years of age and 200 feet (60 m) in height. Conspicuous among the giants inhabiting these forests are Douglas-fir *(Pseudotsuga menziesii)*, Western Hemlock *(Tsuga heterophylla)*, Sitka Spruce *(Picea sitchensis)*, and Redwood *(Sequoia sempervirens)*.

Characteristic birds of these forests include the Chestnut-backed Chickadee *(Poecile rufescens)*, Varied Thrush *(Ixoreus naevius)*, and Townsend's Warbler *(Dendroica townsendi)*. Perhaps the best-known avian residents are the Spotted Owl *(Strix occidentalis)* and Marbled Murrelet *(Brachyramphus marmoratus)*, two species that have become symbols of the fight to save old-growth forest in the region.

Cordilleran Forests Cordilleran forest generally refers to mid-elevation mixed conifer forests growing on mountain slopes of the Sierra Nevada–Cascade chain, the Rocky Mountains, and many smaller mountain ranges in western North America. Summers tend to be hot and dry, with most rain and snow falling in winter. The western slopes of the Sierra Nevada have moist, relatively mild winters, similar to those of the northwestern coastal forest, but farther east the climate is drier and the winters are much colder.

Forests and woodlands. Habitats dominated by trees occur widely and in great variety across the continent. As with all habitats, the boundaries between forest types are rarely sharp transitions. Habitats are often distributed unevenly within the mapped areas and exhibit many local variations. Riparian and subtropical forest habitats cover relatively small areas and are not shown.

Boreal forests
Northwestern coastal forests
Cordilleran forests
Open oak woodlands
Pinyon-Juniper woodlands
Northern hardwood forests
Mixed deciduous forests
Coastal plain pine-oak forests

Among the most diverse conifer forests in the world, cordilleran forests include a number of distinctive plant communities. Besides conifers, these forests contain many deciduous trees, including nut- and seed-producing species that help sustain local bird populations. For example, acorns from oak trees provide food for Band-tailed Pigeons *(Columba fasciata)* and Steller's Jays *(Cyanocitta stelleri)*. The broad meadows scattered throughout these forests further enhance habitat diversity.

The combined effect of these conditions contributes to the region's long list of resident and breeding birds, including the Blue Grouse *(Dendragapus obscurus),* Northern Pygmy-Owl *(Glaucidium gnoma),* Broad-tailed Hummingbird *(Selasphorus platycercus),* Western Tanager *(Piranga ludoviciana),* and Cassin's Finch *(Carpodacus cassinii).*

The forests in the southern mountain ranges of Arizona, New Mexico, and Texas are similar to those found in parts of Mexico and are home to many plants and animals that occur nowhere else north of the Mexican border. These "southwestern specialties" include the Buff-breasted Flycatcher *(Empidonax fulvifrons),* Mexican Chickadee *(Poecile sclateri),* and Olive Warbler *(Peucedramus taeniatus).*

Open Oak Woodlands Open oak woodlands flourish in parts of the West where rainfall is insufficient to support denser forest. Evergreen live oaks dominate the open-canopy woodlands of California's foothill country, where annual precipitation is fairly limited and falls primarily during winter. These woodlands support birds such as the Oak Titmouse *(Baeolophus inornatus)* and Western Bluebird *(Sialia mexicana).* Acorns are a mainstay for other species that dwell here, including the Acorn Woodpecker *(Melanerpes formicivorus)* and Western Scrub-Jay *(Aphelocoma californica).*

Open oak woodlands also occur in Arizona, New Mexico, and Colorado. The oak-pine woodlands of southeastern Arizona and southwestern New Mexico are home to several southwestern specialties, most notably the Arizona Woodpecker *(Picoides arizonae)* and Mexican Jay *(Aphelocoma ultramarina).*

Pinyon-Juniper Woodlands Relatively few bird species are found in the arid, sparse pinyon-juniper woodlands of the Great Basin and southern Rocky Mountains. Representative bird species include the Juniper Titmouse *(Baeolophus ridgwayi)* and Pinyon Jay *(Gymnorhinus cyanocephalus)*, which are found in this area year-round, while the Gray Vireo *(Vireo vicinior)* occurs in summer in the southern portions of this habitat.

Eastern Forests

East of the prairies and south of the boreal forest, moist weather systems from the Gulf of Mexico and Canada produce sufficient rainfall throughout the year to support extensive forests. The growing season lasts up to 200 days, and temperatures exceed 50° F (10° C) for at least half the year. These conditions favor broad-leaved foliage, and many trees in eastern forests are deciduous.

Ecologists recognize several categories of eastern forest, each composed of particular tree species. Regional factors, such as rainfall, temperature, soil composition, drainage, elevation, and historical patterns of glaciation, determine the distribution of each forest type. Many eastern woodland birds occur in multiple forest types and are distributed throughout the region.

Northern Hardwood Forests The northernmost tier of eastern forest is the northern hardwood forest, famous for its extraordinarily colored autumn foliage. Northern hardwood forest occurs in a broad belt, in places several hundred miles wide, from the Great Lakes region to New England and Canada's Maritime Provinces. This zone is generally warmer than the boreal forest. Although temperatures can dip well below freezing in winter, they also can climb to over 100° F (38° C) in summer. There is ample rain, much of which falls during the four- to five-month growing season.

Many tree species are near the edge of their range in this transition forest; several conifers reach their southern limit, and many deciduous trees are at the northern extremes of their range. Typical species include Yellow Birch *(Betula alleghaniensis)*, American Beech *(Fagus grandifolia)*, Sugar Maple *(Acer saccharum)*, Eastern Hemlock *(Tsuga canadensis)*, Eastern White Pine *(Pinus strobus)*, and Northern Red Oak *(Quercus rubra)*.

As in the boreal forest, food availability is seasonal, and many of the birds inhabiting northern hardwood forests are migrants. Characteristic species include the Blue-headed Vireo *(Vireo solitarius)*, Black-throated Green Warbler *(Dendroica virens)*, Mourning Warbler, and White-throated Sparrow *(Zonotrichia albicollis)*.

Mixed Deciduous Forests South of the northern hardwood forest lies a complex array of habitats, known collectively as mixed deciduous forest. These habitats extend from the prairie states eastward through the Mississippi and Ohio River valleys, and across the Appalachians, merging finally into the pine-oak forests of the Atlantic coastal plain. Mixed deciduous forests grow in regions where there are four seasons of about equal length and moderate to high levels of precipitation distributed evenly throughout the year.

Because of their central location and ample food resources, mixed deciduous forests serve both as nesting habitat during summer and migratory stopover habitat for birds that breed farther north. Oak-hickory forest predominates toward the west, with various other oak-dominated assemblages farther east. Typical birds of these forests include the Blue Jay *(Cyanocitta cristata)*, Ovenbird, American Redstart *(Setophaga ruticilla)*, and Scarlet Tanager *(Piranga olivacea)*. Farther to the south and east a milder climate supports a greater diversity of trees and additional bird species such as the Worm-eating Warbler *(Helmitheros vermivorus)*, Swainson's Warbler *(Limnothlypis swainsonii)*, and Summer Tanager *(P. rubra)*.

Coastal Plain Pine-Oak Forests The pine-oak forests that grow on the coastal plain from southern New England south to Florida and west into eastern Texas are well suited to sandy, well-drained, relatively infertile coastal soil, and are maintained largely by fire.

Northern pine-oak forest, which grows from Massachusetts to Virginia, typically takes the form of pine barrens dominated by Pitch Pine *(Pinus rigida)* and a dense understory of low, leathery-leaved scrub oaks. This habitat supports many Brown Thrashers and Eastern Towhees *(Pipilo erythrophthalmus)*, as well as a variety of other characteristic species.

Southern pine-oak forest, which occurs from Virginia south to Florida and west to Texas, differs floristically from its northern counterpart. In these southern forests, several species of pine occur along with oaks and various southern broad-leaved trees. Grasses rather than shrubs are often abundant in the understory. The bird life also is distinctive and includes such species as the Brown-headed Nuthatch *(Sitta pusilla)* and Yellow-throated Warbler *(Dendroica dominica)*. Some pine specialists such as the Pine Warbler *(D. pinus)* are found in both northern and southern pine-oak forests.

In low-lying areas with standing water interspersed within the pine-oak forest, one can find swamp forests dominated by cypress and tupelo trees. Characteristic bird species include the Barred Owl *(Strix varia)*, Northern Parula *(Parula americana)*, and Prothonotary Warbler *(Protonotaria citrea)*. The majestic Bald-cypresses *(Taxodium distichum)*, often the tallest trees in the forest, can provide nest sites for the endangered Wood Stork *(Mycteria americana)* and other colonial waterbirds.

Farther south in Florida, dry winter weather, along with the porous sand and limestone that underlie much of the peninsula, creates locally arid conditions. In elevated areas localized oak scrub is mixed with abundant Saw Palmetto *(Serenoa repens)*. In the remnants of this habitat that have not been cleared for housing or agriculture, one can find the threatened Florida Scrub-Jay *(Aphelocoma coerulescens)*.

Savannas

In the Midwest and the southeastern United States, frequent fires have historically maintained a mixture of grasslands and scattered trees, especially oaks or pines, called savanna. Similar habitats occur in other areas where grassland merges gradually into forest—for example, in the aspen parkland of Canada and in the foothills of California. Savannas support a mixture of grassland and woodland birds.

In the southeastern states, mature stands of Longleaf Pine *(Pinus palustris)* form pine savanna that once covered millions of acres from Virginia to eastern Texas. These "piney woods" support pine specialists like the Red-cockaded Woodpecker *(Picoides borealis)* and Bachman's Sparrow *(Aimophila aestivalis)*, along with birds now associated with open fields such as the Prairie Warbler *(Dendroica discolor)* and Indigo Bunting *(Passerina cyanea)*. Today the pine savanna has disappeared from much of its historical range.

In the Midwest, savannas formed when fires suppressed the regeneration of oaks and allowed grasses and forbs to grow. The bird species most associated with these "oak openings" is the Red-headed Woodpecker *(Melanerpes erythrocephalus)*. Open savannas have become rare in the Midwest, where the land-management policy of suppressing fires allows woody plants to dominate. This practice results in the gradual conversion of savanna to closed-canopy woodland, with the resulting loss of most of the savanna birds.

Subtropical Forests

In southern Florida and southern Texas, small areas of forest support subtropical species of trees, a much greater diversity of tree species than found in more northerly habitats, and a number of unusual southern bird species.

Florida Subtropical Hammocks Woody vegetation in extreme southern Florida grows in patches on slightly higher ground than do the surrounding sawgrass marshes, cypress swamps, and mangrove forests. This vegetation—including many species of trees found nowhere else in North America, such as the Gumbo Limbo *(Bursera simaruba)*—forms dense shaded clumps known as hammocks, where bird species such as the White-crowned Pigeon *(Columba leucocephala)* and the elusive Mangrove Cuckoo *(Coccyzus minor)* are found. These hammocks are perhaps most notable ornithologically for the great diversity of insectivorous birds that they support during winter. In particular, many wood-warbler species that winter nowhere else in North America regularly spend the winter in southern Florida.

Mangrove Swamps The mangrove forests along the coasts of Florida and the Gulf of Mexico are technically swamps, since they contain woody vegetation and are regularly inundated with water. Because mangrove forests, like saltmarshes, benefit from the flushing of tidal action, they can be extremely productive and serve as "nurseries" for many marine organisms. This productivity provides rich feeding for many bird species, particularly waterbirds such as herons, egrets, and ibises. In Florida, mangrove forests harbor tropical species such as the Mangrove Cuckoo and Black-whiskered Vireo *(Vireo altiloquus)*.

South Texas Mesquite In the hot, arid climate of extreme southern Texas a distinct brushy habitat exists. The dominant plant is mesquite, which creates a forest that is at its most profuse in this region. Other thorny shrubs also grow, along with a ground cover of grasses and cacti, and scattered stands of oaks. Along rivers and streams a number of other tree species may be found, including subtropical species such as the Texas Ebony *(Pithecellobium flexicaule)*. In this habitat many Mexican birds reach their northern limit, including the White-tailed Hawk *(Buteo albicaudatus)*, Ferruginous Pygmy-Owl *(Glaucidium brasilianum)*, and Tropical Parula *(Parula pitiayumi)*.

Grasslands

Permanent grasslands occur worldwide, mostly in dry temperate or subtropical regions with relatively little rainfall. Such grassland is found in an intermediate zone between drier desert and moister forest habitats. Gradual transition zones often lie along grassland boundaries, making exact demarcation between the habitats difficult. In most North American grasslands, especially in the northern Great Plains, rainfall is distinctly seasonal, and temperatures can vary widely from very hot in summer to bitter cold in winter.

In North America, permanent grasslands occur primarily in the middle of the continent. In generations past, visitors to the Great Plains were awestruck by the sight of the vast, unbroken prairie, much of which today has been converted to farmland. Smaller areas of permanent grassland also occur in California, the interior Northwest, and along the Texas coast. Although grasslands might appear quite uniform, about 7,500 native plant species occur in North American grasslands, and much diversity can be seen by anyone who walks for a few minutes through a wild prairie.

Successional grasslands form in wetter, more typically forested areas as an early successional stage following disturbance. If disturbance occurs frequently, grasslands can persist for long periods in these areas. Fire, wind, and grazing by large mammals all prevent woody plants from encroaching into grassland habitats.

Prairie Grasslands

Prairie grasslands can be divided into three basic types: tallgrass, mixed-grass, and shortgrass. Each has a characteristic set of dominant plants, which are adapted to particular soil types and rainfall patterns. Especially to the east, maintenance of prairie grasslands depends on frequent fires or on herds of grazing and browsing mammals such as elk and bison, which slow the spread of woody plants. The transition from

tallgrass prairie in the east to shortgrass prairie in the west parallels a decline in annual rainfall.

An important feature of the northern Great Plains grasslands is the presence of numerous glacial depressions that are now small ponds called potholes. These small wetlands dot the prairie landscape and serve as important breeding areas for waterfowl and other marsh-dwelling species.

Tallgrass Prairie Tallgrass prairie originally covered the eastern edge of the Great Plains. Annual rainfall in tallgrass prairie averages 40 inches (100 cm) per year, about half of which occurs during the summer growing season. Dominant plants in this ecosystem include Indian Grass *(Sorghastrum nutans)* and, especially, Big Bluestem *(Andropogon gerardi)*.

Despite the name, tallgrass prairie is not tall year-round. Each winter the grasses die down, allowing a profusion of low-growing spring wildflowers to bloom. By midsummer, however, Big Bluestem grass can grow as tall as 5 to 12 feet (1.5–3.5 m). Today almost the entire original tallgrass prairie has been plowed under for farming and other development, and only scattered pieces remain.

Characteristic birds of tallgrass prairie include the Greater Prairie-Chicken *(Tympanuchus cupido)*, Dickcissel *(Spiza americana)*, and Henslow's Sparrow *(Ammodramus henslowii)*.

Mixed-grass Prairie Mixed-grass prairie, intermediate between tallgrass and shortgrass prairie, extends from Texas into southern Canada; a transition zone

farther north, the fescue prairie, melds into aspen parkland and eventually the boreal forest. Precipitation averages are lower than in tallgrass prairie, about 20 inches (50 cm) annually, and higher wind speeds increase evaporation and add to the region's aridity.

Various hardy grasses dominate mixed prairies. Little Bluestem *(Andropogon scoparius)*, among the most common, grows to a midsummer height of 2 to 3 feet (60–90 cm). Mixed-grass prairie attracts bird species associated with tallgrass or shortgrass prairies, such as the Dickcissel and the Lark Bunting *(Calamospiza melanocorys)*, respectively. The Chestnut-collared Longspur *(Calcarius ornatus)* is a typical mixed-grass breeder, as is Baird's Sparrow *(Ammodramus bairdii)* in the north.

Shortgrass Prairie Shortgrass prairie makes up the remainder of the central prairie region. The eastern boundary is a broad transition zone with mixed-grass prairie, but the western edge ends abruptly at the foothills of the Rockies. Besides being drier than mixed-grass prairie, with annual rainfall as low as 10 inches (25 cm), shortgrass prairie is windier and hence especially arid.

Shortgrass prairies generally exhaust the moisture they receive by the end of the summer growing season, at which time resident grasses become dormant. Grama Grass *(Bouteloua gracilis)* and Buffalo Grass *(Buchloe dactyloides)*, while nutritious forage, grow only in sparse patches. Vegetation is generally no taller than 2 feet (60 cm), and most plants rise just a few inches off the ground.

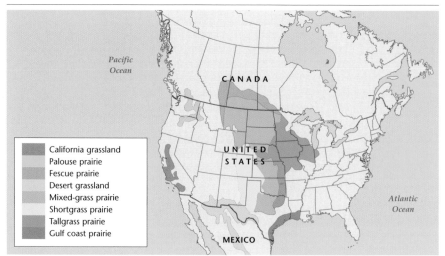

Grasslands. *North America's grasslands can be subdivided into distinct types; this map shows their historical distributions. To the east and north, especially, grasslands transition into open woodlands over a broad area. Today much of this grassland habitat has been converted to farmland, and only a small fraction of some habitats remains. Also scattered throughout the continent are constantly shifting patches of successional grassland.*

Breeding birds of the shortgrass prairie include shorebirds such as the Mountain Plover *(Charadrius montanus)* and Long-billed Curlew *(Numenius americanus),* as well as McCown's Longspur *(Calcarius mccownii)* and the Lark Bunting. In the southern plains, the Lesser Prairie-Chicken *(Tympanuchus pallidicinctus)* is a characteristic species.

Desert Grasslands

Apart from prairies, there are several other, less extensive permanent grassland habitats in North America. Among them, the desert grasslands of the southwestern United States are particularly rich in bird species with small ranges, and these grasslands also serve as important wintering grounds for many birds that nest in the Great Plains. This type of grassland is dominated by bunchgrasses such as Sideoats Grama *(Bouteloua curtipendula)* and Grama Grass that grow in clumps rather than forming sod.

Many of the birds that live in desert grassland breed late in the summer when intense rainstorms called monsoons occur; monsoons are unpredictable and may not occur at all in some years.

Species such as Botteri's *(Aimophila botterii),* Rufous-winged *(A. carpalis),* and Cassin's *(A. cassinii)* Sparrows wait for the monsoons before they breed, and they begin singing and nest-building within days, sometimes hours, of the start of the rains. Summer rains affect seed abundance for wintering birds, and in years of low rainfall many migratory sparrows bypass the southwestern grasslands and winter farther south.

The desert grasslands of Texas, New Mexico, and Arizona are also home to several quail species, including the Scaled Quail *(Callipepla squamata)* and the "Masked" Bobwhite *(Colinus virginianus ridgwayi),* an endangered subspecies of the Northern Bobwhite.

Shrublands

Intermediate between woodlands and grasslands are shrub-dominated habitats. Shrubland often forms where environmental conditions, particularly water availability, are midway between those that support trees and grasses, or as a successional stage in places where forests will eventually dominate. Shrubland habitats occur throughout North America, from Arctic tundra to the southwestern deserts and southeastern coastal plain.

Chaparral

Perhaps the most distinctive shrubland habitat is chaparral, a dense, brushy habitat consisting of woody shrubs with small, thick, evergreen leaves. Chaparral occurs primarily along the California coast, where cold waters close to shore generate little moisture, creating a marked dry season in summer. It extends east from the coastal hills as conditions permit and frequently is found in locations too rocky or steep for grassland. Chaparral is also sometimes called "Mediterranean scrub" because similar habitat is found around the Mediterranean Sea in Europe.

To cope with dry-season aridity, chaparral plants have developed deep taproots and moisture-conserving foliage. The dry, resin-filled chaparral shrubs are highly flammable, and hot fires burn the habitat every few decades. Far from killing the plants, however, these fires generate the release of nutrients, causing a flush of new growth. Rich in insects and berry-producing shrubs, chaparral supports many birds. Resident species include the California Thrasher *(Toxostoma redivivum)* and the Wrentit *(Chamaea fasciata)*, a skulking, secretive chaparral specialist that is heard more often than seen.

Another shrubland habitat—coastal sage scrub—also occurs along the southern California coast, typically at lower elevations and drier sites than chaparral. There has been a great reduction in coastal sage scrub as cities along the coast expand; however, the presence of threatened species, particluarly the California Gnatcatcher *(Polioptila californica)*, has slowed development in some areas.

Other Shrublands

Shrubland is a difficult category to define, since much of this habitat can also be classified as either woodland or desert, or simply as a narrow transitional habitat between low-growing vegetation and forest. The most common shrubland habitat in much of North America is successional shrubland. Permanent shrublands include the vast areas of sagebrush, saltbush, and greasewood habitats found in arid parts of the intermountain West.

Deserts

Deserts are areas that experience an annual water deficit caused by low rainfall, high evaporation rates, or a combination of the two. Most deserts are also characterized by sparse ground cover and extreme temperature fluctuations, with cold nights and hot days. While a strict definition of desert would include many high-latitude areas of tundra and ice cover, this discussion is confined to low-latitude deserts.

Because of the limited ground cover, desert soil generally contains little organic matter. In areas surrounded by mountains, surface water drains into low

Pacific Coast chaparral. *This dense, shrubby habitat grows in the relatively dry, mild climate of the southern Pacific coast. Within the green area shown, chaparral is interspersed among various forest, grassland, and desert habitats. Increasingly urban and suburban development is replacing chaparral, especially in the south. Similar brushy habitat is found on mountain slopes in Arizona and in Mexico.*

basins and quickly evaporates. This process concentrates mineral residues and creates barren salt flats, or playas, with highly saline or alkaline soils. In wet years, these flats can become shallow lakes that provide important habitat for waterbirds.

There are four main deserts in North America, each of which comprises a variety of habitats.

Great Basin Desert

The Great Basin Desert, a high-elevation desert that lies largely in Nevada and Utah, with small portions in California, Oregon, Idaho, and Wyoming, lies in the rain shadow of the Sierra Nevada and Cascade Mountains. Some 60 percent of the precipitation in the Great Basin occurs in winter, much in the form of snow. Although the Great Basin can experience severely hot temperatures during summer, the very cold winters prevent many desert-adapted succulents, such as cacti, from flourishing.

In Pleistocene times (about 2 million years ago) the Great Basin contained a vast network of lakes, including Lakes Bonneville and Lahontan, which occupied thousands of square miles. The largest remnant of these lakes, Great Salt Lake in Utah, covers a tiny fraction of the area once flooded. This and other permanent bodies of water that remain often have high mineral concentrations due to evaporation; Great Salt Lake, for example, is much saltier than seawater, making it uninhabitable for fish.

Perhaps surprisingly, the region supports dense concentrations of waterbirds, which feed on brine shrimp and alkali flies, and on the fish that are found in the less saline lakes and marshes. Substantial colonies of American White Pelicans *(Pelecanus erythrorhynchos)* and California Gulls *(Larus californicus)* nest on islands in the larger lakes. Saline lakes provide migratory stopovers for hundreds of thousands of phalaropes and Eared Grebes *(Podiceps nigricollis),* and large numbers of migratory and breeding shorebirds and waterfowl visit freshwater marshes associated with lakes. Desert salt flats are mostly devoid of vegetation but do provide nesting habitat for the Snowy Plover *(Charadrius alexandrinus).*

Sagebrush shrublands dominate the surrounding desert. Sagebrush-steppe extends to the north and east of the Great Basin and is characterized by perennial bunchgrasses and herbs interspersed among the sagebrush. Farther south, Great Basin sagebrush habitats are more arid, with fewer bunchgrasses. Salt-desert scrub, dominated by saltbush and greasewood plants, occurs in areas where sagebrush is absent and the soil is especially dry and salty, such as the dried-up beds of former lakes.

Bird diversity in all these habitats is low, but a number of characteristic species are far more common here than elsewhere; these include the Greater Sage-Grouse *(Centrocercus urophasianus),* Sage Thrasher *(Oreoscoptes montanus),* and Brewer's Sparrow *(Spizella breweri).*

Mojave Desert

The Mojave, which extends from southern California through southern Nevada to western Arizona and southwestern Utah, is the smallest of the North American deserts. Its border with the Great Basin Desert to the north is indistinct. In the Mojave, most of the rain falls in winter, but there is occasional summer precipitation as well, particularly to the east. The topography of the Mojave is highly variable and includes Death Valley, one of the hottest and driest locations on Earth, with an average annual rainfall of less than 2 inches (5 cm) and temperatures that have reached 134° F (56° C). During periods of such intense heat, resident birds may retreat up the mountain slopes that border the valley for relief.

The Creosote Bush (Larrea tridentata) flats and mesquite washes of the Mojave are similar to those found in other desert regions, but many of the plants that grow here occur nowhere else. The most distinctive of the Mojave's plants is the Joshua Tree (Yucca brevifolia), the tallest of the yuccas, which has many shaggy branches and grows up to 40 feet (12 m) high. The Mojave's desolate saltbush flats are home to few birds, but they are a good place to find the secretive Le Conte's Thrasher (Toxostoma lecontei).

Sonoran Desert

Much of the Sonoran Desert lies in Mexico, but portions extend northward into extreme southern California and Arizona. Overall this is the hottest and driest of North American deserts; however, parts of its eastern expanse in the United States receive quite a lot of rain, both in winter and summer, sufficient in places for desert grasslands to form. The summer monsoons bring widely scattered afternoon thundershowers, with much of the rain falling in the mountain ranges that dot the region, making mountain canyons incongruously lush.

The many plant communities in the Sonoran Desert host an exceptional variety of cacti, the best-known being the Saguaro (Carnegiea gigantea). A southwestern race of Purple Martin (Progne subis hesperia) specializes in nesting among the giant cactus limbs, often in holes excavated by the Gila Woodpecker (Melanerpes uropygialis) or Gilded Flicker (Colaptes chrysoides). Harris's Hawk (Parabuteo unicinctus) and the Elf Owl (Micrathene whitneyi) also use the Saguaro for nesting.

Desert habitats. Deserts are arid, sparsely vegetated regions. North America has four distinctive deserts. The Mojave, Sonoran, and Chihuahuan are referred to as "warm" deserts, whereas the more northerly Great Basin Desert is considered a "cold" desert because of frigid winter temperatures. Nested within these broad regions are a variety of grassland, shrubland, and montane forest types, in addition to typical desert plant communities.

Great Basin Desert
Mojave Desert
Sonoran Desert
Chihuahuan Desert

Chihuahuan Desert

The high-elevation Chihuahuan Desert lies in the continental interior, mostly in Mexico, but extending into southeastern Arizona, New Mexico, and western Texas. The elevation of the Chihuahuan Desert generally exceeds 3,500 feet (1,000 m), and the region can experience freezing temperatures in winter, despite its southerly location. Most of the rainfall (65–80 percent) occurs in summer and originates to the east over the Gulf of Mexico. (These same storm patterns provide much of the summer rain to the eastern Sonoran Desert.)

A principal indicator plant of the Chihuahuan Desert is the Lechuguilla (*Agave lecheguilla*), a type of agave or century plant that grows in profusion on the arid slopes. Characteristic birds of the Chihuahuan Desert include the Scaled Quail, Lucifer Hummingbird *(Calothorax lucifer)*, and Chihuahuan Raven *(Corvus cryptoleucus)*.

Tundra

Tundra habitats are areas beyond the treeline that lack a permanent cover of ice or snow. They occur around the world at high latitudes and high altitudes (the word "tundra" derives from the Finnish *tunturi*, for "treeless heights"). Tree growth is limited on tundra habitats by low water availability, low temperatures, high winds, and shallow soils; the point at which trees can no longer grow varies regionally depending on these factors. Along the southern shores of Hudson Bay, for example, trees grow only as far as a latitude of 55°N, whereas in northwestern Canada they extend to 70°N.

Despite their somewhat different provenance, alpine and Arctic tundra are very similar in appearance, with many closely related resident plants and animals. Alpine plants that grow near the summit of Mount Washington in New Hampshire, such as Diapensia *(Diapensia lapponica)*, have no close relatives in the New England woods below; rather, their nearest kin grow hundreds of miles away in Arctic Canada. Such disjunct tundra "islands" are relics from the last Ice Age, when the northern tundra extended farther south.

Several bird species breed in both alpine and Arctic tundra, including the American Pipit *(Anthus rubescens)*, White-crowned Sparrow *(Zonotrichia leucophrys)*, and Gray-crowned Rosy-Finch *(Leucosticte tephrocotis)*.

Arctic Tundra

A defining feature of Arctic tundra is *permafrost,* a permanently frozen layer beneath the surface that may reach depths of 1,500 feet (450 m); permafrost also underlies some alpine tundra. Each summer, warm temperatures thaw an "active layer" of soil near the surface, usually to a depth of 1 to 3 feet (30–90 cm). Because of the frozen permafrost below, drainage is poor, causing many shallow ponds to form in summer.

The Arctic growing season lasts for only about six weeks to four months, and frost is possible year-round. Average temperatures range from 37° to 54° F (3–12° C) during summer, and –20° to –30° F (–29° to –34° C) in winter. Adding to the frigid temperatures, the flat terrain provides little shelter from wind, and the windchill can be especially brutal.

The Arctic as a whole receives little precipitation; annual totals can be as low as in the southwestern deserts, although some places receive as much as 40 inches (100 cm). The diversity of animal life in the Arctic is markedly lower than in tropical or temperate regions. The large populations of many Arctic-dwelling species offset low species diversity to some extent, but the fact remains that the tundra is a difficult environment in which to eke out a living. The limited number of resident bird species includes the Gyrfalcon *(Falco rusticolus)*, Willow *(Lagopus lagopus)* and Rock *(L. mutus)* Ptarmigan, Snowy Owl *(Nyctea scandiaca)*, and Common Raven *(Corvus corax)*.

Most Arctic-dwelling birds use the tundra as a breeding ground during summer and leave in winter when conditions become unfavorable. Worldwide, about a hundred bird species migrate to the Arctic to breed, including many species of waterfowl and shorebirds as well as some northern passerines, most of which are members of the families Emberizidae (New World sparrows) and Fringillidae (finches and allies).

Low-Arctic Tundra Low-Arctic tundra occurs beyond the treeline, usually in areas near the coast or inland at low elevations. The soil is relatively moist and supports abundant low-growing plants, including grasses, sedges, heaths, mosses, and lichens. Low-growing shrubs such as willows, dwarf birches, and alders form an Arctic scrub habitat that is most common in protected areas and along streams. Contrary to the prevailing image of tundra as a barren wasteland, the Lilliputian forests of the low-Arctic tundra can have dense, if short, cover.

Birds associated with low-Arctic tundra include the Willow Ptarmigan, Parasitic Jaeger *(Stercorarius parasiticus)*, Common Redpoll *(Carduelis flammea)*, American Tree Sparrow *(Spizella arborea)*, and many shorebirds. In the transition zone between the low-Arctic tundra and the boreal forest, characteristic species include Smith's Longspur *(Calcarius pictus)* and Harris's Sparrow *(Zonotrichia querula)*.

High-Arctic Tundra The image of a polar desert most accurately evokes high-Arctic tundra, which occurs in the very far north and also on exposed ridges farther

south. The high Arctic is colder, drier, and less productive than the low Arctic. The growing season is too short to support much plant life, and mosses and lichens often dominate the ground cover. There is little, if any, soil here; much of the ground surface consists of little more than bare rock. Few organisms are able to survive in this region.

A number of tundra-breeding birds nest in dry, rocky areas of the high Arctic, including the Surfbird *(Aphriza virgata)*, Northern Wheatear *(Oenanthe oenanthe)*, and Gray-crowned Rosy-Finch. The Rock Ptarmigan resides in the high-Arctic habitat type, replacing its low-Arctic relative, the Willow Ptarmigan. As conditions become more severe, fewer species occur, with passerines becoming especially uncommon; the Snow Bunting *(Plectrophenax nivalis)* is among the few small birds that can breed in the most extreme Arctic conditions.

Alpine Tundra
Plants and animals that inhabit alpine tundra share many of the biological adaptations found in polar residents. Both environments have a harsh and unpredictable climate, strong winds, a limited growing season, and low year-round temperatures. Although average temperatures are usually higher and drainage is typically better in alpine tundra than in the Arctic, the rigors of life at high altitudes negate any sense of moderation. In flat areas, alpine soil may accumulate, resulting in lush mountain meadows, but where the topography is

rougher or more exposed, only mosses, lichens, and the toughest of cushion plants may survive.

Alpine tundra does not appear abruptly as one moves up a mountain slope. Just as there is a transition zone where boreal forest thins to Arctic tundra, continuous subalpine forest thins into open-canopy woodland at higher elevations before reaching the treeline. The treeline occurs at around 11,500 feet (3,500 m) in the mid-latitude mountains of the Sierra Nevada and Rocky Mountain ranges. In the Northeast, alpine tundra occurs at much lower elevations on mountain ridges and peaks that barely top 6,000 feet (1,800 m). The transitional zone is home to species such as the White-crowned Sparrow in the West and Bicknell's Thrush *(Catharus bicknelli)* in the East.

Few birds are associated with alpine tundra, and most of these retreat down the slopes in winter. In the Rocky Mountains, the only year-round resident of alpine tundra is the White-tailed Ptarmigan *(Lagopus leucurus)*. In the West, typical breeders include the American Pipit, ptarmigan, and all three species of rosy-finch.

Wetland and Aquatic Habitats

Wetlands are highly productive ecosystems, supporting both a variety and an abundance of organisms. Plant matter production in saltmarshes, for example, can equal the best results of human agriculture. Wetlands are especially attractive to birders because of the sheer number of birds it is possible to see in a day. Aquatic habitats are highly diverse, including fresh- and saltwater systems; still and moving water; and areas of permanent or seasonal flooding, with damp ground or water hundreds of feet deep. Aquatic plant communities range from microscopic plankton to cypress forests. Many wetland birds occur in a range of these aquatic settings.

Freshwater Marshes

For many, the term "wetland" conjures up the image of a marsh, a habitat that is particularly important to birds. Marshes are wetlands dominated by emergent, nonwoody vegetation such as reeds, cattails, and sedges. (Emergent vegetation is rooted underwater but has foliage extending above the water's surface.)

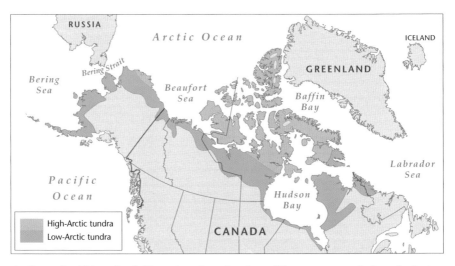

Arctic tundra. *This treeless habitat exists where climatic conditions are so severe that woody plants grow in stunted forms or not at all. Most of the birds associated with tundra visit for a few months in summer to nest and raise young, then migrate south to warmer areas. Alpine tundra occurs on mountain ridges south of the Arctic.*

Deeper and more permanent marshes also support floating aquatic plants.

Freshwater marshes most often occur in poorly drained depressions along slow-moving streams and rivers or in the shallow fringes of lakes and ponds, prairie swales or potholes, and similar environments. The long list of birds that breed in these marshes includes wading birds, waterfowl, rails, shorebirds, gulls, terns, wrens, blackbirds, and sparrows.

Saltmarshes and Tidal Flats

Saltwater marshes form along sheltered river estuaries, in lagoons behind coastal barrier islands, and along shallow coastal stretches where wave action is mild. Saltmarsh vegetation is dominated by grasses such as *Spartina* species and saltgrass, as well as rushes, sedges, and *Salicornia* (or glasswort) species. Tidal action of salt water creates a gradient from lower (and wetter) to higher (and drier) plant communities, as well as from salty water (near the ocean) to brackish and eventually fresh water (away from the ocean). These gradients influence the distribution of birds within the saltmarsh.

Estuaries—the tidally active, brackish zones at river mouths—and their associated marshes and tidal flats provide important feeding areas for waterbirds. Waterfowl, wading birds, shorebirds, and gulls can gather in immense numbers, especially during the nonbreeding season, to feed on exposed mudflats. The tidal cycle determines the daily activities of these birds, which must concentrate their feeding at low tide; often birds congregate in dense roosts to rest when feeding areas are inundated. Estuaries are exceptionally productive wetlands, with fresh nutrients brought in continuously by associated rivers and waste materials flushed out twice a day by the tides.

Breeding species include the Clapper Rail *(Rallus longirostris),* Saltmarsh Sharp-tailed Sparrow *(Ammodramus caudacutus),* Seaside Sparrow *(A. maritimus),* and "Belding's" Savannah Sparrow *(Passerculus sandwichensis beldingi).* Predators such as the Short-eared Owl *(Asio flammeus)* and Peregrine Falcon *(Falco peregrinus)* frequently hunt over saltmarshes and estuaries in winter.

Lakes and Ponds

Lakes and ponds are familiar places to find swimming birds such as loons, grebes, and waterfowl, and lake islands often provide predator-free breeding sites for colonial species such as the Ring-billed Gull *(Larus delawarensis)* and Double-crested Cormorant *(Phalacrocorax auritus).* The main foods here are fish, aquatic invertebrates, and the leaves, seeds, and roots of aquatic plants.

Artificial lakes and ponds can resemble natural deepwater bodies, but reservoirs that are heavily treated with chemicals or that are drained regularly often lack abundant plant and animal life, and

their steep sides hamper the development of nearshore plant communities, further reducing their value to birds.

Rivers and Streams

There are several major river drainages in North America, with thousands of associated streams and tributaries. Although all are characterized by flowing water, they vary considerably, ranging from cold, tumbling mountain creeks to warmer less turbulent lowland streams to the deep, broad rivers that meander across the coastal plain. Characteristics of these watercourses depend on both rainfall and the topography and underlying geology of the watershed, and they may be influenced by conditions hundreds of miles away. In arid regions such as the desert Southwest, even large rivers may dry out between seasonal rains.

Riparian zones provide habitat for many terrestrial species (discussed above under Riparian Woodlands), as well as generalist waterbirds, but there also are a few river specialists. The American Dipper *(Cinclus mexicanus)*, found along mountain streams in the West, is one of the few truly aquatic passerines, and the Harlequin Duck *(Histrionicus histrionicus)* also occurs along fast-flowing rivers where few other waterfowl regularly breed. Other species rely upon riverine features; for example, the Belted Kingfisher *(Ceryle alcyon)* and Bank Swallow *(Riparia riparia)* build their nest burrows in exposed sandy riverbanks.

Ocean Habitats

To the casual onlooker, oceans may seem like vast, undifferentiated tracts of water, but in reality they comprise many varying conditions that are just as significant as the subdivisions within habitats on land. These regions are defined by distance from land, latitude, and physical and biological characteristics of the water. As on land, different bird species associate with different habitats.

The *littoral zone* is the narrow strip of land along the immediate coast. The *neritic zone* comprises the relatively shallow waters that overlie the *continental shelf,* which lies along the edges of continents and can extend tens of miles offshore. At the edge of this shelf, at the *continental slope,* the seafloor drops away sharply into the deep waters of the *oceanic zone.*

Loons, grebes, cormorants, and sea ducks typically stay near shore in neritic waters, while gulls spend much of their time in the littoral zone. In contrast, gadfly petrels, fulmars, and albatrosses are more oceanic, especially during the nonbreeding season. Birds that spend most of their lives over the open ocean often are referred to as *pelagic,* and such species may rarely be seen from land.

Water Masses and Currents

Ocean waters can be subdivided into distinct water masses that differ in temperature, salinity, nutrient availability, and attendant biological communities.

Unlike terrestrial habitats, the location of particular water masses can change over very short time spans as a result of ocean currents, thus making it difficult for scientists to study the habitat selection of individual species or to predict where they might occur.

The Gulf Stream is a broad, blue "river" of warm water that originates in the Caribbean basin and flows north along the eastern coast of North America. The Gulf Stream is large and strong, in places carrying more than a billion cubic feet of water per second. Such tropical species as the Black-capped Petrel (Pterodroma hasitata) travel in the Gulf Stream as it flows north to meet the colder, less saline Labrador Current, which flows south from the Arctic and deflects the Gulf Stream east toward Europe.

Off North America's western coast, the cool California Current flows from north to south, while northward intrusions of warm equatorial waters sometimes bring tropical species, such as the Magnificent Frigatebird (Fregata magnificens), north. The relatively warm Alaska Current circles counterclockwise in the Gulf of Alaska, and there are several other distinct water masses in the Bering Sea.

Upwelling

Many of the world's most productive ocean waters are in areas of upwelling, where deep waters rich in nutrients rise to the surface. Upwelling occurs where ocean currents sweeping along the seafloor encounter an obstruction—such as a seamount, a shallow bank, or the continental slope—that deflects the current toward the surface. Along the coast, prevailing winds can also push surface water offshore, causing water from below to rise and replace the surface water.

Phytoplankton, the tiny plants that constitute the base of the ocean food chain, require both nutrients and sunlight to grow, but nutrients tend to settle to the ocean floor, where sunlight is not strong enough to support photosynthesis. Areas of high productivity occur where upwelling brings nutrients back toward the surface. The masses of phytoplankton then consume these nutrients and are in turn consumed by zooplankton, such as protozoans, crustaceans, and larval fish. These zooplankton then become food for birds and other predators.

Tropical seas are generally less productive than more northerly oceans because less mixing occurs between the surface

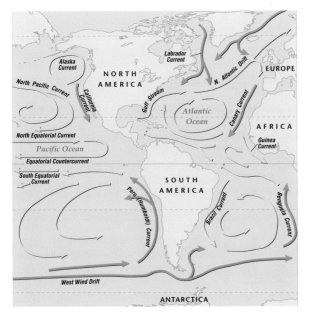

Ocean currents. The water in the world's major oceans cycles in broad currents, which carry warm water away from the equator and cold water away from the poles. Where these currents brush against continents or each other, or where water passes over underwater features, such as canyons and seamounts, they generate upwelling. This upward movement of water brings nutrients to the surface, increasing biological productivity. Many of the world's best places to watch seabirds are in areas of upwelling.

→ Warm current
→ Cold current

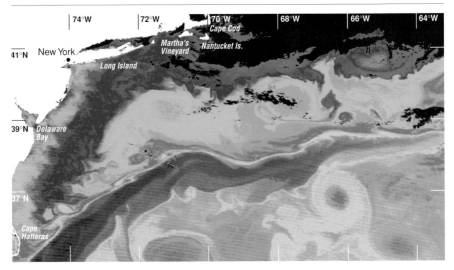

Gulf Stream. The warm Gulf Stream flows northeast along the Atlantic coast of North America until it meets the cold water of the southbound Labrador Current. The sharp gradient between warm and cold water is clearly visible in this infrared satellite image, in which the coldest waters are shown as black and purple, with blue, green, yellow, and red representing progressively warmer waters; temperatures range from about 45° F (7° C) to about 72° F (22° C). Sometimes this front can be seen with the naked eye as a razor-sharp boundary between the tropical blue Gulf Stream water and the distinctly greenish water of the Labrador Current. Bird species associated with warm water are found in the main current as well as in warm eddies that swirl off the edges of the current. Other species are found mainly along the edges, where floating algae and debris are concentrated and local upwelling brings nutrients to the surface.

and deeper waters. The consistently hot temperatures of the tropics warm the ocean's surface water, making it less dense than the deeper water. This density gradient effectively creates a "lid" that traps nutrients in the poorly lit depths where phytoplankton cannot use them. The colder, well-mixed waters of the northern oceans, in contrast, allow the movement of nutrients to the surface, where photosynthesis can occur.

Upwelling accounts for the biological productivity of the Grand Banks and Georges Bank in the North Atlantic and the nutrient-rich waters of Monterey Bay in California. In Monterey Bay, steep underwater canyons provide distinct areas of upwelling caused by the flow of the California Current. The abundance of small marine organisms in Monterey Bay provides ample food for seabirds, large fish, and marine mammals, which is why this has become a premier site in North America for seeing seabirds.

Fronts

The boundaries between water masses are referred to as fronts and are similar to the meteorological fronts that represent abrupt changes in atmospheric conditions. Oceanic fronts are characterized by distinct changes in temperature and salinity over a short distance. In some cases, fronts can be highly productive places for birds to feed because they can cause upwelling and concentrate prey.

The waters off Cape Hatteras in North Carolina are another of North America's top sites to see ocean birds. Although these waters lack the massive nutrient upwelling of Monterey Bay's underwater canyons, there is upwelling along the continental slope. Perhaps more important, the northbound Gulf Stream meets the southbound Labrador Current in this region; the confluence of these two water masses creates local upwelling and concentrates the pelagic drift community, which consists of large mats of the marine alga sargassum as well as numerous fish, crustaceans, mollusks, other invertebrates, and even juvenile sea turtles.

This concentration of prey along the front attracts birds such as the Red-necked Phalarope *(Phalaropus lobatus),* Bridled Tern *(Sterna anaethetus),* and Audubon's Shearwater *(Puffinus lherminieri),* as well as schools of predatory fish.

Predatory Fish and Marine Mammals

In all oceans, there is a strong association between seabirds and predatory fish or marine mammals. Many seabird species have learned to follow schools of dolphins and large fishes such as tuna or Bluefish. These animals often drive schools of smaller fish to the surface while feeding, making them vulnerable prey for seabirds flying overhead. Occasionally, diving seabirds such as the Marbled Murrelet will hunt in a similar way to the dolphins and tuna—a fact that is not lost on surface-feeding Black-legged Kittiwakes *(Rissa tridactyla).*

Some seabirds also associate with whales. In the Bering Sea, researchers have found that two-thirds of all Gray Whales were attended by birds, mostly flocks of Red Phalaropes *(Phalaropus fulicaria),* Thick-billed Murres *(Uria lomvia),* Northern Fulmars *(Fulmarus glacialis),* and Black-legged Kittiwakes. These birds appear to be drawn to mud plumes produced by the whales feeding on the seafloor; as these plumes rise to the surface they bring with them invertebrates that would otherwise be unavailable or much more difficult for the birds to obtain.

Human-created Habitats

Every habitat type and virtually every square inch of North America has been impacted by humans. By logging forests, plowing and grazing grasslands, draining wetlands, channelizing streams, diverting water for human use, stabilizing beaches, depleting fish populations, polluting the air and water, introducing invasive exotic species, and building roads, houses, and cities, our influence has been profound. All of these human activities have brought about changes in bird populations.

Humans have not only altered natural habitats, but they also have created entirely new habitats through development and agriculture. While we generally presume these changes to be harmful to wildlife—and most of them certainly are—there are some species that have thrived as a result of human activities. Human-created habitats range from cities of concrete and glass that barely resemble anything in nature to rice paddies and orchards that are at least superficially reminiscent of the natural habitats they have replaced.

Houses, roads, and other structures built in the midst of the many habitats described in this chapter introduce new features and eliminate others. Some such changes benefit certain species of birds, some cause harm, and others have more mixed effects. For example, road construction creates open roadside verges where hawks can hunt as well as bridges where swallows can nest; but cars also kill many birds, and the combination of noise, pollution, human activity, and introduced plants, predators, and parasites associated with roads can reduce bird numbers in adjacent habitat. The effects of structures—such as radio towers and glass skyscrapers, which kill millions of migrating birds annually—are especially insidious.

Agricultural Lands

Historically the earliest and perhaps the most widespread impact that humans have had on natural habitats has been the conversion of land for farming. Vast areas of grassland have been plowed, wetlands drained, and forests cleared, and these natural habitats have been largely replaced with cropland. Even by the mid-1700s much of southern New England had been cleared for farming.

As devastating as these changes have been, however, agricultural lands do provide habitat for birds. Millions of wintering waterfowl visit winter-flooded rice paddies in California and the Gulf coast states annually, attracted to the grain left after harvest. Shorebirds, rails, herons, and ibises join them in droves to eat aquatic invertebrates. Blackbirds and sparrows gather wherever cereal crops grow. Raptors, in turn, are attracted by the abundance of birds and small mammals that intensive agriculture supports. In orchards, thrushes eat fallen fruit and sparrows hide in brush piles. Cornfields support flocks of cranes and geese, damp pastures and bare fields provide food for shorebirds, and many passerines use weedy irrigation ditches.

While these species seem to thrive in agricultural settings, many of the native species that used the land before agricultural development cannot survive in the new habitat. Even for the species that do use agricultural lands, modern trends toward monoculture and the increasing use of pesticides and fertilizers have negative effects.

While intensive modern agricultural practices reduce diversity, farmland still provides some benefit to open-country species, and the loss of farmland to housing or even forest can be equally devastating to certain species. The Barn Owl *(Tyto alba)* and American Kestrel *(Falco sparverius),* for example, are disappearing from the Northeast, where farming has declined and forest has increased, but they remain common in the intensively cultivated Central Valley of California.

Suburbs

Many people begin birding in the suburbs, usually in their backyard or local park. Even the most aggressively planned and manicured residential areas provide habitat for species such as the Northern Mockingbird, House Finch *(Carpodacus mexicanus),* and American Goldfinch *(Carduelis tristis).* Hummingbirds feed at garden flowers and on sugar-water in

backyard feeders. Other birds come to feeders filled with seeds and fat, especially during the winter months.

The Eastern Screech-Owl *(Otus asio)* in Texas has greater reproductive success in the suburbs than at rural sites, perhaps because more food is available there. Golf courses provide open-country habitats used by familiar birds, such as the Killdeer *(Charadrius vociferus),* American Robin *(Turdus migratorius),* and Eastern Bluebird *(Sialia sialis),* as well as more unusual species like the Burrowing Owl *(Athene cunicularia)* and Mississippi Kite *(Ictinia mississippiensis).* In desert regions, well-watered golf courses and park lawns attract all kinds of birds to drink and feed on insects.

Cities

Cities are generally thought to be the complete antithesis of wildlife habitat, but there are species that prosper in these concrete jungles. The most successful inhabitants of cities are introduced birds like the Rock Dove *(Columba livia)* and House Sparrow *(Passer domesticus),* but native species also occur. Peregrine Falcons nest on the window ledges of skyscrapers and feed on doves, living just as they would in the more natural setting of a northeastern Atlantic sea cliff.

City garbage dumps are some of the best places in North America to watch gulls, regularly attracting rarities among throngs of the more usual species. Sewage-treatment ponds attract tremendous numbers and variety of waterbirds, and offer some of the most exciting bird-watching available in parts of the arid West. Mallards *(Anas platyrhynchos)* and domesticated geese are common on city lakes, often joined by an array of other waterfowl, grebes, loons, cormorants, and gulls. City parks throughout the continent can provide spectacular birding, as these little oases concentrate birds into small areas.

Rick Cech, David Allen Sibley,
Chris Elphick, and John B. Dunning, Jr.

Populations and Conservation

Every birder has observed changes in bird abundance, whether it is the gradual disappearance of some familiar feeder bird, the arrival of a new species into an area, or the cyclical fluctuations of certain species on the National Audubon Society's Christmas Bird Counts. Studies of population dynamics have taught us much about the many factors that determine the abundance of different species and about the causes behind population changes. Moreover, understanding the role played by variables such as habitat quantity and quality, competition, predation, disease, and abiotic (nonbiological) conditions in determining species abundance has become increasingly necessary for conservationists and land managers working to save endangered species and to reverse the declines of species that are disappearing from the landscape.

What Determines Bird Population Sizes?

Scientists assess a bird's global population size by examining both its density and its geographic range, or distribution, both of which are influenced by the suitability and distribution of different habitats. The *density* of a species is a measure of the number of birds in a standard area, and the *geographic range* is the area over which the species occurs. Density can vary considerably throughout the range of a species, but the average density multiplied by the size of the range gives a rough estimate of the overall population of the species.

The commonest species are those with a combination of high densities and large ranges, and the rarest species are those with low densities and small ranges. Most species lie somewhere between these extremes.

Global population sizes can reach staggering numbers in some species. For example, the European Starling *(Sturnus vulgaris)*, House Sparrow *(Passer domesticus)*, and Red-winged Blackbird *(Agelaius phoeniceus)* each have populations numbering many millions of individuals. European Starlings and House Sparrows have achieved these numbers partly through their enormous geographic distributions, which have been expanded through introductions by humans into many areas outside their native ranges in the Old World. The Red-winged Blackbird has a more limited, though still large, distribution but can attain extremely high population densities; these

Abundant species. It has been estimated that there are close to 200 million Red-winged Blackbirds in North America. During the nonbreeding season, these birds form flocks that feed on waste grain in farmland during the day; feeding flocks coalesce into massive roosting congregations at dusk.

birds nest in dense concentrations and form large feeding flocks that benefit from the abundant grain supplies produced by human agriculture.

At the other end of the abundance spectrum are species nearing extinction, such as the California Condor *(Gymnogyps californianus)*. Some uncommon species, including condors, have probably always been relatively rare, although human actions have undoubtedly exacerbated their decline. Other species, such as the Eskimo Curlew *(Numenius borealis)* and the now extinct Passenger Pigeon *(Ectopistes migratorius)*, were once very abundant but became rare largely because of humans. Given the extent to which humans alter the environment, all rare species, even those that are naturally rare, require active protection to prevent their extinction.

Population density is generally related to a species' body size. Large species, such as hawks, tend to occur at lower densities than small species, such as sparrows. Peak densities occur in species that are about the size of a Northern Cardinal *(Cardinalis cardinalis)* or a Spotted Towhee *(Pipilo maculatus)*.

It is not surprising that population density tends to decline as body size increases because large animals need more food and therefore larger areas in which to forage than smaller species. Scientists are less sure why the smallest birds (such

Abundance and body size. *Bird abundance varies with body size. Big birds, such as the Red-tailed Hawk* (Buteo jamaicensis, *left), tend to be much less numerous than smaller species, such as the Northern Cardinal (right).*

as hummingbirds and kinglets) also have lower population densities, although they believe that diet plays a role; most small birds feed on insects or nectar, and their densities might reflect the availability and distribution of these foods. Exceptions to this pattern linking body size to population density are common, and there are rare species of all body sizes, but the general relationship is consistent.

Habitat Quantity and Quality

Foremost among the factors that determine population size are habitat quantity and quality. Beginning birders soon learn that each species has its favored habitat: The Bobolink *(Dolichonyx oryzivorus)*, for example, dwells in grasslands, while the Red-eyed Vireo *(Vireo olivaceus)* is found in deciduous or mixed forests. Some species are decidedly more specialized than others, and the level of specialization influences population size because the variety of habitats a species can use determines the size of its range. For example, breeding Kirtland's Warblers *(Dendroica kirtlandii)* are largely restricted to the young Jack Pine *(Pinus banksiana)* forests that develop following large fires in northern Michigan. The apparent inability of this species to use other habitats is presumably part of the reason that its population is so small.

Specialization also means that large-scale habitat changes can dramatically affect the populations and ranges of particular species. A species' abundance usually increases when more suitable habitat becomes available and decreases when habitat is lost. Species with very particular requirements are especially likely to be affected by habitat changes. In eastern North America, for instance, forest regrowth and fire suppression are eliminating grasslands across the entire region; as a result, grassland birds such as the Bobolink are disappearing. As one habitat decreases, however, others expand, so habitat changes typically involve exchanging one group of species for another. Thus, just as Bobolinks are declining from the Northeast, Red-eyed

Vireos are increasing as trees spread across the landscape.

The abundance and sometimes even the presence of a species can depend on the size and surroundings of a particular piece of habitat. In some cases, a patch of seemingly appropriate habitat may be too small to attract certain species, such as the Henslow's Sparrow *(Ammodramus henslowii)* or the Greater Prairie-Chicken *(Tympanuchus cupido)*. These *area-sensitive* species avoid patches of their habitat below some minimum size or suffer from reduced breeding success in small patches. In other cases, apparently suitable habitat might be poorly located. In general, a piece of woodland surrounded by urban development will attract fewer forest interior species and have lower population densities than a similar patch of woodland surrounded by shrubland, which in turn will have fewer forest birds than a third woodland patch surrounded by other forest types.

Although habitat quality can depend on many variables, high-quality sites are ultimately those where birds can achieve high rates of reproductive success and survival. Assessing habitat quality, however, can be very difficult. Regular occurrence or breeding in an area, alone, does not necessarily indicate high habitat quality because birds are sometimes forced into suboptimal habitat or mistakenly select poor habitat. Instead, it is necessary to determine that a population is self-sustaining and can produce sufficient young birds to replace the adults that die each year.

Those sites where a population is able to produce an excess of young are often called *sources,* and populations in such sites will persist as long as the habitat is not destroyed. Other sites, called *sinks,* do not support self-sustaining populations and rely on immigration of excess birds from source populations to replace those that succumb to disease, predators, and the like. If the flow of immigrants moving into these sites declines, then the population will go extinct even if the habitat remains unchanged.

Unfortunately for conservationists trying to protect the best habitat patches, it is normally very difficult to determine whether a particular habitat patch acts as a source or a sink. Moreover, even sink habitats may play a conservation role by providing habitat for young birds or as migratory stopover sites.

Competition

Competition occurs whenever a resource is in limited supply. Competition can take place between individuals of the same species (called *intraspecific competition*) or between individuals of different species *(interspecific competition),* and birds may compete for a variety of resources, including food, nest sites, and mates. As the density of birds increases, competition becomes increasingly likely and eventually may limit the size of a population because there is simply not enough of the resource to go around. Competition takes two forms: direct conflict, in which a bird actively excludes others from obtaining resources through activities such as territoriality and stealing; or indirect exploitation, whereby the supply is gradually depleted, thus preventing others from using a resource.

A common way in which birds engage in direct competition is through territorial behavior. Especially during the breeding season, many birds maintain some sort of territory, which can range in size from a few square feet in colonially nesting seabirds to hundreds of acres in some birds of prey. Birds may form territories to defend various types of resources; food is perhaps the most common, but other reasons to defend territories include ensuring access to good nest sites and attracting mates.

Territory sizes are not necessarily fixed and may vary according to habitat quality. For example, territory size depends on food availability in species such as the Vesper Sparrow *(Pooecetes gramineus),* which has an all-purpose territory that is used for nesting, foraging, and rearing young. When food is scarce, territories are larger (and thus bird densities lower) than when food is abundant because each bird needs to defend a larger area to ensure that it has enough food.

Even when a territory is not being defended birds may compete directly. For instance, some birds engage in physical tussles when competing for mates, while others will fight over food. Such direct conflict can easily be observed while watching gulls feeding at the local garbage dump.

Although less overt, indirect competition, whereby individuals simply use up a resource, can have just as great an influence on a population as direct competition. For example, a flock of geese grazing in a field will gradually reduce the amount of food. The larger the goose flock, the more rapidly the food will be depleted, and even though there is no defense or direct conflict involved, access to food is nonetheless diminished.

Competition between individuals of different species can also influence population sizes, since different species often use the same resources. The effects of interspecific competition are easiest to detect when the species composition of an area changes. For example, the introduction of European Starlings into North America has been viewed as a reason for the declines of some native bird species that nest in tree cavities because starlings compete aggressively for the same nest sites as the native birds.

The effects of competition can also be seen on islands. Islands often have fewer bird species than are found on the nearby mainland because island populations tend to be smaller and more likely to go extinct than those on the mainland. The species that survive on islands, however, often occur at higher densities and use a wider variety of habitats than they achieve on the mainland. For example, Song Sparrows (Melospiza melodia) occur at much higher densities on certain islands off the coast of British Columbia than they do at some mainland sites. This phenomenon possibly arises because the species living on the island do not have to compete with as many species as they would encounter on the mainland.

Predation

Mammals, reptiles, and some birds prey upon birds and their eggs, killing considerable numbers every year. Foxes, raccoons, and cats are among the most common predatory mammals in North America, and chipmunks and mice are important egg predators in some habitats. The potential for predatory mammals to decrease bird populations is readily apparent from a British study that showed that, during a single year, the 70 pet cats in one small village killed and brought home over a thousand wild birds and mammals representing 37 species. Since other studies have shown that cats bring home only about half of their kills, these results suggest that domestic cats in Britain could kill up to 200 million birds and mammals each year. There are 60 million domestic cats in the United States, 10 times more than in Britain, and while their potential impact on birds is huge, the threat they pose goes largely unnoticed.

Predatory birds also take large numbers of small birds. Best known are hawks, falcons, and owls, but shrikes, herons, gulls, and skuas all prey upon other birds. Crows, jays, and grackles are also important predators, taking both eggs and young from nests. Snakes frequently take eggs from bird nests, and snapping turtles will take waterbirds that get too close. Even large fish will prey on birds, taking ducklings and small seabirds as they swim on the water's surface.

Disease

Diseases caused by protozoa, bacteria, viruses, and fungi can profoundly affect bird populations. While these diseases typically exist at low levels in the environment, or even within the birds themselves, when population densities are high or when environmental conditions are right, they can spread rapidly and kill many individuals. For example, botulism and avian cholera, which often affect waterbirds, can kill thousands of individuals in one outbreak. Unless a disease wipes out a population, however, the impacts are typically short-term, and populations bounce back.

People who put out bird feeders are in a position to detect some types of diseases. For example, in western North America the House Finch *(Carpodacus mexicanus)* is affected by foot pox, a virus that creates swellings and often causes birds to lose toes. In the East, House Finches have also suffered large population declines due to a bacterial disease that affects their eyes.

Sometimes birds carry diseases that can harm humans; these include salmonella, aspergillosis, and influenza. Direct transmission from wild birds to humans, however, is very rare. West Nile virus, which appeared in North America in the late 1990s and which humans get from mosquitoes, has been found in numerous birds and rapidly kills some species. Birds also are a host species for young ticks and can carry the bacteria that cause Lyme disease.

Both predation and disease can have their greatest effects on islands where birds have not evolved defenses against them. In Hawaii, for example, humans inadvertently introduced avian malaria by bringing in infected mosquitoes and exotic birds. While the malaria has had little effect on the introduced bird species with which it evolved, it has devastated native Hawaiian birds. Many native

Disease. In western North America, the House Finch, shown here, and some other species commonly seen at feeders suffer from foot pox, a disease that causes abnormal swellings on the feet and often results in lost toes.

Hawaiian species are today restricted to high elevations or dry areas where the mosquitoes cannot thrive. Many lowland forest birds became extinct after malaria was introduced to Hawaii in the 1800s.

Abiotic Factors

Abiotic, or nonbiological, factors such as weather, fire, and hydrology can influence population size, either directly by impacting the birds themselves, or indirectly by affecting the food supply or habitat availability.

Weather, especially temperature and rainfall, affects habitats and food supplies in many ways. Climate greatly influences the nature and productivity of an area's plant community, which in turn determines the availability of food, nest sites, and shelter. Weather can also influence bird populations over short time periods. For example, a rainstorm can cause waterbirds' nests to flood, while a late-spring snowstorm can kill both eggs and nestlings.

Hurricanes can destroy habitat and devastate bird populations. In 1989, Hurricane Hugo hit South Carolina's Francis Marion National Forest, home to the world's second-largest population of the endangered Red-cockaded Woodpecker *(Picoides borealis).* Sixty-three percent of the woodpeckers died as a result, and the storm also destroyed 87 percent of their nest trees. Even when birds survive a hurricane, many succumb later because the damaged plant communities cannot produce the necessary foods, such as fruit and nectar, to support them.

Fire is another example of an important abiotic agent. Many natural habitats depend on periodic burns in order to persist. If fire frequency, or intensity, is altered, then the quality of the habitat for certain species (such as Red-cockaded Woodpeckers and Bachman's Sparrows, *Aimophila aestivalis,* in southeastern pine forests) can change. As conditions are altered, bird populations may increase or decrease depending on a species' needs. For example, birds that require an open understory can disappear from some forests in the absence of fire. Also, fire suppression in grassland habitats can result in succession to shrubland, and eventually forest encroachment, to the detriment of grassland birds. Black-backed Woodpeckers *(Picoides arcticus)* are particularly dependent on fire; they converge on recently burned forest stands to feed on the rich supply of beetle grubs in charred dead trees.

Many other abiotic aspects of the environment can affect bird populations. Geology, soil types, and hydrology influence plant communities and habitat types. Ocean currents determine the distribution and accessibility of food in the sea. Tides dictate access to submerged prey along the coast. These are just a few of the ways in which abiotic conditions can impinge on bird numbers.

Population Regulation

Determining the relative importance of different factors, such as those discussed above, on a population's size is not straightforward. This is because all of these factors can affect populations simultaneously and because the effects of one factor can alter the effects of another. To complicate things further, the effects of different variables can vary depending on the size of the population.

To give just one example, one might expect that the exclusion of predators from an area would result in an increase in prey populations, but this is not necessarily the case. Whether or not predators affect a population's size depends on whether the birds they kill would otherwise have lived and reproduced or whether they would have died anyway from some other cause. Less predation may cause a short-term increase in numbers, but this in turn may result in intensified competition or may facilitate the spread of diseases, which could bring population size back down again over the longer term.

At high population densities, breeding is often less successful and survival rates lower than at moderate densities. Conse-

quently, increasing populations do not increase forever, but instead reach an upper limit to their size. In contrast, when populations crash, the amount of competition, disease, and predation may decline, enabling more successful breeding and better survival, which would allow the population to increase again.

Sometimes the biological features of a species facilitates recovery after a population crash. For example, the Florida Scrub-Jay *(Aphelocoma coerulescens)* practices cooperative breeding, in which adults that are unable to obtain a breeding territory help raise the young of other adults (usually their parents) rather than breed themselves. In one case, a population with about 70 breeding scrub-jays that had been studied for 10 years at the Archbold Biological Station in Florida suffered a sudden die-off. Adult survival dropped from 82 percent to 55 percent and fledgling survival fell below 5 percent. No bodies were found (though this is not unusual for small birds), so the cause of the die-off was unknown, but it was likely due to predation or disease. Yet in less than two years the number of breeding birds was back to normal, and the only noticeable impact was fewer helpers. Such rapid recovery was possible because former helpers had taken advantage of the population decline by occupying available territories and becoming breeders.

It cannot be taken for granted, however, that a declining population will recover on its own. In some cases, a population goes extinct before it has time to rebound. In other situations, the cause of the crash may not allow for recovery—as when an ecological community undergoes a permanent change such as the destruction of too much habitat.

Understanding Population Trends

Over time, bird population sizes fluctuate, sometimes exhibiting a steady increase or decrease and sometimes cyclically rising and falling. For years, many species of migrant birds that breed in forest interiors and grasslands have been declining as a result of steady habitat loss and degradation. On the other hand, the Eastern Bluebird *(Sialia sialis)* has been increasing steadily because of habitat enhancement—specifically, the extensive placement of nest boxes. Other species, such as some grouse, undergo cycles of alternating increases and declines.

The dynamics of a population can be hard to predict, especially when several factors exert pressure on the population, some acting to increase it and others to deplete it. Small or isolated populations, though, are particularly vulnerable. An excellent example is the now extinct eastern subspecies of the Greater Prairie-Chicken, the Heath Hen *(Tympanuchus cupido cupido)*. The last population of Heath Hens lived on Martha's Vineyard, Massachusetts, and disappeared in 1932. After a sudden population increase during 1915 and 1916 to an apparently secure size of about 2,000 birds, the population quickly crashed due to a combination of events, including a fire that destroyed cover and foraging areas, a gale, a cold winter, late frosts that killed eggs, a sudden upsurge in predators, and continued hunting by humans.

It can be especially difficult to determine the cause of population changes in migratory species because all the factors mentioned above can affect migrant birds on both their breeding and wintering grounds as well as during migration. Thus a migratory species might decline on its breeding grounds because of something that is happening thousands of miles away where it winters, or vice versa. Understanding the reasons for population changes in migratory species consequently requires a careful consideration of conditions in all the places where the species spends part of its life.

For example, when large-scale population declines of migrant forest birds came to the public's attention during the late 1970s and early 1980s, researchers initially blamed the declines on habitat loss on the tropical wintering grounds. Subsequent studies, however, have shown that habitat loss and other factors

Neotropical migrants. Many songbird species that breed in North America and winter in the tropics are experiencing steep population declines. Initially the destruction of tropical rain forest was blamed for these declines, but increasingly scientists are recognizing that habitat loss and fragmentation on the breeding grounds also play an important role. The Wood Thrush (Hylocichla mustelina), shown here, declined by almost 2 percent annually between 1966 and 1999, according to the Breeding Bird Survey.

on the breeding grounds have been at least partly responsible for these declines, and may be the primary cause of declines in many species.

Conservation Threats

The primary causes of species declines in North America, as elsewhere, are the loss, fragmentation, and degradation of habitat. One element these factors have in common is that they are almost exclusively direct or indirect consequences of human actions. Persecution by humans is another problem, although the direct killing of birds is now far less common and much better regulated in North America than it was in the past. Also, as humans have altered habitats they have changed the distribution and abundance of many plant and animal species, including predators, brood parasites, and introduced invasive species, all of which can adversely affect the lives of birds.

Habitat Loss

Habitat loss is a tremendous problem for many bird species, particularly for habitat specialists whose ecosystems have been very hard hit. For example, in North

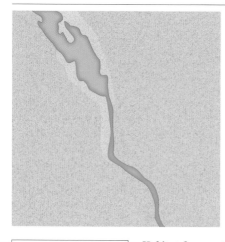

Forest
Lake/waterway
Floodplain meadows
Cultivated land
Housing subdivision
Powerline clearing
Roads

Habitat fragmentation. When continuous habitat is subdivided into ever smaller parcels it is not just the lost habitat that causes bird numbers to decline. Even when very small amounts of habitat are removed, the effects can be large if they fragment the habitat. Simply building roads and clearing vegetation where powerlines cut through forested habitat can allow brood parasites and species that prey on bird eggs and chicks to enter an area, often with devastating consequences for woodland songbirds. Here an area of forest is shown before and after human settlement.

America, 99 percent of tallgrass prairie has vanished due to conversion to agricultural use, fire suppression, and the elimination of native grasses. Other grassland habitats have suffered a similar fate, and it is no surprise that many grassland bird species have experienced widespread population declines as a result. North American wetlands are also persistently threatened, depleted by water diversion for use by agriculture and cities, and filled in to create land for development. In the coterminous United States, more than half of the wetlands have disappeared in the last 200 years; in California less than 10 percent remain.

On the other hand, North American forests are expanding at a rate of about 2 percent each year. Not all of this land is mature natural forest, however, as many estimates of forest area include clear-cuts that will eventually grow into older forest and plantations where trees are grown for harvest. In clear-cut areas and plantations, the trees are of a uniform age, and plantations tend to be stands of only a single (often exotic) tree species. The structurally simple, homogeneous stands of trees that result from intensive forestry typically have a lower diversity of birds than do natural forests.

As the forest area increases, early successional habitats such as grasslands and shrublands are lost. The loss of shrub habitats in the East is particularly acute as the natural disturbances that historically created these habitats no longer occur. Many shrubland birds are declining as a result.

Habitat Fragmentation

When habitat is destroyed in a piecemeal fashion, leaving only fragments of habitat in small patches, direct habitat loss is just one of the conservation problems that arise. In addition, bird populations must contend with the consequences of increased patch isolation and the myriad problems that result from increasing the amount of "edge" between habitats.

Patch isolation decreases the likelihood that birds will move from their birthplace into a new patch to mate. Immigration is important for maintaining small populations, which are especially vulnerable to extinction if there is no periodic exchange of individuals between sites. In order to reduce isolation, many land managers favor the practice of connecting patches with corridors of appropriate habitat.

Habitat fragmentation also increases the amount of *edge,* which occurs where two habitat types meet—for example, at the boundary between a field and a forest. An edge often constitutes a particular habitat in itself, and certain species thrive at these boundaries. Indeed, for many years land managers tried to increase the amount of edge habitat because these habitats benefit certain game species. While some specialists benefit from increased edge habitat, there are often negative consequences for other species that dwell in the fragmented habitat. These include increases in predation and brood parasitism as well as changes in abiotic conditions.

For example, in forest habitats, many predators of bird eggs and nestlings are more abundant near forest edges than in the forest's interior, and breeding success is subsequently reduced in fragmented areas where more of the forest is close to an edge than in continuous stands. In other situations, some predators will follow the boundaries between habitats, increasing the vulnerability of birds in these edge habitats. Habitat fragmentation also favors the Brown-headed Cowbird *(Molothrus ater),* a brood parasite of concern to conservationists (see the Blackbirds, Orioles, and Allies chapter), which generally occupies open habitats but will travel up to a mile into a forest to lay its eggs in another bird's nest. Thus birds in fragmented forests, where much of the habitat is close to an opening, are much more vulnerable to brood parasitism than are birds in large forest tracts.

Research has also shown that changes in abiotic conditions, such as temperature or the amount of wind, near edges might affect both the availability of food and nest site suitability for forest interior birds. One study showed that the density of insects in the leaf litter was lower near

forest edges, reducing the food supply for Ovenbirds *(Seiurus aurocapillus).* Abiotic effects can extend hundreds of yards into a fragmented habitat; consequently, small habitat patches might be entirely subject to edge effects.

Brood Parasites, Predators, and Exotic Species

Habitat changes have not been bad for all bird species. Those that can thrive in conditions that suit humans often benefit as land is converted from one state to another. Unfortunately, some of the species that have benefited from modern habitat changes have lifestyles that exacerbate the declines of species already suffering from habitat losses.

For example, in some fragmented landscapes, the Brown-headed Cowbird can parasitize all the nests of certain species. Some bird species recognize and destroy cowbird eggs that they find in their nests, but others, such as the endangered Kirtland's Warbler, do not; management plans for Kirtland's Warbler and other species now include trapping and removing cowbirds from the nesting area. Two other significant brood parasites are the Bronzed Cowbird *(Molothrus aeneus)* and the Shiny Cowbird

Brood parasites. *Brood parasites, such as this female Brown-headed Cowbird, have been blamed for the reduced breeding success of many North American songbirds. The underlying problem, however, has been the changes that humans have wrought on the landscape: Fragmentation of forest habitat and the keeping of livestock have improved conditions for cowbirds and allowed their populations to spread.*

(M. bonariensis), both of which are expanding their ranges in the southern United States.

Populations of many medium-size mammal and bird predators, including Coyotes, raccoons, skunks, crows, and jays, have increased in recent decades for several reasons: There is less persecution of these species; human settlement provides them with extra food in the form of crops and garbage; and in some cases predators, such as wolves, that would have kept their numbers in check are now gone. An unwelcome consequence of increased predator populations is that these species prey voraciously on eggs and nestlings, and their abundance now threatens some bird populations.

Another important threat to some North American bird populations are introduced exotic birds, which can compete with native species. For instance, the aggressive Mute Swan *(Cygnus olor)* is suspected of displacing native waterbirds from breeding and foraging sites. Most modern introductions of exotic birds involve species that are commonly kept as pets; since many of these species originate in tropical countries, introduced birds are most likely to become established in southern urban areas, such as coastal Florida and southern California. Exotic species, however, occur throughout the continent, and it is difficult to predict which will become established and cause problems.

Introduced birds are not the only exotic species that threaten bird populations. Whether it is introduced insects threatening forest habitats, introduced grasses altering the fire regime of western grasslands, or introduced parasites and diseases threatening to infect bird populations, all changes in a region's biota present the potential to affect at least some bird species. As human travel and transcontinental trade increase, the world's plants and animals are increasingly likely to spread to new areas, typically with unknown consequences.

Pollution

A wide range of pollutants adversely affects bird populations. Perhaps the most obvious are calamitous oil spills, such as that caused by the *Exxon Valdez* oiltanker when it ran aground in Prince William Sound, Alaska, in March 1989, killing hundreds of thousands of seabirds. Much additional oil enters the environment through small spills and the deliberate flushing of fuel tanks on ships, and it is quite common to see oiled waterbirds even when there has been no major spill.

Numerous industrial chemicals also find their way into natural habitats, by either accident or intent. Although many regulations exist to prevent such contamination, much chemical pollution predates the legislation and remains in the environment; often the technology to clean up these problems does not exist

Predators. *Opportunistic predators, such as the Blue Jay* (Cyanocitta cristata), *have always eaten eggs, and egg theft is a natural hazard that small songbirds have always faced. Humans can indirectly affect this relationship by, for example, providing bird feeders or reducing the numbers of predators that attack jays, thus allowing the jay population to increase.*

Pollution. Pollutants such as oil can have devastating effects on birds. Even a small amount of oil eliminates the insulating value of a bird's feathers and can result in death from exposure or from ingesting the oil as the bird tries to remove it. Shown is an oiled Western Gull (Larus occidentalis).

even when there is a will to improve conditions.

Other sources of pollution include sewage treatment plants, livestock barns, paper mills, mines, garbage dumps, factories, and traffic. In urban areas, rainwater flowing across the streets picks up oil and washes it into drains and eventually to watercourses. Agricultural runoff also carries excess nutrients and pesticides into bodies of water; this type of pollution is especially difficult to control because the pollutants originate over a broad area rather than from a single discrete place.

Pesticides can be particularly insidious pollutants, because releases of even small amounts can result in high concentrations in the food of predators, due to an accumulative process as the chemicals pass up the food chain. This *bioaccumulation* occurs because the chemicals are not excreted from the body and consequently build up over time. The results of bioaccumulation can include eggshell thinning (which reduces hatching success), deformed hatchlings, and even the deaths of adult birds. In 1962 the publication of *Silent Spring,* by Rachel Carson, focused public attention on this problem and helped launch the modern environmental movement.

Although pesticides are now more closely regulated than in the past, they continue to threaten bird populations. Some, such as DDT, are no longer used in the United States or Canada but continue to affect birds, including North American migrants, that encounter them in parts of the world where they are still used (for example, to combat malaria). Also, it has been found that even very small amounts of some pesticides and other chemicals can disrupt the actions of reproductive hormones, causing breeding failure.

Naturally occurring chemicals also produce problems at times. In the arid West, for example, water diversion for agriculture has created increased concentrations of salts and heavy metals in many wetlands. In one case, water diversions in California's Central Valley drained natural wetlands and increased selenium concentrations at Kesterson National Wildlife Refuge, causing deformities and deaths in waterbird chicks, as well as in other wildlife and domestic animals. Eventually it became necessary to fill in the toxic wetlands on this refuge in order to keep birds away.

Other forms of pollution are not widely recognized as such. For example, light pollution from outdoor lighting installations can create problems for night-migrating land birds and nocturnal seabirds. These birds are attracted to lights and often collide with structures on which the lights are mounted. In addition, night lighting can disrupt the diurnal rhythms of birds that live nearby and increase their visibility to nocturnal predators.

Persecution

Historically, direct persecution through hunting has had enormous effects on bird populations. Market hunting helped exterminate the Passenger Pigeon and greatly reduced populations of many shorebirds and waterfowl during the late 19th century, and the demands of the fashion industry's feather trade peaked at about the same time. Species that nest in colonies or migrate in large flocks were particularly vulnerable, and populations of many species, including herons, egrets, and terns, declined dramatically as wild birds were converted into fashion accessories. This overexploitation, which mobilized concerned citizens and scientists, was instrumental in the founding of such groups as the National Audubon Society and the American Society for the Prevention of Cruelty to Animals.

The feather trade no longer threatens birds in North America, thanks to increased public interest in conservation and the introduction of protective legislation. Similarly, although hunting is an emotionally charged issue, most modern hunting in North America is heavily regulated, and there is little evidence that it contributes to population declines of most game species. In fact, money derived from hunting pays for many conservation activities in North America. On the other hand, unregulated hunting by indigenous populations has been implicated in the declines of some species of Arctic-nesting waterbirds.

Although direct killing of birds by humans has generally declined over the last century, it nonetheless continues for

Hunting. In the heyday of market hunting, in the late 1800s, many North American bird species were greatly reduced in numbers. Many populations have now recovered, and species that are hunted today are carefully monitored so that hunting does not threaten their numbers. More fortunate than its now extinct cousin, the Passenger Pigeon, the Mourning Dove (Zenaida macroura), shown here, remains common throughout the continent despite the harvest of millions of birds annually.

some species. For example, fish-eating birds, such as cormorants and terns, are often targeted by fishermen who blame the birds for declining fish stocks, even in cases where there is little evidence supporting their claims.

Another threat that has not gone away is the illegal trade in live birds, which remains a multimillion-dollar industry. Particularly vulnerable are parrots and their relatives, which are captured for the pet trade, and hawks and falcons, which are used in falconry. Although most of these birds are taken from the wild elsewhere in the world, North American collectors certainly play a role in sustaining the trade.

Indirect persecution through disturbance is yet another problem; for example, disturbance threatens such species as the Least Tern *(Sterna antillarum)*, which nests on beaches that are often used by off-road vehicles and beachgoers.

Climate Change

Possibly the most significant factor that will alter future bird populations is global climate change. Scientists expect that global warming due to the burning of fossil fuels will affect both temperature and rainfall, two factors that largely determine habitat distribution and food availability. The timing of breeding has already shifted in some species as a result of changing climate, and such changes might cause problems, especially in migratory species that need to synchronize breeding with the availability of resources in other areas of the world where they spend parts of their lives.

The distributions of predators and disease are also likely to change if weather patterns are altered. Although birds have adapted to dramatic climate changes in the past, the changes occurring today appear to be taking place at an unprecedented rate and are combined with widespread habitat destruction. However, the ultimate impacts of global warming on birds in general or on particular species are mostly unknown and will be extremely difficult to predict.

Tracking Bird Populations in North America

In order to determine whether these numerous threats actually influence the size of bird populations, it is necessary for researchers to track bird numbers through regular censuses. All populations vary in size, however, even under natural conditions, and discerning a short-term decline that is part of a normal pattern of fluctuating abundance from a decline that indicates a conservation concern can be difficult and may require many years of information.

Long-term monitoring programs are especially valuable, as they help to determine whether declines are sustained over long periods. The two largest nationwide bird counts in North America are the Breeding Bird Survey (BBS) and the Christmas Bird Count (CBC). The BBS, conducted in the United States by the U.S. Geological Survey and in Canada by the Canadian Wildlife Service, involves thousands of volunteer birders. Observers drive along predetermined routes during the breeding season, stopping at regular intervals to watch and listen for birds; at each stop they count all the birds they detect within a fixed time period. This project has been running since the 1960s and is unequaled in its ability to track populations of hundreds of species on a continental scale.

The CBC, sponsored by the National Audubon Society, has operated for more than a century and also relies on volunteer birders. The count occurs in the two-week period around Christmas each year and involves teams of birders counting all the birds they can find within a series of count circles that are distributed across the continent. Although the CBC is less rigorous scientifically than the BBS (the CBC's data collection is less well standardized), it remains enormously useful because of the sheer scope of the effort and the long time period over which it has been operating. For many species not well covered by the BBS—including Arctic and subarctic breeders,

Disturbance. In many places birds may be affected simply by the presence of human activity. Particularly vulnerable are beach-nesting birds, such as the Least Tern, shown here. Beachgoers trample nests, scare adult birds into leaving their young unprotected, and discard trash that attracts predators into nesting areas.

colonial species, and birds that nest in specialized habitats not easily observed from roadsides—the CBC is by far the best monitoring tool now available to conservationists.

Although both surveys lack complete coverage in some regions and do not adequately monitor all North American birds, they have been key to identifying declines of many species and will be crucial in determining whether those declines are reversed in the future.

Many other monitoring programs augment the BBS and the CBC. Waterfowl populations are surveyed annually by the U.S. Fish and Wildlife Service and the Canadian Wildlife Service, and waterfowl are among the most carefully monitored species in North America. Many hawk and falcon populations are monitored at sites throughout the continent where migrating raptors are concentrated. The International Shorebird Survey, conducted by the Manomet Center for Conservation Sciences, and the Maritimes Shorebird Survey, conducted in eastern Canada, have been used to examine shorebird population trends. Locally, many other monitoring schemes—typically sponsored by state or provincial governments—focus on species, such as raptors and colonial breeders, that are of special interest because they are endangered, hunted, or considered vulnerable.

Protecting North American Birds

In North America, a variety of international, national, and local laws protect birds. One of the most important is the Migratory Bird Treaty Act, an international treaty prohibiting activities harmful to species that migrate across international borders within North America.

The Convention on International Trade in Endangered Species of Wild Fauna and Flora (CITES) polices the illegal trade in plants and animals thought to be at risk of extinction. Its growing list currently comprises more than 1,500 species of birds from around the world, including the Peregrine Falcon *(Falco peregrinus)*, favored by falconers, and almost all of the world's species of parrots.

In the United States, the Endangered Species Act protects threatened and endangered species, subspecies, and unique populations of vertebrates and their habitats. States and provinces also have their own laws governing threatened and endangered species, as well as game birds. Typically, local laws protect a wider array of species than do national laws because they include locally threatened birds that are not of national concern.

In recent years, a growing number of international cooperative ventures have been formed to help protect migratory birds. Perhaps the most prominent is Partners in Flight, a group that includes members from government agencies, local community groups, and nongovernmental conservation organizations; it coordinates various activities aimed primarily at conserving migratory land birds. Another such venture is the Western Hemisphere Shorebird Reserve Network, which identifies key sites for shorebird conservation throughout the Americas.

These organizations have formulated lists of species and sites that warrant particular attention from conservationists. For example, the WatchList, produced by Partners in Flight and the National Audubon Society, identifies species that are likely to become endangered unless

Trade in wild birds. The live bird trade presents a quandary for conservationists. Worldwide, parrots and other species are taken from the wild to support the multimillion-dollar pet trade, and many birds of prey are taken for falconry. Despite protection efforts, these activities continue to threaten many species. On the other hand, captive breeding by aviculturalists can play an important role in species protection. For example, the recovery of North American populations of the Peregrine Falcon, shown here, has been greatly aided by the activities of falconers dedicated to raptor conservation.

protection is put into place. Partners in Flight is also developing a series of regional conservation plans for each part of North America that will identify conservation needs for all bird species.

The North American Waterfowl Management Plan, which sets forth a strategy for protecting ducks, geese, and swans, has resulted in extensive wetland protection since its establishment in 1986. Following this model, a United States Shorebird Conservation Plan was completed in 2000, and a North American Waterbird Conservation Plan will follow shortly.

The goals of these various plans are becoming increasingly integrated through the North American Bird Conservation Initiative (NABCI). This umbrella initiative has formed to coordinate activities conducted under the auspices of the separate bird conservation plans and to ensure that no species or conservation issue falls between the cracks. If successful, NABCI will provide a framework for North American bird conservation in the 21st century.

J. Michael Reed and Chris Elphick

PART II

BIRD FAMILIES OF
NORTH AMERICA

Loons

 Loons, called "divers" outside of North America, are large, bulky waterbirds with wingspans that range from 3 feet to 4 feet 1 inch (90–124 cm). Superficially they resemble certain grebes, or even small geese, but the combination of a dagger-like bill, short neck, long wings, and legs set far back on the body give them a distinctive shape. Loons are perhaps best known for their haunting wails and elaborate displays during the breeding season. Most birders, however, encounter these northern breeders during migration or winter, when they frequent lakes, reservoirs, coastal bays, and open ocean coasts in the southern half of North America.

Taxonomy

Loons constitute one of the more ancient bird lineages; fossil evidence of loon-like birds dates back well over 70 million years to the late Cretaceous period, and birds resembling modern loons are known to have occurred some 20 million years ago during the Miocene epoch. This means that loons survived the great upheavals in Earth's atmosphere that took place between the late Cretaceous and the Tertiary periods.

Relationships of loons to other birds are far from clear. Some studies link loons to auks (murres, puffins, and allies) and gulls, others to grebes. Biochemical studies suggest that tubenoses, penguins (family Sphenisicidae), and frigatebirds may be the loons' closest relatives.

Relationships within the family are less controversial. The two largest species, the Common Loon *(Gavia immer)* and

the Yellow-billed Loon *(G. adamsii)*, are thought to have arisen from populations of an ancestral loon that became isolated in the New World. This same ancestor also gave rise to the Arctic Loon *(G. arctica)* in the Old World. More recently, it seems, the Old World lineage founded a new population in the Americas, from which the Pacific Loon *(G. pacifica)* evolved. Given the similarities between the Common and Yellow-billed Loons and the Arctic and Pacific Loons, some researchers consider each pair a superspecies; the latter two loons are similar enough that taxonomists do not always consider them to be separate species.

The Red-throated Loon *(Gavia stellata)* is the most distinctive species, with a very different appearance during the breeding season and distinct breeding behaviors, such as a territorial duetting song given by both members of a pair and its habit of foraging far from the nesting pond when feeding chicks. Researchers believe this species arose in the Old World and subsequently colonized the Americas.

Food and Foraging

Loons mainly eat a wide variety of medium-size fish up to about 10 inches (25 cm) long.

Whether at sea or on lakes and rivers, loons dive for their prey. They hunt first from the water's surface, peering down with bill and eyes submerged. A dive lasts an average of 40 seconds in larger species and can be as deep as 250 feet

Gaviid diversity. The five species of loons in the world all occur in North America and are structurally quite similar except in size. Their plumages are also similar, although in summer the Red-throated Loon (top) looks quite unlike the other species (represented here by the Common Loon, bottom).

Common Loon diving for prey. Swimming loons often peer beneath the water's surface to look for fish. They dive using only their large, powerful feet for propulsion and the tail and wings occasionally for steering. They hold the neck coiled, ready to strike forward if a fish comes within range.

(75 m), although most prey are probably caught near the surface. Because loons hunt underwater primarily by sight, they usually inhabit clear water. When foraging for slow-moving prey in turbid water, loons occasionally hunt tactilely, probing around vegetation or objects in the water column or on the bottom.

During the breeding season, a pair of loons and their young may consume up to 2,000 pounds (900 kg) of fish, a great quantity that is probably necessary because of the birds' large size and the energetic demands of living in a cold climate. In order to aid digestion, loons regularly ingest small pebbles, which they hold in the gizzard for grinding hard matter like fish bones and crustacean shells.

Loons are well adapted to living and fishing in fresh- and saltwater environments. Their legs and feet are set far back on the body for propulsion while swimming and diving, and they have flattened tarsi to reduce drag. Loons have good underwater vision, denser bones

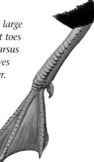

Loon foot. Loons have large feet with the three front toes fully webbed and the tarsus flattened so that it moves easily through the water. The Pacific Loon is shown.

than most birds to help them dive, and dense plumage to keep them waterproof and warm.

These adaptations to life on the water make loons ungainly on land. The setback position of their legs makes walking almost impossible, and they move mostly by pushing themselves along on their breasts. The larger loons cannot take flight from land; their wing-loading (total body weight per unit of wing area) is so high that they must beat their wings rapidly and patter along the water's surface for considerable distances to get airborne. Larger loons forced down in inclement weather during overland migration sometimes perish if they "wreck" on very small lakes or roads they mistake for waterways.

Breeding

Loons prefer to nest on undisturbed lakes from boreal to Arctic zones. Larger species, such as the Common and Yellow-billed Loons, require a long "runway" of open water to become airborne and typically nest on large lakes. The smaller Red-throated Loon can take flight more easily and nests on small pools, often leaving to forage elsewhere. In addition to nesting on lakes, the Arctic, Red-throated, and Yellow-billed Loons also nest along river shores, and on the coast of the Arctic Ocean.

Courtship and nesting behaviors vary considerably among the species. Most loons have synchronous displays, in

Loon head and bill. A loon uses its dagger-like bill to capture fish underwater but not to spear them. The pointed shape may improve the bird's streamlining as it forages underwater. The Common Loon is shown.

which the male and female chase, dive, swim, and lower their bills into the water together. These displays can culminate in the female assuming a posture inviting copulation, in which she lies flat with her neck flush to the ground, sometimes poking the ground with her bill. Repeated copulation at one place on the ground, especially common among smaller species, often creates a depression referred to as a "false nest."

The nest consists of a mound of vegetation 1 to 5 inches (2.5–13 cm) high, placed on the edge of a small island or the shore. The nest site is rarely more than a few feet from the water's edge and allows a clear view of the surrounding area and enough open water for an incubating bird to escape by quickly getting airborne.

Loons often return to former nest sites and are very territorial. In most species, the male signals that he is occupying a territory with a loud yodeling call that can be heard several miles away. Male and female Red-throated Loons vocalize together and often return to the nest site calling loudly. Loons call mainly during the breeding season but occasionally on calm, foggy days at other times of the year. Arctic Loons in Europe have distinctive calls that allow them to be identified as individuals.

Nesting loons engage in stereotyped displays to drive off or threaten any adult loons or other waterbirds that stray into their territories. These displays often resemble those of courtship but also involve chases and circular movements in which the birds maneuver close to one another with necks extended and throat patches or necklaces exposed. Males rarely fight over territories, but when they do, the fights can result in serious wounding or death. Loons are not territorial away from their breeding areas.

Adult loons have few natural predators, but gulls, crows, ravens, raccoons, skunks, minks and weasels, snapping turtles, and large fish such as pike are all known to take loon eggs or chicks. Loons may be vulnerable to large marine predators, such as marine mammals and

Worldwide Family Features

- 21–36" (53–90 cm) waterbirds.
- 5 species in 1 genus worldwide; found throughout Northern Hemisphere. All 5 species occur in North America; breed in continent's northern half; winter primarily along coasts.
- Eat mostly fish caught in underwater pursuit; also crustaceans, amphibians, insects, leeches, aquatic vegetation.
- Solitary pairs defend breeding grounds. Sometimes gather in large flocks when not breeding. Monogamous; thought to pair for life. Migratory.
- Breed first at 2 or 3 years old.
- Both sexes build nest that is mass of vegetation with shallow depression, placed on ground along shoreline. May reuse nests from previous years.

- 1–3 (typically 2) greenish-brown, subelliptical to oval eggs with darker speckling; if lost early in season, replaced with smaller clutch. Both parents incubate, for 24–31 days. Hatching asynchronous. 1 brood per year.
- Precocial young have downy coat; both parents brood 1–3 days at nest, after which young swim and ride on either parent's back. Fledge at 49 days to 11 weeks. Both parents feed, even after fledging.
- Adult annual survival little known; thought to be about 90%. Many live 10 or more years. Among oldest on record: 28 years (Arctic Loon).

Common Loon territorial display. *Territorial displays of loons are elaborate and varied. The display shown here, rearing up in the water with bill pointed down and sometimes advancing across the water in this position, is directed toward other loons intruding on the territory.*

sharks; on rare occasions Sea Otters have been seen eating loons.

Movements

Most loons winter in coastal waters as far south as central Mexico, with numbers peaking at a latitude of about 35°N. A few individuals winter on lakes. Overland migration appears to be common, although the routes are still poorly known. During spring, Walker Lake, in the Nevada desert, supports one of the largest-known concentrations of migrating Common Loons in western North America, with peaks of more than one thousand birds.

South of the breeding range, migrating loons are often found on freshwater lakes during October and November. A few nonbreeders oversummer on these lakes or in the coastal habitats in which they winter. On their wintering grounds, loons are flightless for a period of several weeks—during late fall for the Red-throated Loon, later in the other species—while they molt their flight feathers. Large numbers of Common Loons in eastern areas spend this period in protected coastal waters or in the shallow waters over the continental shelf.

Conservation

Like most waterbirds, loons face a wide array of threats that have resulted from human activities. However, no loon species is considered endangered. Common Loons nesting at the lowest latitudes must contend with human disturbance and development on many once-secluded lakes. A far greater problem on lakes in New England, upstate New York, and eastern Canada is acid rain; as lakes acidify, phytoplankton die, causing food chains to collapse, leaving nothing for the loons to eat. These factors have resulted in substantial declines in some Common Loon populations.

Industrial pollutants dumped directly into lakes, rivers, bays, and oceans also contaminate prey, especially in highly acidic waters, where heavy metals like mercury can dissolve and rapidly pass up the food chain. These chemicals accumulate in the birds' bodies and eventually can cause poisoning. Large-scale die-offs, involving thousands of loons, have occurred on both the Gulf and Atlantic coasts. These deaths have been attributed to various causes, including parasite infections and starvation, but an increased susceptibility to these problems caused by mercury poisoning may be the underlying problem.

Lead poisoning, which results when the birds ingest lead sinkers on discarded fishing lines, and entanglement in fishing nets are other causes of mortality.

Worldwide, many thousands of loons die in oil spills, usually because their plumage becomes saturated by floating oil and they are unable to dive, swim, fly, or keep warm. The oil from the spills also poisons the fish that are the birds' chief prey. Because of their flightless state during part of the winter, loons are particularly vulnerable to spills.

Edward S. Brinkley
and Alec Humann

Grebes

 Grebes are small to medium-size waterbirds. These sleek diving birds share many characteristics with the loons, which they superficially resemble, but are a more diverse group and occupy a wider variety of aquatic habitats, ranging from seasonally flooded scrubland and roadside ditches to deep lakes and coastal bays. Most species have sharp, pointed bills, fairly long necks, short wings, almost no tail, and lobed toes on legs set far back on the body. Grebes are generally dark brown to black above and paler below; a few species have reddish-orange feathers on their necks and flanks. During the breeding season, some have colorful head plumes that complement their elaborate breeding displays.

Taxonomy

Fossil representatives of the order Podicipediformes from as far back as the late Cretaceous period, some 80 million years ago, have been found in Chile; scientists think that grebes originated in this general vicinity. The modern genus *Podiceps* is known from the Oligocene epoch, more than 30 million years ago. Podicipedidae is the only living family in the order.

The evolutionary relationships between Podicipediformes and other bird orders are unclear. Traditionally grebes were thought to be closely related to loons, but more recent analyses suggest that this is not the case. DNA–DNA hybridization studies group the grebes with the families that make up the Pelecaniformes, Procellariiformes, and Ciconiiformes, but suggest that the relationships with these groups are quite ancient.

In North America, there are seven grebe species in four genera. *Tachybaptus* is mainly an Old World genus, but it includes the Least Grebe *(T. dominicus)* of the New World; species in this genus are sometimes referred to as "dabchicks." Three species of *Podiceps* grebes occur in North America—the Red-necked *(P. grisegena)*, Eared *(P. nigricollis)*, and Horned Grebes *(P. auritus)*.

Following the recent extinction of the Atitlan Grebe *(Podilymbus gigas)* in Guatemala, the Pied-billed Grebe *(P. podiceps)* is the world's only living member of the genus *Podilymbus*.

The *Aechmophorus* grebes—the Western Grebe *(A. occidentalis)* and Clark's Grebe *(A. clarkii)*—were considered to be color morphs of the same species until the 1980s. Now taxonomists recognize them as two separate species, citing evidence of different "advertising" calls, genetic differences, and the demonstration of

Podicipedid diversity. *North American grebes represent four genera:* Podilymbus *(represented here by the Pied-billed Grebe, top left),* Tachybaptus *(Least Grebe, bottom left),* Podiceps *(Horned Grebe, top right), and* Aechmophorus *(Clark's Grebe, bottom right).*

assortative mating, whereby individuals of one form preferentially pair with others of the same form.

Habitats

Grebes are closely tied to water, as are loons, and both groups have legs set far back on the body, an adaptation to a life of swimming underwater to catch prey. As a consequence, grebes walk poorly and are rarely found on land. Most species nest on freshwater lakes and ponds with abundant aquatic vegetation; some species also nest along rivers and ocean coasts in sheltered locations. Pied-billed and Least Grebes can nest in ephemeral pools and on small artificial ponds if they contain enough prey.

Pied-billed Grebe standing. Like loons, grebes have legs set far back on their bodies. This arrangement makes for efficient underwater propulsion but makes movement on land difficult and ungainly.

Grebes that migrate along the coast tend to remain close to shore. In overland migration, grebes rely on stopover sites such as lakes, reservoirs, and rivers. Some species, especially the Eared Grebe, take advantage of settling ponds at sewage treatment plants, landfill ponds, and other artificial environments. Unfortunately, the noxious waters of sewage lagoons can damage the waterproofing ability of grebes' feathers.

During migration and in winter, large aggregations of some grebe species can be seen along the California coast and at desert lakes; Eared Grebes congregate at saline lakes, especially Mono Lake, California, and Great Salt Lake, Utah, while Western and Clark's Grebes occur at fresher lakes with fish. In the nonbreeding months, rivers, lakes, and ocean bays provide habitat; the larger species are sometimes found far from land on the open ocean. Microhabitat selection may differ between Western and Clark's Grebes; when the two feed together, Clark's tend to forage farther from shore, in deeper water.

Worldwide Family Features

- 8–29" (20–73 cm) waterbirds.
- 22 species in 6 genera worldwide, of which 2 presumed extinct; found in all regions except Antarctica. North America has 7 species in 4 genera; found throughout most of continent.
- Small species eat mostly aquatic invertebrates; also small fish, amphibians, aquatic vegetation. Larger species eat mostly fish. Catch most prey during underwater pursuit.
- Most species nest in solitary pairs and are territorial on breeding grounds; a few species are colonial. Monogamous; some may pair for life. Many species migratory; some gregarious when not breeding.
- Breed first at 1 or 2 years old.
- Both sexes build nest: floating mass of vegetation, sometimes in reeds or on shoreline. Some species may reuse nests.
- 1–10 (usually 2–7) long elliptical to subelliptical eggs; off-white or pale blue, becoming brown with staining; replaced if lost. Hatching asynchronous after 20–30 days' incubation by both parents. 1 or 2 broods per year, occasionally more.
- Precocial young have downy coat. Brood at nest, with young on parents' backs, between wing and mantle. Abandon nest after last chick hatches. Both adults tend young in sheltered waters; adults or even older siblings sometimes feed young after fledging at 44 days to 11½ weeks.
- Little information on survival, but probably high once birds reach adulthood. Among oldest on record: 14 years (Western Grebe).

Food and Foraging

Smaller grebe species with short bills take mostly aquatic invertebrates, including various insects and their larvae, crayfish, and shrimp; they also eat small fish, amphibians, and aquatic vegetation. The larger species, with long, dagger-like bills and long necks, eat mostly fish. Grebes usually grab fish with the bill, but in some cases they spear them. The birds tend to eat small prey while still underwater but may bring larger food items to the surface before eating them.

Grebe heads and bills. *Bill shapes of grebes vary from the long, dagger-like shape of the Western (top) and Clark's Grebes, which eat mostly fish, to the short and relatively blunt-tipped bill of the Pied-billed Grebe (bottom), which eats mostly aquatic invertebrates.*

Well adapted for aquatic life, grebes have lobed toes similar to those of coots for propulsion and steering underwater. Like loons, they have sleek bodies and dense bones for diving, reduced tails and flattened tarsi to cut down on drag, and flexible necks suited to the pursuit of prey underwater.

Typically grebes forage near or at the water's surface. However, they can dive to depths of 90 feet (27 m), particularly larger species during the nonbreeding season, when they are at sea or on large lakes. By contracting their abdominal muscles and thereby compressing their plumage, while at the same time exhaling, small grebes can submerge themselves from a resting posture on the water's surface without diving. In this manner they can also adjust their buoyancy, for hunting

or concealment from predators; small grebes are often seen with only the head or bill above the surface.

The larger grebes tend to dive conventionally, sometimes with a small upward leap, presumably to attain greater depths. Dives are usually short, most lasting from 10 to 40 seconds.

Large grebes may consume a pound (0.5 kg) of fish in a day, and where present in large numbers, grebes can have a significant impact on prey resources. For example, Eared Grebes can cause large-scale prey depletion at saline lakes, where their staple is brine shrimp. At Mono Lake in California, well over 1 million Eared Grebes gather during fall migration to molt.

Like loons, grebes replace their flight feathers simultaneously and become flightless for a period of several weeks. At this time, Eared Grebes' flight muscles, especially those in the breast, lose up to half their mass, while the birds simultaneously become obese from their diet of shrimp. Researchers have found that brine shrimp populations "crash" during this period, and observers estimate that up to 83 percent of the decline could result from grebe predation. As shrimp become less available late in the fall, the birds begin to do more and more flapping

Grebe foot. *Grebes have lobed toes—not webbed feet—that are superficially similar to those of coots and phalaropes, but with more webbing between the toes and other subtle but distinctive differences. The Horned Grebe is shown.*

Grebe courtship. *The grebes have some remarkable courtship displays; two of the Eared Grebe's displays are shown here. These are known as the mutual penguin-dance (left) and the mutual parallel rush in penguin posture (right). The birds perform courtship displays on their arrival at the nesting area; the displays end abruptly when actual nesting activities begin.*

exercises. They complete their molt, body fat decreases, and their breast muscles regain mass, allowing them to continue their southward migration.

The reasons for this atrophy and rebuilding of muscle are not well understood. Studies of other species, especially the Great Crested Grebe *(Podiceps cristatus)* in the Netherlands, have led researchers to suggest that this cycle of atrophy and rebuilding is simply a response to the reduced use of the chest muscles while the birds undergo a simultaneous molt of their flight feathers. It also is possible that proteins lost from breast muscle are used in the synthesis of new flight feathers.

Another peculiarity of grebe biology, more prevalent in fish-eating species, is the birds' regular ingestion of large numbers of their own feathers, mostly taken from the belly and flanks. The feathers may protect the stomach from puncture by indigestible parts of the grebe's prey and prevent hard items from entering the intestines. They also provide the base material of regurgitated pellets that contain undigested material such as fish bones. Pellet-casting has the additional benefit of removing parasites from the digestive tract. Least Grebes, which eat few fish, also eat few feathers.

Breeding

Grebes have some of the most elaborate, stereotyped, and captivating courtship displays of all birds. The different phases of their displays correspond to the progressive stages of breeding: pair-bond formation, selection of nest site, territory establishment and maintenance, copulation, incubation, and chick-rearing. Some theories hold that the most intensive displays, as seen in the Western and Clark's Grebes, have their origin in the management of aggression, and that the reciprocity in postures and initiative between the sexes relates not just to pair-bonding but also to conflicts between males.

Indeed, the famous ballet-like rushing display of the *Aechmophorus* grebes—in which two birds rear up on their feet, necks kinked, wings swept back, and race across the lake surface—is performed not just by mated pairs but by two males or sometimes two males and one female. This suggests multiple functions for the display.

Grebe nests, comprised of decaying vegetation, are usually anchored on aquatic plants, quite unlike those of most loons, which are built on shorelines or small islands. The nest platform is a key location for grebes, serving also as the site of copulation, which may begin long before egg-laying. Early in the courtship, the female regularly mounts the male in a kind of mock copulation.

Copulation is invited by the female lying flat, neck to the ground (as in loons) and calling. After a brief mount, the male exits forward, over the head and neck of the mate, and returns to the water, often calling.

Chicks are able to swim and dive from birth. Their crowns have bare spots that are usually yellow but become vivid red when the chick is alarmed, endangered, or begging. Studies of Eared Grebes have shown that communication occurs between unhatched chicks and incubating adults. Called a "care-soliciting signal," the peeping of the embryo prompts adult Eared Grebes to respond: They turn the eggs more, build up the nest mound, bring food to the nest, and spend more time incubating or near the nest when "off duty."

As in loons, adults carry chicks on their backs to shelter, protect, and brood them. Sometimes the parents will even swim underwater with the young in this position, especially to avoid danger.

Colonial species, such as Western Grebes, occasionally nest in close proximity to colonies of gulls or terns, which may act as sentries and warn against approaching predators. Natural predators of grebes and their chicks include

Red-necked Grebe with chick on back. Young grebes frequently hitch a ride on the backs of their parents, where they can shelter between the adults' wings and keep warm.

large fishes such as bass and pike, turtles, herons, gulls, crows, coots, raccoons, and minks and other mustelids.

Conservation

One of the main causes of the worldwide decline of many grebe species has been the alteration of nesting and feeding areas, particularly interior lakes. These water bodies suffer from human activities such as development, boating, clearing of surrounding vegetation, acidification, many types of pollution, alteration of water levels, and draining. Even subtle changes in the acidity, alkalinity, or salinity of a lake, such as those caused by agriculture or water engineering projects, can quickly and drastically alter the availability of prey items and aquatic plant life.

Like other birds that eat aquatic animals, grebes have been affected by toxins such as PCBs and organochlorine pesticides, which concentrate in the birds' eggshells, causing breakage and nesting failure. Replacement clutches are usually less successful than the first ones, if they are attempted at all. As with loons and other divers, oil spills and entanglement in fishing nets also take their toll on grebes.

The introduction of large predatory fish into some lakes has reduced grebe populations, because the fish either prey on chicks or compete with adult grebes for other prey. At the turn of the 20th century, tens of thousands of Western and Clark's Grebes were slaughtered for their "fur," which was used for hats and coats.

From counts in migration and wintering areas, it appears that Western, Clark's, and Horned Grebes are declining and that Eared Grebes may be increasing, while Pied-billed and Red-necked Grebe populations are stable. Little is known about the status of the Least Grebe.

Edward S. Brinkley
and Alec Humann

Albatrosses

Albatrosses are among the largest seabirds, with very long, narrow wings and relatively long bills. They have webbed feet, short legs, short tails, stout necks, and compact bodies. Worldwide, albatross wingspans range from 5 feet 10 inches (1.75 m) to 12 feet (3.7 m) in the Wandering Albatross *(Diomedea exulans)* of the Southern Hemisphere, which has the largest wingspan of any bird. Plumages are generally a combination of black, white, and gray; adults of several species have bright orange, gold, or peach tones in the head feathers. The complex, tube-nosed bills also may be brightly colored with red, yellow, blue, peach, gray, or orange patches or stripes.

Taxonomy

The nearest relatives of the albatrosses include the storm-petrels and the shearwaters and petrels, which are also in the Procellariiformes; the fourth family in the order is Pelecanoididae, the diving-petrels of the Southern Hemisphere. Albatrosses are larger than most other members of the order and are unlikely to be confused with any species except the giant-petrels (*Macronectes* species in the family Procellariidae) of the Southern Hemisphere or a gannet or booby.

The Procellariiformes are separated from other avian species by the tubular sheaths (naricorns) on the upper bill, which encase the nasal openings and give the group their colloquial name "tubenoses." Albatross bills have a distinct construction, with several hard plates not found in the shearwaters and petrels or the storm-petrels, and with the nasal tubes separated rather than fused.

Based on recent biochemical studies, albatrosses are now placed in four genera rather than two. The "great albatrosses," the largest of seabirds, remain in *Diomedea*, but the smaller albatrosses (often called "mollymawks" in the Southern Hemisphere) have been placed in *Thalassarche*, and the three North Pacific species are now in *Phoebastria*. The two "sooty-albatrosses" remain in *Phoebetria*. Species of all four genera have been reported in North American waters, but only the three *Phoebastria* species—the Black-footed (*P. nigripes*), Laysan *(P. immutabilis)*, and Short-tailed Albatrosses *(P. albatrus)*—occur regularly.

Habitats

Like other seabirds, albatrosses at sea are usually found around prey concentrations. Sometimes these locations are quite predictable, especially when they are created by permanent upwellings. Other conditions that concentrate food are more ephemeral, such as shifting seawater fronts, cetacean herds, and floating carrion. Many habitat types are not apparent to the human eye.

An important habitat feature for albatrosses is the reliable presence of wind. All but four species are found principally in the wind belt between the southern end of the austral continents and the Antarctic, where high wind speeds are the norm. Their diet of squid means that in many areas albatrosses are highly pelagic, foraging from the continental slope seaward. Some species, such as the

Diomedeid diversity. *The three regularly occurring albatrosses in North America all belong to the North Pacific genus* Phoebastria. *Three Southern Hemisphere genera also occur rarely in North America and differ in details of structure and habits. The Black-footed Albatross is shown.*

Black-footed, are occasionally seen from land in the nonbreeding season, particularly where the continental shelf is narrow.

Albatrosses come to land only to nest, and then exclusively to islands, from small coral-sand atolls to islands as large as those of the Hawaiian archipelago. Black-footed and Laysan Albatrosses breed on islands in the Hawaiian chain. Black-footeds usually nest in sandier areas, and Laysans in grassier areas or near shrubs, although the nesting habitats of the two species overlap in many places. The rare Short-tailed Albatross nests on islands off Japan.

Food, Foraging, and Flight

Albatrosses are omnivores, although most species take little vegetable matter and eat mainly squid. The Black-footed and Laysan Albatrosses also consume large amounts of flyingfish roe, crustaceans, and fish. The large size and strong bills of albatrosses may enable them to scavenge at sea more effectively than the smaller shearwaters and petrels; all manner of floating debris, including trash and parts of penguins and smaller tubenoses, have been found in their stomachs.

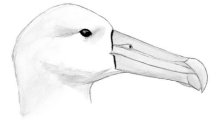

Albatross head and bill. The bill of the Short-tailed Albatross is typical of the family: massive and hooked, composed of several horny plates, with a separate tubular nostril on each side of the culmen.

Albatrosses also follow ships habitually, in part to take advantage of the displacement of air (lift) off the vessels' sides and superstructures, but also to feed on scraps of garbage. Albatrosses also feed on large carcasses, such as those of whales or seals.

Many scavenger species, including albatrosses and giant-petrels, change color with age. Some observers have suggested that because scavengers feed on carrion and compete vigorously, they establish feeding hierarchies. Age-specific plumages would allow individuals to determine the rank of others and minimize conflicts.

Worldwide Family Features

- 28–53" (70–135 cm) seabirds.
- About 14 species in 4 genera worldwide; over all oceans, with greatest diversity in Southern Hemisphere. In North America, 3 species in 1 genus are regular visitors to Pacific coast; plus 5 accidental species—3 on Pacific coast and 2 on Atlantic.
- Eat mainly squid; also many fish and roe, krill, crabs, amphipods, copepods, other invertebrates; occasionally marine algae, offal, carrion. Prey caught with bill at surface or in shallow dives.
- Colonial. Monogamous for life; seek new mates rarely, when breeding attempts repeatedly fail. Travel widely, usually alone, when at sea.
- Breed first at 5–12 years old.
- Most species build nest, constructed by both sexes. Typically cone-shaped structure up to 40" (1 m) tall, with central depression, out of mud, mosses, grasses; North Pacific species build less elaborate nests. Nest sites often reused year after year.
- 1 large, white, subelliptical egg; not replaced if lost. Both sexes incubate, for 7–11 weeks (longest in southern species). At most, 1 chick per year; some species breed only in alternate years.
- Young altricial, covered with down in 2 stages; brood 28–35 days at most; fledge at 19–40 weeks, longest in southern species.
- Adult annual survival very high, up to 97% in some species. Among oldest on record: 66 years (Royal Albatross of the Southern Ocean); older birds likely.

Albatrosses typically grasp prey with the bill at the water's surface or just below it, and all make shallow dives. The shortest-winged species can dive to the greatest depths; the Black-browed Albatross *(Thalassarche melanophris)* of the Southern Ocean can reach 15 feet (4.5 m).

With their long, narrow wings, albatrosses must maintain fast gliding speeds to stay aloft and lack maneuverability in flight. Thus most albatrosses must feed while sitting on the ocean's surface rather than in flight. The Light-mantled Albatross *(Phoebetria palpebrata)* and the Sooty Albatross *(P. fusca)* of the Southern Ocean, which have relatively light wing-loadings, may occasionally forage on the wing. (For more on the physical characteristics that relate to flight dynamics, see Seabird Wings and Flight, in the Shearwaters and Petrels chapter.)

The wings of albatrosses are supremely adapted to life at sea, and the birds cover large expanses of ocean as a matter of course. Some Royal Albatrosses *(Diomedea epomophora)* encircle the globe annually over the Southern Ocean, and breeding Wandering Albatrosses have been known to travel about 9,500 miles (15,000 km) while on a 30-day feeding trip. The biggest drawback to having such long wings, particularly in the great albatrosses, is their inability to fly in

calm conditions. Because of this limitation, some observers speculate, southern albatrosses that reach the Northern Hemisphere may become "trapped," unable to return across the windless doldrums around the equator.

Breeding

Although often capable of reproducing after their third or fourth year, albatrosses usually do not breed until they are several years older. A breeding cycle in the largest species may take more than a year, so nesting is attempted only in alternate years; even species with shorter cycles may not nest every year. Such postponement of breeding may be necessary if birds are to complete their energetically expensive molts.

Albatrosses nest in colonies ranging in size from several hundred to more than 100,000 birds. Typically nests are spaced far enough apart that initial territorial conflicts settle down after a few weeks; thereafter, defense of the site is limited largely to bill-snapping at passersby.

Albatrosses have elaborate visual and vocal courtship rituals on land and sometimes at sea. These consist of a series of stylized, exaggerated postures repeated in sequence; such displays decrease in intensity and duration as the pair bond

Black-footed Albatross breeding display. *Usually seen only on the breeding grounds (such as in Hawaii), the courtship dances of albatrosses are strangely graceful—a series of highly stylized, or stereotyped, postures repeated in sequence by both members of a pair.*

strengthens over the years. After court-ship and copulation, the pair returns to sea to feed; the male lays on fat for his long first turn at incubation, which can last from two to four weeks, and the female takes on bulk for egg formation. The single large egg can weigh well over a pound (0.5 kg), or more than 10 per-cent of the female's body weight; she departs the nest site soon after laying to feed again while the male incubates.

The parents then alternate incubation duties and brooding, feeding the chick a paste of partly digested prey and stom-ach oil. When incubating, the birds forage in areas significantly closer to the nest site than at other times. Breeding success is as high as 60 percent, though about 70 percent of young albatrosses may die in the first year of life.

Conservation

Albatrosses have low reproductive rates and long maturation periods; many species nest only every other year; the one egg they lay cannot be replaced; and the loss of one parent usually means death for an unfledged chick—all factors that make them vulnerable to population declines. The Short-tailed Albatross of the North Pa-cific and the Amsterdam Island Albatross (Diomedea amsterdamensis) of the southern Indian Ocean each have tiny populations in single breeding colonies and are ex-tremely vulnerable to extinction.

Albatrosses were massacred in the hey-day of the plume industry, with more than 300,000 killed in 1909 on Midway and Laysan Islands alone. The expansion of military bases in the tropical Pacific has also taken a huge toll. On Midway during the 20th century, hundreds of thousands were killed in collisions with antennae and planes or were slaughtered to reduce hazards to aircraft. Naval flight operations at Midway ended in 1993, and in 1997 the atoll became a National Wildlife Refuge.

Chief among the current problems for all tubenoses is the fishing industry, which reduces the birds' prey base and is re-sponsible for an enormous "by-catch" of seabirds. Birds become hooked on long-lines, ensnared and drowned in drift-nets and gill-nets, and entangled in cables. In 1990, the salmon and squid industries killed more than 17,500 Laysan Alba-trosses and more than 4,500 Black-footed Albatrosses. The by-catch of all manner of seabirds, particularly in gill-nets, numbers in the millions each year. Extinctions are inevitable unless this trend is reversed.

The body tissues of many procellari-iforms are contaminated with pollutants. Black-footed Albatrosses have high con-centrations of numerous pesticides and mercury in their bodies. The concentra-tions of such chemicals is lower in Laysan Albatrosses, possibly because they eat less offal and garbage. Seabirds ingest an abundance of floating plastic objects. Oil spills that contaminate prey resources and damage plumage also are a constant threat.

Accidental Species

Several Southern Hemisphere species have occurred rarely in North American waters. The Wandering Albatross and the Light-mantled Albatross have each been recorded once off California, both in summer. Also in the Pacific, Shy Alba-trosses (Thalassarche cauta) have been seen off the Pacific coast from Washing-ton to California. The taxonomy of this species is complex, and it may soon be split into four species. A recent study suggests North American records can be assigned to two of the proposed species, the "Shy Albatross" (T. "cauta") and the "White-capped Albatross" (T. "steadi").

In the Atlantic, the Yellow-nosed Alba-tross (Thalassarche chlororhynchos) has been seen in several places from eastern Canada to Texas. The Black-browed Alba-tross has been reported several times from Florida to Newfoundland during summer and once in winter off Virginia, the only photographic record from the western North Atlantic.

Edward S. Brinkley
and Alec Humann

Shearwaters and Petrels

The Procellariidae comprises small to relatively large seabirds that are superficially similar to gulls. Most species are dark above and pale below. North American species have wingspans that range from 27 inches to 3 feet 8 inches (68–112 cm). At close range, procellariids are easily distinguished by their naricorns—raised, horny tubes at the base of the upper bill that encase the nostrils. Other members of the order Procellariiformes (see the Albatrosses and Storm-Petrels chapters) also have naricorns—thus their collective nickname "tubenoses." The two tubes of procellariids are fused (unlike those of albatrosses) and in some species appear to be a single tube. Most shearwaters and petrels exude a musky scent, possibly from the preen gland but more likely from their stomach oil, which may act as an important cue for birds seeking their burrows and mates under cover of darkness. The flight of procellariids distinguishes them from most other seabirds. Shearwaters and petrels are extraordinarily adapted for harnessing the wind in a specialized, sailing flight that allows them to cover vast expanses of ocean. Members of this family live exclusively at sea, except when nesting or when driven inland by storms. Many species are as active at night as they are during the day, often feeding mostly at night. On land, most procellariids move awkwardly, though some species are swift runners and remarkably agile climbers, even able to scramble up trees when threatened by predators.

Taxonomy

The family Procellariidae has four basic subgroups: the fulmars and giant-petrels, the gadfly petrels, the shearwaters, and the prions of the Southern Hemisphere. The fulmar group is represented in the Northern Hemisphere solely by the Northern Fulmar *(Fulmarus glacialis)*, a stiff-winged, heavy-bodied flapper. The gadfly petrels of the genus *Pterodroma*, which means "winged-runner," outclass all other family members in the air, executing high, bounding, S-shaped arcs, even in low wind velocities.

The last group found in North American waters is the shearwaters. The smallest shearwaters, sometimes referred to as "black-and-white shearwaters," form a complex within the large genus *Puffinus*; all have dark brown plumages above, white below, and slender black bills with small naricorns. The genus *Calonectris* contains the largest shearwater in the world, Cory's Shearwater *(C. diomedea)*, which can be distinguished in flight by its heavy, lumbering wing flapping.

The family Procellariidae dates back at least to the Oligocene epoch (which began 37 million years ago), from which fossils bearing skeletal similarities to modern petrels have been found. For some time, Procellariidae has been regarded as one of four well-defined families within the order Procellariiformes. Under this scheme, procellariids' nearest living

Procellariid diversity. *The North American procellariids are subdivided into three groups— the fulmars and giant-petrels (represented here by the Northern Fulmar, left), the gadfly petrels (Herald Petrel, center), and the shearwaters (Sooty Shearwater, right). A fourth subgroup, the prions, is restricted to the Southern Hemisphere.*

relatives are the albatrosses, storm-petrels, and diving-petrels (Pelecanoididae, of the Southern Hemisphere).

An alternative classification, based on DNA–DNA hybridization, combines all these groups into a single family within the order Ciconiiformes and merges the shearwaters, prions, fulmars, gadfly petrels, and diving-petrels in the subfamily Procellariinae. This alternative scheme, which has yet to win widespread acceptance, also suggests that tubenoses are closely linked to the loons, frigatebirds, and penguins (family Spheniscidae).

The species-level taxonomy of the Procellariidae is much debated, and much remains to be learned about the degree of reproductive isolation and genetic differentiation among breeding populations. Some species are separated into Pacific and Atlantic forms, while in others even birds from different islands might warrant species status. In some cases, taxonomic uncertainty arises from the distinct color morphs frequently found in the family. For instance, some authors have treated the Flesh-footed Shearwater *(Puffinus carneipes)* as a dark morph of the Pink-footed Shearwater *(P. creatopus).* Similarly, researchers have suggested that the light and dark morphs of the Herald Petrel *(Pterodroma arminjoniana)* in the Pacific be classified as separate species, while others argue for recognition of the Atlantic form *(P. a. arminjoniana)* as a species separate from the Pacific form *(P. a. heraldica).*

The taxonomy of Fea's Petrel *(Pterodroma feae)* also is unsettled. This species and the similar Madeira, or Zino's, Petrel *(P. madeira),* which both breed on islands off northwestern Africa, were recently split from the Soft-plumaged Petrel *(P. mollis)* of the Southern Hemisphere. Work on this complex has suggested that the two northern species may be more closely related to the Bermuda Petrel *(P. cahow)* than to the Soft-plumaged Petrel, but relationships among these taxa remain uncertain. Some authorities even advocate species status for the *feae* and *deserta* subspecies of Fea's Petrel.

Some European authorities also split Cory's Shearwaters of different populations into separate species. Individuals of both the Mediterranean *(Calonectris diomedea diomedea)* and the northwestern Atlantic *(C. d. borealis)* forms have occurred in North American waters.

Variation

Although there can be considerable intraspecific variation in some species of Procellariidae, it generally is not possible

---

Worldwide Family Features

- 10–39" (25–98 cm) seabirds.
- About 79 species in about 13 genera worldwide; over all oceans, with greatest diversity in Southern Hemisphere. 17 species in 4 genera occur in North America, along all coasts (only 2 species breed); plus at least 6 accidental species.
- Carnivorous; eat mainly fish, crustaceans, cephalopods, shrimp, mollusks. Catch most prey at surface or during shallow dives.
- Mostly colonial. Monogamous; most species mate for life; new pairs form if mate is lost. Most species travel widely during nonbreeding season, some in long migrations; some species very gregarious at sea, others solitary.
- Breed first usually at 5 or 6 years old (can be 3–12 years old, sometimes older).

- Nest is little more than a scrape, sometimes lined with sparse vegetation; placed on cliff, in recess, or in burrow. Both sexes may help build nest. Often reuse nests.
- 1 white, oval to elliptical egg. Typically both sexes incubate, for 6–9 (usually 7–8) weeks. 1 chick per year.
- Altricial young covered with natal down. Both parents care for young; brooding lasts 2–20 days. Fledge at 43 days to 19 weeks.
- Generally long-lived, with adult annual survival often well over 90%. Many birds probably live 15–20 years; several species have lived over 30 years. Among oldest on record: more than 50 years (Northern Fulmar).

to distinguish the sexes in the field. In some gadfly petrel species, males tend to have longer, deeper, and broader bills. Similarly, the bills of male Cory's Shearwaters are a bit larger than those of females. However, these differences are difficult to see in the field.

Young procellariids closely resemble older birds, unlike many albatrosses. Upon close scrutiny, some birds at sea reveal crisp, fresh plumage, with paler or darker edges to the upperwing or upper-tail coverts. These markings usually indicate newly fledged juveniles. The wing proportions (especially the width) in such birds sometimes appear different in the field from those of adults as well. Otherwise, determining the age of birds in the field is impossible.

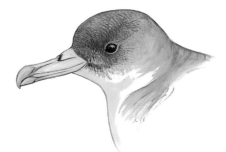

Procellariid head and bill. *The head and bill of Cory's Shearwater (shown here) are typical of the family: a bulbous head and a relatively long bill with a prominent hook at the tip. Characteristic of all procellariiforms are the small tubes on top of the bill encasing the nostrils.*

Plumage polymorphism is commonly seen in the Northern Fulmar, the Herald Petrel, and the Wedge-tailed Shearwater *(Puffinus pacificus),* which is accidental in North America. Variation in the ventral patterns of Sooty *(P. griseus)* and Short-tailed *(P. tenuirostris)* Shearwaters also occurs but is probably not a true poly-morphism.

All tubenoses vary noticeably in appear-ance when molting, especially when molting their flight feathers, coverts, and tail feathers. Worn feathers look paler and less resplendent than new feathers. Ambient light can influence an observer's impression of color as well: A bird that looks black in heavily overcast condi-tions may look golden brown in bright sunshine, thanks to a peculiar reflective quality in the plumage of most tubenoses.

Food and Foraging

Procellariids probably detect prey by a combination of sight and smell. Tube-noses appear to have a well-developed ol-factory sense for detecting prey by day or night. Prey detection by smell is uncom-mon in birds (see also the New World Vultures and Flight, Form, and Function chapters); in tubenoses it seems to in-volve "scanning" the breeze for wind-borne scents while in flight. Larger

species are known to zigzag through the odor plume while flying into the wind to pinpoint the source.

The naricorns of tubenoses are thought to play a role in this well-developed sense of smell and may also enable birds to detect subtle differences in air pressure and wind direction. These structures also direct secretions from the birds' salt glands away from the eyes. The salt glands are located above the bill and serve to reduce the amount of salt in the birds' blood, enabling them to drink sea-water and live entirely at sea. Tubenoses never drink fresh water.

Diets vary greatly among species of Procellariidae, though the birds mostly eat small marine organisms—predomi-nantly small fish, cephalopods (squid and cuttlefish), and crustaceans (shrimp, euphausiids, amphipods). Some species scavenge on marine carrion, and all may be opportunistic in this way, especially around commercial fishing and shell-fishing operations. In the 19th and 20th centuries, Northern Fulmar populations increased dramatically, owing first to the whaling industry and later to the advent of factory ships for fishing.

Many procellariid species, especially those with long migration routes, have diets that vary seasonally. However, like many shorebirds, they return to the same foraging grounds annually, hence the vital importance of marine sanctuaries for their survival. Differences in diet according to age or sex have been well documented in a few species. In gadfly petrels, the smaller-billed juveniles and females take smaller prey than adult males, and in several species the sexes forage separately.

Some Procellariidae species are easy to observe while they forage—for example, Sooty Shearwaters gobbling up anchovies in the Pacific surf during the day. Others, such as many gadfly petrels, feed mainly at night or during twilight hours, when deepwater prey species rise to the surface. (These prey species exhibit a nightly "vertical migration" through the water column presumably because they must come up to feed on the more abundant food near the surface but cannot remain there during the day, as the risk of predation is too great.)

Most procellariids have dark plumage surrounding the eye, which reduces glare off the ocean's surface, making it easier for the birds to feed by day. Most can also probably forage well in low light conditions—on moonlit nights, for example. Species thought to forage mostly at night, such as some of the gadfly petrels, have large eyes with high levels of rhodopsin, a visual pigment that facilitates night vision. Nocturnal species can also exploit the bioluminescence of some of their prey, especially squid. Many procellariids also may use smell to help them find food at night.

For birds that feed near shore, tidal activity and its effect on prey availability may influence feeding behavior more than the time of day does; elsewhere, local upwellings, fronts, or the habits of predatory fish (all of which can concentrate prey) may be more important than the hour. Procellariids may feed in enormous aggregations, small associations, or alone, depending on the species and the distribution of prey.

Many procellariids are surface-seizers, grasping slippery prey with their sharp-edged bills at the water's surface or just below it. Some species dive from the surface to pursue prey underwater. Using their wings for propulsion, some dive to depths of 40 to 60 feet (12–18 m); more typical forays last only a few seconds, as with Audubon's Shearwater *(Puffinus lherminieri)*, which often dives into gulf-weed *(Sargassum* species) to hunt small prey. Some species execute shallow plunges from very low altitudes while airborne. Gadfly petrels feed on the wing as well as from the ocean's surface. The plumage of a shearwater or petrel is very soft to the touch, and some observers believe such plumage may help procellariids capture prey such as squid, which might otherwise be able to grasp the birds with their tentacles.

Shearwaters and petrels are fast fliers and, with a few exceptions, are not strongly attracted to boats, even when tempted with chum. Larger species use various foraging strategies. Some, such as Cory's Shearwater, follow schools of large predatory fish, dipping or alighting occasionally to capture prey fish driven to the surface. A few, such as the Greater Shearwater *(Puffinus gravis)*, regularly follow

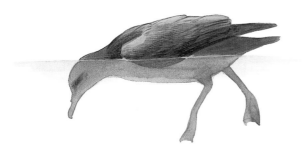

Procellariid foraging.
Shearwaters and petrels feed mainly on prey captured at the surface of the water, but some species dive underwater to pursue prey, using their partially extended wings for propulsion. Some species do this more than others and may even plunge from several feet up in the air directly into the water. Here a Sooty Shearwater peers underwater with wings slightly open, preparing to dive.

Seabird Wings and Flight

The most underdescribed field characteristics of Procellariiformes are their flight behaviors, yet for many seabird enthusiasts, the most arresting adaptation of the tubenoses is their aerial prowess. As described in the chapter Flight, Form, and Function (see the Aerodynamics section), the demands of getting into the air and staying there have shaped birds in very distinctive ways. A procellariiform's flight patterns and wing shape relate to its entire natural history, from its migration and feeding habits to its nesting area.

Wing Shape

Many procellariiforms, especially albatrosses, have heavy wing-loading that is offset by a high aspect ratio. These large, heavy birds have trouble getting off the ground and must move fast to stay aloft, but their long, narrow wings create considerable lift, allowing them to glide for long distances with little flapping and thus minimal energy expenditure.

In contrast, diving-petrels and auks, which spend a lot of time swimming underwater, have short, relatively wider wings. Like albatrosses and the shearwaters and petrels, these diving birds have small wing areas relative to their body mass and are heavily wing-loaded. They do not, however, have long, narrow wings with high aspect ratios because the advantages of such wings in flight are offset by their disadvantages underwater. Thus diving-petrels and auks must flap their short wings almost constantly and fly fast to stay airborne.

Wingbeat Frequency

Wing length and shape influence wingbeat frequency in all birds, and these can be particularly useful for identification in seabirds. Compared to gadfly petrels of similar size, Black-vented and Audubon's Shearwaters have low aspect ratios and so travel shorter distances between bouts of flapping. Sooty and Short-tailed Shearwaters, which migrate thousands of miles, have wings with aspect ratios as high as those of the gadfly petrels. But they have heavier wing-loadings, and to stay aloft they must flap more rapidly between glides than gadfly petrels with similar wing lengths.

Like the much larger albatrosses, large shearwaters such as the Pink-footed and Cory's have evolved more as gliders; they typically flap less rapidly and less often than smaller shearwaters. Gadfly petrels use wind energy to traverse great distances over areas of open ocean; their wings and bodies have high aspect ratios,

Procellariid flight styles. *Flight styles of the procellariids are governed by aspect ratio and wing-loading. Audubon's Shearwater (left) has a low aspect ratio and high wing-loading; its flight is direct and low, with frequent flapping. On the other hand, the Black-capped Petrel (right) has a comparatively high aspect ratio and low wing-loading; its flight is graceful, and it often makes high arcs, with relatively infrequent wingbeats under most wind conditions.*

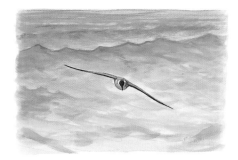

Greater Shearwater slope soaring. *As a wave moves through the water, it forces air up ahead of it; this tiny updraft is often enough to keep a shearwater aloft with no wing flapping. The bird can ride on this cushion of air, essentially surfing on the wave, indefinitely.*

Pink-footed Shearwater in running takeoff. All procellariids have relatively high wing-loading and must achieve and maintain high airspeeds to get, and stay, airborne. Because it is difficult to flap their long, narrow wings rapidly enough to attain these critical speeds, members of this family must run across the surface of the water when taking off in calm conditions.

and they are lightly wing-loaded. In high winds, gadfly petrels can appear to move along on fixed wings without a flap. These adaptations enable them to exploit areas of low productivity, where birds must travel long distances to find food, even while feeding young.

Types of Soaring

Much of the energy that moves seabirds along comes from the interaction of wind and sea. Many procellariiforms, such as the Black-capped Petrel, rely on *dynamic soaring.* Imagine a petrel flying high in the air, into the wind, making relatively little headway and receiving little lift from the head wind. As the bird loses altitude and moves seaward, it converts the potential energy from its altitude into an increased gliding speed and forward motion.

As it dips into the wave trough, the bird encounters slower air caused by both shelter from the wind and friction between air and water. By turning upward, the petrel crosses through a gradient of increasing airspeed that helps lift it back up high above the waves, ready to restart the cycle. The classic form of this maneuver looks like the sinusoidal curve of a roller coaster, but many variations are seen at sea.

Dynamic soaring is often combined with *slope soaring.* As wind passes over a wave it is deflected upward, causing an updraft. The bird uses the updraft off the side of a wave to travel along the wave trough. Some species use the updraft created by ships as they move forward, displacing air. In high winds, gulls, gannets, jaegers, and skuas also use dynamic and slope soaring.

Black-capped Petrel dynamic soaring. The dynamic soaring of the Pterodroma *petrels is one of the most thrilling sights in birding. In strong winds the birds gain altitude, then use gravity to make a long, gradual glide down to water level, where, by turning into the wind, they can increase their airspeed and gain enough lift to rise up again and repeat the process. In this manner, they can travel for miles at high speed without ever flapping. Here, this flight path is shown from the side (top) and as it appears when a bird is flying toward an observer (bottom).*

boats and take bait and fish; others, such as the Northern Fulmar, gather in large groups around carcasses of marine mammals or large squid. However, most species forage independently of ships, cetaceans, or schools of large fish.

Most procellariiforms are very plainly plumaged, in hues of brown, gray, and white, and the majority are countershaded—dark above and pale below. Several possible explanations for the evolution of countershading have been proposed. One suggestion is that it provides protection against the intense ultraviolet radiation at sea; it may also make seabirds harder for prey to detect. In some cases, more cryptic patterning may protect smaller species from predators, whereas more striking patterns, as in the white uppertail coverts of the Black-capped Petrel *(Pterodroma hasitata)*, may foster visual communication with members of the bird's own species across great distances.

Although there is variation, solitary species, which mostly eat squid, tend to be more distinctively patterned than the darker gregarious species, such as the Sooty and Short-tailed Shearwaters.

Breeding

All well-studied procellariid species seem to pair for life, unless a mate is lost, in which case the remaining bird seeks a new partner. Divorces are rare and often associated with nest failure. Nest site fidelity is typically very high; most pairs return to the same site year after year. Birds of several species, however, may sometimes take "sabbatical years," in which a pair either visits the colony but does not nest or simply does not return for several years in a row. These skipped years may be associated with periods when prey is scarce.

Most procellariid species nest once a year (sometimes more often near the equator), usually beginning in the local spring or summer. Almost all form large breeding aggregations, and many are restricted to only a few sites, making them quite vulnerable (see Conservation).

Seabird coloration. Most procellariids are countershaded—dark above and pale below— and many have striking patterning on the upperparts. The pale underparts may function as camouflage, making it difficult for prey to see the bird above them. Buller's Shearwater is shown.

Relatively graceless on land, most shearwaters and petrels are most vulnerable to predation while in breeding colonies, and many move about the colonies only at night, to court, to exchange nest duties, or to feed young.

Males and females generally return to the breeding area at the same time and rendezvous at their previous nest site. Observers believe the birds recognize each other by voice and possibly by scent. They renew pair bonds through diurnal or nocturnal courtship flights, often with antiphonal calling between them, and through mutual preening and calling at the nest prior to copulation. In most well-studied species, the female can be distinguished from the male by her lower-pitched calls.

While breeding adults are renewing their pair bonds, competition for nest sites is low. Adults, however, may squabble among themselves, hissing, calling, adopting threat postures, and dueling with their bills to defend or dispute a territory. Later in the breeding season, large groups of subadults may arrive at the colony and begin "practicing" courtship and territory selection, though they may not nest for several more years.

The sharp-edged bills of some species, especially fulmars and gadfly petrels, are used mostly for hunting at sea. However, they can also be formidable weapons that the birds can employ with considerable force in territorial conflicts and in encounters with predators (especially mammals introduced by human settlers).

Nests

Nest sites vary among species. Many species nest underground, either in an elaborate, multi-chambered burrow housing several pairs or in a single burrow. Sometimes old rabbit burrows are used, but species such as the Manx Shearwater *(Puffinus puffinus)* excavate their own nest holes. Some ground-nesters, such as the Mottled Petrel *(Pterodroma inexpectata),* use burrows in forested areas. Many species also use natural recesses in sea stacks, islets, or mountain cliffs. The Northern Fulmar is one of a few species that nest aboveground, favoring inaccessible ledges on sea cliffs.

Most species are strictly nocturnal on the nesting grounds, except when the area is free of predators. In such rare cases, species such as Murphy's Petrel *(Pterodroma ultima),* which breeds on remote islands in the South Pacific, are diurnal and even nest in the open. However, most procellariids select nest sites such as burrows or steep cliffs to reduce predation and competition with other seabird species. Burrows also serve to regulate temperature for the incubating adults and the nestling.

After copulation and, in some species, rudimentary nest-building, in which a few pieces of vegetation, feathers, or small stones are used to line the nest scrape, the birds make an exodus to sea, often not returning for two or three weeks. During this time females obtain the nutrients they need for egg-laying, while males build energy reserves to last through the first incubation stint.

Eggs and Young

After the adults return from their foraging dispersal, the female lays a single large egg that the male (except in fulmars) begins to incubate, alternating with the female in shifts that range in length from two to 14 days.

On hatching, the chick is covered with thick down. Parents brood the chick only until it can regulate its own body temperature; then they visit the chick intermittently to feed it a thick, oily paste comprised of partly digested prey. For nocturnal species, visits to the nest site are sometimes governed by the amount of moonlight; a bright night gives an advantage to predators.

Shearwater and petrel young gain weight rapidly and surpass the weight of adults before their feathers are fully grown. At their heaviest, chicks can weigh considerably more than their parents. By putting on extra fat, chicks increase their ability to survive short periods of food shortage while in the nest and also enhance their chance of surviving after they fledge. A week or two before the chick leaves the nest, the adults begin to bring food less frequently, often deserting the young bird altogether. During this time, the chick's weight drops as it uses up much of the stored fat to complete its growth.

Manx Shearwater at nest burrow. Awkward on land and potentially easy prey for birds and mammals, many procellariids nest in burrows they visit only at night. Here a Manx Shearwater makes a nocturnal visit to its burrow.

As the chick approaches fledging, it will often test its wings, increasing its activity outside the nest at night after its parents' final visits. Left on its own, the chick must learn to fly, find its way to sea (sometimes from mountains quite distant from the ocean), and learn to forage without help from its parents.

Movements

Members of the Procellariidae can cover large distances during the nonbreeding season. Short-tailed Shearwaters, which breed on islands off the coast of Australia, make a transequatorial migration that takes them to the Bering Sea each year, while Manx Shearwaters, which breed in the North Atlantic, head in the other direction to winter off the eastern coast of South America.

Species that breed in more tropical climes have less distinct migrations but may still spread out over large areas of ocean. Even these species may travel along somewhat predictable routes while away from their breeding sites, as evidenced by our increasing ability to predict when certain species will occur in North American waters; observers have recently discovered the regular presence of Murphy's Petrel off California and Fea's Petrel off North Carolina in the spring.

Though little is understood about how tubenoses accomplish long-range homing, their ability to navigate over great distances is legendary. A Manx Shearwater, for instance, taken from its burrow in Wales and released in Boston, Massachusetts, returned to its burrow in 12½ days, covering 3,200 miles (5,150 km) of ocean. Similar experiments, with comparable results, have been made with the Wandering Albatross *(Diomedea exulans)* and Leach's Storm-Petrel *(Oceanodroma leucorhoa)*.

Conservation

Among procellariid species, a strange dichotomy exists between the abundant and the endangered: At least 15 species have populations of more than 2 million,

while as many as 20 others worldwide may be in danger. In species such as the Northern Fulmar, a large population, successful breeding, and high adult survival rates help maintain population growth. In others, such as the Bermuda Petrel and the Chatham Islands Petrel *(Pterodroma axillaris)* of New Zealand, the remaining populations are extremely small and vulnerable to extinction.

Even abundant species can be vulnerable if breeding populations are restricted to a few colonies in a small area. For example, most of the world's Buller's Shearwaters *(Puffinus bulleri)* breed on one small island group in New Zealand and, despite numbering in the millions, could be drastically reduced in number by a single oil spill or introduced predator species.

Abundant species are also viewed with concern because of increasing mortality, especially of adults, which can have devastating effects on populations over a very short period. As with other seabird groups, many procellariids die as a result of fishing activities (see also the Albatrosses chapter). Additionally, species such as the Pink-footed Shearwater and Cook's Petrel *(Pterodroma cookii)* are vulnerable to the effects of predators, often introduced by humans, at breeding colonies.

Direct harvest by humans also plays a role. Annually species such as the Greater, Sooty, and Short-tailed Shearwaters are taken from their subantarctic breeding sites by the thousands, for use as bait, food, oil, and animal feed; their feathers are even used as sleeping bag insulation. Closer to home, the harvest of adults, chicks, and eggs at breeding sites has reduced local populations of Audubon's Shearwaters in the Caribbean and Cory's Shearwaters in the North Atlantic. Fortunately, some colonies have now been declared reserves and harvests have been reduced.

The most endangered species likely to be encountered in North American waters is the Bermuda Petrel. In fewer than 100 years of human exploitation in the 17th century, the population was reduced from a half million pairs to a handful. Until 1951 the species was considered extinct, but a few surviving birds were found nesting in rocky crevices on rat-free islets off Bermuda. Protection efforts, including rat control and the provisioning of nest boxes designed to prevent competition from White-tailed Tropicbirds *(Phaethon lepturus)*, have resulted in a slow but steady increase in the population.

Not so fortunate was the "Jamaican Petrel," which bred on Jamaica and probably foraged in or strayed into North American waters. Formerly considered a dark morph of the Black-capped Petrel, it is now thought to have been a separate species, *Pterodroma "caribbaea,"* possibly more closely related to Fea's Petrel. It was last documented in 1876 and is now considered extinct.

The WatchList includes the Black-capped Petrel and the Black-vented Shearwater *(Puffinus opisthomelas)*.

Despite conservation advances in some areas, the family will most likely suffer further population reductions in the future. Researchers have found that many procellariids are contaminated with pollutants such as organochlorine pesticides and mercury. While it is still unclear how seabirds are affected by sublethal levels of such chemicals, the history of DDT in other birds suggests that these toxins could devastate species already imperiled and, in the long run, take a large toll in other as yet unaffected species.

Yet another potential threat comes from global warming, a process undoubtedly accelerated by human activity. Climate changes can cause shifts in oceanic circulation patterns that, in turn, may alter food supplies that seabirds rely on. Such changes have been suggested as a possible cause of a reduction of up to 90 percent of the Sooty Shearwaters in the eastern North Pacific over the past two decades. An alternative explanation for these declines is the massive by-catch of procellariiforms by the fishing industry.

Accidental Species

In addition to the regularly occurring species, several additional members of the Procellariidae have wandered into North American waters. The Streaked Shearwater *(Calonectris leucomelas)*, Wedge-tailed Shearwater, Dark-rumped Petrel *(Pterodroma phaeopygia)*, and Stejneger's Petrel *(P. longirostris)* have all been seen off the West Coast of North America, with most reports coming from California during late summer and fall. The Streaked Shearwater is typically found in the western Pacific, and the Wedge-tailed Shearwater is widespread in tropical and subtropical waters of the Pacific and Indian Oceans. Dark-rumped Petrels breed on the Hawaiian and Galápagos Islands, and Stejneger's Petrels migrate between breeding grounds off Chile and the central North Pacific.

Little Shearwaters *(Puffinus assimilis)*, which are found throughout the Southern Ocean and on islands off northern Africa in the Atlantic, have occurred onshore, as wrecked birds, in Nova Scotia and South Carolina. Perhaps most remarkable, given its rarity, the Bermuda Petrel has been seen in Gulf Stream waters off North Carolina in spring and summer more than 10 times between 1993 and 2000.

Providing further evidence of the variety of species that may be encountered in North American waters, several other species have been reported recently but are not yet officially accepted: the Great-winged Petrel *(Pterodroma macroptera)* of the subantarctic and Parkinson's Petrel *(Procellaria parkinsoni)* of the tropical Pacific, off California; the White-chinned Petrel *(Procellaria aequinoctialis)*, also of the subantarctic, off North Carolina; and the pantropical Bulwer's Petrel *(Bulweria bulwerii)*, off both California and North Carolina.

Edward S. Brinkley
and Alec Humann

Storm-Petrels

Storm-petrels are small seabirds with dark or countershaded plumage, often white rectrix coverts, and distinctive flight and foraging behaviors. They have the compact form, webbed feet, and bill adaptations of the other tubenose families (see the Albatrosses and Shearwaters and Petrels chapters) but are much smaller. Known in many world languages as "sea swallows," storm-petrels are more likely to be confused at sea with swallows than with other tubenoses. The Least Storm-Petrel *(Oceanodroma microsoma)*, the world's smallest tubenose, is only as large as a sparrow. Storm-petrels nest colonially, usually on remote islands, and feed offshore throughout the world's oceans.

Taxonomy

The storm-petrels are closely related to the albatrosses and the shearwaters and petrels, and as with the latter two groups, there are several uncertainties about the family's taxonomy. Some authorities split the group into two subfamilies: the Hydrobatinae, which breed mainly in the Northern Hemisphere, and the Oceanitinae, which breed mainly in the Southern Hemisphere. Other taxonomies, including the AOU Check-list, do not make this division.

Four of the world's seven genera of storm-petrels have been reported in North American waters. For the most part, these genera exhibit noticeable differences in shape and modes of flight, so that field observers, aided by the study of plumage, can identify most storm-petrels to the level of genus, if not always easily to species.

As with other tubenoses, distinguishing between subspecies and species is complex, and many island populations may prove to be reproductively isolated as they are studied more thoroughly. The most complex example is Leach's Storm-Petrel *(Oceanodroma leucorhoa)*, which is abundant in the North Pacific and North Atlantic basins through most of the warmer months.

Several subspecies of Leach's Storm-Petrel are recognized, the exact number depending on the authority. In addition, Swinhoe's Storm-Petrel *(Oceanodroma monorhis)* and the now extinct Guadalupe

Storm-Petrel *(O. macrodactyla)* were formerly considered subspecies of Leach's. Swinhoe's Storm-Petrel occurs in the western Pacific and Indian Oceans, and in the 1990s was also found to occur in the Atlantic from western Africa to Norway. It also has been reported off the North Carolina coast. Most ornithologists currently classify Swinhoe's as a distinct species, within a superspecies with the Ashy *(O. homochroa)* and Leach's Storm-Petrels.

The most widespread subspecies of Leach's Storm-Petrel is the nominate race *(Oceanodroma leucorhoa leucorhoa)*, which

Hydrobatid diversity. *Storm-petrels can be divided into two main evolutionary branches: the Southern Hemisphere breeders, such as the White-faced (left) and Wilson's (center), which have relatively long legs and short "arms," and the Northern Hemisphere breeders, such as the Fork-tailed Storm-Petrel (right), with shorter legs and longer "arms." These differences in structure relate to differences in flight and foraging styles.*

is found throughout much of the Atlantic and Pacific Oceans. In the Pacific, differentiation has occurred between northern and southern nesters, with a gradual decline in wing and leg length and in bill size from north to south. Rump color is also variable in the Pacific. Northern birds have white rumps, like those in the Atlantic, but dark-rumped individuals become increasingly common toward the southern end of the range.

Off the western coast of Mexico things become more complicated. A springtime birder on a boat in this area might see as many as four different forms of Leach's Storm-Petrel: the nominate race and birds from three populations that breed locally. The birds that nest on the Coronados and San Benito Islands have been ascribed to the subspecies *Oceanodroma leucorhoa chapmani*, those nesting on Guadalupe Island during winter to the subspecies *O. l. cheimomnestes*, and those nesting on islets offshore from Guadalupe during summer to the subspecies *O. l. socorroensis*. Whether these forms are completely isolated reproductively remains uncertain. To complicate things further, some taxonomists believe the last form is a subspecies of Swinhoe's Storm-Petrel.

Storm-petrel head and bill. *Storm-petrels, the smallest of the tubenoses (order Procellariiformes), have a short, hooked bill with tubular nostrils on top. The tube directs salt excretions from the salt glands away from the body. Recent research suggests that storm-petrels use smell to find food on the surface of the trackless ocean, and the tubes may also play a role in localizing scents. The Fork-tailed Storm-Petrel is shown.*

Rump color also varies within these three Mexican subspecies, although *cheimomnestes* are mostly white-rumped and the other two forms mostly dark-rumped. Identifying these forms at sea is probably not possible.

Food, Foraging, and Flight

Storm-petrels feed primarily on the wing, and their flight styles and foraging methods can be helpful in distinguishing species. In general, these birds fly just above the water's surface, where they can

Worldwide Family Features

- 5–10" (13–25 cm) seabirds.
- About 20 species in 7 genera worldwide; found over all oceans. 8 species (including 4 breeding species) in 3 genera occur in North America, found offshore along Atlantic and Pacific coasts; plus at least 2 accidental species.
- Eat mostly crustaceans, small squid and octopus, fish, jellyfish, offal. Catch most prey on the wing or when resting on water's surface.
- Colonial. Monogamous, though not always for life; same pair usually nests in successive years at same site. Most species travel widely during nonbreeding season, some migrating long distances; range from very gregarious to solitary when at sea.
- Breed first probably at 4 or 5 years old, but little is known.

- Most species dig burrow nests, built by male in some species, both sexes in others; several nest in crevices, sometimes lined with plant matter. Typically reuse nests year after year.
- 1 elliptical to subelliptical, mostly white egg that weighs up to 30% of female's weight. Both parents incubate, in shifts lasting several days, for 38 days to 8½ weeks. 1 brood per year.
- Altricial young covered with gray down. Both parents care for young, which are usually brooded for a week or less but fed for longer. Fledge at 52 days to 17 weeks.
- Adult annual survival 80–95%, suggesting many birds may live 5–20 years after reaching adulthood. Among oldest on record: 36 years (Leach's Storm-Petrel).

pick off small crustaceans and other prey. Some species are more flexible: Fork-tailed Storm-Petrels *(Oceanodroma furcata)* will sit on the surface, picking off prey, and will gather to feed around dead whales. Several species follow ships or visit fishing boats; some will feed on human refuse. Many storm-petrels feed at night, when prey rise to the surface, but some, such as the Band-rumped Storm-Petrel *(O. castro)*, will feed during the day.

Some storm-petrels feed by pattering the water's surface with their feet while remaining stationary over the prey—by fluttering rapidly or by setting their wings into the wind to anchor themselves in place. Foot-pattering may facilitate prey capture, either by alarming prey and causing them to move or by attracting them. The behavior is especially common in Wilson's Storm-Petrels *(Oceanites oceanicus)*, and the webbed feet of this species may enhance the effect of the pattering movements.

Recent research has shown that Wilson's Storm-Petrels can use the presence of aromatic chemicals (produced when zooplankton eat their phytoplankton prey) to identify areas containing high densities of food. These results have led to the suggestion that storm-petrels may perceive the ocean as a landscape of smells and that they use gradients in the concentrations of odors to find feeding areas.

Storm-petrel foot. Storm-petrels have long, slender legs and relatively small feet with webbing between three toes. In Wilson's Storm-Petrel (shown), the webbing is yellow and contrasts with the black toes and legs.

The typical locomotion of the White-faced Storm-Petrel *(Pelagodroma marina)* is unmistakable: The bird holds its wide, sail-like wings up at an angle, lowers its long legs, and, with its enormous feet, pushes off the side of a wave to coast on open wings. Its unusual flight pattern has prompted observers to liken it to an airborne kangaroo.

The *Oceanodroma* storm-petrels are the true aerialists of the family. With proportionately longer, thinner wings than members of *Pelagodroma* and *Oceanites*, the birds are shaped more like the smallest procellariids or even nighthawks. In average winds, this group tends to travel by dynamic soaring, arcing over the waves rather than moving along troughs by slope soaring alone. (See Seabird Wings and Flight, in the Shearwaters and Petrels chapter.)

Wilson's Storm-Petrel foot-pattering. *While foraging, some storm-petrels touch their feet to the water at least occasionally. This paddling may help them hold their position over a particular spot, or it might attract or frighten prey, making them easier to see and capture.*

Leach's Storm-Petrel nest and young. All storm-petrels nest underground, in either a burrow or a crevice. In some species, the young bird remains in the burrow up to 17 weeks, eventually growing nearly twice as heavy as an adult bird. Finding their own burrow at night in a crowded colony is a challenge for the parents, who rely on sound, calling to their mate or young while flying over the colony, and perhaps also on smell.

Breeding

Unlike many seabirds, some storm-petrel species can be difficult to see at their breeding colonies because they restrict their visits to nighttime in order to reduce the risk of predation. Nonetheless, they sometimes nest in enormous numbers; colonies of Leach's Storm-Petrel in both the Atlantic and the Pacific have been estimated to contain more than a million birds. Storm-petrel colonies, like those of gadfly petrels and some shearwaters, can come alive at night with aerial calling and displaying by males and females engaged in chase-flights and by small groups comprised mostly of subadults, which, along with nonbreeders, may attend colonies during the breeding season.

Most species nest in burrows or underground rock crevices, another response to the risk of predation by larger seabirds. Male Leach's Storm-Petrels dig nest burrows using the feet and bill, but birds will also use old rabbit holes, natural crevices, or burrows built in previous years. Ashy Storm-Petrels nest in natural rock cavities and may share holes with other breeding seabirds, such as Cassin's Auklets (*Ptychoramphus aleuticus*). Nests may be sparsely lined with vegetation and debris, and are often used by the same birds for many years in succession. Copulation and courtship activities—mutual preening, singing duets, and stroking—take place in the burrow. After copulation, the female departs to feed intensively for several weeks.

Unlike most other tubenoses, storm-petrels develop a sizable brood patch to incubate their proportionately large egg. Although data are available for only a few species, their breeding success, on average, is much lower than that of other tubenoses: As few as half of the eggs storm-petrels lay may hatch, and as few as half of the chicks may fledge. Annual adult mortality—about 5 to 20 percent—can be three times higher than that of larger tubenoses, making lifetime monogamy (the breeding system of larger tubenoses) less feasible for storm-petrels.

Both parents take care of their offspring. By six to eight weeks of age, a chick may weigh as much as 80 percent more than an adult. Much of this excess weight is lost during the period immediately before fledging. Unlike some members of the shearwaters and petrels family, young storm-petrels are not abandoned by their parents and do not fast at this time, although the rate at which parents bring food may decline.

Conservation

It is difficult to obtain accurate population trend data on species that are so elusive and nocturnal on the nesting grounds as storm-petrels. Counts of Wilson's Storm-Petrels off the Atlantic coast of North America have fallen off sharply since the 1970s, but this may or may not indicate a population decline for this species, which has traditionally (though perhaps incorrectly) been accorded the

Storm-petrel egg size.
Storm-petrels lay eggs that
are relatively large, up to 30
percent of the female's body
weight. Here the egg of a
Leach's Storm-Petrel (left)
is compared to the eggs of two
species of similar weight: the
Western Kingbird (Tyrannus
verticalis; *right), which has*
altricial young, and the
Semipalmated Plover
(Charadrius semipalmatus;
center), which has precocial
young.

status of one of the most abundant species on Earth. It is possible that birds have simply moved elsewhere in response to changes in local environmental conditions.

As is true for most tubenoses, storm-petrels have evolved with few predators. However, the introduction of mammals onto islands with storm-petrels, starting with the colonization of Pacific Ocean islands by the Polynesians and continuing in the centuries since then, has in many cases had a devastating effect. Rats, cats, dogs, minks, mongooses, and various ungulates prey upon adults, young, and eggs; even mice can kill an adult storm-petrel. In addition, cattle, sheep, and horses trample the birds in their burrows or overgraze nesting areas, causing erosion that collapses burrows. Introduced pigs root out the burrows, eating eggs, nestlings, and adults.

Storm-petrels are also vulnerable to avian predators, such as gulls, jaegers, skuas, owls, hawks, and corvids. The substantial increase in populations of large predatory gulls in the last century, a result of the increased food availability in landfills and dumps, has probably affected storm-petrel populations.

The Guadalupe Storm-Petrel, which nested on northwestern Mexico's Guadalupe Island until about 1912 and probably foraged in North American waters, now appears to be extinct. Of the extant species, one of the most vulnerable is the Ashy Storm-Petrel. Although the population does not seem to be declining, it consists of only a few thousand birds concentrated at a handful of breeding colonies located close to the major ports of Los Angeles and San Francisco, where an oil spill could devastate the population. A similar risk threatens the small U.S. population of Black Storm-Petrels (*Oceanodroma melania*), although much larger populations of this species exist in Mexico.

The WatchList includes both the Ashy Storm-Petrel and the Black Storm-Petrel.

Accidental Species

In California, Wedge-rumped Storm-Petrels (*Oceanodroma tethys*) have been reported at various times of year, mainly far offshore; these birds have wandered north beyond their typical nonbreeding range, which extends from southern Baja California to Chile. Another wanderer was a European Storm-Petrel (*Hydrobates pelagicus*) found on Sable Island, Nova Scotia, during August. This species breeds in the northeastern Atlantic as close as Iceland and typically winters south to southern Africa. Finally, there are recent summer reports of Swinhoe's Storm-Petrel from North Carolina and Markham's Storm-Petrel (*O. markhami*), of the tropical eastern Pacific, in California; both have yet to be officially accepted.

Edward S. Brinkley
and Alec Humann

Tropicbirds

Tropicbirds are medium-size seabirds, predominantly white with black patterning on the back, wings, and face. They have thick, pointed bills, red or orange in color, that are slightly decurved. Their most striking feature is their extremely long and narrow central tail feathers, which can be 11 to 22 inches (28–55 cm) long, almost equaling (and occasionally exceeding) the bird's body length. Their wingspans average 35 inches to 3 feet 8 inches (88–112 cm). Superficially tropicbirds resemble terns. Tropicbirds are highly pelagic foragers in tropical and subtropical oceans, coming to land mainly to breed.

Taxonomy

The family Phaethontidae's oldest fossil remains, of an extinct fourth species of tropicbird, date back about 50 million years to the Eocene epoch. Though their pelvic structure is similar to that of frigatebirds, tropicbirds are no more closely related to the Fregatidae than to other families of pelecaniforms. Indeed, some taxonomists separate the tropicbirds into their own suborder; among other differences, tropicbirds lack a naked gular pouch, and their young hatch with down, unlike those of other pelecaniforms.

Taxonomists have often subdivided each tropicbird species into several subspecies. However, recent research suggests that many of the current subspecies may be color morphs and that fewer subspecies should be recognized.

Food and Foraging

Tropicbirds feed mostly around dawn and dusk, when their prey is closest to the surface. Searching for prey, they fly long distances at heights of 30 to 60 feet (9–18 m) or more. Their rapid wingbeats, more akin to those of a pigeon than to the flap-gliding or gliding of other pelecaniforms, give them a distinctive appearance at sea.

Phaethontid diversity. *The world's three species of tropicbirds are very similar and are characterized by their stout bills, short legs, mostly white plumage, and very long central tail feather streamers. The White-tailed Tropicbird is shown.*

Worldwide Family Features

• 15–19½" (38–49 cm) seabirds. (Lengths exclude tail-streamers.)
• 3 species in 1 genus worldwide; pantropical. 2 species occur in North America, off southern U.S. coasts; plus 1 accidental species.
• Eat mainly flyingfish, squid; also other fish, crustaceans. Usually catch prey by plunge-diving.
• Loosely colonial where nesting areas permit. Monogamous, often for life; may seek new mates following nest failure. Generally solitary when not breeding. No regular migrations known, but travel widely.

• Breed first probably at 2–4 years old, but little is known.
• Nest is scrape in crevice or burrow, or on ground; made by both sexes. Reuse nests from year to year.
• 1 oval egg; white, red, brown, or gray with dark scrawlings. Both sexes incubate, for 40–46 days. 1 or 2 broods a year.
• Young semi-altricial, with downy coat at hatching. Both parents provide care. Fledge at 9½–15½ weeks.
• Adult annual survival presumed to be high, but little information. Among oldest on record: 28 years, 6 months (Red-tailed Tropicbird).

Upon locating food, tropicbirds hover briefly, fold their wings, and plunge into the ocean in pursuit. Like other pelecaniforms, tropicbirds have air sacs under the skin around the head and neck that absorb the concussive shock associated with plunge-diving. Their serrated bill edges help to secure prey, which they swallow before taking flight. When pursuing flyingfish, tropicbirds sometimes hunt frigatebird-fashion, gliding low over the water behind the airborne fish and taking them on the wing.

Tropicbirds can plunge-dive to depths of several yards, but they are not known to "swim" with their wings underwater in pursuit of prey, as many seabirds do. Usually they feed singly, though sometimes they hunt in pairs and less commonly in larger groups. Occasionally they join pelagic terns and shearwaters foraging over shoals of fish.

Tropicbirds have a distinctive look when sitting on the water, with their tails cocked at an upward angle. The vivid black-and-white pattern of the upperparts of the White-tailed Tropicbird *(Phaethon lepturus)* may help the bird advertise its presence to others of its kind, possibly providing information about the location of prey concentrations. The eye-catching reflective quality of the upperparts is completely absent below, probably an adaptation to conceal the birds from underwater prey.

Breeding

In equatorial regions tropicbirds nest year-round; at higher latitudes they nest only in warmer months. The birds commonly nest as isolated pairs, although colonies exist where nest sites are numerous. Competition for nest sites can be fierce, and birds sometimes evict their own kind or smaller seabirds. Pairs bond through spectacular, synchronized aerial displays, with strident, repetitive vocalizations. They copulate at the nest site.

Nesting areas are located mostly on remote islands, rarely on mainland cliffs. White-tailed and Red-billed *(Phaethon aethereus)* Tropicbirds favor burrows and crevices for nest sites, preferably with entrances shaded by vegetative or rock overhangs. On some islands, the White-tailed Tropicbird will nest in tree cavities, the only pelecaniform to do so. The Red-tailed Tropicbird *(P. rubricauda)* of the tropical Pacific Ocean nests in more open areas but requires vegetation to conceal its nest. Tropicbird pairs may excavate

White-tailed Tropicbird at nest. *Tropicbirds come to land only to nest, and their short legs make walking so difficult that they must choose a nest site with easy access for the birds but not for predators. In most places, this means a cliff crevice, which the birds can fly to but which is difficult for predators to reach.*

Tropicbird head and bill. The bills of tropicbirds are stout, brightly colored, and pointed, with slight serrations along the edges of the jaws for gripping slippery fish and squid. The Red-billed Tropicbird is shown.

their own burrows but generally use existing burrows, crevices, or ledges. With webbed feet set far back on the body, tropicbirds are poor walkers and prefer to land directly at the nest site.

Tropicbirds lay a single egg but may nest year-round, which allows a breeding pair to raise up to two young per year. Both sexes incubate the egg, with the non-incubating adult sporadically feeding the sitting bird. The downy chick, which remains at the nest for two months or more, is fed a regurgitant of semi-digested invertebrates. Later the parents feed the young bird squid and fish. The young are independent immediately upon fledging.

Movements

Tropicbirds are among the most pelagic of birds and wander widely when not at their nest sites. At midday, tropicbirds can be spotted at great heights, even above the large cumulus clouds that form over warm water. They rely less on thermals or prevailing wind currents than other high-fliers, such as frigatebirds, instead flying by means of rapid, flapping wingbeats. Observers at sea often first note tropicbirds flying high overhead.

Because of their pantropical distribution in open ocean, the birds must be able to cope with the powerful cyclones that arise in the tropics. Tropicbirds may "wreck" less than other pelagic species during hurricanes because they rely less on soaring, and therefore upon prevailing wind currents, to travel.

Nevertheless, as a result of Atlantic hurricanes, 31 White-tailed Tropicbirds were recorded along the coast or in the interior of eastern North America between 1870 and 1995; some of the storm-swept birds ended up as far north as Nova Scotia. These birds may have become trapped in a hurricane's windless eye, or they may have come ashore as the storm made landfall.

Conservation

As with most tropical seabirds, human introductions of mammals to remote islands have been devastating to tropicbirds. In some areas, feral cats, rats, and mustelids can cause total nesting failure. On some islands, local people collect the birds and eggs for food. Nonetheless, many current populations appear to be stable, and none of the three species is in danger of extinction.

Young tropicbirds typically breed close to the site where they were born; consequently, it is unlikely that areas will be recolonized naturally following local extirpations, at least not in the short term. The removal of introduced predators and the provision of artificial nest boxes in predator-free areas near existing colonies may help prevent extirpations from occurring.

Accidental Species

Red-tailed Tropicbirds occasionally are seen offshore along the Pacific coast of North America, primarily off California between July and January.

Edward S. Brinkley
and Alec Humann

Boobies and Gannets

The Sulidae, comprising the tropical boobies and the more temperate gannets, is a family of large seabirds found throughout the world's oceans. Most species have pale or white bodies with darker feathering on the wings, back, or head. All have long, pointed wings and tail, a heavy, pointed bill, and completely webbed feet. In several species the feet and bill are brightly colored and play an important role in elaborate breeding displays. Wingspans average 4 feet 9 inches to 6 feet (1.4–1.8 m). All boobies occur in tropical and subtropical climes; the Northern Gannet *(Morus bassanus)*, the only gannet to occur in North America, is found over colder water in the North Atlantic.

Taxonomy

Probably most closely related to cormorants and darters, the sulids have been split into the genera *Morus* (gannets) and *Sula* (boobies), with Abbott's Booby *(Papasula abbotti)* of the Indian Ocean sometimes separated into a distinct genus. Differences between these groups are small, and some authorities combine them into a single genus.

The world's three gannet species are similar in appearance and were once considered to be a single species. Boobies are more variable, and several species show sufficient geographic variation to be separated into subspecies. In some cases, researchers have proposed that allopatric subspecies be considered separate species. Recently the Nazca Booby *(Sula granti),* which nests from western Mexico to Chile and may have occurred in California, was split from the Masked Booby *(S. dactylatra).*

Sulid diversity. *The Sulidae can be divided into two main groups—gannets in temperate waters and boobies in tropical waters—that differ in bill structure. The Red-footed Booby is shown.*

Worldwide Family Features

• 25–40" (63–100 cm) seabirds.
• 10 species in up to 3 genera worldwide; found in all oceans, tropical to subarctic. 5 species in 2 genera occur in North America; occur along Atlantic coast, rarely on Pacific coast.
• Eat mainly fish; also squid. Capture prey mainly by plunge-diving.
• Highly colonial. Monogamous; often pair for life. Often feed in large flocks during nonbreeding season. Some species migratory; others wander widely but less predictably.
• Breed first at 2–6 years old.
• Nest is scrape in ground rimmed with guano, sometimes placed on broad cliff ledges or flat, rocky plateaus; or platform made of sticks and other plant matter, cemented by guano, placed in small trees or shrubs. Male brings materials; female arranges and builds. Do not reuse nests.
• 1–3 (usually 1) pale green, blue, or whitish, oval to subelliptical eggs. Both sexes incubate, for 41 days to 8 weeks, in turns of up to 3 days. Hatching asynchronous. Clutch replaced if lost within first 21–28 days of incubation. Usually 1 brood per year.
• Young altricial and near-naked at hatch. Brooded on top of parents' feet for several days; attended constantly in 1st month. Fledge at 12–25 weeks; remain dependent for up to 9 months after fledging. Both parents provide care.
• Adult annual survival typically greater than 90%. Among oldest on record: 27 years, 2 months (Brown Booby).

Food and Foraging

Boobies and gannets eat a wide variety of small schooling fishes, including mackerels, anchovies, pilchards, and flyingfishes; some boobies also eat squid. The birds forage at sea and may spend months without returning to land.

Sulids feed by plunge-diving, often gathering in large groups over a school of fish. Because they dive from heights of up to 300 feet (90 m), gannets and the larger boobies can catch prey at depths inaccessible to surface-feeding seabirds, up to 30 feet (9 m) or so below the surface. Like the diving Brown Pelican *(Pelecanus occidentalis)*, boobies and gannets enter the water with wings held backward, in line with the body, which thus takes the shape of a large dart. In some cases, sulids "swim" with their wings underwater; gannets reportedly reach depths of 75 feet (23 m).

Keen binocular vision helps sulids forage. They may take prey at any point during the dive: just after impact, during swimming pursuit, or as the bird begins to surface. They consume smaller prey underwater.

In tropical seas above schools of fish, smaller boobies such as the Red-footed *(Sula sula)* and the Brown *(S. leucogaster)* often associate with other seabirds, especially shearwaters and tropical terns such as the Sooty Tern *(Sterna fuscata)* and the Brown Noddy *(Anous stolidus)*. Masked Boobies are more pelagic in their foraging and often associate with schools of tuna, which drive the birds' preferred

Sulid foraging. All sulids capture fish and other prey by plunge-diving from the air into the water. When a Northern Gannet (shown here) sights prey, it begins a steep descent; just before entering the water, the bird lays its wings back, fully extended but flat against the body, so that body and wings form a long, straight dart that pierces the water with almost no splash.

prey to the surface. The smaller sulids also dive from the water's surface, chase prey on foot (in shallows), and often snag flyingfish in the air.

Breeding

Sulids perform some of the most elaborate, stereotyped, and amusing courtship displays of any seabirds. The name "booby" probably refers both to their fearlessness of humans on their nesting grounds and to their comical appearance during courtship. Gannets, which form the strongest pair bonds among the sulids, may begin nuptials months before nesting.

Among the many poses male sulids strike during territorial advertisement, defense, and courtship are the "stretched-neck sky-point," often with the tail raised skyward; the "yes-no" headshake; and the "slow parade," in which they conspicuously display their feet (which are brightly colored in the smaller species) and often present females with

Sulid head and bill. Boobies and gannets have heavy, wedge-shaped bills and heads, creating a streamlined form for piercing the water when diving after fish. The sharp edges of the bill grip slippery prey. The Masked Booby is shown.

Sulid display. Sulids perform elaborate dancing displays around the nest site. In the part of the greeting ceremony of the Northern Gannet shown here, the pair face each other breast to breast and, while stretching their necks straight up, gently "fence" with their bills.

small "gifts" such as rocks or feathers. Some species also perform aerial displays over the nest site, which is found in locations ranging from flat ground to cliff faces to small trees and shrubs.

Boobies are well known among biologists for their practice of siblicide, in which the first chick to hatch kills its younger sibling. In some species, such as the Masked Booby, the older, larger chick invariably pushes from the nest the smaller chick, which is taken by predators or dies of exposure. Adult boobies also frequently kill unguarded chicks. For breeding Masked Boobies, siblicide serves as an insurance mechanism; a pair can never raise more than one chick, but laying two eggs provides insurance against one failing to hatch. On the other hand, Blue-footed Boobies *(Sula nebouxii),*

Sulid feet. Like all members of the order Pelecaniformes, the boobies and gannets have totipalmate feet, with all four toes joined by webbing. Some boobies have brightly colored red, yellow, or blue feet that they use prominently in displays; the Northern Gannet (shown here) has neatly marked pale green lines along the leg and each toe.

which face variable environmental conditions (in particular, rapid changes in seawater temperatures along the Pacific coast that radically alter the stocks of their prey), "hedge their bets" by hatching two eggs. If conditions are good, they can raise both chicks; if not, the older chick kills the other.

Conservation

Habitat destruction in the tropics, particularly on islands, threatens many booby species, even though direct human exploitation of the birds decreased in the latter part of the 20th century. Many colonies are not protected, and pressure on the birds, particularly by egg-hunters, remains high in places; several local extirpations occurred in the 20th century. Red-footed Boobies in the Caribbean have also been disturbed by the growth of tourism. On the other hand, most colonies of Northern Gannets enjoy legal protection and have steadily increased their numbers in recent decades.

Boobies and gannets often follow vessels engaged in large-scale fishing operations, scavenging surplus fish or squid brought to the surface. But many birds are killed by collisions with or entanglements in fishing gear; they also are easily hooked on fishing lines. The greater long-term threat to sulids is the overfishing of their key prey species.

Edward S. Brinkley
and Alec Humann

Pelicans

Pelicans are very large waterbirds, easily identified by their huge bills and large, distensible pouches, which they use to capture prey. Most are white with black flight feathers; the Brown Pelican *(Pelecanus occidentalis)* is much darker. Pelicans have large, webbed feet and wingspans that range from 6 feet 7 inches to 9 feet (2–2.7 m). Often gregarious, pelicans are found at lakes and marshes and in coastal areas throughout the tropics and warmer temperate zones.

Taxonomy

The order Pelecaniformes has traditionally included pelicans, cormorants, tropic-birds, frigatebirds, darters, and boobies and gannets, based on similarities in toe-webbing and the gular pouch. However, recent research has raised questions about this grouping. DNA–DNA hybridization studies, for example, place pelicans and the Shoebill *(Balaeniceps rex)* of Africa together as each other's closest relatives and split up the order Pelecaniformes. Other research has supported a more traditional grouping, with the Shoebill placed in the order Ciconiiformes instead.

Food and Foraging

Pelicans primarily eat fish. The Brown Pelican occurs in marine habitats and takes such saltwater fishes as anchovies, menhaden, and sardines. The American White Pelican *(Pelecanus erythrorhynchos)* is typically found in fresh water, where it consumes perch, chub, trout, and carp, as well as crayfish and large salamanders.

The two species typically employ very different foraging strategies. Groups of American White Pelicans use highly co-ordinated feeding strategies, typically in water up to 8 feet (2.4 m) deep. Sometimes

Pelecanid diversity. *The world's seven species of pelicans are remarkably uniform in appearance, differing only in details of size and plumage. All share the very long bill and expandable pouch under the bill. The Brown Pelican is shown.*

Worldwide Family Features

- 41–72" (105–183 cm) waterbirds.
- About 7 species in 1 genus worldwide; found on all continents except Antarctica. 2 species breed in North America; occur along Atlantic and Pacific coasts of North America and at lakes in interior, north to central Canada.
- Primarily eat fish caught while swimming or plunge-diving.
- Usually colonial nesters. Apparently monogamous, but keep mates for only 1 breeding season. Gregarious during nonbreeding season; some populations migratory.
- Breed first at 2–5 years old.

- Both sexes build nest: scrape or debris mound on ground, or stick nest in tree.
- 1–6 (usually 2 or 3) long subelliptical, off-white eggs, replaced if lost early in incubation. Both parents incubate, for 28–36 days. Hatching asynchronous. 1 brood per year.
- Young altricial, naked at birth, with down coat by 3–8 days; after 7–14 days, parents brood mostly at night. Both parents care for young. Young of ground-nesting species form crèches after 30 days; fledge at 9–12 weeks.
- Adult annual survival may exceed 80%. Among oldest on record: over 27 years (Brown Pelican).

American White Pelicans foraging. American White Pelicans swim in a group when foraging, advancing slowly across the water and thrusting their bills into the water ahead of them, sometimes in synchrony.

the birds swim in a linear or semicircular formation, moving the fish toward a shoreline, where they are more easily caught. The same strategy is used by two groups of pelicans "mirroring" each other and driving the fish into the narrowing space between them. In other circumstances, a large nonlinear group moves in unison across the water with bills submerged, leaving the prey few escape routes.

During these "fish drives" the birds may coordinate activities such as the lowering of bills into the water or wing-beating to alarm and direct the fleeing fish. Capture rates are highest during coordinated fishing.

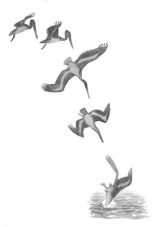

Brown Pelican plunge-diving. The Brown Pelican forages by plunge-diving from the air into the water. When it sights prey, the bird begins a steep dive and enters the water head-first with wings stretched back. The body does not completely submerge and creates a considerable splash, unlike the way sulids enter the water. When the splash subsides, the bird is visible sitting calmly on the water's surface, slowly pulling up its bill as water drains from the pouch.

The smaller Brown Pelican forages primarily by plunge-diving, often from heights of up to 65 feet (20 m). When diving, a Brown Pelican first brings its legs in against its body and retracts its head, then slowly extends the neck and angles the wings backward. The head remains stable during these maneuvers, so that the bird can sight prey along the length of its bill.

On contact with the water, the pelican draws back its wings and opens its bill, centering the prey between its jaws. Its pouch distends rapidly to an enormous size, capable of holding about 21 pints (10 liters), or about 17½ pounds (8 kg), of water, and closes around the fish.

Bill Adaptations

Thought by early naturalists to be a fish-storage device, the gular pouch serves primarily to capture fish, which the pelicans typically swallow immediately. The pouch is so sensitive that the American White Pelican can fish by "feel" on dark nights. The pouch is also richly supplied with blood vessels; pelicans can dissipate body heat through gular fluttering.

To maintain the elasticity of the pouch, pelicans perform pouch exercises, throwing the head back with the bill open, or even tucking the head down and turning the pouch inside-out over the breast. Like other pelecaniforms, pelicans use their pouches in breeding displays that involve lifting the head to show off the pouch or inflating it with air. During the display period, the pouch becomes brightly colored.

The American White Pelican has a fibrous epidermal plate on top of the bill, toward the tip, that grows in the breeding season but is much reduced at other times; it is probably important in displays.

Breeding

Pelicans are colonial nesters; they require predator-free sites, often on islands and close to foraging areas, to nest successfully. The male displays at the colony to attract a female, who chooses the nest site. Ground-nesting Brown Pelicans use a simple scrape nest, and construction does not take long. Where Brown Pelicans nest in trees or on cliffs, they assemble a relatively elaborate stick platform. The American White Pelican, which nests on the ground, may construct a sizable mound of debris for its nest and needs more time for construction than the ground-nesting Browns.

Most copulation occurs at the nest site. Usually females lay two or three eggs, rarely up to six eggs. Single clutches are the rule, although pelicans may replace eggs lost or taken by predators early in the season. Pelicans, like most pelecaniforms, do not have a brood patch and incubate their eggs on their feet.

Eggs hatch in the order laid, and when food is scarce, the smaller, younger chicks

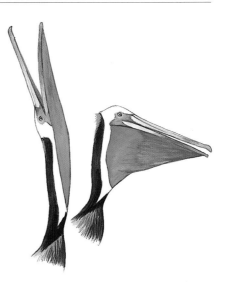

Pouch exercise. Pelicans stretch the pouch frequently to keep the skin flexible. Shown here is a Brown Pelican performing the longitudinal stretch, in which the head is thrown back.

may starve to death, a common occurrence in Brown Pelican broods. After about a month, chicks gather into tight groups (crèches) of up to 100 birds, probably to help regulate their body temperatures and for increased defense against predators.

Conservation

Although most pelican species worldwide are in decline, populations of American White Pelicans appear to be stable, and Brown Pelican numbers are growing in North America.

Brown Pelican populations crashed in the 1960s and 1970s as a result of contamination by dieldrin and DDT, which interfered with eggshell production and caused birds to lay thin-shelled eggs prone to premature breakage.

With the signing of the Endangered Species Act in 1973, the Brown Pelican was officially listed as endangered in the United States. This protection, combined with the banning of DDT, has resulted in recovery in many areas.

Edward S. Brinkley
and Alec Humann

Pelican head and bill. A pelican's bill consists of a long, narrow upper jaw and a matching lower jaw formed by two long, flexible bones supporting a deep pouch of skin. When the open bill is thrust quickly into water, the pouch expands like a balloon, bending the two flexible lower bones outward to create a wide opening. After the initial thrust, the bones return to their parallel position, fitting tightly against the upper jaw. Water drains out of the bill slowly, but the prey are trapped inside and swallowed. The American White Pelican is shown.

Cormorants

Shaped like elongated geese, cormorants are large waterbirds with webbed feet, a long neck, and a long, hooked bill that they use to snag aquatic prey while swimming underwater. Their wingspans range from 3 feet 3 inches to 5 feet 3 inches (99–160 cm). Most species are predominantly black, but some have white patches, especially on their underparts. Cormorants are found on inland lakes and rivers and in coastal marine habitats.

Taxonomy

The taxonomy of the cormorants, the largest of the world's pelecaniform families, is unsettled. Traditionally all species are grouped in a single genus, *Phalacrocorax*. However, some authors divide the family into three genera: *Nannopterum* for the Flightless Cormorant *(P. harrisi)* of the Galápagos, either *Microcarbo* or *Halietor* for a group of small, long-tailed species found in Eurasia, Africa, and Australasia, and *Phalacrocorax* for the remaining species. Still other proposals would split the family into as many as nine genera.

Even the distinction between cormorants and shags is not clear-cut. The name "shag" is often used for smaller species, especially those found in the Southern Hemisphere, but "shag" and "cormorant" do not necessarily refer to taxonomically distinct groups within the family. A recent suggestion to split the family into two subfamilies, with the species in one named cormorants (Phalacrocoracinae) and those in the other named shags

(Leucocarboninae), might clear up the confusion, although it would result in name changes for many species.

The closest relatives of the Phalacrocoracidae are the darters, which have sometimes been combined with the cormorants in one family, and the boobies and gannets. Common ancestors of these families can be found in the fossil record dating back some 60 million years, and the divergence of cormorants and darters dates back at least half that long.

In the early 1990s, a study of bone remains from Amchitka Island in the Aleutians led to the suggestion that a previously undescribed species of cormorant had lived in Alaska until at least the 1950s. This species was described as morphologically similar to the Pelagic Cormorant *(Phalacrocorax pelagicus)* but smaller, and was presumed to have become extinct very recently. The new cormorant has been called "Kenyon's Shag" or the "Amchitka Cormorant" *(P. "kenyoni")*, but it has not been accepted by the AOU's Check-list committee. Indeed, a more recent analysis has shown that Pelagic Cormorants in the central Aleutians are smaller than elsewhere in their range and that the bones ascribed to the new species could have come from a small female Pelagic Cormorant.

Phalacrocoracid diversity. Aside from subtle differences in proportions and habits, all of the world's cormorant species are quite similar. All the North American species are glossy blackish with relatively long tails, short legs, long necks, and long, hooked bills. The Great Cormorant is shown.

Habitats

Cormorants are highly adapted to aquatic environments, both freshwater and marine. Red-faced *(Phalacrocorax urile)*, Brandt's *(P. penicillatus)*, and Pelagic Cormorants are restricted to marine habitats along the Pacific coast, whereas the widespread Double-crested Cormorant

Cormorant head and bill. *Cormorants have a relatively long and slender bill with a sharp hook at the tip. All cormorants also have an area of bare skin, on an expandable gular pouch on the throat, that becomes more brightly colored during the breeding season. The Red-faced Cormorant is shown.*

(*P. auritus*) is more of a generalist, using virtually any open water for foraging, from swamp to open ocean.

The Neotropic Cormorant *(Phalacrocorax brasilianus)* also uses a wide variety of aquatic habitats, in North America mainly in the western Gulf of Mexico and areas bordering Mexico. This species, more partial to rivers and smaller lakes and ponds, occurs less often on salt water than the Double-crested. During their summer and early fall movements, Neotropics are found on inland reservoirs and rivers. The Great Cormorant *(P.*

carbo), which has expanded its range southward along the Atlantic coast in recent decades, rarely strays from marine habitats with rocky substrates in North America. In Eurasia it occurs in freshwater habitats, and a few individuals have been recorded on the Great Lakes and on interior lakes in the Atlantic coastal plain.

Food and Foraging

Cormorants are adept divers, and all North American species consume mostly small fish. The Great Cormorant sometimes tackles much larger prey, taking eels more than 24 inches (60 cm) long and fish over 18 inches (45 cm) long. Cormorants take most of their prey during underwater pursuit, propelling themselves mostly with their webbed feet rather than with their wings. In addition to diving from the water's surface, the Neotropic Cormorant can plunge-dive with closed wings from the air or a perch. The Great Cormorant may kleptoparasitize Northern Gannets *(Morus bassanus)* or follow ships for discarded fish or invertebrates.

Once cormorants catch their prey, they bring it to the surface, maneuver it

Worldwide Family Features

- 18–40" (45–100 cm) waterbirds.
- About 37 species in 1 genus worldwide; found on all continents. 6 species occur in North America; found along coasts north to Arctic Alaska and Newfoundland and throughout much of interior.
- Eat mainly fish and marine invertebrates; in fresh water also eat insects, reptiles, amphibians. Catch prey mostly through underwater pursuit.
- Colonial. Usually monogamous during breeding season, but often change mates annually. During nonbreeding season, generally feed alone, but may roost and travel in groups. Some migratory, others sedentary; most winter in coastal areas.
- Breed first at 2–5 years old; timing may depend on food supply.
- On cliffs, islands, or rocky islets, nest is scrape with some vegetation (sticks,

seaweed) and debris (feathers, bones). In trees, nest is a constructed platform of sticks. Both parents build nest. Nest sites often reused year after year.
- 1–7 (usually 3 or 4) long subelliptical, pale blue or green eggs. Both parents incubate, for 23–35 days, beginning with 1st egg laid. Hatching asynchronous. Lay replacement clutch if 1st clutch lost early in incubation. 1 brood per year.
- Altricial young grow layer of down after 7 days. Both parents brood young continuously during early weeks. Young of some species form crèches after 21–28 days; fledge at 35 days to 10 weeks.
- Adult annual survival estimated at greater than 80%. Among oldest on record: at least 18 years (Brandt's Cormorant, Great Cormorant).

Cormorants foraging. Along the Pacific coast, where up to three species of cormorants overlap in range, the species are segregated by foraging habits. The typical cormorant diving motion is shown at the surface. The Double-crested Cormorant (center) pursues schools of fish in open water, Brandt's (bottom left) targets fish close to the bottom, and the Pelagic (bottom right) forages for small fish and other animals among rocks.

head-first toward the gullet, and swallow it. Sometimes they have to kill struggling prey with repeated blows and bites, then masticate it before swallowing. Cormorants usually fish alone, but where prey is abundant, some species form large groups.

After feeding, cormorants frequently perch in the sun with their wings spread. Studies of the Double-crested Cormorant have revealed no correlation between the spread-wing posture and air temperature or solar intensity, and research on the Flightless Cormorant has shown no significant change in body temperature as a result of the posture. These studies suggest that cormorants, which have a layer of waterproof, insulating feathers against the skin to protect against chilling, spread their wings simply to dry them rather than to regulate their body temperature.

Double-crested Cormorants in the Pacific forage on schooling fish, well above flat bottoms. Brandt's and Pelagic Cormorants, though they feed on similar species, forage very differently. Pelagics take solitary prey among underwater rocks at depths of up to 150 feet (45 m). Brandt's takes similar prey on or just above either rocky or flat-bottomed areas. Brandt's, however, uses rocky substrates less often in the northern part of its range, where Pelagics occur, suggesting that Pelagics may competitively exclude Brandt's from rocky habitats in areas where the species overlap.

Much of what we know about the diet of cormorants comes from their pellets—regurgitated capsules containing fish otoliths (tiny bones from the inner ear) and indigestible parts of invertebrates. The cormorant ejects the pellet through

Cormorant pellet. Like many other species that consume animal prey whole, cormorants periodically regurgitate the indigestible parts in the form of pellets. Cormorant pellets are short ovals, combining small fragments that may include fish bones and shellfish exoskeletons.

the mouth, usually just before dawn. Only adults and subadults produce pellets; nestlings do not, probably because they are not fed the hard items that form the core of the pellets.

Breeding

Cormorants nest in colonies that range in size from a few pairs to many thousands of pairs. They sometimes nest only with their own species, but more usually they nest in mixed colonies with other seabirds or herons. Cormorants that forage entirely in marine habitats nest on islands, sea cliffs, or other areas of remote coastline, situating their nests on the ground. Species nesting in the interior nest on the ground on lake islands or build stick nests in trees.

Displays

During the breeding season, the bare skin on the face of many cormorants becomes brightly colored, and birds of some species develop elongated filoplumes on the head. These plumes are less gaudy than those of herons and egrets but more striking than those of other pelecaniforms.

Males display for females from a nest site selected by the male, often employing a raised-wing posture similar to that of darters. During breeding displays male Great Cormorants raise and lower their wings to alternately expose and conceal their white thigh patches; the white throat patch is also displayed.

The males of some species, including the Great Cormorant, also perform "gargle" displays when soliciting a female's attention, throwing the head and neck all the way back to the rump and uttering low, guttural calls. In Pelagic Cormorants, members of a pair greet each other with a "gape" display that involves exposing the mouth-lining and quickly bobbing the head. Brandt's Cormorants have a similar display in which they inflate the gular pouch.

Nests and Young

As in other pelecaniforms, the male cormorant brings nesting material to the female; she builds the nest, usually a platform of sticks and other plant matter sometimes held together with aquatic vegetation and excrement. The birds copulate at the nest site, which they defend by displays of snapping and head-waving with open bills.

Both parents brood and feed the chicks, which may differ greatly in size; the smallest birds (the last to hatch) usually die in the first few days of life. Cormorants have larger clutch sizes than most other pelecaniforms (up to seven eggs; typically three or four), and in some cases, a relatively low mortality rate among nestlings. Both factors enable populations to increase rapidly during years of abundant food, reducing the

"Gargle" display. A common breeding display of cormorants (performed here by a Great Cormorant) is the so-called gargle display, in which the head is thrown back to display the brightly colored gular skin while low, guttural calls are given.

likelihood of local extinctions due to fluctuating food supplies.

A successful nest generally produces one to three fledglings. Like ground-nesting pelicans, cormorant chicks may form small groups called crèches. By joining a group, individuals may gain thermoregulatory advantages and also may reduce their risk of being preyed upon. In some species, such as Brandt's Cormorant, these groups may begin to form when the chicks are only about ten days old, as neighboring families coalesce. Older chicks then form larger groups, until, at the age of about one month, they belong to very large crèches; adults still come to feed their offspring in these super-crèches, and the young birds also begin to make brief sallies into the ocean.

Conservation

Pallas's Cormorant (*Phalacrocorax perspicillatus*), discovered in the Commander Islands of the Bering Sea in 1741, was hunted into extinction by the mid-1800s. Many other cormorant species around the world have small populations, restricted to just a few islands, and are equally vulnerable.

Populations of North American cormorants, however, are faring much better, so much so that concerns have developed over the rate of increase of some species' populations. In 1989, the legislature of Quebec passed a law authorizing the extermination of 10,000 Double-crested Cormorants nesting on islands of the St. Lawrence River. The rationale was that the birds' nesting habits were destroying the vegetation on these islands and making them unsuitable for other species.

In 1997 and 1998, laws were passed in the United States that permitted the killing of cormorants found nesting on islands in the Great Lakes or feeding in aquaculture farms. These laws affect mostly Double-crested Cormorants, but other species such as the Neotropic Cormorant and the Anhinga (*Anhinga anhinga*) may be affected.

Much of the impetus behind the recent legislation has come from fishermen, who see cormorants as competitors, and from fish farmers, who see cormorants as marauders. In some cases, though not all, the assumptions of fishermen about cormorants have proved false, as the birds often take fish of no commercial value. Such findings, however, have not always been heeded by lawmakers.

This recent legislation is all the more surprising in light of the fact that during the middle of the 20th century, Double-crested Cormorant populations were seriously reduced by DDT and other toxins, and those of Great Cormorants in the North Atlantic were reduced by mercury and PCBs. Once organochlorine pesticides were banned in North America, these populations increased rapidly, particularly in New England, the Canadian Maritime Provinces, and the Great Lakes, resulting in the current conflicts.

There are many other threats to cormorants. As island nesters, they face the same introduced mammalian predators that menace other seabirds. Human disturbance can cause panic in a colony, with eggs lost to gulls or to trampling by fleeing adults. Cormorants frequently perish in inshore fishing nets, and tens of thousands have been lost to oil spills.

El Niño brings unusually warm waters to the eastern Pacific every few years, reducing available prey and significantly lowering populations of species such as Brandt's Cormorant. Populations of Pelagic Cormorants also fluctuate but appear stable. Red-faced Cormorants have increased in number during the latter half of the 20th century, though they remain on the WatchList because of their small range.

Edward S. Brinkley
and Alec Humann

Darters (Anhinga)

Darters are large, cormorant-like waterbirds with mostly dark plumage, a long tail, a long, sinuous neck, and a dagger-like bill. Their wingspan is typically about 3 feet 9 inches (1.1 m). They are able to swim low in the water, with only their slender necks and heads showing—hence their colloquial name "snake-bird." The only North American species, the Anhinga *(Anhinga anhinga)*, is found in various freshwater wetlands with open, shallow waters, but it can also live in brackish and even saltwater habitats, as it does in Florida.

Taxonomy

The oldest Anhinga remains have been found in Florida and date from the Pleistocene epoch, more than 1 million years ago, although fossils of other species of Anhingidae date back at least 18 million years. In the past, scientists have included the darters in the cormorant family, despite significant differences in morpho-

Anhinga. Darters are extremely similar, and many authorities treat all the Old World forms as a single species. Only one species, the Anhinga, occurs in the Americas.

logy, behavior, and physiology, including the darters' single carotid artery, a feature unique among birds. Today darters are generally recognized as belonging to a distinct family. In the Americas, the Anhinga ranges from the southeastern United States to northern Argentina and has two subspecies.

Food and Foraging

On contact with water, the Anhinga's plumage becomes saturated more rapidly than that of other waterbirds. This permits the bird to swim with its body submerged and its neck above water. Like Pied-billed Grebes *(Podilymbus podiceps)*, Anhingas can submerge without diving, by regulating their buoyancy; an observer may see one simply stretch its neck forward and quietly disappear underwater. While submerged, the Anhinga uses only

Worldwide Family Features

- 32–39" (80–98 cm) waterbirds.
- Up to 4 species in 1 genus worldwide; occur throughout tropics and subtropics. 1 species occurs in southeastern U.S.
- Eat mostly freshwater fish; also reptiles, amphibians, insects, crustaceans. Prey typically speared underwater or near water.
- Not highly gregarious, but loose associations of nesting or feeding birds are common. Breeders are territorial and monogamous, possibly re-pairing annually. Only northernmost populations migratory.
- Breed first probably at 2 or 3 years old, but little is known.

- Nest is stick platform lined with twigs and leaves, constructed rapidly by both parents, usually near or over water. Sometimes use old heron nests.
- 2–6 (average 4) bluish or greenish, subelliptical eggs, laid at intervals of 1–3 days. Both sexes incubate, for 25–30 days, beginning when 1st egg is laid. Hatching asynchronous. 1 brood per year.
- Young altricial, with down coat after several days; leave nest at 21 days, fly at 6–7 weeks. Both parents provide care.
- Little information on adult annual survival, but presumed to be high. Among oldest on record: almost 12 years (Anhinga).

its feet for propulsion, rarely "swimming" with its wings.

A special adaptation of the eighth and ninth cervical vertebrae allows an Anhinga to retract its long neck into an S-shape and then thrust it forward like a spear, so that the bird can snare its prey without engaging in the underwater pursuit typical of cormorants. Anhingas may spread their wings when underwater to lure fish into the shade their wings create, a hunting technique known as "canopy-feeding" that is also used by herons standing over the water.

The Anhinga's long bill has internal barbs directed inward, so that it can hold fish easily. Occasionally the bird spears fish from above the water's surface, like a heron. After securing its prey, the Anhinga generally surfaces, tosses the prey into the air, and catches it head-first, to make swallowing easier.

The plumage of darters, like that of cormorants, becomes very wet when they dive, but not because their feathers lack waterproofing oils; rather, the microstructure of the feathers lets water into tiny spaces inside them. The resulting loss of buoyancy helps birds submerge and forage.

After feeding, darters, like cormorants, frequently perch in the sun with their wings spread. Unlike cormorants, which have a layer of waterproof, insulating feathers against the skin to protect against chilling, darters have poor insulation and rather low metabolic rates; thus they keep their wings spread even after they dry to maximize solar-energy gain, which warms up their bodies.

Anhinga head and bill. *The very sharp and straight bill of the Anhinga is externally similar to the bills of herons and egrets. Unlike those species, the Anhinga's bill has fine serrations directed inward so that slippery fish cannot escape.*

Underwater feeding. *The Anhinga is unusual among aquatic birds in that it does not sit on the water's surface, instead swimming largely submerged, with only the head and upper neck exposed. While underwater, it acts much like herons and egrets do above water, moving slowly with the neck coiled and spearing fish with a quick, forward thrust of the bill.*

Breeding

The male Anhinga uses several elaborate courtship displays: peering around with the head raised and moving side to side; wing-waving, in which both wings are spread, first in unison, then alternately, with great vigor; and reverse bowing, with the head, neck, and tail folded onto the back, followed by a forward bow and sometimes a snap, in which the two parts of the bill clap together, occasionally on a twig. Territorial displays include a spiraling flight over the nest site.

The male gathers the nesting material (sticks, twigs, and leaves), which it frequently incorporates into its courtship displays; the female constructs the nest. Like other young pelecaniforms, Anhinga chicks are initially fed regurgitated pastes of partially digested prey items; later the parents bring them whole prey.

Conservation

In the Anhinga's North American range, its populations seem relatively stable. However, local extirpations have resulted from drainage and development of wetlands. Anhingas have been adversely affected by DDT and DDE, which are associated with poor hatching success, but not as severely as some other species.

*Edward S. Brinkley
and Alec Humann*

Frigatebirds

Frigatebirds are large but extremely light seabirds. Their long, narrow wings and tail allow for agile flight. Female frigatebirds are up to 25 percent heavier than males and, unlike most seabirds, have different plumage coloration. All frigatebirds are predominantly black, with variable patches of white, mostly on the underparts; the white patches are more extensive on females and immatures. Males have a large, inflatable red pouch below the bill that they puff up like a balloon during breeding displays. The birds' feet are small and webbed, and the bill is long and hooked. Frigatebirds feed over open ocean, coming to land primarily to breed and roost, usually in trees on islands. The Magnificent Frigatebird *(Fregata magnificens)* generally stays closer to shore and is the only species found regularly in North America; some pairs breed in the Florida Keys.

Taxonomy

The earliest frigatebird fossils date from the Eocene epoch, 50 million years ago.

Frigatebirds share a short, wide, and shallow pelvic structure with tropicbirds, and the two families have been considered closely related in the past. Today most researchers consider frigatebirds to be more closely related to the other four families in the Pelecaniformes than they are to tropicbirds, which are sometimes separated into a distinct suborder (see Tropicbirds). An alternative view, based on DNA–DNA hybridization studies, is that frigatebirds are more closely related to penguins (family Spheniscidae), loons, and tubenoses than to any of the other pelecaniform families.

Frigatebird species are very similar to one another and difficult to identify away from their colonies.

Magnificent Frigatebird. *The world's five frigatebird species are so similar in appearance that most were not recognized as distinct species until the early 1900s. All have very long, black wings and tail, and a long, hooked bill.*

Flight

Observers typically see frigatebirds soaring high in the sky in the middle of the day, often not flapping at all. The birds' very light bodies, low wing-loading, and high aspect ratio allow them to soar even under calm conditions; a fused breastbone provides structural strength for this kind of flight. The Magnificent Frigatebird has the lowest wing-loading of any bird, a product of its light weight of 2½ to 3½ pounds (1.1–1.6 kg) and its broad wingspan—5 feet 7 inches to 8 feet (1.7–2.4 m). A Bald Eagle *(Haliaeetus leucocephalus)* has a similar wingspan but is three to four times heavier.

Frigatebirds routinely travel on trade winds, which are more reliable at sea than thermals. Trade winds are faster at higher altitudes, so frigatebirds are often seen high up, where few seabirds fly. Most return to a terrestrial roost at dusk; researchers believe they seldom fly at night.

Frigatebirds are not well designed for sustained flapping, but they can employ deep, deliberate wingbeats when needed. As kleptoparasites, they are extremely agile, able to execute sharp turns in pursuit of victims, often nipping at the pursued bird's tail or wing. The frigatebird uses its long, deeply forked tail for braking and changing course abruptly.

Although frigatebirds are capable of riding out tropical storms and can travel

*Frigatebird feeding.
Frigatebirds steal much of their
food from other seabirds. A
favorite strategy is to soar over
a seabird nesting colony and
pursue boobies or other species
as they return, forcing them to
regurgitate the food they are
bringing back to the nest. At
sea, frigatebirds acquire much
of their own food, which they
snatch from the water's surface,
getting only the bill wet. The
Magnificent Frigatebird is
shown.*

across vast expanses of ocean, their light-weight design puts them at the mercy of high winds; cyclonic storms often carry frigatebirds far beyond their normal range. Hurricane Gilbert of 1988, for example, sent hundreds of Magnificent Frigatebirds into the interior of North America, producing records from New Mexico to Ontario.

Food and Foraging

Frigatebirds are superbly built to forage over open ocean. Their distribution seems limited only by the presence of flyingfish and steady, reliable wind currents, habitat requirements that confine them to tropical marine environments. Their names from centuries past—Man-o'-War Birds, Pirates of the Sea—evoke their kleptoparasitic ways. Frigatebirds

target mostly larger birds, such as boobies, and appear to single out birds with distended crops, a sign the bird is carrying recently captured food.

Frigatebirds also capture prey on their own. They specialize in taking flyingfish, coursing low over the water to snatch a fish by its "wing" as it either emerges from the water or appears just below the surface. They often follow dolphin herds or schools of large predatory fish, which flush flyingfish into the air. Besides skimming swiftly over the water's surface, frigatebirds also soar in large spirals up to great altitudes in order to spot prey or aggregations of fish and mammals below.

These birds seldom alight on water, and when they do, it is only briefly, as their plumage quickly becomes saturated, hampering takeoff and flight. A long bill allows them to avoid much contact with water;

Worldwide Family Features

• 28–45" (70–114 cm) seabirds.
• 5 species in 1 genus worldwide; pantropical. 1 species occurs in North America, along southeastern coast; plus 2 accidental species.
• Eat fish (especially flyingfish), squid, jellyfish, crustaceans; feed opportunistically on hatchling sea turtles, fishing by-catch, and eggs and chicks of other seabirds. Kleptoparasitic; also forage from air at water's surface.
• Colonial nesters. Seasonally monogamous. Nonbreeders may gather together at roost sites. Nonmigratory, but may wander widely.

• Breed first at 5–11 years old.
• Nest is loose platform of sticks atop island vegetation or rocks, or on ground; female builds, using materials male collects.
• 1 white, elliptical to oval egg (rarely 2). Both sexes incubate, for 40–55 days. 1 brood every 1–4 years.
• Altricial young, covered in whitish down after several days. Fledge at 17–30 weeks. Both parents feed young, continuing for 3–18 months after fledging.
• Adult annual survival poorly known, but probably high. Among oldest on record: at least 34 years (pantropical Great Frigatebird).

Frigatebird head and bill. The bill of frigatebirds is long, with a pronounced hook at the tip that is adapted for snatching prey out of the water while flying. Adult males inflate a huge red pouch on the neck when displaying. Two views of the Magnificent Frigatebird are shown: On the left is a first-year bird; on the right, an adult male displaying at the nest site.

in most captures, even the head remains dry. After catching a fish, they juggle it in midair, maneuvering it into a head-first position to ease ingestion. Frigatebirds usually hunt singly or in pairs but may congregate where food is abundant. Unlike many seabirds, frigatebirds drink fresh water when it is available, flying low over the water and drinking on the wing, as swallows do. They will also "splash-bathe" like flycatchers and swallows.

Breeding

Early in the breeding season, male Magnificent Frigatebirds gather on nesting islands to display for mates. With wings outstretched and pointed skyward, and with their large red gular pouches inflated, they compete to attract females. When a female approaches, a male quivers its wings and produces a low, resonant drumming sound by vibrating its bill against its inflated pouch. After choosing a mate, the female joins the male in pair-bonding rituals. In one of these, the male clasps the female's bill in his own; in another, both mates shake their heads in synchrony.

Nest construction soon follows, with the male collecting most of the material and the female building the structure. Most frigatebirds nest on islands with small trees or bushes, but some use mainland sites, especially in mangrove tracts. The female lays a single egg, which both

parents incubate. From this time onward, they guard the nest intently, as the eggs and young chicks are vulnerable to predation by other frigatebirds.

Young Magnificent Frigatebirds typically fledge at 20 to 24 weeks, but when food supplies are low fledging can be delayed for up to two months. The young often do not become independent until they are at least 12 months old. Consequently female frigatebirds breed every other year at most. Males may breed annually where food is plentiful. Unlike most seabirds, frigatebirds tend to remain close to their breeding grounds year-round.

Conservation

The small North American population of the Magnificent Frigatebird is stable, but populations in the Caribbean have undergone long-term declines. The birds' habit of nesting in dense colonies renders them vulnerable to tropical storms, introduced predators such as rats, and human disturbance.

Accidental Species

In North America, the Great Frigatebird (*Fregata minor*) has been recorded in Oklahoma in November and California in March; a Lesser Frigatebird (*F. ariel*) has reached Maine in July. Both species nest and disperse widely in tropical oceans.

Edward S. Brinkley
and Alec Humann

Herons, Egrets, and Bitterns

Family Ardeidae
Order Ciconiiformes

Members of the Ardeidae are medium-size to large wading birds, usually with long legs, necks, and bills; short, rounded tails; and long, broad wings. Their wingspans range from 17 inches to 6 feet (43–182 cm). Upright in stance, they resemble other tall wading birds, such as storks and ibises. Their plumage color varies greatly. Some species are pure white, some predominantly dark, and others patterned with mixtures of black, white, grays, browns, blues, and even yellows and reds. All family members have powder-down breast and rump patches (in some species also on the back and thighs) in which the down disintegrates to a powder the birds use for preening their feathers, often with their pectinate middle toes. Most species are found in coastal and interior wetlands, but some use more terrestrial habitats.

Taxonomy

The ardeids are placed with other families of large wading birds in the order Ciconiiformes, which also includes the storks, the ibises and spoonbills, the New World vultures, and, according to some, the flamingos.

Taxonomists have made numerous changes in the classification of the Ardeidae. Initially the family was divided into two subfamilies—bitterns and all other species. More recently, dividing Ardeidae into four subfamilies has become popular: the typical herons (Ardeinae), the night-herons (Nycticoracinae), the bitterns (Botaurinae), and the tiger-herons (Tigrisomatinae). The first three occur in North America; the tiger-herons are found in the neotropics. Experts disagree over the evolutionary relationships among these groups. Recent DNA–DNA hybridization data suggest that tiger-herons are the oldest group, and that the other three evolved from ancestral stock later.

Over the past 50 years, the trend has been to lump together species and particularly genera in the family, so that more than 90 species have been consolidated into about 60 to 65, and about 35 genera into about 16 to 21, depending on the taxonomy.

The Green Heron *(Butorides virescens)* and the Striated Heron *(B. striatus)*, of Central and South America, were lumped together as the "Green-backed Heron" in the 1970s, then re-split in the 1990s. The original lumping was based on a study of museum specimens that indicated evidence of hybridization between the two taxa, but this hybridization appears to be very limited.

Ardeid diversity. *The family Ardeidae can be divided into four main groups, of which three are found in North America: the secretive, cryptically colored bitterns (for example, the Least Bittern, left); the slender, conspicuous, white or grayish typical herons (such as the Great Egret, center); and the stocky, nocturnal, gray-patterned night-herons (such as the Yellow-crowned Night-Heron, right).*

There is also some disagreement about the taxonomic status of the "Great White" Heron. Most observers consider it a color morph of the Great Blue Heron *(Ardea herodias)* rather than a separate species. Clearly, despite recent research using modern genetic techniques, the taxonomic arrangement of the herons remains uncertain.

S-shaped neck. All ardeids have a long, slender neck with a characteristic S shape. The anatomy of the neck reveals adaptations to foraging techniques. The bones create a coil that is even more exaggerated than the outward S curve, allowing the bird to strike at prey with incredible speed. The esophagus and trachea (shown in red) actually cross over and run behind the vertebrae (shown in blue) on the lower part of the neck. This gives these organs the shortest possible course to the body, but perhaps more importantly protects them from damage in case the foreneck bumps something during a strike.

Habitats

Members of the Ardeidae are mainly tropical birds, but they have spread out to occupy all but extremely high latitudes and elevations. Largely aquatic in their foraging habitats, they usually nest near wetlands. In North America, ardeids can be found along almost every river, pond, or marsh, although their presence may be highly seasonal.

Typical herons are a diverse group and occupy all types of wetlands. The Cattle Egret *(Bubulcus ibis)* is the only North American species that usually forages in dry fields and grasslands, but Great Blue Herons and Great Egrets *(Ardea alba)* also often feed in dry agricultural fields. Some species, such as the Green Heron, can be found in almost any wetland habitat.

Bitterns are normally restricted to freshwater wetlands, where they hide in dense vegetation and can be extremely difficult to see. Like typical herons, Yellow-crowned *(Nyctanassa violacea)* and Black-crowned Night-Herons (*Nycticorax nycticorax)* will use a variety of saltwater and freshwater habitats. As their names suggest, these two species are largely nocturnal; they spend the day roosting in trees, bushes, or dense reedbeds, except in the nesting season, when they sometimes forage during the day.

Food and Foraging

Ardeids are strictly carnivorous and have adaptations for exploiting a wide variety of live prey. Their long legs and necks allow them to forage in aquatic habitats, and their bills are adapted for spearing and grasping prey. Modification of the sixth cervical vertebra lets them draw the neck into an S shape and shoot the head and bill forward with lightning speed.

Most ardeid species specialize in fish and other aquatic animals such as crustaceans and amphibians, but they are generalists and will take almost any live prey available. The Great Blue Heron has been observed taking Black Rails *(Laterallus jamaicensis)* and small mammals such as voles, and the Black-crowned Night-Heron is notorious for taking the chicks and eggs of terns, ibises, and other herons. Many species tend to be gregarious year-round, often congregating in nocturnal roosts, and they may forage in large single-species or mixed-species aggregations when food is concentrated.

Adaptations for Foraging

Several ardeid species have plumage polymorphisms that result in both light and dark-colored individuals. In Little Blue Herons *(Egretta caerulea)*, the variation is age-related, with light-colored young and dark adults; Reddish Egrets *(E. rufescens)* are either white or dark throughout their lives. The reasons for the evolution of plumage polymorphism have been extensively debated. Most explanations link it to foraging efficiency, but other factors, such as the absorption or reflection of heat, may also be involved.

Some observers have proposed that white plumage has a signalling function. They suggest that individuals in search of food may use the presence of white birds, which are easily seen from a distance, to find patches of food. Other researchers point out that being white has disadvantages, including greater visibility to predators.

The cryptically patterned plumage of the American Bittern *(Botaurus lentiginosus)* might provide camouflage from the bird's prey species.

Foraging Behavior

Ardeids have a diverse repertoire of foraging behaviors; researchers have described more than 30. The birds may feed from a crouched or upright posture, sometimes extending their necks and pointing their bills down in a behavior called "peering over," which may reduce

glare and give them a binocular view of prey below the water's surface. Ardeids use a variety of head and neck motions while foraging: swaying, bobbing, and swinging, presumably to compensate for water refraction and to enhance their binocular vision. They may also stand motionless and wait, or move slowly, quickly, or at a run in pursuit of prey.

The Reddish Egret and the Tricolored Heron *(Egretta tricolor)* are active feeders, often prancing and pirouetting with one wing extended while they forage. Active feeding may serve to flush prey, and the open wing may help maintain balance.

Typical herons often try to flush prey from hiding places by wing-flicking, foot-stirring, raking, and paddling. Though they don't often do so, some species, such as the Snowy Egret *(Egretta thula)*, can also forage from the air. Their aerial foraging behavior includes hovering over the water; dipping their bills beneath the surface while flying low; flycatching; and diving from perches or while in flight.

Standing in wait is the most widespread and common foraging behavior. While standing, some species extend one or both wings to shade the water's surface.

Worldwide Family Features

- 11–54" (28–137 cm) wading birds.
- About 65 species in about 21 genera worldwide; on all continents except Antarctica, with greatest number of species in tropics; 13 species in 8 genera occur in North America, found across southern two-thirds of North America; plus 4 accidental species.
- Carnivorous; eat primarily fish, but also amphibians, crustaceans, other invertebrates; some species insectivorous. Most species forage in shallow water, plucking prey from water; some feed on dry land.
- Mostly colonial breeders; defend only area adjacent to nest. Most species seasonally monogamous; some perform elaborate courtship displays. Often feed or roost in groups during nonbreeding season. Some species migratory in some regions.
- Breed first at 2 or 3 years old, occasionally at 1 year old.

- Nest usually a platform of sticks or reeds, built in trees, bushes, or reeds; larger species tend to nest higher than smaller species. Usually male gathers material and female builds nest. Will reuse old nest or pirate one for material.
- 1–10 (usually 2–5) elliptical to subelliptical eggs, typically blue or blue-green, unmarked; brownish in large bitterns. Hatching often asynchronous. Both parents incubate for 14–35 days. 1 brood per year, rarely 2.
- Young altricial, nearly naked at hatch. Fledge at 42 days to 8 weeks in large herons, 28–42 days in smaller species; most young can climb from nest by 14 days and fly short distances to nearby branches. Both parents feed young.
- For some species, adult annual survival about 60%; about 30% during 1st year. In several species, wild birds live more than 20 years. Among oldest on record: 23 years, 3 months (Great Blue Heron).

Reddish Egret foraging. The Reddish Egret has the most active foraging techniques of any ardeid, literally chasing small fish through shallow water. The abrupt, animated actions of a foraging bird— running, flapping, stretching, crouching, spinning—can be comical to watch.

This activity reduces glare off the surface, which may allow birds to see prey more easily; fish may also be attracted to the shade, which would usually indicate safety.

Some typical herons follow other animals, using them as "beaters" to stir up prey. The best example is the Cattle Egret, named for its association with cattle, which disturb grasshoppers and other insects on which the egrets feed. With the advent of modern agriculture, Cattle Egrets also will follow farm equipment, feeding on the insects and small vertebrates disturbed during harvest.

Perhaps the most interesting foraging behavior is "bait-fishing" or "baiting," which is used worldwide by Green and Striated Herons and has been reported in the Black-crowned Night-Heron as well. A bait-fishing heron attracts fish by placing bait—insects, flowers, seeds, twigs, bread, even popcorn—on the water's surface. The Striated Heron may also break off part of a twig to use for bait, making this bird not only one of the few tool-using animals, but one of the very few that actually make their tools.

Bitterns are usually solitary feeders, while typical herons and night-herons are more gregarious and often feed in flocks. Some ardeid species defend feeding territories at certain times of year. Night-herons and bitterns are generally crepuscular and nocturnal feeders, but they do forage in daytime, especially when raising young. Typical herons generally forage during daylight hours.

Breeding

Ardeids are seasonally monogamous and form pair bonds through elaborate courtship displays. Most species are gregarious and breed in colonies; even those that are more solitary, such as the Green Heron and the Least Bittern *(Ixobrychus exilis)*, may nest in loose aggregations. Most ardeids probably do not breed until they are two years old, but there are records of year-old Black-crowned Night-Herons and Little Blue Herons breeding.

Arriving at the colony, males generally select a territory that includes a nest site, then defend it against all others. As more birds arrive, each male's territory shrinks, until he is defending only his nest site and a small perimeter.

Courtship Displays

The legs, bills, and bare parts of ardeids change color during the breeding season and become part of the birds' courtship displays. For example, the dull yellow lores of the Snowy Egret may turn cherry red. The bill of the Cattle Egret turns red; that of the Great Egret, orange.

Most species also develop nuptial plumes. Great and Snowy Egrets, for example, have spectacular head, neck, and scapular plumes, or aigrettes, which they display prominently during courtship. Black-crowned Night-Herons have long, white, lanceolate plumes that help to coordinate pair formation. These and other plumes appear during a prealternate molt.

Males use a variety of displays to entice females to their territories. Their flight displays include a circle flight, in which the male flies powered by slow wingbeats and with neck extended. Another common courtship display is the stretch, in which the bird curves its head and neck over its back until the bill is vertical; legs flexed, it then utters a call and brings its head and neck forward and down. This display emphasizes the specialized plumes of most species, as well as any soft-part coloration.

Still another common display is the snap: The displaying bird stretches its head and neck forward and down, with crown and neck feathers erect, and audibly snaps its bill shut. Agonistic displays include the "upright," in which a bird raises its head and neck upward and straight, and the more aggressive "forward," in which the bird leans forward, often with wings raised, and sometimes stabs at an antagonist with its bill. Females of some species use the stretch display, and most females use the upright and other agonistic displays.

Elements of all these displays may be used in various courtship, appeasement, and aggressive situations throughout the nesting cycle. When a female responds

Bittern cryptic stance. This Least Bittern is adopting the camouflage posture—neck erect and bill pointed up—that allows it to blend in with vegetation. Bitterns adopt this posture frequently, using it to take full advantage of the cryptic color and pattern of their plumage and blend in with grasses and reeds.

to a male's overtures, pair formation is maintained and heightened by bill-clappering and mutual preening.

Vocal displays are most common among those species that need to communicate over long distances or through dense vegetation, where visual displays would be less effective. These displays include the "booming" of bitterns and the *skeow* call of the Green Heron.

Nests

Nests are usually located near water. Islands, including dredge-spoil islands, have become favored colony sites, presumably because they offer enhanced protection against mammalian predators. Ardeids may reuse and improve old nests or build new ones, often using old nests as sources of sticks and twigs. The male usually collects sticks and passes them to the female, who does most of the nest building. There are exceptions: Least Bittern males, for example, do most of the nest construction.

Ardeids may place their nests on the ground or elevate them, using anything from low bushes to tall trees. Nests have even been found in pure stands of Poison Ivy. In some cases, ardeids make their nests out of reeds, but most nests are

Ardeid breeding colors and plumages. In the breeding season, ardeids develop much brighter colors on their bare parts (bill, lores, and legs), and most species also develop showy plumes. The colors of the bare parts reach an intense peak during courtship. Shown here is a typical adult Snowy Egret in nonbreeding condition (drab bare parts, no plumes) and at the peak of the breeding season (red lores, all-black bill, lacy plumes).

made of sticks and twigs woven into a platform. Birds often continue to add to their nests or rearrange sticks throughout the nesting cycle.

When they join mixed-species colonies, larger ardeids tend to nest in trees. The nests of these larger species may, when enhanced for reuse over a period of years, reach massive proportions and be more than 5 feet (1.5 m) across.

Eggs and Young

North American ardeids produce a single brood per year. Clutch size varies from two to seven eggs; most species produce three to five. Incubation typically begins after the first or second egg has been laid; both parents share incubation duties. Pairs "changing shifts" at the nest often perform an elaborate and noisy greeting ceremony.

When birds begin incubating before the clutch is complete, the first eggs laid get a head start, resulting in asynchronous hatching and chicks of different sizes. Siblicide is common in some species; even when it doesn't occur, the smallest chick is often outcompeted by its older and larger siblings and starves. During years when food is abundant, the "extra" chick can be successfully raised. It may also serve as an "insurance" chick to replace an older sibling that dies or an egg that doesn't hatch.

Ardeid chicks are nidicolous, born nearly naked, and with their eyes tightly closed. The chicks emit food-begging calls persistently, contributing to the constant noise typical of a heronry. Their parents bring them food and regurgitate it, whole or partially digested, onto the nest platform or directly into the open mouths of the chicks. Items too large for chicks to swallow are re-swallowed by the adults for further processing— one observer reported an adult Black-crowned Night-Heron re-swallowing a 10-inch (25-cm) goldfish twice.

When the young are able to maintain a constant body temperature without brooding, both adults are free to forage, leaving the chicks alone. Unprotected nestlings of some species will assume a "bittern stance" when humans or other potential predators approach the nest, extending their necks and pointing their bills upward, mimicking the sticks of the nest site they inhabit. Adult bitterns assume this stance when alarmed, blending in with the surrounding vegetation.

By two weeks of age, most chicks can leave the nest and perch in nearby branches (hence the term "branchers"). Humans approaching a nesting tree may find chicks from a half-dozen nests crowded together near its top.

Movements

Ardeids engage in post-breeding dispersal, perhaps in response to the ephemeral conditions in which they live. Many

Ardeid display at nest. *Courtship displays are performed mainly at the nest and involve various bowing and stretching motions to show off the plumes. Here a Little Blue Heron performs part of a stretch display in which the head is alternately tossed over the back and pointed down between the legs, all the time with plumes spread to best advantage. Other species perform various versions of this display. The nest shown here—a sloppy platform of heavy sticks and twigs—is typical of all herons and egrets.*

wetlands have historically experienced seasonal or episodic drying; more recently, they have been subject to the vagaries of human water-management practices. Dispersing birds may travel in any direction, resulting in individuals occasionally occurring in areas where they are not normally recorded.

Possibly because of their penchant for dispersal, ardeids are predisposed to vagrancy, and in some cases the vagrants have remained and founded breeding populations. Early in the 20th century, the Cattle Egret spread from Africa to South America, where forested areas had been cleared and grazing animals introduced; the species first arrived in the United States in the early 1950s and has since become widespread and common in North America. The same pattern may repeat itself with the Little Egret *(Egretta garzetta)*; this species' increasing rate of occurrence in North America comes at a time when it is also expanding its range in western Europe.

As fall approaches, birds from more northerly colonies begin a southward migration. Many of them winter in the southern United States; others migrate to the Caribbean, Mexico, or Central and South America.

Conservation

In the past, ardeids were shot for food, but only a few are currently shot—as a control measure at fish farms or when a colony achieves "pest" status. Many, particularly those bearing fancy plumes, such as the Great and Snowy Egrets, were reduced almost to extinction by plume-hunters in the late 19th and early 20th centuries. Their slaughter spawned the conservation movement in the United States, including the establishment of the National Audubon Society and eventually protective legislation for most birds. Populations of the hardest-hit species have rebounded substantially, and Great and Snowy Egrets now breed as far north as Maine.

After World War Two, the use of persistent pesticides, especially DDT, caused eggshell thinning and related reproductive problems in some species, such as the Black-crowned Night-Heron. With the banning of these pesticides in the early 1970s, the reproductive problems have declined, although pesticide residues still show up in some birds, particularly those that winter in Central and South America, where DDT is still used. Because of their position at the top of the food chain, ardeids are considered excellent biological indicators of the health of wetland ecosystems.

While some species, such as the Green Heron, are stable or increasing and do not currently warrant conservation priority, most ardeids have been affected locally by wetland drainage associated with urbanization and agricultural expansion. For example, changed water regimes in Florida have led to the relocation or decline of several species, including the Little Blue Heron.

Because colonial breeding concentrates large numbers of birds in small areas, many ardeid species are especially vulnerable to hurricanes, oil spills, and other catastrophes. Many species appear on local lists of threatened species, and the Reddish Egret is on the WatchList. The white morph of the Great Blue Heron, because of its restricted range in Florida, is vulnerable to hurricanes.

The alteration of their habitat remains the greatest threat to most species today.

Accidental Species

The Yellow Bittern *(Ixobrychus sinensis)*, Chinese Egret *(Egretta eulophotes)*, and Chinese Pond-Heron *(Ardeola bacchus)*, all from eastern Asia, have each been recorded once during spring or summer in the Bering Sea islands of Alaska. There also is a summer record of a Western Reef-Heron *(E. gularis)* from Nantucket Island, Massachusetts; this species usually ranges along coastal areas from Africa to India.

William E. Davis, Jr.

Ibises and Spoonbills

Family Threskiornithidae
Order Ciconiiformes

Ibises and spoonbills are medium-size to large aquatic waders with long legs and necks, duck-like bodies, and wingspans that range from 3 feet to 4 feet 2 inches (91–127 cm). Their distinctive bills and striking plumage colors make them among the most remarkable birds in North America. They occur in a wide variety of wetlands, including freshwater marshes, flooded fields, estuaries, coastal marshes, and tidal mudflats. Highly gregarious, these birds are often found in large groups.

Taxonomy

Ibises and spoonbills are classified in the same order as herons, storks, and New World vultures, but there are clear morphological and behavioral differences between the families.

The ibises, which have a long, thin, and downcurved bill, are placed in the subfamily Threskiornithinae; the spoonbills, with their long, flattened, spatulate bills, are in the subfamily Plataleinae. Members of the two groups are closely related and will even hybridize.

Worldwide, species-level taxonomy is controversial; there is even dispute over the family name, with some taxonomists preferring the name Plataleidae. The White-faced Ibis *(Plegadis chihi)* was once considered a subspecies of the more widespread Glossy Ibis *(P. falcinellus)*, but hybridization is not known in Louisiana, where the species' ranges overlap. In contrast, the Scarlet Ibis *(Eudocimus ruber),* which is native to northern South America and has escaped into the wild in Florida, does hybridize with the White Ibis *(E. albus)* in the wild, leading to suggestions that the two species be combined as one.

Food and Foraging

Ibises are highly gregarious and typically feed in flocks, often alongside other wading birds. When the birds are not feeding, they spend most of their time resting and preening. In general, spoonbills are less gregarious, often feeding alone or in small flocks.

Ibises and spoonbills eat various aquatic prey, which they capture while wading in shallow water or probing in the mud. In addition to aquatic insects, mollusks, crustaceans, small fish, and amphibians, they also will occasionally eat small grains and other plant matter.

The differences in bill structure between the two subfamilies result in different foraging techniques, although both forage primarily by touch. A spoonbill generally feeds by bill-sweeping, moving its bill from side to side in an arc through the water, grasping prey items that its bill touches. An ibis usually probes in mud for its prey. However, both groups may use either method.

In the Eurasian Spoonbill *(Platalea leucorodia)*, which occurs from Europe to China, the shape of the bill is known to work as a hydrofoil, serving to move prey items off the feeding substrate so they can be grasped and swallowed. The bills of other spoonbills, such as the Roseate Spoonbill *(Ajaia ajaja)* of North America, presumably function in a similar way.

Threskiornithid diversity. The four species of Threskiornithidae in North America, all long-legged wading birds, are in two distinctive subfamilies: the Threskiornithinae (ibises) and the Plataleinae (spoonbills), which differ mainly in bill shape and foraging habits. On the left is the Glossy Ibis; on the right, the Roseate Spoonbill.

Breeding

Ibises and spoonbills are socially monogamous, although some species, such as the White Ibis, will engage in extra-pair copulations. Most species breed in colonies and often mingle with other nesting species. Usually the male arrives on the breeding grounds first and establishes a small territory, defending his potential nest site from other males by engaging in threat displays.

Threskiornithid heads and bills. Ibises (such as the White-faced Ibis, left) have a long, tapering, downcurved bill. The bill of spoonbills (Roseate Spoonbill, right) is flattened and spoon-shaped.

Once females arrive, courtship begins. The birds use various displays to establish and maintain pair bonds. Pairs will preen each other, rub heads together and entwine necks, and simultaneously grasp vegetation in their bills and shake their heads. Large flocks of White Ibises will engage in complex aerial displays high above the colony. Ibises and spoonbills of both sexes have bare areas on the face that become brightly colored during pair formation and that are displayed in courtship.

The nest is constructed from plant material and placed in a tree, a bush, or low brush, almost always near water. Generally the male gathers material and the female constructs the nest.

Egg-laying coincides with good water conditions and high prey availability. In North American species, incubation lasts for 20 to 24 days. Both sexes incubate, although the female contributes more hours. A change in incubation duty, which occurs at least once every 24 hours, is often marked by displays involving an exchange of nest material.

Hungry chicks place their heads inside the parent's bill to receive regurgitated food. For the first few weeks, parents guard the chicks constantly as they slowly become more independent.

Movements

Most ibis and spoonbill species are able to wander widely. The North American

---

Worldwide Family Features

- 18–44" (45–112 cm) wading birds.
- About 33 species in 14 genera worldwide; on all continents but Antarctica, with greatest diversity in tropics. 4 species in 3 genera occur in North America, from southern coasts to southern Canada; plus 1 escaped species.
- Eat aquatic invertebrates, small vertebrates, occasionally vegetation; grasp prey while probing in mud or from water column.
- Most are colonial breeders and gregarious year-round. Monogamous; pair bonds last 1 breeding season. Northern populations migratory, usually traveling in groups.
- Breed first at 2–4 years old, sometimes older.

- Nest is large pile of sticks and other vegetation, placed on ground in marshes or in bushes or trees near water; some use old heron nests. Both parents build nest. Occasionally reuse nests.
- 1–7 (usually 2–4) subelliptical, pale blue, green, or white eggs, some with light speckling. Both parents incubate for 20–31 days. Hatching asynchronous. 1 brood per year; may lay replacement clutch if eggs are lost.
- Semi-altricial young immobile and downy, with eyes open at hatching. Both parents feed chicks. Fledge at 23–56 days; independent 7–28 days later.
- Adult annual survival fairly high, but little data. Among oldest on record: 28 years (Eurasian Spoonbill).

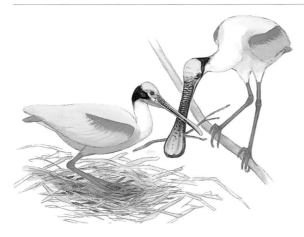

Roseate Spoonbill stick presentation display. The male brings a stick to the female on the nest and presents it with various bowing and head-tossing displays and grunting calls. Similar displays are used by ibises and many other species in maintaining the pair bond.

species are all at least partial migrants and will move long distances in response to changes in water conditions that would hinder reproduction. All are periodically found far outside their normal ranges. This propensity to wander aided the rapid range expansion of Glossy Ibises along the Atlantic coast in the second half of the 20th century.

White-faced Ibises that breed in the continent's interior winter in the southern United States and Mexico. Similarly, North Atlantic populations of Glossy Ibis travel south for the winter. Such a wholesale departure from large parts of the breeding range is not found in the White Ibis or the Roseate Spoonbill, which have more southerly breeding ranges, although many individual birds winter in Mexico and Central America.

Ibises also make daily movements, between their daytime feeding sites and nocturnal roosts. Birds leave the roosts in groups at dawn, often flying in V formation, and spread out to look for food. In the evening they return; up to tens of thousands of birds may pack into a small area of trees or marsh for the night.

Conservation

In North America, ibis and spoonbill populations fluctuated considerably during the 20th century. Hunting for the plume trade reduced Roseate Spoonbill populations early in the century, but they recovered after the introduction of protective legislation. Eggshell thinning caused by DDT has affected some populations. Although banned in the United States and Canada, DDT continues to be used in the birds' wintering areas farther south; its effects continue after the birds return to their North American breeding sites. Ultimately the biggest threats to ibis and spoonbill populations are the dwindling numbers of suitable wetlands and nesting sites, caused by habitat destruction and human disturbance.

William J. Seng

Bill shape of nestlings. Newly hatched ibis and spoonbill young have similar bill shapes, reinforcing the idea that the two subfamilies are closely related. The bill of the Roseate Spoonbill chick (left) is slightly broader and more duck-like than that of the Glossy Ibis (right). Within weeks, the bills grow into the shapes characteristic of each subfamily.

Storks

Family Ciconiidae
Order Ciconiiformes

Storks are large, long-legged wading birds superficially similar to herons and ibises, but heavier. The Wood Stork *(Mycteria americana)* differs from herons and ibises in its heavier, slightly decurved bill, bare head and neck, and lack of ornamental plumes. Its wingspan averages 5 feet 1 inch (1.5 m). It also has very different feeding behavior, often standing perfectly still with the bill submerged. Storks often soar with vultures or other birds, and they always fly with neck and legs extended (herons fly with the neck coiled and never soar). The adults produce no vocal sounds other than occasional hissing. Storks occur in various fresh- and saltwater wetland habitats, including marshes, mangroves, estuaries, and riversides.

Taxonomy

Although storks, particularly the genus *Mycteria*, bear many similarities to the herons and ibises (the Wood Stork was once called the "Wood Ibis"), they are separated from these groups by structural features and by their foraging habits, and form a well-defined family.

There has been much debate over the relationships between storks and herons, ibises, and, especially, New World vultures. The AOU now considers storks and vultures to be each other's closest relatives, based on evidence from studies of morphology, anatomy, behavior, and various genetic measures.

Food and Foraging

Wood Storks feed mainly on live fish captured in shallow water, but nearly any small animal is fair game, and the

Wood Stork. *Taxonomists separate the storks into three groups, with one representative of each found in the Americas. Only the Wood Stork occurs regularly in North America.*

birds are not above scavenging dead fish or other carrion. They also frequently take crustaceans (crayfish and shrimp), reptiles, frogs, tadpoles, and occasionally small mammals or birds.

They typically capture prey in shallow water, normally holding the bill slightly open and submerged while standing still or walking slowly and swinging the bill from side to side. The posture of a foraging stork, hunched over and moving methodically or not at all, is unique.

When feeding, Wood Storks typically stand and wait for something to swim between their bill tips. To increase their chances of catching fish, they may stir the water with one foot or open their wings, all the while with the bill in the water. These techniques presumably rouse prey from hiding places. Similarly, a small group of storks may walk in close formation back and forth across a pond, "flushing" the fish in their path.

When a Wood Stork touches prey with its bill, it can snap the bill shut in 0.025 seconds—one of the fastest reaction times known in vertebrates. Presumably the bill is very sensitive to touch, as storks with their eyes experimentally covered capture fish at the same rate as those that can see.

Hunting by touch allows storks to find prey in muddy, opaque water where herons and other visual feeders would be unable to hunt. Some researchers suggest that a trigger mechanism is used in prey capture, with the bill "cocked open" under

180

Wood Storks foraging. Wood Storks forage by touch, submerging their bills and waiting for prey to swim between the open bill tips. To increase the chances of this happening, they often forage in groups, advancing slowly across a pond and stirring the water with one foot or opening one or both wings, presumably to scare fish out of hiding.

tension and snapping shut upon contact with prey. However, the birds can find fish in tangled vegetation and select fish of certain sizes, suggesting that more than a simple trigger is involved.

Hunting by touch is not unique to storks; spoonbills, ibises, shorebirds, and others also do it, but most species that feel for prey probe in the mud for worms and other slow movers. Storks are trying to catch fish, and they have had to overcome the challenges presented by agile, fast-moving prey.

Breeding

The entire life cycle, and especially the breeding cycle, of Wood Storks is closely tied to changes in prey availability. To forage effectively with their specialized technique, storks require a high density of prey, which occurs most reliably when ponds dry up and concentrate fish in ever smaller pools.

Young birds can consume 50 to 60 percent of their body weight in food daily for the first few weeks of life. Consequently, adults time nesting so that hatching occurs as ponds are drying up. When the system works, more young survive and the young fledge sooner and are heavier at fledging.

If the timing is off, the birds will abandon their nests and even their young. If there is too much rain, prey will not be concentrated enough for the adults to feed the young. Too little rain during the winter causes ponds to dry up completely

Worldwide Family Features

- 30–60" (75–152 cm) wading birds.
- 19 species in 6 genera worldwide; found on all continents except Antarctica, with greatest diversity in Old World tropics. 1 species occurs regularly in southeastern U.S.; plus 1 accidental species.
- Eat mainly fish and other aquatic vertebrates caught in shallow water.
- Most colonial; some solitary. Monogamous; usually form new pairs every year; noncolonial species may pair for life. May roost in groups, but often feed alone. Some species migratory; others move in response to changing water conditions.
- Breed first at 2–7 (usually 3–5) years old.
- Build platform nest of sticks, usually in tree; some species nest on buildings, cliffs, or ground. Male usually collects

material, often stolen from nearby nests; female places material. Reuse nests rarely.
- 1–7 (usually 2–5) elliptical to subelliptical, whitish eggs. Both parents incubate, beginning with 1st or 2nd egg. Hatching asynchronous about 27–38 days after incubation starts. 1 brood per year.
- Altricial young soon covered with white down. Both sexes provide care, bringing food several times a day; regurgitate food onto nest floor. Fledge at 55 days to 16½ weeks; young visit nest to be fed for several weeks more but are soon independent.
- Adult annual survival high, but data are limited. Among oldest on record: 33 years (White Stork, *Ciconia ciconia,* of Europe and Africa); 16 years, 8 months (Wood Stork).

Wood Stork head and bill. *The strong, slightly decurved bill of the Wood Stork is sensitive to touch, allowing birds to feed in murky water. The naked head solves the problem of dirtying feathers when foraging in muddy conditions.*

before the young are grown. Recently established colonies of storks near tidal saltmarshes have circumvented this problem to some extent, as the ebb and flow of the tides concentrates prey twice a day and is much more predictable.

To find enough food even during good years, Wood Storks must travel long distances daily. As excellent soaring birds, they are well adapted for this. They can climb to several thousand feet (about 1,000 m), scan for miles to locate potential feeding sites (often by spotting egrets and other storks there), and, if necessary, travel 50 miles (80 km) from the nest for food.

Movements

Wood Storks leave the northern portions of their range in winter, and on occasion more remarkable movements occur, tied to the availability of food. Post-breeding dispersal routinely brings hundreds of storks from Mexico to southern California and coastal Texas. Following a disastrous nesting season in southern Florida in 1950–1951 and poor breeding success in the next few years, Wood Storks traveled as far as Oklahoma, Ohio,

and Massachusetts. Other wanderers have reached the Yukon Territories. The northward expansion in the species' breeding range in the late 20th century probably owes much to these nomadic tendencies.

Conservation

North American Wood Stork populations plummeted from an estimated 150,000 individuals in the early 1900s to about 15,000 today. The species is considered endangered in the United States but maintains healthy populations in Central and South America. The decline probably resulted from such factors as pesticide accumulation and the loss of foraging areas and nest sites. Colonies usually occur in large trees, often cypresses, in standing water; cypresses were heavily logged early in the 1900s.

The single most dramatic drop in Wood Stork numbers probably came from the building of outflow channels in the Florida Everglades. This huge area of marsh formerly supported most of the North American stork population, but after much water was drained for agriculture and development, or diverted to the growing cities on Florida's coasts, it now supports only a few thousand storks.

Recently the Wood Stork has shifted most of its breeding activity out of southern Florida and into northern Florida, Georgia, and southern South Carolina. In these areas the birds have established a number of smaller colonies, and the overall population appears to be stable.

Accidental Species

The neotropical Jabiru (*Jabiru mycteria*) has been recorded several times in North America, with most records from Texas between July and October. The species' normal range is from southern Mexico south to northern South America.

David Allen Sibley

New World Vultures

The New World vultures are large to massive, soaring scavengers with wingspans of 4 feet 11 inches to 9 feet 1 inch (1.5–2.8 m). In flight, vultures resemble eagles or large hawks, but they are in fact more closely related to storks than to members of the hawk family. Their plumage is mostly dark, and their heads are bare and often brightly colored. Perching birds often sit with their wings spread wide like a cormorant. Vultures soar long distances searching for carrion and are familiar sights along North American highways and roads. One or more species occur over most of North America, living wherever there is a steady supply of carrion, as well as sites for roosting and nesting.

Taxonomy

Although the New World vultures resemble the Old World vultures and other members of the family Accipitridae, they are more closely related to the storks. In recognition of this relationship, the AOU now places the Cathartidae in the order Ciconiiformes.

The close affinities of the Cathartidae and the storks is supported by recent studies using DNA–DNA hybridization and mitochondrial DNA and by older descriptions of anatomical and behavioral similarities. As one example, both groups practice urohydrosis, in which they squirt liquid excrement onto their legs; the evaporation of the liquid has a cooling effect.

In contrast, many behavioral differences separate the Old World and New World vultures. There is no current or

Cathartid head and bill. All of the New World vultures have an unfeathered head and neck; in most species the bare skin is bright reddish or orange, as on the California Condor shown here. The bare skin is more easily cleaned and maintained than feathers would be, a useful trait given that vultures often stick their heads into very messy carcasses.

fossil anatomical evidence to suggest a close common ancestor. American vultures do not build stick nests, do not have true vocalizations, and do not nest colonially, as do many Old World vultures.

Both Old World and New World vultures have naked heads and necks, which prevents the fouling of feathers while the birds feed on decaying carcasses. Bald heads may also be an adaptation that helps the birds regulate body temperature. Both groups have meat-tearing beaks and feet adapted to walking on the ground. Both feed their young by regurgitation. But these similarities are now attributed to convergent evolution. The two groups have similar lifestyles, and their adaptations for a diet of carrion evolved independently.

Cathartid diversity. Although superficially similar to one another, the New World vultures form several distinct genera that may be quite distantly related to one another. Three of these genera are found in North America, ranging in size from the massive California Condor (left) to the relatively small Black Vulture (right).

Food and Foraging

Because vultures and condors eat carrion, how much and how often they eat can be highly unpredictable, and this unpredictability of diet shapes many aspects of their lives. If necessary, cathartids can rapidly ingest large quantities of food and then go for many days without feeding.

Generally cathartids prefer the meat of freshly dead animals, but they will eat meat in various stages of putrefaction and appear to have excellent resistance to the microbes and toxins found in decaying flesh. On occasion, the Black Vulture *(Coragyps atratus)* and the Turkey Vulture *(Cathartes aura)* will also take live prey, such as nestling herons, and there are records of Black Vultures feeding on living newborn calves and baby turtles.

The Black Vulture and the California Condor *(Gymnogyps californianus)* feed on larger carcasses than does the Turkey Vulture. Both Black and Turkey Vultures feed on roadkills, and they visit farms, ranches, landfills, shorelines, hunting grounds, and other areas where carrion can be found. Black Vultures sometimes become campground pests, quickly descending on unguarded picnic coolers and gobbling raw eggs and meat. In winter, Turkey Vultures glean small dead

Cathartid foot. Like other New World vultures, the Turkey Vulture (shown here) has relatively long legs and toes adapted for walking, with weak claws unlike the predatory feet of hawks but very similar to the feet of storks. Vultures even have a vestige of webbing between the toes. The legs and feet are usually whitish because of the feces that vultures (like storks) spray onto the legs for evaporative cooling.

mammals from burned-over cane fields in the South. In recent decades, California Condors have foraged in rural farms and ranchlands in southern California.

All the New World vultures search for food in flight, making use of good wind conditions to travel. The California Condor can travel up to 140 miles (225 km) a day when searching for food. In general, New World vultures search for food visually; however, the Turkey Vulture can

Worldwide Family Features

- 22–53" (55–135 cm) soaring scavengers.
- 7 species in 5 genera; found throughout temperate and tropical Americas. 3 species in 3 genera occur in North America; found north to southern Canada.
- Eat primarily carrion located visually or by smell.
- Solitary nesters; territorial and monogamous, with long-term partnerships in at least some species. Social away from nests. Roost and may forage communally. Northern populations migratory.
- Breed first at 6–8 years old.
- Nest in caves, hollow trees. Do not build nests: Condors make shallow, rimmed scrape; vultures lay directly on substrate. Reuse nest sites for years.
- Eggs subelliptical. Condors lay 1 pale

blue-green, unmarked egg; vultures lay 1–4 (usually 2) eggs; tan or dull white, with variable dark markings. Vultures incubate 35–40 days; California Condor, 8 weeks. Both sexes incubate. 1 brood per year in vultures, 1 every other year in condors.
- Altricial young hatch with heavy down. Vultures fledge at 8–13 weeks, condors at about 6 months. Both adults care for young; fledglings have prolonged dependency on adults, up to 1 year in condors.
- Adult annual survival in wild little known, but probably quite high: 75–90% in vultures, 75% in recent years for declining California Condor population. Among oldest on record: 45 years (California Condor).

Cathartid foraging. New World vultures feed almost exclusively on carrion, and small groups will gather at a carcass; shown here are a Black Vulture (left) and two Turkey Vultures. Turkey Vultures have lighter wing-loading and fly more easily under their own power, and so rise earlier than Black Vultures; they fly low and locate food by smell. Black Vultures rise later, after warm thermals have developed to aid their soaring flight; they fly higher and find food mainly by sight, often by locating groups of feeding Turkey Vultures.

also quickly locate carcasses by smell, a trait that is unusual among birds.

Turkey Vultures can reliably locate dead chickens hidden by researchers on the forest floor. With their light wing-loading, they are superb soarers, and with their keen sense of smell they are well adapted to foraging over forests.

In contrast, species with heavier wing-loading, such as the California Condor and the Black Vulture, are more likely to feed on large corpses in open habitats. Cathartids follow birds of their own species as well as other avian scavengers to food, quickly forming large feeding aggregations and fighting for dominance with conspecifics as well as with different species. Subordinate only to the Golden Eagle *(Aquila chrysaetos)*, California Condors easily supplant Turkey Vultures at a carcass. In the eastern United States, Black Vultures easily dominate Turkey Vultures at carcasses, while Crested Caracaras *(Caracara cheriway)* of the falcon family dominate Black Vultures.

Cathartids sometimes cooperate when foraging. Coalitions of several pairs of Black Vultures and their offspring, for example, may roost together and will follow one another from a roost to a previously located carcass. They also watch and follow Turkey Vultures and other scavengers homing in on food.

Cathartids use their strong beaks to rip meat off a carcass while holding it down with a foot. To reach internal organs, they can insert their heads and necks entirely into an orifice. If a carcass has become tough, two birds may stand opposite each other and tug at it as a team. Vultures may drag food around while feeding, but they rarely carry it more than a short distance in their beaks. Their feet are not adapted to carrying either; they carry food to the nest only inside their crops, from which they regurgitate it to their young.

Breeding

New World vultures form long-term monogamous pair bonds but may pair again upon the death of a mate. They are solitary nesters, using caves and deep crevices in cliffs. Nest caves that have been used for many years acquire a powerful odor.

Some birds also nest in large, hollow trees and, in Florida, on the ground in palmetto thickets. Both Turkey and Black Vultures occasionally nest in man-made structures such as abandoned buildings.

Sunning. New World vultures, such as this Turkey Vulture, all spend time sunning their spread wings. They apparently adopt this posture to warm the body and to dry nighttime dew from the feathers. The posture may also help them realign their flight feathers, which can become misshapen while soaring.

For several weeks before the female lays eggs, a pair of condors investigates potential nest sites and engages in courtship and territorial displays. Pair flights, in which both birds glide high above their nesting site in a steady and coordinated fashion, their wingtips nearly touching, may signal to neighboring pairs that the area is occupied. In courtship, the male puts on a stately display, standing upright before his mate, partially spreading his wings, strutting theatrically, and bobbing his head. Other cathartids perform similar follow flights, in which members of the pair coordinate movements and soar close together and perform perched courtship displays with raised wings and feet.

Cathartid chicks are altricial. One parent attends them closely during the first few weeks. Vulture chicks fledge at eight to 13 weeks of age; condor chicks, at about six months. The chicks associate with one or both parents for months after fledging, flying to and from roost and foraging areas together and being fed by adults.

Conservation

The California Condor has been the target of an intensive conservation program since the early 1980s, when fewer than 20 individuals remained in the wild. Lead poisoning from the ingestion of bullet fragments in carcasses was a major cause of the condor's decline. By 1987 all the wild birds had been captured; thanks to the subsequent captive-breeding program, their numbers have steadily increased. By 2000, there were more than 165 birds, and between 1992 and 1998, 66 condors were released into the wild at sites in California and Arizona.

Reintroduced birds have continued to die from lead poisoning, and it may not be possible to reestablish the species until lead bullets are replaced with nontoxic alternatives now available. In addition, some birds have been lost to collisions with overhead wires. Young condors reared by their parents have done much better at avoiding human environments than young raised by humans. By 2000, none of the released birds had bred in the wild.

Large, walk-in vulture traps put up by ranchers in Florida and Texas formerly caused the deaths of many thousands of Black and Turkey Vultures, which were trapped to reduce the threat they posed to newborn calves. Subsequently, both species have shown continent-wide population increases, although threats do remain. In the Southeast, modern forestry practices have severely reduced the number of hollow-log nest sites available for Black Vultures. Better sanitation on farms and ranches has reduced the availability of carcasses, but both species have expanded their ranges in the Northeast, apparently to exploit roadkills.

Helen Snyder

Flamingos

Family Phoenicopteridae
Order Phoenicopteriformes

Flamingos are among the tallest and most distinctive-looking aquatic waders. They have long legs and necks, a wingspan of 5 feet (1.5 m), dazzling pink plumage, and peculiarly shaped, deep, downcurved bills. Colonies are usually located on saline lakes, coastal lagoons, or salt ponds, and the birds can withstand high temperatures and very alkaline waters that many wetland species cannot tolerate. Flamingos will also use habitats such as freshwater wetlands, flooded rice paddies, and tidal mudflats. The Greater Flamingo *(Phoenicopterus ruber)* is seen occasionally along the southeastern Atlantic and Gulf coasts, and more rarely elsewhere in North America. Many of these birds are escapees from captivity, but the mobility of flamingos suggests that wild birds may wander north from breeding colonies in the Caribbean and northern Mexico.

Taxonomy

Superficially flamingos resemble storks, cranes, and spoonbills, which occur in similar habitats and have a similar body structure. Close inspection, however, reveals a strange mixture of features in flamingos. They have a highly specialized bill unlike that of any other bird, a neck and legs that are proportionately longer than in other avian families, and unmistakable pink feathering. Flamingos are tall like herons, have webbed toes like ducks, and give honking calls to keep their flock together like geese; they even secrete a milk-like substance to feed their young, like pigeons. Not surprisingly, their taxonomic position is an uncertain and much disputed topic.

Traditionally flamingos have been grouped with the Ciconiiformes, which include the herons, storks, and ibises, based upon similarities between the pelvic and rib bones of flamingos and storks and between the egg-white proteins of flamingos and herons. Recent DNA–DNA hybridization studies also support this placement.

Another school of thought suggests that flamingos are more closely related to the Anseriformes (ducks, geese, and swans); both groups have webbed feet and waterproof plumage, and they share similarities in bill structure. Recent research has also revealed similarities in the chemical makeup of the bile of flamingos and geese. A third hypothesis proposes that flamingos may be related to avocets and stilts, based on fossil evidence and anatomical and behavioral similarities between flamingos and the Banded Stilt *(Cladorhynchus leucocephalus)* of Australia.

Currently flamingos are placed within their own order, between the Ciconiiformes and the Anseriformes. Debate over their classification will undoubtedly continue.

Greater Flamingo. *Flamingos are unmistakable: They are almost grotesquely slender and have awkwardly angled bills. Although the world's five flamingo species are sometimes separated into three genera, they are very similar, and many taxonomists combine them into a single genus.*

Food and Foraging

Flamingos are omnivorous, feeding on a wide variety of small insects, crustaceans, mollusks and other invertebrates, algae, and small seeds. They feed primarily by filtering prey out of shallow water but also will grasp larger prey in their bill. When ponds dry up, flamingos may

187

ingest mud, from which they extract nutrients. Outside of the breeding season, they feed mostly at night and use daylight hours for sleep and leisure.

Flamingos typically feed with the head submerged, upside down and facing backward, with the top, curved portion of the bill parallel to the bottom substrate. While feeding in this position, a bird may swing its bill from side to side in order to increase the area it covers. A flamingo's long legs and neck allow it to feed in deep water, and its webbed toes lend support when walking on mud and also facilitate swimming. While swimming, a flamingo is able to upend like a dabbling duck in order to reach food that is far below the surface.

Flamingos have a complex bill that is specialized to filter small items suspended in the water. The bill curves so that there is a small gap of equal size along its entire length. This gap houses the tongue, which is moved to pump water in and out of the bill during feeding. The edges of the bill are lined with rows of lamellae, which are like the teeth of a comb and collectively act as an effective filtering structure. When the bird is feeding it takes a mouthful of

Greater Flamingo head and bill. The flamingo's bill is unique: large and stout, with a sharp bend in the middle. It is designed so that the outer (downturned) portion of the culmen will be parallel to the ground when the head is down in foraging posture.

water and food, and then uses its tongue as a piston to push water out through the lamellae, which trap the prey on the inside. Spines on the tongue and palate move the food particles to the throat.

Breeding

Flamingos breed only in years when environmental conditions are conducive to rearing offspring. Months before breeding, the birds devote substantial time to

---

Worldwide Family Features

- 32–57" (80–145 cm) wading birds.
- 5 species in 1–3 genera worldwide; occurs in Central and South America, southern Eurasia, and Africa. 1 species occurs occasionally in Florida and rarely north to Nova Scotia or west to the Pacific. Most records, including all reports of other species, probably involve escapees from captivity.
- Eat mostly small invertebrates and algae. Filter-feed in shallow water, using highly specialized bill.
- Highly gregarious throughout year; massive groups conduct elaborate displays to synchronize breeding within colonies. Monogamous; pair bonds may last for multiple breeding seasons. May move considerable distances during nonbreeding season.
- Breed first usually at 3–6 years old; most birds fail at first breeding attempt.
- Cone-shaped mud nest mound, 6–18"

(15–45 cm) high, with small depression on top. Both parents build, usually on mudflat. Often reuse old nests.
- 1 chalky white, oval egg (rarely 2). Both parents incubate, for 27–31 days. 1 brood per year; sometimes lay replacement clutch if 1st is lost early in incubation.
- Semi-precocial young down-covered at hatching; usually stay on nest mound for several days before leaving to group with other chicks in crèches tended by a few adults. Both parents feed young with milky secretion. Young can feed independently at 28–42 days, fledge at 9–13 weeks; parents will feed until fledging.
- Adult annual survival high; birds often live 20–30 years. Among oldest on record: at least 33 years in the wild, more than 44 years in captivity (Greater Flamingo).

Flamingo display. Flamingos engage in several distinctive group displays that are virtually always performed by many birds en masse. Here a number of Greater Flamingos perform a head-flagging display, standing tall and walking slowly while turning their heads back and forth.

group displays that synchronize breeding activities within a colony. Displays include wing-saluting, wing-leg stretching, twist-preening, head-flagging, and marching.

Birds often will not display unless they are part of a large group. Researchers have induced small groups of captive Lesser Flamingos *(Phoenicopterus minor),* which normally occur in Africa and India, to display by using mirrors to trick the birds into thinking they were part of a larger ensemble.

Flamingos typically breed in large colonies and build their nest mounds close together. Each pair rarely produces more than one egg, although a second may be laid if the first is lost to predators or natural disaster. Parents share the incubating, with stints lasting from one hour to several days, depending on the distance to feeding sites.

After hatching, the young remain in the nest for several days, unless predation or flooding requires an earlier evacuation. After five to 12 days, the chicks leave the nest, although they still depend on their parents for food. Both parents produce a milk-like secretion in the digestive tract, which they drip from the bill into the chick's mouth. Even though chicks are able to feed themselves at four to six weeks, the parents may continue to provide this secretion until the chicks fledge, many weeks later. When they fledge, the young look much like their parents, although it takes several years for them to obtain the pink color of adults.

Conservation

Caribbean populations of the Greater Flamingo have declined considerably. Although the population is estimated to number about 80,000 individuals, most breed at only four colonies. The main reasons for the population declines are probably habitat destruction and human disturbance; the capture of birds for zoos also may have played a role in the past.

If flamingos do not receive a proper diet, their color fades and they may die. Consequently, early attempts to keep flamingos in captivity resulted in repeated collection from the wild to replace birds that had lost their pink color or died from improper diets. The propensity for flamingo feathers to fade once they are plucked, however, protected populations from the ravages of the plume trade in the early 1900s.

William J. Seng

Ducks, Geese, and Swans

Family Anatidae
Order Anseriformes

The Anatidae (collectively called waterfowl in North America and wildfowl in Britain) is a varied group of medium-size to very large waterbirds that includes true ducks, geese, swans, and whistling-ducks. Members of this family have large heads with conspicuous and often horizontally flattened bills, long necks, heavy bodies, relatively short tails, long wings, and webbed feet for swimming. Wingspans range from 17 inches to 6 feet 8 inches (43 cm–2 m). Plumage coloration of most Northern Hemisphere ducks ranges from the bright colors and conspicuous patterns of the breeding male to the female's highly camouflaging mixture of browns and grays. The appearance of other anatid species varies less with sex, age, or season. Waterfowl live in a variety of aquatic habitats, including marshes, lakes, and rivers; seasonally flooded grasslands, shrublands, and forests; coastal estuaries; and shallow ocean bays. More so than most families, they have a close relationship with humans and are important for food and recreational hunting; several domesticated species are of great economic value.

Taxonomy

The family Anatidae is a large, complex taxonomic group. Species range from the cosmopolitan Mallard *(Anas platyrhynchos)* of the Northern Hemisphere, with its long-distance migrations, to flightless or near-flightless single-island endemic species. The antiquity, wide distributions, isolation on islands, and diverse social behavior of waterfowl have re-sulted in the evolution of many unusual taxa.

Family classification varies greatly in treatises and field guides, depending on the date of publication. Plumages of the downy young and courtship displays, as well as more typical anatomical and genetic approaches, have been important in creating such classifications. Currently North American species are grouped into three subfamilies. Most biologists now

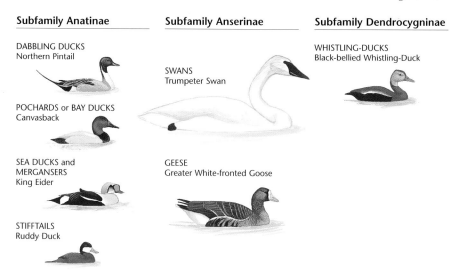

Subfamily Anatinae

DABBLING DUCKS
Northern Pintail

POCHARDS or BAY DUCKS
Canvasback

SEA DUCKS and
MERGANSERS
King Eider

STIFFTAILS
Ruddy Duck

Subfamily Anserinae

SWANS
Trumpeter Swan

GEESE
Greater White-fronted Goose

Subfamily Dendrocygninae

WHISTLING-DUCKS
Black-bellied Whistling-Duck

Anatid diversity. North American waterfowl include representatives of seven tribes in three subfamilies. The subfamily Anatinae includes the dabbling ducks, pochards (bay ducks), sea ducks and mergansers, and stifftails. Anserinae comprises the swans and geese. Dendrocygninae is the whistling-ducks.

place the whistling-ducks in a separate subfamily, the Dendrocygninae. Geese and swans are in the subfamily Anserinae, which formerly included the whistling-ducks in some taxonomies. The Anserinae are subdivided into two tribes: the Anserini (geese) and the Cygnini (swans). The true ducks are in the subfamily Anatinae, which is split into several tribes, of which four occur in North America: the Anatini (dabbling or surface-feeding ducks), the Aythyini (pochards or bay ducks), the Mergini (sea ducks and mergansers), and the Oxyurini (stifftails). At least three other subfamilies occur elsewhere in the world.

The closest relatives of the Anatidae are the screamers (family Anhimidae) of South America and the Magpie Goose *(Anseranas semipalmata)* of tropical Australia and New Guinea, which is placed in the family Anseranatidae.

Subfamily Dendrocygninae (Whistling-Ducks)

The whistling-ducks of the Dendrocygninae occur in diverse warm temperate to tropical habitats around the world. Their general appearance lies somewhere between that of a goose and a true duck; males and females are similar in color and size. Two species regularly occur in

Worldwide Family Features

- 12–71" (30–180 cm) waterfowl.
- About 154 species in at least 45 genera. Found on all continents and many isolated islands; range from tropical to Arctic and subantarctic regions. 50 species in 19 genera occur in North America, of which 1 species is introduced; 1 additional species is extinct. An additional 9 species have occurred as accidentals. Escapees from avicultural collections are common and occasionally form small breeding populations. Family occurs throughout North America.
- Omnivorous, herbivorous, or carnivorous. Most swans and geese feed on plants year-round; whistling-ducks and most true ducks eat animal foods during breeding and prebreeding periods and as juveniles, with plant foods more common at other times. Sea ducks eat large invertebrates, shellfish, fish eggs, or fish year-round.
- Territorial; some species are colonial. Whistling-ducks, swans, and geese generally monogamous, with long-lasting pair bonds. Pairing seasonal in true ducks. Extra-pair copulation common in some species. Highly social during nonbreeding season. Northern species migratory.
- Breed first at 1 or 2 years old in most species, 2 or 3 years old in sea ducks and geese, and 3–5 years old in swans.
- Nests vary from those requiring no construction (tree holes, cliff ledges, shallow burrows) to simple scrapes in soil hidden by herbaceous vegetation to interwoven bowls with canopies concealed in dense vegetation, often over water. Female typically builds nest; among whistling-ducks and swans, male may help. Eggs usually insulated with heavy down. A few species may reuse nest sites and materials.
- Typically 3–8 eggs in swans and geese, 3–14 in ducks; parasitic laying, common in some species, results in even larger clutches. Eggs plain off-white, buff, or pale olive. Shape variable but usually elliptical or subelliptical. In most species, female alone incubates; exceptions include whistling-ducks and some swans. Clutch hatches within 24–36 hours after 21–40 days of incubation. Normally 1 brood per year.
- Young precocial and covered with down at hatching. Most ducklings remain with female until near flight; geese and swan families may stay together through migration south and even to following spring. Age at 1st flight ranges from 25 days in Green-winged Teal to 24 weeks in some swans.
- Survival extremely variable among populations. Up to 65–80% of ducks may die in 1st year; survival rate higher thereafter, although most birds that reach adulthood live only for another 1–2 years. Survival higher among geese and especially swans, whose life expectancy after 1st year can be at least 4 years. In wild, many species have lived more than 20 years. Among oldest on record: more than 28 years (Canada Goose, Brant); more than 26 years (Mute Swan, Snow Goose, American Black Duck, Mallard).

North America: the Fulvous Whistling-Duck *(Dendrocygna bicolor)* and the Black-bellied Whistling-Duck *(D. autumnalis)*.

Subfamily Anserinae (Geese and Swans)

Members of the Anserinae show no sexual differences in plumage coloration, but males and females often differ in size and voice.

Tribe Anserini (Geese) Geese are especially common at northerly latitudes and are well adapted to cold weather. Six species breed in North America. A seventh species, the Barnacle Goose *(Branta leucopsis)*, does not breed in North America but occurs rarely, although some records may involve birds escaped from captivity.

Tribe Cygnini (Swans) Of seven species of swans worldwide, North America has two regularly breeding native species: the Tundra Swan *(Cygnus columbianus)* of the high Arctic and the more temperate Trumpeter Swan *(C. buccinator)*, which is now increasing in numbers after extirpation from many areas. In addition, the Whooper Swan *(C. cygnus)* occurs rarely, especially in Alaska, where it has bred in the Aleutian Islands. The Mute Swan *(C. olor)* has been introduced from Eurasia and now breeds in several parts of North America.

Subfamily Anatinae (True Ducks)

The subfamily Anatinae is dominated by species with plumages that show conspicuous sexual dichromatism that varies seasonally. Seasonal changes in plumage color are more common in Northern than in Southern Hemisphere species.

Tribe Anatini (Dabbling Ducks) Also known as surface-feeding ducks, dabbling ducks number more than 50 species worldwide, of which 12 are native breeders in North America. Two species found throughout Eurasia, the Eurasian Wigeon *(Anas penelope)* and the Garganey

Anatid foot. The feet of all waterfowl are completely webbed between the three front toes. Geese (as in the Greater White-fronted Goose, shown here) have relatively long legs and walk easily. Diving ducks have shorter legs and a lobed hind toe.

(A. querquedula), also occur regularly in North America, but breeding has not been documented. The dabbling ducks include species with a diverse array of plumage patterns; males are often bright and colorful, while females are typically colored with a mixture of mottled browns. Whereas members of the other three Anatinae tribes found in North America feed mainly by diving, dabblers primarily feed on the water's surface by straining water through the bill; by up-ending to reach deeper food items; and while walking on land, by picking up food with the nail of the bill or stripping seed heads and foliage with the edge of the bill.

In addition to typical dabblers—like the Mallard, the Northern Pintail *(Anas acuta)*, and the teals—such forest-loving, cavity-nesting ducks as the Wood Duck *(Aix sponsa)* and the Muscovy Duck *(Cairina moschata)* have now been placed in the Anatini. (Muscovy Ducks that have escaped from captivity have been reported as breeding in Texas and Florida; wild birds from Mexico also have occurred in southern Texas.) Recently a free-living breeding population of Mandarin Ducks *(Aix galericulata)* has become established in California, but this species has not yet been added to the AOU Check-list.

Tribe Aythyini (Pochards or Bay Ducks) Of the 15 species of pochards worldwide, five have widespread breeding populations in North America. The Tufted Duck *(Aythya fuligula)* also occurs in small numbers during winter. Members of this group are distinguished from the dabblers by their diving behavior, shorter bills, rounded heads, plumper bodies, and simpler color patterns.

Tribe Mergini (Sea Ducks and Mergansers) All nine genera and 15 of the world's 19 species of sea ducks and mergansers breed in North America. The extinct Labrador Duck *(Camptorhynchus labradorius)* is also in this group. The term "sea ducks" refers to a collection of species often associated with coastal waters: eiders, scoters, goldeneyes, the Bufflehead *(Bucephala albeola)*, the Harlequin Duck *(Histrionicus histrionicus)*, and the Long-tailed Duck *(Clangula hyemalis,* formerly called the Oldsquaw). Sea ducks and mergansers share diving skills, tolerance of salt water (at least in winter), compact plumage with heavy down that is suitable for cold climates, a prevalence in northern temperate or subarctic areas, and a preference for animal foods.

Tribe Oxyurini (Stifftails) Only two species of stifftails occur in North America: the widespread Ruddy Duck *(Oxyura jamaicensis)* and the Masked Duck *(Nomonyx dominicus),* which periodically occurs and occasionally breeds in freshwater ponds in Texas and other Gulf coast states. Members of this tribe are quite distinctive, with their small size and long, stiff, often vertically pointing tail feathers that give them their common name.

Variation

Many species of Anatidae vary greatly in plumage patterns and body size, presumably because of the extensive and often geographically separated ranges of these long-distance migrants. For example, there is considerable size variation among

Canada Geese *(Branta canadensis),* with birds of the largest races more than twice the size of those of the smaller races. At least 11 subspecies of the Canada Goose have been recognized by taxonomists, and other distinct populations exist.

Color variations also occur in some species. The white and blue morphs of the Snow Goose *(Chen caerulescens)* appear distinct enough that they were once considered separate species. Now considered a genetic variant, the blue morph, or "Blue Goose," is especially common in eastern populations of the "Lesser" Snow Goose *(C. c. atlanticus)* and occurs rarely in both the larger eastern race often called the "Greater" Snow Goose *(C. c. caerulescens)* and in the diminutive white Ross's Goose *(C. rossii).*

The Mallard group contains many taxa, some more differentiated than others; they range widely throughout the Northern Hemisphere and vary from a large form, resident in southern Greenland (the "Greenland" Mallard, *Anas platyrhynchos conboschas),* to a non-dimorphic southern race of the arid Southwest, the "Mexican" Duck *(A. p. diazi),* both considered subspecies. In the past, the Mottled Duck *(Anas fulvigula),* the American Black Duck *(A. rubripes),* and two Hawaiian island endemics, the Laysan Duck *(A. laysanensis)* and the Hawaiian Duck *(A. wyvilliana),* all have been treated as Mallard subspecies.

Several species with circumpolar distributions show clear differences between North American and Eurasian populations. In the past the Tundra Swan has been separated into two species—the "Whistling Swan" *(Cygnus "columbianus")* in North America and "Bewick's Swan" *(C. "bewickii")* in Eurasia—but these are now considered to be a single species. In contrast, it has been proposed that the White-winged Scoter *(Melanitta fusca),* the Black Scoter *(M. nigra),* and the Green-winged Teal *(Anas crecca)* should each be split into North American and Eurasian forms.

Hybrids are very common in many species of ducks, especially in captivity,

Hybrid duck. Hybrids are relatively frequent in this family. Most hybrids involve closely related species-pairs, such as the two wigeons or the Blue-winged and Cinnamon Teal. A number of other combinations have been recorded, including some unusual ones like this male Wood Duck × Ring-necked Duck.

and escapees create major identification problems. Hybrids have been reported mostly among dabbling ducks and among pochards. Some of these hybrids have proved to be fertile, leading to further identification problems for birders in the field.

Molts and Plumages

Difficulties in identifying ducks often result from birders not recognizing their variable appearance. The dramatic differences in sexual dichromatism of most Northern Hemisphere species can be confusing for beginning birders; in fact, some males and females of the same species were classified as different species by early naturalists. The basic plumages of males, acquired after the breeding season, make them look much like females. Also confusing is the reduced sexual differentiation in juveniles of all species and in second-year, nonbreeding sea ducks.

The American Black Duck, the Mottled Duck, and isolated southern races of the Mallard (such as the "Mexican" Duck) lack extreme sexual dichromatism.

Although duck plumages were once considered unique among birds, ducks are now thought to follow the same sequence of plumages and molts as most birds, although most ducks differ in the timing and duration and of their plumages.

Newly hatched waterfowl are covered with dense down. This natal plumage provides excellent insulation and traps air that makes the hatchling buoyant. Color patterns of the down differ dramatically among species; consequently, the young of many species can be identified at a very early age. Between two weeks of age and the flight stage, the juvenal plumage, which has more rigid contour feathers, replaces the natal down.

As in all aquatic birds, feathering develops first on the underparts. As down feathers are pushed out of their bases, they sometimes remain attached to the shafts of the new feathers and can serve as a guide to the age of the bird. In almost grown young, remnant fluffy down on the head may identify a young bird nearly ready for flight. The shafts of natal tail feathers also are continuous with the shafts of the growing juvenal feathers, resulting in a notch in the tip of the vane, which is used by banders to distinguish young of the year from older birds. With the exception of some stifftails, the juvenal flight feathers are not shed until the following summer, often providing a means of distinguishing young of the year from adults.

Young males of most true duck species then have a partial prebasic molt that results in a briefly held first basic body plumage that is usually similar in color to the juvenal plumage. In some cases, however, the appearance of immature males is intermediate between juveniles and adults, as in the Canvasback (Aythya valisineria). The females also acquire an extensive first basic plumage, but differences in female color or feather patterns are less easily recognized in the field than those of males.

Subsequently, adult North American ducks have at least two body plumages per breeding cycle that may differ markedly in color according to sex, season, or both. In Ruddy Ducks, molts in both sexes are almost equally spaced in time so that the alternate plumage occurs in summer and the basic plumage occurs in winter, a pattern similar to that of many songbirds. But in adults of most species of ducks, males attain their duller basic plumage after breeding and keep it for only a few months, from midsummer to fall. At this time, wing feathers and tail are replaced, and the birds become temporarily flightless. Presumably their nondescript appearance at this time, termed "eclipse plumage," helps male ducks avoid predators.

Most male dabblers acquire a bright alternate plumage in late fall or early winter; courtship usually is initiated at wintering or migration sites, and they retain this plumage until after they abandon nesting females during the wing molt. The Blue-winged Teal *(Anas discors)* is unusual among Northern Hemisphere dabbling ducks in retaining its basic plumage well into winter after migration.

Plumages of most female dabblers and pochards in the Northern Hemisphere differ less in color by season than do those of males, and changes are therefore less obvious and are difficult to document without individually marked feathers. Those species that have been studied—the Mallard, Northern Pintail, Gadwall *(Anas strepera)*, Ring-necked Duck *(Aythya collaris)*, and Redhead *(Aythya americana)*—have two plumages per annual cycle, but molts may differ in timing from males, and in each molt only certain feathers are replaced. Thus females may have several generations of feathers, acquired during different molts, at any one time. Females begin their molt into basic plumage prior to nesting, when they replace head feathers and some or most of their body feathers, as well as acquiring longer and fluffier down. At this time, however, they do not molt their flight feathers. Later in summer, after nesting, they complete their basic molt and replace the flight feathers and any remaining old body feathers. Soon after, females begin to acquire new alternate plumage feathers.

Age-related appearance is more complicated in sea ducks, which do not breed until they are two or three years old. As subadults, male sea ducks look more like

Molt of flight feathers. *Most ducks have an unusual molt schedule that differs from that of most other birds. The males wear a drab basic (eclipse) plumage (as shown on these male Wood Ducks) from midsummer to fall and a brighter alternate plumage during the rest of the year. They attain the alternate plumage much earlier than most birds because ducks start to display and form pair bonds in winter. During the prebasic molt, in late summer, birds lose all their flight feathers at once and become flightless for a period of a few weeks. During this vulnerable period the birds are secretive, congregating in areas with rich food sources and good protection from predators.*

Long-tailed Duck. The molt pattern of the Long-tailed Duck is among the most complex of any bird. It is based on the standard pattern of two molts per year, as in other ducks, but in the Long-tailed Duck each molt is interrupted, producing four partial molts each year, while the scapulars and head feathers are molted three times a year. The "winter" plumage shown here arises from the complete molt in summer, followed by a September–October molt of much of the head and body, and an additional molt of head and neck feathers in October–November.

juveniles or adult females than adult males. In most species, though, age can be determined: in some, like the Surf Scoter *(Melanitta perspicillata),* by their more colorful bills; in others, like the Common Merganser *(Mergus merganser),* by the amount of white in the wing. The Long-tailed Duck has an extra plumage between the basic and alternate, with some feathers replaced three times during the annual cycle, further complicating age and sex determination in this species.

In whistling-ducks, geese, and swans, as in true ducks, the natal down is followed within a few weeks by a juvenal plumage, which usually is duller and less patterned than the natal down. It is gradually replaced with a first basic plumage, which looks like that of an adult. This molt involves replacement of tail feathers but not wing flight feathers. Thereafter these birds generally have only one plumage per annual cycle, acquired after the breeding season; however, some head molt has been noted in a number of species of geese during spring.

In geese with strong family bonds, large body size, and good terrestrial locomotion, adults normally undergo wing molt as their offspring are learning to fly.

Habitats

Although some geese regularly use upland habitats, members of the Anatidae generally breed near aquatic habitats. Waterfowl use most wetland types, but habitat suitability varies with season, vegetation, and water characteristics. High-latitude (Arctic) or high-elevation (alpine) wetlands are useful to waterfowl only in warm weather. In all areas, but especially in warmer arid areas, the natural drying of wetlands may make some habitats unsuitable for waterfowl; drying may also create new habitats, such as mudflats that attract waterfowl that eat invertebrates and seeds. Flooding can make marginal areas more attractive to waterfowl but can also wash out nests and inundate nesting cover.

Waterfowl use bodies of water that range from fresh to hypersaline. Freshwater areas, which can occur almost anywhere due to rainfall and snow-melt, are generally favored by waterfowl for breeding, as hatchlings do not survive drinking salty water. This is apparently because their specialized salt glands—which extract salts from saline water, making it drinkable—are poorly developed. Even extremely marine species, such as the King Eider *(Somateria spectabilis),* nest in freshwater tundra ponds. During nonbreeding periods, many species of waterfowl use saline as well as freshwater areas.

The once-glaciated "prairie pothole region" of the northern Great Plains at one time had enormous numbers of lakes and smaller wetlands, of which only 50 percent remain today. A large proportion of the ducks in North America breed in this region. Many dabbling species, such as the Mallard, Northern Pintail, teals, Northern Shoveler *(Anas clypeata),* and Gadwall, nest at wetland edges in this region or in its uplands. Redheads, Ruddy Ducks, Canvasbacks, and the "Giant" race of the Canada Goose *(Branta canadensis maxima)* nest in aquatic vegetation in its waters.

More northerly wooded areas are frequented by mergansers, goldeneyes, and the Bufflehead. Farther north, colder tundra dominated by cold-climate grasses and sedges is occupied by the Long-tailed Duck, some eiders, the Northern Pintail, Snow Goose, Brant *(Branta bernicla)*, Greater White-fronted Goose *(Anser albifrons)*, smaller races of Canada Goose, and Tundra Swan.

American Black Ducks are common in the marshes of the northeast coast of North America, and Mottled Ducks use Gulf coast marshes. Brants, eiders, scoters, and mergansers often gather in large groups in marine habitats during the nonbreeding season in order to take advantage of the abundant food available. Deciduous forest wetlands form ideal nesting habitat for Wood Ducks and Hooded Mergansers *(Lophodytes cucullatus)*, and Common Mergansers also are found in forested areas, breeding along northern rivers and lakes. Harlequin Ducks select breeding sites on fast-flowing rivers, and in winter they feed and loaf along wave-battered, rocky ocean shores.

Food and Foraging

Different tribes and species of waterfowl often select different foods. Patterns of food use and feeding behavior are closely linked to the foods available in a given season and the nutritional demands of a bird's life stage.

Diet

Plant foods typically available in wetlands include seeds, underground tubers, green herbaceous foliage of aquatic grasses and sedges, sea grasses, and submerged pondweeds. Animal foods range from tiny crustaceans and fish eggs to large invertebrates (for example, clams) and fish.

The larger-bodied geese and swans tend to be herbivores. Most ducks, especially abundant, wide-ranging species, are omnivorous. But some ducks, depending on their genus, can be mainly herbivores or mainly carnivores.

Depending on their nutritional demands (for breeding, feather growth, migration, and so on), ducks eat different foods in different seasons. Many species of dabbling ducks and pochards shift to

Dabbling versus diving. One of the primary distinctions between the tribes of the Anatinae is the primary foraging methods of each. Anatini feed mainly by "dabbling," either filtering the surface water or mud with the bill (as does the Northern Shoveler, left) or upending to reach submerged vegetation a few inches below the surface (Mallard, center). The other tribes forage mainly by diving; most species use only their feet for propulsion underwater (Ring-necked Duck, right), but many of the Mergini use their wings and feet together.

an invertebrate diet prior to breeding or molting in order to acquire minerals and proteins necessary to produce eggs and replace feathers. They then return to a diet of plant foliage and seeds in the fall. Young ducks eat mainly insects, and even newly hatched goslings take invertebrates opportunistically. But as ducklings grow, they shift their diet more and more toward foods eaten by their parents in the nonbreeding period.

Field-feeding on agricultural crops is common among most geese, some swans, and Mallards, American Black Ducks, Northern Pintails, and sometimes other dabbling ducks.

Mergansers, eiders, scoters, and the Greater Scaup *(Aythya marila)* are animal specialists and feed on fish or large invertebrates year-round.

Despite the family's diversity, unrelated species often feed in the same manner on the same foods. For example, in winter the American Wigeon *(Anas americana)*, Redhead, and Brant all forage in shallow estuaries by dabbling and uprooting eelgrass.

Body Forms and Postures

The body form and standing or swimming posture of a waterfowl species is dictated by its typical foraging behavior. Geese, swans, and whistling-ducks, which often feed on dry land, tend to hold their bodies horizontally when standing

Swimming postures. Members of different waterfowl groups differ in bouyancy and typical swimming posture. Geese and swans (such as the Snow Goose, top) ride high in the water. Diving ducks (Surf Scoter, center) ride very low, especially when actively foraging. Dabbling ducks (Cinnamon Teal, bottom) are intermediate.

because they have legs placed centrally on the body to facilitate walking and running. The extremely long necks of swans enable them to reach far underwater when feeding. Diving ducks of the pochard and sea duck tribes stand more vertically because their feet are nearer the tail, a requirement for powerful diving and swimming underwater. Because stifftails have heavy bodies and feet placed near the tail, they stand poorly, usually resting on their bellies like loons. Typical dabbling ducks are more intermediate in leg placement and body posture, resembling geese more than diving ducks.

Body postures on land. Geese, swans, and whistling-ducks (represented here by the Canada Goose, left) tend to have large, horizontally held bodies and long necks; the central position of the legs on the body facilitates walking when grazing on land. The pochards, sea ducks, and mergansers (represented by the Common Goldeneye, second from left) stand more vertically because their feet are nearer the tail, a feature that helps them to dive and swim underwater. Stifftails (such as the Ruddy Duck, third from left) stand poorly and infrequently; their short legs are also set back on their bodies to help them dive. Dabbling ducks (such as the Northern Pintail, right) are intermediate in leg placement and body posture, resembling geese more than diving ducks.

On the water, geese and swans ride very high; divers ride low, especially when in an active diving mode with feathers compressed to expel air and reduce buoyancy; and dabblers are intermediate. Divers have larger feet than dabblers relative to body size, as is evident when comparing the dabbling Cinnamon Teal *(Anas cyanoptera)* and the diving Ruddy Duck; the larger feet help with underwater propulsion.

Bills

The bill designs of waterfowl may be specialized for foraging on certain foods, but all are flexible enough to exploit alternate foods when necessary. The Canada Goose has a generalized bill suitable for clipping grasses and taking seeds, while the bill of the Snow Goose is a tool made for digging out and cutting off the tubers and roots of marsh plants. Swans have flatter bills suitable for taking submerged vegetation and straining for seeds.

The bills of dabbling ducks may seem alike but range from generalized to specialized. Mallard bills are well adapted for straining invertebrates or picking up marsh seeds or agricultural grains. The short, high bills of American and Eurasian Wigeons allow them to clip or dig up vegetation on land. The bill of the Green-winged Teal has tiny lamellae, which form finely toothed, comb-like structures suitable for straining almost microscopic invertebrates from mud.

The spatulate bill of the Northern Shoveler has long lamellae ideal for straining aquatic invertebrates of various sizes. Like phalaropes, which follow shovelers and other ducks to capture disturbed invertebrates, shovelers will follow swans and other waterfowl to capitalize on invertebrates brought to the surface by the paddling action of the swans' feet.

Mergansers all have elongated bills, with the lamellae reduced to sharp projections or serrations ideal for gripping live fish and invertebrates. Most other sea ducks have short and sturdy bills for probing in dense sand or between rocks for shellfish. In all waterfowl species, the prominent nail at the tip of the upper bill is ideal for gripping large prey and stripping seeds from seed heads; it is also used in defense.

Breeding

Pair bonds and other social and sexual relationships vary markedly among anatid subfamilies and tribes. Whistling-ducks, swans, and geese have long pair bonds that often last for life, and both sexes tend to share in brood care. In some geese, family bonds may last through the winter and even until the start of the following breeding season. Some yearling Canada Geese and swans, which do not breed, may return to their family groups after nesting is over.

Anatid heads and bills. *Although all anatids share a similar overall bill structure, there are many small variations on the basic plan of a long, broad, flattened bill. Most species have comb-like lamellae along the sides of the bill for straining small items from mud or water; these have reached their greatest development in the Northern Shoveler (left), which also has a very broad bill adapted for sifting large amounts of muddy water. The bill of a Common Merganser (center) is long and slender, and the lamellae are reduced to small, tooth-like points adapted for gripping small fish. The bill of a Surf Scoter (right) is hard and stout, for pulling shellfish from rocks underwater; the elaborate pattern of the Surf Scoter's bill probably functions in displays.*

Among ducks, new pair bonds are established each year in most migratory species that have been studied; this commonly occurs on the wintering grounds or at northward migration stopovers. Ducks of low mobility, like Mottled Ducks, probably remain paired or pair again with the same mate. Males often follow females to their breeding areas, making genetic mixing more common in populations of ducks than in geese.

Most sea ducks do not mature until they are at least two years old. Subadult males, however, may participate in courtship parties and establish territorial areas, although they rarely win mates or complete the nesting cycle; reported displays by "female-like" sea ducks are actually displays by immature males. Subadult geese and swans either are chased from nesting areas or voluntarily abandon them for communal feeding sites; thus they play little role in reproduction but may gain some breeding experience. Some subadult geese may form bonds with other birds of their age and even establish favored sites, but they do not breed, and they abandon the site early in the breeding cycle.

During the breeding season, distribution of mated pairs depends on the social and territorial behavior of the species. Greater White-fronted Geese often nest alone. Races of Canada Geese vary in their sociability at breeding time; smaller races are highly colonial, whereas the "Giant" race is often solitary. Snow Geese and Brants are highly social, yet they are strongly territorial in defending small nest areas in a large colony; they defend feeding areas less vigorously. Swans also vary in how close to one another they nest, perhaps influenced by food availability.

As a subfamily, true ducks are less social breeders than geese, but they too vary in their territorial behavior. The sociability of nesting ducks is probably dictated by the distribution of resources in their wetland habitats, with lesser distances between nesting pairs where resources are abundant. Male Mallards, Northern Shovelers, and Blue-winged

Teals defend territories and females strenuously while the female is locating the nest site and laying, and during early incubation. Males of these and probably most other species abandon females during incubation, but some may remain in the area in small groups as they begin their body molt; this pool of potential mates allows for re-mating, with the same or a different partner, if first nests are destroyed. Aggression and chasing are less conspicuous in the Redhead and Gadwall, which nest almost socially in some places and as isolated pairs elsewhere. Other species, like the Common Eider (*Somateria mollissima*), are highly social, nesting in dense colonies and defending only the nest.

Nests

In dabbling ducks, geese, and some swans, which build nests on the ground at wetland edges, nest-building begins with a simple scrape in the soil or the pulling together of nearby nest material. Species that nest over water, such as the Redhead, Canvasback, Ring-necked Duck, Lesser Scaup (*Aythya affinis*), and Ruddy Duck, typically choose a dense clump of aquatic vegetation where leaves can be bent over to form a substrate; some will use the nursery nests of American Coots (*Fulica americana*) or the feeding stations of muskrats. They construct their nests using nearby material that they can reach and pull under their sitting bodies, rather than carry material to the nest, as many other bird species do.

Duck nests tend to be well concealed. Some species that build in dense and tall vegetation pull leaves over the top of the nest while they are incubating, forming a canopy that conceals the incubating bird.

Mallards, Gadwalls, and Blue-winged Teals commonly nest on the ground in dense vegetation that varies from damp sedges at the edge of wetlands to dry grasses and even shrubs. Northern Pintails and Mallards often nest in agricultural fields, where they may perish due to farming operations. Some incubating females, such as field-nesting Northern

Anatid nests. *Most waterfowl nest on the ground, but the nest itself varies from nothing more than a shallow scrape to a carefully concealed, feather-lined bowl with an overhanging canopy (such as that of the Northern Pintail, near left). A few species, such as the Common Goldeneye (far left), nest in tree cavities, a strategy that requires the downy young to leap to the ground and follow their mother to water just hours after they hatch.*

Pintails and tundra-nesting Greater White-fronted Geese, are exposed to predators due to the sparseness of vegetation, but they are protected either by their location on islets or by their camouflaged color and behavior. Snow Geese, Brants, and eiders also nest on small islands where they are protected from ground predators.

Wood Ducks are perhaps best known for nesting in tree cavities and man-made nest boxes, but they are not alone in that practice. Mandarin Ducks, Muscovy Ducks, Black-bellied Whistling-Ducks, Hooded and Common Mergansers, both goldeneyes, and the Bufflehead all nest in tree holes. More unusual nest sites include those of Canada Geese, which will nest on rock shelves on cliffs or in old eagle or Osprey *(Pandion haliaetus)* nests. Red-breasted Mergansers *(Mergus serrator)* and Barrow's Goldeneyes *(Bucephala islandica)* nest occasionally in ground burrows or crevices. Mallards and Canada Geese nest on top of beaver and muskrat lodges.

Eggs

Waterfowl eggs are unspotted and dull white, buff, or pale olive in color. They vary considerably in shape, size, and color, even among individual birds. Incubation may begin before the clutch is completed. Clutch size varies among species; swans and geese lay fewer eggs than ducks. The number of eggs laid also depends on location, time of year, and whether or not it is the first nesting attempt of the season.

Parasitic egg-laying, both within and between species, is common in waterfowl and is practiced by Redheads, Ruddy Ducks, whistling-ducks, Wood Ducks, Common Goldeneyes *(Bucephala clangula)*, and some eiders, and by Canada and Snow Geese. Because of parasitism, one nest may hold masses of eggs—60 were recorded in one Fulvous Whistling-Duck nest and more than 80 in a Redhead nest. In these extreme situations, hatching success is reduced because of poor incubation or because of increased nest failure due to predation or nest abandonment. The mixed broods that often result from parasitism are cared for by the foster parent.

Egg and nest success tends to be very low in ground-nesting species such as the Blue-winged Teal, Mallard, Northern Pintail, eiders, and the Long-tailed Duck due mainly to predation by skunks, minks, and foxes. Nest success in a local population of these species commonly is less than 40 percent, and in some years high predator populations may cause total nesting failure. Temperate-zone breeders, which nest in regions with longer seasons, commonly lay replacement clutches, but northern tundra species may not renest. Because pochards often nest in aquatic vegetation over water, their nest success may be higher (up to 70 percent), but they too can experience total loss due to flooding or aerial predators such as crows and large gulls. Renesting is much less common in pochards and sea ducks than among dabblers.

Downy young. Newly hatched ducks and geese are remarkably precocious. They can walk, swim, and feed themselves just hours after hatching. In some species, such as the Ruddy Duck, all parental care ends just a few days after hatching, while families of geese may stay together for more than a year. Shown here is a family of Mallards; the young are just a few days old.

In ducks and geese, only the female incubates. Both sexes do so in the Black-bellied Whistling-Duck and probably the Fulvous Whistling-Duck. Males of most swan species defend the nest and may assist in building it but do not incubate; male Mute Swans may cover the eggs when the mate is absent.

Young

Hatching of the entire clutch takes from 24 to 36 hours, and parents may lead young away from the nest as soon as all or most are dry. Unhatched eggs may be abandoned once the majority of the downy young are active.

The imprinting of downy young on their parents is especially striking in waterfowl. While on the nest, females initiate low calls, and the young, still in the eggshell, call back. Downy young cluster near one another as they hatch and demonstrate their bond as a brood by swimming in a tight group.

Waterfowl young are known for their heavy down insulation and their precocity. Wood Duck broods have been seen swimming across the Mississippi River shortly after jumping to the ground from their tree-hole nest; goslings hatching in old eagle nests or on cliffs reach the ground in the same manner. By marking brood members with colored dye or by tracking marked females, researchers have been able to determine brood movements in many species. Many broods soon leave the scene of hatching, especially if disturbed, and select new feeding sites, which can be up to 5 miles (8 km) away.

Waterfowl parents brood and defend the young against predators but do not feed them directly, as the young can feed themselves from the time they hatch. Young whistling-ducks remain with both parents until they can fly, and family bonds last even longer in geese and swans. Typically, female ducks remain with their ducklings until the young are near flight, but pochards abandon their young earlier. Ruddy Ducks may abandon theirs after only a few days, and these downy young show amazing precocity, feeding themselves and diving skillfully shortly after hatching.

Eiders, goldeneyes, and scoters abandon their young after a few weeks; young of mixed ages then form crèches that may be attended by one or more adults.

Movements

Waterfowl species vary greatly in their breeding and wintering ranges, and thus in the extent and direction of their migrations. The long-distance movements of waterfowl are well known; most North American species depart much of their breeding ranges to winter to the south. Not all waterfowl are strongly migratory. Those in warmer temperate areas, where freezing is not a problem, might remain in the same small area year-round; other populations may move opportunistically, tracking favorable conditions. Whistling-ducks and Mottled Ducks along the Texas coast vary in number and distribution but are present year-round; although many seem to stay paired all year, they still may form flocks in fall and go where food and feeding conditions are favorable. These birds probably move hundreds rather than thousands of miles.

Seasonal movements by other species may also depend on conditions in a given year. Whether and how far such birds migrate is probably determined by the availability of food and water. Some species, such as the Masked Duck, are considered erratic or nomadic at the margins of their range, their unpredictable occurrence depending on their prospects for finding water and food. Masked Ducks have been much more common in southern Texas after heavy rainfall and when wetlands are densely vegetated.

High-altitude migration is common; migratory geese regularly move over land areas at altitudes of 1,000 to 5,000 feet (300–1,500 m), and there are records of Snow Geese observed at 20,000 feet (6,000 m) and swans at nearly 27,000 feet (8,200 m).

Molt and Migration

After breeding and in anticipation of molting, adult male ducks, and probably females that were unsuccessful at nesting, become more social and mobile, moving to areas that provide food and protection from predators. Some species that undertake such molt-migrations fly considerable distances to traditional sites with deep water where they can lose and regrow their flight feathers in safety. Among Redheads and Canvasbacks in the prairie pothole region, such traditional molting areas commonly are hundreds of miles north of breeding sites, in large lakes where the birds can capitalize on late-summer foods while the days are still long.

During mid- to late summer, food is abundant, and the males undergo the complete prebasic molt, which includes the simultaneous loss of all wing feathers. This molt leaves birds flightless for up to five weeks, and during this time they are vulnerable to predation. Their chances of surviving are enhanced if they have selected areas with reliable water supplies and rich food resources. At this time many female ducks complete their prebasic molt, started before nesting, by shedding their flight feathers, and then initiate a prealternate molt that produces a definitive alternate plumage in fall.

In North America, wing molt usually occurs prior to the southward fall migration to wintering areas. However, several species of eiders and probably the Fulvous Whistling-Duck seem to molt after moving south; this would help Arctic species avoid being caught by an early freeze-up when they are flightless, while southern species would avoid marshes that are drying. Many nesting female ducks do not undergo wing molt until they have abandoned their broods; others seem to molt on the breeding area.

Timing of Migration

Different species migrate at different times, and the timing of the annual migration varies greatly among individuals from year to year, perhaps because of variable climatic conditions, such as the times of thawing and freezing. Spring migration may differ in geographic pattern and timing from that of fall, presumably because of climatic conditions and food resources.

The smaller western or "Lesser" race of the Snow Goose gathers in subarctic areas for long periods in the fall, and then completes its southward move to the Gulf coast quickly, making long flights with few periods of rest. The birds' migration northward is more leisurely and involves a more westerly route with numerous "refueling" stops—an approach that allows the birds to avoid carrying excess weight.

Canada Geese and divers like the Lesser Scaup also seem to remain in the north as long as water is open, arriving at wintering sites in November; some even remain at mid-latitudes as long as open water and foods are available. Blue-winged Teals from southern pothole prairies and Northern Pintails from more northerly areas are both early migrants, arriving on the Gulf coast in mid- to late August.

The time of day when migration occurs differs among species and groups. Dabbling ducks and pochards typically fly at night after gaining orientation in late evening to set their course. Individual dabbling ducks have been recorded at the same stopovers annually and even tend to fly similar distances each year in their nightly flights south. Sea duck migrations along coastlines seem to be more commonly diurnal.

Canada Geese seem more likely than ducks to migrate during the day, and Snow Geese migrate during day or night. In fact, when the wind is favorable, many species of a regional community may leave an area within several days and cover much of the distance from breeding areas to wintering grounds without regard for the time of day.

Routes

Migratory waterfowl once were thought to use one of four continental "flyways"—labeled Atlantic, Mississippi, Central, and Pacific—that correspond to major topographic features, such as coasts, mountains, and rivers. However, band recovery data have shown that birds do not necessarily conform to such a simple scheme.

For example, birds that winter on the Atlantic coast are not necessarily derived from breeding populations in northern areas along that coast. Redheads may move to Chesapeake Bay from breeding areas throughout the Prairie Provinces of Canada, and others from the same region may winter in Texas or at the Salton Sea in California. Some Northern Pintails from Alaska and the Northwest Territories move southeastward across the Pacific Flyway to Texas, which is in the Central Flyway. Tundra Swans commonly move from Alaska to the Atlantic coast.

Some species that nest at high latitudes are well adapted to cold conditions and move relatively short distances south in the fall. Eiders travel from inland and near-coastal breeding areas to coastal and even offshore marine areas that remain ice-free all winter; at these sites they can feed on large invertebrates. Using satellite radio-tracking, scientists have recently found that Spectacled Eiders *(Somateria fischeri)* will winter at polynyas (areas of open water in sea ice) in the Bering Sea.

Another coastal marine species, the Brant, feeds on estuarine plants and travels to the cool but ice-free regions of the

Waterfowl movements. Historically, waterfowl movements have been portrayed as though birds simply travel north and south within four continental flyways (shown here with arrows from left to right: Pacific, Central, Mississippi, and Atlantic). Based on banding studies, biologists now know that there is also much movement between flyways during both migration and dispersal. Nonetheless, the flyways concept remains useful and is the basis for much waterfowl management. This map shows locations where Green-winged Teals banded in Kansas (blue) and Quebec (red) were subsequently found. Banding sites are shown with large squares.

Spectacled Eiders in winter. One of the last great mysteries of North American bird distribution involved the wintering grounds of the Spectacled Eider. In 1993, thanks to satellite tracking of birds carrying radio-packs, the eiders were found on patches of open water within the pack ice of the northern Bering Sea, just below the Arctic Circle. Apparently much of the world's population winters in this area.

northeast coast of the United States or to Pacific coast areas where upwelling cold waters off California and Mexico produce extensive eelgrass beds. Brants make extended flights over water while migrating. Similarly, Canada Geese breeding in the Aleutian Islands must cross open ocean while traveling to and from the coast of the Pacific Northwest.

Other Arctic species, such as the Snow Goose and some races of the Canada Goose, move long distances overland to coastal wetlands of the Gulf of Mexico, and Northern Pintails move into Mexico or Central America. Inland freshwater species of the prairie pothole region, such as Mallards, move along large rivers to southeastern rice fields and swamps, and most Blue-winged Teals move still farther into Central America and northern South America.

Many dabbling ducks and pochards that breed in Canada and the northwestern United States move toward the Pacific coast via intermountain basin and river valley wetlands. Green-winged Teals, American Wigeons, mergansers, and goldeneyes breeding in the forested wetlands of eastern Canada move along the Atlantic coast to large estuaries and some to southern freshwater swamps.

Because breeding areas sometimes change due to water conditions, travel routes and stopovers also must shift. Banded Northern Pintails have, during years of extended droughts, abandoned former nesting areas in the prairies and moved to Alaska and Siberia, where their survival, if not nesting success, would be less in doubt. When water returns to the prairies, so do the ducks.

A number of waterfowl species also have shifted migration routes, presumably because of changes in habitat conditions. The Canvasback has bypassed perennial fall gathering areas when food supplies were eliminated by sedimentation and pollution in Minnesota and Illinois, opting instead for new habitats created by impoundments along the Mississippi River. The "Black" Brant *(Branta bernicla nigricans)*, the Pacific race of the Brant, has shifted to coastal stopover and wintering areas farther south in Mexico, apparently because of sedimentation and boating activity in California estuaries.

Band recoveries have shown that individual Canvasbacks and Redheads will switch wintering areas from the Atlantic Flyway to the Mississippi Flyway. Such switches could occur if populations of these species mix in northern molting areas prior to southward migration, or if males in these areas pair with females of another population and return with them to their previous breeding area.

Conservation and Management

Many early conservationists lamented that enormous numbers of waterfowl once existed but suffered major declines during the drought years of the 1930s. This brought attention to the plight of many waterfowl species and resulted in efforts by federal and state agencies, as well as private organizations, to protect habitat. Additionally, the development of annual surveys in breeding and wintering areas has allowed agencies to follow continental populations more closely, and to alert wildlife managers to species of concern.

These efforts have resulted in a variety of conservation and management actions, including the elimination of market hunting and egg collection, greater federal regulation over sport hunting, active population management, and public education efforts to foster awareness and acceptance of conservation measures. A gradual shift from single-species management to a focus on waterfowl-rich habitats as a whole has benefited many other species besides waterfowl.

Population Trends

Since the development in 1986 of the North American Waterfowl Management Plan, a continent-wide conservation program designed to restore waterfowl populations, many duck populations have increased substantially. Yet there are exceptions. For example, populations of scaup and American Black Ducks continue to decline, and there are concerns about Northern Pintails and Mottled Ducks. The reasons these species have not increased have not been clearly identified. In addition, the status of many sea ducks is poorly known, as these species are difficult to monitor.

That long-term trends in duck populations are related to the availability of

Scaup conservation. Although populations of many waterfowl species have increased considerably since the mid-1980s, others continue to experience declines. Scaup numbers have declined steadily since at least the late 1970s, and the reasons for this decline are not well known. Currently most surveys do not distinguish between the two scaup species, so it is particularly difficult to determine the status of Greater Scaup (shown here), which are thought to make up only about 10 percent of the North American scaup population.

quality wetlands is obvious. Rainfall cycles have a major influence on the reproductive success and population size of ducks. It is at the extremes of habitat—dry or flooded—that the status of wetlands seems to have the most impact on duck populations; areas that are too wet may produce as few waterfowl as areas that are too dry, because preferred foods are less available and nest sites may be flooded. The recovery of depleted breeding populations also lags behind apparent improvements in habitat conditions, probably because complete recovery of wetland plants and invertebrates is not immediate.

Northern Hemisphere goose species fared well during the late 20th century. However, for some species the situation is complex, as different populations follow different trajectories. For example, while Canada Goose populations have increased to the point that the species is viewed as a pest in many areas, concerns remain about some races that still have low numbers, such as the "Dusky" Canada Goose *(Branta canadensis occidentalis)* of the Pacific Northwest.

"Greater" and "Lesser" Snow Geese and Ross's Goose populations have increased dramatically throughout much of their ranges, largely due to the increased availability of wintering habitat in agricultural areas. Populations of the Brant, Greater White-fronted Goose, and

Emperor Goose *(Chen canagica)* are stable or increasing.

Populations of the Tundra Swan have increased throughout the continent and continue to grow in the West. Trumpeter Swans also are increasing in number following extensive efforts to restore populations in areas where this species had been extirpated.

Natural Mortality Factors

Waterfowl have survived despite predation, disease, and other forms of natural mortality for thousands of years. Their populations undoubtedly rise and fall due to such external pressures and because of fluctuation in wetland water conditions. Egg predators (corvids, gulls, snakes, foxes, coyotes, skunks) and predators on nesting females (foxes, coyotes, minks, hawks, owls) have long been blamed for major waterfowl losses. Despite generally attentive parental care, great loss of young is common due to aquatic, aerial, and terrestrial predators.

A 40-percent loss of brood members has been recorded in Mallards, 41 percent in Wood Ducks, and 80 percent in Common Eiders. Such losses have prompted efforts to control if not eliminate predators in breeding areas. While studies suggest that such control programs reduce egg loss and increase brood production locally, they are costly, and their success on a regional scale is difficult to demonstrate. Moreover, the strategy has become increasingly controversial as ecosystem management and long-term views of wetland habitat management have supplanted a short-term, species-oriented, and regional perspective.

One of the more conspicuous and catastrophic causes of mortality has been botulism, a disease that has had great impacts on waterfowl in arid western areas and that occurs throughout the world. Typically botulism strikes waterfowl during natural periods of wetland drying, when dead invertebrates and organic matter provide a substrate for the botulism bacteria, which release a toxin into the water. Where water-level control is an option, maintaining higher water levels has reduced outbreaks of the disease. However, deep water may also affect plant succession patterns, which are important in maintaining the suitability of wetlands for future use by all waterbirds.

Other diseases affecting waterfowl directly include avian cholera, aspergillosis (a fungal disease), and duck plague (duck viral enteritis). Naturally occurring plant diseases can also adversely affect waterfowl populations. For example, eelgrass blight has created periods of food scarcity that reduced populations and distribution of Brants, wigeons, and swans, especially in the 1930s and to a lesser degree in the 1950s.

Some evidence suggests that reproductive success and the impact of predation fluctuate with population size. In one Canada Goose population, more losses of nests due to parasitism, predation, and nest abandonment occurred at high nesting densities than at low densities. In Snow Geese, clutch sizes tend to be lower when populations of nesting adults are high. In the Blue-winged Teal, at higher population levels predation impacts are high and nest success is low. These observations suggest that losses due to predation may simply reflect rates of annual reproduction and emphasize the importance of a broad perspective.

Impact of Human Activities

Human activities have affected many breeding areas, migration stopover sites, and wintering sites used by waterfowl. Drainage for agriculture has been the major cause of wetland loss. More than half the wetlands that existed when the future contiguous United States was settled by Europeans are gone; though the rate of wetland loss has slowed, it continues. Drainage or filling of wetlands has eliminated many smaller basins and has reduced diversity within wetland complexes. Moreover, some protected wetlands lack the surrounding upland vegetation that is so important for maintaining high water quality and nesting habitat for dabbling ducks.

Tagging. The management of waterfowl populations for hunting requires information on numbers, reproduction, and movements. Traditionally most information on movements came from banding, placing numbered aluminum rings on the legs of thousands of ducks and hoping some bands would be recovered from recaptured or shot birds. Other studies use more visible markers such as nasal saddles and neck collars that can be seen and read at a distance. More recently, radio transmitters have prompted much research on daily movements and migration patterns of individual birds. Shown here are a Canada Goose with neck collar and leg band (left) and a Ring-necked Duck with a nasal saddle (right).

Water diversion, especially widespread in the arid West, has caused the drying of interior freshwater areas as well as the flooding of lower-elevation and larger wetlands, both of which can adversely affect waterfowl feeding opportunities and nesting success. Additionally, floodwaters in certain soils may concentrate natural toxins such as selenium and arsenic, inducing direct mortality and embryonic abnormalities in waterfowl and other nesting waterbirds.

Intense grazing, especially by cattle, is common in many wetlands and tends to eliminate vegetation of importance for nesting; light to moderate grazing seems compatible with nesting by many prairie ducks, however. Overgrazing and tilling also lead to sedimentation of wetlands, influencing both water quality and water basin depth.

Fertilizers and sedimentation from urban and agricultural drainage cause declines in pondweeds in large lakes and in sea grasses consumed by Canvasbacks, Redheads, wigeons, and Brants in Chesapeake Bay and other estuaries. Oxygen depletion (hypoxia) is currently a matter of concern for the entire Gulf of Mexico, with the potential for damaging impacts on all marine life. Acidification resulting from mining and industrial products can also reduce wetland food resources.

Although in the United States lead shotgun pellets have been replaced by less poisonous steel shot for hunting waterfowl, the residual lead in substrates still accounts for about 3 percent of waterfowl mortality, possibly more in some areas.

While efforts to increase waterfowl numbers have been widely applauded, in some cases populations have become so large that they have caused conflicts with human activities. Depredation of wheat and other grains, especially by ducks, and of forage crops by wigeons, geese, and swans do not endear these birds to farmers. Persecution of mergansers and other sea ducks is common worldwide because of their perceived impact on both captive-reared and wild fish. Fouling of park lake water, mostly by Mallards and Canada Geese, and the fouling of lawns and interference with humans on golf courses by Canada Geese are major wildlife management problems in some areas. Control methods include trapping and moving the birds, using them as food for needy people, and hunting them.

In some cases, waterfowl have adapted to new food resources as their natural habitats decline, with unexpected consequences. Snow Goose populations, for example, have increased dramatically due to increased winter survival as the birds feed on rice and other agricultural crops. These population increases have caused the destruction of natural plant communities on the coastal tundra, where the geese breed. Ultimately these "eat-outs" may reduce reproductive success rates and the survival of goslings; they also adversely affect other tundra birds, mammals, and plants.

The accidental or ill-conceived introduction of exotic plants has seriously affected waterfowl habitat. Water Hyacinth *(Eichornia crassipes)*, a floating plant introduced to southern freshwater basins and channels, has eliminated the open water essential for some species and shaded out underwater plants. The exotic Hydrilla *(Hydrilla verticillata)* is a submergent plant favored as food by Blue-winged Teals and Ring-necked Ducks, but the plant soon dominates native vegetation, becoming extremely dense and eventually reducing open water even for these species; moreover, it inhibits the growth of a more diverse aquatic plant community, thereby reducing food for all waterbirds. Invasive emergent plant species, such as Purple Loosestrife *(Lythrum salicaria)*, outcompete native wetland plants important as food for many waterbirds and degrade marshes by reducing plant diversity.

Introduced exotic animals have affected waterfowl in various ways. Exotic fish like the Common Carp *(Cyprinus carpio)* compete directly with waterfowl for invertebrate and plant foods; they also increase turbidity, to the detriment of submerged plants. The use of northern prairie wetlands in summer and south-ern ponds in winter as growth areas for stocked trout creates the potential for competition for food between fish and waterfowl. Zebra Mussels *(Dreissena polymorpha)* now provide food for many diving ducks and have caused dramatic shifts in the winter distribution of some species.

The expansion of species' ranges, aided by human introductions and habitat changes, can create problems when new species compete or hybridize with native species. For instance, Mallards have spread in eastern North America after introductions into parks and forest clearings, and now hybridize extensively with American Black Ducks. Competition with Mallards may have also contributed to American Black Duck declines. In a similar way, human introductions of Canada Geese into new areas have resulted in genetic mixing among races and confounded historical distribution patterns.

Mute Swans from Europe have been introduced or have escaped from captivity all around the world. Free-living populations now occur in scattered locations in temperate and coastal areas of North America. At least one small-scale study has found no measurable negative impacts of this bird on local species, but the topic is controversial because of swans' aggressive behavior toward other species. In addition, Mute Swans feed on aquatic plants and, as populations continue to increase, may outcompete other species for food. The reintroduction of the Trumpeter Swan to eastern North America raises similar concerns.

Aggressive Mute Swan. Mute Swans are frequently admired for their regal poise and snow-white plumage. However, they are not native to North America, and many biologists are concerned about their effects on native species. They are voracious herbivores and can be very aggressive during the breeding season, raising concerns that they might outcompete smaller waterbirds.

Waterfowl Management

Early conservation efforts in North America focused on wetland habitat protection through direct land purchase for refuges, sanctuaries, and preserves. There are now more than 500 National Wildlife Refuges operated by the U.S. Fish and Wildlife Service that protect many millions of acres. Much of this effort has been focused on preserving wetlands for waterfowl, especially during migration and winter. Land acquisition and protection has also increased in Canada, where Ducks Unlimited and government agencies have protected wetlands since the drought years of the late 1930s. Recent government action in the United States has made funds available to purchase land for waterfowl in Canada and Mexico. But currently protected areas still constitute a small percentage of the original area that once supported waterfowl.

Data on breeding populations have been obtained annually in North America by federal, state, and provincial wildlife agencies since the late 1930s. Banding programs and the subsequent band returns from hunters have been used to estimate annual mortality rates by age and sex. These have resulted in a better understanding of population dynamics, which has in turn helped wildlife agencies establish hunting regulations for each species to prevent overkill. The most extensive data, those available for Mallards, demonstrate that hunting can be detrimental at certain population levels and in some areas, but that, nationwide, Mallard populations can tolerate hunting as long as limits are imposed and habitat conditions are favorable.

Various forms of population management have been used to protect declining or threatened species. These have included the elimination or reduction of hunting seasons at various times for the Trumpeter Swan, Wood Duck, Canvasback, and Ross's Goose; reduced bag limits for the Redhead and Northern Pintail; and the closing of hunting areas for the "Aleutian" *(Branta canadensis leucopareia)* and "Dusky" races of the Canada Goose.

Species, Races, and Populations of Concern

The only North American waterfowl species to become extinct in modern times is the Labrador Duck, which was seen and shot in the Canadian Maritime Provinces into the early to mid-1800s; the last confirmed record in the wild was from New York in 1878. It seems that the species was either always rare or isolated on the Canadian northeast coast and perhaps the St. Lawrence estuary. Although hunting and collection of the bird's eggs for food were blamed, the cause of its extinction probably will never be known. The loss of the Labrador Duck was one of several factors that inspired the conservation movement in North America and pointed to the need for international cooperation.

Such cooperation will be vital in dealing with such pressing problems as the decline of Steller's Eider *(Polysticta stelleri)* and the Spectacled Eider, which is of great concern in Alaska and Russia; both species are also considered threatened in the United States. These sea ducks have declined drastically in their restricted breeding areas, but the causes are unknown. Egging and local killing have been suspected. Another Arctic nesting species, the Emperor Goose, is on the WatchList, along with the Trumpeter Swan, Ross's Goose, Brant, Mottled Duck,

Labrador Duck. The only North American waterfowl species to become extinct in modern times, this species was poorly known and was probably never common. The last specimen was recorded in 1878 in New York.

and American Black Duck. The eastern population of the Harlequin Duck is on the Canadian list of endangered species.

Among geese, the "Aleutian" Canada Goose population declined following the introduction of foxes for the fur industry to the Aleutian Islands and is considered threatened. Recovery efforts, however, have been successful, and in 2001 it was removed from the U.S. Endangered Species List. The subspecies of Greater White-fronted Goose known as the "Tule" White-front *(Anser albifrons elgasi)* is still a cause for concern, but data are difficult to gather and assess because of the bird's isolated breeding areas in southern Alaska.

Escaped waterfowl. Many of the world's waterfowl species, such as this Common Shelduck, are kept in captivity in North America, and these birds frequently escape into the wild. Their appearance far out of their native range presents a challenge for record-keepers, as it is often impossible to determine whether an individual bird is a wild visitor or a local escapee.

Accidental Species and Escapees

In part because of their powerful flight, their long migrations, and their extensive ranges in the Northern Hemisphere, waterfowl regularly appear far outside their normal ranges. In addition, many captive-reared birds escape and are reported by careful observers. The frequency of escapes often makes it difficult to determine whether unusual species are of natural or captive origin.

The Bean Goose *(Anser fabalis)*, Lesser White-fronted Goose *(Anser erythropus)*, Baikal Teal *(Anas formosa)*, Falcated Duck *(Anas falcata)*, Spot-billed Duck *(Anas poecilorhyncha)*, Common Pochard *(Aythya ferina)*, and Smew *(Mergellus albellus)* have all been recorded in the western Aleutians or elsewhere in Alaska, where a captive origin is unlikely; most of these records are from the spring. These species are all native to much of Eurasia, or just to parts of eastern Asia. While some of these species are very rare in Alaska, others are regular. Many of these species have also been recorded elsewhere in North America; some records, especially those from close to the Pacific coast, are considered to involve natural wanderings.

On the Atlantic coast, the Pink-footed Goose *(Anser brachyrhynchus)*, which breeds in Iceland, Svalbard (Spitzbergen), and Greenland and winters in western Europe, has been found on several occasions. Most records from eastern Canada are likely to involve wild birds. Reports from farther south are more difficult to evaluate. White-cheeked Pintails *(Anas bahamensis)*, of the West Indies and South America, have been found regularly in Florida, where they are generally considered to have a wild origin. Other reports as far west as Texas and north to Wisconsin, Ontario, and Quebec most likely refer to escaped captives; even in Florida at least some records could involve escapees.

There have been several Florida records of the West Indian Whistling-Duck *(Dendrocygna arborea)*. The Red-breasted Goose *(Branta ruficollis)*, Common Shelduck *(Tadorna tadorna)*, and Ruddy Shelduck *(T. ferruginea)*, all from Eurasia, have been found at scattered locations throughout North America. Reports of these species, and the less common sightings of other species far from their usual ranges, are presumed to refer to escaped birds. The migratory patterns and history of vagrancy from areas where escapees are unlikely (for example, Greenland), however, make some of these species potential candidates for natural occurrence in North America.

Milton W. Weller

Hawks and Allies

The North American accipitrids are medium-size to very large diurnal raptors with hooked beaks for tearing flesh, and strong legs and sharp talons for grasping, holding, and in some cases killing their prey. Their wingspans range from 23 inches to 6 feet 8 inches (58 cm–2 m). Generally colored to blend in with their environment, species in this family lack brilliant plumage. Most are predominantly brown, gray, or black above, often with paler underparts barred or streaked with brown. Members of this family have eyesight that is four to eight times better than that of humans, enabling them to spot prey from great distances. Accipitrids occur in most terrestrial habitats and are regularly seen soaring overhead. Unlike many birds, their long-distance migrations occur during the day, allowing observers to view this spectacle at sites throughout the continent where migrating birds concentrate.

Taxonomy

The Accipitridae is a large, diverse family that includes most of the world's diurnal raptors. They are closely related to the falcons, but only distantly related to the owls and New World vultures. Despite the family's diversity, biochemical evidence suggests that the members of the Accipitridae share a common ancestor.

The AOU currently includes the Osprey *(Pandion haliaetus)* in the Accipitridae but places it in a separate subfamily (Pan-

dioninae); other authorities place the Osprey in a separate family. The AOU combines the rest of the family into a single subfamily, the Accipitrinae. The relationships among genera within this subfamily are under active study and revision; meanwhile, the North American members of this group can be subdivided into five groups based on their anatomy and appearance.

The largest group is the buteo hawks and their allies. This group includes familiar, widespread species such as the

Worldwide Family Features

- 8–59" (20–150 cm) diurnal raptors.
- About 235 species in 66 genera; found worldwide except for high Arctic and Antarctic. 24 species in 14 genera occur throughout North America; plus 4 accidental species.
- Eat mammals, birds, fish, reptiles, amphibians, and invertebrates they capture with talons in flight, often after a dive; occasionally eat carrion.
- Territorial; mostly solitary or semi-colonial. Most species monogamous, often for life. Some species highly migratory, often traveling in groups; others more sedentary.
- Breed first from 9 months (Snail Kite) to several years old (eagles).
- Nest built of sticks and lined with other vegetation. Usually in tree or bush or on cliff, occasionally on ground. Both sexes build. Regularly reuse nests.
- 1–9 (usually 1–4) rounded, short sub-elliptical to elliptical eggs; generally white,

pale, or cream, sometimes with variable dark markings. Both sexes, but mostly female, incubate for 25 days–8½ weeks. Multiple egg clutches usually hatch asynchronously. Usually 1 brood per year.
- Altricial young downy at hatch; eyes open at hatching or soon after. Young fledge after as few as 22 days in smaller species to more than 6 months in large tropical species. Female defends nest and cares for young when chicks are small; male hunts and brings back food; both adults hunt toward end of nestling period. Adults provide food for young after fledging.
- Adult annual survival variable, ranging from as low as 65% for smaller species to well over 90% in larger species. Average lifespan 1–2 years in many hawks, older in some species. Among oldest on record: 38 years in wild, more than 50 years in captivity (Golden Eagle).

212

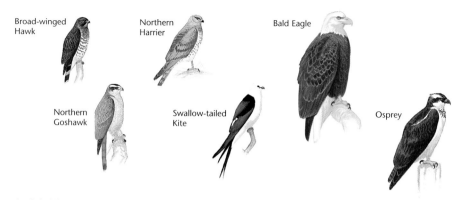

Broad-winged Hawk   Northern Harrier   Bald Eagle

Northern Goshawk   Swallow-tailed Kite   Osprey

Accipitrid diversity. The 24 North American species of accipitrids can be divided into six fairly well-defined groups based on general appearance. Buteos, such as the Broad-winged Hawk, are stocky and short-tailed. The mainly bird-eating accipiters (Northern Goshawk) are more slender, long-legged, and long-tailed. The harriers, represented in North America only by the Northern Harrier, are very slender, with long legs and tail and an owl-like facial disc. The kites (Swallow-tailed Kite) are a diverse group of smallish hawks that feed mainly on insects (three species) or snails (two species). The two eagles are large, bulky, and superficially similar, though quite distantly related to one another; the Bald Eagle is a member of the fish-eagle group. The Osprey, sometimes placed in its own family, is a distinctive, fish-eating species.

Broad-winged Hawk *(Buteo platypterus)* as well as members of the smaller genera *Buteogallus, Parabuteo,* and *Asturina;* the Gray Hawk *(Asturina nitida)* is sometimes included in the genus *Buteo.* In Europe, members of the genus *Buteo* are called "buzzards," a name sometimes applied to vultures in North America.

Accipiter is another large genus of hawks with a worldwide distribution, although only three species occur in North America. Old World members of this genus are often called "sparrowhawks," a term that also was formerly applied to the American Kestrel *(Falco sparverius)* in the family Falconidae. A third group, the harriers, is represented by just one species in North America, the Northern Harrier *(Circus cyaneus);* more harrier species occur elsewhere in the world.

Finally, there are the kites and the eagles. Each of the five North American species of kites is placed in a different genus, but all are grouped together. In contrast, the two eagle genera, although often considered together, are quite distantly related within the family Accipitridae. In fact, The Golden Eagle *(Aquila chrysaetos)* is the only North American member of a large worldwide group,

sometimes called "booted" or true eagles, that are thought to be closely related to the buteos. The Bald Eagle *(Haliaeetus leucocephalus)* is a member of a group known as fish-eagles, which are thought to be more closely related to the kites.

Some species of Accipitridae are morphologically variable over part or all of their ranges. The Red-tailed Hawk *(Buteo jamaicensis)* shows the most variation in plumage and also the highest incidence of partial albinism among accipitrids.

Traditionally the family Cathartidae, the New World vultures, was classified alongside the Accipitridae in the order Falconiformes. However, recent research suggests that the New World vultures are more closely related to the Ciconiidae, the storks, than to the hawks and eagles. *The Sibley Guide to Birds* maintains the traditional positioning of the vultures alongside hawks and eagles because of the strong (even if only superficial) resemblance between the groups. This volume follows the current AOU sequence and places the Cathartidae chapter following the chapter on the storks, within the order Ciconiiformes.

The species has been split into as many as 16 subspecies by various authorities, but much of the variation is clinal. Only "Harlan's" Red-tailed Hawk *(B. j. harlani)* is clearly distinctive.

In the past, taxonomists considered the White-tailed Kite *(Elanus leucurus)* to be the same species as the Black-winged Kite *(E. caeruleus)* of Europe, Africa, and Asia and the Black-shouldered Kite *(E. axillaris)* of Australia. However, new information on morphological and behavioral differences has recently led taxonomists to separate these three similar species.

Variation

In addition to geographic variation, the sexes differ in size and sometimes also in plumage. Young birds often can be distinguished from older birds, and there is polymorphism in some species.

Reversed Sexual Size Dimorphism

Most accipitrids show some degree of reversed sexual size dimorphism; that is, females are larger than males. The reason for this size difference and why it is the reverse of the usual pattern in the avian world has been much debated, but no consensus has emerged. Any useful hypothesis must explain not only why such size dimorphism occurs in many avian raptors but also why in some species, such as certain owls, it does not.

Researchers have established that the degree of size dimorphism increases with the tendency of a species to take other birds as prey; carrion-feeders show little dimorphism, while bird-eating raptors show the most. Thus the Sharp-shinned Hawk *(Accipiter striatus)* and the Peregrine Falcon *(Falco peregrinus,* in the family Falconidae) are more dimorphic than buteos and kites. In the most dimorphic accipiters, the size difference between the male and female of a mated pair leads each to select prey of different sizes and different species, and to seek food in different habitats, effectively allowing one pair to exploit two ecological niches.

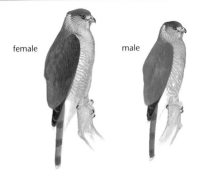

Size dimorphism. *The accipitrids are well known for their reversed sexual size dimorphism, in which females are noticeably larger than males, a characteristic shared by other raptors such as falcons and owls. Theories to explain this dimorphism focus on the mated pair's ability to exploit different food sources, as well as the female's need for greater body mass both to produce large eggs and then to incubate them during cold weather. Cooper's Hawk is shown.*

In the Accipitridae and Falconidae, eggs are large relative to the bird's body size, and producing a clutch places high energy demands on the female. A large size gives females an advantage both in the hard work of egg-laying and in warming the clutch through incubation. After the young hatch, the larger female can better attack intruders; thus females, rather than the smaller males, typically defend the young. However, it is not clear whether this is a cause of reversed sexual dimorphism or simply a by-product of it.

Many factors probably limit the extent of sexual size dimorphism. Among these would be the male's inability to copulate with a female almost twice his size.

Age Variation

During their first year, most Accipitridae species look quite different from their parents. While adults of different species often have quite distinctive plumages, the juveniles are more similar to one another: brown, sometimes mottled with pale spots, above; and lighter with brown streaks below. The Zone-tailed Hawk *(Buteo albonotatus)* is an exception, with juveniles looking very much like adults; only their finely barred tails and a few

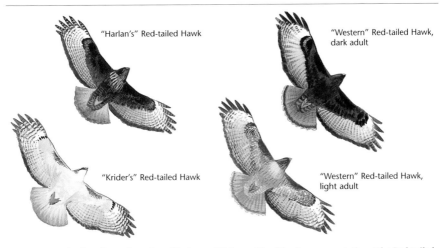

"Harlan's" Red-tailed Hawk

"Western" Red-tailed Hawk, dark adult

"Krider's" Red-tailed Hawk

"Western" Red-tailed Hawk, light adult

Plumage variation. *Several species of buteos exhibit considerable plumage variation. The Red-tailed Hawk is one of the most variable. Geographic variation within the species ranges from the very dark "Harlan's" to the very pale "Krider's" (left). Within a given population there also might be strikingly different color morphs. The light and dark adults shown at the right are found within a single western subspecies.*

spots of white on the breast differentiate them. Older age classes may be identified in a few species. Second-year White-tailed Hawks *(Buteo albicaudatus)* are easily recognized, and the age of some other second-year buteos can be determined by carefully examining molt patterns and feather shapes. Eagles take several years and several plumage changes to attain their full adult appearance.

By the time young raptors reach independence, they often look larger than adults due to their longer feathers, and they may indeed weigh more. The longer feathers may compensate for the extra wear and tear a young bird exerts on its plumage as it becomes proficient in flying and hunting during the first year of life.

Plumage Polymorphism

Several raptor species exhibit polymorphism—distinct, nonclinal light and dark plumages that may occur within a brood. No satisfactory explanation has been offered for this phenomenon, which is found among few birds. The buteos that exhibit it are open-country birds—Swainson's *(Buteo swainsoni)*, Ferruginous *(B. regalis)*, and Rough-legged *(B. lagopus)*

Hawks. Another open-country raptor, the Gyrfalcon *(Falco rusticolus)*, also exhibits polymorphism.

Food, Foraging, and Flight

As a group, members of the Accipitridae eat a wide variety of prey, including birds, mammals, reptiles, amphibians, fish, carrion, and many invertebrates. Some individual species have a varied diet; the Common Black-Hawk *(Buteogallus anthracinus)*, for instance, takes everything from birds, fish, and crayfish to aquatic insect larvae. Other species eat a narrow range of prey. Most buteos feed predominantly on small mammals but will also take other small vertebrates and invertebrates. Accipiters prey mostly on birds and have long legs, long, thin toes, and long tails that increase their maneuverability as they chase prey through the trees.

Other species are very specialized. Ospreys feed almost entirely on fish and have feet that are well adapted for grasping slippery, wet prey. Among the most specialized foragers of all birds is the Snail Kite *(Rostrhamus sociabilis)*, which feeds on apple snails and has a long, thin, curved beak and feet with long, curved claws that allow it to grip the snails and extract them from their shells.

Accipiters hunt in forests and open woodlands and along forest edges; they make short flights between concealed perches, dodging through cover to stay out of sight, then sit in a semi-concealed spot for a minute or more to search for moving prey. During a kill, an accipiter grabs the prey with its feet, extends its long legs away from the body to protect its head and eyes, and repeatedly punctures the victim with its long, penetrating claws until the prey stops struggling. An accipiter does not use its beak in killing, but only for plucking and feeding on prey once it is dead.

Buteos frequently practice sit-and-wait hunting from a perch. They often choose open perching sites, sometimes high on snag tops and power poles, sometimes much lower on fence posts. Buteos take prey in a similar manner to accipiters, catching and killing victims with their feet.

Some buteo species hunt regularly on the wing. Zone-tailed Hawks hunt while circle-soaring in a vulture-like manner;

Accipitrid head and bill. Accipitrids are well known for their strongly hooked bill. This fearsome-looking weapon is actually used almost exclusively for tearing apart prey when eating. It is the feet that are used for killing, carrying, and holding prey, as well as for defense against enemies. Also shown in this illustration, which depicts a Golden Eagle, is the family's typically large eye, shaded by a bony supraorbital ridge. Hawks and eagles have eyesight up to eight times sharper than humans, and they can easily spot prey such as small mammals from a mile away.

Accipitrid foot. The feet of the accipitrids are characterized by strong toes and very sharp talons that birds use to grip and kill prey. Foot structure varies considerably within the family, depending on a species' hunting methods and preferred prey. The Northern Goshawk (shown here) has the relatively long legs and toes that accipiters typically use to capture agile prey in flight.

Short-tailed Hawks *(Buteo brachyurus)* hunt while hanging in an updraft; and both Rough-legged and Red-tailed Hawks will hunt by hovering while actively flapping their wings. Swainson's Hawk hunts rodents and insects both from perches and while in flight. Soaring buteos, which flap less frequently than accipiters or kites, often flap to initiate a diving attack on an intruder or prey.

In flight, accipiters and forest buteos, such as the Red-shouldered Hawk *(Buteo lineatus)*, alternate rapid bouts of flapping with short glides. Their wings appear rounded, and their notched outermost primaries are very hard to see except when they soar, circling upward to gain altitude. Soaring buteos taking advantage of thermals for lift typically look wide-winged and short-tailed, with their notched primaries showing as separate "fingers" when the wings are fully spread. The notched primaries of buteos and other soaring birds serve to reduce drag at the outer end of the wing, which allows them to travel at lower speeds and remain airborne.

Harriers hunt on the wing, cruising close to the ground over flat terrain, wings held in a shallow V, face pointed toward the ground in front of them. They forage in open habitats, such as marshes, grasslands, and fields, and are usually seen in flight or standing on the ground or a fence post rather than perched in a tree.

Eagles and Ospreys hunt both from perches and from high in the air, taking prey in spectacular dives. The Osprey hunts fish by hovering over water and plunging in head- and feet-first.

Kites have varied hunting methods. Snail Kites and Hook-billed Kites *(Chondrohierax uncinatus)* both specialize in snails, catching them by dropping down from a perch in a tree; Snail Kites will also hunt on the wing. White-tailed Kites feed largely on rodents, frequently hovering in the air as they search for movements below, and Mississippi Kites *(Ictinia mississippiensis)* and Swallow-tailed Kites *(Elanoides forficatus)* eat large quantities of insects caught on the wing.

However they hunt, most accipitrids do not reveal their presence to prey until the instant of capture. The Zone-tailed Hawk is an exception. In flight this bird closely resembles the Turkey Vulture *(Cathartes aura)* and may in fact mimic

Stooping. *The foraging methods of hawks and eagles are as diverse as the species themselves, and all species are somewhat opportunistic, taking advantage of whatever prey is readily available. Many species employ a steep dive known as a "stoop" to surprise prey. After soaring high above, the hawk simply folds its wings (as this Sharp-shinned Hawk is doing) and plummets toward its prey. At the last second the hawk swings its feet forward and swerves to capture the prey.*

one. Like a vulture, the Zone-tailed Hawk holds its wings above its body in a shallow V and rocks from side to side in flight. The hawk's coloring and shape are also similar to the vulture's and, in combination with flight behavior, may allow the hawk to closely approach sharp-eyed prey habituated to the presence of vultures. Upon sighting a victim, the hawk continues to soar, maintaining its vulture-like behavior while watching the prey closely. As it circles, the hawk passes out of view behind a bush or rock, then emerges from cover and quickly flips into a falcon-like dive to snatch up its prey.

Accipitrids usually hunt alone but occasionally will team up with others in apparent cooperation. Team-hunting is well documented in the social Harris's Hawk *(Parabuteo unicinctus)*; close relatives form hunting parties to search for, capture, and share prey. Hunting cooperatively allows Harris's Hawks to take large jackrabbits weighing more than an individual bird. Young accipiters will sometimes hunt in the company of siblings after becoming independent, but such hunting is not as obviously cooperative as that of Harris's Hawks.

Primary "fingers." *Most large soaring birds (such as the hawks, vultures, and storks) have long, narrow outer primaries that separate into "fingers" when the wings are fully spread. These "fingers" provide an aerodynamic advantage in allowing the birds to fly at lower speeds without stalling. The Northern Goshawk is shown.*

Breeding

Accipitrids are usually solitary nesters, defending their nesting territories from members of their own species. Some species just defend an area around the nest, whereas others defend a larger feeding territory, the size of which varies with food supplies. Open-country species tend to chase off conspecific trespassers in their foraging range, while forest-dwellers do not, probably because it is more difficult to detect intruders in the forest.

Members of the Accipitridae are generally monogamous. They remain with a mate throughout a breeding season and often pair for life, seeking a new mate only if their original partner is lost. North American exceptions are Harris's Hawks, which sometimes breed in cooperative groups and are occasionally polyandrous, and Northern Harriers and Ospreys, which are sometimes polygynous.

The Snail Kite diverges from the typical Accipitridae breeding system in several ways. The shallow-water habitats required by this species are constantly changing, and it has developed several adaptations to exploit good breeding conditions. Birds may abandon the pre-

Osprey diving. The Osprey, one of the most specialized hawks, finds its fish prey by hovering high over open water, then plunging head- and feet-first into the water. Special barbed pads on the soles of its feet help to grip the slippery fish, which the bird carries to a nearby tree to eat.

vious season's nesting area and move about in response to changing water levels. They may nest in loose groups and roost communally near good feeding areas. When food is abundant, they may nest throughout the year and as young as nine months of age. The male or female of a pair often abandons an active nest midway through the chick phase to start a new nest with another adult, leaving its original mate to rear their young alone.

Displays

Breeding-season displays advertise the reproductive readiness of one individual to another as well as the presence of a mated pair to conspecifics. Golden Eagles and buteos have an undulating flight display in which a bird, usually the male, powers up into the sky, closes its wings, and topples downward for several seconds in an accelerating dive toward the ground, then opens its wings to rise and repeat the process. This display is performed high above the bird's territory and is visible for miles.

Accipiters have a similar flight display, executing J-shaped dives that eventually end with a descent into the forest canopy near the nest. In another accipiter flight

Flycatching. The Mississippi Kite (shown here) and the Swallow-tailed Kite feed almost entirely on insects such as dragonflies and cicadas that they capture and consume in flight. Other species of hawks (and some falcons) also practice this method of hunting, with varying frequency and varying success.

display, the male or female flies harrier-like, cruising slowly on a horizontal plane above its territory, slowly beating its long, stiffened wings and fluffing out its conspicuous undertail coverts.

Some display flights are performed by a pair, as when Red-tailed Hawks circle together and chase off an intruder. After such a display, the male floats down to the female from above and behind, dangling his feet and white thighs. As he approaches, the female dangles her feet in the same way, and the pair parachutes a few inches apart in a stately descent to a perch near their nest. Often, early in the nesting season, this display immediately precedes a copulation.

Calls

Hawks are not often heard outside the breeding season or away from the nest. In the breeding season, they may call to signal alarm or location, to beg for food, to solicit copulation, or while engaged in aggressive encounters and territorial defense. In general, forest-dwelling species are more vocal than open-country species. Juveniles, on the wing but still dependent on their parents to bring them food, may call incessantly when hungry.

Nests

All members of the Accipitridae build nests out of vegetation. Most species build substantial stick nests, and they may reuse the same one for years. Pairs typically have alternate nests in their territory, and they may switch nests occasionally, especially in the year after a brood failure or a parasite infestation. Eagles build huge nests that may grow to weigh hundreds of pounds, the result of thousands of deliveries of woody nesting material over the years. At the other extreme, kites' nests are often small and flimsy because they are built of grasses, weed stalks, and twigs. Kites have relatively weak beaks and feet and are perhaps less able to carry heavier building materials.

Nests generally are lined with finer materials to provide insulation and cushioning and to help keep eggs from wedging between the twigs that make up the bottom of the nest cup. Accipiters line their nests with pieces of outer bark from trees, whereas buteos often use more fibrous materials, such as the inner bark of trees and frayed palm or agave leaf bases. Bald Eagles and Ospreys sometimes use a lining of seaweed.

Buteos are primarily tree-nesters, although some of the trees they select may be very short. Red-tailed, Ferruginous, and Zone-tailed Hawks will also occasionally nest on cliffs, and Rough-legged Hawks in far-northern regions nest on the ground. Ospreys, eagles, and kites also nest in trees, although Ospreys are quite versatile and will use a variety of tall structures, including cacti, rock towers, and, increasingly, nest platforms built by humans. Eagles also may nest on cliffs. The Northern Harrier builds its nest directly on the ground, sometimes under the shelter of a small shrub.

Nest-building involves the investment of considerable time and energy. An inferior nest can cost a pair their reproductive effort for the entire year if it collapses late in the season under the weight of a full-grown brood. A pair typically works on its nest for several weeks to months, and may spend several hours a day in construction. Both members of the pair build the nest, delivering sticks individually in the feet or beak. If they choose to reuse an old nest, they refurbish it with new sticks and lining. As egg-laying approaches, the male does most of the stick selection and active fetching, while the female carefully shapes the cup.

Most accipitrids bring fresh green leaves or conifer needle clusters to the nest during the breeding season. The reason for this is a matter of speculation; the vegetation may provide concealment from above, may serve as a natural "coolant," or may reduce odors and fungal growths. In addition, conifer needles contain aromatic chemicals, called terpenes, that may repel insects and prevent aspergillosis (a fungal disease). Depositing fresh vegetation in the nest early in the breeding season may even send a sophisticated signal to passing migrants that a nest is occupied when its owners are away hunting. New vegetation is often a sign that an old nest has been reoccupied.

In forested areas, other raptors may depend on hawks for their nesting structures. One such species, the Great Horned Owl *(Bubo virginianus)*, begins nesting a month or more before hawks do, perhaps to gain an edge in competing with resident accipitrids for an old nest. Barred Owls *(Strix varia)* often use the old nests of Red-shouldered Hawks, while Merlins *(Falco columbarius)* and Aplomado Falcons *(F. femoralis)* take over the nests of both hawks and corvids. Northern Goshawks *(Accipiter gentilis)*, Cooper's Hawks *(A. cooperii)*, Red-tailed Hawks, and Zone-tailed Hawks all have been observed using old nests built by other accipitrid species.

Eggs

Accipitrids usually lay one egg every other day until the clutch is complete. The energy requirements for egg production are high, and a female may produce up to 30 percent of her body weight in eggs in just a few weeks. To conserve energy, she defers her molt until after egg-laying, and as egg-laying approaches she sits fluffed and immobile near the nest for many hours at a time. Meanwhile, the male works on the nest, copulates with the female, and hunts for himself and his mate.

Clutch size varies with species, food supply, and latitude. Clutches are larger in the north than nearer the equator. The eggs of some accipitrids are plain and light-colored. Exceptions include those of Golden Eagles, Sharp-shinned Hawks, and Snail Kites, which have dark streaks and splotches. Incubation lasts 28 to 35 days for most species, longer for eagles.

Golden Eagles at nest.
Hawks and eagles generally build a large and bulky stick nest on a cliff ledge, in a tree, or on the ground. Here two young Golden Eagles occupy a cliff nest. One young bird exercises its wings, a common activity, while the other rests in the nest. Such cliff nests can be located from a great distance by looking for the tell-tale "banner" of whitewash (excrement) that builds up on the cliff just below the nest. In the Arctic, this banner is usually orange, as the guano provides nutrients for a species of bright orange, phosphorous-loving lichen.

*Rough-legged Hawk nest.
Accipitrid eggs hatch a day
or two apart, in the sequence
laid. In periods of food shortage
the older, stronger chicks
outcompete their younger
siblings for food brought by the
parents. This system of brood
reduction insures that scarce
food goes first to the strongest
nestlings, even as the youngest
and weakest nestlings die. In
seasons of abundant food all
the nestlings may survive.*

Both sexes incubate, although in such highly dimorphic species as the Sharp-shinned Hawk, the role of the smaller male is limited simply to squatting lightly over the eggs or perching on the side of the nest for a few minutes several times a day, while the female feeds on kills he has brought her. Presumably the male's small size prevents him from effectively heating the clutch; also, by trying to squat over a clutch too wide for him, he risks puncturing an egg with a talon. The male is most effective simply guarding the eggs for short periods from jays and other potential egg thieves.

Some species defend their nests vigorously against intruders. For example, Northern Goshawks are notorious for knocking off loggers' hard hats and unseating horseback riders, and Red-tailed and Zone-tailed Hawks will make repeated dives at intruders. Other species may abandon the nest if the area is disturbed during incubation or even during the early chick stage. Buteos that experience nesting failure soon after egg-laying may renest that season, although eagles and accipiters generally do not.

Accipitrids begin incubation before the clutch is complete, producing an asynchronous hatch and chicks of different sizes. Brood reduction is common, especially if food is limited, when the youngest

(and weakest) chick will often starve. In some cases, older chicks may hasten the demise of a smaller sibling by attacking it. Golden Eagles, which normally rear only one offspring a year, often lay two eggs, but the smaller offspring is routinely killed and eaten by its older sibling. In this system, the main purpose of the second egg may be insurance against any defect or accident involving the first egg.

Young

Chicks hatch with a coat of down, which is soon replaced by more down. Pinfeathers start to emerge after several weeks. Most chicks have bright white down at first, but Ospreys, Snail Kites, and Harris's Hawks are cryptically colored at hatching. The eyes are open at birth, and the hatchlings are able to hold their heads up and feed by sight from the very first hours of life.

The female does most of the chick-feeding, waving tidbits of meat in front of the tiny beaks until the bite is accepted. She watches attentively, and if a chick tries to swallow something too big, she retrieves the mouthful and swallows it herself. Males do most of the hunting and bring food to the nest many times a day during the chicks' peak growth period. Females stay on or near the nest for much of the nesting period to defend their young from predators and extremes of weather. They begin to hunt away from the nest area when the chicks have body feathers and can effectively regulate their temperature.

Females will vigorously attack large owls, mammals, and snakes that approach the nest. Accipiters may shield the nest contents from the view of predators flying overhead by sliding their bodies over the eggs or young and drooping their wings and tail downward. Newly hatched chicks can easily die from exposure, and females quickly respond to cries of discomfort from their offspring by shading their broods on sunny days and covering them in the rain.

Nest sanitation is a potential problem for meat-eating birds, whose young produce copious amounts of ammonia-rich excrement. Adults never defecate on the nest. In most species, the young face the center of the nest and then back away from it to defecate, expelling their excrement over the edge. Swallow-tailed Kite chicks, which lack the strength to clear the nest, defecate on the rim, into a large layer of vegetation brought by the adults. Birders can often spot eagles' nests on cliffs from miles away, thanks to the coating of "whitewash" below the nest site, produced by the young.

If the young do not completely consume their food, the female may cache it away from the nest until the next feeding. After each meal, the female inspects the chicks' heads and backs, as well as the nest rim and floor, for bits of food, and tugs and shakes the twigs at the bottom of the nest, perhaps to clean it.

After about a month, the chicks begin to hop out onto nearby branches or ledges. They flap and jump back and forth between perch and nest, gradually increasing the distance they travel until they can make short flights across openings to nearby perches. They return to the nest to feed, then leave again. Baby hawks out of the nest may appear to have been abandoned, but their parents are usually away hunting and are adept at locating their young when they return with food.

After the young fledge, the adults continue to hunt and bring food to the nest for many weeks. The young thus learn to fly, land, dodge, and maneuver through their environment while being subsidized by their parents. They may even begin making inefficient attacks on potential prey during this time. When the parents bring food to the nest, the hungriest of the brood tend to get there first and grab the meal. When the next delivery occurs, the one who ate well last time is apt to stay away; thus food is apportioned among the chicks. The hungriest birds call the most, and adults may carry food toward the most persistently calling youngster. Eventually the offspring start to make their own kills and leave the nesting area.

Movements

Many North American raptors vacate some or all of their breeding range in winter, and every autumn great waves of hawks, kites, harriers, eagles, Ospreys, and falcons roll across the continent in synchrony with advancing weather systems. Unlike many birds, these raptors migrate by day, presumably because the wind conditions that speed their travel are better in the daytime. Indeed, the preference of many predators for daytime travel may explain why much of the avian world migrates by night. On average, immatures usually migrate at different times than adults and may winter in separate areas. Weather and food conditions also affect the timing and distance of flights.

Some species gather in large flocks before starting to fly south. For example, thousands of Swallow-tailed Kites gather along the western shore of Lake Okeechobee in central Florida every autumn before departing for their wintering grounds in South America. Swainson's Hawks make one of the longest journeys, traveling several thousand miles in loose flocks from the United States and Canada southward to Argentina and back every year.

Other Accipitridae species and most falcons travel south individually but are often guided by topographic features such as mountain ridges and peninsulas that concentrate birds into rivers of raptors. Migrant hawks avoid traversing open water, as the thermals on which they soar are less well developed there than over land. They gather in large numbers on capes and other points of land that minimize the distance they must travel over water and will often stall to gain altitude or await optimal flight conditions before making a water crossing.

Most fall migration occurs between mid-August and November: in the East on days following the passage of a cold front, and in the West just before the passage of

Migration of Swainson's Hawk. Perhaps the most ambitious migration of any accipitrid is performed by Swainson's Hawk. This species breeds in western North America (orange), with isolated populations north of the main breeding range, and migrates in flocks through Central America to Argentina (yellow; the exact migration route across the Amazon basin is unknown). The main wintering grounds (blue) are poorly documented and may be shifting north as deforestation creates more suitable habitat in Brazil.

a low-pressure system. During such times thousands of birds may pass overhead in some places. In years gone by, hundreds of migrating raptors were shot every fall at sites in the eastern United States. Today, however, hunting raptors is illegal and the predictable migration affords outstanding public viewing at locations throughout the continent.

Sites such as Hawk Mountain in Pennsylvania, Cape May in New Jersey, and coastal Veracruz state in Mexico have been developed to accommodate crowds of observers. Many major sites also provide important research and educational opportunities, and maintain regular counting, trapping, and banding stations, whose work tells us much about where the birds come from and where they go.

In addition to regular migrations, periodic invasions of species such as the Northern Goshawk and the Rough-legged Hawk may occur in some winters. These northern species often subsist on only a few different prey species, whose numbers fluctuate considerably. Periodic crashes in populations of Snowshoe Hares and voles can lead to major invasions of these birds into areas south of their usual winter range.

Conservation

Over the years, members of the Accipitridae have faced many threats, ranging from deliberate extermination campaigns in which they have been shot, poisoned, and trapped, to such inadvertent threats as electrocution when birds contact power lines, collisions with vehicles, and poisoning from the ingestion of pesticides. Today the loss of nesting and foraging habitat is probably the single biggest threat to these birds.

Between the 1940s and the 1960s, organochlorine pesticides caused global population declines in many raptors through direct mortality or eggshell thinning. These chemicals become concentrated in lipids and are passed up the food chain to concentrate in carnivorous species at the top. Many organochlorine chemicals were banned in North America in the early 1970s, although they are still used in the tropics and "imported" into North America every spring in migrant songbirds.

New threats arise continually. In the past decade, a shift from grazing to crop farming on the Argentine wintering grounds of Swainson's Hawk has led to the poisoning of hundreds of these birds by pesticides used to control grasshoppers. Wind farms in California, which generate power with extensive arrays of spinning blades, have also killed hundreds of birds.

In general, however, things are looking up for the Accipitridae. Data from the Breeding Bird Survey suggest that populations of many species are increasing continent-wide. Bald Eagle and Osprey populations, for example, which suffered severe reductions from organochlorine pesticides, have made significant recoveries. Bald Eagle protection measures mandated by the U.S. Endangered Species Act have been so successful that the species is no longer endangered.

A few species still generate concern. The Swallow-tailed Kite, Snail Kite, and Short-tailed Hawk are all currently on the WatchList, primarily because of their limited ranges in the southeastern United States. The Snail Kite, listed as endangered in the United States, is particularly at risk because of its specialized diet and its vulnerability to changing water management practices in Florida's wetlands. The Gray Hawk and the Common Black-Hawk are vulnerable to the loss of riparian habitat in the Southwest; the Northern Goshawk is considered a sensitive species in the West and upper Midwest, although investigations have found that it does not warrant protection under the Endangered Species Act; and the Ferruginous Hawk is a species of concern in parts of its range where it can suffer from programs to poison ground squirrels and prairie dogs. Other species are of concern locally; for example, the Mississippi Kite, the Northern Harrier, and the Red-shouldered Hawk are all on the endangered species lists of certain states.

Public attitudes toward raptors have changed greatly over the past century, due in part to environmental education in schools as well as television programming that has featured species in trouble. Intensive conservation efforts to pull species like the Bald Eagle back from the brink of extinction have gained major public support. Just as significant has been the commitment of individuals to protect locally important patches of wildlife habitat and the dedication of rehabilitators who care for injured and orphaned birds with the goal of returning them to the wild.

Accidental Species

The White-tailed Eagle *(Haliaeetus albicilla)*, which occurs in Eurasia from Greenland to the Bering Sea, and Steller's Sea-Eagle *(H. pelagicus)* of northeastern Asia have each occurred in North America several times; most records are from islands in the Bering Sea. The White-tailed Eagle has nested on Attu in Alaska's Aleutian Island chain and has occurred elsewhere in that state, as well as in the northeastern United States, during winter. A Steller's Sea-Eagle found in southeastern Alaska remained there for several years and apparently paired with a Bald Eagle.

Two species typically found from Mexico to South America, the Crane Hawk *(Geranospiza caerulescens)* and the Roadside Hawk *(Buteo magnirostris)*, have occurred in extreme southern Texas during winter.

Helen Snyder

Falcons and Caracaras

Family Falconidae
Order Falconiformes

Falcons are compact, fast-flying diurnal raptors with long, pointed wings. Small to quite large in size, they are anatomically well adapted to dashing level flights, twisting maneuvers, and high-speed dives in pursuit of live prey. Falcon wingspans range from 22 inches to 3 feet 11 inches (55–119 cm). Their upperparts vary from reddish-brown to blue-gray to black; most are paler below, with dark barring or streaks. Most falcons can be recognized by their distinctive dark moustachial stripes. Falcons have long toes with sharp talons for grasping prey items, and hooked, notched beaks for killing and eating them. Female falcons are larger than males (see the section on reversed sexual size dimorphism in Hawks and Allies). Caracaras have a longer neck and longer legs than falcons, and long, rounded wings with wingspans of at least 4 feet 1 inch (1.25 m); the only North American species, the Crested Caracara *(Caracara cheriway)* eats both carrion and live food and is capable of long, steady flights, but not great speed, while it searches for carrion. Falconids are generally associated with open habitats such as coastal marshes, farmlands, grasslands, prairies, deserts, tidal flats, and Arctic tundra.

Taxonomy

There are three major subdivisions within the Falconidae: the true falcons (subfamily Falconinae), the caracaras (Caracarinae), and the forest-falcons (Micrasturinae); no forest-falcons occur regularly north of Mexico.

Taxonomists place the falcons and the caracaras together in the Falconidae because of many basic anatomical and biochemical affinities between them. The carrion-feeding caracaras, however, have several features that are superficially unlike those of falcons, such as rounded wings, feet adapted for walking, and a semi-bare face—all results of convergent evolution with other scavenging birds.

All falcons share many similarities in morphology, molt, external parasites, and DNA, which suggests that they are closely related. They differ from the accipitrids in having long, pointed wings, a notched bill, and a small, peg-like bony projection (or tubercle) in the nostril. They are also unlike accipitrids in their killing behavior, using the notched beak as their primary killing tool to crush the neck vertebrae of their prey; in their use of the beak (as well as the feet) when defending themselves; and in the fact that they do not build stick nests.

Falconid diversity. *The family Falconidae is represented in North America by two strikingly different subfamilies: the caracaras and the true falcons. On the left is the Crested Caracara; on the right, the Prairie Falcon.*

Habitats

North American falconids are open-country birds found in a wide variety of habitats, ranging from tundra to southern deserts. The American Kestrel *(Falco sparverius)*, the most widespread species, occurs throughout all but the northernmost reaches of North America. Its habitats include pastures, fields, and golf courses.

Peregrine Falcons *(Falco peregrinus)* and Merlins *(F. columbarius)* also are widespread, occurring in various habitats.

Nesting Merlins range from open tundra to forested landscapes, while Peregrines can be found breeding in western deserts and on sea cliffs, and are expanding into urban areas throughout North America. Prairie Falcons *(F. mexicanus)* are more restricted and are found primarily in the prairies and deserts of western North America. Gyrfalcons *(F. rusticolus)* occur in tundra habitats north to Ellesmere Island in the high Arctic. The Aplomado Falcon *(F. femoralis)* and Crested Caracara are the most tropical North American species, found in open range and pasturelands with scattered large trees and semi-desert grasslands.

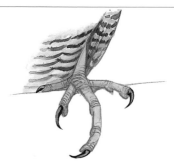

Falcon foot. True falcons, such as this Peregrine Falcon, have relatively long toes, with sharp and strongly curved talons. Falcons generally use their feet to capture prey in the air or to simply knock prey down; in both cases the large feet and long toes are an advantage, providing a powerful blow and a strong grip. Unlike true falcons, caracaras have long legs well suited to walking on the ground.

Northern falcons migrate south in winter and concentrate in open habitats with abundant prey, perches, and cover for roosting. Peregrine Falcons and Gyrfalcons often winter at estuaries, inland lakes, and wetlands, where waterbird concentrations provide a reliable food supply. Merlins winter in many lowland habitats; they are found regularly in coastal habitats, California chaparral, and the high deserts of the continent's interior. American Kestrels from northern states winter by the thousands in Florida, avoid-ing the resident kestrels, which maintain territories year-round.

Food and Foraging

True falcons are specialized for chasing and catching their prey in flight. The larger species usually hunt on the move, taking vulnerable prey that cannot make it

Worldwide Family Features

- 9–25" (23–63 cm) diurnal raptors.
- About 64 species in 11 genera worldwide, found on every continent except Antarctica. 7 species in 2 genera regular throughout North America; plus 3 accidental species.
- Falcons eat live-caught birds, sometimes mammals and insects; generally catch prey in flight or on ground after aerial dive. Caracaras eat carrion, sometimes small animals. Occasionally cache food and kleptoparasitize other birds.
- Most species territorial and solitary, a few colonial. Generally monogamous, often for many years; some species remate seasonally. Generally solitary during nonbreeding season. Northern populations migratory.
- Breed first at 1–3 years old.
- Falcons do not build nests; use other species' stick nests or nest in tree cavities or caves or on cliff ledges. In caracaras,

both sexes help build large, twiggy nest in trees. Often reuse nest sites.
- 1–7 (usually 2–5) short subelliptical to elliptical eggs; base color pale, but often heavily marked with reddish-brown spots. Incubation 26–46 days, by both parents or predominantly by female, with male bringing her food. Hatching often quite synchronous. Usually 1 brood per year, rarely 2.
- Altricial young downy and helpless at hatching; eyes closed at birth, open in a few days. Female provides most care at nest, while male hunts for brood. Fledge at 25–56 days. Both parents care for brood until young are flying well.
- Most mortality in 1st year. Adult annual survival varies from 65–80%, perhaps higher in some populations. Among oldest on record: 22 years (Crested Caracara, Peregrine Falcon).

Falcon foraging. The hunting success of the true falcons depends largely on surprise, and that surprise is aided by great speed. Some species stoop from high in the air, descending on their unsuspecting victims at speeds that have been estimated at more than 100 miles per hour (160 km/h). Other species, such as the Gyrfalcon (shown here), usually approach prey at high speed at ground level, hiding behind low ridges or bushes until the last possible moment.

to cover in time. They either grab prey in flight or deliver a stunning blow to a flying bird with their feet and then quickly return to snatch the tumbling prey from the air. Merlins often will fly low using tree lines and hedgerows as cover to hide their approach. Falcons dispatch their prey quickly by biting through the neck and breaking it; their beaks have a specialized tooth-and-notch structure for this purpose that is visible at close range.

The Peregrine Falcon is a supreme bird hunter, catching its prey at the bottom of vertical dives launched from high in the air. Peregrines take birds ranging in size from songbirds up to ducks, geese, and even herons, but most of their victims are the size of doves and pigeons. In the Grand Canyon, Peregrine Falcons take many bats and are almost entirely crepuscular. Young Peregrines sometimes soar high above the ground for hours, catching and eating dragonflies.

Gyrfalcons and Prairie Falcons capture prey on open ground, surprising the animals with a fast approach. Gyrfalcons take ptarmigan (genus *Lagopus*), hares, and ground squirrels, as well as lemmings when their numbers are high. Prairie Falcons feed mainly on rodents, such as ground squirrels, and terrestrial birds, such as meadowlarks (genus *Sturnella*). In hotter deserts, where such prey are inactive for much of the day, they take lizards, large insects, and occasionally Desert Tortoises.

The larger North American falcons rarely hunt from perches. American Kestrels and Aplomado Falcons, however, will hunt in this way, and kestrels will perch on a utility line, waiting to drop onto prey below. These species catch many small birds, mammals, lizards, and insects; kestrels wintering in Florida even take crayfish. Kestrels sometimes hover before dropping down when they see potential prey. After landing on a perch, they often give a few tail-bobs, a characteristic behavior useful in separating this species at a distance from other perched falcons.

Pairs of Aplomado Falcons may hunt cooperatively. The male drives a small bird into the cover of an isolated tree or large shrub. While the male darts around the outside of the plant to prevent the

Falcon head and bill. True falcons have a short and strongly hooked bill that has a small "tooth" near the tip of the upper jaw (for cutting the spinal cord of prey) and a round peg in the center of the nostril (thought to be for disrupting airflow to allow breathing at high speed). The Gyrfalcon is shown.

Falcon nest. True falcons do not build their own nests; instead they usually lay eggs either on a bare cliff ledge or in an old stick nest of some other species, or, in the case of the American Kestrel, in cavities. The Merlin (shown here) is particularly adaptable; it nests on cliff ledges or on the ground, or uses stick nests as available.

prey's escape, the female plunges in and chases the intended victim until it bolts for other cover, whereupon the male captures it just outside the tree.

Crested Caracaras are primarily scavengers, but they will also take fish, turtles, snakes, and other terrestrial animals. In the first hours of daylight, they systematically patrol the highways in search of roadkills. When a carcass is found, a breeding bird will strip off bits of meat and lay them to one side until it builds a small pile, which it then carries off to the nest in its beak. Caracaras forage before most other avian scavengers are active and can displace vultures at a carcass. Caracaras also forage for small animals by walking about on the ground, especially later in the day, making them less visible than more aerial raptors.

Breeding

True falcons do not build their own nests. The three largest species—the Peregrine Falcon, Prairie Falcon, and Gyrfalcon—are cliff-nesters, breeding in areas with high cliffs that have protected holes or ledges. American Kestrels usually nest in tree cavities, and Merlins and Aplomado Falcons will use the old nests of other raptors and crows. Merlins are especially adaptable, using cliff ledges and, rarely, tree holes in some areas and even nesting on the ground if elevated sites are unavailable. In recent decades, Merlins and Peregrines have also moved into cities, where Merlins use old corvid nests in trees and Peregrines nest on office buildings, bridges, and skyscrapers. Caracaras, in contrast, build their own stick nests.

True falcons select nest sites early in spring, and their courtship consists of spectacular diving displays by the male, in which he streaks toward the ground in front of the nest cliff, then rises sharply and dives again. Most adult falcons vocalize only around the nest site. The young call incessantly after fledging. Nesting adults and begging young give long, wailing cries, and adults give a sharp note during nest site selection. Both sexes give sharp *kek kek kek* calls at intruders.

True falcons usually lay three or four eggs, occasionally more, while caracaras typically lay two or three eggs. Crested Caracaras breed early in the year, laying eggs in January or February in Florida. Their eggs hatch quite quickly, given the bird's size, but the young take up to a week longer to fledge than even the larger falcons. The adults of all falconid species continue to bring food to the young after they fledge and help supplement their offspring's diet while they learn to hunt. Young begin to disperse several weeks after they first leave the nest. Caracara young remain in the nest area for several months, perching inconspicuously on the ground or in low vegetation.

Conservation

Many grim forces threaten North American raptors. Besides succumbing to electrocution by utility wires and shooting, and having their numbers depleted by habitat loss, they frequently must face fresh and insidious threats, including new pesticides and new wildlife diseases introduced by escaped or translocated animals.

However, not all the news is bad. The Peregrine Falcon has become a symbol of successful conservation and in 1999 was removed from the Endangered Species List in the United States.

In the late 1940s, however, Peregrine Falcons began to suffer steep population declines worldwide, even in the Arctic, where human influence was presumed to be small. At that time, all falcons, but especially those that feed on birds, such as Peregrines, suffered from the devastating impact of organochlorine pesticides. These deadly compounds were consumed by insects and became more concentrated in animal fat at each higher level on the food chain. The migratory birds in a Peregrine's diet not only carried high concentrations of these pesticides but spread the contaminants worldwide. Soon Peregrine Falcons became among the most contaminated of all birds, and many died from dieldrin poisoning. Others suffered repeated and catastrophic nesting failure due to DDT–induced eggshell thinning, which caused the eggs to crack prematurely. Local extinctions followed rapidly across the globe.

The Peregrine Falcon's beauty and its popularity among falconers were its salvation. Once the use of organochlorine pesticides was curtailed in the 1970s, the bird's admirers began intensive restoration efforts. Falconers and raptor experts perfected techniques for the captive breeding of Peregrines and for "hacking," in which birds released into the wild are provisioned with food while they gradually become independent. Much of the Peregrine's recovery can be attributed to private conservation efforts.

Other species of North American falcons, especially the Merlin, were also affected by organochlorine pesticides, though to a lesser extent. Today most Merlin populations are stable or increasing, and the species is expanding its breeding range into New England and northern New York. American Kestrels are surviving well in many areas but are vulnerable locally. Populations in Florida and New England have declined, and the species is considered endangered in some areas.

The endangered Aplomado Falcon was a regular nesting bird in the southwestern United States in the late 1880s but had vanished by the early 20th century for unknown reasons. It still occurs in Mexico near the U.S. border, where it can be found in open range and pasturelands with scattered large trees, and in semi-desert grasslands containing yucca and mesquite trees similar to the habitats that it once occupied in southern Arizona, New Mexico, and Texas. Efforts are under way to reintroduce captive-bred Aplomado Falcons to parts of the bird's former range in Texas, using the captive-breeding and reintroduction techniques developed with the Peregrine Falcon.

Crested Caracara populations in the United States seem stable, although they have declined in the past. The Florida population is currently listed as threatened under the Endangered Species Act and numbers only a few hundred birds. Development and habitat fragmentation pose future threats to these birds.

Accidental Species

Both the Eurasian Kestrel *(Falco tinnunculus)* and the Eurasian Hobby *(F. subbuteo)*, which occur throughout much of Eurasia and parts of Africa, have been recorded several times in the western Aleutian Islands of Alaska. Eurasian Kestrels have also occurred in eastern North America and the Pacific Northwest, and a Eurasian Hobby was reported from a ship 300 miles (500 km) east of Newfoundland. Both species have been seen in spring and fall, although the kestrel has occurred most frequently in the fall, while most hobby records are from the spring.

The Collared Forest-Falcon *(Micrastur semitorquatus)*, which ranges from central Mexico to Argentina, has been reported once in winter, in extreme southern Texas. Other falcons and falcon hybrids are occasionally reported in North America after escaping from falconers.

Helen Snyder

Chachalacas and Allies

Cracids are medium-size to large birds found primarily in the neo-tropics. The family has typical galliform characteristics: legs well developed for walking, rounded wings for bursts of flight, long necks, small heads, bulky bodies, and long tails. Their coloration varies, but most are predominantly brown or black, often with pale underparts and brightly colored bare areas of red, blue, or yellow on the throat or face. Unlike most galliforms, cracids have an elongated hind toe, presumably an adaptation for perching in trees, where the birds nest, roost, sing, and do most of their foraging. The tropical curassows and guans are forest birds, but chachalacas occupy more open woodlands, forest edges and clearings, and second-growth forests as long as they provide dense thickets and brush. Many species, including the Plain Chachalaca *(Ortalis vetula)*, the only species to occur north of Mexico, are well known for their extremely noisy vocalizations.

Taxonomy

The Cracidae are most closely related to the megapodes (Megapodiidae) of Austral-asia. Fossil records date back at least 50 million years to the middle Eocene epoch. The family consists of three sub-groups: the chachalacas, the guans, and the curassows.

The chachalacas and guans are rather similar to one another. They are medium-size birds, more slender than curassows, and most lack horny growths on the beak or head. Curassows are larger, heav-ily built birds with stout beaks. Many

species have brightly colored knobs growing from the beak or forehead.

Chachalacas are usually regarded as the most primitive cracids, in part because of their drab plumage and their lack of elab-orate head and face ornaments, which are found in other cracids. Instead they have relatively simple patches of bare skin around the eyes and on the throat.

The number of chachalaca species is unresolved and ranges from six to 17, de-pending on the authority. For example, the Plain Chachalaca has previously been lumped with the West Mexican Chacha-laca *(Ortalis poliocephala)* and White-

---

Worldwide Family Features

- 17–36" (43–90 cm) arboreal birds.
- 50 species in 11 genera worldwide; found throughout neotropics. 1 species in North America, in southern Texas.
- Largely vegetarian, but occasionally take animal prey; pluck food from vegetation or ground.
- Generally territorial and seasonally monogamous, but some species presumed to be polygynous; may be highly gregarious when feeding or roosting. Nonmigratory.
- Breed first probably at 1 year old in chachalacas, 2 or 3 years old in other species.
- Build flimsy nest of twigs, grasses, and leaves, often lined with green leaves; usually placed in dense vegetation 5–23' (1.5–7 m) above ground. Both members

of pair build nest. Do not reuse nests.
- 2–4 subelliptical to oval, creamy white eggs. Female incubates for 22–36 days; hatching synchronous. Probably 1 brood per year, sometimes 2.
- Precocial young covered with down at hatch, cryptically colored; mobile within hours of hatching. In chachalacas and most guans, both sexes care for young; in curassows, female only. Parents feed young whole or regurgitated food for days or weeks after hatch. Young can fly short distances within a few days.
- Adult annual survival little known, but thought to be high once birds reach maturity. Among oldest on record: more than 8 years, 10 months in wild (Plain Chachalaca); up to 24 years in captivity (curassows).

Plain Chachalaca. The Plain Chachalaca is the only North American representative of the neotropical family Cracidae. It differs from members of the Phasianidae in its long, broad, rounded tail, raucous voice, longer hind toe, and plain plumage coloration.

bellied Chachalaca *(O. leucogastra)* of Mexico and Central America.

Food and Foraging

Primarily vegetarian, cracids eat leaves, seeds, nuts, flowers, twigs, and buds. They are unusual among birds in that they will eat coarse, older leaves in addition to young ones. They also take invertebrates such as snails, worms, caterpillars, and other insects, along with occasional vertebrates, such as salamanders and tree frogs. Cracids forage mostly in trees but will take food from the ground.

Fleshy fruits such as hackberries and wild grapes make up a large portion of the Plain Chachalaca's diet. It will occasionally feed on agricultural crops such as melons, citrus, sorghum, and lettuce.

Vocalizations

Plain Chachalacas are well known for their extraordinary bouts of vocalization, especially around sunrise and sunset. Their choruses are a regular feature during the breeding season, but they also occur intermittently at other times of year. Because calling birds incite others to call, many individuals in an area often join together in a chorus that may last as long as two hours.

A male and female often will perform antiphonal duets in which the birds sing in unison, each coordinating its vocalizations with those of its mate. The name

"chachalaca" itself is onomatopoetic, mimicking the loud calls of this species.

In Plain Chachalacas and many other cracid species, the male's voice is lower and louder than the female's because of a curious anatomical trait found in the male. Much of the trachea (windpipe) of the male lies between the breast muscle and the skin and forms a long loop, running from the neck down to the belly and back up to the base of the neck before entering the body cavity. In Plain Chachalacas, the trachea of an adult male is more than twice the length of the adult female's trachea due to this loop. Also, the inner diameter is wider in males. Presumably the lengthening and widening of the trachea changes pitch, much as length and width change pitch in musical wind instruments. The voice of a male Plain Chachalaca can be an octave lower than that of the female. Together with the birds' duetting and choruses, this unusual anatomical feature

Chachalaca head and bill. The bill of chachalacas is quite chicken-like, similar to that of phasianids but relatively longer. The Plain Chachalaca is shown.

Plain Chachalacas in a tree.
Chachalacas are quite social, traveling in small parties that can often be seen resting on tree branches within their brushy woodland habitat. Pairs nest in trees, or in vines supported by trees, often by refurbishing former nests of Yellow-billed Cuckoos (Coccyzus americanus), *Groove-billed Anis* (Crotophaga sulcirostris), *and other tree-nesting species. Typically, nesting trees are alive and covered with Spanish Moss and vines that help conceal the nests.*

suggests that vocalization plays a critical social role for chachalacas.

Breeding

Although many cracids are extremely gregarious, their primary social unit appears to be the breeding pair. In Plain Chachalacas, pairs stop caring for their young after about six to eight weeks, when the offspring are about half their adult size, but pairs remain together during the nonbreeding season.

Unlike other galliforms, which usually build their nests on the ground, cracids place their nests up to 23 feet (7 m) high in trees. Cracids also have smaller clutches than other galliforms, typically with two to four eggs. The eggs are relatively large for the birds' size, and the chicks are well developed at hatching.

Females incubate alone, but in chachalacas and most guans, males help with brooding. The Plain Chachalaca, which nests in April and May in Texas, incubates for 22 to 27 days. Once hatched, the young continue to develop rapidly, their wing and tail feathers emerging within a

week. Unlike other galliforms, cracid parents feed their chicks. Chachalacas and guans regurgitate food onto the ground, while curassows hold food items in the bill for the chicks to take.

Conservation

Mechanized agriculture and intensive land use have eliminated Plain Chachalacas from most of their former range in the lower Rio Grande Valley of Texas. They now persist in Texas primarily in protected reserves, with the largest and densest population at the Santa Ana National Wildlife Refuge. Efforts to expand the overall population in southern Texas are under way, and birds are being relocated to establish new populations.

Cracids are often subject to heavy hunting pressure outside the United States, but even where they are hunted, habitat destruction appears to be more damaging to their survival. Because Plain Chachalacas are able to use disturbed sites, they are often the last cracid species to disappear following the transformation of habitat by humans.

David J. Delehanty

Grouse, Turkeys, and Allies

Family Phasianidae
Order Galliformes

Members of the Phasianidae are well designed for terrestrial life. They range from small, round, plump birds with short legs, neck, and tail and cryptic brown plumage to very large, sleek, brilliantly plumaged birds with long legs, neck, and tail. All phasianids have legs well developed for walking, three long, forward-pointing toes used for scratching earth, and a small hind toe. In many species, adults (especially males) have one or more sharp, rear-facing spurs above the hind toe that are used to rake opponents during fights. Phasianid flight typically consists of bursts of wingbeats interrupted by brief glides. Many species can turn and dodge sharply in flight, but most return to the ground rather quickly after being flushed. The habitats of phasianids are extremely varied, ranging from arid deserts to dense rain forests; the birds occupy elevations from below sea level to above 19,000 feet (5,800 m).

Taxonomy

Currently the large family Phasianidae includes four distinct subfamilies: pheasants and partridges (Phasianinae), grouse (Tetraoninae), turkeys (Meleagridinae), and guineafowl (Numidinae). Until recently the New World quail also were included in the family.

Researchers have long debated whether all the diverse forms of the four subfamilies ought to be included in one family. All the species share key skeletal features, which supports their current classification. Nevertheless, many experts contend that each of the four subfamilies merits elevation to family status.

The subfamily Phasianinae is an Old World group but is represented in North America by several species introduced as game birds. The most prominent of these are the Ring-necked Pheasant *(Phasianus colchicus),* the Gray Partridge *(Perdix perdix),* and the Chukar *(Alectoris chukar).* Pheasants originated in Asia, Indonesia, and the Indian subcontinent; the partridges are primarily Eurasian, but many species occur in Australia and Africa.

The distinction between pheasants and partridges is not always clear. In general, sexually monomorphic and monogamous species are assigned to the partridge group, while sexually dimorphic and polygynous species are considered pheasants. While

Phasianid diversity. Phasianidae is a diverse family that is often split into several families. Two subfamilies are native to North America: The Tetraoninae is the grouse subfamily, which includes the ptarmigan and prairie-chickens (the Sharp-tailed Grouse is shown at left). The Meleagridinae is the turkey subfamily (Wild Turkey, center). A third subfamily, the Phasianinae, is not native to the Americas but is widespread following introductions; this subfamily includes partridges, pheasants, snowcocks, francolins, and peafowl (Gray Partridge, right). A fourth subfamily, the Numidinae, is represented by feral populations of guineafowl (not shown).

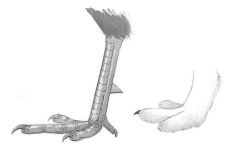

Phasianid feet. The legs and feet of phasianids (including the domestic chicken) are strong and well developed for walking. The feet of several species are feathered to varying degrees, most notably in ptarmigan (genus Lagopus*), which have stiff, bristly feathers covering the legs and toes so that the feet act as snowshoes and are insulated in the very cold environment of these species. The illustration shows the leg and foot of the Ring-necked Pheasant (left) and of the Willow Ptarmigan (right).*

this practice may be reasonable based on the existing evidence, it may oversimplify the true variation in form and life history among pheasants and partridges and may not accurately reflect evolutionary relationships.

Grouse are found throughout the Northern Hemisphere and form a clear taxonomic group. They have pectinate toes, which have membranous, comb-like structures extending from their lateral edges, and feathered nostrils and legs.

Restricted to North and Central America, the two modern species of turkeys arose from a pheasant-like lineage in Central America 10 million to 15 million

years ago. They are large, dark, and bareheaded; based on genetic information, they are more closely related to pheasants than to other galliforms.

The subfamily Numidinae is native to Africa, but one species, the Helmeted Guineafowl *(Numida meleagris)*, occasionally is found in semi-feral flocks in rural parts of North America.

A great deal of variation is found within many Phasianidae species. Perhaps because these are mainly sedentary birds with little genetic mixing among populations, subspecies with distinctive plumage characteristics are quite common. Many subspecies formerly were regarded as

Worldwide Family Features

- 5–98" (13–249 cm) terrestrial birds. (Maximum length includes tail elaborations.)
- About 183 species in 48 genera worldwide. Occur on all continents except South America and Antarctica; many species widespread due to introductions and domestication. 12 species in 7 genera native to North America; at least 7 introduced species may also occur. Found throughout continent.
- Primarily herbivorous, but animal prey often important. Eat leaves, fruit, flowers, nuts, tubers, bulbs, other plant matter; a few species eat mostly invertebrates they take from vegetation or the ground.
- Monogamous to highly polygynous; pair bonds last more than 1 breeding season in some monogamous species. Usually territorial; some species form leks. Several species form large winter flocks, others more solitary. Mostly nonmigratory.
- Breed first at 1 or 2 years old.
- Nest typically a scrape in ground lined with dry vegetation; usually concealed in

vegetation. Built by female in polygynous species, by both sexes in monogamous species. Do not reuse nests.
- 1–24 subelliptical to oval eggs; unmarked white to olive or brown with dark spots. Incubation lasts 14–30 days; by female in most species, male in some. Hatching synchronous. Usually 1 brood per year.
- Highly precocial young downy at hatch, often with primaries already formed. Able to forage soon; attain flight rapidly. Often capable of short flight within 7–14 days. Parental care highly variable: In monogamous species, both sexes usually remain with brood until fledging, although in several species male or female rears brood independently; in polygynous species, female typically provides all parental care.
- Adult annual survival varies greatly among species and, within species, from year to year. Generally short-lived; most birds probably live less than 1 year in smaller species; up to 5 years in large species. Among oldest on record: 13 years, 6 months (Lesser Prairie-Chicken).

Phasianid head and bill. All phasianids have relatively short, blunt-tipped bills. In grouse, head features play an important role in spectacular courtship rituals, during which the birds display colorful air sacs and ornamental feathers that are otherwise hidden. This male Lesser Prairie-Chicken is shown with the pinnae (long feathers on the sides of the neck) laid down against the neck in the normal relaxed position (left), and raised and pushed forward with air sacs inflated in the display position (right).

distinct species; for example, "Franklin's" Grouse is now considered the western form of the Spruce Grouse *(Falcipennis canadensis)*. Not all analyses have resulted in geographic forms being merged into single species. Genetic, morphological, and behavioral evidence has shown that the Gunnison Sage-Grouse *(Centrocercus minimus)* is distinct from the Greater Sage-Grouse *(C. urophasianus)*, and in 2000 the two forms were split into separate species. The smaller Gunnison Sage-Grouse, which occurs only in a small area of Colorado and Utah, was not even recognized as a subspecies prior to the split.

Variation, Molt, and Plumages

Phasianids, with their astonishing array of distinctive plumage features and dermal ornaments, include some of the world's most bizarre-looking birds. This eccentricity of appearance reaches its extreme among males of the sexually dimorphic pheasants and peafowl of Asia and the Indian subcontinent. The Wild Turkey *(Meleagris gallopavo)* of North America also ranks high as a striking example of avian ornamentation.

Grouse are sexually dimorphic, with males larger than females, and their plumages afford them good camouflage. Both sexes of most species are cryptically colored, and have mottled black, brown, gray, and white feathering. To avoid compromising this camouflage, the male's brightly colored combs, air sacs, and elongated feathers remain largely hidden except when the bird is displaying during courtship.

The importance of camouflage is vividly evident in ptarmigan. Molt sequences make these birds snow white in winter, mottled brown in summer, and broken brown and white during periods with partial snow cover. Some ptarmigan populations in areas lacking extensive winter snow cover—for example, the subspecies of Willow Ptarmigan *(Lagopus*

Willow Ptarmigan molt sequence coloration. Ptarmigan molt almost continuously from spring until late fall, changing their appearance to match the colors of their habitat. In Willow Ptarmigan, the plumage is entirely white during winter (left); in early spring, males acquire a rufous head and neck for the courtship season (center); then, during the snow-free summer, brown feathers cover the body (right). In late summer, many body feathers are replaced again by a more grayish-buff plumage to match the fall tundra and finally by all-white as the winter snows begin. The timing and extent of these molts varies by region to match the local seasonal cycle.

lagopus) that occurs in the British Isles (called the Red Grouse, *L. l. scoticus*)—does not attain white winter plumage.

The Ring-necked Pheasant and Gray Partridge have plumage patterns typical of pheasants and partridges, respectively. Male pheasants are brightly colored year-round, with red wattles, shimmering multicolored feathers, and very long tails. Females are a cryptic mottled brown. In partridges, the sexes are more alike, although in some species the larger males can be distinguished from females. Other than small combs over the eyes or other small patches of bare skin in some species, partridges tend not to have special ornaments.

The turkeys and guineafowl all are large, dark-plumaged birds whose bare heads and upper necks are adorned with colorful ornaments used in sexual displays. The bare skin appears to help these large-bodied birds cool down during thermal stress.

The male Wild Turkey also has a "beard"—an odd, hair-like structure that hangs in front of the breast plumage. The beard is thought to be a male sexual ornament; it is never molted and grows continuously from the breast, its length limited only by the continuous wear it receives from rubbing against vegetation and the ground. About 10 percent of adult female turkeys grow a thin beard.

Wild Turkey ornamentation. *The male Wild Turkey is heavily ornamented, with a colorful bare head, skin elaborations, and a "beard." These features are thought to play a role in attracting mates. A displaying male is shown.*

Notch on wing's trailing edge. *The Chukar, like most phasianids, has a distinct "notch" on the trailing edge of the wing where some flight feathers are unusually short. This gives the bird an aerodynamic advantage and allows it to make the explosive takeoff so characteristic of the family.*

Feathers

The primaries and secondaries of a phasianid's mid-wing are shorter than those closer to the wingtip and the body, resulting in a "notch" on the wing's trailing edge. This notch, along with a short, rounded wing and a rapid wingbeat, allows for an explosive takeoff and short accelerated flight before the bird lands and disappears into cover.

Adult phasianids do not grow down feathers, but like other galliforms their contour feathers have an after-shaft, a well-developed second feather emanating from the shaft of a body feather. The typical after-shaft is soft and often downy, and is probably very important in maintaining warmth. Many birds have after-shafts, although in most they are not as well developed as in the galliforms.

Habitats

In North America, members of this family can be found in most upland habitats. Members of the Tetraoninae present excellent examples of how species change from one ecosystem to another. In the far north, Rock Ptarmigan *(Lagopus mutus)* use open, rocky tundra. Willow Ptarmigan occur farther south, where woody vegetation is more common. White-tailed Ptarmigan *(L. leucurus)* use alpine tundra with scattered shrubs or windswept, stunted trees.

Within the boreal zone, Spruce Grouse occupy closed conifer forests, while Blue

After-shaft feather. The body feathers of phasianids have a very well developed after-shaft, an extra feather that grows from the base of the main feather. This structure is thought to provide additional insulation.

Grouse *(Dendragapus obscurus)* use open conifer forests. These species give way to Ruffed Grouse *(Bonasa umbellus)* where the forest grades into a mixture of conifers and hardwoods or outright hardwood stands. In turn, where forest gives way to prairie other species occupy the land. Sharp-tailed Grouse *(Tympanuchus phasianellus)* use a wide range of open country in which woody brush mixes with grass. Greater Prairie-Chickens *(T. cupido)* occupy tallgrass and mixed-grass prairie, especially where grassland is interspersed with stands of oak, and Lesser Prairie-Chickens *(T. pallidicinctus)* are found in more southerly, arid grasslands.

The several subspecies of Wild Turkey occupy a range of habitats across the United States. All subspecies, however, require secure, elevated nocturnal roosts, usually in woodland. In winter, many Wild Turkeys seek nut-bearing trees for food, although they also often eat waste grain in agricultural areas. They also need relatively dense foliage for nesting and rearing chicks. Turkey chicks rely heavily on insect prey; thus females with chicks typically seek grass cover.

In North America, Ring-necked Pheasants and Gray Partridges are birds of agricultural regions, particularly where row crops and small grains are grown. Pheasants are especially abundant in the corn belt of the midwestern and prairie states and in the grain regions of central California, Oregon, and Washington.

The Gray Partridge thrives around small-grain crops such as wheat, oats, barley, and rye, especially if there is short grass cover nearby.

Chukars thrive in the arid American West, particularly where grazing practices have led to the replacement of native perennial grasses by exotic Eurasian annual grasses.

Food and Foraging

Phasianids typically forage on the ground, although some species also feed in trees. The birds obtain their food through walking searches, often scratching plant litter with the feet or beak. Chicks usually depend on a diet of invertebrate prey during the first few weeks of life, but the young become increasingly herbivorous as they mature. Adults are mainly herbivorous, but invertebrate prey remains important to them.

Phasianids have a well-developed crop located at the base of the neck, in which they store food during foraging. The birds then return to their roosts, where the food steadily advances to the stomach for digestion while they rest. Phasianids have powerful gizzards for grinding hard foods such as seeds and nuts; they consume a lot of grit to help with the grinding.

Grouse are more herbivorous than most other phasianids. They are unusual in their ability to digest plant foods with high concentrations of secondary compounds, bitter and sometimes toxic chemicals that the plants produce to deter herbivores. This ability to process the chemicals enables grouse to survive harsh winters in northern parts of their range, where more succulent food is unavailable. The Greater Sage-Grouse, for example, consumes large amounts of sagebrush, which is high in nutrients but contains aromatic oils that can kill microorganisms in the digestive tracts of most animals. Blue and Spruce Grouse eat conifer needles, while the Ruffed Grouse feeds on aspen buds. Ptarmigan eat willow and birch buds and catkins. During the spring, the grouse diet shifts to green leaves and insects, supplemented by fruits and seeds as they become available.

Wild Turkeys, Ring-necked Pheasants, and Gray Partridges feed mainly on the ground. After the first few weeks of life, Wild Turkeys primarily eat nuts, fruits, leaves, and tubers. They will scratch the leaf litter extensively in search of nuts; where populations are dense, large tracts of the forest floor bear the signs of turkey foraging.

Ring-necked Pheasants are omnivorous and opportunistic. Although pheasant chicks are primarily insectivorous and adult birds primarily granivorous, adult pheasants will feed heavily on insects such as grasshoppers in warm autumns. In many areas, Ring-necked Pheasants and Gray Partridges take advantage of waste grains, such as corn and rice, left in fields after the harvest. Besides agricultural grains, Gray Partridges eat various wild seeds and prey on small invertebrates such as aphids. In autumn, these birds feed heavily on green vegetation by tearing small pieces of leaves from plants such as clovers and grasses.

Breeding and Territoriality

Breeding season territoriality in the Phasianidae is complex and diverse, defying simple generalities. The grouse are perhaps most complex.

Grouse

Except for ptarmigan, grouse are generally polygynous. Many species form leks, aggregations of males visited by females only for the purpose of mating. At grouse leks, such as those of the Sharp-tailed Grouse, males gather together, each defending a display area 12 to 50 feet (3.7–15 m) in diameter that only females may enter.

In lekking species, females generally choose to mate with males that occupy central display territories within the lek. This leads to intense competition among males seeking to occupy central positions. The often bizarre and complex behaviors of displaying males include foot-drumming; "hooting" with inflatable, pigmented esophageal air sacs; feather-rattling, accomplished by shaking heavy tail or wing feathers against one another; feather-scraping (very pronounced in Greater Sage-Grouse, which scrape the leading edge of their wings against short, bristle-like feathers on their inflatable air sacs to produce loud, rasping sounds); bowing with arched wings and fanned tails; aerial leaps; and wing-fluttering and wing-beating. Each grouse species has a characteristic suite of displays.

Forest grouse do not form the tight leks typical of open-country species. In Spruce Grouse, for example, males display alone, scattered throughout suitable habitat and without a tendency to aggregate. Other species employ an intermediate strategy, forming "dispersed" or "exploded" leks, in which displaying males are somewhat clustered within suitable habitat but each male still has a rather large territory. Blue Grouse often are regarded as forming dispersed leks. Male Ruffed Grouse defend a "core area" around their display site within their much larger home range

Ruffed Grouse display. The grouse are well known for their elaborate, stereotyped breeding displays. Ruffed Grouse have a thumping display (left) that is performed by rapidly beating the wings while standing on a log or on the ground. Once a female is in sight, the males begin more elaborate display posturing (right), reminiscent of the displays of lekking species.

Prairie-chicken lek. Several species of grouse (such as these Greater Prairie-Chickens) have a lek mating system, in which males gather on a communal display ground and try to attract females, who visit the lek to choose a mate. Activity is usually most intense just after sunrise, with males hooting, shaking their wings, leaping in the air, and performing other displays to try to capture the interest of females.

against intrusions by other males. In all cases, females visit displaying males to choose their mates.

Often a female grouse copulates with more than one male before nesting, then moves away from the display grounds to a preferred nesting area, where she raises the young alone.

Ptarmigan tend to be monogamous, forming a pair bond prior to copulation and maintaining it through the nesting cycle. During this period, males watch for predators while females forage. Females incubate the eggs, brood young chicks, and lead them to food sources.

Turkeys, Pheasants, and Partridges

The Wild Turkey and Ring-necked Pheasant are polygynous, and males take no part in incubation or brood-rearing.

Male turkeys compete for copulations in what is sometimes described as a mobile lek. The males perform gobble calls to advertise their availability to females; when a female calls back, one or more males will congregate around her and solicit copulations by displaying with a fanned tail, arched wings, raised plumage, feather-rattling, and gobble calls—much like a male grouse on a typical lek.

Ring-necked Pheasants follow a different reproductive strategy. Males crow to advertise their status to other males and females, and aggressively defend territorial boundaries against intrusions by other males. Male territories encompass all or part of the home range of several females, and males seek to establish harems of breeding females from which other males are excluded. Dominant males will mate with many females; less dominant males may not breed at all.

Female pheasants are persistent re-nesters if their clutches are destroyed. However, it is believed that once chicks hatch females cease nesting for that season, even if the brood is lost.

Partridges, which generally are monogamous, employ yet another form of space defense, a "mobile territory" or zone of intolerance that moves with the bird. In the Gray Partridge and, less so, the Chukar, once a pair bond has formed the male becomes intolerant of other males and the female intolerant of other females. Both sexes will aggressively defend their immediate surroundings against occupation by other breeding adults.

The Gray Partridge produces some of the largest clutches of any bird, averaging 15 to 17 eggs and sometimes as many as two dozen. The female does most of the incubating, but occasionally the male assists. Both sexes help rear the chicks.

Family Flocks

As the breeding season closes, many phasianid species become more gregarious. Their large broods form small "family flocks" that usually remain together through summer and often longer. It is not unusual for several family groups to coalesce, forming large winter flocks that aggregate around quality foraging or roosting habitat. Even the grouse, which are most prone to being solitary, can form flocks of hundreds of migrating birds. Social intolerance increases as the breeding season approaches.

Movements

Perhaps because grouse tend to be quite sedentary, their ability to move long distances is sometimes overlooked. Greater Sage-Grouse in Idaho will move 100 miles (160 km) between their wintering and breeding areas. In autumn, after the long-distance dispersal of juvenile Ruffed Grouse, the young grouse suddenly appear tens of miles from the nearest breeding areas.

Ptarmigan in particular will undertake lengthy migrations. Northern populations of the Willow Ptarmigan and populations of the Rock Ptarmigan in Iceland and Greenland regularly form migratory flocks during severe winters and move to areas with adequate food sources.

Wild Turkeys are capable of long movements, but they generally remain on their breeding grounds if their needs are being met. Young males remain with their mother for the first year of life, departing, often as a group of brothers, when they become sexually mature. Females leave their mother during their first breeding season to nest as yearlings and disperse farther than males.

Rare Introduced Species

Many members of the Phasianidae have been introduced to areas outside their native ranges. Most introductions fail, but some result in self-sustaining populations. In addition to the Ring-necked Pheasant, Gray Partridge, and Chukar, small populations of other introduced species persist in North America.

Himalayan Snowcocks *(Tetraogallus himalayensis)*, native to central Asia, can be found at high elevations in the Ruby Mountains of northeastern Nevada, where the birds are well suited to survive on the sparse vegetation of the steep, rocky slopes. Small numbers of Black Francolins *(Francolinus francolinus)* were introduced from Asia to Florida and southwestern Louisiana, but these populations seem to have died out. Free-ranging, semi-feral groups of Helmeted Guineafowl from Africa and Common Peafowl *(Pavo cristatus)* from India may also be found, especially in rural parts of North America.

Many other phasianid species, such as the Red-legged Partridge *(Alectoris rufa)* of southern Europe and the Green Pheasant *(Phasianus colchicus versicolor)* of Japan, have been released by private and government organizations, but none of these species has established a feral population.

Conservation

While many galliforms coexist well with humans, others have suffered greatly from habitat loss. Globally at least 78 species and subspecies of Phasianinae and Numidinae are considered vulnerable to extinction. Many of these taxa are critically threatened; some, like the Himalayan Quail *(Ophrysia superciliosa)* of northern India, are probably extinct already. Many more taxa may be seriously threatened, but reliable population data do not exist. Deforestation, grazing, tillage, and other forms of habitat destruction associated with expanding human populations are the primary causes of pheasant, partridge, and guineafowl population declines.

Grouse, too, are the subjects of serious conservation concern. In the United States, the Heath Hen *(Tympanuchus cupido cupido)*, a subspecies of the Greater Prairie-Chicken that once occurred along the Atlantic seaboard, is now extinct; the last confirmed record in the wild was from

Heath Hen. *Ornithologists still debate whether the Heath Hen was a full species or simply a distinctive Atlantic coast population of the Greater Prairie-Chicken, but there is no doubt that the population is extinct. Formerly common in pine barrens habitat ranging from New Jersey to Massachusetts, the Heath Hen was last seen in the wild on Martha's Vineyard, Massachusetts, in 1931.*

1931 in Massachusetts. "Attwater's" Prairie-Chicken *(T. c. attwateri),* a subspecies that once occupied what is now the intensively farmed land of southern Texas, was reduced from more than 1 million individuals early in the 20th century to fewer than 50 in the wild by 1999.

Greater and Lesser Prairie-Chickens and Sharp-tailed Grouse (especially the subspecies *columbianus,* which is found from southern British Columbia to Colorado) now occur largely as scattered vestigial populations. Without the restoration of major tracts of habitat, an unlikely prospect given agricultural demands, these species will probably never regain their former abundance. The Greater Sage-Grouse, once ubiquitous across the sagebrush steppe of the arid American West, has declined severely in range and population density because of grazing practices that remove native grasses and forbs. Of even greater concern is the recently described Gunnison Sage-Grouse, which apparently is restricted to a tiny area and is a likely candidate for listing under the U.S. Endangered Species Act in the near future.

Even the widespread introduced species have experienced significant population declines in recent decades. The decline of Ring-necked Pheasants is due to the agricultural practice of growing large, clean fields of a single crop, with few brushy edges where birds can feed and hide. Autumn plowing, which buries residual crop vegetation and waste grain, also negatively affects Ring-necked Pheasants and Gray Partridges in North America.

European studies have linked agricultural pesticide use to brood failure in galliform birds. Young chicks rely heavily on a diet of insects. The paucity of insects or the consumption of insects contaminated with pesticides may result in brood failure, a possibility that merits investigation in North America. It is not yet clear if the expansion and contraction of Chukar populations in western North America represent normal fluctuations or if this relatively newly introduced species has yet to establish its definitive range.

There are success stories. The Wild Turkey once again occupies most of its historic range and more, thanks to hunting regulations during the 20th century, extensive reintroductions of the bird into areas where it had been extirpated, and "turkey friendly" public land management.

Similarly, the Ruffed Grouse has benefited from forestry practices that create stands of mixed-age hardwood trees with brushy openings. Ruffed Grouse have also been introduced beyond their historic range (into Nevada and Missouri, for example). Blue and Spruce Grouse use mature pine forests, and populations can be harmed by extensive logging. Nevertheless, robust populations of both remain, in part because these species use forests that currently are not being logged for economic reasons.

Much of the Rocky Mountain montane habitat of the White-tailed Ptarmigan is public land and thus probably secure. Similarly, vast tracts of the Arctic habitat of Rock and Willow Ptarmigan remain relatively undisturbed.

David J. Delehanty

New World Quail

The New World quail are small to medium-size galliforms. All have a stout, decurved, sharply pointed, chicken-like bill. Most species have an erectile crest on the crown. The scimitar-shaped crest of six or more tightly fitted feathers in the California Quail *(Callipepla californica)* and Gambel's Quail *(C. gambelii)* is referred to as a topknot, while the lance-like feather ornament of the Mountain Quail *(Oreortyx pictus)* is often called a plume. New World quail have short necks and tails and round breasts. Long tail coverts and flank plumage contribute to the birds' plump appearance. Their short, rounded wings give quail the capacity for explosive takeoffs and rapid bursts of flight. All species have featherless tarsi and legs well developed for walking and running. They use their three long, forward-pointing toes for scratching the earth and leaf litter when foraging. These birds are highly terrestrial, usually occupying brushy habitats and other low, dense foliage.

Taxonomy

The relationship of New World quail to other galliforms is unresolved. Most current treatments give the New World quail family status based on morphologic and genetic characteristics. The family, Odontophoridae, is named for the serrations on the lower beak, a trait absent among other galliforms. The New World quail also lack the tarsal spurs found in some phasianids.

Past treatments often classified New World quail as a subfamily (Odontophorinae) within the large family Phasianidae (grouse, turkeys, pheasants, and partridges). This, together with the shared use of the name "quail" to describe a multitude of small, short-necked, short-tailed Old World phasianid species, has led to confusion about relationships. Old World quail—such as the Common Quail *(Coturnix coturnix)* of Eurasia—are part of the partridge complex and are more closely related to such phasianid species as the Gray Partridge *(Perdix perdix)* than to any New World quail.

Habitats

The six quail species found north of Mexico use brushy habitats. The precise nature of these habitats varies considerably, even within the range of a single species. The Mountain Quail, for example, uses the moist western slopes of the Sierra Nevada and Cascade Mountains; the arid, high-elevation brush on the eastern slopes of these ranges and the Great Basin mountains; mixed desert scrub in the Mojave Desert; and chaparral in southern California. In each case, the presence of dense brush appears critical, but apart from that general requirement, the Mountain Quail is not associated with any specific plant community.

If brushy edges remain around cultivated fields, the California Quail adapts well to agricultural settings in which irrigation water is brought into arid lands. The wide distribution of the Northern Bobwhite *(Colinus virginianus)* is a tribute to its ability to use a range of plant communities; however, the bird must have early successional forbs and brush for food and cover. These requirements are

Odontophorid diversity. *The New World quail are represented in North America by six species in four genera. All have striking but cryptic patterns. Three species have distinctive head ornaments, as shown by the California Quail (left). The Montezuma Quail (right) is a more intricately patterned species with bold facial markings.*

met in the desert scrub of eastern Texas, the open pine forests of the American Southeast, and wherever row-crop agriculture creates small fields with brushy edges. Gambel's Quail and the Scaled Quail *(Callipepla squamata)* also use desert scrub effectively.

The Montezuma Quail *(Cyrtonyx montezumae)* is perhaps more of a habitat specialist. It relies heavily on underground bulbs and tubers found in dense grass and open pine-oak scrub at mid- to high elevations in the American Southwest. Because the Montezuma Quail can dig for moist bulbs during dry months, it does not need to have free water within its home range.

Despite the ability of North American quail to occupy arid environments, all require seasonal precipitation, which appears to cue the birds to reproduce, especially in desert habitats. More than 50 years ago, observers first noted that Northern Bobwhites in eastern Texas reproduced more prolifically after abundant spring rains. The Scaled Quail breeds in summer rather than spring, following the summer rains characteristic of its Chihuahuan Desert habitat. The Montezuma Quail also breeds after summer rains.

Robust reproduction following spring rains is regularly seen among California and Mountain Quail, and probably occurs in Gambel's Quail as well. Scientists seeking to explain this phenomenon have recently advanced the hypothesis that female quail respond physiologically to plant pigments in their diet when fresh green vegetation becomes available after desert rains.

Food and Foraging

New World quail are scratchers and diggers. Most of their foraging occurs on the ground, though they occasionally take food from trees and bushes. The birds are expert at sifting through plant litter and loose soil, using sideways kicking motions to expose seeds and insects. They also tear pieces of leaves and flowers from living plants, and they jump up and grab hanging fruits and seeds. Several species dig for underground bulbs and tubers using the long claws of their front toes.

Prior to and during the breeding season, New World quail incorporate a large

Worldwide Family Features

- 7–15" (18–37 cm) terrestrial birds.
- About 31 species in 9 genera worldwide; native to New World only, but some species introduced elsewhere. 6 species in 4 genera occur in North America, where family is found throughout much of U.S. and just reaches southern Canada.
- Eat mainly plant foods, especially seeds, but also forb and grass leaves, flowers, fruit, nuts, roots, tubers. Also often eat invertebrates, such as insects. Peck food off ground and vegetation.
- Usually labeled monogamous, but polygyny and polyandry increasingly reported; mostly seasonal pair bonds. Highly social and gregarious, except during breeding season, when pairs do not tolerate other adults; not territorial. Generally nonmigratory.
- Breed first at 1 year old.
- Nest is scrape on ground lined with vegetation, usually placed in dense vegetation with thick overhead cover;

some species build canopy over nest. Both sexes build nest, which birds do not reuse.
- 3–15 oval to subelliptical or short pyriform eggs that are white, cream, buff, or reddish; spotted brown or reddish in some species. Depending on mating system, either parent incubates for 21–26 days, though 16 to perhaps 30 days in poorly studied tropical species. Hatching synchronous. 1–3 broods per year.
- Highly precocial young downy at hatch; juvenal plumage begins erupting within days. Walk and forage within hours; capable of short flights within 14 days. Both parents provide care.
- High mortality rate at all ages; among northern species, adult annual survival 20–40%. Longevity not well studied, but average probably less than 1 year. Among oldest on record: 6 years, 11 months (California Quail).

New World quail foot. *Members of the Odontophoridae are characterized by relatively short legs and chicken-like feet. They lack the tarsal spur found on the males of many phasianid species. Gambel's Quail is shown.*

percentage of green vegetation into their diet and also consume insects, flowers, and new fruits. The proportion of animal food taken varies greatly among species. For example, Mountain Quail are highly herbivorous year-round, even as chicks, while the adult Montezuma Quail forages heavily on insects during moist months. In the Northern Bobwhite, as in most New World quail species, the chicks' diet is composed largely of insects, and insects remain an important food source for breeding adults.

As summer advances, most species rely increasingly on the seeds of forbs and shrubs and, in agricultural settings, on waste grain. Northern Bobwhites probably expanded northward with the advent of small-grain agriculture in the Midwest, only to retreat southward again as agriculture modernized.

New World quail bill. *The short, chicken-like bill of the New World quail is similar to that of the phasianids, but close inspection reveals tiny serrations near the tip of the lower bill, presumably used in cutting vegetation. The serrations are not found in phasianids. The bill of the Mountain Quail is shown.*

Sociality

New World quail are gregarious, typically found in groups except when nesting. After the young hatch, social groups called coveys form. Usually coveys consist of one or two adults and their chicks, but in years of poor reproduction coveys may consist of birds from various families. The mixing of families continues as the breeding season progresses into autumn and winter. Coveys also merge to form large flocks, especially around food sources.

The degree to which coveys merge varies considerably among species. For example, winter flocks of more than 1,000 California Quail have been reported, while flocks of Mountain Quail usually contain no more than 10 to 20 individuals. Northern Bobwhites usually roost on the ground, often in a tight circle of 5 to 15 outward-facing birds. Roosting coveys may be essential for survival in this species, since lone bobwhites may not generate enough warmth to survive a cold night.

Breeding

Although New World quail traditionally have been considered monogamous, it now appears that their mating patterns are more complex. Even the well-studied Northern Bobwhite has provided researchers with some surprises. Perhaps the most interesting is that incubation and chick-rearing by Northern Bobwhite males is far more common than previously thought. The species was studied for more than 100 years before this was recognized.

Researchers are now observing male incubation, polygyny, and polyandry, and have even noted parents ceasing to care for half-grown broods in favor of renesting. New World quail appear to possess complex and flexible mating behaviors, which allow them to adjust to the availability of mates and prevailing environmental conditions in order to maximize their annual reproduction.

Vocalizations and Displays

Male New World quail use distinct vocalizations during the breeding season—for example, the *bob WHITE* whistle of the Northern Bobwhite or the crowing of the Mountain Quail. Unmated males call frequently, presumably advertising for a female. But even mated males will call, a behavior that may help maintain the pair bond. Males give these loud calls from prominent perches and are intolerant of one another. Nevertheless, New World quail generally do not defend fixed spaces during the breeding season the way highly territorial birds do.

Little is known about the breeding displays of most New World quail. Often these displays occur in the concealment of heavy cover, where they are difficult to observe. Studies of captive birds have provided most of our current information. Unmated Mountain Quail males will display in front of a female by strutting, puffing their body feathers, fanning their tails, and cupping their wings.

Both male and female Mountain Quail perform a ritualized nesting display called straw-tossing, in which they throw small bits of vegetation into the air. Both sexes also perform an unusual display in which they crouch low at the feet of a potential mate, apparently in ritualized submission. Many New World quail

Mountain Quail courtship display. One of the most interesting displays of the Mountain Quail (not known in any other species) is the stand/crouch display shown here. One bird crouches flat on the ground, hiding its contrasting flank markings, while the other stands above it. This display is used in courtship; both males and females will assume either position.

perform "tidbitting," in which an adult, usually a male, picks and dabbles with food and ruffles its feathers in front of a potential mate. In some species, especially those of the tropics, males and females sing duets with each other.

Movements

In general, New World quail are highly sedentary. They thrive in habitats where summer and winter food, water, and protective cover lie near one another. The Mountain Quail is less sedentary than other North American quail due to its summertime use of mountain habitat that becomes covered with snow in winter. Mountain Quail make annual elevational migrations, descending below the snow line during the winter months and returning to higher habitats each spring to breed, moving 20 miles (32 km) or more in the process. The Montezuma Quail is also thought to make periodic elevational movements.

Conservation

Robust populations of all six North American species exist. Nevertheless, several species are declining in portions of their range due to changes in land use. Significant reductions in population densities of Northern Bobwhites have been linked to large-scale agricultural changes that reduce the amount of weedy vegetation found around fields throughout the southern United States, changes in forestry practices, and the invasion of fire ants, which disrupt incubation by adults and may kill young chicks.

Mountain Quail numbers declined severely during the 20th century in the intermountain West, probably because of changes in range conditions following heavy grazing and concomitant changes in fire regimes. The Montezuma Quail is very sensitive to overgrazing and has declined throughout its limited range in the United States.

David J. Delehanty

Rails, Gallinules, and Coots

The rallids are small to medium-size, short-tailed, stubby-winged birds that are mostly solitary and shy. Rails have laterally compressed bodies and are marked with black, grays, and browns that range from rich rufous to dusky olive to light buff. Coots, moorhens, and gallinules range in color from pale grayish (juveniles) to purple or black, and are more easily seen than rails. Coots are much plumper and more gregarious than the other species. In North America, rallids are found in wetland habitats ranging from saltmarsh and mangroves to mountain lake vegetation.

Taxonomy

The Rallidae is by far the largest family in the order Gruiformes. Within the order relationships are not well known, but the rallids are often grouped close to the other North American gruiforms—the cranes and the Limpkin *(Aramus guarauna)*. Recent DNA–DNA hybridization studies, however, suggest that rallids are quite different from all other families in the order.

Various arrangements of species within the family have been proposed, some with up to five subfamilies. However, differences are small, and the AOU does not recognize any subfamilies.

Among North American species, only the classification of the King Rail *(Rallus elegans)* and the Clapper Rail *(R. longirostris)*

Rallid diversity. The nine North American species of rallids are placed in seven genera. Relationships among genera are poorly known, but the family is usually separated into three groups based on general appearance and behavior. The rails and crakes (such as the King Rail, top left) are much more secretive than the coots (American Coot, bottom). Moorhens and gallinules (Purple Gallinule, top right) are intermediate between the two groups.

is controversial. Some experts maintain that they are two species; others, that they are subspecies of one form. There are differences in size, plumage, and voice, as well as habitat choice, but observers can find the two species very difficult to distinguish. Mitochondrial DNA studies have also found only small differences between these two rails, and hybrids occur where the two species' ranges overlap.

Adaptations to Lifestyle

Rallids are well suited to their wetland habitats. North American rails are cryptically colored and blend into their surroundings. When one views a rail head-on, it becomes clear how the expression "thin as a rail" originated. The laterally compressed bodies of rails enable them to move about nimbly in dense marsh vegetation, squeezing among stems without rustling the plants; such movements would give a bird's position away to predators.

To facilitate movement in dense vegetation, members of this family place one foot directly in front of the other and so leave a single line of tracks. Their dense habitat also explains the frequent and loud vocalizations the birds perform in establishing their territories; in densely vegetated conditions birds cannot communicate visually and must call regularly.

Though rallids seem to be weak fliers when flushed, they are notorious for straying well beyond their normal range, and members of some populations migrate great distances—perhaps a response to the ephemeral habitats in which they reside.

The abnormally large clutch sizes and semi-precocial chicks, which allow members of this family to produce as many young as they can as quickly as possible, also may have evolved in response to the vulnerability of their habitat.

Food and Foraging

Rallids are opportunistic omnivores. They mostly eat a wide variety of invertebrates and plant matter but will also eat small vertebrates and carrion. Gallinules and coots may feed on berries and fruit and are generally more vegetarian than rails. Soras *(Porzana carolina)* have been seen working heads of grass stems through their bills, removing seeds as they go.

What rallids eat, and how much, depends largely on the time of year and what is available seasonally. They eat more plant matter during the winter and more animal matter in the warmer months. A study of the diet of King Rails revealed that 95 percent of their food in spring was animal matter, compared to 58 percent in winter. Ornithologists believe that adults feed the young mostly

"Thin as a rail." The bodies of rails are laterally compressed (flattened), and the feathers can be held tightly against the body when necessary to allow the bird to slip easily through very narrow spaces. The Clapper Rail is shown.

animal food, but little information is available.

Rallids can be active throughout the day, but some are mostly crepuscular or nocturnal. Many rails feed during the day in areas where they can remain out of sight. The longer-billed rails probe while the smaller-billed species peck at water, plant, and mud surfaces. Some observers believe that rails use the pathways of mice

Worldwide Family Features

- 5–25" (13–63 cm) mostly marsh birds, although some species terrestrial.
- About 143 species in 34 genera worldwide; absent only from Arctic and Antarctic. 9 species in 7 genera breed in North America; occur from west-central Canada through Maritimes south to U.S.–Mexico border; plus about 5 accidental species and 1 escapee.
- Omnivorous: feed on wide variety of plant and animal matter, by probing or pecking.
- Highly territorial; vocalize frequently and, in some cases, persistently in breeding season to define territory boundaries. Generally form seasonal, monogamous pair bonds, but some species polygynous or polyandrous. Cooperative breeding found in several species. A few species mate for life. Many temperate species migratory; tend to wander far. Most tropical species nonmigratory.
- Breed first usually at 1 year old, some tropical species after as little as 6 months.

- Cup- or dome-shaped nests built from vegetation in nest area, usually on ground or over water; constructed by both sexes or female alone. Occasionally use old nests of other bird species.
- 1–18 (typically 5–10) subelliptical to oval eggs; range from off-white to brown, with blotches or spotting. Intraspecific brood parasitism in some species. Incubation 13–34 days; often performed by both sexes, sometimes just female. In many species, male incubates during day and female at night. Hatching can be synchronous or asynchronous. 1–3 broods per year, sometimes more in tropical species.
- Semi-precocial young are downy; entirely or mostly black. In most species, both parents feed young. Fledge at 19 days to 10 weeks.
- Adult annual survival 50–88% in the few species studied. Among oldest on record: 22 years, 4 months (American Coot).

when foraging in dense vegetation, but little is actually known about their foraging patterns.

Coots, gallinules, and moorhens spend more time out in the open than rails, and coots will gather in large flocks on open bodies of water to feed. Coots are highly aggressive and will steal food from dabbling ducks and even from humans at campsites. They are the only members of this family that regularly dive for their food, reaching depths of 3 to 6 feet (1–2 m).

Breeding

Most rallids are thought to form monogamous pair bonds that last for the breeding season, though only in coots and gallinules have the processes of courtship and pair-bonding been well studied. Pair bonds of the Common Moorhen *(Gallinula chloropus)* are usually seasonal but can last for several years. In other cases, Common Moorhens may breed cooperatively, with two females sharing a nest and a male partner, or in polyandrous trios. Polygyny has also been observed in captive Yellow Rails *(Coturnicops noveboracensis)*.

Members of the Rallidae are territorial through the breeding season, and some may extend the maintenance of their territories longer. Rallids fight with each other on occasion, especially if one member of a species intrudes on another member's territory. They utter growls and

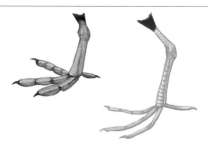

Rallid feet. The feet of the American Coot (left) and the Purple Gallinule (right) show the range of variation in the family. The lobed toes of the coots (with fleshy flanges mainly along the inside of each toe) are unique in this family, but the grebes and the phalaropes have a similar foot structure. The Purple Gallinule, the Common Moorhen, and all rails have long, slender toes with a long hind toe; the toes are especially elongated in the Purple Gallinule, which spends much time walking on floating vegetation.

assume an antagonistic posture, with tail cocked and wings spread over the back, to try to drive out unwelcome visitors.

Most rallid species probably attempt two broods; however, the American Coot *(Fulica americana)* usually has only one, and the Common Moorhen may attempt as many as three. Intraspecific brood parasitism occurs quite often in Common Moorhens.

Vocalizations and Displays

Most rails communicate primarily by vocalizations rather than through visual displays, which would be difficult to see in their densely vegetated habitats. Some species call throughout the year, while others remain mostly silent except during the breeding season. At the start of the breeding season, calling intensifies as territory boundaries are formed.

Copulation is often preceded by a male or female bird chasing the other. The male Virginia Rail *(Rallus limicola)* dances around the female with the head extended and the wings held high. The male King Rail circles the female with the tail cocked, while puffing out its white undertail coverts. Purple Gallinule *(Porphyrula martinica)* pairs perform a combination of bowing and swaying moves during their courtship.

Rallid heads and bills. The bills of the American Coot (left) and the Clapper Rail (right) show the range of variation in the family. Rails of the genus Rallus (such as the Clapper Rail) have relatively long bills, while other species in the family have short or triangular bills like that of the American Coot.

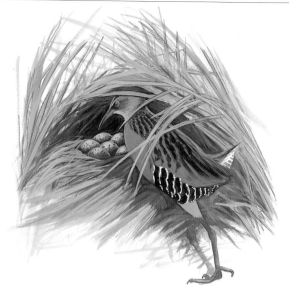

Virginia Rail approaching nest. Nesting rallids usually build a platform of grass and reeds on the ground, hidden among vegetation. The birds often pull together overhanging grasses and weave them over the nest to create a canopy, and some species lay down material to form an "entrance ramp." The more aquatic species, such as American Coots, often nest over water, weaving together emergent plant stems. Common Moorhens will even nest in trees on occasion.

Coots and moorhens may court while in the water but usually copulate on land. Many species of Rallidae display their boldly patterned flanks or contrasting undertail covert feathers during courtship rituals. Feeding of the female by the male and vice versa is common. Most species also allopreen.

Nests

Solitary nesters, rallids do not form colonies, though they may have small territories. Common Moorhen pairs nest in close proximity, often within 25 to 30 feet (8 m) of each other. Males of many species choose where the nest will be constructed, and nests are often hidden in areas of dense wetland vegetation, usually a short distance from water. They are made of plant material found in and around the nest site and are bowl-shaped, well lined with grasses, and sometimes quite deep.

Some species build ramps up to the nest entrance, and some build floating nests. Black *(Laterallus jamaicensis)* and Yellow Rails build dome nests with a canopy to cover them.

Eggs and Young

North American rallids usually lay 5 to 12 spotted eggs that vary in color from off-white to brown. Some 24 to 48 hours

may elapse between the laying of one egg and the next. Nesting females will replace clutches as many as four times after losing eggs to predators or flooding.

Incubation often begins early in the laying sequence, causing chicks to hatch asynchronously. In Soras the oldest chicks may hatch two weeks before the last egg, resulting in young of very different sizes. Since not all chicks must be fed at once, the parents can concentrate on a few birds at a time, rather than struggling to satisfy all of them simultaneously.

The semi-precocial rallid chicks hatch in all-black or mostly black down. After one to three days, they are capable of leaving the nest for short forays. American Coot hatchlings with more conspicuous head plumes than their siblings are fed more frequently by their parents.

Freshly hatched rail chicks are capable of swimming if faced with danger, but they cannot remain in water long without perishing. They roost during the night, or in inclement weather, in the egg nest or in a different "nursery" nest constructed by the parents as an alternative shelter or brooding place. The parents feed the young from bill to bill for the first few days, but the semi-precocial offspring start to forage on their own, under the watchful eye of a parent, soon thereafter.

The Virginia Rail sometimes moves young and eggs to a new nest, using its bill, if the first nest area is threatened. Similarly, Purple Gallinules have been observed transporting young in flight, carrying them in their bills.

Body feathers in rallids begin to replace the nestling down within 6 to 15 days after hatching. The legs and feet grow quickly and attain full growth before the rest of the body. These large feet keep the young birds from sinking into moist terrain and make them able runners. Tails take the longest to grow, and the head and neck is usually the last area to obtain immature feathering.

Most rallid species can extend their breeding season if sufficient food is available. The offspring are often independent before they fledge and may be driven out of the territory by their parents.

Sometimes the offspring of rallids do not disperse immediately. Immature Purple Gallinules may remain in their natal territories to help in the maintenance of succeeding broods. Common Moorhen nests may be attended to by immatures from a previous brood and even by one or two other adult birds, which aid the nest pair in the feeding of the young.

Conservation

Worldwide, the greatest threat to continental rallids is the loss of suitable habitat. Flooding or droughts, changes in water quality, erosion, pollution, pesticides, and dikes (constructed to manage mosquitoes and water levels) easily disturb wetlands and marshes where rallids occur.

Globally there are many island-endemic rallid species and subspecies. Many are flightless, and they have suffered considerably as humans have colonized remote islands, especially in the Pacific. It is estimated that prior to human expansion, there was at least one unique rail species on every island in the Pacific. Many have become extinct, and others are critically endangered as a result of predation by rats, cats, snakes, and other species introduced by humans.

In North America, the Black and Yellow Rails are viewed as vulnerable because of small ranges and threatened habitat and are on the WatchList. Both North American races of the Black Rail (*Laterallus jamaicensis jamaicensis* and *L. j. coturniculus*) are considered threatened or endangered in most states where they are found. The three western races of the Clapper Rail (*Rallus longirostris yumanensis*, *R. l. levipes*, and *R. l. obsoletus*) are considered endangered at state and federal levels. The family as a whole is vulnerable to disturbance because of the sensitivity of its habitat. The Black Rail is more vulnerable than other species because it inhabits the edges of wetlands, where habitat degradation usually begins.

Accidental Species

Long-distance vagrancy is quite common among the rallids (see Adaptations to Lifestyle), and several species from elsewhere in the world have wandered to North America. The Corn Crake (*Crex crex*) of Eurasia formerly strayed to eastern North America with some regularity but is now extremely rare. Another wanderer from Eurasia, the Eurasian Coot (*Fulica atra*), has occurred in the Canadian Maritimes and the Pribilof Islands. A third Old World species, Baillon's Crake (*Porzana pusilla*) was recently reported from Attu but has yet to be officially accepted.

Three species from South or Central America have also occurred in North America. Paint-billed Crakes (*Neocrex erythrops*) have been found in Virginia and Texas, the Spotted Rail (*Pardirallus maculatus*) in Pennsylvania and Texas, and the Azure Gallinule (*Porphyrula flavirostris*) has been recorded once on Long Island, New York; the last was most likely a bird that had escaped from captivity.

Finally, Purple Swamphens (*Porphyrio porphyrio*), native to areas from southern Europe to Australia, have recently escaped from captivity and established a small breeding population in Florida.

George L. Armistead

Limpkin

Named for its odd "limping" walk, the Limpkin *(Aramus guarauna)* is a medium-size, dark brown bird heavily spotted and streaked with white. It has long legs, a long, slender neck, and a long, slightly drooping bill. The Limpkin prefers to walk or run, often pumping its tail, and avoids flying if possible. In flight it appears short-tailed; its wings are broad and rounded, with a wingspan of 3 feet 4 inches (1 m). A furtive species, the Limpkin is more often heard than seen; its most common call, a raucous *kwEEEeeer*, may be repeated several times or echoed by nearby Limpkins. The bird is found mostly in freshwater wetlands.

Taxonomy

In geological ages past, members of the family Aramidae could be found around the globe. Today only the Limpkin remains. Superficially the Limpkin bears a resemblance to some ibis species, but it lacks their dramatic, sickle-like bill. In the past, the Limpkin has been grouped variously with ibises and spoonbills, herons, shorebirds, or galliforms. Current taxonomy places it between the rails and the cranes, as physical appearance would suggest. DNA–DNA hybridization studies suggest that Limpkins are most closely related to the sungrebes (Heliornithidae), a tropical gruiform family.

Until 1934 the Limpkin was split into two species, one in South America and one in North and Central America. Since these forms were lumped, four subspecies have been recognized. The northernmost form, *Aramus guarauna pictus* of Florida and southern Georgia, formerly was called the "Courlan."

Limpkin. *The family Aramidae includes only one species, which is related to the cranes and the rails but distinctive in many respects.*

Food and Foraging

Apple snails of the genus *Pomacea* are the staple of the Limpkin diet, and the Limpkin in North America is found primarily in habitats conducive to a healthy population of this prey. These include freshwater marshes, wooded swamps, and edges of rivers and ponds. The snails need a requisite amount of submerged aquatic vegetation, proper depth and hardness of the water, and emergent vegetation where they can lay eggs.

Limpkins are able swimmers but usually feed in water shallow enough for wading. Typically solitary feeders, they forage by sight and touch. Although they commonly probe mud surfaces and water in search of snails, Limpkins also snatch them from vegetation.

Once a Limpkin captures a snail, it takes it to solid ground, where it uses its laterally compressed bill to remove the snail from its shell. Limpkins can remove snails from their encasements in less than 20 seconds, and where prey is ample a Limpkin can capture, extract, and eat a snail every two to three minutes.

Breeding

Limpkins are not typically colonial nesters, but they sometimes gather in loose groups. They are territorial, and territories that provide good feeding areas with stable water levels may be defended year-round. Poorer territories are defended only during the breeding season. Males perform most territorial defense, flying at unwelcome visitors while calling loudly. Boundaries are further defined by territorial calling of the nest pair.

During courtship, pairs rest and feed together. In one courtship display, a female looks on as a male extracts a snail from its shell and presents it to her; she crouches or stands by his side and then takes the snail from his bill.

Limpkins build saucer-shaped nests, up to 2 feet (60 cm) across, in a variety of sites, from ground level to high up in a tree. Nests are usually placed over water in marshes, swampy woodlands, or mangroves. Limpkins have even used old Osprey *(Pandion haliaetus)* nests and large cavities as nest sites.

Limpkin nests are composed of plant matter from the surrounding habitat. A foundation of twigs is covered by weavings of dried, hollowed rushes and cattails, and lined with grasses. Limpkins also build a brooding platform just before their eggs hatch, from which the young can forage. The parents share nest duties, and soon after hatching, the precocial young are guided to the brooding platform.

Conservation

Locally common throughout its range, the Limpkin has endured substantial pressure and even extirpation in some areas, such as Puerto Rico.

By the early 1900s, the Limpkin was nearly extinct in Florida. It made a good

Limpkin head and bill. The Limpkin's bill is long and heavy. Several adaptations aid the bird in extracting apple snails. About half an inch (1 cm) from the tip there is a distinct curve to the right, allowing it to fit into the right-hand curve of the snail's shell; the tip of the lower bill is twisted 90 degrees, with the sharpened edge fitting against the upper bill and used to cut the snail's operculum from its body. In addition, the long tongue has a stiff, barbed tip that the bird presumably uses to extract the snail.

meal and was loud, tame, and slow in flight and thus an easy target. Massive drainage and irrigation also took a serious toll on this population. Greater environmental awareness and wetland restoration has helped the species to persist, and the population today is mostly stable. Hunting, land development, irrigation, poor water quality, and the introduction of exotic plants that could affect the reproduction of apple snails pose the biggest threats to the Limpkin's survival.

George L. Armistead

Worldwide Family Features

- 22–28" (56–70 cm) wading bird.
- 1 species worldwide; ranges from temperate South America to southern Georgia.
- In wetland habitat, eats mainly apple snails, occasionally freshwater mussels and other aquatic prey, small reptiles, and land snails. Plucks prey from ground or vegetation or probes items from mud.
- Territorial, but territories may be aggregated. Solitary feeder, though feeds in flocks if food is plentiful. Generally monogamous; some females polyandrous. Does not migrate.

- Breeds first at 1 year old.
- Both parents build saucer-shaped nest of plant matter, over open water to heights of 50' (15 m). May reuse nests.
- 4–8 subelliptical eggs, light to olive buff and blotched with brown. Both parents incubate, for 25–28 days. Hatching synchronous. 2 broods per year.
- Precocial young, with brownish or black down, are adept swimmers and runners almost upon hatching. Fledge at 12–17 weeks. Parents share care.
- Little survival information. Among oldest on record: 12 years.

Cranes

Cranes are large, elegant wading birds with long necks and legs, and wingspans ranging from 6 feet to 7 feet 3 inches (1.8–2.2 m). Most species are predominantly pale gray or white, with patches of red on the face. Their grace and their elaborate "dance" displays have inspired artists, choreographers, and biologists alike. They inhabit a variety of freshwater wetlands and uplands, including agricultural tracts, but are typically restricted to open habitats. Outside the breeding season they often gather in large flocks. Huge congregations of migrating Sandhill Cranes *(Grus canadensis)* attract birders to Nebraska and other staging areas every spring.

Taxonomy

The cranes comprise two subfamilies: the Balearicinae, with two species of crowned cranes from Africa, and the Gruinae, with 13 species of typical cranes. The genus *Grus* contains both North American species: the Whooping Crane (*G. americana*) and the Sandhill Crane. Researchers currently recognize six subspecies of Sandhill Crane, although all have been combined as a single taxonomic unit in the past, and there is much intergradation in appearance among subspecies.

Superficially cranes resemble herons, storks, and flamingos; all have long legs and necks, and all occur in wetland habitats. Cranes, however, are only distantly related to these families and are classified instead in the order Gruiformes, along with the rails and the Limpkin (*Aramus guarauna*), as well as several groups not found in North America.

Gruid diversity. *Structurally most cranes are very similar, with a straight, stout bill; long, curved tertials forming a "bustle"; a straight neck; and bare facial skin, as shown in this Sandhill Crane.*

Crane head and bill. *Cranes have long, straight bills that are superficially heron-like, but stouter and less pointed. They are used for picking among vegetation and probing in the mud. The Whooping Crane is shown.*

Food and Foraging

Most cranes have a varied diet and are opportunistic, taking whatever food is available. They typically feed by pecking at the ground or probing the mud as they walk along. In the wetlands where they are usually seen, Whooping Cranes eat crabs, clams, various other aquatic invertebrates, and small vertebrates such as fish, frogs, and snakes. They will also forage in upland habitats, eating acorns and agricultural grains if available. Sandhill Cranes often feed on seeds in farm fields but will also eat berries, leaves, tubers, various invertebrates, and small vertebrates.

Displays

All cranes engage in complex "dance" displays, which typically consist of synchronized dips, bows, head swings, wing spreads, leaps, and flaps. Birds also will occasionally pick items off the ground and toss them into the air.

Dancing is an important component of courtship and is especially common among subadult birds that have yet to breed. It often occurs early in the morning and during spring migration, when dancing activity can spread contagiously through a flock, creating a spectacular show. Older birds typically retain their mates from the previous breeding season and dance less frequently.

Cranes also engage in a variety of aggressive behaviors that are used to defend breeding territories or feeding areas. Sometimes these aggressive displays are incorporated into dances.

Breeding

Both North American cranes build a simple platform of vegetation in a marshy area, gathering materials from the area immediately around the nest to form a "moat." Males and females both incubate, although the female does about 70 percent of the job. At the time of hatching, young cranes are covered with down and are mobile, but they depend on their parents for food. The young leave the nest within hours after hatching and follow the parents on foot. As they grow, they increasingly feed themselves, although they continue to solicit their parents for food until they become independent, several months after hatching. The young cranes stay with their parents in a family group until the end of their first spring.

Movements

Cranes from northern populations generally undertake tremendous migrations, with some birds logging thousands of miles a year. Cranes may spend weeks at staging areas socializing and fattening up before migration begins. Typically birds start migrating a few hours after sunrise, when thermals begin to develop.

Most Sandhill Cranes fly at altitudes of 500 to 2,500 feet (150–750 m) when they migrate, but some have reached 12,000 feet (3,600 m). After achieving "cruising" height, cranes often fly in a V formation, gliding up to 500 miles (800 km) in nine or ten hours. Young cranes rely on their parents to teach them the route to the wintering grounds.

Conservation

The Whooping Crane is one of the most endangered bird species in North America. The wild population is now restricted to one small breeding area in Canada's Northwest Territories and winters only in Texas. Numbers hit a low point in 1941, when only 15 or 16 birds remained. Luckily, conservation measures taken in

Worldwide Family Features

- 36–69" (90–176 cm) wading birds.
- 15 species in at least 2 genera worldwide; on all continents except Antarctica and South America, with greatest diversity in Old World. 2 species in 1 genus breed in North America, 1 species found throughout continent; plus 1 accidental species.
- Eat wide variety of plant material and small animals, picked off ground or dug up with bill.
- Territorial. Monogamous; pairs bond for life. All perform "dancing" displays. Temperate zone species migratory.
- Breed first at 2–6 years old, but early breeding attempts usually fail.

- Nest is large platform on the ground with surrounding "moat"; built by both parents from adjacent vegetation. Nests are rarely reused.
- Usually 2 variably colored, subelliptical eggs. Both parents incubate during day, female at night. Hatching asynchronous, after 28–36 days. 1 brood per year.
- Precocial young mobile, covered with down at hatching. Both parents feed. Fledge at 50 days–18½ weeks.
- Adult annual survival typically exceeds 80%. Among oldest on record: 23 years in wild (Sandhill Crane); more than 40 years in captivity (Whooping Crane).

Cranes dancing. Cranes are renowned for their courtship "dances": dipping, bowing, leaping, and flapping while giving wild, bugling cries. The Sandhill Crane is shown.

earlier years helped the population survive. Although Wood Buffalo National Park, in Canada, was established to protect bison, it also protected the last Whooping Crane breeding grounds.

Attempts to revive crane populations have been successful but slow-going. Wild cranes often lay two eggs, but they rarely raise more than one young. Birds in captivity can be induced to lay extra eggs each year; consequently, biologists have been able to collect hundreds of surplus eggs to form captive populations. Many birds hatched from these eggs have been successfully reintroduced into the wild.

Whooping Cranes are especially vulnerable because of their small geographic range, and the creation of other breeding populations has been a high conservation priority. Early attempts involved placing Whooping Crane eggs in the nests of "Greater" Sandhill Cranes *(Grus canadensis tabida)* in Idaho. Initially the program went well, with the foster parents raising their wards and the young Whooping Cranes successfully learning migration routes from the Sandhill Cranes. Ultimately, however, the young Whooping Cranes did not form pair bonds with each other.

Similar problems have arisen with cranes hand-reared by humans; it seems that young birds that imprint on foster parents have trouble recognizing members of their own species as potential mates. Biologists now use a combination of techniques to minimize exposing the captive birds to people. These include caretakers using crane puppets and models when feeding young chicks and dressing in crane costumes when approaching older birds.

As a result of conservation efforts, the wild Whooping Crane population has risen to about 150 birds. Initial attempts to introduce a nonmigratory population in Florida also appear to be working.

Sandhill Cranes are much more numerous than Whooping Cranes. Nonetheless, the "Mississippi" Sandhill Crane *(Grus canadensis pulla)* numbers fewer than 100 birds and is considered endangered. Captive breeding has also been used in the management of this population, and most of the birds currently in the wild were born in captivity.

Accidental Species

The Common Crane *(Grus grus)* of Eurasia has been recorded in North America several times, with sightings scattered across the continent and at various times of year. Some of these birds may have migrated to North America with "Lesser" Sandhill Cranes *(G. canadensis canadensis)* from Siberian nesting populations.

William J. Seng

Thick-knees

Family Burhinidae
Order Charadriiformes

A distinctive family of medium-size to large shorebirds that occur in dry, open country with scattered vegetation, thick-knees are characterized by large, staring eyes, a broad head, a stout bill, and long legs with the enlarged "knee" joint (really the ankle) that gives them their name. All are largely nocturnal; they spend the day resting on the ground, where their cryptic coloration allows them to go unnoticed. Thick-knees will almost always walk or run away from an observer rather than fly. Though rarely heard by day, their vocalizations are loud and elaborate, and include plaintive wails and other sounds.

The relationship of the family to others is unclear. Previously placed alongside the bustards (family Otididae) of the Old World in the order Gruiformes, thick-knees are now recognized as shorebirds; the plovers and the avocets and stilts are thought to be their closest relatives.

Two species occur in the Americas. One, the Double-striped Thick-knee *(Burhinus bistriatus)*, is typically found from central Mexico to northern Brazil but has strayed to southern Texas once in winter. An Arizona record is thought to have been an escapee. This species is not very well known, in part because of its nocturnal habits. It feeds mostly on invertebrates but will also take small lizards and mammals. In the species' normal range Double-striped Thick-knees are sometimes kept semi-domesticated on ranches, where they are said to be effective insect-controllers.

David Allen Sibley

Double-striped Thick-knee. This species is typical of the family—all nine species are quite similar in appearance and habits. Their tall structure allows thick-knees to see over vegetation in their arid grassland habitats, their sandy-brown colors help to provide camouflage, and their large eyes presumably provide good night vision.

Worldwide Family Features

- 13–24" (33–60 cm) shorebirds of arid, open country.
- 9 species in at least 1 genus; largely tropical, but found on all continents except Antarctica. 1 species accidental in Texas.
- Eat primarily insects and other invertebrates, but also birds' eggs, reptiles, and small mammals. Prey generally plucked from ground with plover-like action.
- Generally solitary when breeding, but may be semi-colonial; form small flocks at other times. Monogamous; some pair for life. Most species do not migrate.

- Breed first probably at 2 or 3 years old, rarely when 1 year old.
- Nest is scrape on ground, placed in the open or under a bush; built by both adults, often lined with pebbles or shells.
- 1–3 (typically 2) rounded oval eggs that are white or buff with brown marks. Both parents incubate, for 24–30 days. 2nd egg usually hatches within 24 hours of 1st. 1 brood per year.
- Young precocial, covered with down at hatch; leave nest on 1st day. Parents provide protection until fledging, at 36 days to 12 weeks.
- Little information on survival or longevity.

Plovers and Lapwings

Family Charadriidae
Order Charadriiformes

Plovers and lapwings are small to medium-size shorebirds with upright posture, large eyes, rounded heads, thick necks, short, rather thick bills, and medium-length legs; their feet have vestigial hind toes. Plovers have long, narrow, sharply pointed wings perfectly suited for rapid, direct, long-distance flight; lapwings have broader, more rounded wings. Members of this family are found in open habitats, including tundra, shortgrass prairies, plowed fields, interior lake and coastal shorelines, coastal estuaries, and mudflats.

Taxonomy

The Charadriidae is the second-largest family of shorebirds. Although it is often assumed that Charadriidae has a close relationship with the family Scolopacidae, which includes sandpipers, phalaropes, and their allies, several recent studies suggest that plovers and lapwings may be more closely allied to gulls and terns. It also appears that stilts, avocets, and oystercatchers may have derived from a plover-like ancestor. Another theory that remains to be verified is that all of these groups, and most other living birds, are descended from an ancestral shorebird that survived the large-scale extinctions at the end of the Cretaceous period nearly 65 million years ago.

Members of the Charadriidae tend to be similar to one another in shape, form, and overall behavior; even plumages and plumage sequences are remarkably consistent among the various species. Unlike scolopacids, these shorebirds have very small or vestigial hind toes, and their bills are decidedly uniform; most bills are short, straight, and blunt, with a slight swelling at the tip and a constriction in the middle. The bill length of most plovers and lapwings never exceeds the distance from the base of the bill to the back of the eye.

The family is split into two subfamilies, the Vanellinae (lapwings) and the Charadriinae (plovers). North American members of the Charadriinae fall into two very distinct genera and thus can be further subdivided into *Charadrius* and *Pluvialis* plovers. There is general agreement that the lapwings and the *Charadrius* plovers probably evolved in the tropics of the Southern Hemisphere, while the older *Pluvialis* plovers originated in the Northern Hemisphere.

For the most part, the species-level taxonomy of the Charadriidae is fairly stable. Some authors have suggested that the Snowy Plover *(Charadrius alexandrinus)* of the Americas should be classified as a species distinct from the Kentish Plover of the Old World, but most taxonomies continue to treat these birds as a single species. Before the 1990s, there

Charadriid diversity. North American members of the Charadriidae can be subdivided into three groups: the Charadrius *plovers (including Wilson's Plover, left), which are relatively small, with pointed wings; the* Pluvialis *plovers (such as the Pacific Golden-Plover, center), relatively large birds with pointed wings; and the lapwings, which are relatively large, with rounded wings and ornamental plumage (one species, the Northern Lapwing, shown at right, occurs as a rare visitor but does not breed).*

was also uncertainty about the taxonomic status of North American golden-plovers. But studies of their breeding vocalizations, nesting habitat, and assortative mating behavior in coastal Alaska has revealed that what was once thought to be a single species is actually two species: the American Golden-Plover *(Pluvialis dominica)* and the Pacific Golden-Plover *(P. fulva).*

Charadriid head and bill. Plovers and lapwings are characterized by relatively large eyes and short bills that are straight but slightly swollen at the tip. The Semipalmated Plover is shown.

Variation and Molt

Many lapwing species have conspicuous crests on their heads, colorful facial wattles, and horny spurs on their wings that they use in combat with other lapwings or territorial intruders. These features are most highly developed in males, which are also larger and more aggressive than females. Their relatively long legs enable them to move about readily in grassland habitats. Lapwings have broad, rounded wings unsuited for long-distance migration, and most species are sedentary. An exception is the migratory Northern Lapwing *(Vanellus vanellus)*, which has occurred in eastern North America.

Adult *Charadrius* plovers often have one or more completely dark, usually black, breast bands or distinct dark markings at the sides of the chest. They also display prominent black-and-white head and facial markings, which, along with their dark chest collars, create effective camouflage within their preferred haunts. Plover species whose nesting habitats tend to have a uniform appearance, such as sandy beaches, have incomplete breast

Charadriid foot. Plovers and lapwings have three forward toes that are sometimes partially webbed and a vestigial hind toe. The Black-bellied Plover is shown.

bands. Complete breast bands are worn by plovers in habitats with more variably colored backgrounds, such as the shingle beaches where Common Ringed Plovers *(C. hiaticula)* breed. Besides aiding in camouflage, these striking head and breast markings also appear to function in courtship display and during aggressive encounters between plover species in the nonbreeding season.

Adult *Pluvialis* plovers have black underparts when breeding; the black feathering is lost after nesting, so adults and juveniles are similar in appearance in winter. Ordinarily the black on the underparts is more extensive and more intense in males than in females, and immatures do not usually develop completely black underparts until their second spring. Age and individual variation, however, often make it difficult to reliably tell the sex of Black-bellied Plovers *(P. squatarola)* and golden-plovers in the field. Similarly, the sexes are close enough in size in all plover species to make size of little value in determining the sex of birds in the field.

Once on the wintering grounds, adult plovers normally undergo a complete prebasic molt. In some species, this molt begins while the birds are still on the breeding grounds and continues during autumn migration. If wing molt begins before migration, however, it is usually suspended and finished after the birds arrive on their wintering grounds. Sometime before nesting, there is a partial prealternate molt involving only the contour feathers; during this molt, adults acquire their breeding colors.

Habitats

Lapwings and plovers generally live in open habitats. Lapwings occupy farmlands, pastures, grasslands, mountain steppes, river edges, and marshlands in temperate, tropical, and arid regions. Since most lapwings are sedentary, their habitat use changes little from season to season; even migratory lapwing species tend to occupy similar habitats throughout the year.

Plovers, especially the highly migratory *Pluvialis* group, show greater seasonal diversity in their choice of habitats. In the Arctic, Black-bellied Plovers and golden-plovers are birds of open heathlands, hummock tundra, high rocky domes, and barrens covered with lichens and studded with Arctic wildflowers. During migration and in winter, golden-plovers prefer plowed fields, closely grazed pastures, and grasslands, while Black-bellied Plovers use intertidal coastal habitats.

The *Charadrius* plovers also use a variety of habitats. Snowy Plovers occupy interior alkaline lakeshores and sandy or coralline beaches along the coast, while Semipalmated Plovers *(C. semipalmatus)* nest on subarctic gravel ridges and tundra river bars, and occupy lakeshores and intertidal mudflats during migration. Mountain Plovers *(C. montanus)* are relatively specialized, breeding only in arid shortgrass prairies and wintering in agricultural fields and heavily grazed rangelands. Killdeer *(C. vociferus)* nest in habitats ranging from the desert surrounding Great Basin wetlands to plowed fields, golf courses, and gravel rooftops; during the nonbreeding season, they occupy farmland and shortgrass habitats.

When not breeding, plovers and lapwings are gregarious, often mingling with other shorebirds at foraging sites during migration and in winter. They often roost in flocks of their own kind, although at coastal sites Black-bellied and Semipalmated Plovers routinely join flocks of roosting sandpipers. Most species tend not to travel great distances between feeding and roosting areas unless they are regularly disturbed or tidal conditions force them to use distant

Worldwide Family Features

- 5–15" (12–38 cm) shorebirds.
- About 66 species in about 10 genera worldwide, with cosmopolitan distribution. North America has 12 breeding species and 2 regular but rare visitors in 3 genera; found throughout all of North America; plus 2 accidental species.
- Eat mainly invertebrates, especially polychaete worms; also small crustaceans, aquatic insect larvae, occasionally seeds, berries. Typically locate food visually and pluck prey from substrate with bill.
- Mostly seasonally monogamous; a few species polygynous or sequentially polyandrous; some form long-term pair bonds. Most species solitary nesters; a few semi-colonial. Male engages in territorial defense mostly when breeding. May flock during nonbreeding season, especially at roost sites. A few species maintain winter territories. Many species migratory; some tropical species sedentary.
- Breed first at 1–3 years old.

- Nest is shallow scrape created by male, often modified by female; sometimes lined with shells, pebbles, leaves, lichens, mosses. Usually on sandy beach, lakeshore, gravel, open tundra; some species build nests in marshes on raised mounds. Some species use same site from year to year; occasionally reuse old nests.
- 2–4 oval to pyriform eggs, usually with whitish, beige, or greenish background; covered with dark spots and scribbles of variable size and density. Incubation generally by both sexes, for 18–36 days. Hatching usually synchronous or within 2 days. Usually 1 brood per year; may replace lost clutches; some temperate-zone species raise up to 3 broods.
- Cryptically colored downy chicks are precocial; leave immediate vicinity of nest soon after hatching; may wander up to several hundred yards per day. Usually tended by both parents or just the male. Fledge at 22 days–9 weeks.
- Adult annual survival 70–90%. Among oldest on record: more than 20 years (Black-bellied Plover, Mongolian Plover).

roost sites. Unlike scolopacids, lapwings and plovers rarely perch or roost in trees, undoubtedly due to the absence of functional hind toes on their feet, which may also explain why they tend not to forage on rocky shores.

Food and Foraging

Plovers and lapwings are specialized feeders that rely on vision to locate their prey, which includes all manner of invertebrates, such as earthworms, adult and larval insects, amphipods, isopods, tiny crabs and shrimp, polychaete worms, and occasionally small mollusks; some species also regularly eat berries. Regardless of their prey, the birds' foraging techniques are highly stereotyped. Typical charadriid feeding strategy involves running, almost robin-like, for distances ranging from a few steps to a few yards, and periodically stopping with head held high. During such standstills, these birds use their large eyes to scan the substrate for movement, which, if detected, elicits an abrupt peck at the surface.

Plovers and lapwings never employ the tactile probing of scolopacids. Presumably because they rely more on visual foraging, they have significantly larger optic brain lobes than do tactile-feeding shorebirds. Some Charadriidae species routinely feed at night despite their reliance on visual foraging. This may be explained by the high density of retinal rod cells in their eyes; rod cells are sensitive to low light and facilitate night vision. (Scolopacids, which are less reliant on visual cues for nocturnal feeding, have lower densities of rod cells.) Various researchers have suggested that lapwings and plovers feed at night to avoid predation, to reduce competition from other diurnal foragers, to increase their odds of finding certain prey items, or to ensure that they obtain enough food daily. It is likely that all of these factors play some role.

An interesting feeding ploy used by lapwings and plovers involves foot-trembling and foot-tapping. On intertidal mudflats, plovers will often slightly raise one leg and vibrate it rapidly so the toes disturb the substrate, causing small prey to move and become easier to see and capture. The same technique used in grassland habitats may mimic the sound of either rain or subterranean burrowing predators, causing prey such as earthworms to come to the surface.

Flocks of plovers invariably scatter when foraging, almost never feeding in the closely ranked flocks characteristic of many sandpipers. A few species, including the golden-plovers and the Black-bellied and Semipalmated Plovers, defend feeding territories during the non-breeding season. Sometimes a bird will defend a feeding territory throughout an

Charadriid foraging motions. The foraging motions of plovers and lapwings are similar to those of thrushes, another group of visual hunters. In both families, birds stand alert and upright watching for prey, then run quickly to another spot. Plovers and lapwings employ a trick known as foot-trembling (left), in which they stand still on one leg with the other foot held loosely, slightly forward, and vibrating against the ground. Presumably this affects their prey in some way, either scaring concealed prey out of hiding or attracting prey to the vibrations. At other times, the birds just stand and wait (center); when prey is sighted close by, they dip abruptly to peck at it (right). The American Golden-Plover is shown.

entire nonbreeding season; other defensive stands last only a few days or even a few hours.

Breeding

Most plovers and lapwings are seasonally monogamous; species like the European Golden-Plover *(Pluvialis apricaria)* sometimes mate for life. Despite this, studies using color-marked populations of Northern Lapwings and Snowy Plovers have revealed that, at least in these species, there may be more extra-pair mating behavior than previously suspected.

Unusual plover breeding strategies include various types of sequential polyandry. Female Mountain Plovers abandon their mate shortly after laying eggs, leaving the male to complete incubation. Meanwhile, the female produces another clutch, sometimes after copulating with a second male, and incubates it herself.

A more elaborate strategy occurs in the Eurasian Dotterel *(Charadrius morinellus)*, a rare breeder in Alaska. After leaving her first mate to complete incubation and rear the young, a female dotterel mates with another male, whom she also typically abandons after egg-laying. In this species, females rarely help rear the young. Remarkably, though, during certain years or in situations where dotterel sex ratios are out of balance, this system shifts, and the birds are polygynous rather than polyandrous.

Whatever the breeding system, most plover and lapwing species maintain individual breeding territories, although in some semi-colonial lapwing species, several pairs may work together to defend communal territories against predators.

Vocalizations and Displays

The evocative calls of lapwings and plovers have been described as plaintive, mournful, strident, whistled, and melodious. During the late 19th century, untold numbers of plovers were killed by market-gunners, who had no trouble attracting the birds by mimicking their calls. For the few species whose voices

Broken-wing display. *Broken-wing distraction displays are performed by many ground-nesting species. The bird distracts a potential predator by acting injured and appearing to be easy prey, thus drawing attention away from a nearby nest or young. Plover nests are merely a shallow scrape on open ground, sometimes surrounded by bits of debris for camouflage. The only chance of avoiding predation at such nests is to escape detection, and the birds and eggs have evolved to be virtually invisible in their habitat. The Snowy Plover is shown.*

have been analyzed, different calls can be categorized according to their context: warning, alarm-threat, pair-contact, nest-scraping, copulation, settling-on-nest, distraction, all-clear, location, contentment, and distress. The precise function of the different calls is suggested by their names.

Of the vocalizations produced by these birds, few are more impressive than the flight songs that accompany courtship display flights. These vocalizations are especially impressive in the aerial songs of the *Pluvialis* plovers and the Northern Lapwing. The ritualized, stiff-winged, "butterfly flights" of displaying golden-plovers are accompanied by haunting and protracted vocalizations. Lapwings use a series of eerie vocalizations with various different display-flight modes, including spectacular steep ascents and vertical dives executed in series.

Among the vocalizations that birds use in defending their nests and chicks, distraction calls are particularly interesting. These are unusually loud, strident, and persistent, and ordinarily are accompanied by distraction behavior, most notably the broken-wing display, during which an adult feigns injury in an attempt to lure a would-be predator away from its nest or chicks.

Semipalmated Plovers commonly use a low, accelerating *churtle* call that is usually accompanied by partially drooped wings, raised back feathers, lowered head, and fanned tail. This combination of vocalization and posture is aggressive in nature; the birds use it in defending breeding territories and nonbreeding feeding territories. The display calls of the Semipalmated Plover are important in allowing observers to distinguish the species from the Common Ringed Plover, which breeds in Greenland and far northern Canada but is primarily an Old World species.

Piping Plover brooding. Young plovers are precocial and very mobile just hours after hatching. They follow their parents during their first weeks and rely on their cryptic coloration to escape predation. They have a relatively low metabolism and need their parents to brood them frequently for the first two weeks until they are able to maintain their own body temperature.

Nests

Plover nests can be located almost anywhere on the ground—from the tops of tussocks on open tundra, to gravel bars in braided streams, to furrows in plowed fields and dune hollows on sandy beaches. The nests are typically shallow scrapes created by the male or by both sexes together. These scrapes are usually lined with a few pebbles, shell fragments, grass strips, bits of lichen, or moss fragments. Lapwings that nest in marshlands fashion vegetation into nests atop mounds raised above the waterline. All species show strong site fidelity, and Black-bellied Plovers and golden-plovers occasionally occupy previously used nest scrapes.

Eggs

Charadriid eggs are similar to those of other shorebirds: oval to pyriform and cryptically colored, with a whitish, beige, or greenish background, and heavily marked with dark scrawls and speckles. Plovers and lapwings, particularly Arctic-nesting species, normally nest once a year. Many species will replace sets of eggs that are lost, and *Charadrius* plovers, such as the Killdeer, that nest at temperate latitudes often produce two or more broods. Snowy Plovers are unusual in that they sometimes move considerable distances (up to hundreds of miles) between nesting attempts.

Clutch size in this family ranges from two to four eggs; three or four are most common. Because of the large size of shorebird eggs, a clutch of more than three or four may not be incubated successfully, and females never lay more than four eggs in a clutch. As ground-nesting shorebirds experience high rates of nest predation, another possible explanation for their small clutch size is that small clutches are less vulnerable to predators as they take less time to produce; they are also easier to replace if lost.

Plovers produce eggs at intervals of one to two days. In some species, incubation sometimes begins when the third egg is laid, but more often the clutch is completed before incubation begins in earnest. The incubation period is long (21 to 30 days in North American species) for birds the size of most plovers, but may be needed to allow for development of fully precocial young at hatching.

In most species, both parents maintain nearly continuous incubation to keep the eggs from getting chilled, especially in Arctic regions, or overheated in tropical and desert environments. Killdeer that breed in torrid environments actually soak their belly feathers to cool the nest and eggs during incubation. For single-parent incubators such as Eurasian Dotterels and

Mountain Plovers, the problem of maintaining appropriate egg temperatures can be especially challenging.

Young

Plover and lapwing chicks are beautifully cryptic, with distinctive patterns. Shortly after hatching, they are fully precocial and capable of foraging on their own. They grow rather slowly, however, and tend to have comparatively low metabolic rates. Although a low metabolic rate may reduce the energy demands associated with growth and allow the young to better cope with food shortages or inclement weather, it is not without costs. During cold weather, chicks need to be brooded regularly in order to maintain their body temperature. Brooding is especially important during the first two weeks of life when the young cannot maintain a proper body temperature on their own.

Despite the apparent independence of the young at hatching, fledging does not occur until 21 to 36 days after hatching in North American species; in some cases, the young remain with their parents for even longer. Northern Lapwings and *Charadrius* plovers reach sexual maturity within a year, while *Pluvialis* plovers typically do not breed until they are two or three years old.

Movements

Few shorebird travels rival the epic migrations undertaken by American and Pacific Golden-Plovers. In the fall, after a period of almost continuous feeding, small to medium-size flocks of fat-laden American Golden-Plovers depart from eastern Canada in a southeasterly direction on a heading that takes many of them over the Atlantic Ocean to northern South America—a distance of some 2,500 miles (4,000 km) or more. Pacific Golden-Plovers departing from Alaska make equally dazzling nonstop flights of 2,000 miles (3,200 km) or more to islands in the Pacific. Radar studies confirm that these migrants regularly travel at altitudes of 15,000 to 20,000 feet (4,500–6,000 m) and at speeds of at least 50 miles per hour (80 km/h). Even at this rate, some golden-plovers have to fly continuously for at least a day or two.

The birds attempt to optimize flying conditions by departing with favoring tailwinds on a course that will offer the least flight resistance. One way American Golden-Plovers accomplish this is by setting a southeasterly flight trajectory that intercepts the westerly trade winds, helping to deflect their flight toward the South American mainland. Once they reach northern South America, the plovers rest and refuel at suitable stopover locations before completing their migration. Pacific Golden-Plovers island-hop until they reach Polynesia and Australia.

During their spring migration, American Golden-Plovers follow a different route. Instead of flying over the Atlantic, they take an inland course that brings them across the Gulf of Mexico to the coast of Texas, then onward through the prairies to their Arctic nesting grounds. This elliptical configuration—offshore in fall and inland in spring—is a route used by many North American shorebirds. This strategy allows the birds to exploit the abundance of food in the prairies in spring, and to take advantage of trade winds to assist them in reaching the South American coastline after departing from eastern Canada in autumn.

The energy and physiological abilities required for long-distance, over-water migrations on the scale undertaken by golden-plovers are amazing. One prerequisite for long-distance migration is the ability to accumulate subcutaneous body fat that can be metabolized rapidly during sustained flight. To meet the energy demands of a flight of a thousand miles or more, these plovers spend up to two months at strategic staging areas with food resources that allow them to pack on the fat they need for sustained flying. For American Golden-Plovers during autumn migration, the western coasts of Hudson Bay and James Bay are critical staging areas.

While no other plovers and no lapwings attempt the transoceanic flights of the golden-plovers, other species are nonetheless migratory. Many Black-bellied Plovers, Wilson's Plovers *(Charadrius wilsonia)*, and Semipalmated Plovers regularly make their way to the Southern Hemisphere, and many Eurasian Dotterels travel from the Eurasian tundra to North Africa and the Middle East. The Mongolian Plover *(C. mongolus)*, a rare but regular visitor to North America, typically migrates from Siberian breeding grounds to as far south as Australia; this species is capable of making it to the East Coast of North America on occasion. Other species move less far: Even after migration, many Mountain and Piping *(C. melodus)* Plovers remain within North America.

Migration path of American Golden-Plover.
The American Golden-Plover performs one of the most remarkable migrations of any bird. In fall the birds leave their breeding grounds (orange) and stage at rich feeding areas around Hudson Bay and Labrador, where they fatten up in preparation for a 2,500-mile (4,000-km) nonstop flight over the Atlantic Ocean to South America. Ultimately they reach their wintering grounds in Argentina (blue); in the spring, they return north via a more westerly route. The map shows the primary migration corridors (yellow), but small numbers of birds occur elsewhere throughout the Americas.

Conservation

Plover conservation in North America needs to be addressed on several fronts. Coastal nesters—especially the Piping Plover, which is on the U.S. Endangered Species List, but also Snowy and Wilson's Plovers—are in particular need of protective efforts as coastal development and the increased use of recreational vehicles on beaches continue to have a discouraging impact on populations. Additionally, changing water levels have affected interior lake-nesting populations of Piping and Snowy Plovers.

On the arid, shortgrass plains of western North America, Mountain Plover numbers have fallen precipitously as once-suitable grasslands are converted to agricultural use or become overgrown by alien grasses and cultivated crops. Changes in grassland ecology brought about by the absence of grazers like bison and prairie dogs contribute to this loss of habitat. Killdeer populations have also shown significant declines that have been linked to agricultural and other land-use changes, and declines in Black-bellied Plovers have been detected in parts of eastern North America.

The Snowy and Mountain Plovers are on the WatchList.

On the positive side, the success of federal recovery efforts centering on improved beach management is reflected in the recent steady increase in the population of Piping Plovers along the Atlantic coast. Over a longer period, American Golden-Plover populations have greatly increased since their near-demise at the hands of market-gunners at the end of the 19th century.

Accidental Species

Two species of plovers have been recorded as accidentals in North America. A Collared Plover *(Charadrius collaris)*, usually found in Central and South America, has occurred in Texas in May, and Little Ringed Plovers *(C. dubius)* from Eurasia have been seen in the western Aleutian Islands during late spring.

Wayne R. Petersen

Oystercatchers

The oystercatchers are large, bulky, black or predominantly black-and-white shorebirds. They have long, laterally compressed, reddish-orange bills and yellow eyes with reddish-orange eye-rings. Oystercatchers are typically found on rocky coasts or extensive tidal flats. During the breeding season, these birds are especially conspicuous because of their loud, piping calls and their distinctive territorial, courtship, and distraction displays.

Taxonomy

Recent systematic work suggests that oystercatchers are closely allied to the stilts and avocets and the gulls and terns, and that they evolved from a plover-like ancestor. The relationship of oystercatcher species to one another is poorly understood; the sole genus, *Haematopus*, is thought to be comprised of as few as five to as many as 11 species, one of which—the Canary Islands Oystercatcher *(H. meadewaldoi)*—is almost certainly extinct.

Oystercatchers can be divided into two groups based on plumage coloration. Some species—for example, the Black Oystercatcher *(Haematopus bachmani)*—are all-black; others, including the American Oystercatcher *(H. palliatus)*, have pied black-and-white plumage.

Historically, geographically distinct populations of all-black oystercatchers have been treated as separate species. In contrast, most pied oystercatchers have been viewed as subspecies of two widespread species: the Eurasian Oystercatcher *(Haematopus ostralegus)* in the Old World or the American Oystercatcher in the New World. Currently, however, geographically separate populations of both all-black and pied oystercatchers are usually considered separate species.

Variation

On average, female oystercatchers are slightly larger than males and have longer bills. Male American Oystercatchers tend to have blacker backs and redder bills than females. Juveniles of both North American species are distinctive in having dusky-tipped bills, and scapulars and wing coverts dotted and edged with buff. The juvenal plumage is usually recognizable for up to four months, and some birds retain the dusky-tipped bill for more than a year.

Habitats

Worldwide, all-black oystercatchers tend to be associated with rocky shores, and pied oystercatchers with sandy or muddy substrates. The North American species tend not to occur inland.

There is little seasonal variation in habitat use by North American oystercatchers, largely due to their relatively sedentary nature. However, Black Oystercatchers occasionally forage on soft substrates during the nonbreeding season.

At high tide and at night, especially in the nonbreeding season, American Oystercatchers tend to gather in communal roosts that may contain a hundred or more individuals. Black Oystercatchers are considerably less gregarious but may be seen in small groups.

Haematopodid diversity. The two North American species of the family Haematopodidae are virtually identical to each other except in plumage color; in fact, all the world's species of oystercatchers are similar in appearance and habits. The American Oystercatcher is shown.

Food and Foraging

Oystercatchers feed mainly on mollusks. They also eat polychaete worms, amphipods, crabs, barnacles, echinoderms, and occasionally small fish.

The foraging techniques of oystercatchers are especially interesting to watch as the birds use their stout red bills to pry, probe, hammer, or stab in order to open or crush the shell or exoskeleton of a desired morsel. Individual oystercatchers may specialize as "hammerers" or "stabbers." The "hammerers" break

Oystercatcher bill. Oystercatchers' bills are long, straight, laterally flattened, and chisel-shaped. The birds use them to pry or hammer open bivalve shells, or to remove limpets and other shellfish from rocks. The Black Oystercatcher is shown.

shells open by pounding on them and have blunt-tipped bills. "Stabbers" have more pointed-tipped bills that they use to pry apart shells. These feeding differences are best studied in Eurasian Oystercatchers, but both techniques appear to be used by North American species.

Certain subtle prey differences exist between the sexes, possibly a reflection of the differences in bill size and structure between males and females. Seasonal dietary shifts may result from fluctuations in the availability of prey.

Breeding

During the breeding season, oystercatchers are monogamous and very territorial. They are also extremely site-faithful; it is routine for a pair to occupy the same territory for many years in succession.

Oystercatcher displays involve spectacular vocal and visual antics. The most characteristic vocalization is a loud, piping call that is variously used as a greeting between pair members, as an aggressive call when neighboring pairs confront each other in territorial disputes, and possibly to establish dominance hierarchies in feeding areas.

Worldwide Family Features

- 16–20" (40–51 cm) coastal shorebirds.
- Up to 10 extant species in 1 genus worldwide; cosmopolitan, but absent in polar areas, rare in tropical Africa and Asia. 2 species breed in North America; occur along most coasts south of the Arctic; plus 1 accidental species.
- Eat mainly bivalve mollusks, plus variety of other invertebrates; catch prey by probing in mud or prying items from rocks with bill; occasionally catch small fish.
- Monogamous; strong territory and mate fidelity over many years. In nonbreeding season, some species gather in flocks; others are solitary and territorial. Many are nonmigratory; northernmost breeders migrate south.
- Breed first at 3 or 4 years old, sometimes much older.

- Nest is a scrape, usually on a beach, rocky shore, or saltmarsh; sometimes lined with pebbles or plant matter. Male builds, usually at location determined by female. Occasionally reuse nest scrapes.
- 1–4 (usually 2 or 3) subelliptical to oval eggs; grayish or buffy, variously marked with dark spots or streaks. Incubation 24–39 days, by both sexes; often begins with laying of 2nd egg. Hatching asynchronous. 1 brood per year.
- Precocial young downy at hatch; usually leave nest within 24 hours. Fed by both parents at least until fledging at 34–49 days; may remain with parents for up to 6 months.
- Adult annual survival exceeds 80%. Among oldest on record: 43 years, 6 months (Eurasian Oystercatcher); 14 years (American Oystercatcher).

American Oystercatcher pair in nuptial flight. In the spring, pairs of oystercatchers of both North American species circle their territory together, calling loudly. During these flights, birds from adjacent territories may join the initial pair, and small groups of two or three pairs may display in unison, creating quite a commotion.

Unlike scolopacids (sandpipers, phalaropes, and their relatives), oystercatchers do not have elaborate flight displays. Courtship involves both members of a pair walking and posturing side by side, or flying together in low-level flight, making piping calls as they go.

Oystercatcher nests are usually located in the open, often on a beach, amid sand dunes, or on rocky shingle. American Oystercatchers sometimes nest in saltmarshes, and Black Oystercatchers will nest on rocky shores or offshore boulders. The nest is a scrape made by the male and is sometimes lined with a few bits of debris, small pebbles, or shells.

American and Black Oystercatchers both usually lay two or three eggs. They often replace clutches lost early in the nesting season, but replacement clutches are on average smaller than the first clutches.

Unlike most shorebirds, oystercatcher chicks are fed by their parents for up to a month or more. Young may stay with

Oystercatcher leg and foot. Oystercatchers have thick, sturdy legs and toes. Like their close relatives the stilts and avocets and the gulls and terns, they have webbing between their toes. The Black Oystercatcher is shown.

adults for up to six months before becoming fully independent and probably migrate with their parents. During this period young apparently learn foraging techniques from their parents.

After nesting, the northernmost breeding birds move a short distance south, but many individuals are nonmigratory.

Conservation

American Oystercatchers are widespread in the Americas and might once have bred as far north as Labrador, but by the early 20th century they no longer nested north of Virginia. The population has recovered somewhat and has steadily spread northward along the Atlantic coast. By 1997 the species had reached Nova Scotia as a breeding bird. Yet the North Atlantic population remains quite small, and nesting birds are vulnerable to beach development. Black Oystercatchers also are widely distributed, and most populations are apparently stable. However, they have declined locally in some areas, such as southern California, and the species is on the WatchList. It is also vulnerable to oil spills in important breeding areas, such as Prince William Sound.

Accidental Species

The Eurasian Oystercatcher, which breeds from Iceland to eastern Russia, has been found in northeastern North America several times in spring.

Wayne R. Petersen

Stilts and Avocets

Family Recurvirostridae
Order Charadriiformes

The stilts and avocets are tall, slim shorebirds with long, thin bills, very long, slender legs, long necks, and striking black-and-white plumage. Stilts have straight bills, while those of avocets are prominently re-curved. Their habitats include shallow freshwater or saline wetlands, lakeshores, and coastal estuaries. Stilts and avocets often wade in deep water, either pecking at prey items or sweeping their bills through the water. Both species give loud, strident calls, especially when breeding or in flight.

Taxonomy

Biologists believe that stilts and avocets are closely related to oystercatchers, plovers, and thick-knees, as well as to the peculiar Ibisbill *(Ibidorhyncha struthersii)* of central Asia. Indeed, the Ibisbill is sufficiently similar to the stilts and avo-cets that it is sometimes classified as a subfamily of the Recurvirostridae, but usually it is placed in its own family, the Ibidorhynchidae.

The Recurvirostridae has three genera: *Himantopus* and *Recurvirostra*, which occur throughout much of the world, and the single-species genus *Cladorhyn-chus* in Australia. The two species that breed in North America are the Black-necked Stilt *(H. mexicanus)* and the American Avocet *(R. americana)*.

The taxonomy of the cosmopolitan Black-winged Stilt *(Himantopus himanto-pus)* group (which includes the Black-necked Stilt) is complex, and the number of species within it uncertain. At one extreme, five separate species are recog-nized; at the other, the entire group is combined as a single species. Most North American ornithologists treat the Black-necked Stilt as a full species, though it is often classified as a subspecies of the Black-winged Stilt elsewhere in the world. The endangered "Hawaiian" Stilt *(H. mexi-canus knudseni)* is also generally considered a subspecies of the Black-necked Stilt but is a potential candidate for full species status.

The American Avocet is one of four avocet species worldwide; all are widely considered to be separate species.

Variation

Field identification of North American stilts and avocets is straightforward, and neither species is likely to be confused with any other shorebird. The sexes can usually be distinguished in the field in both species (unlike most shorebirds). Fe-male Black-necked Stilts differ from adult males in being brownish rather than glossy black on the back; juvenile stilts are also browner-backed.

The plumages of female American Avo-cets are similar to those of males, but fe-

Recurvirostrid diversity. The two North American species of Recurvirostridae, which are quite different from each other in appearance, represent the two main genera of the family worldwide. The American Avocet is shown at the left, the Black-necked Stilt at the right.

American Avocet leg and foot. Long legs, partial webbing between three toes, and a tiny hind toe characterize the American Avocet. The Black-necked Stilt has similar but longer legs with far less webbing, only between the inner and middle toes on each foot.

males usually have shorter, more recurved bills. The reason for this difference is not clear, but it may be related to foraging ecology or some form of sexual selection.

Juvenile American Avocets are unusual in having a plumage similar to that of breeding adults, with orange feathers appearing on the head and neck soon after hatching. It has been suggested that this "adult mimicry" may afford the young increased protection from predators that do not recognize them as helpless chicks unable to fly. Careful observers can distinguish young birds by their slightly smaller size, more swollen ankle joints, and fluffier appearance.

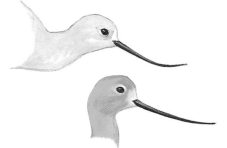

American Avocet bills. In many bird species, male and female differ in bill size and body proportions. The American Avocet is one of very few species in which the sexes differ in bill shape. The male's bill (bottom) is somewhat longer and is less strongly curved.

Habitats and Feeding

Stilts and avocets use a wide variety of habitats for feeding. During most of the year, the two North American species may be found together in shallow inland wetlands, both fresh and alkaline, as well as along lakeshores and prairie ponds, and on coastal mudflats. American Avocets are much more common than stilts in the most saline waters.

Prey typically consists of aquatic invertebrates, especially crustaceans and insects, but both species are somewhat opportunistic. American Avocets have been seen eating prey as large as a Tiger Salamander.

Stilts and avocets employ both tactile and visual feeding strategies. Perhaps most dramatic is the side-to-side swinging of the head and bill used by American Avocets as they glean organisms from shallow water or soft mud. Often groups of avocets advance in shallow water, sweeping their bills in unison.

Avocets, which have well-developed toe webbing, are among the few shorebirds other than phalaropes that regularly venture into water deep enough to require swimming.

Worldwide Family Features

- 14–20" (35–51 cm) shorebirds.
- About 9 species in 3 genera worldwide; found in most tropical and temperate regions. 2 species in 2 genera breed in North America, in western U.S. north to southern Prairie Provinces of Canada and along southern half of continent's Atlantic coast; plus 1 accidental species.
- Eat invertebrates and small vertebrates, caught with bill as birds wade in shallow water or mud. Avocets often swim in shallow water to pursue prey.
- Often nest in loose colonies. Seasonally monogamous. Often gregarious in non-breeding season. North-temperate populations migratory; others may move in response to habitat availability.
- Breed first at 2 or 3 years old, occasionally 1 year old.

- Nest generally a scrape on bare, open ground near water; sometimes lined with pebbles or debris; built by both sexes. In wet areas, build nest of mounded vegetation. Occasionally reuse nests.
- Usually 4 subelliptical to oval eggs with pale brownish-buff background, variably blotched with scattering of black and brown markings. Both sexes incubate, for 19–26 days. Most eggs hatch within 1–2 days of one another. 1 brood per year.
- Precocial young covered with down at hatch; generally leave nest within 24 hours. Both adults provide care. Chicks feed themselves; can fly after 28–55 days.
- Adult annual survival estimated at 80–90%. Among oldest on record: 24 years (Pied Avocet, *Recurvirostra avosetta,* of Europe); 14 years (Black-necked Stilt).

Recurvirostrid nest. The nests of the Black-necked Stilt (shown here) and the American Avocet are simple, varying from little more than a few grass stems around a shallow scrape to a larger mound of grassy vegetation when built near water. If rising water levels threaten the nest, the birds quickly add material to raise the level of the nest.

Breeding

Stilts and avocets tend to be seasonally monogamous. They are unusual among shorebirds in that they often breed in loose colonies, sometimes mixing with other waterbirds, including gulls, terns, and grebes. Both North American species will also breed as isolated pairs.

Before copulation, the birds perform elaborate preening and bill-dipping displays; afterward, they cross their bills and walk together for a short distance.

Depending upon the latitude, nesting begins in April or May. Nest-building is shared by the sexes. The nest is a scrape sparsely lined with pebbles or debris and located in the open on bare ground, usually near water. In wet areas, the birds may build more substantial nests out of vegetation. The four eggs are pale brownish buff, variably blotched with black and brown markings. Incubation lasts 22 to 25 days; both sexes share in the task.

Adult stilts and avocets use a variety of distraction displays, including "false brooding" behavior, a broken-wing act, and direct attacks, to lead or chase predators away from nests and young. The precocial chicks can feed themselves and may leave the nest within a few hours of hatching. At first they rely on their parents for brooding and warnings against predators but soon become independent and are able to fly after four to six weeks.

Conservation

Populations of both North American species are relatively large and thought to be stable. Locally, however, problems have arisen, especially in parts of the western United States where agriculture and wildlife compete for water. American Avocet populations, for example, have suffered in arid areas, where the accumulation of heavy metals such as selenium has caused horrific deformities in chicks.

American Avocet mating display. The American Avocet engages in a number of intricate displays. One of the most endearing is shown here: After copulation, the pair walks together a few paces with bills crossed and with the male's wing draped over the female's back.

Accidental Species

The Black-winged Stilt of Eurasia has occurred once on Nizki Island in the western Aleutians in late spring.

Wayne R. Petersen

Jacanas

The Jacanidae is a well-defined family of small to medium-size shorebirds with extremely long toes and claws. The birds' large feet spread their weight and allow them to walk on floating plants, from which they pick food items. Jacanas typically occur in shallow freshwater habitats with extensive aquatic vegetation, living their lives on the unsteady foundations of floating water plants. They have predominantly dark or reddish-brown plumage and stout, brightly colored bills; some have bare facial shields and wattles. Females are generally larger than males and may be twice as heavy in some species.

Taxonomy

Superficially jacanas appear similar to coots and rails, with which they have been grouped in the past. Studies of morphology, DNA–DNA hybridization, and behavior, however, show the jacanas to be shorebirds, most closely related to the painted-snipes (Rostratulidae) of South America, Africa, Asia, and Australia.

The only extant species to occur north of Mexico is the Northern Jacana *(Jacana spinosa)*; fossil evidence shows that at least one other species, now extinct, once occurred in Florida. Northern Jacanas normally range from central Mexico south to Panama and only rarely wander north to the southern United States.

Food and Foraging

Jacanas feed in various ways, but usually they can be seen inspecting the surfaces of aquatic plants for small invertebrates. They turn over floating plants with their feet and bills, searching for tiny insects

Northern Jacana. The eight species of jacanas in the world all share a somewhat stocky, coot-like bill and amazingly long toes that allow them to walk on floating vegetation.

Worldwide Family Features

- 6–12" (15–31 cm) shorebirds. (Maximum length excludes 12"/30 cm tail of one species.)
- 8 species in 6 genera worldwide; found throughout tropics and subtropics. 1 species has bred in southern U.S.
- Eat primarily insects gleaned from aquatic vegetation with bill; occasionally eat small fish, vegetation, seeds, even ticks off hippopotamuses.
- Territorial when breeding, often gregarious at other times. Females of most species polyandrous. Generally nonmigratory, but may make long-distance movements.
- Breed first probably at 2 years old or older.
- Nest is simple platform of plant matter on floating vegetation. Built primarily by male. Nests are not reused.

- 3 or 4 relatively small, subelliptical to oval eggs; brown with shades of yellow, green, or rufous; most have heavy, blackish markings and glossy surface. Male incubates, for 22–28 days. Hatching synchronous, although 1 egg can hatch early. Nests often fail; replacement clutches common. Polyandrous females may have several broods per year.
- Precocial young down-covered at hatch; cared for mostly by male. Develop slowly, fledging at 50 days–11½ weeks. May stay on male's territory through 1st year.
- Little known about adult survival or longevity. Presumed to be long-lived. Among oldest on record: 8 years (Northern Jacana), but older birds likely.

Northern Jacana foraging. The extremely long toes and claws of jacanas distribute their weight widely enough to allow them to walk on floating vegetation such as lily pads. Here a Northern Jacana uses a typical foraging method: turning over a lily pad with one foot to expose snails and insect larvae hidden on the underside of the leaf.

and creatures hiding on the undersurface. All jacana species occasionally eat plant matter. Northern Jacanas eat water-lily flowers opened up by other foraging species, such as Purple Gallinules *(Porphyrula martinica)* and Common Moorhens *(Gallinula chloropus).*

Breeding

Jacanas are territorial breeders, and both males and females defend territories against members of the same sex. Females typically have larger territories that encompass the territories of several males. The polyandrous females may be mated to as many as four males simultaneously and can lay clutches as frequently as every nine days.

Aggressive disputes over territories are common among females, and ownership changes frequently, especially when few males are around and competition for good mates to raise young is high. Consequently a male may be sequentially polygynous, changing mates whenever a new female moves into his territory. An intruding female that successfully ousts a resident female from her territory sometimes destroys the existing nests and kills any chicks. This infanticide presumably benefits the newcomer because it reduces the responsibilities of the resident males and increases the chance that they will mate immediately and devote time to raising young for the new female.

Males perform most of the chores of nest-building and chick-rearing, while females provide defense against predators. Males may build several platforms to be used for solicitation displays and copulation; subsequently one of these platforms is usually used as the nest.

The frequent, unpredictable flooding of wetland habitats, together with heavy predation, leads to high rates of clutch loss among Northern Jacanas. Nest predators include Purple Gallinules, Spectacled Caimans, and probably nocturnal snakes and mammals. Nests built on floating mats of vegetation are vulnerable should the plants begin to break apart. When this happens, the male will sometimes build another nest nearby and move the eggs to the new site.

Conservation

As a group, jacanas do not face major conservation threats. All species are relatively abundant throughout their ranges, and Northern Jacanas are common at shallow, vegetated wetlands throughout much of Central America. In the southern United States, Northern Jacanas are rare, as is typical for species near the periphery of their ranges. Nonetheless, local populations face threats from wetland loss, removal of emergent plants, and the reduction of food supplies by pesticides. The loss of wetland plants may be especially hard on jacanas, which rely on floating walkways to get around in their aquatic habitats.

David Allen Sibley and Chris Elphick

Sandpipers, Phalaropes, and Allies

Family Scolopacidae
Order Charadriiformes

Scolopacidae, the largest family within the order Charadriiformes, is a group of small to large shorebirds with long toes; long, tapered wings; and necks and legs that vary considerably in length. All scolopacids except the Sanderling *(Calidris alba)* have a short, elevated hind toe that distinguishes them from the plovers, with which they closely associate. Their bills, typically more slender than those of plovers, range from short to extremely long and can be decurved, recurved, straight, or even spatulate. The plumage of most species is a mixture of browns, grays, and white, often with reds and oranges in the breeding season. Males and females generally look alike, particularly in winter. Scolopacids usually occur near water but can be found in a wide variety of habitats, from arid grasslands to forests to open oceans.

Taxonomy

Scolopacidae is one of four major shorebird families found in North America, along with the plover and lapwing, oystercatcher, and stilt and avocet families. Taxonomists have traditionally placed these families in the order Charadriiformes along with gulls, terns, and auks.

The scolopacids are typically compared to plovers, and these two families are often thought to be each others' closest relatives. Osteological evidence and DNA–DNA hybridization studies, however, indicate that the painted-snipes (family Rostratulidae, of South America, Africa, Asia, and Australia) and the jacanas are the scolopacids' closest relatives.

While several research efforts support the idea that scolopacids are derived from a common ancestor, the family's fossil history is scant. The earliest fossils date to the late Eocene epoch, about 40 million years ago, and most have been found in North America or Europe.

Modern-day scolopacids are divided into different groups, although controversy still exists as to the relationships among groups. North American species are subdivided into nine groups, which are variously classified as either subfamilies or tribes. The two largest groups are the calidridine and tringine sandpipers. The calidridine group includes species such as Baird's Sandpiper *(Calidris bairdii)*, the Dunlin *(C. alpina)*, Sanderling, Red Knot

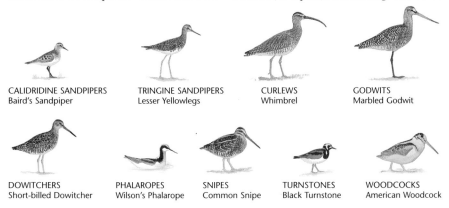

| CALIDRIDINE SANDPIPERS | TRINGINE SANDPIPERS | CURLEWS | GODWITS |
| Baird's Sandpiper | Lesser Yellowlegs | Whimbrel | Marbled Godwit |

| DOWITCHERS | PHALAROPES | SNIPES | TURNSTONES | WOODCOCKS |
| Short-billed Dowitcher | Wilson's Phalarope | Common Snipe | Black Turnstone | American Woodcock |

Scolopacid diversity. The 43 species of scolopacids in North America sort into nine groups. The calidridine sandpipers and the tringine sandpipers are the two largest groups, with 19 and seven species, respectively. The curlews and the godwits each have four North American species, and the nine remaining species are split among the other five groups.

273

Scolopacid head and bill. Most scolopacids have a relatively long and slender bill often used to probe in mud or sand to extract food. Within the family, however, the range of variation in bill length and shape is truly remarkable. The Stilt Sandpiper, shown here, has an "average" bill, moderately long and slightly drooped.

single group, as are the snipes and the dowitchers. Finally there are the woodcocks, the turnstones, and the phalaropes.

Species-level taxonomy within the family Scolopacidae has been relatively stable for some time. The most recent change among the North American species occurred in the early 1950s, when researchers recognized that the Long-billed Dowitcher *(Limnodromus scolopaceus)* and Short-billed Dowitcher *(L. griseus)* were distinct species.

Recent genetic and morphometric analyses, however, have revealed differences within the currently recognized scolopacid species that indicate the potential for future species splits. One such split may be to separate the North American subspecies of the Whimbrel from

(C. canutus), and Surfbird *(Aphriza virgata),* as well as rare visitors from Eurasia, such as the Little Stint *(C. minuta)* and Ruff *(Philomachus pugnax).* The smaller species in this group are often called "peeps" because of their peep-like calls.

The tringine sandpipers include the Lesser Yellowlegs *(Tringa flavipes),* Spotted Redshank *(T. erythropus),* Willet *(Catoptrophorus semipalmatus),* Wandering Tattler *(Heteroscelus incanus),* and Spotted Sandpiper *(Actitis macularia).*

The curlews—which include the Whimbrel *(Numenius phaeopus)* and the Upland Sandpiper *(Bartramia longicauda)*—and the godwits sometimes are combined in a

Scolopacid foot. Sandpipers and their allies have relatively long legs and slender toes with little or no webbing. The hind toe is reduced and raised so that it barely touches the ground, and in one species (the Sanderling) it is absent altogether. The Western Sandpiper is shown.

Worldwide Family Features

- 5–26" (13–66 cm) shorebirds.
- 87 species in 21 genera; found worldwide. 43 species in 16 genera regular in North America; plus 20 accidental species; 1 other species probably extinct. Family occurs throughout continent.
- Eat a wide variety of invertebrates; some species eat small amphibians, fish, seeds, fruit. Obtain prey by locating it visually and plucking it from water, ground, or other surfaces, or by probing in mud.
- Territorial when breeding; some species colonial. Monogamous, polygynous, or polyandrous; pair bonds usually last for 1 breeding season or less. Generally gregarious when not breeding. Most species migratory.
- Breed first at 1 year old in smaller species, 2 or 3 years old in larger species.
- Nest usually a scrape in the ground

lined with grasses and leaves, often near water. Male generally builds initial scrape; female finishes nest and adds lining. Occasionally reuse nests; a few species use old passerine nests in trees.
- 2–4 (generally 4) pyriform to oval eggs; often off-white, light buff, or olive, marked with black or brown. Both parents incubate for 17–32 days. Hatching synchronous. Usually 1 brood per year; more in polygamous species.
- Precocial young covered with down at hatching; leave nest within hours to forage with at least 1 parent (usually the male). Fledge at 14–45 days.
- Adult annual survival typically 60–70% in small species, 85–95% in larger species. In 1st year, survival often less than 50%. Among oldest on record: 32 years (Eurasian Curlew); 29 years (Marbled Godwit).

the European and Siberian subspecies (both have occurred in North America). Within scolopacid species in North America there are a number of subspecies that can be identified through plumage and other morphological differences. In North America, there are three sub-species each of the Dunlin, Red Knot, Rock Sandpiper *(Calidris ptilocnemis)*, and Short-billed Dowitcher. One Short-billed Dowitcher subspecies breeds in Canada, mainly east of Hudson Bay, another in Canada from Hudson Bay west, and the third mainly in Alaska.

In addition to breeding in different areas, different subspecies often segregate in winter. For instance, one subspecies of the Red Knot breeds in the high Arctic of Canada and winters in Europe, while a second breeds in the low Arctic of Canada and winters in southern South America.

Research on vocalization differences between the two subspecies of Willet shows that eastern birds discriminate between the songs of the eastern and western subspecies, suggesting that these subspecies have attained an intermediate stage of speciation.

Rarely sandpipers will hybridize, adding to the identification problems of this al-ready difficult group. "Cox's Sandpiper," a bird that has been reported in Massa-chusetts, was originally thought to be an extremely rare species that wintered in Australia and presumably bred somewhere in Siberia. Genetic studies, however, have revealed it to be a hybrid between the Curlew Sandpiper *(Calidris ferruginea)* and the Pectoral Sandpiper *(C. melanotos)*.

Molts and Plumages

The habits and habitats of scolopacids make them easy birds to observe. Most shorebirds roost, forage, nest, and raise their young in relatively open, flat areas. When not breeding they regularly occur in large numbers. Many allow observers to approach within several feet. Species identification can still be difficult, how-ever, especially among the smaller peeps and the dowitchers. There are many clues

Feather wear. *As with other birds, the feathers of shorebirds are subject to a great deal of wear over time. Here, the Whimbrel feather on the left is fresh, while the one on the right is very worn. The pale portions of the feather abrade more quickly than the dark areas, giving rise to the dark appearance of worn birds. Even the shapes of individual feathers change, following the contours of dark markings.*

birders can use to accurately identify a difficult species, including relative size, foraging style, and microhabitat choice. Recognizing age-specific plumages can also aid in identification. In addition, the presence and stage of molt is a valuable key to the age and identity of many shorebird species.

Scolopacids have 11 primaries on each wing, with the outermost feather greatly reduced, and 8 to 14 secondaries. Gener-ally they have 12 tail feathers, but some species have more; certain snipes have as many as 28. In adult scolopacids, these flight feathers are typically replaced once a year, usually during the prebasic molt in late summer or fall. Body feathers are usually replaced twice a year, during both the prebasic molt and a spring prealter-nate molt.

In adult scolopacids, flight feather molt often starts with the inner primaries and continues toward the outermost pri-mary. After about half of these feathers have been dropped, the bird begins molt-ing the secondaries, starting with the feather farthest from the body and molt-ing progressively inward. Often the secondary closest to the body molts at the same time as the outermost secondary, and the molt simultaneously progresses toward the center. During this time, the rectrices are also molted, usually from the center outward, but often in irregular sequences.

Juvenile scolopacids generally do not replace their primaries and secondaries during their first prebasic molt; instead, these feathers are retained for 13 to 18 months until the second prebasic molt.

Feather characteristics often differ according to age. While some of these differences are visible in the field, others require study of a captured bird. The feathers of young birds are structurally weaker, and they wear much faster than those of adults. The difference in wear that results from the combination of weaker feathers retained for a longer period can be quite dramatic and is a useful characteristic for determining the age of birds. Juveniles tend to have paler brown primaries with more ragged edges compared to the neater, dark blackish-brown primaries of adults.

There are several other clues that can be used to tell the age of shorebirds. In a juvenile's wing, where all the primaries grow at the same time, wear on the feathers tends to increase from the protected inner primaries toward the outer primaries. In an adult bird that has completed a full primary molt, the wear is initially more uniform, as the inner primaries are several weeks older than the outer ones. A juvenile's primaries, secondaries, and tail feathers tend to be pointed and relatively narrow, in contrast to the broader, more rounded adult feathers. Juveniles also usually have inner median coverts edged with buff, a characteristic that often can be used to distinguish between juvenile and adult birds in the hand.

Scolopacid Plumage Changes

The appearance of scolopacids, such as the Western Sandpiper shown here, changes throughout their lives as a result of both molt and feather wear. Young birds exchange the down they are born with for their juvenal plumage within a few weeks of birth. As summer turns into fall, the juvenal feathers become worn and the body feathers (but not the flight feathers) are replaced by the first basic plumage.

The next spring, the body feathers are replaced again, this time by the first alternate plumage. At this time, these birds still retain their juvenal flight feathers, which appear much more worn than those of older individuals. During the bird's second fall it replaces its body feathers yet again and, for the first time, its flight feathers, during a complete molt into definitive basic plumage. Thereafter, birds undergo a partial molt each spring, replacing only body feathers, to attain the definitive alternate plumage, and a complete molt each fall to revert to definitive basic plumage.

Appearance also changes with feather wear; for example, birds may become darker over the summer as the pale feather edges are abraded.

fresh juvenal   worn juvenal   first basic

first alternate   definitive basic   fresh definitive alternate   worn definitive alternate

The adults of most North American scolopacids molt their flight feathers either at a staging site during migration or on their wintering grounds. Exceptions are some populations of Purple Sandpipers *(Calidris maritima)*, Dunlins, Common Snipes *(Gallinago gallinago)*, and American Woodcocks *(Scolopax minor)*, which molt their flight feathers on or near their breeding grounds. A few species, such as the Greater Yellowlegs *(Tringa melanoleuca)* and the Long-billed Dowitcher, may begin their flight feather molt on the breeding grounds, suspend molt during migration, then resume it once again when they reach the wintering grounds.

The primary molt usually takes from 50 to 130 days; in general, the farther north a sandpiper winters, the shorter the duration of its molt. The primary molt is typically a gradual process; however, about half of all Bristle-thighed Curlews *(Numenius tahitiensis)* become flightless by simultaneously dropping their flight feathers while on their Pacific Island wintering grounds, which are generally free of predators and disturbance.

Habitats

Members of the Scolopacidae occupy a tremendous variety of habitats over the course of a year, ranging from small oases in the middle of deserts to islands in the middle of oceans to mountaintops to open ocean. Almost all North American species spend at least part of their time near water, where they commonly feed and breed. The American Woodcock is unique among the North American species in that it spends the majority of its life in woodlands.

Breeding Habitats
Worldwide only 11 of the 87 species of scolopacids breed in tropical latitudes. Most members of the family breed in taiga or tundra habitats, with 37 different species nesting in Alaska alone. In North America, many species breed in low-lying tundra, at such places as the

Yukon–Kuskokwim Delta in Alaska and Canada's Hudson Bay region.

Red Phalaropes *(Phalaropus fulicaria)*, Red-necked Phalaropes *(P. lobatus)*, Long-billed Dowitchers, Hudsonian Godwits *(Limosa haemastica)*, Bar-tailed Godwits *(L. lapponica)*, and many species of calidridine sandpipers breed in grass-dominated, moist to wet, low-lying tundra, usually near bodies of fresh water.

Other species—including both yellowlegs, the Short-billed Dowitcher, the Solitary Sandpiper *(Tringa solitaria)*, and, to some degree, the Least Sandpiper *(Calidris minutilla)* and Whimbrel—breed mainly in subarctic taiga regions, mostly within and near muskeg wetlands. A few species breed only on windswept, alpine tundra in Alaska and Canada; these include the Surfbird and the Wandering Tattler. The real high-Arctic breeders—Sanderlings, Red Knots, and some Ruddy Turnstones *(Arenaria interpres)*—breed in moist and grassy to dry and barren tundra.

Not all scolopacids breed at high latitudes; for example, five species breed near freshwater wetlands within the arid Great Basin in the western United States. Grasslands and wet meadows in the central United States and south-central Canada support breeding Long-billed Curlews *(Numenius americanus)*, Willets, Marbled Godwits *(Limosa fedoa)*, Upland Sandpipers, and Wilson's Phalaropes *(Phalaropus tricolor)*. Spotted Sandpipers breed along rivers and lakeshores throughout the continent. The eastern subspecies of Willet breeds in coastal saltmarshes along the Atlantic, a very different habitat from the grasslands and Great Basin deserts used by the western subspecies.

Migration and Winter Habitats
The varied habitats used by scolopacids during the nonbreeding season are also usually associated with water. By November, when most migration is over, scolopacids wintering in North America are generally found at temperate coastal sites or in areas where extensive wetlands lie relatively close to the coast. The Willamette Valley of Oregon, the Central Valley

of California, and the rice-growing regions of Louisiana and Texas support large numbers of wintering shorebirds.

Along North American coastlines, estuaries with large expanses of mudflats often attract concentrations of peeps, dowitchers, and godwits. Within estuaries, different species occupy different water depths and substrate types, although there can be some overlap. Dunlins and dowitchers prefer the muddiest areas, while Red Knots, Sanderlings, and Western Sandpipers (Calidris mauri) feed in sandier substrates and at differing water depths. The birds' use of coastal estuaries, bays, and beaches is largely dictated by tidal cycles.

Dunlin on one leg. *"One-legged" shorebirds are often seen awkwardly hopping about. In almost all cases these birds are not actually missing a leg, but simply have one leg tucked up against the belly, hidden by feathers, to conserve heat.*

When feeding, shorebirds often segregate by species, offering useful clues for identification. Least Sandpipers generally feed in the moist mud close to marsh edges or within marsh vegetation. Dunlins favor areas just below the falling tide line, where they wade up to their chests, while godwits and Willets occur in deeper waters. Dowitcher species often segregate by water salinity, with the Short-billeds typically occurring in saltier waters than Long-billeds.

Favorite coastal roosting areas include beaches at the high-tide line, barrier reefs, jetties, barrier islands, logjams, and even cliff ledges. In areas where estuaries lie near agricultural fields and lawns, birds often leave the mudflats during inclement weather and high tides to forage and roost in the fields. Some species, including the Red Knot and the Dunlin, have been observed flying in large flocks during the entire high-tide period, presumably to escape predators.

Commercial salt production can create important nonbreeding habitats for scolopacids. In California, salt ponds are especially favored by the smaller calidrine sandpipers, dowitchers, Willets, Marbled Godwits, and phalaropes.

Rocky shores, especially at more northerly latitudes in North America, are favored by such species as Purple Sandpipers, Rock Sandpipers, Wandering Tattlers, Surfbirds, Ruddy Turnstones, and Black Turnstones (Arenaria melanocephala).

During migration, scolopacids gather, sometimes in enormous concentrations, at interior sites with water in North America. Areas that attract the highest numbers of birds are typically shallow, extensive bodies of water, including managed wetlands, rice fields and other temporarily flooded fields, lakes and reservoirs, and sewage ponds.

Phalaropes spend the nonbreeding season on alkaline lakes or on open ocean far from land. Wilson's Phalaropes gather to winter at alkaline lakes in the

Habitat segregation of shorebirds. *Flocks of foraging shorebirds often include more than one species, but the species often segregate by subtle habitat differences. In this example, the habitat changes from the high, dry mudflats with grassy vegetation on the left to relatively deep water on the right. The typical species also change along that gradient. Species shown, from left to right, are the Least Sandpiper, Semipalmated Sandpiper, Western Sandpiper, Dunlin, and Short-billed Dowitcher.*

Long-billed Curlews foraging. The Long-billed Curlew uses its prodigious bill to probe deep into mud and sand, following the burrows of fiddler crabs, crayfish, and other crustaceans, and bringing prey up to be consumed at the surface.

Andes, while Red-necked and Red Phalaropes concentrate in areas of upwelling in the southern Atlantic and Pacific Oceans. The large alkaline lakes of the West and the Great Plains, such as Utah's Great Salt Lake, California's Mono Lake, and Oregon's Lake Abert, attract spectacular concentrations of migrating birds, especially Red-necked and Wilson's Phalaropes. Hundreds of thousands of dowitchers, mostly Long-billed, use managed wetlands where water levels have been lowered to create shorebird habitat. Such sites include the Carson Sink in Nevada and Cheyenne Bottoms, Kansas.

Food and Foraging

Within the family Scolopacidae there is extreme variability in bill morphology that results in a wide variety of feeding habits. Many species have straight bills for making rapid thrusts through soft substrates or for picking prey off the water's surface. Species that probe in firm soils generally have straighter bills than those that feed in softer sediment. Dowitchers probe with a rapid up-and-down movement, referred to as "stitching" because it resembles the motion of a sewing machine. The decurved bills of species like the Long-billed Curlew and the Whimbrel are used to remove long, soft-bodied prey from mudflats, and these birds can be seen angling their bills deep into invertebrate burrows.

Many scolopacids have bills with tactile and chemo-sensitive nerve receptors at the tips that allow them to locate prey through touch, smell, and pressure gradients. The use of these senses opens up feeding options unavailable to the more exclusively visual plovers. Species with these sensory adaptations are as active at night as they are during the day.

Phalaropes and other scolopacids transport small prey items along their bills using the surface tension of water drops. The bird captures a drop of water containing a prey item in its bill tip and then opens its jaws so that the drop moves toward the mouth, taking the food with it. When the water drop reaches the mouth, the bird closes its jaws, squeezes and shakes the water from its bill, and consumes the prey. With this method, prey transport can occur in a hundredth of a second.

Phalaropes also use a distinctive foraging technique while swimming in open water. They spin around in tight circles on the surface to create an upwelling plume of water. This plume transports small invertebrate prey items from the water column below up to the surface, where the birds can reach them.

During the breeding season, most scolopacids forage in low-lying, moist areas for freshwater zooplankton and the larvae and pupae of various insects, including midges, crane flies, and muscid flies. They also feed on spiders, plant seeds, and adult insects.

The Buff-breasted Sandpiper *(Tryngites subruficollis)* and other species that remain

Red-necked Phalarope spinning. Swimming phalaropes often spin in tight circles while foraging. Spinning creates a small upwelling of water under the bird, transporting prey items to the surface. Individual phalaropes consistently spin in only one direction—to either the left or the right.

on the drier upland areas of tundra are more dependent on adult insects. Some Arctic-breeding species, such as the Bristle-thighed Curlew, rely heavily on low-bush berries. Farther south, grassland species like the Upland Sandpiper eat insects, invertebrates, and seeds, while the Spotted Sandpiper forages for a variety of organisms, including annelid worms, fish, spiders, crustaceans, carrion, and terrestrial and aquatic insects. The American Woodcock specializes in earthworms, probing the soil and extracting the worms with its long bill.

The array of organisms scolopacids consume during the nonbreeding season is as varied as the habitats they occupy. Coastal species such as Dunlins, peeps, Willets, godwits, dowitchers, and Long-billed Curlews forage for bottom-dwelling invertebrates in the muddy intertidal areas of estuaries and bays. Main prey items include polychaete worms, small clams, gastropods, and amphipods.

Greater Yellowlegs often chase and catch small fish in puddles of water. Along the rocky intertidal zone, Whimbrels, Surfbirds, and Wandering Tattlers search for mussels, polychaetes, and crustaceans. Bristle-thighed Curlews and Ruddy Turnstones wintering on oceanic islands will even eat seabird eggs.

Territoriality and Flocking

On the breeding grounds, scolopacids generally defend some type of territory, even if it is only the area immediately around the nest. Territorial aggression tends to be more bluff than action, although birds will commonly rush and bump other birds with their bodies. Occasionally birds will actually lock bills and fight, and aggressive encounters can sometimes be intense. Fights between breeding Spotted Sandpipers have resulted in serious injuries, and a fight observed between two Western Sandpipers reportedly lasted six hours.

Away from the breeding grounds, social behavior ranges from individuals defending feeding territories to large, tightly integrated foraging flocks. Some species, such as the Spotted and Solitary Sandpipers, only rarely form groups of more than a few individuals, while others, such as the Western Sandpiper, often occur in flocks numbering in the tens of thousands. Some species, such as the Sanderling, may temporarily defend resource-rich areas but abandon them when Merlins *(Falco columbarius)* or other predators arrive.

When food is superabundant or very scarce, scolopacids stop defending their territories, either because the territory becomes too large to defend or because the birds spend more energy being territorial than they gain by excluding competitors from feeding areas.

Many scolopacid species are faithful to specific wintering sites, returning year after year to the same lagoon or estuary.

Shorebirds often gather in flocks for protection; one of the most spectacular events a birder can witness is a falcon attacking a swirling mass of birds. Falcons typically try to separate a bird from its flock, presumably because a single bird is easier to follow and attack. When attacked, birds form dense, coordinated flocks that twist and turn in synchrony

Aggressive display. Many species of shorebirds defend small feeding territories during migration and winter. The two Semipalmated Sandpipers shown here have faced off in a common threat display: lowering one wing and raising the back feathers to appear bigger. Most such displays end when one bird simply walks away.

at high speeds, generating "waves" of motion. The wave action appears to be initiated by birds on the outside of the flock that rotate into the center.

Based on experimental work on the Dunlin, it has been suggested that abrupt changes in direction and speed of the waves are possible because individual birds are prepared to turn well before their immediate neighbors turn. This allows them to time the turn to coincide with the arrival of the wave, much like a human chorus line.

Least Sandpiper aerial display. On the tundra breeding grounds, where raised perches are nonexistent, displaying sandpipers broadcast their songs from the air. The Least Sandpiper sails 15 to 20 feet (4.5–6 m) over the tundra with gently fluttering wings and sings its trilling song.

Breeding

Most North American scolopacid species are monogamous, with both sexes defending territories and incubating eggs. The mating systems of some species, however, are much more complex.

The Buff-breasted Sandpiper is the only shorebird regularly breeding in North America that forms leks. Up to 20 Buff-breasted males may gather at a lek site on the breeding grounds to display to females (see Vocalizations and Displays, below). The female selects a male to mate with and then leaves to lay eggs and raise the young alone. The Ruff, which breeds only rarely in Alaska, also forms leks.

White-rumped Sandpipers *(Calidris fuscicollis)*, Pectoral Sandpipers, American Woodcocks, and several other species are polygynous. Individual males will defend a territory and pair either simultaneously or sequentially with several females. In these species, pair bonds are typically brief or nonexistent.

Conversely, if enough males are available, the Spotted Sandpiper and all three phalarope species will engage in polyandrous behavior, in which a female mates and lays eggs with several different males. The males of these species generally incubate the eggs, although in the case of the Spotted Sandpiper the female often helps.

Vocalizations and Displays

Scolopacids signal extensively with sound, but their acoustic communications are not as well studied as those of passerines. Scolopacid vocalizations tend to suit the open nature of their habitats; the birds employ loud, low-frequency, repeated sounds during aerial displays to attract mates and defend territories.

Vocalizations vary greatly among individuals, and even a single bird uses different sounds in different situations. For example, many species of *Calidris* sandpipers produce a variety of sounds during display flights, including a chattering call often associated with aggression, a rhythmically repeated call, and a song. Some scolopacid species will sing fragments of breeding songs at spring migration stopovers, thousands of miles away from the breeding grounds.

Scolopacids also communicate with aerial and ground displays. Aerial displays are especially suited to the birds' open habitats, since they can be viewed without obstruction over long distances. Aerial displays can vary in height, direction, wing-beat amplitude, frequency, and calls given during flight. Most species engage in some type of aerial breeding display. The American Woodcock generally flies in a woodland opening, while Arctic breeders like dowitchers and Dunlins fly and sing in the air above the tundra. Turnstones, however, have few aerial displays.

The Common Snipe's winnowing display is probably the most commonly observed scolopacid aerial display in North America. In this display, special muscles fan out the tail feathers; as the snipe plunges toward the ground, the tail feathers vibrate in the wind, creating a distinctive winnowing noise. Perhaps as a result of these displays, Common Snipes have either 14 or 16 tail feathers (depending on the subspecies) instead of the 12 tail feathers of most scolopacids.

The breeding displays of other scolopacids also can be quite complex. Male Pectoral and White-rumped Sandpipers inflate special breast sacs to create unusual noises. The male Pectoral flies low over the tundra, its inflated breast sac hanging low and heavy, producing a distinctive deep, hooting noise.

The male Buff-breasted Sandpiper engages in one of the most entertaining breeding displays of any shorebird. The males gather at leks; when a female approaches, they begin lifting one or both wings into the air, flashing their white wing-linings while jumping up off the ground, and then fluttering back down. Studies have found that females seem to prefer males with more extensive white patches, typically found on older birds. The Buff-breasted Sandpiper will occasionally display at migration stopovers.

In the phalaropes, typical avian sex roles are reversed. Males, which are responsible for incubating the eggs and raising the young, do not defend territories and exhibit little in the way of displays and songs. Instead females can be seen chasing males, displaying, and soliciting copulations.

Common Snipe winnowing display. One of the more unusual displays of any shorebird is the winnowing flight display of the Common Snipe. The male flies high up into the air and spends minutes performing a series of steep dives, during which the air rushing past the spread tail feathers produces a low, throbbing whistle.

If a predator advances too near to a nest, birds may use several defensive display tactics to divert its attention, including feigning an injury. Parents are easily provoked into broken-wing displays, in which they spread and drag a wing or tail while slowly fluttering away from the nest; they may also flash brightly contrasting feathers such as wing-bars.

In the rodent-run display, which mimics a small running mammal, the bird drags its wings to create the illusion of a second pair of legs, erects its feathers to resemble fur, and squeals while zigzagging along the ground. This behavior is performed mainly by the smaller *Calidris* sandpipers.

Nests

Most scolopacids build crude scrapes in the ground that are bare or sparsely lined with small leaves, grasses, and mosses. Nests are often located near water and are often overhung or concealed by grass tussocks. Many species place the nest near the base of a tree or shrub, when available.

In the majority of scolopacids, the initial scrape is built by the male, and then the nest cup is altered by the female, who often shapes the cup with her legs and breast. Nest sites are occasionally reused, although this varies among species. Fifteen percent of Stilt Sandpipers *(Calidris himantopus)* have been found to reuse nest cups from previous years. The Solitary Sandpiper is North America's only regular tree-nesting shorebird, readily reusing the nests of such birds as the American Robin *(Turdus migratorius)* and the Cedar Waxwing *(Bombycilla cedrorum).*

Eggs

Members of the family Scolopacidae lay from two to four eggs, with four-egg clutches by far the most common. Scolopacid eggs are cryptically colored to blend in with their surroundings. The base color is often pale olive, buff, or off-white, but it can range from reddish to

Solitary Sandpiper at nest. Most shorebirds nest on the ground, but there are exceptions. Solitary Sandpipers typically nest in trees, reusing the old nests of passerines such as the American Robin.

purple. Almost all eggs are covered with medium to dark (usually black, brown, or olive) splotches, dots, and streaks, with the markings heavier toward the round end. The eggs generally have a slightly glossy finish.

Until full clutches are laid and full-time incubation begins, eggs can survive for days in the cold without suffering damage. However, eggs exposed to temperatures greater than 104° F (40° C), even for a short period of time, are at risk of embryonic damage, a fact birders should keep in mind when approaching nesting birds during hot, sunny weather. Incubation periods usually range from 18 to 22 days, although the Long-billed Curlew incubates for 27 or 28 days.

Depending on the species, either the male, the female, or both sexes incubate the eggs. In monogamous scolopacids, both parents provide care, although the male often does most of the incubating as the eggs get closer to hatching. In some species, including the American Woodcock and the Buff-breasted, White-rumped, and Pectoral Sandpipers, only the female incubates. In polyandrous species, the male does most of the incubating. All the eggs in a scolopacid clutch tend to hatch within a 24-hour period.

Young

Within hours of hatching, the precocial chicks are out of the nest and foraging. Wilson's Phalarope chicks can swim at the ripe old age of one hour. Sometimes chicks spend their first night in the nest brooded by an adult; in bad weather, chicks will remain in the nest with the adults brooding them until conditions improve. American Woodcocks and Common Snipes are the only North American scolopacids that feed their chicks.

Chicks are able to move several miles within a few days. At least one parent, usually the male, remains with the chicks during the first weeks. Researchers speculate that the female often leaves the majority of the chick-rearing to the male so she can fatten up and regain the energy expended during egg production.

Chicks are often brooded for the first week or so following hatching, after which the adults act mainly as sentinels watching for predators. The young of smaller species are able to fly in 14 to 26 days, while larger species take longer; Long-billed Curlews fly after 41 to 45 days. Flight usually marks the onset of independence in scolopacids.

Movements

Almost all scolopacids have long wings with pointed tips and sleek, tapered bodies that aid them in rapid flight and migration. The American Woodcock is an exception; like many of the larger forest-dwelling birds, it has rounded wings to facilitate movement in its obstacle-filled environment. Most members of the family are somewhat migratory, and some are capable of tremendous migrations covering thousands of miles in a single flight.

For example, the White-rumped Sandpiper typically breeds in the high Arctic and winters in southern South America, and a few individuals even reach the Antarctic. The birds appear to achieve this migration in a series of long-distance jumps that cover stretches of up to 2,500 miles (4,000 km) at a time. Other species move much shorter distances; some

Spotted Sandpiper at nest.
The Spotted Sandpiper, like
many scolopacids, nests on the
ground in a grassy cup
concealed near tall grasses. The
eggs are relatively large and are
speckled with a cryptic pattern.
The Spotted Sandpiper is
unusual in that the male cares
for the eggs and young, while
each female may mate with
several different males.

subspecies of Rock and Purple Sandpipers spend their entire lives in relatively restricted areas along the subarctic coast.

Scolopacids engaging in long-distance migrations often turn up in unusual places; Black Turnstones have been known to wander to Wisconsin and American Woodcocks to New Mexico. Both the Sharp-tailed Sandpiper *(Calidris acuminata)* and the Red-necked Stint *(C. ruficollis)* primarily breed in northern Siberia and winter in Australasia and southern Asia (the stint rarely breeds in Alaska as well). Yet displaced birds of both species regularly occur on the East Coast of North America, especially during fall migration. Black-tailed Godwits *(Limosa limosa)* from Eurasia have wandered to eastern North America on occasion, and Hudsonian Godwits are found annually in New Zealand; all four of the world's godwits have even appeared together in New Jersey.

There can be a great deal of variation in how the birds migrate, even within a species. Of two subspecies of Dunlin breeding in Alaska, one subspecies winters in Asia, while the other winters in western North America. Within the latter subspecies some individuals may spend the winter in coastal Alaska near their breeding grounds, while others winter as far south as the western coast of Mexico.

Often males winter farther north than females. For instance, 70 to 80 percent of the Western Sandpipers that winter in California, Texas, and northern Mexico are males; in Central and South America the percentage of females is higher. While it is not entirely clear why this is true, one explanation is that males stay closer to the breeding grounds so they can return and set up breeding territories before the best sites are taken.

Some species perform elliptical migrations, using one route as they head south and another as they head north. For instance, many of the world's Semipalmated Sandpipers *(Calidris pusilla)* fly east in the fall from their Arctic breeding grounds toward the Bay of Fundy in southeastern Canada, where they fatten up before embarking on a nonstop transatlantic flight to South America. When returning to the breeding grounds, many of these birds fly across the Gulf of Mexico and head north through the Great Plains.

The spring migration period is typically shorter than the fall migration. In fall, the earliest birds to be seen on migration, beginning in late June, are typically the failed breeders. They are followed by adult females that have successfully bred, then adult males, and lastly juveniles, which arrive at migratory stopovers from August onward. Because determining the age of individuals is often an important step in the identification process, understanding this pattern of migration by different birds can be helpful in distinguishing species.

Weather conditions often play an important role in shorebird migration, especially as they affect wind patterns.

Radar studies have revealed that sco-lopacids will migrate at altitudes where favorable wind conditions exist, ranging from just above sea level to more than 20,000 feet (6,000 m), where they compete for airspace with low-flying commercial airplanes. Migratory movements can be seen at all times of day but generally begin in the late afternoon or early evening; at coastal locations, birds often depart on rising tides.

Often the birds will form whirling pre-departure flocks in which there is much calling. Migrating flocks range from fewer than 10 to more than 500 individuals and typically consist of a single species.

Flight speeds during migration can be impressive, with many birds traveling at speeds of 25 miles per hour (40 km/h) or more. A 1-ounce (28-gm) Western Sandpiper carrying a small radio transmitter flew about 1,900 miles (3,000 km) from San Francisco to the Copper River Delta in Alaska in less than 42 hours, averaging about 40 miles per hour (64 km/h). A Semipalmated Sandpiper of similar size averaged close to that flight speed, traveling from Maine to Guyana in two days.

For most scolopacid species, having access to a series of stopover sites along a migration flyway is vital. Some of the most exciting bird-watching experiences occur at sites where migrating shorebirds stop and concentrate. At some sites it is possible to see up to a million birds pack into relatively small areas over the course of a few days. Well-known North American staging areas include the Bay of Fundy, Delaware Bay, Cheyenne Bottoms in Kansas, Great Salt Lake, San Francisco Bay, and the Copper River Delta, Alaska.

Inclement weather can stimulate the movements of birds. In California, Dunlins that normally winter on the coast will move more than 100 miles (160 km) inland into the Central Valley during wet years, presumably to feed in newly flooded fields and seasonal wetlands. During coastal storms, shorebirds commonly move to nearby agricultural fields to roost and feed.

Freezing temperatures and snow will also stimulate movements. For example, American Woodcocks wintering in Gulf coast states move to coastal marshes in cold winters; local abundance of this species in the southern United States can vary greatly depending on winter temperatures farther north.

In preparation for migration, scolopacids sometimes undergo remarkable physiological changes. For example, Wilson's Phalaropes and Bar-tailed Godwits can add up to 55 percent of their body mass in fat prior to migration. Some Wilson's Phalaropes become so fat that they cannot walk and swimming birds need a long "runway" in order to take off. In Red Knots and Bar-tailed Godwits the digestive organs can reduce in size prior to long flights, presumably to reduce unnecessary weight during migration.

Conservation

The conservation and management of shorebirds is complicated by the fact that these birds use a wide variety of habitats and areas over the course of a year. They are largely migratory species, requiring a series of interconnected areas of suitable habitat to successfully complete their annual movements. Formulating a comprehensive conservation and management plan for migratory shorebirds is especially challenging at ephemeral interior wetlands that can dry up completely in some years. In wet years these sites can be too deep for shorebirds, but in years with ample shallow water they may be used by hundreds of thousands of birds.

The Eskimo Curlew (Numenius borealis) is perhaps the most recent North American bird to become extinct. It is the only member of the family presently listed as endangered in the United States and Canada. Historically this bird bred in Arctic Canada and wintered in South America, but there have been few verified sightings since the 1950s; the last confirmed records in the wild were from Texas in 1962 and Barbados in 1963. Two unconfirmed sightings in Canada's Prairie Provinces in 1996 give faint hope that the species persists.

The IUCN–World Conservation Union's Red List of Threatened Animals includes the Bristle-thighed Curlew as a species of concern, based on its low population numbers and limited distribution. The North American WatchList includes the Bristle-thighed Curlew and 10 additional Scolopacidae species: the Willet, Long-billed Curlew, Hudsonian Godwit, Black Turnstone, Surfbird, Red Knot, Rock Sandpiper, Stilt Sandpiper, Buff-breasted Sandpiper, and Short-billed Dowitcher. Concerns about these species primarily stem from their small population sizes, their limited distributions, or their propensity to gather at a very few staging sites during migration, rather than from documented population declines.

The lack of information for most scolopacid species makes it difficult to determine population trends. However, in eastern North America significant declines of Least and Semipalmated Sandpipers, Sanderlings, Red Knots, Short-billed Dowitchers, and Whimbrels appear to have occurred in the past 30 years. Along the northern coastal plain of Alaska, significant declines have been detected in the breeding population of Dunlins that winter in Asia. Habitat destruction in Asia is suspected as being a factor in this decline.

The Upland Sandpiper, still considered to be at risk by the U.S. Fish and Wildlife Service, appears to be increasing across the continent. Populations at the edges of the species' range are faring less well, however, and the species is listed as endangered in some areas.

Explanations for population declines in scolopacids are confounded by a variety of issues. Undoubtedly, heavy hunting in the late 1800s severely impacted shorebird populations, especially those using grasslands and marshes in North and South America. Since the passage of the Migratory Bird Treaty Act in 1918, only the Common Snipe and the American Woodcock can be hunted legally in North

Eskimo Curlew. In the early 1800s the Eskimo Curlew was abundant, but it is probably now extinct as a result of overhunting and habitat conversion. Continuing reports hold some hope of its survival, but there have been no confirmed sightings since the 1960s.

America. Upland species, such as the Eskimo Curlew and the Upland Sandpiper, appear to have also suffered from the conversion of native grasslands into agricultural fields and from declines in native insect populations.

Habitat loss in general, through the conversion and degradation of migration and wintering grounds, is perhaps the biggest threat to shorebird populations today. California has lost more than 90 percent of its wetlands since European settlement. Interior wetlands continue to be drained and plowed under and to have their freshwater sources diverted, especially in parts of the arid West. Rising sea levels caused by global warming also could have disastrous effects on shorebird populations due to the potential loss of low-lying coastal habitats.

Species that stage at single sites in large numbers are particularly sensitive to threats to individual wetlands. For instance, in some years more than 70 percent of the world's Western Sandpipers migrate through Alaska's Copper River Delta over a period of three weeks in spring, while an equally large percentage of Semipalmated Sandpipers sometimes use the Bay of Fundy in fall. Anything affecting the way birds use these sites could have dramatic consequences for these species' global populations.

Many major sites along the migration routes have faced serious threats. Mono Lake in California and Cheyenne Bottoms in Kansas have been negatively affected by water diversion, Delaware Bay by horseshoe crab exploitation, and San Francisco Bay by development. The Copper River Delta has been threatened by oil spills within Prince William Sound.

Direct loss of habitat is exacerbated by less visible factors that reduce the quality of remaining habitats. Human disturbance in the form of jet skis, off-road vehicles, airplanes, and even people walking their dogs has been a particular problem for some species as people increasingly head outdoors for recreation. At interior sites, particularly in the West, water diversion has degraded water quality, often by increasing salinity levels and concentrating other contaminants. The introduction of exotic plants and animals has also changed the nature of many wetlands, and the effects on shorebird populations are only just beginning to be understood.

Accidental Species

With their long-distance migrations, shorebirds are good candidates for vagrancy, and many rare species have been found in North America. For example, Wood Sandpipers *(Tringa glareola)*, which range from Siberia to Scotland, are regular migrants in the western and central Aleutian Islands of Alaska in spring and have even stayed on to breed. This species has also occurred elsewhere in Alaska, and even as far east as New York and Bermuda.

In western North America, other Old World species that typically breed in northern Eurasia and winter in Africa, Asia, and Australasia are most likely to be seen in Alaska, and particularly on the Bering Sea islands. These rare species are generally found during migration periods (from mid-May through June and

then again between mid-August and mid-September) and have included the Common Greenshank *(Tringa nebularia)*, Marsh Sandpiper *(T. stagnatilis)*, Green Sandpiper *(T. ochropus)*, Gray-tailed Tattler *(Heteroscelus brevipes)*, Common Sandpiper *(Actitis hypoleucos)*, Terek Sandpiper *(Xenus cinereus)*, Little Curlew *(Numenius minutus)*, Far Eastern Curlew *(N. madagascariensis)*, the Siberian subspecies of the Black-tailed Godwit *(Limosa l. melanuroides)*, Great Knot *(Calidris tenuirostris)*, Temminck's Stint *(C. temminckii)*, Long-toed Stint *(C. subminuta)*, Spoonbill Sandpiper *(Eurynorhynchus pygmeus)*, Broad-billed Sandpiper *(Limicola falcinellus)*, Jack Snipe *(Lymnocryptes minimus)*, and Pin-tailed Snipe *(Gallinago stenura)*. Several of these species also have been found farther south along the Pacific coast of North America.

Old World shorebirds also occur periodically in eastern North America, generally during migration, with most records coming from far eastern Canada and New England. The Eurasian Curlew *(Numenius arquata)* and Common Greenshank have both been found several times in the northeastern corner of the continent. The Common Redshank *(Tringa totanus)* has been seen in Newfoundland, the Slender-billed Curlew *(Numenius tenuirostris)* in Ontario, the Jack Snipe in Labrador, the Terek Sandpiper in Massachusetts and Manitoba, and the Broad-billed Sandpiper in Nova Scotia and New York.

Dunlins of the Greenland subspecies *(Calidris alpina alpina* and *C. a. arctica)* and the Russian subspecies *(C. a. sakhalina)* have been found in several places throughout North America and could easily be missed.

There also are several records from the 1800s of the Eurasian Woodcock *(Scolopax rusticola)* ranging from Newfoundland to Alabama, but this species has not been seen in North America for several decades.

Nils and Sarah Warnock

Coursers and Pratincoles

Family Glareolidae
Order Charadriiformes

Members of the Glareolidae are small to medium-size shorebirds with long, pointed wings and fairly short necks and bills. This exclusively Old World family comprises two distinctive subfamilies—coursers and pratincoles. The two share a short, arched bill and details of leg scaling and nostril structure but are otherwise quite different.

The eight pratincole species of the subfamily Glareolinae are tern-like, with their relatively short legs, extremely long wings, and graceful, buoyant flight. Species in this group are associated with aquatic habitats and feed largely on insects captured in the air. Pratincoles are gregarious at all seasons and can be noisy, giving sharp, tern-like calls.

The nine species of coursers, none of which has occurred in North America, are grouped in four genera within the subfamily Cursoriinae. These birds are generally long-legged and plover-like in appearance and occur in arid terrestrial habitats.

The position of the Glareolidae within the Charadriiformes is unclear. Evidence from DNA–DNA hybridization studies supports a close relationship with the gulls and terns, but morphological analyses suggest that plovers or thick-knees may be more closely related.

Several pratincole species make long-distance migrations; some have occurred as vagrants far outside their typical range. Oriental Pratincoles *(Glareola maldivarum)*, which breed in eastern Asia and winter south to Australia, have occurred twice in Alaska in the summer.

David Allen Sibley

Oriental Pratincole. *The Oriental Pratincole is the only member of the Glareolidae to occur in North America, and it is extremely rare. With its long wings and graceful flight, this species is typical of the pratincoles.*

Worldwide Family Features

- 7–12" (18–30 cm) shorebirds.
- 17 species in 5 genera worldwide; restricted to Old World, with greatest diversity in tropical Africa. 1 species accidental in Alaska.
- Eat primarily insects, especially larger species, including locusts and beetles. Pratincoles feed on the wing; coursers typically catch food on the ground.
- Pratincoles are gregarious and defend small territories within loose colonies. Coursers breed in solitude but may form small flocks. All species presumed monogamous, but little information on pair bonds. Some make long-distance movements; others more sedentary.

- Breed first at 1 year old, when known.
- Nest is scrape or shallow depression in the ground, sometimes lined or ringed with plant material or small stones.
- 1–4 typically rounded elliptical, dull white, yellow, or grayish eggs with dark markings. Incubation shared equally by the sexes; lasts 17–31 days. 1 brood per year.
- Precocial young covered with down at hatching; leave nest within a few days. Both parents provide protection and feed young during first weeks. Fledge at 20–42 days.
- Little information on survival or longevity.

Gulls, Terns, and Allies

The family Laridae is a large group of small to fairly large web-footed waterbirds with very diverse foraging strategies. The group is divided into four subfamilies. Jaegers and skuas have mostly brown plumages and comparatively deep, sturdy bills. Gulls are predominantly white-bodied as adults and gray-brown as immatures. Most terns are also white, although a few species have much darker plumages; most are smaller and have shallow, more sharply pointed bills than gulls. Skimmers are striking, black-and-white birds with outsized red-and-black bills in which the lower jaw, or mandible, is longer than the upper jaw. North American larids have wingspans ranging from 20 inches to 5 feet 5 inches (50–165 cm). Larids are generally found near water, and most species occur in coastal areas. However, members of the family use a wide range of habitats, including beaches, freshwater marshes, open tundra, muskeg swamps, sea cliffs, tropical atolls, and open ocean. Some species have adapted well to humans, especially gulls, which often frequent agricultural fields, urban ponds, and garbage dumps.

Taxonomy

The systematic relationships among skuas, jaegers, gulls, terns, and skimmers are unsettled, as with many large groups of birds. Some researchers split these birds into four families first set forth in 1925 by Jonathan Dwight—Stercorariidae (skuas and jaegers), Laridae (gulls), Sternidae (terns), and Rynchopidae (skimmers).

Currently, however, the AOU considers these four groups to be subfamilies (Stercorariinae, Larinae, Sterninae, and Rynchopinae) within the Laridae. Although this merger may accurately reflect a close evolutionary relationship among the groups, it downplays their substantial differences in morphology and ecology.

Subfamily Origins and Relationships

According to most recent work, gulls and terns are more closely related to each other than either group is to the skimmers, though at least one morphological study suggests that the noddies, which are currently grouped with the terns in the subfamily Sterninae, may be more like skimmers than other terns.

Scientists believe that gulls, and possibly also terns, evolved during the Paleocene epoch (58–65 million years ago) from other groups in the order Charadriiformes. The first gull-like fossils are from the Oligocene epoch (24–37 million years ago), and the first true gulls are found in the fossil record of the lower Miocene epoch (about 15 million years ago). The

Larid diversity. Worldwide this family is divided into four distinctive subfamilies that are sometimes considered separate families. The four groups differ in bill shape, wing shape, and other morphological features, as well as behavioral characteristics. The skuas and jaegers are placed in the subfamily Stercorariinae (Pomarine Jaeger, top left); gulls, including the kittiwakes, in the Larinae (Glaucous Gull, bottom left); terns, including the noddies, in the Sterninae (Royal Tern, top right); and skimmers in the Rynchopinae (Black Skimmer, bottom right). Members of all four subfamilies are found in North America.

fossil record for modern gull species begins in the Pleistocene epoch (10,000 to 1.6 million years ago).

Ancient terns are scarcely found in the fossil record, although recently scientists reevaluating a Miocene-epoch (5–24 million years ago) fossil from Maryland suggested that it may be that of a primitive noddy. Skuas and jaegers are believed to have diverged from their closest allies, the gulls, in the Miocene epoch (about 10 million years ago), but as with other larids, their fossil record is poor. A Pleistocene-epoch skua from Oregon is one of the few known fossils for that group. There are no known skimmer-like fossils.

Genera and Species

Taxonomy at the level of genera and species within the Laridae is controversial in a number of cases. Worldwide there are currently about 78 gull taxa grouped into about 51 species in up to 12 genera; 123 tern taxa are grouped into about 44 species in 3 to 10 genera; the 10

taxa of jaegers and skuas are placed in 6 to 9 species in 1 or 2 genera; and the 5 skimmer taxa are grouped in 3 species in a single genus. In addition to much uncertainty about the exact number of species and genera, the relationships among taxa within these groups are not well known.

Under the AOU's current taxonomy, the larids that regularly occur in North America are classified as 27 gull species in 5 genera; 17 tern species in 3 genera; 5 skua and jaeger species in 1 genus; and 1 skimmer.

Gulls

Traditionally taxonomists have placed most gulls in the genus *Larus* but separated the most distinctive species into other genera. In North America all regularly occurring gulls are currently included in *Larus* except the kittiwakes, which are placed in the genus *Rissa,* the Ivory Gull *(Pagophila eburnea),* Sabine's Gull *(Xema sabini),* and Ross's Gull *(Rhodostethia rosea).*

Worldwide Family Features

- 8–31" (20–78 cm) waterbirds.
- About 104 species in 15 genera worldwide; cosmopolitan. 50 species in 10 genera found throughout North America; plus at least 4 accidental species.
- Gulls, skuas, and jaegers are opportunistic omnivores, eating almost anything. Terns and skimmers mainly eat small fish. Obtain food by various methods, including picking off ground or water surface, plunge-diving, aerial capture, kleptoparasitism, begging from humans.
- Gulls, terns, and skimmers are generally colonial; skuas and jaegers nest alone or in small, loose colonies. Most species are monogamous; many retain mate in successive years. In nonbreeding season some species (especially gulls) are highly gregarious, others (especially skuas and jaegers) are solitary. Many species migratory.
- Age at first breeding highly variable, typically 2–5 years old; small species nest at a younger age than large species. Great Skuas may not breed until 12 years old.
- Nest varies from a large mound, cup, or

mat of vegetation (some gulls) to little more than a scrape, sometimes lined with grasses (beach-nesting terns, skimmers). Typically both parents build nest, usually on ground, but sometimes on sea cliffs, on floating marsh vegetation, in trees, and even on roofs and window ledges. Some species reuse nest sites.
- 1–4 (usually 2 or 3) subelliptical eggs, greenish to buff or cream, marked, sometimes heavily, with spots and flecks. Both parents incubate for 19–32 days. Hatching asynchronous. 1 brood per year, but may replace lost clutches.
- Semi-precocial young hatch with downy coat; brooding at nest lasts up to 14 days. Both parents generally guard young until fledging at 19 days–9 weeks and may provide food for longer periods.
- Adult annual survival high, often exceeding 80%. Mean longevity after attaining adulthood 5–12 years (small gulls and terns), 9–20 years (large gulls). Among oldest on record: more than 20 years (Black Skimmer); 28 years (Herring Gull); 34 years (Arctic Tern, Great Skua); more than 35 years (Sooty Tern).

Larid heads and bills. Bill size and shape varies considerably both within and among Laridae subfamilies. The gulls are most variable, ranging from stout, blunt bills among the large white-headed gulls (Great Black-backed Gull, left) to more delicate, thinner bills among the smaller species (Bonaparte's Gull, center). Terns have longer, more pointed bills than gulls (Elegant Tern, right), although size and shape vary among species. Skuas and jaegers (not shown) have gull-like bills, while skimmers (not shown) more closely resemble terns.

The genus *Larus* is divided into two subgroups. The hooded gulls include Franklin's *(L. pipixcan)*, Laughing *(L. atricilla)*, Little *(L. minutus)*, Bonaparte's *(L. philadelphia)*, and Black-headed *(L. ridibundus)* Gulls; the white-headed gulls encompass all other North American species. In most cases the white-headed gulls are larger and take longer to reach sexual maturity than the hooded gulls.

Gull species are sometimes also grouped by birders according to the number of years it takes to reach sexual maturity. These subdivisions, however, do not strictly reflect taxonomy or the relationships between species. For example, the Western Gull *(Larus occidentalis)* is referred to as a "four-year" gull because it takes four years to mature. In contrast, the Yellow-footed Gull *(L. livens)*, which was once treated as the same species as the Western Gull and is presumed to be a close relative, is a "three-year" gull.

One of the more controversial situations in gull taxonomy involves the status of Thayer's Gull *(Larus thayeri)*. Currently, Thayer's is considered a full species, although at various times it has been viewed as a subspecies of either the Herring *(L. argentatus)* or the Iceland Gull *(L. glaucoides)*. The current classification, however, has been questioned, because of evidence that Thayer's Gulls hybridize with the North American subspecies of the Iceland Gull, known as "Kumlien's" Gull *(L. g. kumlieni)*.

Gull hybridization Hybridization in gulls, especially among white-headed *Larus* gulls, is relatively common and is a major source of the controversy over the species-level classification of these birds. The situation is most complicated in the Northern Hemisphere, which is ringed by a series of taxa that hybridize where their ranges meet. These different taxa are variously considered to be separate species or subspecies, based on morphological differences and described levels of hybridization. However, increasing awareness of the degree of morphological variation within particular taxa, combined with the difficulty of assessing how much hybridization is enough to warrant combining two forms in a single species, makes some of these taxonomic decisions somewhat arbitrary.

Larid leg and foot. Larids typically have rather long, slender legs, with three toes fully webbed and the hind toe reduced. This leg structure allows the birds to walk easily, while the webbed toes allow them to swim. Leg color differs among the many species, from pink in the Herring Gull (shown here) to yellow, black, or red.

The taxonomic problems created by hybridization in the white-headed *Larus* gulls test the concept of treating species as discrete groups of organisms and elucidate the very protean aspects of the speciation process itself. They also highlight what many see as a major problem with the biological species concept, which uses the extent of hybridization as a criterion for distinguishing species.

Studies of isolating mechanisms in sympatrically nesting seabirds of the same family or genus have shown that species with similar coloration of their soft parts, such as the bill or foot, are more likely to hybridize than those with bills or feet of different colors. Moreover, hybrids from the former pairings appear more likely to find mates as adults than do hybrids from the latter. Eye color and orbital ring color may serve as supplementary isolating mechanisms, along with differences in calls and displays.

The relationships among Herring, Lesser Black-backed *(Larus fuscus),* and Yellow-legged *(L. cachinnans)* Gulls are especially complex. Each of these species is subdivided into several subspecies, but in some cases it is unclear which species a particular subspecies belongs with. Some subspecies may even warrant elevation to species level in their own right. Genetic research has shown that these birds diverged relatively recently in evolutionary time, and it appears that there has not been enough time for the different groups to become sufficiently different to prevent hybridization or to make the identification of species limits a simple exercise.

On the Pacific coast of North America, hybridization is commonplace between the Glaucous-winged *(Larus glaucescens)* and Herring Gulls in southern Alaska and British Columbia, and between Western and Glaucous-winged Gulls in Washington and Oregon. In some areas, apparent hybrids may outnumber birds of either parent species.

Researchers have found that Glaucous-winged and Western Gulls hybridize from northwestern Washington state to Oregon, with a "zone of introgression" in which Western Gull genes can be found in Glaucous-winged Gulls extending north to the Queen Charlotte Islands of British Columbia.

The incidence of hybridization has increased in recent decades, although the birds remain more likely to breed with members of their own species. The hybrid zone encompasses a marine ecotone, where conditions change as one ecosystem merges into another. To the north are extensive fjords and estuaries, while to the south conditions are more influenced by upwelling of the California Current. Glaucous-winged Gulls seem better adapted to conditions north of the ecotone, while Western Gulls seem better able to exploit conditions to the south. In the hybrid zone, the hybrid birds enjoy greater reproductive success than either parental species in some years, while Western Gulls do better in other years; Glaucous-winged Gulls generally fare poorly.

Glaucous Gulls *(Larus hyperboreus)* and Herring Gulls also hybridize occasionally, producing a hybrid combination that has been dubbed "Nelson's" Gull. Well-documented, though much less common, instances of other gull hybrids include: Laughing Gull × Ring-billed Gull *(L. delawarensis),* Kelp Gull *(L. dominicanus)* × Herring Gull, Black-headed Gull × Ring-billed Gull, California Gull *(L. californicus)* × Heermann's Gull *(L. heermanni),* Herring Gull × Lesser Black-backed Gull, Franklin's Gull × Ring-billed Gull, and Herring Gull × Great Black-backed Gull *(L. marinus).* In addition, observers have reported apparent hybrids whose parentage is a complete mystery.

Subspecies Much of the variation in gulls is due to differences within rather than between subspecies, and most species have only one subspecies in North America. There are, however, exceptions. The California and Western Gulls are each separated into a northern and a southern subspecies; Black-legged Kittiwakes *(Rissa tridactyla)* are split into Pacific and Atlantic subspecies; and the Sabine's Gulls

Hybridization: Glaucous-winged Gull × Western Gull. The world's large gulls are notorious for their hybridization, and North American species are no exception. The case of the Glaucous-winged and Western Gulls is particularly well studied. These two species interbreed where their ranges overlap along the Washington coast, producing a wide array of hybrids and backcrosses. The birds on the left and right are pure Glaucous-winged and Western Gulls, respectively; the bird in the center is a hybrid.

breeding in Alaska are differentiated from those that nest throughout Arctic Canada.

North American Glaucous Gulls have been subdivided into three subspecies, and the northern Russian race of the Herring Gull, generally known as the "Vega" Gull *(Larus argentatus vegae)*, breeds on St. Lawrence Island in the Bering Sea and has been reported elsewhere during the nonbreeding season. In addition to the "Vega" Gull and the common American subspecies, *L. a. smithsonianus,* two other subspecies of Herring Gulls, both from Europe, have been tentatively identified in North America: the nominate form *(L. a. argentatus),* often called the "Scandinavian" Herring Gull, and the form *L. a. argenteus,* sometimes called the "European" Herring Gull, which nests in western Europe. In addition to North America's nesting subspecies, *brachyrhynchus,* two subspecies of the Mew Gull *(L. canus)* have been found in North America: the "Common" Gull *(L. c. canus)* of Europe and the "Kamchatka" Gull *(L. c. kamtschatschensis)* of Siberia. Most of the plumage and structural characteristics that distinguish these various subspecies are subtle.

Terns

Regular North American tern species are currently grouped into three genera. The largest of the North American tern genera, *Sterna,* includes the predominantly

white species, such as the widespread Forster's Tern *(S. forsteri),* as well as the darker Sooty *(S. fuscata)* and Bridled *(S. anaethetus)* Terns. The genus *Chlidonias,* the marsh terns, includes the Black *(C. niger)* and White-winged *(C. leucopterus)* Terns. The noddies are placed in the genus *Anous.*

Some taxonomists place the Caspian Tern *(Sterna caspia)* and the Gull-billed Tern *(S. nilotica)* in the monotypic genera *Hydroprogne* and *Gelochelidon,* respectively. Both of these species have deep bills that distinguish them from other terns. Taxonomists also sometimes place the Royal *(S. maxima),* Elegant *(S. elegans),* and Sandwich *(S. sandvicensis)* Terns, along with other large crested terns, in the genus *Thalasseus.*

Skuas and Jaegers

Members of this subfamily have long been separated into the genera *Stercorarius* (jaegers) and *Catharacta* (skuas), but the AOU recently merged all species into the genus *Stercorarius.* Genetic evidence, as well as similarities in behavioral displays and skeletal features, suggest that the Pomarine Jaeger *(S. pomarinus)* is more closely related to the large skuas than was previously suspected. The Pomarine Jaeger, it appears, may have arisen from an ancient hybridization of one of the small species with the Great Skua *(S. skua).* An alternative explanation holds that jaegers and skuas evolved as separate groups, but that the mitochondrial DNA of the Pomarine Jaeger was later replaced through hybridization with the Great Skua.

The relationships among the large skuas are unclear. Scientists agree that the Great Skua of the North Atlantic, the Chilean Skua (*Stercorarius chilensis*) of southern South America, and the South Polar Skua (*S. maccormicki*), which breeds throughout the Antarctic, are discrete species. The remaining forms, which are all restricted to the Southern Hemisphere, are variously described as subspecies of the Great Skua or as one, two, or even three additional species.

Variation

In some ways, gulls are ideal subjects for bird enthusiasts. They gather in large numbers, have many age-specific plumages, and can often be studied for long periods at close range, even "chummed," or lured close, with food.

In a brief morning's study of a single flock, a birder can observe considerable variation among gulls of the same species, even of the same age class: the amount of black in the primaries, the degree of wear in various feathers, the progression of molt, the pigmentation of the bill and legs, the amount of streaking on the head and nape. Most of this vari-

ation is normal, and over years of study the veteran larophile develops a feel for such variation and is able to spot the true nonconformists.

The degree of sexual dimorphism in larids varies among subfamilies, possibly in relation to the breeding roles of males and females. In gulls, males are often much larger than females, but in skuas and jaegers, females are larger and have heavier bills than males. In each case, the larger sex plays a greater role in territorial defense. In terns and skimmers, which share breeding duties more evenly, the size difference is much less pronounced.

Like gulls, skuas and jaegers show a bewildering array of plumages, many of them age-related. Unlike other members of the Laridae, however, skuas and jaegers also have distinct color morphs (sometimes called plumage phases) within a species. Usually there is a light morph and a dark morph, but intermediate birds are often found as well. These color variations are most distinctive in Parasitic (*Stercorarius parasiticus*) and Pomarine Jaegers of all ages, in younger Long-tailed Jaegers (*S. longicaudus*), and in older South Polar Skuas. They are least pronounced in other species of skua. Even subadult Great Skuas, which range from dark to light and have varying amounts of rufous, have subtly different morphs: darker and lighter, with varying amounts of rufous pigmentation.

Age-related plumages. Large gulls may take up to four years to attain their definitive plumages, and along the way their appearance changes each year to become gradually more adult-like. Thus at any given moment a birder might encounter up to four different age classes of a large gull such as the Great Black-backed Gull (shown here), not to mention many variations within each age class. It is no wonder that gull identification can be so confusing for beginning birders.

It is thought that the incidence of different color morphs is related to the foraging opportunities available in a particular area. Light-morph birds are expected to be better suited for hunting live prey over tundra and ocean than dark morphs, because their pale underparts provide camouflage from prey looking up at a pale sky. This same explanation is used to explain why gulls, terns, and many other aerial predators are typically pale below, and is supported by a study of Black-headed Gulls, which found that birds whose underparts had been dyed black had lower prey capture rates than birds with normal white coloring below.

Dark-morph jaegers, in contrast, may be better kleptoparasites than light-morph birds because they are harder for a potential victim to see against the dark water and can thus approach more easily. It has also been suggested that birds that look unusual are at an advantage in kleptoparasitic attacks, because the victim does not recognize them as a threat. If seabirds often encounter aggressors with a particular plumage phase, they will quickly learn to associate it with danger, but a bird with a rare plumage phase may not be identified as a jaeger until the attack is already under way. Scientists have used a similar argument to explain the presence of different morphs among the hawks, another predatory group in which different morphs are found.

These proposed explanations for why different phases arise support the idea that light-morph birds should be more common than dark-morph birds, and this is usually the case. In some places, however, dark-morph birds predominate. For example, on the Kola Peninsula in Russia, two-thirds of the Parasitic Jaegers are of the dark morph, quite unlike elsewhere in Arctic Russia, where dark-morph birds are rare. This surprising situation may arise in cases where there are so many opportunities to steal food—for example, when nesting near major seabird colonies—that the advantages of dark plumage outweigh the advantages of having a rare plumage phase. Thus the dark plumage that supposedly benefits kleptoparasites could become quite common. Indeed, in areas where there are a lot of dark-morph birds, kleptoparasitism is a much more important feeding strategy than in areas where few dark birds are found.

All of these theories about plumage phases, however, are very difficult to test. So far, studies of jaegers have not shown that dark birds enjoy greater predatory success than light birds when compared at the same site. Consequently the accuracy of these ideas remains to be verified.

Food and Foraging

Members of the Laridae eat a wide variety of foods and forage in numerous different ways. Gulls, skuas, and jaegers are opportunistic omnivores, eating whatever they can find that will satisfy their nutritional needs. Terns and, especially, skimmers are more specialized in their choice of diet and methods of prey capture.

Gulls

Gulls are remarkable opportunists. In a day, a group of gulls might move from a fleet of fishing boats on the open ocean to the intertidal zone, into agricultural fields, to the parking lot of a fast-food restaurant, to a landfill (and perhaps afterward to a lake in a suburban housing development to bathe), then to a marsh, finally ending up at a freshwater roost well upriver from the sea.

Because of their ability to adapt to human-altered environments, gulls are one of the few avian "success" stories in the 20th century. What has been disastrous for many other species in the developed world—loss of wetlands to landfills, loss of riparian habitat to hydroelectric plants, and the like—has often been a boon for gulls. As opportunistic foragers, gulls adapt rapidly to drastic environmental changes, a quality that sets them apart from their relatives the terns and skimmers.

In natural environments most gulls typically feed on fish and marine invertebrates, but most species, especially the larger gulls, are omnivorous and opportunistic feeders. Their diet can include small mammals, birds (and their eggs and young), reptiles, amphibians, and invertebrates. They are also well adapted to foraging on beach-washed organisms, carrion, dung, waste grain, berries, and much more. In addition to finding their own food, gulls will often resort to harassing other birds that have found food (see Kleptoparasitism, below).

Gulls that nest in the high Arctic, such as Ross's, Ivory, and Sabine's, all feed on marine invertebrates and vertebrates. The Ivory Gull, for example, appears to specialize in carrion and dung, particularly carcasses of seals killed by Polar Bears, as well as the scat of those mammals. The Red-legged Kittiwake *(Rissa brevirostris)*, a highly pelagic species, feeds extensively at night when squid and other prey rise to the water's surface.

Many gulls will also eat food provided, albeit unintentionally, by humans. It is not surprising for gulls to scavenge on the remains of bologna sandwiches, snack cakes, potato chips, and other human leftovers at landfills. Anyone who has set foot into the pungent environment of a dump will immediately understand its importance to scavenging gulls of many species. Gulls feast on garbage throughout the year, particularly in the nonbreeding season.

Several studies have been conducted on gulls at landfills. One study of Herring Gulls in Ohio found that, during the chick-rearing weeks, adults and chicks ate relatively little garbage, but that after fledging, the gulls' consumption of garbage increased substantially. In another study, done in Newfoundland, researchers compared the foraging habits of Herring Gulls in different environments. They found that during the pre-laying and incubation periods, up to 80 percent of the Herring Gulls foraged selectively, specializing either on marine organisms, garbage, or other seabirds; the remaining gulls studied were generalists. Pairs that specialized on organisms in the intertidal zone had larger and heavier clutches and higher rates of hatching (indications of greater reproductive success) than generalists or other specialists.

This and other research suggests that landfills provide a supplemental rather than principal source of food for most

Begging for food. *Gulls are one of the few groups of birds that seem to have benefited from the increasing human population, and many species are more numerous now than 100 years ago. Gulls can be seen in huge numbers at open garbage dumps, and every beachgoer is familiar with the sight and sound of a hovering flock of gulls, like these Laughing Gulls, looking for handouts.*

Red spot on gull bill tip. As adults, most large gulls have a red spot at the tip of the bill, as shown in this Herring Gull. Newborn chicks peck at this spot to stimulate their parents to regurgitate food for the chicks to eat.

species of gulls, which fare better foraging in local marine environments. This appears to be borne out by the observations of birders who have noted that very harsh winter weather drives the largest numbers of gulls, including more adult birds, into landfills. Scavenging at landfills may thus be linked to the local supply of "natural" prey for gulls and to the rigors of the environment.

Because gulls exploit many different niches and use various strategies for foraging, they are often said to be very intelligent. Their habit of dropping mollusks onto hard surfaces from the air, a behavior known in very few birds, is often cited as evidence of how smart they are. Nevertheless, there is a learning curve for this behavior. First-winter Herring Gulls at golf courses (where they often bathe in waterways) can be a nuisance, picking up the odd golf ball and bouncing it off cars and hard-top parking lots; adult gulls rarely try to open such inappropriate objects.

The wing structure of different gulls is tied to their degree of specialization. Whereas the wings of smaller gulls resemble those of the terns—streamlined, pointed at the tip, and highly maneuverable for such tasks as capturing small fish at the water's surface—the larger gulls have broader wings and are less capable of tight maneuvers. Consequently, larger gulls are less likely than the more agile,

smaller species to hunt for insects from the air or to feed by dipping and plunge-diving.

As adults, all of the larger four-year gulls have a red spot toward the bill tip during the nesting season. This spot serves primarily as a focal point for the chicks, which from the first hours of life instinctively peck at the color, stimulating the adult birds to regurgitate food.

The rather small, thin, almost tern-like bills of the smaller gull species are well suited to dealing with small prey such as bait fish, insect larvae, and flying insects, as well as bits of sewage at outflow pipes.

The bills of larger gulls are more formidable, capable of dispatching prey in much the same way as a raptor's bill, though generally only the largest gull species kill prey of any size. For example, the world's largest gull, the Great Black-backed, takes adult Atlantic Puffins *(Fratercula arctica).* Most gulls larger than Bonaparte's Gull take the eggs and chicks of other species, which can be devastating for certain terns and shorebirds that nest in exposed settings. Gulls usually swallow chicks whole, sometimes later ejecting a pellet of feathers and bone from the mouth, much as an owl might do. They also catch passerines when they can, swallowing them whole; Great Black-backed Gulls can swallow prey as large as a Boat-tailed Grackle *(Quiscalus major)* head-first, bill and all.

Terns

Terns have a more delicate appearance than gulls, but they are also hardy birds that practice interspecific and intraspecific kleptoparasitism (see below) and that can adapt to human activities such as agriculture and fishing, feeding opportunistically on insects above crops or on small fish discarded behind fishing boats. Like gulls, they may harass diving species for fish; for example, Royal Terns and Brown Noddies *(Anous stolidus)* are known to harass Brown Pelicans *(Pelecanus occidentalis)* in much the same way as Heermann's Gulls. Also like gulls, they sometimes follow schools of large predatory fish, such as tuna, that periodically flush smaller bait fish to the surface. Some species, notably the Sooty Tern, rely heavily on this food source. The occurrence of such prey patches can be very unpredictable and ephemeral, depending on the behavior of the fish.

In general, terns are more specialized than gulls. For the most part, terns eat small fish found near the water's surface in marshes, rivers, bays, and oceans, although some species, such as the Black and Gull-billed Terns, feed heavily on insects. Most terns capture prey with their sharp, pointed bills by dipping and plunge-diving while in flight. The feeding strategies of different species vary, however; Forster's Terns will dive from a perch, Aleutian Terns *(Sterna aleutica)* apparently never plunge-dive, and Black Noddies *(Anous minutus)* will foot-patter like small gulls or storm-petrels.

Skimmers

The Black Skimmer *(Rynchops niger)* forages for its favored prey, small fish, at shallow coastal bays, rivers, and marshes. To feed, skimmers fly a few inches above the surface of calm waters, with the lower bill partly submerged. When they make contact with a small fish, the bill snaps shut and the fish is plucked from the water. This strategy, which skimmers often repeat many times over the same area of water, can produce capture rates that match or exceed those of terns.

Skimmers feed by touch, which allows them to feed at dawn, dusk, and even at night, when prey may be closer to the water's surface than during the day. They

Diving motions of terns. *Many terns are plunge-divers, as in the case of the Common Tern (left), which hovers over the water before diving head-first, plunging in, and seizing a small fish with its bill. However, about half of North American tern species do not plunge-dive, instead snatching their food from the surface with little contact with the water, as in the Sooty Tern (center). Another method is used by the noddies (Brown Noddy, right), which hover at the surface of the water—sometimes "foot-pattering" like storm-petrels—as they pluck food from the surface.*

Black Skimmer fishing. *One of the most unusual foraging methods in all birds is that of the Black Skimmer. These birds have a laterally flattened (knife-like) bill with an elongated lower jaw. When foraging, the birds fly just above the water's surface with the lower jaw slicing the water. When the lower jaw contacts prey, the head snaps downward and the prey is gripped by the bill, tossed up, and swallowed. This method, which relies entirely on chance contact with fish, requires a high density of prey at the water's surface. Skimmers forage mainly at night when small fish rise to the surface of sheltered waters.*

have relatively small eyes for their body size, but their fully dilated pupils are larger than the pupils of birds that forage by day, giving them the keen night vision they need to navigate shallow coastal waters. The world's three species of skimmer are the only birds known to close their pupils vertically, with a slit very much like that of a cat's eye. This structure, found mostly in aquatic and nocturnal vertebrates, allows a skimmer to close its pupils tightly, which protects the retina in bright sunlight.

Skuas and Jaegers

Skuas and jaegers use the various foraging methods of both gulls and terns, from tern-like aerial dipping for tiny prey by Long-tailed Jaegers to predation on Black-legged Kittiwakes and other birds by Great Skuas. Their diet is almost as varied as that of gulls, including berries, insects, rodents, chicks and eggs of other birds, adult birds, carrion, and offal. Kleptoparasitism (see below) is most common in the skuas and in the Parasitic Jaeger, but Pomarine and Long-tailed Jaegers also often try to pirate a meal from other seabirds. Both Pomarine and Long-tailed Jaegers prey heavily on rodents,

especially lemmings, during the Arctic summer, although the two species use different methods to capture these prey. Long-tailed Jaegers typically hover-hunt for lemmings from the air, whereas the less agile Pomarine Jaegers frequently use their large bills to dig the rodents out of their subterranean hiding places in the tundra.

When pursuing other birds, whether as prey or for their regurgitated food, jaegers usually surprise their host from below, whereas skuas tend to stoop from above, like a Peregrine Falcon *(Falco peregrinus)*, often using their feet and bill to drive the victim to the water's surface. Among jaegers, the large Pomarine is perhaps most likely to kill other birds, although all three species will take passerines and young shorebirds during the breeding season. Skuas also prey on adult birds, although the small South Polar Skua forages largely on fish and penguin eggs and chicks. The larger Great Skua may forage almost exclusively for long periods on adult seabirds and by kleptoparasitism. Great Skuas, like some of the larger gulls, will also cannibalize their neighbors' chicks, at least in lean years.

Pomarine Jaeger with lemming. *During the breeding season Pomarine and Long-tailed Jaegers feed mainly on lemmings, supplemented (especially in Long-taileds) by a variety of other prey.*

All skuas and jaegers forage over the ocean during the nonbreeding season, although Parasitic Jaegers spend the most time in inshore waters and are thus most likely to be seen from land.

Kleptoparasitism

Some species of seabirds, particularly jaegers, skuas, and frigatebirds, regularly engage in kleptoparasitism—the stealing of food from other seabirds, typically by aerial pursuit. Gulls and terns also harass other birds for food, but unlike the "specialist" kleptoparasites, they often attempt to steal food from members of their own species; frigatebirds, jaegers, and skuas generally attack other species.

Kleptoparasitism is profitable only if the attacker can be sure that it is chasing a bird that has something worth stealing. Consequently, the behavior is particularly common around cliffs where adult seabirds are constantly bringing food back to their young. Under these circumstances, potential victims are easy to find because most birds arriving at the colony will be carrying food; in many species, they will be carrying food in their bill, where it can be seen. Some kleptoparasites apparently use subtle visual cues, however, and do not actually need to see the food item. The most specialized of the aerial kleptoparasites, the Parasitic Jaeger, readily discriminates between a Black-legged Kittiwake carrying little or no food and one carrying food in its stomach, and will chase the latter to make it regurgitate its prey.

Kleptoparasitism is unlikely to be worthwhile if a bird can obtain more food by direct foraging. In many cases, about 20 to 25 percent of kleptoparasitic attacks are successful, a rate similar to that found when birds are direct predators. However, comparing the success rates of kleptoparasitic attacks to direct predation is difficult for many reasons. For one thing, the comparison may depend on the individual concerned, because some birds seem to be much more skilled than others at forcing their victims to drop food. Moreover, some pursuit behavior seems to be merely exploratory, and it is difficult to judge whether these chases should be viewed as failures. Finally, it is hard to prove that kleptoparasitism is more energy-efficient than direct foraging, since the two behaviors rarely occur under the same conditions.

It is also difficult to explain why inveterate kleptoparasites such as the Parasitic Jaeger persist in using kleptoparasitism when prey is abundant and accessible at the water's surface. Some researchers have suggested that the bird's falcon-like wing shape, highly adapted for pursuit, may put it at a disadvantage for hovering over and splash-diving into schools of fish when they have to compete with large, dense flocks of terns.

Despite these difficulties, studies at seabird cliffs have yielded many insights into kleptoparasitism, particularly studies of Parasitic Jaegers, which appear to rely on kleptoparasitism more than any other seabird. Studies in Iceland show that Parasitic Jaegers nesting along the coast primarily attack Black-legged Kittiwakes early in the breeding season, switching to Atlantic Puffins later in the season. Indeed, in these areas Parasitic Jaeger chicks hatch at about the same time as puffin chicks, which suggests that jaegers time their egg-laying to coincide with the best time for stealing food. These jaegers also harassed puffins much more often than they harassed murres, even though the murres carry larger loads of food back to their young. It may be that murres, being larger than puffins, are less willing to surrender their food.

Very little is known about kleptoparasitism from the perspective of the host or victim species. One long-term study found that terns were less willing to drop fish to jaegers in years when food was scarce, and that kleptoparasitic chases by gulls were more likely to succeed when terns were enjoying greater reproductive success.

A study conducted along the St. Lawrence River in Quebec during the nonbreeding season found that Parasitic Jaegers chased Common Terns *(Sterna hirundo)* more than they chased Black-legged Kittiwakes and Ring-billed Gulls,

and that Common Terns surrendered fish more readily than kittiwakes. The study also found that the jaegers' opportunities to steal food increased with the number of attackers present, but understandably, the per capita yield for the jaegers decreased. Other studies have found that jaegers' success rates increase with the duration of the chase and when visibility is poor (at dusk or in mist, for example).

Rarely do kleptoparasites take more than 1 percent of their hosts' food over the nesting season, and rarely do they parasitize more than 2 percent of the potential victims in a seabird colony. In an extreme case, a study from Iceland found that up to 6 percent of the puffins in a colony were chased, and about 4 percent robbed, by Parasitic Jaegers. Interestingly, no study has demonstrated that the Parasitic Jaeger, despite its name, is a more successful kleptoparasite than the Great Skua or even the Herring Gull.

Larger species of gulls tend to rely more on kleptoparasitism than do smaller gulls, but a diverse array of species can be involved in parasitic interactions, both as attackers and victims. Herring Gulls, for example, often harass Common Loons *(Gavia immer)* bringing prey to the

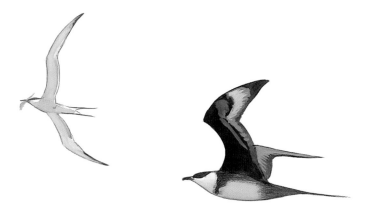

Kleptoparasitism. The jaegers are known for their aggressive attacks, stealing food from other species of seabirds rather than catching their own. The aptly named Parasitic Jaeger, shown here chasing a Common Tern, is the most persistent; it acquires much of its food year-round by stealing from other species. The attack begins with a fast, low, falcon-like approach, followed by a swerving chase as the victim attempts to escape, usually by climbing. This chase usually lasts only a few seconds and ends with the victim dropping its prey, which the jaeger then picks up.

surface, and Bonaparte's Gulls do the same to Razorbills *(Alca torda)*. In all cases, adult birds appear to be more successful kleptoparasites than young birds, which must still learn what situations are likely to yield a meal. When gulls follow ships for offal and discarded fish, they commonly chase other gulls of the same genus or species to steal their food, with the subadults and adults often harrying the youngest birds.

Breeding

Gulls, terns, and skimmers nest mostly in colonies, sometimes in very large ones. Some gulls, however, form only loose colonies, and larger species may nest alone. Inland, for example, a pair of Herring Gulls may occupy an entire lake by itself, and Bonaparte's Gulls will nest in spruce trees at some distance from other pairs, converging with other gulls chiefly to drive predators from the nesting area. Often, skuas and jaegers are also solitary breeders and may vigorously defend large territories against conspecifics.

Within colonies, members of the Laridae are highly territorial, even though a territory may be only a tiny foothold on a cliff, as with the kittiwakes, or a few square feet of beach. All larid species will attack any intruders they perceive as a threat. Despite the birds' small size, a colony's worth of dive-bombing terns can pose a formidable deterrent to a would-be predator. Large skuas have even been known to stoop on, and topple, adult humans.

In some colonial species, breeding is highly synchronized. By laying their eggs at the same time, all the pairs reduce the chances of their eggs and young being eaten by predators, which will have a greater choice of nests to prey upon. Highly colonial nesters tend to have the most elaborate breeding displays, including much sky-pointing, bill-drooping, billing, wing-drooping, and, throughout the nesting season, incessant calling. Indeed, their synchronous return to colonies at the beginning of the breeding season, along with such highly stereotyped and elaborate displays, probably facilitates synchronous nesting. Tropical species, such as the Sooty Tern, do not have an annual breeding cycle and may be found nesting year-round in some places.

Site fidelity among gulls, terns, and skimmers depends on the availability of suitable habitat from year to year. Some

Elegant Tern colony. *Most larids are colonial nesters. Colonies are usually situated on islands where predators are scarce, and nests (which are nothing more than shallow scrapes, sometimes lined with grasses) are densely packed. The entire colony joins in defending nests against predators by swooping, pecking, and defecating on the intruder, as anyone who has walked into a gull or tern colony knows.*

Brown Noddy at nest. *Among the larids nesting in North America, only the Brown Noddy and Bonaparte's Gull nest off the ground in trees or bushes. All other species nest on the ground or on cliffs or rooftops.*

barrier islands, for instance, shift and change a great deal within a year, losing or gaining high areas or clumps of vegetation desired by some species and avoided by others. Other habitats, such as sea cliffs, are more stable, and the birds that nest in such places will often reuse the same site year after year. In most larid species, selection of the nest site is a joint decision, made by the birds after they have formed a pair bond.

Skuas in particular are creatures of habit on the nesting ground, typically occupying a very small patch of land near the nest when not tending eggs or young. Nonbreeding skuas, mostly subadults, are more sociable and occupy a communal loafing area in groups that are known as "clubs." In Great Skuas, these nonbreeding birds gather with breeding adults to form large aggregations at freshwater bathing sites, where hundreds of birds may display, fight, bathe, preen, and rest. Like skuas, gulls will also gather at freshwater sites to drink and bathe.

Most members of the family Laridae are monogamous and pair with the same mate annually, until one partner dies. A few pairs do part, especially if they are unable to raise young successfully. In general, skuas and jaegers are highly monogamous and show strong site fidelity. The Brown Skua *(Stercorarius skua lonnbergi)*, a form of the Great Skua from the Southern Hemisphere that is often considered a separate species, sometimes

forms polyandrous groups of two males and one female. The Pomarine Jaeger is also unusual among larids, often switching mates and nest sites from year to year in response to changes in the abundance of its chief prey item, lemmings.

Displays

Most larid species have well-developed courtship rituals, often accompanied by noisy vocalizations that they use to maintain pair bonds and in territorial defense. Many such displays are common to species throughout the family, but

Gull threat posture. *Larids have an elaborate system of vocalizations and postures for communication within their colonies. The threat display, shown here by a Herring Gull, involves walking stiffly with the neck stretched up and the bill pointed slightly down; this is an aggressive action directed at unwanted visitors.*

Long call. *One of the most conspicuous territorial displays given by larids is the long call. In this display, the bird begins by lowering the bill almost to the ground while giving some low-pitched calls, then raises the bill with the neck outstretched and gives a series of trumpeting calls. The calls and postures of different species vary slightly. The Herring Gull is shown.*

others are found only in certain groups. For example, skuas and the Pomarine Jaeger perform a raised-wing courtship and territorial display in which they expose their white wing-patches and give a "long call." A long call is usually made up of a series of laughing sounds delivered in quick succession, sometimes beginning or ending with a long, strident call. Also given by gulls and the smaller jaegers, long calls are often accompanied by a display in which the bird stretches its neck up and forward.

Courtship feeding occurs in many larid species. In terns, the male presents gifts of small fish to the female. The presentation is often preceeded by a fish flight, in which the male flies above the nesting colony, a fish clasped in his bill, with the female following behind.

The "Lesbian Gull" Mystery

During the 1970s, researchers studying Western Gulls on Santa Barbara Island, California, noticed a very skewed sex ratio in the colonies, with almost four females for every male. Moreover, some

of the "excess" females were pairing with other females, leading the popular press to call the birds "lesbian gulls." However, the reason for both the skewed sex ratio and the female-female pairs turned out not to be sexual "orientation" but chemical alteration of the male gulls' capacity to breed.

The development of male vertebrate embryos can be affected by chemicals, such as the organochlorine pollutant DDT, that mimic natural hormones associated with female sexual development. As adults, these birds may be unable to breed or may fail to develop behaviors necessary for breeding, such as courtship displays and colony attendance, effectively causing a shortage of males at colonies.

The widespread use of DDT in the Los Angeles area over a 20-year period beginning in the 1950s had led to very high concentrations of the contaminant in fish, marine mammals, and seabirds, with the result that many Brown Pelicans and Double-crested Cormorants *(Phalacrocorax auritus)* experienced nesting failure

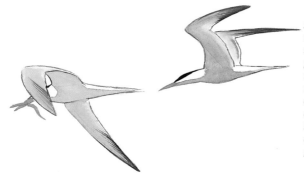

Fish flight. *The courtship of terns involves aerial displays, the most conspicuous of which is the fish flight. The male carries a fish that he exhibits to the female as the pair flies around in an exaggerated and synchronized aerial "ballet," calling as they go. If all goes well, the pair lands, and the male gives the fish to the female. Royal Terns are shown.*

Semi-precocial young. The young of gulls and terns are semi-precocial and can walk soon after hatching, although they continue to rely on the adults for food even after fledging. Since their shallow open nests provide little protection, within a few days of hatching the young birds often move to find shade or shelter nearby. As they grow they follow the parents more and more tenaciously, begging for food. Herring Gulls are shown.

due to DDT–induced eggshell thinning. Gulls' eggshells were less affected by such thinning; instead, they were susceptible to the estrogenic effects of DDT.

Male gull embryos exposed to high levels of DDT showed abnormal development of ovarian tissue and oviducts. This "feminization" probably inhibited breeding behavior in male Western Gulls, which failed to return to the breeding colony on Santa Barbara Island to breed, causing the sex bias that was observed by the scientists.

Females unable to find a mate can still breed by seeking extra-pair fertilizations from an already mated male, but they are unable to raise their young without a partner to share the duties of nest defense and foraging. Such females may team up, laying their eggs together in the same nest and sharing parental responsibilities.

The effects of "environmental estrogens" such as DDT were not isolated to Santa Barbara Island. Female-female pairing has been subsequently found in other gull and tern colonies, and the feminizing effects of estrogen-mimicking chemicals persist in various vertebrate species throughout North America.

Movements

Larids occur in aquatic habitats throughout the world, and many species have wide distributions and make long seasonal movements. Many skuas, jaegers, gulls, and terns have circumpolar distri-

butions; several terns occur throughout equatorial waters. Some species, such as the Sooty Tern, are entirely pelagic for years at a time. Some Sooty Terns may not breed until 10 years of age; these birds probably remain at sea almost until first breeding, returning to colonies—much as subadult tubenoses do—a couple of years before they are ready to breed.

Most skuas and jaegers are fairly long-distance migrants. South Polar Skuas travel from breeding sites in the Antarctic to spend the austral winter in the Northern Hemisphere, while Long-tailed Jaegers make the reverse journey, breeding in the Arctic and wintering in subantarctic waters. Gulls more typically travel shorter distances. Species that nest in the interior of North America move toward the coasts, and few North American gulls travel farther south than Central America. Franklin's and Sabine's Gulls are the only species in which much of the population travels south to equatorial waters or beyond. Nonetheless, there are many species in which rare individuals may wander considerable distances from their typical range. With the boom in new information on gull identification and with perhaps increasing gull populations around the world, species such as the Black-tailed *(Larus crassirostris)* and Slaty-backed *(L. schistisagus)* Gulls, both from eastern Asia, are being found more frequently in North America. This trend seems likely to continue.

Many larids that nest in the southern United States and Central America, such as the Royal Tern and the Black Skimmer, are year-round residents, while others, such as Heermann's Gull, may wander north during the nonbreeding season.

The Black Tern may move in the course of a year from the marshes and lakes of the North American interior, where it nests, to the littoral zone of the Atlantic and Gulf states, to deep Gulf Stream waters in the pelagic zone. Here it mixes with a pelagic specialist, the Bridled Tern, both species feeding on organisms of the pelagic drift community in the gulfweed (or sargassum) while on their way to wintering grounds in western South America.

The World's Greatest Migrant: The Arctic Tern

The world champion among long-distance migrants is the Arctic Tern *(Sterna paradisaea).* From their nesting grounds in the Arctic—which extend as far northward as there is land, to Cape Morris Jesup in Greenland, at latitude 84°N— Arctic Terns move southward to reach, or even circle, the Antarctic pack ice, where they have been noted as far south as latitude 78°S. The round-trip journey from the nesting grounds can be as long as 31,000 miles (50,000 km) per year, or roughly a trip around the world. Some Arctic Terns live as long as 25 years, which translates into perhaps more than 600,000 miles (1,000,000 km) traveled in a lifetime.

During migration and in the nonbreeding months, Arctic Terns are highly pelagic and typically visible from land only during onshore gales. Only in the latter half of the 20th century has some sense of their migratory routes been pieced together, from observations often made thousands of miles apart.

Most Arctic Terns mass in the northeastern North Atlantic before heading south toward wintering areas. Traveling southward past western Africa, some cross the equatorial Atlantic toward northeastern South America, but most move southward offshore of southern Africa. A smaller number of birds travels southward along the west coast of North and South America, joining the Atlantic migrants in Antarctic waters.

A major challenge to the terns are the howling westerly winds found in the Southern Ocean, especially at latitudes of 40°S and beyond. These winds would force a strong eastward drift upon any migrant, but Arctic Terns appear to use them to their advantage: Rather than fighting the winds to reach the closest Antarctic pack ice (their chief "wintering" habitat), the terns move eastward while traveling south, ending up in Antarctic waters east of South Africa, mainly between 60° and 120°E longitude.

While the terns are in Antarctica, they molt their flight feathers and feed heavily on the abundant krill in the pack-ice waters. As the austral spring progresses into summer, the pack ice recedes toward the Antarctic coastline much farther south, where the influence of westerly winds gives way to the opposing easterly flow of air around the South Pole.

Though some terns may encircle the continent during the austral summer, riding the westerlies, most birds appear to reverse course and head west. These birds follow the polar easterlies as far as the Weddell Sea, which lies to the east of the Antarctic Peninsula and the tip of South America. They then use the energy of the westerlies once again to propel them northeastward to southern Africa, whence they make their way northward to their nesting areas.

Young Arctic Terns are a different matter. Like other terns, they do not breed in their first spring and so do not make the long return trip to the nesting areas like the adults. Some subadults spend their first "summer" off the coast of western South America in the Peru (Humboldt) Current. To get to this current, they probably use westerlies to encircle the Antarctic continent in an eastbound direction, rather than trying to cross the Drake Passage between South America and Antarctica, where strong westerly winds would make westbound progress extremely difficult.

Conservation

All larids are vulnerable to the negative effects of oil spills on lakes, seas, rivers, and oceans, whether by damage to their plumage or contamination of their prey. Environmental pollutants that concentrate in the tissues of prey occur in high levels in many larids. Many colonially nesting larids at lower latitudes, especially ground nesters, must also contend with the same host of introduced mammalian hordes that plague other seabird species—rats, cats, dogs, pigs, horses, cattle, and the like.

In past centuries, and even in the early 20th century, gulls were a source of food (adults, chicks, and eggs alike) for North Americans living along the coasts. With all species now enjoying protection—and with the market for gull eggs a thing of the past—many species have expanded their populations, helped in no small part by their remarkable ability to adapt to human-altered environments. There are few threats to gulls nesting on the continent, and no species are listed as endangered or threatened in North America.

Many gull species, on the contrary, are perceived as threats, especially where they congregate in great numbers: as hazards to the airline industry, as potential carriers of disease, and as agricultural and aquacultural pests. Further cause for alarm lies in the predation of gulls on beach-nesting terns and plovers, particularly when populations are perilously low. In some areas, Great Black-backed and Herring Gulls have been culled to protect threatened species such as the Piping Plover *(Charadrius melodus)* and the Roseate Tern *(Sterna dougallii)*.

The Red-legged Kittiwake and Aleutian Tern are both vulnerable because they have small population sizes and are restricted to only a few sites in Alaska and eastern Russia. Red-legged Kittiwake populations have been declining, and although the species is not listed as threatened or endangered, it perhaps should be. Heermann's Gull and the

Sooty Tern migration route.
The Sooty Terns nesting on the Dry Tortugas, off southwestern Florida, have been studied for many years. Tens of thousands have been banded, and band recoveries have given researchers a clear picture of the travels of these birds. After fledging the young birds travel south to Colombia, then east across the Atlantic to waters off western Africa. The young birds stay in this rich feeding area (shown in blue) for three years or more. After they reach sexual maturity the birds fly back across the Atlantic and return to the Tortugas, where they may touch land for the first time in several years. As adults the birds stay relatively close to the islands, leaving the breeding area for only a few months each winter, but remaining mostly within the Caribbean.

Yellow-footed Gull also are both vulnerable because of their small breeding ranges. Ninety percent of all Heermann's Gulls breed at one site in the Gulf of California. Yellow-footed Gulls, which nest in scattered colonies along beaches, are especially vulnerable to disturbance by tourists and egg collectors.

Heerman's, Franklin's and the Yellow-footed Gulls are on the WatchList.

Terns are much more vulnerable than most gulls in their nesting situations, and many tern populations are in decline. Tern feathers, unlike those of gulls, were used extensively in the fashion industry at the turn of the last century, and their eggs were harvested as well. Many tern colonies on the Atlantic coast vanished over a short period toward the end of the 19th century, when hundreds of thousands of terns were slaughtered. Overfishing of inshore waters, too, may affect terns more than gulls, as terns appear less able than gulls to exploit by-catch and discarded fish. Loss of habitat is particularly disastrous for both terns and skimmers; many remote spits that once teemed with terns are now used for human recreation.

The Least Tern (*Sterna antillarum*) is listed as endangered in California and the interior United States. The Black Tern also merits concern; it has undergone population declines in many areas and is clearly declining on the southern edge of its range around the Great Lakes. Probably the most vulnerable tern species is the Roseate Tern, which is on the endangered lists of both the United States and Canada. This species declined in numbers during the latter half of the 20th century; the current population has only a few thousand birds, most concentrated at four breeding colonies.

Skimmers are particularly sensitive to disturbance by humans or animals on their nesting grounds, but they are able to renest rapidly if conditions permit. Their tendency to shift nesting areas regularly has meant that counts of skimmer populations are difficult to interpret. The

Black Skimmer's populations may actually have increased slightly in the 20th century, but the data are ambiguous.

Threats to skimmers' well-being include disturbance by feral dogs, cats, and other mammals; toxins such as PCBs and heavy metals in fish; and the development and recreational use of potential nesting habitat. The protection of nesting areas, even artificial dredge-spoil islands of apparently little value other than to skimmers, will be crucial in keeping their populations healthy.

There seem to be few particular conservation concerns for skuas and jaegers; none is listed as endangered or threatened. If anything, these predatory birds are potential threats to small, sensitive populations of certain petrels in the Southern Hemisphere.

Accidental Species

As gull identification becomes more sophisticated, rare species and subspecies of gulls are being seen with greater frequency in North America. Indeed many such forms are now recognized as regular, if uncommon. Among the extremely rare species are the Band-tailed Gull (*Larus belcheri*), which has been found in Florida and California; the Gray Gull (*L. modestus*), which has occurred once in Louisiana; the Gray-hooded Gull (*L. cirrocephalus*), recorded once in Florida; and the Swallow-tailed Gull (*Creagus furcatus*), which has been seen off the California coast. These four species are all native to the coasts of South America (the Gray-hooded also occurs in Africa). Concerns have been raised about whether these vagrants traveled to North America on board ships, and the last two species are not currently accepted by the AOU.

Another rarity from South America is the Large-billed Tern (*Phaetusa simplex*), which has been found in North America in late spring and summer. In addition, a Eurasian species, the Whiskered Tern (*Chlidonias hybridus*), has occurred in Delaware and New Jersey in the summer.

Edward S. Brinkley and Alec Humann

Auks

The auks, or alcids, are a distinctive family of small to medium-size seabirds. Their plumage is mostly black and white or brown. They have compact, muscular bodies with short wings, tail, and legs, and are normally seen flying rapidly and close to the sea surface with whirring wingbeats. The webbed feet are set well back on the body, and bill size and shape are quite variable. Exclusively marine, auks come ashore only to breed, usually in colonies on isolated islands and coastal cliffs.

Taxonomy

Ecologically the auks are similar to the penguins (family Spheniscidae) and the diving-petrels (Pelecanoididae), their counterparts of the southern oceans, with which they share the habit of wing-propelled pursuit-diving, or "flying" underwater. Auks, penguins, and diving-petrels have shared characteristics that include wings adapted for underwater propulsion, very dense waterproof plumage, and physiological adaptations for diving.

These three groups, however, are not at all closely related and are classified as members of different orders; their similarities result from similar lifestyles. The major difference between auks and penguins is that auks are capable of flight in the air as well as underwater, while all penguins are flightless in air. Cassin's Auklet *(Ptychoramphus aleuticus)* and the Common Diving-Petrel *(Pelecanoides urinatrix)* are particularly similar in appearance and offer an excellent example of convergent evolution.

Although auks are superficially similar to loons and grebes, the latter groups are not closely related to auks, and their underwater diving is entirely propelled by foot rather than wing-propelled.

Auks form an anatomically distinct group of birds, but they have sometimes been classified as a subfamily of the gulls, to which they are most closely related within the order Charadriiformes.

The auks divide into six taxonomic groups, or tribes. Most distinctive are the puffins (including the Rhinoceros Auklet, *Cerorhinca monocerata*), which eat fish and have extraordinarily deep bills, and the small, plankton-eating auklets, which have short, broad-based bills. The Dovekie *(Alle alle)* is superficially similar to the small auklets and also eats plankton but is grouped with the murres and the Razorbill *(Alca torda)*. The guillemots form a fourth tribe, and the murrelets are subdivided into the two remaining tribes: the *Synthliboramphus* murrelets, which look like small murres, and the *Brachyramphus* murrelets, which develop mottled brown plumage during summer.

Alcid diversity. Although the auks are subdivided into six taxonomic groups, they can more simply be thought of as having three main types, based on appearance and diet: the slender-billed, fish-eating species, ranging from the large Common Murre (top left) to the small Xantus's Murrelet (bottom left); the deep-billed, fish-eating puffins (such as the Tufted Puffin, top right); and the stubby-billed, plankton-eating auklets (including the Least Auklet, bottom right).

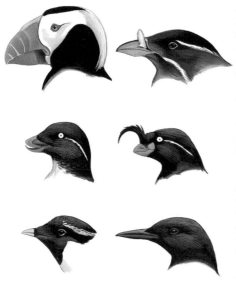

Alcid heads and bills. Members of the Alcidae show more variation in the form of the bill than any other family of North American birds. Some have developed odd bill shapes for foraging; others have elaborate bill and feather ornamentation for courtship. Many have a "normal" straight bill used for capturing fish and other small aquatic animals. The puffins, represented here by the Tufted Puffin (top left), have very deep, laterally compressed bills. The Rhinoceros Auklet (top right) develops a horny growth at the base of the bill in the breeding season. The Parakeet Auklet (center left) has the most remarkable bill shape; it uses its upward-hooked lower jaw to capture jellyfish. The Crested Auklet (center right) has a short, stubby bill like some other auklets but develops horny plates around the bill and facial plumes during the breeding season. The Ancient Murrelet (bottom left) has a small, laterally compressed bill, while other murrelets, the murres, and the guillemots (Pigeon Guillemot, bottom right) have simple, dagger-shaped bills.

This last group includes the Marbled *(B. marmoratus)* and Long-billed *(B. perdix)* Murrelets, which were considered a single species until the late 1990s.

Adaptations to Lifestyle

Because of their small, stiff wings adapted for propulsion underwater, auks fly in a distinctive manner; they never soar and normally fly close to the sea surface, with continuous, whirring wingbeats. Their flight is fast—35 to 50 miles per hour (55–80 km/h)—and direct, but it is also costly in terms of energy expended, and some species encounter difficulties in maneuvering while taking off and landing. All species have fully webbed feet and lack a hind toe.

Auk species vary somewhat in body shape. For example, murres and murrelets have relatively slender bodies and feet set well back, increasing their diving performance at sea at the expense of agility on land, while puffins and auklets have chunkier bodies with larger, more forward-mounted feet, increasing their agility on land at the expense of diving performance at sea. The anatomical specializations for agility likely have resulted from selection related to predation by gulls and raptors at breeding colonies.

Murrelets require less agility on land because they avoid predators by gathering at their colonies at night *(Synthliboramphus* murrelets) or by using dispersed cryptic nest sites *(Brachyramphus* murrelets).

All auks have very dense waterproof plumage and strong bones that can resist crushing water pressures. Their physiological adaptations for diving include the enhanced oxygen-storing capacity of their tissues and the ability to use anaerobic respiration during long dives.

Auk plumage is normally black, white, and gray, countershaded with dark above and light below to minimize the bird's conspicuousness to predators and to prey both on and below the sea surface. Exceptions are the Marbled, Kittlitz's

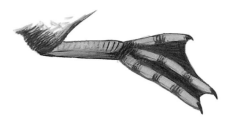

Alcid foot. The foot of the Crested Auklet is typical of the family, with webbed toes and no hind toe. Alcids usually stand on the "heel," with the lower leg resting flat on the ground rather than on the toes.

(Brachyramphus brevirostris), and the Long-billed Murrelets, which nest solitarily in exposed habitats; their very cryptic summer plumage of brown mottled with russet and gray resembles the camouflage worn by nesting shorebirds and ptarmigan. In winter, these murrelets revert to murre-like black-and-white countershaded plumage more appropriate for life at sea. Similarly, guillemots switch from almost entirely black plumage in summer to almost entirely white plumage in winter.

A few species—for example, Xantus's Murrelet *(Synthliboramphus hypoleucus),* the Ancient Murrelet *(S. antiquus),* Cassin's Auklet, and the Whiskered Auklet *(Aethia pygmaea)*—are active at night at their colonies. This adaptation for avoiding daytime predation by gulls and raptors makes them hard to observe on land without a light, but they are readily identifiable by the distinctive nighttime vocalizations they use for sexual display and individual recognition.

Habitats

Like other seabirds, auks face the predicament of a complete separation of their foraging and breeding habitats. While all auk species forage at sea—usually many miles from land in a vast, superficially featureless environment—all species must come to land to breed.

Breeding Habitats

Auk breeding habitat has two important characteristics. First, it provides nesting places that are relatively free of terrestrial predators. Second, it lies close to areas where food to nourish parents and young is predictably available.

Auks are anatomically well adapted for life at sea but less well equipped for life on land. Although their body shapes vary somewhat, their legs are generally set far back on the body, making walking on land difficult, and their wings are small, making rapid acceleration into flight from the ground impossible. Both

Worldwide Family Features

- 6–18" (15–45 cm) seabirds.
- 23 species in about 10 genera worldwide, throughout temperate and Arctic oceans of the Northern Hemisphere. 21 species in 10 genera occur in North America: on Pacific coast from Baja California to Alaska, widely on Arctic coast, and on Atlantic coast from Delaware Bay to Labrador; 1 other species now extinct.
- Eat marine fish and invertebrates, captured through pursuit-diving.
- Most species colonial but defend nest site; *Brachyramphus* murrelets nest solitarily. Monogamous; pair bonds usually last several years, often for life; some species have extra-pair copulations. During winter, move out to sea, away from breeding areas; some species disperse widely to high seas well south of breeding range.
- Breed first at 3 years old (small species) to 8 years old (large species).
- Nest on cliff ledge or rock crevice, or in earth burrow close to sea; solitary murrelet species nest inland in exposed scrape on alpine tundra, or on limb of ancient coniferous tree. Burrow-nesting species may add vegetation such as

grasses to construct rudimentary nest; burrows built by both sexes; other species lay eggs on dirt, collections of small pebbles, or bare rock. Reuse nests.
- 1 (in 16 species) or 2 (in 7 species) eggs, white (in some cavity-nesting species) or light brown, green- or blue-speckled, with dusky markings; shape varies among species, ranging from pyriform to elliptical. Incubation 27–53 days, by both parents; 2-egg clutches hatch synchronously. 1 brood per year, 2 (rarely) in Cassin's Auklet.
- Young hatch covered with down. Development is variable: Some species are semi-precocial, others "intermediate" or precocial. Both parents provide care at nest site only (most species), take chick to sea soon after hatching *(Synthliboramphus* murrelets), or care for chick at nest site until half-grown, after which male parent takes chick to sea (murres, Razorbill). Fledge in 28 days to 8 weeks.
- Adult annual survival 75–95%, highest in larger species. Many birds live 7–25 years. Among oldest on record: 29 years (Thick-billed Murre).

Murre eggs. The eggs of the Common Murre (shown) and Thick-billed Murre are unusual in several respects. They have a strongly pyriform shape, pointed at one end, so they will roll in a tight circle if bumped, and they are unusually variable in color. Both of these features are presumably adaptations to the crowded, cliff-ledge nesting sites of the colonial murres. Eggs can roll around without falling off the ledge, and an individual bird can recognize its own egg, by its patterning, among dozens of others.

these characteristics render auks vulnerable to terrestrial predators such as foxes, minks, raccoons, cats, and rats. This is why colonial auks nest on precipitous sea stacks, cliffs, and remote offshore islands where there are no predators.

For example, murre breeding habitat consists either of cliffs with numerous small ledges or flat offshore islands where as many as 20 or more pairs of birds can nest per square yard, the highest nesting density of any bird. Dovekies and auklets occur in vast colonies where rocky scree slopes or porous lava flows from recent volcanic action provide numerous nesting crevices. Puffins usually choose islands with grassy slopes and deep soil suitable for burrowing.

Marbled and Kittlitz's Murrelets have forsaken the colonial habits of their family and adopted an alternative strategy for selecting breeding habitat and avoiding predators. These species nest well inland where their widely spaced nests can be carefully hidden.

Marbled Murrelets choose broad moss- or litter-covered limbs of massive ancient trees in Pacific coast rain forests, concealing their open nests high above the ground in this natural labyrinth. Nests of this cryptically colored species remained undiscovered by ornithologists until the mid-1970s. Kittlitz's Murrelets nest on open alpine tundra close to snowfields and glaciers, where few predators ever go.

Feeding Habitats

During the nonbreeding season, most auk species are widely distributed well offshore. Birds may be observed, however, as they fly by prominent headlands when there is an onshore wind, especially in the early morning hours. During the summer, they occur closer to land and to breeding areas.

A few species—for example, the Black Guillemot *(Cepphus grylle)*, Pigeon Guillemot *(C. columba)*, Marbled Murrelet, and Razorbill—regularly forage close to shore and in protected waters year-round. Sick, oil-covered, or emaciated auks enter bays and harbors in winter and sometimes can be observed closely. In general, however, auks' foraging habitat is located throughout the open sea. To an auk, the ocean must resemble a vast desert with widely spaced and ephemeral oases where food is available only briefly in quantities that make foraging worthwhile.

Looking out over the ocean for auks, a birder often glimpses small, fast-flying groups of birds moving quickly to the horizon in search of food. These auks are seeking places where their prey is concentrated to many (up to 100 or more) times its average density, perhaps by sensing subtle features on the ocean surface. On an oceanic scale, these can be places where abundant nutrients and phytoplankton nourish many more of the zooplankton and fish upon which auks forage.

On a smaller scale, auks also seek out areas where their prey is concentrated by strong currents flowing over shoals and banks and in passes between islands, or at oceanic fronts where water masses of different density and temperature meet to form an underwater wall against which prey items are trapped.

For example, the violent upwellings and strong currents in passes among the Aleutian Islands off Alaska provide rich feeding grounds for auks. This resource is shared by four auklet species, each exploiting a different food source. Recent field work has shown that the Crested Auklet *(Aethia cristatella)*, the most powerful diver among this group, probes the depths on the upstream side of a pass to intercept helpless krill driven toward the surface by vertical water flow. Whiskered Auklets use the most violent tide rips at the center of the pass, preying on krill and copepods. The Least Auklet *(A. pusilla)* frequents downstream areas where it makes shallow dives to exploit swarms of disoriented copepods. Parakeet Auklets *(A. psittacula)* distribute themselves widely and feed on plankton associated with jellyfish, often even eating jellyfish tentacles.

A few auk species exploit foraging opportunities provided by the activities of other marine predators. The Rhinoceros Auklet and the Common Murre *(Uria aalge)* sometimes exploit schools of prey driven to the surface and concentrated by predatory fish.

Food and Foraging

The auk diet consists of fish and invertebrates, including squid, planktonic crustaceans, gelatinous zooplankton (comb jellies), and polychaete worms that the birds capture by pursuit-diving, propelled by beating the wings underwater.

Colonial auks probably learn where good feeding areas are by watching the flight directions of birds bringing food back to the colony. Once at sea, individual auks seek out patches of prey by looking for foraging birds and probably

for subtle features of the sea surface, such as surface slicks, that might indicate the presence of prey below.

Auks feed entirely by pursuit-diving, in which a bird resting on the sea abruptly tilts forward, opens its wings with the primary feathers oriented backward and parallel to the body, and disappears beneath the surface to begin looking for targets. Once underwater, the bird flaps its wings and "flies" at a speed roughly equivalent to a human's walking speed. This swimming ability allows individual auks considerable freedom when searching for prey.

Ornithologists first became aware of the extraordinary diving ability of auks when they learned that drowned birds had been recovered from gill-nets set 300 feet (90 m) or more below the surface. More recently, information from depth recorders placed on birds at colonies and recovered later has demonstrated that even small species, such as the Dovekie, frequently dive to 150 feet (45 m), while

Underwater diving. *Alcids use only their forelimbs (wings) for underwater propulsion, unlike virtually all other swimming vertebrates. To reduce drag, the relatively small wings are held only partly extended, which reduces their surface area to less than half that used during flight. Well adapted for swimming, these small wings are not particularly well suited for aerial flight. The Great Auk, now extinct, had such small wings that it could no longer fly. The Thick-billed Murre is shown.*

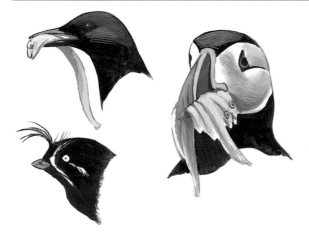

Auks carrying prey. Auks have solved the problem of transporting food to their young in various ways. Guillemots (such as the Pigeon Guillemot, top left) carry a single fish crosswise in the bill. Auklets (such as the Whiskered Auklet, bottom left) fill an expandable throat pouch with planktonic prey. Puffins (like the Atlantic Puffin, right) can carry multiple fish crosswise in the bill.

larger species like murres regularly dive to 300 feet (90 m) and attain maximum depths of more than 600 feet (180 m).

Auk diving behavior is remarkable not just because of the physiological challenges of deep diving, but also because at the depths the birds attain there is so little ambient light that one wonders how they can possibly see their prey. Auks must depend on vision alone, since echolocation or smell as means of locating prey seem implausible. The most likely explanation is that auks can see well in the dark and use bioluminescence as well as ambient light to locate prey. Nevertheless, we have a lot to learn about how auks forage underwater.

Much of what we know about auk foraging ecology has been learned by observing parents feeding their chicks at colonies. Different auk species may bring their chick a single large fish, many small fish, or even hundreds of tiny planktonic crustaceans, such as copepods.

Murres and guillemots invariably deliver a single item, usually a fish, held more or less lengthwise in the bill with the head of the fish enclosed in the mouth cavity. They are apparently incapable of carrying larger prey or several items because of constraints on their flying ability posed by their high wingloading. Puffins and Razorbills, which have laterally compressed bills, typically deliver multiple fish held crosswise in their bills. Atlantic Puffins *(Fratercula arctica)* and Horned Puffins *(F. corniculata)* are the champion prey loaders, somehow capable of catching and holding dozens of slender fish (often sand lances) at a time.

While small, energy-rich fish like sand lances, capelin, and herrings are ideal food for growing auk chicks, their delivery to colonies provides an attractive opportunity for kleptoparasitic gulls. In North America, large gulls such as the Herring Gull *(Larus argentatus)*, Great Black-backed Gull *(L. marinus)*, and Glaucous-winged Gull *(L. glaucescens)* specialize in stealing fish from colonial auks, especially puffins.

Growing evidence suggests that although large auks bring their chicks fish, which are easy to carry and represent an efficient energy bundle, they themselves feed more on crustaceans. The smaller auklets, which feed on plankton, bring their chicks food loads containing hundreds of wet but undigested items in their specialized throat pouches.

Even with colonies close to the best feeding locations, the breeding success of auks varies from year to year due to changing environmental conditions. For some species, such as the Tufted Puffin *(Fratercula cirrhata)*, years of reproductive failure may be more common than success. Auks' long life spans (to 25 years or more) buffer the effect of poor breeding years and maintain population stability.

On the Atlantic coast of North America, variability in the distribution and abundance of capelin has profoundly affected auk breeding performance at some colonies. On the Pacific coast, the El Niño phenomenon, with its associated lack of coastal upwellings, has caused breeding failures and has even been linked to population declines of Common Murres and Cassin's Auklets; the latter species declined by 65 percent between 1975 and 1995 at the Farallon Islands, off California.

Breeding

Auks are socially monogamous. Most breeding auks retain their mate from year to year, but divorces occur. In Crested and Least Auklets the divorce rate can reach 30 percent of pairs per year. In larger species, such as murres, divorce is rare and pairs may remain together for many years.

Male and female auks meet and form pair bonds at their breeding colonies; there is no evidence of pairs associating together at sea outside of a brief period just before the laying of eggs. At the beginning of a new nesting season, pairs reunite at their previous years' nest site or display rock.

Although they are socially monogamous, males and females of several auk species pursue extra-pair copulations. Among ledge-nesting murres, females sometimes copulate with nearby males when their mate is away from the colony. Crested and Least Auklets copulate on the sea, and males guard their partner to prevent extra-pair copulation. Rough seas, the approach of a predator, or the disruptive actions of a rival male can interrupt mate-guarding and provide opportunities for females. Least Auklet males are particularly active in disrupting the copulations of other pairs, and paired males respond (and maximize their chances of fathering offspring) by copulating with their mates as frequently as four times per hour.

Pair formation in auks usually starts when a female approaches a male standing near his nest site. Among murres, this often involves a female landing near a suitable nesting ledge occupied by a male; among puffins, a female commonly approaches an unmated male standing near his burrow entrance.

In some species, females respond to elaborate postural or vocal displays performed by unmated males. At first, the female approaches cautiously and carefully inspects the male's appearance. Later, courtship intensifies with lengthy face-to-face contact, coordinated postural displays, and mutual preening.

Courtship Displays

During courtship, many auk species display elaborate visual ornamental traits, such as brightly colored bills (puffins) or plumes and crests (auklets). Both male and female Crested Auklets prefer partners with large ornaments. Since both males and females display these ornaments and have a preference for well-ornamented partners, the evolution of ornaments in auks has likely resulted from mutual sexual selection.

The elaborate visual ornaments of Crested and Whiskered Auklets are augmented by their distinctive citrus-like plumage odor, which probably serves as a mate-attracting perfume. The Crested's odor is strong enough to be detected by birders on boats near large flocks.

Most auks are not vocal at sea; thus vocalizations provide them with no clues to mate identification away from nesting colonies. One exception is the Marbled Murrelet, whose loud *kleeeer* contact calls are often the first clue to the presence of this species at sea; the calls provide an eerie signal of the birds' dawn and dusk flights to their forest nesting areas.

Murres and Razorbills have a rich variety of calls, which are used within pairs and directed toward neighbors at their colonies, including calls used only during copulation. Puffins have the least diverse repertoires and communicate vocally with a few low growls.

Male Razorbills, guillemots, Ancient and Xantus's Murrelets, and auklets perform advertising displays to attract mates. The most conspicuous of these is the advertising call, or song, of the nocturnal Ancient Murrelet. The loud, complex songs—performed by males perched on boughs of large trees in their colonies, just above their own burrows—appear to function in the same way as the songs of passerine birds.

There is no evidence that auks are capable of vocal imitative learning, so each individual's vocal sounds are innate. In several species recognition of close relatives is crucial to the birds' life cycle. All species in which adults care for their young at sea have conspicuous sounds used for communication between parents and chicks. This ability is highly developed in Ancient Murrelets, which lead their chicks to the sea from their burrows, sometimes hundreds of yards from the shoreline. Parents and chicks of this species have individually distinctive calls that are mutually recognized.

Young

Compared to other avian families, auks are unusual in terms of chick development. While birds within all other North American families have a single developmental pattern, the auk family contains species with three distinct modes of chick rearing.

Guillemots, *Brachyramphus* murrelets, puffins, and auklets, like their relatives the gulls and terns, have semi-precocial young that are cared for at the nest site until they are close to adult size, at which point they fledge unaccompanied by their parents. Razorbills and murres have "intermediate" young that are cared for at the nest until half-grown and then depart the colony accompanied by the male parent, who provides additional care at sea. The Ancient Murrelet, Craveri's Murrelet *(Synthliboramphus craveri)*, and Xantus's Murrelet have precocial young that leave the colony when only two days old, accompanied by both parents, who provide the young with extended care at sea.

There are several reasons adult auks might take their chicks to sea at an early age; controversy exists over which are most important. Furthermore, different explanations may account for the evolution of early departure in large and small auk species.

The evolution of an "intermediate" strategy in Razorbills and murres seems to have resulted from the difficulty of retrieving food from distant foraging areas while simultaneously guarding the chick at exposed nest sites. Male murres thus take their offspring to foraging areas to avoid the high energy costs of transporting food home.

The evolution of a precocial departure strategy in the *Synthliboramphus* murrelets probably resulted from the very high predation risk adult murrelets encounter in their nesting colonies. For example, Ancient and Xantus's Murrelet parents take the chicks to sea soon after hatching to avoid their being caught by falcons, eagles, and gulls at the colony.

Conservation

Currently most North American auk populations are faring reasonably well due to the protection of many breeding areas within refuges, and the long average life spans of auks, which allow populations to persist even after years of low reproductive success.

There are, however, exceptions. The Great Auk *(Pinguinus impennis)*, which formerly bred in North America, became extinct in the 19th century; Xantus's Murrelet is probably in danger of extinction; and numbers of the Marbled Murrelet are declining due to habitat destruction. In addition, many populations are threatened, at least locally, by human activities that kill adult birds, both at colonies and at sea.

Like other seabirds, auks have suffered terribly from the introduction of predators onto islands. During the 19th and early 20th centuries, fur farmers brought Arctic Foxes and Red Foxes to 455 islands in Alaska that had been predator-free. These introductions had a devastating impact on seabirds, most notably in the Aleutian Islands, where populations of Ancient Murrelets and Cassin's, Whiskered, Crested, and Least Auklets were decimated, along with other seabird species.

Marbled Murrelet chick at nest. *The remarkable nest site of the Marbled Murrelet, on a moss-covered branch high in a conifer and up to 45 miles (72 km) inland, was first discovered only in 1974. One of many challenges presented by this nesting strategy is that the young bird must remain in the nest until ready to fly to sea. Most other auks nest in burrows or crevices, or on open cliff ledges. Most other species also nest in colonies, unlike the Marbled Murrelet.*

The accidental introduction of rats onto islands has had similarly devastating effects. For example, rats introduced onto Langara Island in the Queen Charlotte Islands of British Columbia wiped out thousands of Ancient Murrelets and Cassin's Auklets that formerly bred there. Rats have recently been removed from Langara, but seabirds throughout the Queen Charlotte Islands are now gravely threatened by recently introduced raccoons, which are invading murrelet and auklet colonies and devouring adults. Programs to remove alien predators from seabird breeding islands, and to prevent introduction of new predators, are essential to the preservation of auk populations.

Many auk breeding colonies are now protected from human disturbance, which should reduce the chance of an extinction similar to that of the Great Auk. This species was wiped out by aggressive hunting for its meat, feathers, fat, and eggs, and for use of its flesh for fish bait by fishermen working near its North Atlantic colonies.

Human interference with breeding areas continues to be intense for Marbled

Murrelets, which nest in large trees in old-growth rain forests in the eastern part of their range, from southeastern Alaska to California. Loss of habitat due to intense logging of coastal forests has led to the disappearance of this species from many localities, and to its legal designation as a threatened species. Little breeding habitat has been set aside in protected reserves for the Marbled Murrelet, as has been done for most other North American seabird species. With much of the Marbled Murrelet's breeding habitat slated for logging, continued population declines are expected.

Auk mortality at sea has received greater attention than the problems auks encounter at colonies. Hunting of auks is no longer as widespread as it was before the 20th century, but a legal hunt of the Thick-billed Murre *(Uria lomvia)* and the Common Murre in Newfoundland involved kills of up to a million birds in a single season during the 1980s, one of the largest bird hunts ever in North America. This hunt has not been closely regulated (a bag limit was introduced only in 1995) and its potential impact on murre populations is of great concern. Furthermore, Razorbills, the rarest North American Atlantic auk, are illegally killed in large numbers during this hunt.

Hunting of auks by native peoples probably has had negligible impact on most auk populations, except in western Greenland, where subsistence hunting has decimated several murre colonies.

Accidental oil spills, such as the *Exxon Valdez* spill in Alaska's Prince William Sound in 1989, have caused several devastating auk die-offs. Auks are extremely vulnerable to contact with petroleum or vegetable oils, because oil immediately destroys the insulating capacity of their feathers, leading to death by exposure. Petroleum also causes damage to the liver and other internal organs when the birds attempt to preen themselves and ingest the oil.

An estimated 350,000 or more seabirds (mostly Common Murres and other auks) died as a result of the *Exxon Valdez* oil spill. Even more auks are killed each year by numerous small oil spills and deliberate (often legal) dumping of oil by careless vessel operators. Although the long-term impact of such catastrophes on auk populations has not been well quantified, the response of the public and the media has often been intense. However, it has had little effect in changing shipping regulations or increasing enforcement of existing rules, which would reduce the death toll.

Instead, public-relations efforts by government and industry have focused largely on the so-called rehabilitation of oil-soaked birds. For example, after the *Exxon Valdez* spill, $41 million was spent on cleaning 800 birds (mostly Common Murres). But survival of rehabilitated auks after their release has been extremely low. For example, the average survival time after release was estimated as less than 10 days in one study.

Other than oil spills, the major cause of auk mortality at sea is commercial fishing. The main problem relates to the use of monofilament gill-nets, which are normally set in productive areas of ocean frequented by auks, and which form a nearly invisible underwater death trap for diving birds. Experience has shown that auk populations cannot coexist with intensive monofilament gill-net fishing. Gill-netting has had documented impacts on Razorbills, puffins, both murre species, and Marbled Murrelets.

Commercial fisheries and other operations that employ bright lights at sea, such as offshore drilling platforms, are dangerous to nocturnal species, particularly Ancient and Xantus's Murrelets and Whiskered and Cassin's Auklets. These auks can become dazzled by bright lights, particularly on foggy nights, and are killed by collision with vessels or predation by the swarms of gulls that often accompany fishing boats. Death as a result of light attraction is a problem when brightly lit vessels anchor near seabird colonies.

Great Auk. Formerly abundant, breeding on islands in the northwest Atlantic, this flightless species was wiped out by hunting in the early 1800s. The last confirmed records in the wild came from off Newfoundland in the 1830s and off Iceland in 1844.

Extreme conservation concerns now focus on Xantus's Murrelet; the species' total population amounts to only a few thousand pairs nesting on islands off southern California and along the western coast of Baja California. Xantus's Murrelets have recently been extirpated from several islands by a combination of predation by introduced cats (on adults and chicks) and mice (on eggs and chicks), and by habitat degradation by introduced domestic animals.

At the species' largest colony on Santa Barbara Island, California, the population of Xantus's Murrelets rose from a few hundred to about 1,500 birds after cats were removed from the island. But one major oil spill from a ship using the nearby ports of Long Beach or Los Angeles could eliminate the U.S. population.

An additional threat is mortality due to light attraction at fishing vessels that regularly anchor close to this colony. Efforts to remove predators from other Xantus's Murrelet colonies are likely to be helpful, but in the absence of major conservation efforts, prospects for this species' long-term survival seem grim.

Ian L. Jones

Pigeons and Doves

Pigeons and doves are small to medium-size birds with short legs and necks and small heads. Although the plumage coloration of North American species is dominated by tones of tan and gray, many species have scaling or barring on the wings and tail, and some exhibit prominent, showy iridescent patches on the nape. Their short bills are soft at the base and hard at the tip, often with a naked, swollen cere at the base of the upper bill. Columbids commonly occur in open habitats, including fields, croplands, grasslands, deserts, woodland edges, suburbs, and cities. A few species, such as the Band-tailed Pigeon *(Columba fasciata),* inhabit woodlands. Two of the more familiar members of the family are the introduced Rock Dove *(C. livia),* which is well known as the common, city-dwelling "pigeon," and the abundant Mourning Dove *(Zenaida macroura),* which lives in suburban and agricultural areas as well as in more natural habitats.

Taxonomy

The family Columbidae is part of the order Columbiformes, which includes the family Raphidae, a now-extinct group of large, flightless birds, such as the Dodo *(Raphus cucullatus),* that once inhabited several islands in the Indian Ocean. Also sometimes included in this order are the sandgrouse (Pteroclididae) of arid regions of Africa and Eurasia. The classification of the sandgrouse remains uncertain, but taxonomists no longer see them as close relatives of pigeons and doves.

Six genera of pigeons and doves are represented in North America. The relatively large *Columba* species—usually, but not always, referred to as pigeons—occur worldwide; this genus includes the

Band-tailed Pigeon and the Rock Dove. The *Zenaida* doves are a group of medium-size, relatively long-tailed birds that includes the Mourning and White-winged *(Z. asiatica)* Doves. The inclusion of White-winged Doves in this genus has been questioned, based on their songs and display behaviors; instead they may be more closely related to the genus *Columba,* but more study of this possibility is needed.

Representatives of three largely neotropical genera are found in the southern United States: the tiny *Columbina* ground-doves; the widespread genus *Leptotila,* whose single North American representative is the White-tipped Dove *(L. verreauxi);* and the *Geotrygon* quail-doves, which include the Key West Quail-Dove *(G. chrysia),* a rare visitor to Florida.

Finally, the *Streptopelia* doves are represented by three introduced Old World species that are similar in shape and size to the Mourning Dove. One, the Ringed Turtle-Dove *(S. risoria),* is a domesticated variety thought to have been derived from the African Collared-Dove *(S. roseogrisea)* of northern Africa. Ringed Turtle-Doves are sometimes also called "Barbary Doves."

The terms "pigeon" and "dove" do not refer to separate taxonomic groupings within the family, although "pigeon" is often used to describe larger species, while "dove" is used for smaller species.

Columbid diversity. In North America, the family Columbidae includes pigeons of the genus Columba *and the smaller doves of various genera. The extremes are shown here in the large Band-tailed Pigeon (left) and the diminutive Common Ground-Dove (right).*

319

Variation

Most members of the Columbidae show only minor variation in plumage. One exception is the Rock Dove, which has considerable plumage variation ranging from slaty blue-gray to mottled browns to white and black. This variety can be attributed to the release or escape of domestic birds that were originally bred for particular colors, plumage characteristics, or behaviors. There is no known geographic pattern in the variation among Rock Doves; the Cornell Laboratory of Ornithology's Project PigeonWatch is collecting data to determine whether such a pattern exists.

Columbid head and bill. The Red-billed Pigeon shows the typical bill structure of the family; the bill is rather soft at the base and hardened at the tip. The nostril is covered by a raised cere.

Food and Foraging

Most North American pigeons and doves forage in open habitats for grains, seeds, and fruit. Their small, soft-based bills are better suited to picking seeds from the ground or removing fruits and nuts from trees or bushes, rather than hammering or tearing at their food.

Columbids store food in a large crop, then grind it up with the aid of grit in the muscular gizzard. Their ability to store relatively large amounts of food in the crop may allow the birds to forage briefly in areas that put them at risk from predators, then process the ingested food in a safer location. Indeed, in areas with ample food supplies, individuals often spend long periods of time roosting between brief, concentrated feeding bouts.

Most pigeons and doves, especially those that feed mainly on dry seeds and grains, drink relatively large volumes of water. Laboratory studies have shown that some species drink as much as 10 to 15 percent of their body weight in water each day. Species that regularly eat fleshy

Worldwide Family Features

- 6–33" (15–83 cm) landbirds.
- About 312 species in about 40 genera worldwide; found everywhere except polar regions. Highest diversity in South America, Australasia, Pacific Islands. 14 species in 6 genera occur in North America (of which 4 species are introduced); found throughout continent, with highest diversity in southwestern U.S. and Texas; plus 4 or 5 accidental species and 1 extinct species.
- Eat primarily seeds and fruit; some species also eat insects. Forage on ground or glean food from trees and bushes.
- Monogamous; sometimes pairs stay together for successive breeding seasons. Typically defend area immediately around nest during breeding season; form flocks in winter and at foraging sites. Some species migratory.

- Breed first at 6–12 months old, sometimes even earlier.
- Nest a simple, flat platform of twigs or plant fibers; placed in tree or bush, sometimes on ledge (especially Rock Doves), on the ground, or in a tree or rock cavity. Male supplies material, female constructs nest. Reuse nests repeatedly.
- 1 or 2 pale, unmarked, elliptical eggs. Both parents incubate, for 11–30 days, longer in larger species. Hatching synchronous or asynchronous, depending on species. Some species have up to 5 broods a year.
- Semi-altricial young with sparse, coarse down at hatching. Fledge at 11–30 days. Both parents feed young "crop milk" at first, seeds and fruit thereafter.
- Adult annual survival 40–65% (Mourning Dove, Rock Dove). Among oldest on record: 19 years, 4 months (Mourning Dove).

fruits and berries may fulfill most of their water requirements from their food.

All columbids share an interesting adaptation that allows them to drink by immersing the bill and sucking. Most other bird species must scoop up water with the bill and throw back the head to swallow. A columbid's ability to suck up water may allow it to drink rapidly, thereby lessening the amount of time it spends in dangerous locations.

During the nonbreeding season, most columbid species form flocks that sometimes number in the hundreds or even thousands, with members competing for food at favored locations and coming together in large communal roosts at night. Birds may travel as far as 13 miles (20 km) from roosting sites to feeding areas.

In some cases, sociality may help birds to save energy. Inca Doves *(Columbina inca)* have an interesting behavioral adaptation for staying warm on cold winter days, in which groups of up to 12 birds stand on each others' backs in several tiers to form a pyramid. Every several minutes the birds rotate positions, with individuals on the bottom tier moving to the top. A group may maintain a pyramid for as long as an hour.

Band-tailed Pigeon drinking. Pigeons and doves, such as this Band-tailed Pigeon, are the only North American birds capable of suctioning water into the esophagus, so they can drink without raising their heads (other birds must dip the bill into water and raise it to let the water run down the throat). Related to this ability is the fact that columbids have an unusual need for water, drinking up to 15 percent of their body weight each day.

Breeding

Pigeons and doves are monogamous, and some Mourning Dove pairs may remain together for more than one breeding season. Most species have multiple broods each year, sometimes as many as four or five in the Rock and Mourning Doves.

In many species, pairs nest closely together, often forming loose colonies. The now-extinct Passenger Pigeon *(Ectopistes migratorius)*, which once inhabited deciduous forests of eastern North America, nested in immense colonies that stretched for miles. A colony discovered in Wisconsin in 1871 covered 850 square miles and contained an estimated 136 million birds, with as many as 100 nests in a single tree. More recently, White-winged Doves were found in Texas breeding in colonies as dense as 200 to 400 nests per acre. White-winged Doves in desert cities such as Tucson, Arizona, will also breed in high densities, nesting in exotic pine trees in parks and yards.

Pigeons and doves do not defend an extended territory, but rather an area immediately around the nest site. Birds will repel not only intruders of their own species, but also snakes and other predators, striking them briskly and repeatedly with the wings.

Vocalizations and Displays

Pigeons and doves produce a fairly low-frequency cooing sound, with distinctive variations among species. Because many species have rather extended breeding seasons, they can be heard throughout much of the year.

The most commonly heard vocalization is the male's advertising song, typically given repeatedly over long periods. Females of some species occasionally give a muted version of this vocalization. Males also use specific vocalizations during courtship displays.

In a common courtship display, the male struts around the female, bowing and puffing his neck and breast feathers while cooing. Some species also perform display flights that involve exaggerated

Rock Dove courtship display. *The Rock Dove, like most other columbids, engages in a number of displays during courtship, including bowing, puffing, and strutting in front of a potential mate. This species' display flight involves wing-clapping and gliding. Some of the many domestic varieties of Rock Dove have been bred to exaggerate specific parts of the courtship display.*

flapping and clapping of the wings. For example, breeding Rock Dove males engage in a display in which they alternate between physically hitting the wings together to make a clapping sound, and gliding with the tail spread and the wings held in a V shape above the body. Mourning Doves, White-winged Doves, and Band-tailed Pigeons also have distinctive aerial displays.

Nests

Pigeons and doves build rather simple platform nests from stiff twigs; most have no lining, although some species add a rudimentary lining of fine rootlets or pine needles. The nests are located on the ground, on ledges, and in cacti, bushes, or trees, usually 5 to 40 feet (1.5–12 m) above the ground and occasionally as high as 80 feet (24 m); Rock Doves' nests can be much higher. A number of species regularly build their nests on top of the old, abandoned nests of other birds.

Nest-building typically takes two to four days. Usually the male selects the nest location and brings materials to the female, who assembles them into the platform. Males of some species present the nest-building materials while standing on the females' backs.

Birds will reuse nests repeatedly, a practice that sometimes results in a buildup of fecal material in and around the nest.

Eggs and Young

Pigeons and doves normally lay one or two white or whitish, unmarked eggs. Up to four eggs are found, rarely, in Rock

Dove and Mourning Dove nests, but these are typically the result of two females laying in the same nest.

Both sexes incubate, with the male incubating for a portion of the daylight hours and the female incubating through the night. Before egg-laying takes place, Rock Doves (and possibly others) "pseudo-incubate" the empty nests for periods of up to one and a half hours. Incubation begins after the first egg is laid but is erratic until the clutch is complete. Most North American species incubate for 12 to 14 days; some larger species, such as the Band-tailed Pigeon and the Rock Dove, incubate for as long as 16 to 20 days. The hatching process takes a chick about one day.

Within a few hours of hatching, parents feed the altricial chicks "crop milk," or "pigeon milk," derived from sloughed-off, liquid-filled cells that line the crops of both male and female adults. Rich in fats and proteins, crop milk meets the nutritional needs of young pigeons and doves in the same way that insects and animal protein do for the young of most other bird species. A chick feeds by placing its head inside the adult's open mouth, which causes the adult to produce the crop milk. Incubation stimulates crop milk production, which generally continues for 5 to 10 days after hatching, after which the chicks begin to eat regurgitated seeds or fruits.

The young leave the nest 11 to 16 days after hatching, with the exception of the larger *Columba* species, which can take up to 30 days. Parents (particularly the male if a second clutch is initiated) continue to feed the fledglings until they are as old as 30 to 40 days. As the young become more competent fliers, they begin to associate with other immatures and join mixed feeding flocks of adults and immatures. They may, however, remain in the nest vicinity for part of the day and at night. When the adults eventually stop feeding them, the chicks begin to spend more time with their feeding flocks, roaming substantial distances in search of food. Immatures attain adult plumage within several months after fledging.

Movements

In North America, only four columbids show regular migratory behavior—the Mourning Dove, White-winged Dove, Band-tailed Pigeon, and White-crowned Pigeon *(Columba leucocephala)*. All are thought to be diurnal migrants, although occasionally Mourning Doves have been found in surveys of communications tower kills, suggesting that this species sometimes migrates nocturnally. In one instance, thousands of migrating Mourning Doves perished during a rainy night when they became disoriented by a high-power light beam at a military base and flew into the ground. Such events, which have occurred in other bird species that migrate at night, are the result of con-

fusion similar to that experienced by airplane pilots in foggy or rainy conditions.

Large numbers of Mourning Doves, White-winged Doves, and Band-tailed Pigeons move south to spend the winter in Mexico and Central America. Smaller populations of wintering birds continue to occupy their North American breeding grounds, although most individuals withdraw from the northern edges of the range.

Individual White-winged Dove and Band-tailed Pigeon vagrants are occasionally discovered far to the east of their normal range, with annual records from New England and the Maritime Provinces of Canada. A few White-crowned Pigeons remain to winter in the Florida Keys, although most leave, presumably to winter in the Caribbean islands.

Immature Mourning Doves are the first to begin the southward movement, followed by adult males, then adult females. In contrast, adult White-winged Doves leave before the immature birds.

Rock Doves show a strong attachment to their hatching site, and they will attempt to return there if captured and released, even some distance away. Well known for their homing abilities, members of this species have been bred specifically for this purpose and used as homing pigeons or racing pigeons. Much of what is known about the orientation

Feeding "milk" to young at nest. For the first ten days or so after columbid young hatch, the parents feed them "crop milk," a substance that is secreted by the walls of the crop. (Flamingos also feed their young a milk-like substance.) Pigeons and doves, such as this White-winged Dove, are known for their flimsy nests. Often simply a few sticks laid across branches, the nest sometimes seems too weak to hold the eggs. Frequently birds build on top of the old nests of other, unrelated species.

and navigation of birds was learned through experiments with Rock Doves. Rock Doves apparently orient themselves by using the position of the sun, Earth's magnetic field, and in some cases possibly distinctive odors, low-frequency sounds, and polarized light. Other columbids presumably use similar means to navigate. In certain areas of Earth's surface where there are unusual geomagnetic anomalies, released homing pigeons often become disoriented and lose their way.

Throughout history, homing pigeons have been used to carry messages quickly over long distances. During World War One, several homing pigeons were celebrated for saving American troops by carrying messages tied to their legs through heavy artillery fire, even after sustaining severe injuries.

Introduced Species

Four of the North American species of doves were introduced to the Americas by humans. The Rock Dove of Europe and northern Africa was introduced in the early 17th century and has spread throughout North America; it is extremely common, especially in urban areas. More recently, the Eurasian Collared-Dove *(Streptopelia decaocto)* of Europe and Asia was introduced in the Bahamas in 1974 and has since spread into the southeastern United States and beyond. After dispersing from the Bahamas to Florida in the late 1970s, this species began rapidly expanding its range. It is now found west to Louisiana and north into the Carolinas, with local populations in Pennsylvania, Arkansas, Texas, Colorado, New Mexico, and California. Records have been reported from as far away as Montana, and it seems possible that this species will continue to spread into new territory much as it did in Europe during the 20th century.

The Spotted Dove *(Streptopelia chinensis)* of Asia was first released near Hollywood in 1917 or 1918, and by the 1960s the species occurred in urban areas through-

Spotted Dove. Doves, like parrots and finches, are popular cage birds, and several species have escaped frequently enough to establish feral populations. The Spotted Dove of Asia was released in 1917 or 1918 and had occupied urban areas throughout southern California by the 1960s; it has since declined in numbers.

out much of southern California. However, according to more recent Christmas Bird Count data, the numbers are now quite low. Throughout the 20th century, the Ringed Turtle-Dove occasionally escaped from cages or was released from captivity; it now breeds in small numbers in several southern cities. Both the Spotted Dove and the Ringed Turtle-Dove have shown virtually no range expansion beyond their urban introduction sites.

Conservation

Most species of pigeons and doves with large breeding ranges in North America are abundant. For example, Mourning Doves are estimated to number in the hundreds of millions; tens of millions are harvested by North American hunters each year, and yet the species remains very common.

The Passenger Pigeon, declared extinct in 1914 (the last confirmed record in the wild was from Ohio in 1900), was once considered perhaps the most abundant bird species in the world, with flocks estimated to contain as many as 2 billion birds. From the 1820s to the 1870s, however, they were hunted mercilessly, without any thought about sustaining the species. Professional hunters killed millions and shipped them by rail to city markets in the eastern United States.

They also raided breeding colonies, supplying enormous numbers of chicks (squabs) for market. The species was unable to maintain itself in the face of such concentrated persecution.

The fate of the Passenger Pigeon has raised conservation concerns about the Band-tailed Pigeon, White-winged Dove, and White-crowned Pigeon, all of which are heavily hunted in their Mexican, Central American, and Caribbean ranges. The Band-tailed Pigeon has shown a significant decrease in the United States and Canada over the last 30 years, according to Breeding Bird Survey data; nevertheless, they are still legally hunted in some areas. Many recovered bird bands from White-winged Doves come from birds shot for food in Mexico during the winter. The White-crowned Pigeon is listed as a threatened species in Florida, based on concerns over population declines as well as the loss of its hardwood forest feeding habitat. Both Band-tailed and White-crowned Pigeons are on the WatchList.

Common Ground-Doves *(Columbina passerina)* showed a long-term decline from 1966 to 1979, according to Breeding Bird Survey data. Since the 1980s, the

Passenger Pigeon. Early in the 19th century, ornithologist Alexander Wilson reported a flock of more than 2 billion migrating Passenger Pigeons, but by 1914 the species was extinct. This bird remains a powerful symbol of the natural riches of the New World, and of the wanton destruction carried out by market-hunters and colonists.

species has increased in number; however, decreasing trends in some southeastern states continue to be of concern. The Ruddy Ground-Dove *(C. talpacoti)*, in contrast, was formerly a rare visitor to the U.S.–Mexico border but has started to occur regularly in the Southwest. Both Inca and White-winged Doves have stable or increasing population trends in North America. As the White-tipped Dove and Red-billed Pigeon *(Columba flavirostris)* have only a small portion of their range north of Mexico, their population status depends largely on conditions in Mexico.

Accidental Species

The Scaly-naped Pigeon *(Columba squamosa)*, a Caribbean species, has two old specimen records (1898 and 1929), both from Key West, Florida. Given that its nearest source populations are in Cuba, where the species is now uncommon, further records are unlikely.

The Zenaida Dove *(Zenaida aurita)* is another Caribbean species and is similar in appearance to the Mourning Dove. It was documented in southern Florida fewer than ten times between 1940 and 2000 but may once have been a resident breeder in the Florida Keys.

The Ruddy Quail-Dove *(Geotrygon montana)*, which occurs from the West Indies and Mexico through South America, has also been found several times in southern Florida and, more rarely, in southern Texas.

The Oriental Turtle-Dove *(Streptopelia orientalis)*, a migratory Asian species, has been reported from the Pribilof and Aleutian Islands of Alaska, and from British Columbia (although the latter record may have involved an escapee from captivity). A close relative of this species, the European Turtle-Dove *(S. turtur)*, was found in the Florida Keys in 1990. This bird is suspected of being an escapee, but the species is a long-distance migrant, and the record is currently included in the AOU Check-list.

Jeffrey V. Wells and Allison Childs Wells

Parrots and Allies

Family Psittacidae
Order Psittaciformes

Parrots are forest birds with an almost instantly recognizable shape: a large head and short neck, a strongly hooked bill, and short legs. Parrots exist in a variety of sizes. Their plumages are usually dominated by brilliant greens but also contain splashes of red, yellow, blue, white, black, or gray. They have a bare, fleshy cere, sparse feathering with much powder down, zygodactyl feet, and a muscular tongue. Parrots typically flock in large numbers in their native forest, forest edge, or savanna habitats, where they fly high between foraging and roosting sites. Many species are kept in captivity, and through the release of captive birds, many exotic species have become naturalized in urban areas of southern Florida, southernmost Texas, California, and other locales.

Taxonomy

The parrots form a unique, well-defined group and appear to have no close living relatives. The family constitutes its own order, the Psittaciformes.

While the fossil record of parrot-like birds goes back some 40 million years to the Eocene epoch, little is known of the group's history. The number of parrot species is greatest in Australasia and Central and South America, although there is also a diversity of parrots in tropical Asia, Africa, and the islands of the southwestern Pacific Ocean. Parrots are generally absent from the temperate regions of the Northern Hemisphere.

In the past, the psittaciforms have been subdivided into as many as a dozen separate families. Today most taxonomies recognize only one or two families that are often divided into several subfamilies and tribes. Of these subfamilies, the lories and lorikeets (Loriinae), found in Australasia and the southwestern Pacific Islands, have a unique brushy tongue adapted for gathering pollen and nectar. The cockatoos (Cacatuinae), including the familiar Cockatiel *(Nymphicus hollandicus)* and the spectacular Sulphur-crested Cockatoo *(Cacatua galerita),* are primarily Australasian and most readily distinguished by the presence of erectile crests. Another mainly Australian group is the Australian parakeets and rosellas (Platycercinae), which includes the Budgerigar *(Melopsittacus undulatus),* the familiar cage bird known as the "Budgie." African and some Asian parrots are placed in the Psittacinae, which includes the Rose-ringed Parakeet *(Psittacula krameri),* established in southern Florida and in California.

Psittacid diversity. *The species of parrots seen most frequently in North America fall into four subfamilies, shown here from left to right: Cacatuinae (the cockatoos, represented here by the Sulphur-crested Cockatoo), Psittacinae (typical parrots, such as the Rose-ringed Parakeet), Arinae (New World parrots, such as the Green Parakeet), and Platycercinae (the Australian parakeets, such as the Budgerigar).*

All native New World parrots belong to the Arinae, which includes the spectacular macaws, the *Amazona* parrots, and many parakeets and conures. Examples of these groups that have been seen free-flying in North American cities are the Chestnut-fronted Macaw *(Ara severa)*, the Yellow-naped Parrot *(Amazona auropalliata)*, and the Dusky-headed Parakeet *(Aratinga weddellii)*, respectively.

The species-level taxonomy of some established North American parrots is in flux. One example, the "Canary-winged Parakeet," has recently been split into the White-winged Parakeet *(Brotogeris versicolurus)* and the Yellow-chevroned Parakeet *(B. chiriri)*. These two species normally occupy different ranges in central South America, but they both have been introduced in southern Florida and coastal California. In both areas the Yellow-chevroned Parakeet seems to be increasing, while the White-winged is decreasing.

While the two species of parrot historically found in the United States are no longer present (see Conservation, below),

Psittacid head and bill. All parrots have powerful hooked beaks with a short, squarish lower bill. Their beaks are adapted for a diet of seeds, nuts, and fruit. The larger species are able to crack seeds that are impossible for most other birds to open. The Monk Parakeet is shown.

there are probably some birds that have arrived here without direct human intervention. Many ornithologists believe that at least some of the Red-crowned Parrots *(Amazona viridigenalis)* and Green Parakeets *(Aratinga holochlora)* that are now well established in southernmost Texas are wanderers from the core ranges of these species, which extend as far north as the neighboring states of Tamaulipas and Nuevo León, Mexico.

Worldwide Family Features

- 4–39" (10–98 cm) arboreal birds.
- About 360 species in 80 genera worldwide; found in all tropical and subtropical regions, and in temperate regions of southern continents; most diverse in South America and Australasia. In North America, historically 2 native species in 2 genera, but 1 now extinct, the other extirpated. Native species formerly found throughout eastern U.S., plus southeastern Arizona and southwestern New Mexico. At least 27 exotic species in 12 genera found regularly, many others occasionally. Exotic species concentrated in urban centers, especially in southern U.S.
- Eat fruit, seeds, nectar of trees and shrubs, including many exotic species.
- Social; often form large feeding flocks and roosting aggregations; often found in pairs within these flocks. Generally monogamous, most species for life. Most nonmigratory, but may range far from breeding sites in nonbreeding season.
- Breed first usually at 2–4 years old (but as young as 6 months in Budgerigar).

- Nest in tree cavities, skirts of dead palm fronds, or nest boxes and other artificial cavities; may enlarge nest cavities by chewing soft wood. Monk Parakeet builds large, communal "apartment" nest out of sticks, twigs, grasses. Both sexes inspect and select nest cavities, and build nest. Often reuse nest cavities.
- White, subelliptical to oval eggs, usually 1–3 in larger species, up to 11 in smaller species. Both parents incubate, for 14–23 days in smaller species, up to 33 days in larger species. Hatching asynchronous over 2 days or more. 1 or 2 broods per year.
- Altricial young hatch naked or with some down; fed by both adults with regurgitated food. Fledge at 18 days to 9 weeks in smaller species, up to 15 weeks in larger species; may be dependent on parents for several weeks after fledging.
- Adult annual survival poorly studied, especially in wild. Many species live 20–30 years in captivity; larger species can live 50–100 years in captivity.

Habitats

In general, parrots are birds of savannas, woodlands, or forests. Escaped or released captive parrots naturalized in North America generally occur where a profusion of exotic (often tropical) flora can be found, frequently in urban and suburban regions of Florida, southern California, and southernmost Texas.

Most species require cavities for nesting, and their distribution and populations may be limited by the availability of nest sites. Budgerigars feed on grass seeds and are most numerous where unmowed grasses are abundant, but they also rely heavily on seed feeders in urban and suburban areas.

Parrots are generally thought of as tropical birds, but some thrive in temperate

---

How Many Parrot Species Occur in North America?

The importation of huge numbers of parrots for the pet industry, and the subsequent release or escape of many individuals, has created numerous naturalized populations of parrots in North America. Determining the number of parrot species in North America is complicated by the establishment of new populations of various species in different regions. Dozens of species occur as escapees, and almost any parrot species may be seen. A recent monograph on the birds of Florida mentions more than 60 parrot species recorded as free-flying within that state. Field identification is further hampered by the failure of most North American field guides to include many of the established species.

Several organizations maintain official lists of North American birds. Most prominent of these lists are those of the American Birding Association and the AOU. Both of these groups consider non-native species to be established in North America only after populations have survived for several generations and have bred successfully. An established population also must be able to persist without continued release of birds from captivity.

In general, it is difficult to tell whether a psittacid population has become established because parrots can live for many years. Even populations that have been present in an area for more than ten years may be entirely composed of birds that originated in captivity. Since few ornithologists study escaped non-native birds, breeding and population stability are often poorly documented. Consequently, in areas where continued escapes or releases of individuals still occur, authorities are hesitant to consider many populations fully established.

Because of this complicated situation, species such as the Red-lored (*Amazona autumnalis*) and White-fronted Parrots (*A. albifrons*), both of Central America, have been present in southern Florida for years but are not considered part of the established North American avifauna. The 1998 AOU Check-list cites 28 psittacids as present in urban areas in the United States but considers only six or seven of them to be established. Other species—such as the Blue-fronted Parrot (*A. aestiva*) and Blue-crowned Parakeet (*Aratinga acuticaudata*), both South American natives—are easily found in southern Florida but are not even mentioned in the Check-list.

Blue-crowned Parakeet. *The Blue-crowned Parakeet is an example of a species that has frequently escaped from captivity; this species has been recorded breeding in the wild as far north as New Jersey. The challenge for bird checklist committees is to decide when such records constitute viable feral populations, rather than just incidental escapees, and thus deserve a place on the official bird list for a region.*

climates, including the Monk Parakeet *(Myiopsitta monachus)*; native to temperate South America, it has established populations as far north as New York City, Chicago, and Portland, Oregon. In their native range, Monk Parakeets are considered agricultural pests.

Food and Foraging

Most parrot species are highly social. The birds usually feed in flocks, and the pre-roosting aggregations of some species may number in the hundreds. The roosts may serve in part as centers where parrots might share information on the location of productive feeding sites.

Parrot feeding. This Red-crowned Parrot has just transferred a small fruit from its foot to its mouth. Most parrots are left-footed; they can deftly pick up a small food item and transfer it to their equally dexterous mouth. In the bill, the short muscular tongue manipulates the food item, while the powerful and sharp-edged bill shears off hard husks or removes pits from fruit.

Most species present in North America eat fruit and seeds, feeding mainly in exotic trees and shrubs and at feeders. Studies in California show that parrots use some native trees, such as sycamores, for feeding, but that exotic plant species dominate parrot diets, which include nuts (walnuts and pecans), fruit (apricots, figs, and cherries), seeds, nectar, and blossoms—the last two from such plants as eucalyptus and coral trees.

Parrots are seed predators, in that they generally destroy rather than disperse the seeds they eat. Parrots often eat only part of each fruit, tossing the rest on the ground; their sloppy feeding habits result in much waste. Some 15 percent of the world's parrot species are, at least in some places, seen as crop pests.

Parrots have an array of feeding adaptations, including a hooked bill for grasping, a muscular, versatile tongue that is often fleshy and prehensile for food manipulation, strong jaw muscles for cracking nuts, and highly coordinated feet for handling food. They climb about in trees using both the feet and the bill for grasping. Their predominantly green plumage provides excellent camouflage and makes silent parrots virtually impossible to spot within a tree's foliage.

Parrot foot. Parrots have zygodactyl feet—two toes forward and two back—and are able to use their toes very dexterously to climb on branches and to bring food to the beak. The Red-crowned Parrot is shown.

Vocalizations

The contact calls of most parrots are loud and raucous; they can carry for great distances. The calls may vary from loud, grating screeches and cawing sounds to inflected whistles, depending on the species. Parrots have a complex vocal repertoire of calls for various social interactions, courtship, and mating. However, most parrots are relatively silent while feeding during the day; they vocalize mostly at roost-site gatherings and while commuting to and from foraging sites. Fledged young often have distinctive, repetitive begging calls.

Breeding

Researchers believe that all established parrot species in North America are monogamous and form persistent pair bonds; most may remain paired for life. Most parrot species are highly social while feeding and roosting, but within flocks there are many monogamous pairs; nesting pairs may be solitary and very inconspicuous.

Breeding parrots are not strongly territorial—only the immediate nest area is defended. Many pairs may breed close to one another when nest sites are abundant, as happens with *Amazona* parrots in the suburbs of Los Angeles. The Monk Parakeet is a colonial and perhaps cooperative breeder, with several pairs sharing a large, apartment-like nest structure.

Parrots generally place their nests in a cavity—either a natural hollow in a tree trunk or branch, or a cavity drilled by a woodpecker. They can enlarge existing cavities and their entrances by chewing with their bills. The Monk Parakeet is a notable exception to the cavity-nesting habit; the apartment-like stick nests this species builds also serve as winter roosts.

In a given year, the proportion of birds in a population that actually breed can be low. Indeed, some species breed only every other year or every few years.

Thick-billed Parrots at a nest hole. Most parrots nest in cavities, mainly in old woodpecker holes in trees. Like other cavity-nesting birds, their distribution and abundance may be limited by the availability of suitable nest holes, and it has been suggested that Thick-billed Parrot numbers have declined in part because of the recent extinction of the Imperial Woodpecker, which shared the same range in Mexico and excavated many suitable nest sites for the parrots.

Movements

Most North American parrots make daily "commutes" between their roost sites and feeding areas, sometimes covering several miles. No naturalized parrot species in North America are migratory; most populations are sedentary, apart from their daily movements. Individuals found well away from naturalized populations in North America are almost certainly locally escaped or released birds.

Conservation

About one-fourth of the world's parrot species are globally threatened, mainly because of habitat modification and de-struction, and the trapping of wild birds for the pet industry.

Hundreds of thousands of parrots were legally imported into the United States from the 1960s through the 1980s, and many more were illegally imported. The trapping and export of parrots create a major drain on many natural populations. A large percentage of trapped birds die during capture, shipment, or quarantine. Even when a country bans the export of parrots, the birds may be illegally transported to a neighboring country that permits their export. Australia has enforced its total ban on the export of parrots very successfully. Other countries with export bans, such as Mexico, have faced greater challenges in enforcement.

The United States has recently enacted the Wild Bird Conservation Act, which greatly restricts the legal importation of live birds into the country. The Convention on the International Trade of Endangered Species (CITES) further restricts the import and export of parrots. Many conservation biologists feel that the key to preserving parrot populations lies in creating an economic incentive for local people to preserve parrot populations and their habitats.

North America lost its only native breeding parrot, the Carolina Parakeet *(Conuropsis carolinensis)*, early in the 20th century; the last confirmed record in the wild was from Missouri in 1905. This species lived in forested river valleys of the midwestern and southeastern United States. Its numbers had fallen sharply by the mid-1800s, and the last known individual died in captivity in 1918. The best evidence suggests that direct human persecution caused the bird's extinction. Because Carolina Parakeets raided orchards, flocks were routinely slaughtered. Like the Passenger Pigeon *(Ectopistes migratorius)*, which became extinct around the same time, the Carolina Parakeet was a highly social species and was probably doomed to extinction once its numbers were significantly reduced.

The Thick-billed Parrot *(Rhynchopsitta pachyrhyncha)* also occurred naturally in the United States. Native to western Mexico, where it specializes in pinecone seeds and requires mature pines for nest holes, this species occasionally made incursions into the mountains of southeastern Arizona and southwestern New Mexico, presumably when food levels in its normal range were low. Some evidence suggests that Thick-billed Parrots may have bred within these mountains on occasion.

The extensive destruction of mature pine forests in the mountains of northern Mexico and the extinction of the Imperial Woodpecker *(Campephilus imperialis)*, which excavated the cavities that provided nest sites for the parrots, have greatly reduced populations of the

Carolina Parakeet. *The Carolina Parakeet was North America's only native breeding parrot. Found over most of the midwestern and southeastern United States, it was considered good eating and a pest at fruit orchards, and its numbers quickly declined with the settling of the frontier. John James Audubon reported in 1831 that numbers had declined precipitously in the previous decade. The last known living individual died in the Cincinnati Zoo in 1918.*

Thick-billed Parrot, which is not known to have occurred naturally in the United States since 1938. Attempted reintroductions in the 1980s were hampered by the poor adjustment of captive-bred birds to the wild and high levels of predation by Northern Goshawks *(Accipiter gentilis)* and other predators. Efforts to reintroduce Thick-billed Parrots into the United States have now been suspended, and it appears that no released birds remain.

Some parrot species that have been established in North America are declining in their native ranges, particularly the Yellow-headed Parrot *(Amazona oratrix)* and the Red-crowned Parrot in Mexico; these declines are due mainly to habitat loss and the capture of birds for the pet trade.

Kimball L. Garrett and John B. Dunning, Jr.

Cuckoos, Roadrunners, and Anis

Family Cuculidae
Order Cuculiformes

The Cuculidae is a diverse family of medium-size birds with no known close relatives. Cuculids have zygodactyl feet, and most species are relatively slim, with long, decurved bills and tails that measure at least half the bird's total length. Plumage coloration and patterning vary considerably. Many Old World cuckoos are well known for parasitizing other birds by laying eggs in their nests and leaving the hosts to raise their young. Only three New World species (all found in Central and South America) are regularly parasitic. Members of the family are found in habitats ranging from deserts to forested wetlands to tropical rain forests.

Taxonomy

This family is an old group of birds; fossils date to the Oligocene epoch (24–37 million years ago) and possibly earlier. The six cuculid species that breed in North America represent three genera, each so distinct that it is in a separate subfamily.

The Yellow-billed Cuckoo *(Coccyzus americanus)*, the Black-billed Cuckoo *(C. erythropthalmus)*, and the Mangrove Cuckoo *(C. minor)* are all currently classified in the Coccyzinae subfamily. They are slender, streamlined birds, generally dark above and light below, with white

spots on the underside of the tail; the females are about 5 percent larger than the males.

The Neomorphinae subfamily includes the distinctive Greater Roadrunner *(Geococcyx californianus)* a familiar sight in the desert Southwest. The Crotophaginae subfamily contains the Groove-billed Ani *(Crotophaga sulcirostris)* and the Smooth-billed Ani *(C. ani)*, tropical species whose ranges just reach our region—in Texas and Florida, respectively. Anis are characterized by long tails, black color, and distinctive bills that are laterally flattened (like puffins) yet decurved.

Food and Foraging

Cuculids typically forage at a slow pace, spending much time sitting and scanning for insects or other prey. When the Greater Roadrunner and the *Coccyzus* cuckoos spot prey, they pounce on it with great speed.

In the East, Yellow-billed Cuckoos specialize in tent caterpillars, sometimes eating more than 100 from one web at a sitting. In the West, their primary prey are sphinx moth caterpillars, katydids, grasshoppers, and tree frogs. Both Yellow-billed and Black-billed Cuckoos move into areas where cicada outbreaks are underway, to capitalize on the feeding windfall. *Coccyzus* cuckoos forage mainly in the foliage of trees, but they will dive out to catch flying insects or hop on the ground to capture tree frogs and grasshoppers.

Cuculid diversity. The six regularly occurring members of the cuculid family in North America belong to three quite distinctive subfamilies: Coccyzinae (New World cuckoos, such as the Black-billed Cuckoo, top), Neomorphinae (roadrunners, Greater Roadrunner, center), and Crotophaginae (anis, Smooth-billed Ani, bottom).

The Greater Roadrunner feeds on large insects, scorpions, lizards, snakes, small rodents, and small birds, including nestlings and hummingbirds. In pursuit of its prey, the bird runs very fast—up to 18 miles per hour (30 km/h)—and can outrun many lizards. Unlike cuckoos and roadrunners, anis forage in loose flocks, moving through tall grass and bushes, feeding primarily on insects and spiders.

Cuckoos are among the few birds that regularly eat hairy caterpillars; the hairs remain in their stomachs and form pellets that the birds later regurgitate. *Coccyzus* cuckoos and Greater Roadrunners hold large prey items in their bills and hammer them on branches or rocks until they are dead. Cuckoos often soften prey items by mashing them with their bill tips before swallowing the food themselves or feeding it to their young. The widely held belief that Yellow-billed Cuckoos eat the eggs of other birds is based on dubious reports.

Cuculid head and bill. Cuckoos of the genus Coccyzus, such as this Mangrove Cuckoo, have the fairly long, sturdy, decurved bill typical of the family. Other North American cuculids have bills that are longer (Greater Roadrunner) or much deeper (anis).

Cuculid foot. All cuculids share a similar zygodactyl foot structure, with two toes forward and two back. In anis and cuckoos (the Black-billed Cuckoo is shown), the legs are short, and the feet are used only for perching; the birds do not walk or hop easily. The Greater Roadrunner, in contrast, has long, strong legs and is one of the fastest-running birds, often preferring to run rather than fly.

Worldwide Family Features

- 6½–28" (16–70 cm) forest- and ground-dwelling birds.
- About 142 species in about 30 genera worldwide; on all continents except Antarctica; greatest diversity in Old World tropics; one-third of species in Americas. North America has 6 breeding species in 3 genera, found from southern Canada to Mexico; plus 2 or 3 accidental species.
- Omnivorous, though most species eat mainly caterpillars; many larger ground-dwelling cuckoos eat lizards, snakes.
- Generally territorial and monogamous; long-term pair bonds found in at least some species. Communal nesting and nest helpers also found in some species. Nonbreeders usually solitary; anis found in small flocks year-round. Many species migratory; others, especially in tropics, are permanent residents.
- Breed first at 1 year old. In some species young males act as helpers and defer breeding.
- In nonparasitic species, both sexes build loose stick nest, generally in dense foliage in bush or tree. Parasitic species lay eggs in other birds' nests and do not raise their own young.
- 2–6 elliptical to subelliptical eggs per clutch; some parasitic species can lay more than 25 eggs per year. In nonparasitic species, eggs generally white to blue; in parasitic species, color often matches host's eggs. In nonparasitic species, parents share incubation, which lasts 11–18 days. Hatching asynchronous. 1 or 2 (rarely 3) broods per year.
- Altricial young naked at hatching; in many species, young develop rapidly; in some species, young leave nest after less than a week. Young can fly after 17–30 days, but may be fed by parent for several weeks more. In all North American species, both sexes care for young; male sometimes takes over feeding duties while female starts 2nd nest.
- Little information on adult annual survival. Among oldest on record: at least 7 years (Greater Roadrunner).

Breeding

When courting, many male cuculids attract the female with cooing calls and then offer her food. Mating occurs when a female accepts the male's offering; food is often exchanged during copulation.

All North American cuculids build stick nests, with both parents building the nest, incubating, and tending the young. Clutch size varies from two to six eggs and depends on the available food supply. Anis often nest communally, with up to four pairs laying eggs in the same nest; up to 20 eggs may be found together. The dominant female in a nest will toss out the eggs of other females until she begins to lay her own; at that time, females sharing the nest will lay simultaneously until their clutches are complete.

Communal nesting behavior has also been observed occasionally in Yellow-billed Cuckoos. Typical of all cuckoos that raise their own young, the male incubates and broods all night, while the female and male divide incubation and brooding equally during the day.

The incubation and nestling period is relatively short; for example, Yellow-billed Cuckoo eggs hatch in 11 to 12 days, and young fledge in 5 to 8 days. Incubation begins when the first egg is laid, so the young hatch asynchronously. In the case of the Yellow-billed Cuckoo, the oldest young can be near to fledging when the youngest has just hatched.

Asynchronous hatching can lead to chick mortality if the food supply declines during the breeding season. Under such conditions, the parents may stop incubating later eggs after one or more young hatch, in which case the unhatched young die in the egg. Another possibility, sometimes seen in Greater Roadrunners, is the parents eating weak young chicks or feeding them to older siblings. In times of food stress, male Yellow-billed Cuckoos may remove the youngest chick from the nest.

When young cuckoos leave the nest, they are about half the size of their parents. At this time they cannot fly, and the parents feed them for another three to six weeks until they are entirely independent. Ani young often stay with their families for the first winter and sometimes remain as helpers indefinitely.

Yellow-billed and Black-billed Cuckoos occasionally parasitize other birds' nests when food is abundant. Some observers assume that overly abundant food, as in a cicada emergence, throws off the synchrony between nest-building and egg-laying and leads to opportunistic parasitism. In some cases, these "parasitized" nests are really interspecific communal nests, with adult cuckoos sharing duties with other species, such as the American Robin *(Turdus migratorius)* and the Mourning Dove *(Zenaida macroura)*.

Nesting Yellow-billed Cuckoos sometimes have apparently unrelated helper

Greater Roadrunners hunting. The Greater Roadrunner eats mainly lizards and snakes, and is one of the only animals known to attack rattlesnakes. Pairs sometimes hunt rattlesnakes cooperatively—one bird distracts the snake while the other sneaks up and pins its head. They then kill the snake by bashing its head against a rock.

Cuculid nest and young. All nonparasitic cuculids build a messy platform of sticks for a nest. In Coccyzus *cuckoos, the platform is built of only a few sticks (like the nests of doves), and sometimes eggs can be seen from below through the floor of the nest. Cuculid young develop quickly and fledge early, often when only half the size of adults. Early fledging means less susceptibility to in-nest predation, and in parasitic species rapid development gives the young cuckoos an advantage over their host parents' offspring. Yellow-billed Cuckoos are shown.*

males that can supply the young with up to 40 percent of their food, allowing the dominant pair to raise a second brood.

Greater Roadrunners and Yellow-billed Cuckoos double-brood regularly; during years of exceptionally high food abundance, Yellow-billeds have raised three broods in a season. Male Yellow-billed Cuckoos tend the young of the first nest, and a second clutch is initiated as soon as the young leave that nest; this can happen before the young are a week old.

Conservation

In the West, Yellow-billed Cuckoos are now extremely uncommon. Fewer than 50 pairs remain in California, mostly in the valleys of the Sacramento and Kern Rivers. The U.S. Fish and Wildlife Service has been petitioned twice to list the western subspecies as endangered. The first petition was denied because the validity of the subspecies was questioned. The second petition, based on the importance of regional populations, is under consideration. The subspecies is listed as endangered by all state wildlife agencies where the birds occur.

Yellow-billed Cuckoos are vulnerable to extirpation because of habitat fragmentation. In the West, where they are restricted to riparian habitats, they seldom breed at sites smaller than 25 acres (10 ha). In the East, both Yellow-billed and Black-billed Cuckoos are still relatively common but have declined 45 and 42 percent, respectively, since 1980, according to Breeding Bird Survey data.

Greater Roadrunner populations appear stable across their range, but in southern California they are one of the first species to disappear when chaparral and coastal sage scrub habitat is fragmented. Smooth-billed Anis have declined dramatically over their range in southern Florida since 1980, but the cause is unknown. Little is known about the population status of Groove-billed Anis and Mangrove Cuckoos.

Accidental Species

The Common Cuckoo (*Cuculus canorus*), which breeds from the British Isles to eastern Russia, occurs regularly in early summer during migration in the western Alaskan islands and was found once in Massachusetts. The Oriental Cuckoo (*C. saturatus*), which breeds from central Russia to Japan and south to Malaysia, is a rare vagrant from May to July in the Bering Sea islands. Finally, a Dark-billed Cuckoo (*Coccyzus melacoryphus*) from southern Texas is under review by the AOU Check-list committee.

Stephen A. Laymon

Barn Owls

Members of the family Tytonidae are slim, medium-size owls with long, sparsely feathered legs and wingspans of about 3 feet 6 inches (1.1 m). The discs of the heart-shaped face form a ruff that funnels sounds into asymmetrical ear openings. The sole North American species, the Barn Owl *(Tyto alba)*, is characteristic of most of the family, with pale plumage that gives the bird a ghostly appearance. The Barn Owl is one of the world's most widespread birds, occurring in North America especially in open farmland with scattered buildings for nesting.

Taxonomy

The order Strigiformes includes two families: the Tytonidae, whose members are collectively known as barn owls, and the Strigidae, or typical owls. All owls share strong, downturned bills; forward-facing, immovable eyeballs surrounded by a disc of feathers; zygodactyl feet with arching claws; nostrils covered by bristly feathers; and other skeletal, muscular, and circulatory similarities.

These mainly nocturnal families are not closely related to the predominantly diurnal birds of prey (hawks, falcons, and their allies), despite superficial similarities in appearance and lifestyle. Many morphological features separate these groups: Unlike hawks, owls lack a crop and have large, forward-facing eyes, nostrils located in front of the cere, an outer toe that can rotate backward, and usually asymmetrical ear openings.

Compared to the typical owls, the barn owls have a narrow skull behind a distinctly heart-shaped face that has been described as monkey-like, and their tails are neither long nor rounded. Barn owls also lack the ear-tufts characteristic of many typical owls. Their legs are long, with inner and middle toes of equal length (the inner toe is shorter in typical owls); the middle toe has a pectinate (comb-like) claw.

Worldwide the family Tytonidae has between 13 and 17 species, depending on the taxonomy. Most species are Australasian in distribution; only two breed in the New World: the Barn Owl, which is widespread, and the Ashy-faced Owl *(Tyto glaucops)* of Hispaniola.

Food and Foraging

Members of both owl families have numerous adaptations for nocturnal feeding, although these features have been best studied in the Barn Owl. When hunting, most owls use a combination of sight and hearing to detect their prey. The sound of their approach is minimized by modified edges on their flight feathers that allow silent flight.

Like humans, owls have forward-facing eyes and binocular vision. Unlike humans, however, birds cannot rotate their eyes in their eye sockets; owls compensate for this limitation by bobbing their heads up

Barn Owl. The family Tytonidae includes up to 17 species worldwide. The 15 species in the genus Tyto are all very similar to the sole North American representative of the family, the Barn Owl.

Barn Owl foot. The Barn Owl has feathered tarsi, long legs and toes, and a pectinate (comb-like) middle claw that is typical of the family.

—— pectinate claw

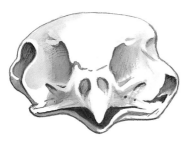

Owl ears. Many owls have asymmetrical ear openings, with the opening on one side of the head higher than the other. In some species, this asymmetry extends to the skull shape, as in this skull of a Northern Saw-whet Owl (Aegolius acadicus), a member of the family Strigidae. The size, shape, and location of the ears can all be asymmetrical, depending on the genus. Even in owls with symmetrical skulls, the fleshy outer ears can be markedly asymmetrical. In the Barn Owl, the ear opening is higher on the left side of the head.

and down and from side to side. This provides an enhanced stereoscopic view and improves the birds' ability to estimate distances.

For a night-hunting bird, the Barn Owl does not have large eyes, suggesting that it relies more on sound than sight, and indeed this species has the most acute hearing of any animal tested. Unlike the facial feathers of typical owls, those on a Barn Owl's face make a heart-shaped ruff. On each side of the face, there is a movable ear flap that changes the shape of the ruff. The ruff forms cones that funnel and amplify sounds into troughs leading to the bony ear canals. The movable ear flaps and the openings of these canals are placed asymmetrically, which greatly enhances hearing and prey location by allowing birds to triangulate on sounds made by their prey.

In the Barn Owl, the opening on the left side of the head angles downward, while the lower opening on the right angles up. With this arrangement, the two ears are more sensitive to sounds from different directions. In addition, each ear is "tuned" to perceive slightly different frequencies. Barn Owls use the differences in the tim-

ing and pitch of sounds reaching each ear, along with their ability to memorize the noises made by various prey, to calculate the speed, position, and orientation of each strike. These adaptations allow them to capture prey in total darkness or when leaf litter or snow obscures the prey.

Barn Owls sometimes hunt during the day, perhaps most often to feed a hungry brood. They fly close to the ground, at times making short flights from fence post to fence post, appearing to examine the ground.

Breeding

Barn Owls employ many displays, most often accompanied by calls that consist of clicks, simple harsh screeches, or whistles. These calls are quite unlike the rhythmic hooting or clear, whistled calls of typical owls. During the nesting season, Barn Owl displays include a rising and falling courtship flight by the male; noisy chasing during courting; the male hovering in front of the female, showing her a nest site and bringing food to her; and both sexes crouching and vibrating their wings before copulation.

Barn Owl in flight. Colored areas show the direction of most sensitive hearing, a product of the asymmetrical orientation of the ears. Having ears on either side of the head enables owls to locate sounds along the horizontal axis (right to left), and asymmetrical ear openings allow them to determine locations on the vertical axis (up and down). Precisely locating sounds on the vertical axis is impossible for animals with symmetrical ear openings.

The Barn Owl's worldwide distribution is due in part to its adaptability when nesting. It uses a multitude of sites that include ledges, caves and lava tubes, wells, tree cavities, tunnels the bird digs itself, and a host of structures built by humans, including barns, steeples, abandoned buildings, stacked hay bales, deer blinds, and duck nest boxes. Some enclosed nest sites are so small that they barely accommodate the incubating female. Despite the Barn Owl's flexibility, manicured agricultural lands may be devoid of suitable nest sites and hunting perches for this species.

Barn Owls have a long breeding season and may nest in any month. Territory sizes and reproductive success vary greatly from site to site and year to year, depending on food availability. When conditions are good, birds produce large broods and may lay multiple clutches. If insufficient food is available, the youngest chicks are often outcompeted by older siblings, which may eat the younger chicks after they die. After fledging, the young disperse broadly, occasionally traveling more than 1,000 miles (1,600 km), though typically much less.

Conservation

Although the Barn Owl is locally common throughout much of North America, its populations appear to be in a state of slow decline. It is now absent or nearly so from parts of the Midwest where habitat has been converted to row crops such as corn and soybeans. In the Northeast, habitat has been lost as forests regenerate.

In some locales, the loss of nest sites from the clearing of old buildings and better sealing of barns and silos has made Barn Owls rare. Where enough prey is available, supplying nest boxes or platforms has dramatically increased Barn Owl populations.

Large-scale reintroduction programs in the central United States have been unsuccessful, suggesting that either nest sites or food availability limit the population size. Chemical control of dense row crops may keep small mammal populations too low to support owls; however, the weedy character of harvested rice fields supports rodents and songbirds suitable as prey items for this and other owl species. Many birds, usually dispersing young, die in collisions with cars.

Robert A. Behrstock

Worldwide Family Features

- 9–23" (23–57 cm) nocturnal predators.
- Up to 17 species in 2 genera worldwide, primarily in Australasia. 1 species widespread in North America, from extreme southern Canada southward.
- Eat mainly mammals the size of shrews to small rabbits; also small numbers of birds, reptiles, amphibians, insects. Hunt on the wing or from perches, typically dropping on prey and grasping with feet.
- Territorial. Usually monogamous; pairs may remain together until mate dies. Occasionally polygynous. Generally solitary when not breeding. Nonmigratory or partially migratory; some emigrate during food shortages.
- Breed first at 1 year old or less.
- Nests in cavities in cliffs, hollow trees, buildings, other sites. Some species nest on ground in grassy areas. May lay eggs on bed of shredded pellets containing

prey remains regurgitated by female, or directly on substrate. Good sites reused annually, though often by new birds.
- Typically 2–8 (up to 13 in favorable prey years) white, long subelliptical to elliptical eggs, laid at 2- to 3-day intervals. Hatch in 29–42 days. Female incubates alone, beginning with 1st egg; hatching asynchronous. Usually 1 brood per year, sometimes 2, rarely 3.
- Altricial young hatch with closed eyes, sparse pale gray down. Female broods alone. Initially only male brings food to nest; female joins in foraging when young about 2 weeks old. Fledge at 42 days to 13 weeks; dependent upon adults several weeks longer.
- Adult annual survival 40–60%. 1st year survival can be as low as 25%. Most birds live less than 2 years. Little data for species other than Barn Owl. Among oldest on record: 34 years (Barn Owl).

Typical Owls

Strigids are small to large predatory birds with dark brown, gray, black, or reddish plumage. Most species are colored with a mixture of different shades in various patterns of streaks and bars. This mottled appearance, along with an upright stance and elevated ear-tufts, helps the birds to remain concealed during the day. Species that feed in the open are often countershaded, with pale underparts. Owls generally have round heads with flat faces and movable ear-like or horn-like feathers that function in camouflage and display. Most species are nocturnal and well adapted to catching prey in the dark. Their wingspans range from 12 inches to 4 feet 4 inches (30–132 cm). Owls are found on many islands and in virtually all terrestrial habitats, including deserts, rain forests, plains, Arctic tundra, farmland, and cities.

Taxonomy

Both the Falconiformes (hawks, eagles, and falcons) and the Caprimulgiformes (nighthawks and nightjars and their allies) have been proposed as the closest relatives of owls. Biochemical evidence derived from DNA–DNA hybridization and egg-white protein analyses supports a close relationship to the nighthawks and nightjars but none to the hawks. Similarities between the Falconiformes and Strigiformes apparently result from convergent evolution associated with similar feeding methods. Within the Strigiformes, the Strigidae and the Tytonidae (barn owls) are closely related and share many features.

North American typical owls may be divided into several groups. Five genera that have many species worldwide are found on the continent: *Otus* (screech-owls) and *Glaucidium* (pygmy-owls) both comprise small species; *Asio* owls are medium-size, and *Strix* and *Bubo* contain larger species. Three species belong to genera with only a single species worldwide: the large Snowy Owl *(Nyctea scandiaca)*, the medium-size Northern Hawk Owl *(Surnia ulula)*, and the diminutive Elf Owl *(Micrathene whitneyi)*.

Another American species, the Burrowing Owl *(Athene cunicularia)*, has sometimes been placed in the monotypic genus *Speotyto* but is currently classified in the genus *Athene*, along with three Old World species. Skeletal and genetic evidence, however, suggest that it may warrant being placed again in *Speotyto*. Finally, two of the world's four *Aegolius* species—the Boreal Owl *(A. funereus)* and the Northern Saw-whet Owl *(A. acadicus)*—are found in North America.

Many owl genera are widely distributed. For example, the Great Horned Owl *(Bubo virginianus)*, which occurs throughout the Americas and is represented by many subspecies, is in the same genus as the eagle-owls of the Old World. A number of North American owl species, especially those found at high latitudes, also occur throughout northern Europe and Asia; these include the Snowy Owl,

Strigid diversity. *Typical owls in North America represent 10 genera and range from the large, mammal-eating Great Horned Owl (left) to the tiny, insectivorous Elf Owl (top right) to the hawk-like, diurnal Northern Hawk Owl (bottom right), which preys largely on small rodents.*

Owl relatives. Although owls share many behavioral and morphological characteristics with hawks, these two groups are quite distantly related. Instead the owls are most closely related to another group of largely nocturnal birds, the nighthawks and nightjars and their allies. Here, a Barred Owl (center) is shown with a Red-shouldered Hawk (Buteo lineatus, left) and a Chuck-will's-widow (Caprimulgus carolinensis, right).

Northern Hawk Owl, Great Gray Owl *(Strix nebulosa)*, Long-eared Owl *(Asio otus)*, Short-eared Owl *(A. flammeus)*, and Boreal Owl. (English speakers in Eurasia call the last Tengmalm's Owl.)

The number of species in the Strigidae varies considerably depending on the taxonomic treatment. This variation is due largely to uncertainties about the classification of the screech-owls and pygmy-owls. The taxonomic status of tropical forms in these two large genera are under constant revision. Vocal differences, which seem more pronounced than plumage differences in this family, are just being discovered and have led to the splitting of several species.

In North America, the Eastern *(Otus asio)* and Western *(O. kennicottii)* Screech-Owls were considered a single species until 1983, when they were formally split. The occasional occurrence of mixed pairs has led to questions about this split, but differences in vocalizations and DNA support the separation. Additionally, the Western Screech-Owl lacks the red morph found in some populations of the Eastern Screech-Owl.

Worldwide Family Features

- 5½–29" (14–73 cm) nocturnal predators.
- About 164 species in about 24 genera worldwide; on all continents except Antarctica; most species in tropics. 18 species in 10 genera breed in North America; present throughout continent; plus 3 accidental species.
- Carnivorous; eat wide array of invertebrates and vertebrates. Most feed at night, some during day. Generally catch prey with feet after aerial approach.
- Territories often overlap. Typically monogamous; polygyny rare. May retain mate or change from year to year; some remain paired until mate's death. Most species solitary when not breeding, but some form roosting groups. Some species migratory; others permanent residents.
- Several species breed first at 1 year old, others not until at least 3 years old.
- Nest is natural or artificial cavity or platform; some species nest on ground,

one species in burrows; may use nest boxes. Add little or no nesting material to nest sites. Platform nesters often reuse old hawk nests. May reuse cavities.
- Usually 2–8 eggs; white or with slight pastel tint and elliptical to nearly rounded; laid at 1- to 2-day intervals. Female incubates, for 21–35 days; male delivers food to her. Incubation begins after 1st or 2nd egg is laid. Hatching asynchronous. Most species raise 1 brood per year.
- Altricial young hatch with closed eyes, sparse down, unable to lift head. Fledge in 28 days to 3 months. Leave nests after 12–36 days, often long before capable of flight. Young may depend on adults for several weeks after fledging. Both parents provide care.
- 1st-year mortality high; adult annual survival 45–90%. Among oldest on record: 27 years, 7 months (Great Horned Owl).

Northern Saw-whet Owl facial disc. Profuse bristles surrounding the base of the bill and the radiating feathers around the eye create the "facial disc" that is characteristic of all owls. The function of the bristles is debated, but they may serve to provide tactile information about nearby objects. The facial disc is composed of stiff, lacy feathers similar to the ear coverts of all birds, but covering a much larger area in owls.

Northern Pygmy-Owl *(Glaucidium gnoma)* taxonomy is also complex. Currently considered a single species by the AOU, this owl is subdivided into as many as four different species by some authorities, based largely on vocal differences. Two of these putative species occur in North America, with birds from southeastern Arizona and southwestern New Mexico *(G. g. gnoma;* variously called either the "Mountain" or the "Mexican" Pygmy-Owl) considered distinct from more northerly birds.

There is decided subspecies variation in several other North American owls. The smaller, lighter "Mexican" Spotted Owl *(Strix occidentalis lucida)* is genetically distinct from the "California" Spotted Owl *(S. o. occidentalis)* of the West Coast; these Pacific coast birds are sometimes further subdivided, with the northern birds called the "Northern" Spotted Owl *(S. o. caurina).* Short-eared Owls from the Caribbean, which occasionally occur in Florida, are sufficiently different from those found throughout North America to have been considered a separate species in the past. The Burrowing Owls in Florida also differ in various plumage details from those in western North America.

Food and Foraging

See the Barn Owls chapter for a discussion of adaptations for feeding among all owls, including modifications of the flight feathers, vision adaptations, and positioning of the ears.

Many owls avoid competition with diurnal predators, such as hawks, by feeding exclusively at night. A few species feed during both day and night, or concentrate their foraging at dawn and dusk, but only the Northern Hawk Owl, the pygmy-owls, and to a lesser extent the Snowy, Burrowing, and Short-eared Owls are normally active in daylight.

Nocturnal species typically spend their days concealed at a roost site, where they are unlikely to be seen unless the scolds of mobbing jays, crows, chickadees, or other birds alert a passerby to their presence. During winter, Long-eared and Short-eared Owls may roost in groups of several dozen individuals—Long-eareds

Cryptic posture. Most owls spend the day concealed in vegetation or cavities, with eyes closed, body feathers compressed, and ear-tufts raised to blend with tree bark, as shown in the Flammulated Owl (red morph) on the left. At night they present a very different appearance, with eyes wide open, ear-tufts down, and body feathers relaxed, as shown in the gray morph of the same species, on the right.

Section of a typical owl's primary feather (magnified view). The soft, comb-like leading edge of the feather and the fuzzy upper surface muffle sounds as the feather moves through air and against other feathers. The auditory hunting of owls is effective only in a quiet environment. Some owls that hunt in daylight and do not require sensitive hearing—for example the pygmy-owls—lack these feather adaptations.

usually close together in trees, Short-eareds more dispersed in tall grass. Also in winter, groups of Short-eared Owls may feed together in the same area.

Diet

Owls vary greatly in body size and habitat choice, and they take a wide range of prey items, including moths, beetles, earthworms, crayfish, and other invertebrates; reptiles, amphibians, and fish; various birds up to the size of grouse, geese, and even other owls; and mammals ranging in size from shrews and bats to cats and skunks. The degree of diet specialization varies. The Eastern Screech-Owl is an omnivore whose diverse diet enhances its ability to survive in many different habitats. In contrast, Flammulated Owls (Otus flammeolus) eat insects almost exclusively. Some populations of Burrowing Owls also subsist primarily on invertebrates, while some birds in some other populations eat many small mammals.

Most owls take prey commensurate with their body size, but this is not always the case. Pygmy-owls eat moths, beetles, and grasshoppers but frequently take small mammals, including bats and birds as large as towhees. Great Horned

Owls typically eat prey ranging in size from rats to skunks, but some prey on insect larvae, small frogs, or insects attracted to lights.

Anatomical proportions often provide a clue to the size of prey favored by a species. For example, the Western Screech-Owl's relatively large feet allow for a strong grip, enabling the bird to capture mammals and birds. The Flammulated Owl's much daintier feet reflect its arthropod diet. Intermediate in foot size is the Whiskered Screech-Owl (Otus trichopsis), which feeds primarily on large invertebrates but occasionally takes rodents.

Species of similar size may coexist by partitioning food resources. In a zone of overlap, the Northern Saw-whet Owl and the Northern Pygmy-Owl took warm-blooded prey of similar size; however, the pygmy-owl's diet was about one-third birds, and the saw-whet's was almost totally mammals.

Capture and Consumption of Prey

Owls take most prey items from the ground, trees, or shrubbery, though some species, including the Elf Owl, Eastern Screech-Owl, and Snowy Owl, also snatch food from the water or in aerial pursuit. Owls' powerful feet have outer toes that can rotate so that two toes point forward and two backward. This arrangement

Owl left foot. Owls have zygodactyl feet, with the outer toe capable of pivoting back and forth. Vertebrate-eating species, such as the Great Horned Owl (shown here), generally have large, strong feet well suited for grasping large, squirming prey. Insect eaters often have proportionately daintier feet.

Owl feet from below. The illustrations show the positions possible through rotation of the outer toe: (a) three toes forward and one back; (b) two front and two back; and (c) toes fully spread on both feet in preparation for capture of prey. Note that the rotation of the toes allows the two feet to create a complete "web" of talons for efficient prey capture.

permits a strong, symmetrical grip on squirming prey. Owls share this anatomical feature with the Osprey *(Pandion haliaetus)* and the turacos (family Musophagidae) of Africa.

Most owls avoid interactions with predators and competitors by gulping down prey whole (occasionally first removing a vertebrate's head or the spiny legs of an insect) and returning to cover, rather than sitting in the open and eating slowly, as hawks are more likely to do. Snowy Owls, on the other hand, always feed in the open, quickly eating several small mammals whole, then more slowly dissecting subsequent kills as they become sated.

Rather than grinding or dissolving indigestible materials, the owl's digestive system compacts fur, bones, and the

Owl pellets. Owls swallow their prey whole and, about eight hours later, regurgitate the inedible fur, feathers, and bones as a compact pellet. Pellets litter the ground beneath favored roost sites, providing clues to the owls' roosting locations and diet. Shown here are pellets of the Great Horned Owl (top; about 5 inches long) and the Northern Saw-whet Owl (bottom; about 1 inch long).

chitinous (exoskeletal) remains of invertebrates into a pellet. Each day, an owl ejects one or two pellets through the mouth. Piles of these pellets can be a useful clue to the location of a regular roost site. Prey remains in owl pellets provide detailed information on prey species and have been used by researchers to reconstruct the diets of owls and to study foraging patterns.

Breeding

In owls, the pair bond is typically monogamous; polygyny is rare but has been noted in Boreal and Northern Saw-whet Owls. Rarely a female Boreal Owl will raise two broods fathered by different males during the same season. Several species, including the Flammulated, Eastern Screech-, Spotted *(Strix occidentalis),* and Great Horned Owls, may retain their mate from year to year, and some pairs remain together until one bird dies. Other species change mates annually. Some Snowy Owls, in response to their nomadic lifestyle, change both mate and territory in successive years.

Sexual displays of owls are poorly known. At night, vocalizations are probably more important than visual displays. Males advertise and females respond with various calls. Pairs of many species rub bills and allopreen; males pass food to females. The male Burrowing Owl has been observed in swooping display flights of about 130 feet (40 m) in diameter, quickly ascending to a height of

Long-eared Owl at nest with recently hatched young. Owls do not build nests, instead using the abandoned nests of crows or hawks, as well as tree cavities, cliff ledges, and man-made structures. The Burrowing Owl uses old animal burrows. The young are helpless at first but leave the nest after as little as 12 days in the ground-nesting Short-eared Owls and as long as 36 days in several other species.

about 100 feet (30 m); the owl hovers five to ten seconds, quickly descends partway, then repeats its ascent.

Small owls are cavity nesters and use both natural and artificial sites; many species, including the Northern Pygmy-Owl, Flammulated Owl, and Boreal Owl, favor woodpecker nest holes. Larger species may occupy stick nests built by eagles, hawks, or ravens, or may nest on the top of a stump or snag, in a niche between diverging branches or palm fronds, in a cave in a cliff face, or in an old building. Owls often reuse sites, especially where there is a limited number of cavities. Many species, both large and small, readily use nest boxes.

The unusual Burrowing Owl nests in tunnels 6 to 10 feet (2–3 m) long that have been dug by a tortoise or a burrowing mammal. Less frequently, these owls dig their own burrows, using the beak to shape the tunnel and nest chamber, which they may later line with mammal dung. The nests of Burrowing Owls contain more feathers, grasses, and other materials than do those of most owls.

Owls lay eggs at one- to two-day intervals. When food resources are favorable, some pairs lay additional eggs or fledge extra young. Species with more flexible nesting strategies lay larger clutches when prey is very abundant; Boreal Owls may increase clutch size from three or four to nine. The insectivorous Flammulated Owl, which has a less variable food supply, lays a small clutch of two to four eggs with little variation.

Incubation, which the female performs while the male delivers food to her, begins after the first or second egg is laid. The incubation period ranges from as little as 21 days in the tiny Elf Owl to 35 days in the much larger Great Horned Owl. Hatching is asynchronous; in many clutches, the last chicks to hatch are outcompeted and ultimately consumed by their larger siblings. The fledging period lasts four to five weeks in the smaller species and up to three months in Great Horned Owls.

Downy young Long-eared Owl. Young owls frequently leave the nest when still unable to fly. Young Long-eareds move onto nearby branches at about 24 days and begin to fly at 30 to 40 days. The parents continue to deliver food to the young each night for up to 60 days.

Juvenile Great Horned Owl displaying. *The presumed intent of this threat posture, with head down and wings raised and spread in a broad fan, is to deter potential predators by increasing the apparent size of the owl.*

During incubation and brooding, the male delivers food to the nest. Occasionally the female may leave the nest briefly to take prey items from the male. When the young are larger and food demands become greater, the female joins in the foraging.

Although species such as the Burrowing Owl may infrequently rear a second brood, most North American owls raise one brood per year. The energy demands of the late-summer molt may make raising another brood impractical; hunting to provide enough food for the female and the young would be difficult while the male is replacing his wing and tail feathers. In northern climes, short summers do not allow for two complete cycles of laying, incubating, brooding, and caring for fledglings.

Movements

Owls may be permanent residents, migratory, or nomadic, and in some species there are individuals in all three categories. Broadly speaking, the screech-owls, the Barred Owl *(Strix varia)*, the Ferruginous Pygmy-Owl *(Glaucidium brasilianum)*, the Great Horned Owl, and most Spotted Owls maintain permanent territories. At least some populations of the remaining North American owl species are migratory, or undertake sporadic invasive movements, also known as irruptions, in some years.

Migration

Northern populations of Burrowing, Long-eared, and Short-eared Owls are migratory, as are the insectivorous Elf and Flammulated Owls, which move south every winter toward more certain insect supplies. The Northern Saw-whet Owl is migratory in parts of its range. Depending on such variables as temperature, snow characteristics, and food availability, the Northern Pygmy-Owl makes elevational migrations, moving up- and downslope.

Within some species, different populations of owls exhibit differing migratory behaviors. As winter approaches, for example, the adaptable Burrowing Owl leaves the northern portion of its range to seek warmer conditions; en route many individuals wander, appearing on coastal jetties, islands, even offshore oil platforms and ships at sea. This tendency to cross water is unusual among other birds of prey but is shared by several owl species.

Differences occur even among sexes. In the Snowy Owl, the larger adult females are able to winter farther north than immatures and males, and do not migrate as far south. In Boreal Owls, however, the considerably larger females are prone to migratory or nomadic movements; the smaller males are more sedentary, exhibiting greater fidelity to their nesting territories throughout their adulthood.

Irruptions

Northern owls—including the Boreal, Snowy, and to a lesser extent the Great Gray and Northern Hawk Owls—make invasive winter movements in certain years and can be found in large numbers far south of their normal winter ranges. In some areas as many as ten owl species may concentrate at sites with abundant prey (often voles).

Irruptions are often thought to be related to plunges in the availability of prey, especially lemmings and voles, farther north. Fluctuations in mammal populations, however, do not completely explain regional differences in owl abundance; other factors—including patchiness of prey populations, snow cover and crust characteristics, and temperature—also must be taken into account.

Following irruptions, Snowy Owls and Boreal Owls are known to remain and breed in areas far from their previous nesting sites; some Boreals have nested more than 425 miles (680 km) from the site they used the previous year.

Dispersal

The most universal type of movement among owls is the dispersal of young. In fall, adults reestablish their winter feeding territories, driving away their now self-sufficient offspring. Species such as the Eastern Screech-Owl signify this territoriality with vocalizations that differ from their spring breeding songs. Young of even small species may travel 10 miles (16 km) or more, and some turn up hundreds of miles from their nest sites. The dispersal period is a perilous time for the naive offspring, and many are killed by cars or other birds of prey. Juvenile mortality during the dispersal period has been identified as one of the main factors contributing to the decline of Spotted Owls.

Conservation

Many cavity-nesting owls have declined in numbers after logging operations deprived them of nest sites; however, the provision of nest boxes has resulted in dramatic rebounds, especially in rejuvenating forests where natural cavities are not yet available. Today certain populations of species such as the Boreal Owl are largely dependent on artificial nest sites. Logging, especially the practice of clear-cutting, also removes hunting and roosting perches, as well as the sub-canopy and ground-cover vegetation required by some prey species.

Habitat loss associated with human residential development has had an impact, usually a detrimental one, on many species. However, Eastern Screech-Owls inhabiting neighborhoods with mature trees may have higher survival rates than countryside populations, thanks to a lower diversity of predators, greater availability of water and of prey attracted to bird feeders and garbage cans, the suitability of lawns as hunting areas, and the warmer conditions associated with urban enclaves.

In western North America, some populations of Burrowing Owls have declined as a result of urban sprawl and agricultural intensification, falling victim to insecticides, the widespread poisoning of burrow-providing prairie dogs, and the plowing of remaining burrows. The situation is particularly dire in the Great Plains, where this species is listed as endangered or threatened in several states and provinces. The fate of Burrowing Owls is viewed as one of the highest avian conservation concerns in the Canadian prairies.

In contrast, Florida populations of these owls have spread, thanks to human occupation, as land has been made available through the drainage of wetlands and turned into good hunting territory by grazing and mowing; in the late 1990s Florida populations were highest in residential and industrial sites.

The Spotted Owl rivals the Bald Eagle (Haliaeetus leucocephalus) as North America's highest-profile bird of prey. The owl's fate has been at the center of bitter disputes among government agencies, legal and illegal timber cutters, logging

"Mexican" Spotted Owl. The Spotted Owl is considered threatened in the Pacific Northwest and the interior West and has been the center of bitter disputes between environmentalists and foresters. The birds in these two areas belong to genetically distinct populations and are known as the "Northern" and "Mexican" Spotted Owls, respectively.

companies, land managers, economists, and researchers. The "Northern" and "Mexican" Spotted Owls are listed as threatened in the United States; the former is listed as endangered in British Columbia. The species' continued survival in the Pacific Northwest is put at risk by tree harvest practices aimed at extracting the last vestiges of valuable timber from ancient old-growth forests. In portions of the Spotted Owl's range, virtually all of its habitat has been lost to the chain saw.

In addition, the Spotted Owl is threatened by the westward spread of the Barred Owl, an aggressive and more adaptable species that does not depend upon the continued presence of old-growth forest. Barred Owls are closely related to Spotted Owls, and the two species hybridize where their ranges overlap.

Concern exists for populations of several other owl species, at least locally. The Long-eared Owl is viewed as a species of management concern in New England, the upper Midwest, and California, and is listed as threatened or endangered in some states. Short-eared Owls also are viewed with concern in some areas and are on the WatchList

because of steep population declines and threats associated with the disappearance of grassland habitats.

The Ferruginous Pygmy-Owl is also the focus of some conservation interest because it has small North American populations; although common farther south in Central America, it is proposed for threatened status in the United States. The Elf Owl is another species of concern on the WatchList; its very limited breeding and wintering ranges render it highly sensitive to habitat disturbances.

Chemicals meant for other organisms, such as insecticides, rodenticides, and other toxic mammal baits, may not kill owls outright, but they cause abnormal eggs, small clutches, and poor fledging success. Both the direct effect of these chemicals accumulating in owls at the top of the food chain and the indirect effect of decreased prey availability contribute to owl population declines. Species that nest or feed along roads—especially Burrowing Owls and Barn Owls *(Tyto alba)*, but others as well—may experience high mortality from traffic. Owls are still shot in some areas, and small populations may be susceptible to malicious and illegal hunting pressure. Feral and domestic cats may kill smaller species, especially as the young are fledging.

Accidental Species

Three accidental species have been documented in North America. In Alaska, remains of the small, migratory Oriental Scops-Owl *(Otus sunia)* of northeastern Asia have been recovered twice in the Aleutian Islands during summer. In the Rio Grande Valley of southern Texas, the Stygian Owl *(Asio stygius)* has been seen twice, and a dead Mottled Owl *(Ciccaba virgata)* has been found. All three reports were from Bentsen–Rio Grande Valley State Park during winter. Both species normally occur in Central and South America north into Mexico.

Robert A. Behrstock

Nighthawks and Nightjars

Nighthawks and nightjars are superficially similar, medium-size crepuscular or nocturnal birds whose presence and identity are best revealed by voice. These birds are collectively referred to as "goatsuckers," after the old, erroneous belief that they would fly into barns at night and suck dry the teats of goats. Goatsuckers are typically dark, cryptically colored, and intricately patterned. They are outwardly similar to owls or perhaps small hawks but are easily distinguished by their flight patterns, face and head shape, short legs, and horizontal stance. Goatsuckers live in forests, savannas, beach and desert scrub, and cities, at elevations from sea level or below to about 12,000 feet (3,600 m).

Taxonomy

In most people's minds, goatsuckers are grouped with owls because they share soft, dark, cryptically patterned plumage, nocturnal habits, and commanding voices. Biochemical evidence suggests a fairly close relationship between these groups; however, there are many major differences, and the two groups are typically classified in different orders.

Goatsuckers and other caprimulgiforms are separated from owls by their short legs and weak feet. They also have small bills backed by a broad gape that engulfs flying insects. Owls, in contrast, generally possess strong feet with sharp claws and strong beaks that are designed for capturing and killing vertebrate prey. Unlike goatsuckers, owls have forward-facing eye sockets and often have asymmetrical ear openings.

The Caprimulgidae is the largest of several families of similar-appearing nocturnal birds in the order Caprimulgiformes; the other families are largely restricted to the tropics. Two of these occur in the New World: Nyctibiidae, which comprises the potoos, and Steatornithidae, which includes just the Oilbird *(Steatornis caripensis)*, an unusual species that eats fruit and can echolocate. The remaining families in the order are restricted to the Old World.

Caprimulgid species inhabit all continents except Antarctica and are absent from only the highest elevations and latitudes. Their greatest diversity is in the tropics, and the family includes many island species. The family is subdivided into two subfamilies: the Chordeilinae (nighthawks), which are confined to the Americas, and the more cosmopolitan Caprimulginae (nightjars).

Caprimulgid diversity. The eight species of caprimulgids in North America fall into two main groups: the nightjars (three genera, but most species in Caprimulgus*), such as the Whip-poor-will (left); and the nighthawks (genus* Chordeiles*), such as the Common Nighthawk (right).*

Caprimulgid foot. The weak feet and very short legs of caprimulgids are best suited for perching, and the birds walk awkwardly, with a shuffling gait. All have partial webbing between the toes and a pectinate (comb-like) claw on the middle toe. Chuck-will's-widow is shown.

348

Of the four genera of nighthawks, only *Chordeiles* occurs in North America. All three North American species are mainly crepuscular, as indicated by the Greek-derived genus name, which suggests "music in the evening." They will also feed on cloudy days or around lights at night. The plumage of nighthawks is countershaded, unlike that of the uniformly darker nightjars.

The eyes of nighthawks are large, but smaller than those of the more nocturnal nightjars. The wings and tail are long, like those of falcons and swifts, and allow fast, sustained aerial feeding in open habitats. Nighthawks are easily distinguished from these other birds by their erratic flight, which has been considered bat-like and has given the Common Nighthawk *(Chordeiles minor)* the colloquial name "Bullbat." As the birds roost, usually lengthwise on an elevated limb, their long, unbarred wings extend to or beyond the tip of the tail.

The subfamily Caprimulginae consists of about ten similar genera, three of which occur north of Mexico. The Common Pauraque *(Nyctidromus albicollis)* and Common Poorwill *(Phalaenoptilus*

nuttallii) are each the sole members of their genera, with the remaining North American species in the large genus *Caprimulgus*.

Unlike nighthawks, nightjars are infrequently seen during the day, instead emerging to feed after sunset or before dawn. They do not congregate in well-lit cities, as nighthawks do, nor do the North American species participate in group displays, as do some tropical genera. Their large eyes and long rictal bristles that form a basket-like insect trap around the open mouth are adaptations for feeding in reduced light levels (see Food and Foraging, below).

Nightjars have shorter and more rounded wings than nighthawks, an advantage for hunting in dense vegetation. Among North American species, the wings of roosting nightjars fall short of the tail tip, except in the very short-tailed Common Poorwill.

Plumage and Vocalizations

Never exhibiting the bright colors by which we recognize so many groups of birds, goatsuckers have evolved into an

Worldwide Family Features

- 6–16" (15–40 cm) nocturnal birds. (Length excludes long flight feathers found on some tropical species.)
- About 78 species in 14 genera worldwide; occur on all continents except Antarctica. 8 species in 4 genera breed in North America, found throughout continent, north to central Canada; plus 1 accidental species.
- Eat very small to large flying insects captured by mouth during flight; larger species may take vertebrates, including bats and small songbirds.
- Generally territorial; some may nest in loose colonies. Apparently monogamous, but may change mates during successive years. Nighthawks may roost, feed, and migrate in large groups; nightjars are less social. Most temperate species migratory, tropical species usually nonmigratory.
- Age at first breeding unknown for most; assumed to be 1 year old.
- Most do not build a nest; lay eggs on

ground, rooftops, or other flat substrates; sometimes among pebbles or leaves or shaded by a bush or log. May reuse nest sites.
- 1–3 (usually 2) elliptical eggs, laid on successive days. Color variable; may be white, buff, or pastel, often with fine speckles or blotches for camouflage, others much darker. Incubation begins with 1st egg. Hatching asynchronous, about 16–22 days after incubation begins. Incubation and brooding shared or done mostly by female while male provides food. 1 or 2 broods per year.
- Semi-precocial young hatch with eyes open; brown-and-buff down, with dark spots and bars, renders them virtually invisible. Remain at nest for about 2 days. Fledge at about 14–23 days; often dependent on parents for 1 or 2 weeks more. Both parents feed young.
- Survival rates poorly known. Among oldest on record: 14 years, 10 months (Chuck-will's-widow).

array of species invisible to diurnal predators. Their limited palette of buff, gold, rufous, brown, and black acts to reproduce the earth tones of tree bark, soil, and leaf litter against which the birds sleep throughout the day. These patterns, which camouflage a Common Poorwill against the gravel of a sun-dappled desert wash or allow a Common Pauraque to blend with the fallen leaves of the shadowy forest floor, probably play no part in species recognition. In the dark of night, when these birds become active, it is largely their voices, not their plumage, that they use to recognize one another.

Goatsuckers, like all nocturnal birds, are most easily found and identified by their calls. Many species are more often heard than seen, and most cultures have coined common names such as Whip-poor-will *(Caprimulgus vociferus)* or Chuck-will's-widow *(C. carolinensis)* that mimic the sound and cadence of the bird's familiar vocalization. Birders searching for the rare Buff-collared Nightjar *(C. ridgwayi)* in Arizona and New Mexico usually locate it by hearing its rising, insect-like song. In Florida, knowing that the Cuban name "Querequeté" mimics a quickly delivered set of dry chip notes will enable birders to differentiate a calling Antillean Nighthawk *(Chordeiles gundlachii)* from the very similar-looking Common Nighthawk.

Males use these calls when they establish and defend territories and advertise for females. Other noises include a flight call, as well as a short scold the birds give when flushed. Some clap their wings, and many give a guttural growl, often produced by males in response to the call of another male.

During the nesting season, a novel aspect of the Common Nighthawk's sound repertoire is a loud, humming, whooshing *hoooov*, produced as air rushes through the primary feathers of the diving male. This display may be directed at a female, another male, a young bird, or an intruder.

Food and Foraging

Specialists at sustained, aerial foraging, nighthawks emerge at dusk in great flocks, dispersing far from their roosting areas in search of food and water. Nightjars also typically catch prey in the air, but instead tend to make hops or short flights from the ground or an elevated perch. Some species, including the Common Poorwill, forage most frequently from the ground; others, like Buff-collared Nightjars, typically hunt from atop a tree or large shrub. Nightjars also are more likely to forage alone, near their nest or roost site, and often in or close to concealing vegetation. Some goatsuckers, including the Lesser Nighthawk *(Chordeiles acutipennis)*, drink in flight by skimming the water's surface with an open bill.

While foraging, some goatsuckers sit on roads, using them as hunting corridors and probably benefiting from the retained heat of the day. If an observer looks directly along the line of headlights or a flashlight beam, sitting birds can be detected by their eyeshine, typically a rich, glowing red that is visible at considerable distances. Eyeshine is produced when light bounces off the

Caprimulgids foraging. The two main groups within this family differ in many respects, including their foraging methods. The nightjars, such as the Whip-poor-will (shown below), perch on the ground in open woods or clearings and fly up to capture passing insects, often returning to the same perch. The nighthawks, such as the Common Nighthawk (shown higher in flight, above), fly continuously over treetops, towns, or fields, catching insects in the air as they go.

Caprimulgid head and bill. When closed, the small bill of the Whip-poor-will (shown here) looks insignificant, but it opens to reveal an extremely large mouth surrounded by long, stiff rictal bristles. The large mouth is presumably an advantage when capturing flying insects at night.

tapetum, a reflective surface inside the eye that enhances light absorption.

Goatsuckers have a small beak but a massive gape; when the mouth opens to take an insect, the lower jaw changes shape from a V into a semicircle, creating a surprisingly large area. Although the huge gapes of many species allow them to take large moths, or even small birds, goatsuckers seem to feed with equal facility on winged stages of ants and termites, tiny moths, mosquitoes, and small flies, stuffing immense numbers (as many as 2,000) into their capacious gullets. Some species feed on more unusual prey: Molting Chuck-will's-widows have been observed chasing and capturing small frogs on the ground, possibly because the loss of flight feathers hinders aerial foraging.

Unlike most birds, goatsuckers do not have a bony palate. Some researchers suggest that the unusual soft membrane lining the upper jaw is a sensitive surface that reacts to collisions with tiny insects and causes the mouth to snap shut. More recent studies suggest that the soft membrane is important in thermoregulation, allowing Common Poorwills and Lesser Nighthawks to nest on the blistering desert floor. In hot climates, the large expanse of capillary-rich tissue lining the mouth and throat radiates heat. Gular (throat) fluttering and dog-like panting enhance this heat loss.

Most nightjars have well-developed rictal bristles, which may funnel food into the mouth, protect the bird's eyes from insect legs and wings, or have a tactile function similar to the whiskers of some mammals or the barbels of some fish (see also Tyrant Flycatchers). In nighthawks, these bristles are rudimentary, suggesting perhaps that they are less important for birds foraging at high speed under brighter twilight skies.

Like many insect-eating birds that occur in temperate regions, most North American goatsuckers are migratory. In fall, when insect food supplies become unpredictable, the birds head southward. They return northward in spring to warmer temperatures, longer days, and renewed insect abundance.

Breeding

The sequence in which different species return to the breeding grounds reflects the availability of their favored prey. For example, Common Nighthawks arrive later at their nesting areas and leave earlier than Common Poorwills and Whip-poor-wills, apparently responding to the shortage of aerial prey during cool spring and fall days. Perhaps the more complex environment closer to the ground provides greater warmth for the array of insects upon which the other two species feed.

Once on the nesting grounds, different species employ various breeding strategies. The Whip-poor-will coordinates its nesting with the moon's cycle; its eggs hatch as the moon waxes, providing many hours of moonlight against which the adults may spot the prey they feed to their young. In contrast, the Common Poorwill does not coordinate its breeding activities with the lunar cycle.

Unlike the Whip-poor-will, the Common Poorwill is able to enter torpor as a means of conserving energy resources. When a bird is in torpor, its body temperature regularly falls below 50° F (10° C), a drop of more than 54° F (30° C). There are even reports of Common Poorwills using torpor for extended time periods during winter. By entering torpor, these birds can survive periods of inclement weather and reduced food availability. This ability to save energy may explain why they can nest earlier in the year than some other goatsuckers.

During displays, male goatsuckers fluff up or spread out distinct white regions of their bodies, including collars, wing-patches, and the tips or outer margins of the tail feathers. The size, shape, and position of these marks, often invisible while the birds sleep during the day, provide species-specific signals.

Goatsuckers do not build a nest, although they may lay eggs in a shallow depression scraped in the ground. Nesting substrates include sand and gravel; earth that is bare or covered with leaves or pine needles; flat rocks; and wooden and metallic surfaces. Many goatsuckers nest in forests; others (for example, nighthawks and the Common Poorwill) use open land, such as desert, or burned, logged, or grazed areas. Vegetation or rocks may shade the nest. Some species, especially nighthawks, nest in loose colonies.

Common and Lesser Nighthawks also nest on flat rooftops and have become familiar city birds, congregating by the dozens to capture insects around well-lit billboards or rows of streetlights.

Incubation and brooding are shared by both parents in species such as the Common Poorwill and the Common Nighthawk; in other species (such as the Lesser Nighthawk) the female takes these responsibilities while the male provides food. If the first eggs are lost, the clutch is replaced. A few species raise a second brood. Female Common Poorwills have been known to lay a second clutch while the male feeds the first brood.

Young goatsuckers leave the nest when a few days old. The juvenal plumage is present by their second week, and they fledge when 14 to 23 days old.

Conservation

Assessing population trends among goatsuckers is difficult because of their nocturnal habits. Evidence from Breeding Bird Surveys, however, suggests that both Chuck-will's-widow and the Common Nighthawk are declining throughout their breeding ranges. Whip-poor-will populations have declined in the central part of the bird's range but have increased on the periphery; populations of this species, which lives in dry, open woodlands near fields, are known to fluctuate dramatically in response to the cutting and regeneration of forest. Chuck-will's-widow is on the WatchList.

Widespread in the western United States, the Common Poorwill is not considered threatened, and there is no evidence of general declines, although data are scanty. In western Canada, near the limit of its range, the Common Poorwill receives more attention. Lesser Nighthawk populations are apparently increasing in North America.

The reasons for these trends are not known, but Common Nighthawk declines have been associated with insecticide use, loss of open habitats, road kills, and perhaps increased predation.

Grazing, small-scale logging, and forest fires, all of which create clearings, may increase the nesting and roosting habitat of both the Common Nighthawk and the Common Poorwill. Placing gravel on rubberized roofs encourages urban nesting by Common Nighthawks, which have declined in some cities as builders have shifted to using smooth, rubberized roofs.

Accidental Species

One accidental species has been recorded in North America. The remains of a Jungle Nightjar *(Caprimulgus indicus)*, which normally occurs in eastern Asia, were collected on Buldir Island, Alaska, in May.

Robert A. Behrstock

Swifts

Swifts are small to medium-size aerial foragers with long, sickle-shaped wings and black or dark brown plumage; they often have white or gray patches on the body. Their extremely short legs give swifts their family name, which means "without feet." Members of the Apodidae are the most aerial of birds, spending most of their lives on the wing. They not only capture their food in flight, but also bathe, drink, and sometimes even copulate and spend the night in the air. Their habitats range from deserts to tropical forests. North American habitats include desert canyons, mountain forests, and many urban areas.

Taxonomy

Swifts are considered to be most closely related to the hummingbirds, primarily because the two families share similar wing structures. Both have a very short humerus (the wing's inner portion) and elongated distal elements, characteristics related to their fast wing movements. In most respects, however, the two groups are quite different, and any common ancestry must be quite old.

Superficially swifts are similar to swallows, and the two families share the habit of foraging for flying insects. But several key differences exist. The faster-flying swifts generally have narrower, more swept-back wings than swallows. Swifts do not perch between foraging flights as swallows do, resting only at nests and nocturnal roost sites. Swallows are passerine songbirds; swifts are not. Many anatomical characteristics of the syrinx and skeleton support the separation of swifts and swallows into different orders.

Ornithologists recognize three Apodidae subfamilies, all of which occur in North America. The subfamily Cypseloidinae consists of 13 largely tropical New World species, including the Black Swift *(Cypseloides niger)* of western North America. Their mossy nests are located on dark rock surfaces near or behind waterfalls.

The subfamily Chaeturinae, the spine-tailed swifts, includes the Chimney Swift *(Chaetura pelagica)* and Vaux's Swift *(C. vauxi)*, as well as the swiftlets (genera *Aerodramus* and *Collocalia*) of southeastern Asia and the Pacific Islands. The rectrices of many chaeturine swifts have strong protruding shafts that the birds use as props when roosting in their hollow tree or chimney nesting sites. Both cypseloidine and chaeturine swifts have anisodactyl feet, typical of most birds, with three toes directed forward and one backward.

Members of the subfamily Apodinae lack the stiffened tail shafts of the Chaeturinae, and they possess a unique laterally grasping foot that enables them to cling to their roost or nest substrate. The long, rattling screams of apodine swifts often announce their presence before they can be seen high overhead. The familiar White-throated Swift *(Aeronautes saxatalis)* of western North America and the well-studied Common Swift *(Apus apus)* of Europe belong to this subfamily.

Apodid diversity. *North American swifts include members of three subfamilies that differ in nesting habits, foot structure, and wing and tail-feather shape. Shown here are the adult Chimney Swift (Chaeturinae, top left), the juvenile Black Swift (Cypseloidinae, top right), and the adult White-throated Swift (Apodinae, bottom).*

353

Food and Foraging

Swifts eat a wide array of aerial arthropods, mostly insects, although they also capture ballooning spiders. They generally take whatever prey items are available within the size range a given species can handle. Both large and small species consume many small insects ($\frac{1}{16}$–$\frac{1}{4}$"/2–6 mm long); larger swifts eat larger prey items when these are available. Swifts are quick to exploit temporary prey concentrations, such as nuptial flights of termites, ants, and mayflies. They may aggregate at localized food sources, often accompanied by swallows.

Black Swifts and other cypseloidine swifts forage far from their nest colonies, seeking out swarms of lipid-rich insects, such as winged ants and termites. They store large masses of food in the esophagus to bring back to their chicks, which they feed once or twice a day. Foraging may continue until dusk. The birds regurgitate food to the nestlings over several hours, sometimes continuing well after dark.

Chaeturine and apodine swifts are more generalist foragers, searching over distances of up to several miles. They feed the nestlings typically one to three times per hour, carrying smaller boluses of up to several hundred insects and ballooning spiders that often visibly distend the floor of the mouth. These swifts use

Swift head and bill. The head and bill of a swift are similar to those of a swallow or nightjar, with a tiny bill but a large mouth opening surrounded by stiff rictal bristles. Vaux's Swift is shown.

salivary cement from seasonally enlarged salivary glands to glue the food bolus together. The same cement is used as a glue in nest construction.

Like bats, swiftlets in the genus *Aerodramus* navigate by echolocation, a form of sonar. By emitting audible clicks and then detecting the reflection of the sounds from solid surfaces, they can maneuver in and out of the caves in which they nest and roost. Unlike bats, however, the swiftlets are unable to detect objects as small as their typical prey, and so do not feed at night, except where artificial lighting facilitates prey capture.

Breeding

Distinct differences in breeding biology and nest placement tend to support the current swift subfamily divisions.

Cypseloidine swifts generally breed in damp, dark situations, building their nests of mosses and lichens on ledges or steep rock surfaces near or behind waterfalls. Black Swifts, for example, are often found near waterfalls. Cypseloidine swifts reuse nests for years, adding only a small amount of new material each year. Black Swifts and other *Cypseloides* swifts lay one-egg clutches.

Chaeturine swifts build their half-saucer-shaped nests out of small twigs, which they break off in flight from the tops of dead trees. They use a salivary cement to glue the twigs together and to attach the nest to the wall of their nest chamber, typically within a hollow tree or chimney. The nests of some swiftlets,

Swift feet. Swifts have small but very strong feet, with sharp, curved claws that help them grip upright structures. Species in the subfamilies Cypseloidinae and Chaeturinae have an anisodactyl foot (for example, the Chimney Swift, left), like most birds, with three toes in front and one behind. In contrast, swifts of the subfamily Apodinae (for example, the White-throated Swift, right) have a different foot structure adapted for lateral grasping.

Black Swift at nest. *The nests of the three subfamilies of swifts differ in structure, with each constructed according to their different placement. Black Swifts, in the subfamily Cypseloidinae, build a pad of vegetation on a ledge near a waterfall.*

which local people in Asia carefully harvest and use as the principal ingredient of bird's nest soup, are built entirely out of this hardened saliva. Clutch sizes in the swiftlets are usually only one or two eggs, while Chimney and Vaux's Swifts and other species in this subfamily may lay up to four or five.

Often highly colonial, the apodine swifts build nests of plant material, including plant seed floss, and feathers glued into a felt-like consistency. The nests are situated in narrow, rocky crevices, often on inaccessible cliffs. Some species, particularly in Europe, have readily adapted to nesting in man-made structures (more or less colonially, depending on the number of sites available), while others build bulky colonial nests on the sides of buildings and bridges. Clutch sizes in this subfamily range from one to seven; most species lay two or three eggs.

Chick growth is slow. In some species, a dense coating of downy semi-plume feathers appears before the contour feathers.

Migration

Several swifts that breed in northern latitudes make transequatorial migrations during winter in response to declining insect populations. For example, the Chimney Swift winters in Peru, the Common Swift of Europe in South Africa, and the White-throated Needletail *(Hirundapus caudacutus)* of Siberia in Australia and New Zealand. At least two species from the Southern Hemisphere migrate

Worldwide Family Features

- 3½–9" (9–23 cm) aerial foragers.
- About 100 species in 19 genera worldwide; found on all continents except Antarctica; greatest diversity in tropics. 4 species in 3 genera breed in North America; found throughout continent south of boreal forests; plus 5 accidental species.
- Eat mostly insects but also ballooning spiders, captured in flight; some species specialize in localized swarming insects.
- Often colonial. Typically monogamous; extra-pair helpers in 2 species. Defend territory immediately around nest. Foraging often highly social; large flocks form prior to roosting, particularly during migration, when thousands may use same roost. Often highly migratory.
- Breed first at 2 years old, some species possibly at 1 year old.

- Nest varies by subfamily: pad of vegetation on damp ledge; half-saucer of twigs and saliva glued to wall, hollow tree, or chimney; or mass of plant fibers and feathers in rock crevice or building. Both parents build nest. May reuse nests.
- 1–7 white, long oval eggs (average 2–4 in many species, 1 or 2 in others). Both sexes incubate, for 19–24 days. Hatching nearly synchronous. Typically 1 brood per year.
- Altricial young naked at hatching. Fledge at 28 days to 8½ weeks. Both parents care for young.
- Adult annual survival 65–83%. Among oldest on record: 26 years (Alpine Swift, *Apus melba,* of Old World); 14 years (Chimney Swift).

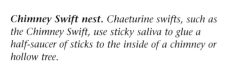

White-throated Swift nest. *The White-throated Swift, in the subfamily Apodinae, uses small amounts of plant material and feathers for its nest, which is typically placed inside a cliff crevice.*

Chimney Swift nest. *Chaeturine swifts, such as the Chimney Swift, use sticky saliva to glue a half-saucer of sticks to the inside of a chimney or hollow tree.*

to the Northern Hemisphere in the austral winter: the Ashy-tailed Swift *(Chaetura andrei)* within South America and the White-rumped Swift *(Apus caffer)* within Africa. Chimney and Black Swifts winter in South America, while Vaux's Swifts seem to go only as far as Central America. White-throated Swifts are migratory only in the northern part of their breeding range.

Prior to migration, Chimney and Vaux's Swifts aggregate at traditional stopover points to accumulate the fat reserves they need to fuel their long migratory flights. Observers at these locations are often treated to a nightly spectacle of several thousand swifts going to roost in a single large chimney.

Conservation

Although several species of swifts live in close association with humans and have been thoroughly studied, others, because of restricted ranges or inaccessible nest sites, are very poorly known. Populations of several species, including Chimney, White-throated, and Black Swifts, seem to be declining. Rangewide, Vaux's Swift numbers seem stable.

Unfortunately, the explanations for suspected population declines are mainly speculative. Chimney Swift declines may be due to recent closings of

household chimneys that were once used for nesting. Artificial chimneys and nest boxes, which have been erected by a local group in Texas and a number of private individuals for use as nest sites, offer great promise for reversing the decline of this species. While the apparent population decline in the Black Swift may simply be a product of inadequate information, the species is on the WatchList.

Accidental Species

The White-collared Swift *(Streptoprocne zonaris)* of Central and South America has occurred as a vagrant along the northern Gulf of Mexico, and in southeastern Florida, northwestern California, and even Michigan. Two Asian species, the Fork-tailed Swift *(Apus pacificus)* and the White-throated Needletail, have each occurred on several occasions on islands off Alaska, with most records in the western Aleutians between May and September.

The single North American record of a Common Swift also comes from the Bering Sea, although unusual swifts reported from elsewhere in North America may have been Common Swifts and certainly involved the genus *Apus.* Finally, the Antillean Palm-Swift *(Tachornis phoenicobia)* has occurred in Florida in the summer.

Charles T. Collins

Hummingbirds

The smallest of all birds, hummingbirds weigh only 0.1 to 0.3 ounces (2.5–8 gm). Their tiny bodies and long, slender bills, and the distinctive blur and hum of their hovering wings, set them apart from all other birds. Males have iridescent feathers, brightly colored throat patches (called gorgets), and flashy courtship and territorial displays. Females and immatures have plainer plumages. Hummingbird habitats range from tropical rain forests to montane meadows to deserts. The family Trochilidae is found only in the Americas, with the greatest number of species in the tropics. In North America, the greatest diversity of hummingbird species is found in the mountains of southeastern Arizona, the most likely place in the United States to see Mexican species such as the Plain-capped Starthroat *(Heliomaster constantii)* and the White-eared Hummingbird *(Hylocharis leucotis).*

Taxonomy

Hummingbirds are unlike any other family of birds. Their extremely small size, their long, slender bills, and their ability to feed while hovering for extended periods of time generally characterize and distinguish them. The family is subdivided into two groups: the hermits of the subfamily Phaethornithinae, a curve-billed tropical group that has not occurred in North America; and the typical hummingbirds (Trochilinae), to which all North American species belong.

Based on various morphological and genetic features, hummingbirds are placed in the order Apodiformes with the swifts. Both hummingbirds and swifts have small, weak feet and legs ("apod-" means "without feet"), but the two groups differ in many ways.

The hummingbird family is one of the largest in the Americas, with over 320

Trochilid diversity. Even though they are split into 12 genera, the 18 species of North American hummingbirds are all quite similar in basic structure. They range in size from the large Blue-throated Hummingbird (left) to the tiny Calliope Hummingbird (right), our smallest bird.

species in more than 100 genera. Most genera contain few species, and none dominates the family. For example, the two largest genera in North America contain only three species each; *Amazilia* is represented by the Violet-crowned *(A. violiceps),* Berylline *(A. beryllina),* and Buff-bellied *(A. yucatanensis)* Hummingbirds and *Selasphorus* by the Rufous *(S. rufus),* Allen's *(S. sasin),* and Broad-tailed *(S. platycercus)* Hummingbirds.

The remaining 12 species are distributed among 10 genera. Two North American species, the Magnificent Hummingbird *(Eugenes fulgens)* and the Calliope Hummingbird *(Stellula calliope),* are considered sufficiently distinct to warrant their own genera. Six other species, including the Plain-capped Starthroat and the Broad-billed Hummingbird *(Cynanthus latirostris),* are the sole North American representatives of genera that occur more widely in Latin America.

Hybridization is common in hummingbirds compared to other families, perhaps as a consequence of their mating system, and many combinations have been reported. Crosses are found both between very closely related species and between species in different genera. For example, Anna's *(Calypte anna)* and Costa's *(C. costae)* Hummingbirds hybridize with each other, and both have also hybridized with Blue-throated Hummingbirds *(Lampornis clemenciae).*

Adaptations to Lifestyle

Hummingbirds have many specializations for their lifestyle as the world's smallest birds. Among these is the ability to feed on nectar while hovering at flowers, a special adaptation made possible by the unique figure-eight motion of their wings. In addition to facilitating hovering flight, this unique wing movement allows hummingbirds to fly forward, backward, sideways, up, down, and even upside down for short distances.

Most of the time hummingbirds maintain their body temperatures at levels normal for birds (104–111° F/40–44° C). At times of food deprivation or cold temperatures, however, they can almost totally suspend body functions by entering a state of torpor. The birds employ this strategy when energy-stressed, such as during cold nights.

While in torpor, hummers can lower their body temperature to 55° F (13° C) or less to conserve energy reserves in their bodies. In this torpid state, the heart beats as little as 50 times per minute, contrasting sharply with the 250 beats per minute of nontorpid hummers at rest. The rate soars to an amazing 1,250 beats per minute while the birds fly and forage.

Food and Foraging

Hummingbirds were once considered to be exclusively nectivores, but the importance of invertebrates in their diet is now recognized. Invertebrate prey includes fruit flies, gnats, mosquitoes, thrips, aphids, spiders, maggots, caterpillars, ants, and insect eggs; hummers will eat almost any arthropod small enough to swallow. Hummingbirds take nectar from a wide variety of flowers and from artificial feeders.

Feeding on Nectar

Hummingbirds have long tongues, which they can extrude far beyond the tips of their bills. This ability enables them to reach the nectaries at the base of flowers. When feeding at flowers hummingbirds rapidly lap up nectar, taking several licks every second. Capillary action, a physical force that causes fluids to rise in small-diameter tubes, carries nectar up tiny grooves running the length of the tongue to the mouth, with no sucking required. The sharp observer at a feeder can sometimes see a bird swallowing constantly while its tongue is submerged in the nectar, and then the tongue being drawn back, whip-like, into the bird's beak.

Worldwide Family Features

- 2–8" (5–20 cm) nectar-feeders.
- About 325 species in 107 genera worldwide; widespread throughout Western Hemisphere. 18 species in 12 genera found in North America; occur from Alaska and southern Canada to Mexican border; plus 5 accidental species.
- Take nectar from flowers and sugar water from feeders; also eat tiny invertebrates.
- Mostly solitary; vigorously defend breeding and feeding territories. Do not form pairs; males breed with as many females as possible. In some tropical species, males compete for mates at leks. North American species mostly migratory; tropical species typically nonmigratory.
- Breed first at 1 year old; sometimes older.
- Nest usually cup-shaped and placed on top of thin branch in tree or bush; built by female from soft, downy materials bound together with spider webs.

Sometimes reused, often by different females.
- Usually 2 long elliptical to long subelliptical, white eggs per clutch; laid 1–3 days apart. Female incubates, for 14–23 (usually 13–19) days. Hatching asynchronous. Commonly 2 broods per year, rarely 3.
- Altricial young born mostly naked. Female does all care; likely regurgitates predigested nectar and insects directly into crops of young for first 5–7 days, undigested food thereafter. Just prior to fledging at 19–30 days (longer in a few species), young perch on edge of nest as female deposits arthropods on nest floor.
- Adult annual survival poorly known; only 30–45% in one study (Ruby-throated Hummingbird). Among oldest on record: more than 12 years (Broad-tailed and Blue-throated Hummingbirds).

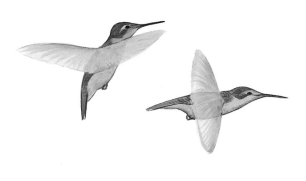

Hummingbird flight. One of the most remarkable features of hummingbirds is their ability to hover and even to fly backward. In hovering flight (left), the body is oriented vertically, and the wings nearly touch in front of and behind the body. In forward flight (right), the wingbeats are shallower and given in short bursts, with intervals of gliding; the birds can reach flying speeds of up to 60 miles per hour (96 km/h). Anna's Hummingbird is shown.

Despite these adaptations for nectar-feeding, hummingbirds are quick to consume any arthropod they encounter. Quickly flitting from flower to flower, they ingest both the fuel (nectar) required for such activity and the insects and spiders that help them meet protein, vitamin, and mineral requirements.

Nectar concentrations vary greatly among the wide variety of flowers hummingbirds visit, but they are typically quite low in sugar. Consequently, it is normally recommended that hummingbird feeders should contain a 20-percent sucrose solution (one part sugar to four parts water). Solutions with higher concentrations do not necessarily benefit hummingbirds, because nectar that is too concentrated cannot travel well through the grooves on the birds' tongues.

Although typically associated with red, tubular flowers, hummingbirds will feed at a variety of plants of different shapes and colors. Flowers that attract hummingbirds have evolved because of the birds' role as pollinator for many plants. By enticing hummingbirds for a meal, the plants further their own reproduction. At least one type of plant, jewelweed (genus *Impatiens*), can even move its pedicels to maximize the amount of pollen that is deposited on the bird's head during a visit to a flower.

Co-evolution, in which the plant and bird species simultaneously evolve characteristics, seems to have played a role in the development of bill and flower shapes. This is especially the case in some tropical species, where the most bizarre hummingbird forms occur. Many common features of hummingbird-pollinated flowers—including their thick walls, tubular shape, and lack of scent—are thought to have evolved to maximize

Hummingbird tongue. Hummingbirds possess a long, slender tongue that can be extended far beyond the tip of the bill. Shown in the diagram on the right is the hyoid apparatus, a forked structure made of a number of small bones and connected muscles that wraps around the back of the skull and controls the tongue extension. (Woodpeckers, with their extensible tongues, have a similar arrangement.) Hummingbirds' tongues have long grooves, and the outer half is divided (forked), although the split is virtually never visible. The Rufous Hummingbird is shown.

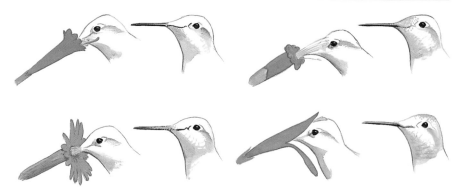

Hummingbirds and flowers. *Each flower species deposits pollen in a specific place on a humming-bird's head to increase the chance that birds visiting the same species of flower will cross-pollinate the flowers. Fuchsias (*Zauschneria *species) deposit pollen on the bird's throat (upper left); pinks (*Silene *species) deposit pollen on the bill (lower left); Ocotillos (*Fouquieria splendens) *deposit pollen on the forehead (upper right); Chuparosas (*Beloperone californica) *deposit pollen on the crown (lower right). Allen's Hummingbird is shown.*

the benefits to hummingbirds by discouraging insects and nectar-robbers that would compete for nectar.

Often hummingbirds will make daily rounds in which they visit patches of flowers and artificial feeders in a predictable sequence; this behavior is known as trap-lining.

Feeders are more attractive to hummingbirds if they are red. An attraction to red is not innate in hummers, but they are quick to associate a vibrant color with a food reward. It is not necessary to color the syrup, however. In fact, since some commercial hummingbird foods use dyes that are suspected carcinogens, it is probably safer to make "hummingbird nectar" out of plain table sugar.

Hawking Insects

Probably the most common method by which hummingbirds hunt insects is hawking, a technique similar to that more commonly seen in tyrant flycatchers. It involves perching on bare, open twigs and scanning for flying insects. When prey is spotted, the perched hummingbird sallies out and engulfs the unsuspecting insect.

Often the birds will hawk around an insect swarm. Ruby-throated Hummingbirds *(Archilochus colubris)* have been observed taking as many as 30 insects in one hovering frenzy. A single Rufous Hummingbird was observed to make a dozen sorties into a swarm of tiny aphids over a period of 20 minutes. In this feeding orgy, the bird appeared to make 130 individual attempts at capturing the hapless prey.

Gleaning

Hummingbirds also feed by gleaning, perhaps most effectively by searching the new leaves found at the very tips of tree branches for tiny moth caterpillars. During spring and fall migration, insect-infested trees can be alive with hummingbirds hovering and foraging on the bountiful supply of prey.

Several methods of gleaning are particularly useful during colder weather, when insect flights are suppressed and hawking is less effective. One method used by hummingbirds—and also employed by creepers and nuthatches—involves hovering near tree trunks and branches, picking insects and their eggs from the cracks and crevices of the bark. When multiple insects or an egg cluster are found at a single location, hummingbirds may cling to the plant and feed.

Gleaning can also involve leaf-rolling, a method often employed by wrens and

***Hummingbird foot.** A hummingbird's feet are small and weak, with very short legs but relatively long toes and long, curved toenails used for preening. The feet are useful only for perching and gripping; even simple maneuvers such as turning around on a perch are accomplished with the wings by hovering briefly. Their foot and leg structure make walking difficult, though the leg musculature allows females to stomp and compact the nest platform during construction in order to make it structurally sound. The Ruby-throated Hummingbird is shown.*

some ground-feeding wood-warblers. The hummingbird disturbs leaves lying on the forest floor with blasts of air from its hovering wings. As the leaves are "rolled over," the bird scours the undersides and curls for arthropods and their eggs. This behavior has been observed in Ruby-throated, Rufous, and Allen's Hummingbirds.

Perhaps the most intriguing type of gleaning that hummingbirds use is really a form of poaching, in which the birds take food resources from other foragers, especially sapsuckers and spiders.

Sapsuckers feed by making small holes in the bark of trees. Once opened, these "wells" weep sap, which contains nutrients used by the tree. The sapsucker taps that food source, not only for those nutrients but also for a wide range of insects that are attracted to it. Hummingbirds use this food supply when it is available. Anna's Hummingbirds use sapsucker wells in California woodlands, while Broad-tailed Hummingbirds feed in this way in riparian woods throughout the arid West. Rufous and Ruby-throated Hummingbirds will even trap-line feed at sapsucker wells.

Spiders, too, are victims of larcenous hummingbirds, which regularly glean small arthropods trapped in a spider's

web. The spiders themselves also constitute a major portion of the hummingbird diet. Not only will hummers eat small adult spiders, but they will gorge on their eggs and young. Hummers also pilfer spider webbing to build their nests. These behaviors are not without risk, as hummingbirds occasionally become entrapped in the sticky spider web and die.

Breeding

First-time breeding probably occurs for most hummingbirds in their first spring. Some late-hatching males, however, may not attain full breeding colors and vocalization skills in time to be effective breeders when only one year old; these individuals are probably the nonterritorial birds noted in some field studies.

Breeding Territories
Males and females both occupy territories, which may be far apart from those of the other sex. Hummingbirds do not form pair bonds; they come together only to mate. Males therefore set up territories where they will encounter many females, while females claim territories with good nesting sites.

In migratory species, males arrive at breeding sites well ahead of females and stake out a territory that they intend to defend. The main component of a male's breeding territory is an ample food resource that will attract females. Breeding territories can range in size from only a couple of hundred to several thousand square yards, depending on food availability and the species involved.

Male territories are occupied only as long as they attract females. If visits by females drop off sharply, the resident male is likely to abandon the territory and establish a new one elsewhere.

Male Breeding Behavior
The male's strategy is simple: He attempts to breed with any females that feed in his territory and makes vigorous and often violent attempts to evict trespassing males. Territorial males use

various strategies in the defense of territories. The first line of defense is vocalization. Under normal conditions, sharp scolding and warning notes are sufficient to warn off intruders. In the event that the interloper does not get the message with the first warning, the tempo is raised by the occupying male. Warnings are given more frequently, and their volume rises to a fevered pitch.

At the same time, the defending male often raises the iridescent feathers of the gorget and, in species such as Anna's and Costa's Hummingbirds, the crown. The male makes frequent use of these brilliant reflective feathers to literally "flash" rivals a warning. The "flashing" is often augmented with a vigorous side-to-side movement of the head.

If the intruder does not leave, the defender will physically assault him, sometimes even driving him to the ground and punctuating the attack with a series of diving aggression displays filled with loud wing sounds and vocalizations. Rarely is permanent physical injury inflicted in these outbursts, although disputes may result in the displacement of the original territory owner.

The focus on mating and the neglect of proper nutrition during breeding takes its toll on males, which lose as much as 20 percent of their body weight during the breeding season and become ragged and weakened as the summer winds down. Only after breeding activity declines do males regain the lost weight and the vigor required for migration. This lifestyle comes with a cost: Female Ruby-throated Hummingbirds live approximately 25 percent longer than males.

Female Breeding Behavior

Breeding females also are territorial, but for different reasons. A female does not necessarily locate her territory close to that of the male she mates with, since her site selection is determined largely by the presence of quality nesting sites, not rich food patches alone.

The most aggressive females will be able to defend their nesting sites against possible predators and food poachers. Ruby-throated Hummingbird females have been observed confronting and harassing tree-climbing snakes, hawks, crows, Blue Jays *(Cyanocitta cristata)*, Carolina Wrens *(Thryothorus ludovicianus)*, and Tufted Titmice *(Baeolophus bicolor)*.

These defending females also regularly "buzz" humans and pets that approach their nests. Such confrontations often consist of U-shaped dive displays accompanied by heightened vocalizations. In addition, females will chase away other hummingbirds seeking a meal in their nesting territory.

Vocalizations and Displays

In many hummingbird species, the male performs a spectacular courtship or territorial defense display. Often the display consists of a steep climb up into the air, followed by a rapid dive toward the ground. The display is often directed at a perched hummingbird—usually a female, but sometimes an intruding male. The climb-and-dive pattern is repeated several times and is followed by side-to-side arcing directly in front of the perched female.

The exact pattern traced in the air can sometimes help separate species. Male Black-chinned Hummingbirds *(Archilochus alexandri)* trace a large U-shaped pattern in the air, while male Anna's Hummingbirds make a steep J-shaped dive, often circling back up to the apex to repeat the display. Male Ruby-throated Hummingbirds are estimated to reach heights of 40 to 50 feet (12–15 m) in their climbs, while Costa's and Calliope Hummingbird males may reach 100 to 130 feet (30–40 m).

Both young males and females can use dive displays as expressions of aggression to other hummingbirds.

In most hummingbird species, male breeding displays can begin as a typical aggressive outburst but can quickly change to a pre-copulation presentation. The final sales pitch takes the form of a very close aerial shuttle display within inches of a perched female.

During this shuttle, the hovering male lowers his head slightly and extends his neck well forward, with the bill pointed directly at the female. His frenzied side-to-side arcing flight is accompanied by constant vocalizations and erection of the brilliant gorget feathers. In addition, the male repeatedly spreads and closes his tail as he shortens the arc and closes in on the female. The fanned and cupped tail may be used to direct and concentrate the wing sounds and vocalizations toward the female.

The female may appear mesmerized, often closing her eyes and becoming frozen in position during the shuttle dis-plays. If courtship is successful, the pair copulates, and the female returns to her territory to tend the nest and young alone.

Adult male Broad-tailed Hummingbirds have tapered outer primaries on their wings, which create a long trill as the air passes through them. This trill is heard whenever the male flies, thus advertising his presence to females, potential rivals, and visiting birders. As the breeding season progresses and the feathers become worn, their shape changes; by the time the males reach their wintering grounds the sound may be greatly reduced or absent.

Iridescence

One of the most striking features of hummingbirds is their iridescent plumage, especially the brightly colored head and gorget feathers of adult males. The structure of these feathers amplifies certain wavelengths of light and reflects them directly in front of the bird, so that a bright flash of color will be seen only when the bird is directly facing the observer, as shown in this Anna's Hummingbird (below).

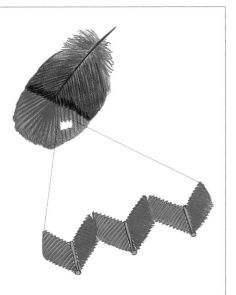

Iridescent colors are produced by a complex of feather features. The feather tip (right, top) is iridescent; here a section of three barbs has been cut out and enlarged (right, bottom) to show their structure in detail. The barbules, which attach to each side of the barb (see the Feathers section in the chapter Flight, Form, and Function), do not lie flat. Instead they are raised upward at an angle to create a 3-D structure with a V-shaped trough running along each barb. In addition to being angled up from the barb, the iridescent surface of each barbule is precisely positioned so that it reflects light directly toward an observer when the bird faces the observer.

Within the iridescent surface of the barbule are layers of microscopic discs, each filled with tiny air bubbles. Each disc has an optical thickness of half the wavelength of the reflected color. Light of the correct wavelength is "added together" and intensified, while other wavelengths mutually "interfere" and are canceled out. Different colors of iridescence in different species of hummingbirds are determined by minute differences in the thickness of the discs and the size of the air bubbles.

Broad-tailed Hummingbird at nest. *Female hummingbirds build nests out of soft, silky materials such as thistle down, bound together by spider webs and caterpillar silk. The nest is usually placed on top of a branch or other support and camouflaged with lichens or bits of bark stuck on the outside.*

Nesting

The female builds the nest on a branch or other supporting structure, constructing it of thistle and dandelion down, hair, feathers, rootlets, fine strips of bark, or any other soft, downy material, including lint and carpet fibers. Spider webs are often used to "glue" materials together, and lichen or small bits of bark are placed on the outside of the nest as camouflage. Nests of Ruby-throated, Rufous, and Calliope Hummingbirds are sometimes reused, but not always by the female that built the nest. Anna's Hummingbirds, in contrast, rarely reuse nests but will recycle materials from old nests when building new nests.

The nesting process can be severely disrupted by heavy and prolonged rains; many nest failures occur after such downpours. The naked young are particularly at risk when the brooding female is forced to leave the nest to forage. In some species, females renest after early nest failures, which can result in the hatching of subsequent broods very late in the season. Occasionally, during cold, wet weather, females apparently starve to death while brooding their young.

Migration

Most North American hummingbirds winter south of the U.S.–Mexico border. Within the last decade, however, extensive research by field ornithologists has documented individuals of a dozen species wintering in the United States. Most species are found in the Southwest, but wintering hummingbirds are becoming more common in the Southeast. The most common species to winter in the East is the Rufous Hummingbird, while smaller numbers of other species, including Black-chinned, Allen's, and Anna's Hummingbirds, are reported each year.

Most migrating hummingbird species travel overland. The vast majority of Ruby-throated Hummingbirds, however, apparently cross the Gulf of Mexico in nonstop flights each spring and fall. Such long-distance flights are possible because these birds can increase their fat reserves and double their weight in as little as seven to ten days before migrating.

Ruby-throated Hummingbirds are nocturnal migrants for most of their journey across the Gulf. Studies using Doppler radar show that in spring the birds depart the Yucatán Peninsula at dusk with huge flocks of passerines and arrive with them the next day along the Gulf coast of the United States.

Banding has demonstrated that migrating hummingbirds have great fidelity to their migration routes. Moreover, the banders' annual encounters with banded birds often occur on the exact same day each year.

The precise guidance system involved in hummingbird migration is not known.

Most of the bird's instructions are surely inherited, however, since young hummingbirds winter where their ancestors have wintered and travel the same routes—even though the young birds have never been there before. Hummingbirds also do not migrate as a group and therefore cannot learn migration routes from each other. When migrating, they are aggressive and unfriendly, yet they share a single migration strategy.

Long-distance vagrancy is relatively common in hummingbirds, even among fairly sedentary species such as Anna's Hummingbird. The Green Violet-ear *(Colibri thalassinus)*, a Central American species that does not breed north of Mexico, has been found at scattered locations across eastern North America, as far north as southern Canada. The widespread use of hummingbird feeders to attract birds no doubt accounts, at least in part, for the increasing number of extralimital hummingbird records.

Conservation

The population status of most hummingbird species is not well known, because their small size, rapid flight, and the soft vocalizations of some species make them difficult to study. Species that have small North American ranges are particularly poorly known, because they are not encountered frequently enough to estimate trends during large-scale monitoring efforts, such as the Breeding Bird Survey.

No hummingbird species is listed as endangered in Canada or the United States, but the WatchList includes the Rufous, Allen's, Buff-bellied, and Lucifer *(Calothorax lucifer)* Hummingbirds. Breeding Bird Survey data suggest that Rufous Hummingbirds are declining throughout much of their range, but the reasons for these declines are not known. The remaining species on the WatchList are viewed with concern, primarily because their small ranges make them vulnerable to habitat losses.

The continuing loss of habitat in Mexico and Central America is a major threat for species such as Magnificent and Berylline Hummingbirds found primarily south of the U.S.–Mexico border. These losses may also affect migratory species such as the Rufous Hummingbird by reducing wintering habitat.

Artificial feeders and the planting of garden flowers may support increased populations in urban and suburban areas, but may also increase mortality due to collisions with windows and encounters with house cats. The overall population effect of these artificial food sources is poorly studied for even the most common hummingbirds. It is known, however, that feeders do not cause migratory species to delay migration and thus cause birds to die, despite folklore to the contrary.

Accidental Species

The Bahama Woodstar *(Calliphlox evelynae)*, which breeds only in the Bahamas, has been reported several times in southeastern Florida, while the Green-breasted Mango *(Anthracothorax prevostii)* of Central and South America has been observed a few times in Texas, mostly in early fall, and once in North Carolina. Xantus's Hummingbird *(Hylocharis xantusii)* is normally found only in southern Baja California, but lone individuals have been found in winter in California and British Columbia.

One Mexican species, the Cinnamon Hummingbird *(Amazilia rutila)*, has been recorded once in southeastern Arizona in July and once in southern New Mexico in September. Another, the Bumblebee Hummingbird *(Atthis heloisa)*, has been found in southeastern Arizona twice. The records of the Cinnamon Hummingbird occurred in recent years and were well documented, but both Bumblebee Hummingbirds were collected (in July) in the 1890s, and some have questioned whether they actually came from Arizona at all.

Robert and Martha Sargent

Trogons

Trogons are medium-size arboreal birds, brightly colored with green or blue-violet above and red, orange, or yellow below. With their long tails, short legs, and short, heavy bills, trogons superficially resemble parrots, but trogons have much smaller bills. Among their unique features is the heterodactyl foot, with the inner front toe turned backward. Elegant Trogons *(Trogon elegans)* occupy moist canyons lined with oaks and sycamores; farther south they occur in thorn scrub and tropical broadleaf forests. Eared Trogons *(Euptilotis neoxenus)* prefer mountain slopes covered with pine-oak woodlands and coniferous forests. Both species are rare in North America, with ranges that barely extend north of the Mexican border.

Taxonomy

Trogons belong to the sole family within the order Trogoniformes and appear to have no close relatives among living birds. As with many tropical bird groups, biologists have conducted few studies of trogons, and large gaps remain in our knowledge of these birds.

Despite their broad distribution, trogons are a remarkably uniform group, with only minor, mostly geographic divisions within the family. The 25 New World and the 11 Asian species are currently assigned to the subfamily Trogoninae, and the three African species are placed in the subfamily Apalodermatinae. Some researchers believe that the five species of quetzals, in the genus *Pharomachrus*, and the closely related Eared Trogon should be separated from the other New World trogons into a distinct tribe or subfamily.

Food and Foraging

Trogons have short legs and weak feet, traits that limit their ability to walk and climb. They are difficult to detect when silent, as they sit virtually motionless, except for short aerial sallies after food.

They eat insects, fruit, and occasionally small vertebrates, usually snatching a prey item off vegetation and swallowing it whole at a nearby perch. Diet can vary seasonally; for example, madrone berries are the main winter fare of Eared Trogons in Arizona. Trogons feed their nestlings mostly insects, supplemented with fruit.

Trogon diversity. *Trogons are a very distinctive group of birds found in tropical forests around the globe. They are characterized by short, stout bills, long, square-tipped tails, and very brightly colored plumage. Although all American trogons are placed in the same subfamily, there are differences in structure, voice, and habits between the typical trogons (represented here by the Elegant Trogon, left) and the quetzals, with which the Eared Trogon (right) is usually grouped.*

Breeding

Both Elegant and Eared Trogons are monogamous, although it is not known whether pairs typically stay together for more than a year. In Arizona and northern Mexico, most Elegant Trogons nest in spring and early summer, but some active nests have been found in late September. Eared Trogons nest during the summer rainy season, which typically begins in July at the northern edge of their range. In both species, one-year-old males probably do not establish pair bonds or maintain territories.

Vocalizations and Displays

Elegant Trogons use variations on their characteristic croaking call to communicate with both mates and rivals. Both sexes (more typically males, although the calls are also given by unpaired females) give a series of loud, nasal *koink, kwa,* or *bwarr* calls to advertise in the breeding season, and both members of mated pairs produce a softer, hoarse version of this call during intimate interactions, such as "discussions" about nest-site selection, contact calls during exchange of nest duties, and calls to the young. Male Eared Trogons advertise with a series of shrill whistles, to which females respond with a nasal *squee* or *kweeeeeeee-chk.*

Elegant Trogons can be aggressive when defending a nest cavity or tending their young. They directly attack competitors and predators—including birds of prey, jays, Sulphur-bellied Flycatchers *(Myiodynastes luteiventris),* Northern Flickers *(Colaptes auratus),* and squirrels —by flying at and striking them with their feet or bills. If a human approaches fledglings too closely, adult trogons will place themselves between the human and their young, behavior inexperienced observers often mistake for curiosity.

Elegant Trogons signal alarm by slowly raising and lowering the tail. Both adults and young give a harsh *bekekekekekek* call when disturbed. Young birds are sluggish and quiet; hungry nestlings and recent fledglings have a soft *tu-u* call.

Eared Trogons are extremely sensitive to disturbance, particularly near the nest. They usually react to human intrusion by giving an emphatic *kweeeeeeee-chk* while raising the tail, or by delivering a harsh cackle—*chikikikik*—in flight.

Trogon foot. *Trogons have a toe arrangement unlike that of any other birds in the world. The basic arrangement of two toes in front and two in back is shared by several other families, but in those birds it is the outermost front toe that points backward. In trogons the inner front toe has rotated to the back. The Eared Trogon is shown.*

Trogon head and bill. *Trogons have rather short, stout bills suited for plucking berries and insects from vegetation. The Elegant Trogon is shown.*

Worldwide Family Features

- 9–16" (23–41 cm) arboreal birds. (Length excludes the long tail coverts of quetzals.)
- 39 species in 6 genera worldwide; pantropical, excluding Australasia. North America has 2 species in 2 genera; restricted to mountains of southern Arizona and New Mexico.
- Eat mostly insects and fruit plucked from vegetation during aerial sallies.
- Monogamous and territorial during breeding season; usually solitary at other times. Duration of pair bonds unknown. Generally nonmigratory, though most U.S. birds migrate short distances.
- Breed first at 1 or 2 years old.
- Nest in cavity, either pre-existing or excavated by both adults. Reuse nest sites.
- 2–4 white or pale blue, short subelliptical eggs. Both parents incubate, for 17–21 days. Hatching presumed to be asynchronous. 1 brood per year.
- Altricial young hatch naked and blind; quickly grow thick coat of down. Fledge at 15–31 days. Both parents feed.
- Adult annual survival and longevity little known.

Nests and Eggs

Elegant and Eared Trogons nest in tree cavities—usually an abandoned woodpecker hole in a dead tree trunk or limb between 8 and 70 feet (2.5–21 m) above the ground—that they often enlarge. They lay their eggs on a bed of accumulated debris.

Elegant Trogon eggs are white, and Eared Trogon eggs are pale blue, like those of quetzals. Both parents begin incubating after the full clutch is laid; incubation continues for 17 to 19 days in these two species. The nestling period lasts 17 to 23 days in Elegant Trogons and probably 24 to 30 days in Eared Trogons. Fledglings stay with one or both parents at least for the first few weeks after independence.

Trogon nest defense. The Elegant Trogon nests in tree cavities; in Arizona these cavities are typically high in sycamore trees. Despite their normally sedate manner, trogons are quite aggressive in defense of their nests and will dive at any threatening intruder, in this case a Mexican Jay (Aphelocoma ultramarina) that is too close to the nest hole.

Movements

Most trogons are sedentary, although Elegant Trogons vacate most of their breeding range in Arizona for the winter. It is unlikely that they move very far; the species is resident in northern Sonora, Mexico, and a few individuals are present year-round in low-elevation drainages on the Arizona–Sonora border.

Eared Trogons are resident throughout their range, although, like quetzals, they often descend to lower elevations in winter. This species first appeared in Arizona in 1977, and a second conspicuous influx followed in 1991. Presumably these arrivals were caused by rare dispersal events, due either to unusually successful reproduction and overwinter survival in preceding seasons or to habitat destruction in Mexico.

Conservation

Although the Elegant Trogon is rare north of Mexico, its broad range and habitat make it one of the most common of all trogons. Numbers in the United States have fluctuated, impacted in the past by human activities such as logging, subsistence hunting, and scientific collecting, as well as by natural factors such as drought, which can reduce populations of large insects that are vital to the species' reproduction. With the exception of growing recreational use, human activities in southeastern Arizona currently present little immediate threat.

The Eared Trogon's range is restricted to the Sierra Madre Occidental of Mexico, and the bird is listed as endangered by the IUCN–The World Conservation Union. At the extreme northern limit of its range in southern Arizona, the Eared Trogon is very rare.

The primary threats to this species are logging of native forests and other related activities. In addition, the Tarahumara people of southern Chihuahua and adjacent states hunt both adults and nestlings for food. Plans to dramatically increase tourism in the Copper Canyon region of Mexico (in southern Chihuahua and neighboring states) threaten to increase disturbance of Eared Trogons. However, tourism could provide an economic incentive to preserve large tracts of wilderness needed not only by Eared Trogons, but also by Thick-billed Parrots (Rhynchopsitta pachyrhyncha) and other Sierra Madrean endemics.

Sheri L. Williamson

Hoopoe

The Eurasian Hoopoe *(Upupa epops)* is a rather bizarre-looking, medium-size bird, with a broad, black-tipped crest, a long, decurved bill, and prominent wing markings that are conspicuous and unmistakable in flight. The black-and-white wing markings contrast with a peculiar brownish-pink body plumage and are shown off during a variety of displays directed at other members of the species. When excited, hoopoes fan their crests and spread their wings, making the birds look remarkably large-headed and dramatically displaying their colors. Hoopoe flight is erratic, suggesting that of a large butterfly. The common name derives from the male's call—*hoop-hoop-hoop*—a pure tone similar to the sound made by blowing across a bottle opening.

The Eurasian Hoopoe is currently placed in its own family in the order Upupiformes, which also includes several other small groups such as the woodhoopoes (family Phoeniculidae) of Africa. Traditionally, this order was subsumed within the Coraciiformes, alongside the kingfishers and their close relatives, in part because all these birds have a syndactyl toe arrangement. Some authorities consider certain African populations of the Eurasian Hoopoe to be a separate species.

Normally, hoopoes are found in open, warm, arid habitats with exposed rock outcrops and bare soil. They are ground foragers, digging deep in the soil and in crevices for invertebrates, especially butterfly and beetle larvae and crickets. Birds are considered tame in areas where they are not hunted, but elusive and shy where they have need to fear humans.

The species is migratory in the northern parts of its range in Europe and Siberia, and frequently overshoots its breeding grounds during spring migration in western Europe. In North America, there is a single fall record from western Alaska.

John B. Dunning, Jr.

Eurasian Hoopoe. *The distinctive Eurasian Hoopoe is the only species in its family. It is extremely rare in North America, with only one record, from the Yukon Delta in western Alaska.*

Worldwide Family Features

- 10–11" (26–28 cm) ground-feeding bird of open, arid country.
- 1 species worldwide; occurs throughout Eurasia and Africa; winters in southern Asia, Africa. Accidental in Alaska.
- Eats large insects, especially larvae and pupae, and other arthropods; detects prey by probing long bill into soil, litter, animal droppings.
- Territorial and monogamous; rarely forms polygynous trios. Pair bonds seasonal. Solitary over much of year. During migration, occurs in small flocks.
- Breeds first probably at 1 year old.

- Nests in natural cavity, dirt embankment, building, or nest box. Cavity may be unlined or lined with grass or leaves. Both sexes excavate or clean out cavity.
- 4–12 (usually 7–8) elliptical eggs; gray, yellow, or olive, unmarked but with prominent pores. Female incubates, for 14–20 days. Hatching asynchronous. 1 or 2 broods per year.
- Altricial young sparsely covered with long, fluffy down at hatch. Fledge at 26–29 days. Female does most brooding; both parents feed.
- Little information on survival or longevity.

Kingfishers

Family Alcedinidae
Order Coraciiformes

Small to medium-size birds, kingfishers are thickset and have short necks and tails, small feet, and large heads with long, strong bills. Worldwide, they display an array of colors and patterns. Most species are boldly marked with blues or greens above and a mixture of orange, red, and white below; many species have a pale collar. The larger American species have a shaggy crest on the back of the head. The outer and middle front toes are partially joined, a characteristic known as syndactyly. North American kingfishers usually live near perennial waters.

Taxonomy

The Alcedinidae is divided into two or three subfamilies, which some experts consider to be families in their own right. The family occurs primarily in the Old World and Australasia, with the greatest diversity in New Guinea.

The "fishing" kingfishers in the subfamily Alcedininae, distributed throughout much of the Old World, are small, have narrow, sharp-pointed bills, and are always found near water. The more diverse "forest" kingfishers of the Daceloninae (sometimes called the family Halcyonidae), which occur mainly in Australasia, are typically larger and have broader and flatter bills; they often live far from water.

The third subfamily, the Cerylinae, includes all six New World species and often is combined with the Alcedininae, although recent evidence suggests that its

members may be more closely related to the Daceloninae. Cerylinae species frequent freshwater riparian habitats, coastal estuaries, and lakes; three are found in North America. The Belted Kingfisher *(Ceryle alcyon)* occurs throughout most of the continent; the Ringed Kingfisher *(C. torquata)* and Green Kingfisher *(Chloroceryle americana)* are widespread in the neotropics but barely extend north into the United States.

Food and Foraging

In the Americas, kingfishers typically are associated with perennial streams, rivers, freshwater ponds, and lakes; they hunt by sight and require clear water to find prey. Kingfishers mainly eat small fish, but they also consume small crustaceans, aquatic insects, reptiles, and amphibians. New World kingfishers typically sit on an exposed perch overhanging water. From

Alcedinid diversity. *The three North American kingfishers, all in the subfamily Cerylinae, are found near water, where they catch fish by plunge-diving. Worldwide, however, kingfishers are a diverse group with a wide range of foraging habits; many species typically occur far from water and do not eat fish. The Green Kingfisher is shown.*

Belted Kingfisher foraging. *All three North American kingfishers feed almost exclusively on small fish that they capture underwater. The birds watch from a prominent perch or hover over open water before plunging head-first after prey.*

the perch a bird surveys the area for food, plunges head-first into the water to capture it, then flies back to kill and consume its prey. Some larger species, such as the Belted Kingfisher, also hover 20 to 30 feet (6–9 m) above the water, then plunge to capture prey in a spearing dive.

Although American kingfishers may appear to have stereotypical feeding behaviors, foraging within the whole family is quite variable. The Laughing Kookaburra *(Dacelo novaeguineae)* of Australia consumes lizards, mice, rats, and even venomous snakes. Other Old World species include a kingfisher that feeds at night, another that eats land snails, and one that digs for invertebrates in the forest floor. In North America, the Green Kingfisher has been recorded up to a mile from water, hunting insects when rivers and streams are muddied during torrential storms.

Breeding

During courtship, the male kingfisher conducts aerial pursuits of the female. The pursuits are followed by courtship feeding in which the female sits upright with her beak in the air, wings drooped and quivering, and gives a begging call. After the male presents her with a fish, the two mate.

Most New World kingfishers nest in burrows in exposed vertical banks along watercourses, in roots of upturned trees, or even in holes in a wall or bridge. Ringed Kingfishers sometimes nest in vertical

Kingfisher foot. The feet of kingfishers are weak and suited only for perching. The outer and middle toes on each foot are partly joined. The Belted Kingfisher is shown.

Kingfisher head and bill. The North American kingfisher species, such as this Ringed Kingfisher, have a large head and a long, heavy bill used for capturing fish underwater after a plunge-dive.

Worldwide Family Features

- 4–18" (10–45 cm) birds of forest, scrub, and aquatic habitats.
- 95 species in 17 genera worldwide; absent only from polar regions and some oceanic islands. 3 species in 2 genera occur in North America; 1 species found throughout most of continent, the other 2 near U.S.–Mexico border.
- Eat diversity of vertebrate and invertebrate prey. Typically feed from perches, dropping onto prey spotted from above. Many species specialize in catching fish by plunge-diving.
- Defend territories year-round. Monogamous; pair for life; establish and maintain pair bond through display and active defense. Most species solitary when not breeding. A few species migrate.

- Breed first typically at 1 year old.
- Nest in tree holes, termite mounds, and unlined burrows in banks of rivers and lakes. Both sexes excavate nest, which can be reused from year to year.
- Typically 2–8 white, elliptical eggs; incubated by both parents, for 14–28 days. Hatching asynchronous. 1 or 2 broods per year.
- Altricial young naked at hatch. Both parents feed regurgitant initially, then fish and other prey. Fledge within 22–40 days.
- Survival and longevity for most species poorly known. Adult annual survival 25–55%. Among oldest on record: 15 years, 5 months (Common Kingfisher, *Alcedo atthis*, of Old World).

Kingfisher at burrow nest.
Kingfishers excavate a long tunnel into a vertical bank of dirt or sand. At the end of the tunnel is a slightly enlarged nest chamber in which the eggs are laid directly on the dirt floor. The Belted Kingfisher is shown.

banks up to a mile (1.6 km) from water. Both sexes build the burrow, chiseling into a dirt bank and creating a tunnel up to 2 inches (5 cm) wide and 3 to 10 feet (1–3 m) deep, depending on the bird's size. The tunnel, which may take up to a week to complete, is generally horizontal or angled upward and ends in a rounded nest chamber. Green Kingfishers conceal their burrow entrances behind overhanging vegetation.

No nesting materials are used within the chamber. Kingfishers ignore nest sanitation, and soon after the young hatch, the nest chamber is littered with prey remains, food remnants, and excrement. Most temperate and some tropical species attempt two nestings each year, but Belted and Ringed Kingfishers rarely attempt a second brood.

Both sexes incubate, switching duties twice each day, with the male typically incubating in the afternoon while the female feeds, and the female incubating at night. Both parents feed the altricial young regurgitant until they are large enough to consume whole prey.

Belted Kingfishers teach their young to fish by dropping dead prey into the water for retrieval. Young Green Kingfishers have been observed playing with sticks, repeatedly dropping them into the water and then retrieving them; these training sessions can be dangerous, and young occasionally drown before they become proficient hunters. The parents feed the young for up to three weeks after fledging but then force the young from their natal area.

Movements

Most kingfishers are permanent residents in the area where they breed. The Belted Kingfisher is the only North American species that regularly migrates and is one of only 11 kingfisher species worldwide that shows seasonal movements. It will winter as far north as it can feed in open water, but many individuals migrate south to seek warmer climates and more abundant prey. Migrating by day, the birds move at low altitude along rivers, lakeshores, and coastlines to suitable winter habitat.

Conservation

Kingfishers are highly specialized and are threatened by habitat alteration and nest disturbance; in particular, these birds, which nest in eroding banks, are deprived of nesting sites as streams are "controlled." Breeding Bird Survey data show an average annual population decline of almost 2 percent for the Belted Kingfisher.

Populations of Ringed and Green Kingfishers, however, appear to be stable; these birds have expanded their ranges in Texas and Arizona, respectively. Human population growth, alteration of habitat, and shooting are the main threats to kingfisher populations worldwide.

David J. Krueper

Woodpeckers and Allies

Family Picidae
Order Piciformes

Woodpeckers are arboreal birds known for creeping up tree trunks and drilling into the wood to find food and excavate nest holes. They have a vertical posture, rounded wings, a chisel-shaped bill, and a characteristic undulating flight pattern. Their strongly contrasting colors—mostly black and white, brown and black, or green and white—are augmented by varying amounts of red or yellow highlights. Woodpeckers live primarily in wooded areas, but worldwide there are species that occur in tundra, deserts, and treeless grasslands. Several species have adapted well to human activities and live in suburban settings, where they visit feeders in winter.

Taxonomy

The family Picidae is one of seven families in the order Piciformes and the only one represented in North America. The other families in this order—the jacamars (Galbulidae), the puffbirds (Bucconidae), and the New World barbets and toucans (Ramphastidae) of Central and South America; and the honeyguides (Indicatoridae) and Old World barbets (Megalaimidae and Lybiidae) of Africa and Asia—are thought to be related to woodpeckers because of similarities in the breastbone, the palate, and the arrangement of foot tendons. Taxonomists disagree about whether all of these families belong in the same order, and some suggest that jacamars and puffbirds should be separated in the order Galbuliformes.

The Picidae includes three subfamilies: Jynginae (wrynecks) has a single tribe and a single genus that is restricted to the Old World. Picumninae (piculets) contains two tribes and three genera that are

found mostly in the tropics of the New and Old Worlds. The Picinae (woodpeckers) is most widespread—occurring throughout the Americas, Europe, Africa, and Asia—and comprises six tribes and 24 genera. Only the Picinae occurs regularly in North America.

Four Picinae tribes are found in North America. The Campephilini is a group of large woodpeckers boldly marked with patches of black, white, and red feathers; the Pileated Woodpecker *(Dryocopus pileatus)* is the only species found north of Mexico. Members of the Colaptini are predominantly brown or green woodpeckers, represented in North America by the flickers, which are largely brown with brightly colored underwings.

The Melanerpini is a varied group of species, including the Acorn *(Melanerpes formicivorus)* and Red-bellied Woodpeckers *(M. carolinus)* and the sapsuckers. As a group these birds are medium-size and at first glance more colorful than other woodpeckers.

Picid diversity. *North American woodpeckers represent four tribes (shown here from left to right): the small to medium-size, black-and-white Campetherini (represented here by the Downy Woodpecker); the medium-size and colorful Melanerpini (Red-bellied Woodpecker); the larger, brown or green Colaptini (Gilded Flicker); and the large, boldly marked Campephilini (Pileated Woodpecker).*

Finally, members of the Campetherini are small to medium-size woodpeckers that are mostly white below and black above, often with considerable white barring. Typical species include the Downy *(Picoides pubescens)*, Ladder-backed *(P. scalaris)*, and Three-toed *(P. tridactylus)* Woodpeckers, but the more strikingly plumaged White-headed Woodpecker *(P. albolarvatus)* is also in this group.

The number of species within the family increases and decreases based on evolving scientific evidence and interpretations. In the 1980s, the Yellow-bellied Sapsucker *(Sphyrapicus varius)* was separated into three species. The two western forms—the Red-breasted Sapsucker *(S. ruber)* and the Red-naped Sapsucker *(S. nuchalis)*—were recognized as distinct species based on their different appearance, limited hybridization, and genetic dissimilarities.

Three North American forms of flicker were lumped into a single species in 1973, based on hybridization between forms where they overlap. More recently, the Gilded Flicker *(Colaptes chrysoides)* was re-split from the Northern Flicker *(C. auratus)* complex because it was recog-

nized that the two species interbreed only rarely and select different habitats where their ranges overlap. The "Red-shafted" and "Yellow-shafted" forms of the Northern Flicker are still combined as one species because they interbreed extensively where their ranges overlap.

For several decades the Arizona Woodpecker *(Picoides arizonae)* was lumped with Strickland's Woodpecker *(P. stricklandi)* of southern Mexico in spite of considerable morphological and habitat differences between the two forms. The combined form was known as either "Strickland's" or the "Brown-backed Woodpecker." The two taxa are now considered separate species.

Variation

Many woodpecker species are sexually dimorphic, but many of the differences involve subtle structural features, like bill length and overall body size; only sexually dichromatic species are easy to distinguish in the field. Color differences between the sexes usually involve differences in head pattern; for example, the males of many species have a red head

---

Worldwide Family Features

- 5–22" (13–55 cm) arboreal birds.
- About 217 species in 28 genera worldwide; found throughout Americas, Eurasia, and Africa, with greatest number of species in New World tropics. North America has 22 breeding species in 5 genera; plus 1 species that is probably extinct and 2 accidental species; family occurs throughout most of continent, with greatest number of species in the northern Sierra Nevada, where ranges of 11 species overlap.
- Eat mainly insects; some species also eat fruit and, in winter, seeds; sapsuckers also eat sap.
- Most species territorial. Largely monogamous; many species have long-term pair bonds; some maintain only seasonal pair bonds. Some species practice cooperative breeding and polygyny. Usually solitary during nonbreeding season. Some species migrate; many do not.

- Breed first at 1 year old.
- Nest is cavity in living or dead tree, usually lined with fresh wood chips. Both sexes build nest. Most excavate new cavity each year.
- 3–12 (usually 4–6) white, elliptical to subelliptical eggs. Both parents incubate, male often at night. Hatching synchronous, after 9–19 days. 1 or 2, rarely 3, broods per year.
- Altricial young are blind and naked at birth. Fledge at 18–30 days. Both sexes care for young; sometimes parents divide brood during foraging. Fledglings may remain with parents until fall, even if not dependent on them; in species that are cooperative breeders, young can remain as helpers for years.
- Adult annual survival estimated at 50–90%. Among oldest on record: at least 16 years (Acorn Woodpecker, Red-cockaded Woodpecker).

patch, while the females do not. In species such as the Ladder-backed Woodpecker the difference is obvious. In contrast, birders trying to determine the sex of a Red-cockaded Woodpecker *(Picoides borealis)* may have trouble seeing the tiny red "cockade" on either side of the male's crown.

The most dramatic sexual differences in any North American woodpecker are found in Williamson's Sapsuckers *(Sphyrapicus thyroideus)*. Females look like the immatures of other sapsucker species; at one time males and females were thought to be separate species.

Sometimes it is possible to determine the sex of a species by observing its feeding habits. Male and female Downy Woodpeckers, whose only structural difference is tongue length, partition resources by concentrating their foraging on different species of trees within their habitat and by using different foraging methods, males more often pecking and females probing. In most parts of its range, the male Red-cockaded Woodpecker feeds high in trees, while the female forages on tree trunks. Male and female Ladder-backed Woodpeckers have the reverse feeding pattern.

Some species, such as the Acorn and Pileated Woodpeckers, vary significantly in size depending on where the birds live, with larger individuals found in more northerly populations. Acorn Woodpeckers also have noticeable but subtle geographic plumage variations. A casual observer would not notice most of this variability, which requires extensive experience or measurements of captured birds to be detected.

Common names often do not reflect obvious field characteristics, in part because birds were named from dead specimens. Birders looking for a cockade on a male Red-cockaded Woodpecker will likely be disappointed. The cockades, which are absent in females, consist of a small red patch on either side of the crown, sometimes with only a few feathers each; they are normally visible only when the bird is bathing or during

Red-breasted Sapsucker foraging. Different woodpecker species have characteristic ways of getting food. Among the most unusual foraging methods is the drilling of rows of "wells" by sapsuckers. The wells leave distinctive scars that serve as a record of a birds' presence for many years.

aggressive encounters when its head feathers are raised. Fledgling males have a variable amount of red in the center of the crown, but this is not the cockade.

The "red" belly of Red-bellied Woodpeckers is difficult to see unless you are close and the belly feathers are ruffled. In the field Downy Woodpeckers do not look soft or downy, nor do Hairy Woodpeckers *(Picoides villosus)* look shaggy.

Habitats

Woodpeckers live mainly in woodlands of all types. Within this broad category, certain species have habitat preferences. For example, burned forests attract Red-headed *(Melanerpes erythrocephalus)*, Lewis's *(M. lewis)*, and Three-toed Woodpeckers, probably because of the insects that invade the damaged trees.

The Northern Flicker often frequents areas around human habitation, where it forages on open ground and drums on artificial surfaces. Sapsuckers in arid regions tend to nest near willows and aspens, feeding in the willows and nesting in the aspens. In the deserts of the southwestern

United States, where there are few trees, Ladder-backed and Gila *(Melanerpes uropygialis)* Woodpeckers feed and nest on tall cacti. The Red-cockaded Woodpecker lives only in old pine savannas.

Food and Foraging

While woodpeckers are primarily insectivorous, some species (for example, flickers) also eat fruit and nuts during the nonbreeding season. Several nonmigrants add seeds to their winter diet, and fledglings of some species eat fruit. Both Gila Woodpeckers and Gilded Flickers will eat great mouthfuls of Saguaro pollen when the cacti are in bloom.

Acorn Woodpecker granary. The Acorn Woodpecker has a unique social system involving small groups that breed cooperatively and store acorns in holes they excavate in trees or posts.

Woodpeckers forage for invertebrates in bark and wood crevices, and excavate them from wood, nuts, and occasionally crops such as corn. They locate prey on bark and in crevices by searching visually and by probing with the tongue. They find prey within wood by listening. Small species, such as the Downy Woodpecker, will also feed on less sturdy uprights, such as cattail leaves in marshes or the stalks of annual plants.

Some woodpeckers use more varied foraging techniques. Sapsuckers mainly eat the inner bark of trees, lap sap that oozes from small wells that the birds drill in a tree trunk, eat invertebrates trapped in the sap produced at these "sapsucker wells," and also flycatch invertebrates. Young sapsuckers learn to make wells by watching adults. There are also reports of Red-headed Woodpeckers wounding trees and eating the sap and inner bark. Other animals feed at sapsucker wells, including mammals, insects, other woodpeckers, orioles, hummingbirds, and warblers.

During the winter, nonmigratory species, such as the Downy Woodpecker, often join mixed-species feeding flocks that move through their territory, leaving the flock at the edge of the territory.

Nine species of North American woodpeckers cache food to eat in winter, storing insects and nuts in holes, crevices, cracks, and bark for future consumption.

The Downy, Hairy, Gila, and Golden-fronted *(Melanerpes aurifrons)* Woodpeckers and the Yellow-bellied Sapsucker sometimes cache food, while the Acorn, Lewis's, Red-headed, and Red-bellied Woodpeckers do so regularly. Sometimes woodpeckers will lodge hard food items into crevices in order to pound them and break them open; this behavior may have been the evolutionary precursor to caching.

When woodpeckers cache food, acorns are the most commonly cached item, although other locally abundant nuts such as pinyon pine nuts, beechnuts, almonds, and pecans are also harvested. With the exception of the Acorn Woodpecker, cachers typically remove the seed's hull and break the nut on a hard surface before storing it.

The Acorn Woodpecker is the only species that regularly drills holes for food storage, caching acorns in trees, telephone poles, or fence posts. These sites are referred to as granaries. The Acorn Woodpecker is a communal, cooperative breeder, with groups of birds filling, using, and defending granaries. The granaries can be quite substantial: One study reported Acorn Woodpeckers storing more than 60,000 acorns in a single granary.

Adaptations to Lifestyle

The woodpecker body is well adapted to the birds' foraging and nesting habits, which require clinging to and hammering into hard vertical surfaces. Deviations from the standard upright body plan reflect deviations from the traditional woodpecker lifestyle.

Woodpeckers use their entire body when excavating in wood, in contrast to drumming (discussed below), which involves mainly the head and neck muscles. The brain case is enlarged, and the frontal bones are more folded at the base of the bill to act as shock absorbers; muscles behind the bill provide a similar advantage.

The nostrils, which are more protected in those species that excavate heavily—such as Downy, Hairy, and Pileated Woodpeckers—are feathered and sometimes narrowed or hidden below a ridge to keep out sawdust. As the birds excavate, they close their eyes just before the bill hits the wood.

Woodpecker tail. A woodpecker uses its tail as a brace while the bird clings to a tree. The central tail feathers (shown in side view at the left) are curved and stiffened with rigid points that flex when the tail is pressed against the trunk (shown at right). Even the molt pattern of the tail is adapted to maintain the climbing function: The all-important central feathers are not dropped until all the other feathers have grown to full length; then the outer feathers can support the bird during climbing while the central feathers regrow. The Downy Woodpecker is shown.

Tail and Feet

A woodpecker uses its tail for support as it moves up and down tree trunks and as a brace as it forages for food or excavates a nest cavity. The tail feathers are stiff and supported by large muscles that allow fine manipulation. The two central feathers are pointed and reinforced by longitudinal ridges; they have barbs that curve inward toward the tree, creating a concave structure that increases the tail's strength. These critical central feathers normally are not molted until all the other new tail feathers have grown in—a molt pattern that is very unusual. The more arboreal the species, the more sharply curved the tail.

Piculets have a horizontal body plan. They forage by pecking or hammering on, and gleaning from, small branches, twigs, and vines, and do not use their fan-shaped tails as props.

Most terrestrial birds have anisodactyl feet, with three toes facing forward and one toe facing backward. In contrast,

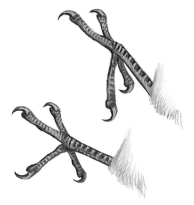

Woodpecker foot. Woodpeckers have zygodactyl feet, with two toes forward and two back (top), but in many instances as a bird is climbing the outer rear toe rotates to the side in an ectropodactyl arrangement (bottom). Black-backed and Three-toed Woodpeckers have only three toes; the inner rear toe is missing, and the outer rear toe always points backward, never rotating as in other woodpeckers. The Red-breasted Sapsucker is shown.

Woodpecker climbing motions. In this series of illustrations a Red-headed Woodpecker takes one "step" up a tree. First the body leans in toward the trunk, taking pressure off the tail. Then a strong push with both legs together moves the body up in a vertical "jump," and the legs quickly swing up to grip the trunk again as the body settles back to rest on the tail.

woodpeckers have zygodactyl feet, generally with two forward-facing and two rear-facing toes. Zygodactyl feet are found throughout the order Piciformes but also occur in some other groups, such as parrots and cuckoos. In woodpeckers, the two rear-facing toes help increase support for clinging to vertical surfaces; sometimes one toe extends laterally (ectropodactyl) as the bird moves up a tree.

The Three-toed and Black-backed *(Picoides arcticus)* Woodpeckers are the only North American land birds with three toes instead of the usual four. In these species, the true hind toe (the inner rear toe in a zygodactyl arrangement) is absent and the remaining rear toe always points backward. Some large woodpecker species, such as the Pileated Woodpecker, have feet that splay out from the body so that the tarsus touches the tree, allowing the heel to act as another support.

A woodpecker's feet and tail work together to support it and propel it up tree trunks. With the feet hopping together and the tail propping the bird during propulsion, woodpeckers have a jerky gait as they ascend a tree.

Bill

A woodpecker's bill is chisel-shaped and sturdy for excavating in wood. (A pointed bill would tend to bind in the wood.) Differences in bill shape correspond with the hardness of the wood a

species excavates and the hammering force it uses. Striking a hard surface with a stiff, curved point would break the point. Species that excavate less during foraging, such as the Northern Flicker, have slightly curved bills; the Pileated Woodpecker, which forages primarily by excavating hard wood, has a stouter, straighter bill.

Tongue

Woodpecker tongues are barbed, sticky, and extremely long for the bird's head size, adaptations that reduce the amount of excavation required for foraging. In some species, the tongue can extend as far as 5 inches (13 cm) out of the bill.

Tongue length correlates with foraging behavior: Species such as the Downy Woodpecker that feed primarily through excavating wood have shorter tongues relative to their body size; those that probe crevices and surface-feed, such as the Northern Flicker, have relatively longer tongues.

In all birds, the tongue contains a set of bones, known collectively as the hyoid apparatus, that provides support, structure, and an attachment point for muscles that allow the birds to move their tongues and manipulate food. The hyoid apparatus ends in two elongated "horns" that sweep off the back of the tongue and wrap under the jaw bone and around the skull in connective tissue sheaths.

Woodpecker heads and bills. All woodpeckers have a strong, straight, chisel-shaped bill, well shown by the Pileated Woodpecker (left). Subtle variations in bill shape are related to foraging habits. Species such as the Pileated Woodpecker, which pound vigorously to excavate holes, have stronger, chisel-shaped bills and more prominent nasal tufts to protect the nostrils from wood chips. The other extreme is represented by the Northern Flicker (right), which forages more by probing and exploring crevices and thus has a more pointed and slightly curved bill, with reduced nasal tufts.

When a bird wants to stick its tongue out, the hyoid horns slide forward in their sheathing, pushing the rest of the hyoid apparatus and thus the whole tongue forward. In woodpeckers extreme tongue extension is possible because of exceptionally long hyoid horns, which wrap completely around the skull and are anchored near the nostril or around the eye, depending on the species.

Woodpecker tongue and hyoid bone. The long, extensible tongue of woodpeckers, like that of hummingbirds, is made possible by the greatly elongated hyoid apparatus, a set of bones and muscles that controls tongue movements. In the Hairy Woodpecker (shown here), this hyoid apparatus wraps around the entire skull and coils around the right eye. When extended, the tongue can reach up to 5 inches (13 cm) in some species. The tip of the tongue is shaped differently in different species but is usually barbed and sticky to help the birds capture insect prey from deep inside wood crevices and tunnels.

Vocalizations, Drumming, and Displays

All woodpeckers use simple calls and drumming to communicate. There are different calls to express alarm, to attract or keep contact with a mate, and to declare a territory, and the birds produce particular calls during agonistic encounters, such as territory defense and mate defense. Nestlings make buzzing calls that reach peak intensity when a parent arrives at a cavity entrance with food.

There are three circumstances under which woodpeckers make noise by beating on wood or other surfaces: cavity excavation, foraging, and drumming. Of these, only drumming is a form of communication. Woodpeckers drum to attract a mate or to declare a territory.

Drumming normally is used to communicate over long distances, so it is done on a surface with good acoustic properties, such as hollow branches or trunks (or stove pipes and rain gutters). Drumming is also fast, while excavation and foraging are slow and deliberate, as well as relatively quiet. Consequently, drumming is readily distinguishable, particularly when the listener is near the bird in question.

Drumming is a seasonal activity, and unlike singing in most passerines, both male and female woodpeckers drum. The Red-cockaded Woodpecker drums more quietly than other species, probably to communicate within its group.

It is often difficult to identify a species based on its drumming pattern. This is due to many factors, including distance to the drummer, the drumming substrate, and the similarity of drumming patterns among species. A study of 11 woodpecker species in California found that the Hairy, Downy, Nuttall's *(Picoides nuttallii),* and Ladder-backed Woodpeckers and the Northern Flicker could not be distinguished reliably based on their drumming pattern.

It is sometimes possible, however, to identify a species by its drumming cadence (beats per second) and rhythm; sapsuckers often can be identified by the irregular rhythm of their drumming. In areas where relatively few species occur, the task of distinguishing woodpeckers by their drumming pattern also becomes much less daunting.

Breeding

Woodpeckers tend to be monogamous and territorial. The majority of species have long-term pair bonds, but some, including the sapsuckers, form only seasonal pair bonds. Unlike most species, Red-cockaded Woodpeckers are cooperative breeders that retain young from previous years to assist in territory defense and the incubation, brooding, and feeding of new young. In late summer they can form groups as large as ten birds, including a breeding pair, four helpers (also called supernumeraries), and four young.

Acorn Woodpeckers are also cooperative breeders: Multiple males and females breed in a group, often with more than one female laying eggs in a single nest; sometimes females remove the eggs of other females before laying. If too many eggs are in the nest, all are not efficiently incubated, and fewer hatch; a female removes another's eggs to increase the chances of her own eggs hatching.

Nests

All woodpeckers are cavity nesters, excavating their own cavities in living or dead wood. A pair may excavate two cavities, one for breeding and one for roosting in the fall. In some species, each adult has a cavity. Territories of nonmigratory species such as Red-cockadeds might contain many cavities, not all of which are used. Cavity excavation takes about two weeks, on average.

In deserts where trees are not available, woodpeckers nest in tree-size cacti such as Saguaros. But the tissue of a Saguaro is primarily a water-storage material, so desert woodpeckers find themselves drilling into a wet, goopy substrate. The plant excretes a protective fluid that hardens into a shell and lines

Woodpecker at nest hole. *Woodpeckers nest in tree cavities they excavate themselves, lining the nest with nothing more than some clean wood chips. The nest hole varies among species; it is made just large enough to admit the species doing the excavating. Some species dig distinctively shaped holes. The most unusual cavities are those of the Red-cockaded Woodpecker (shown here), which may work intermittently for two years on a hole that then may be used for up to 20 years. These cavities are surrounded by a distinctive red or white "plate" that the birds create by continually peeling off bark around the hole to produce a flow of sap, presumably to repel predators and competitors.*

the cavity. This hard shell can outlast the cactus; a nest cavity found on the ground near a decayed cactus is sometimes called a "Saguaro boot" because of it shape.

Most species that nest in living trees choose tree species with soft wood, such as aspens. The tree must be wide enough to allow a cavity without breaching the tree's phloem (the tissue under the bark through which sap flows), which would cause the cavity to partially fill with sap.

Climate affects nest orientation; in cold regions, cavities usually face south and east so they get full sun, whereas in warm climates they usually face north to prevent the eggs and young from overheating. Cavity entrances are never placed on the top of a branch, presumably so they won't fill with rain water.

Cavity construction typically begins with a horizontal tunnel a few inches long, followed by vertical excavation inside the trunk. Most species prepare a bed of fresh wood chips before they lay their eggs.

The size and shape of a cavity varies among species. Cavities of larger species have coarser cutting patterns due to the birds' larger bills. An entrance is usually no larger than is needed for adult birds to pass through. Hence a Northern Flicker cavity is easily distinguished from that of a Hairy Woodpecker, and a Pileated Woodpecker's cavity is unmistakable.

Most woodpeckers do not reuse a cavity in subsequent years. Old nests may no longer be in sufficiently good condition, may harbor nest parasites that would harm the young woodpeckers, and may be especially vulnerable to predation, as mammalian predators are known to remember cavity locations. Species nesting in living trees often build new cavities in the same tree in subsequent years.

Many species of vertebrates and invertebrates inhabit abandoned woodpecker cavities. Flying squirrels and other birds—including other woodpeckers, starlings, and bluebirds—will sometimes usurp occupied cavities. This is a critical problem for the endangered Red-cockaded Woodpecker because of its limited habi-

tat (see the Conservation section, below) and the time this species needs to excavate a new cavity.

The Red-cockaded Woodpecker, which nests in living pines, spends an average of two years excavating its cavity. This is longer than for most species, and is due to excavating in living trees with relatively hard wood. The birds drill "sap wells" around the tree above and below cavity height, creating a flow of sap that provides protection by trapping some predators and irritating others, such as snakes. If the understory grows as high as the cavity, the woodpeckers abandon the nest, presumably to avoid predation by snakes that might avoid the sap barrier by using the shrubs to gain access.

Trees with Red-cockaded Woodpecker cavities can be recognized from a distance either by a red hue, caused when the birds scrape off the top layer of bark, or by a white, candlestick appearance, caused by dried sap. Regular pecking around the cavity to keep sap flowing results in a "plate" where bark is absent, which grows larger over years of use. The only other woodpecker that occasionally makes "plates" is the Black-backed.

Red-cockaded Woodpecker population size is limited by the availability of trees that are large enough to be excavated for cavities. Unlike other woodpeckers, Red-cockadeds may reuse a cavity for more than 20 years. Helper adults, typically related to at least one of the breeders, inherit a territory and its cavities when both breeders die, or if the male breeder dies and the female leaves the site.

Eggs and Young

In woodpeckers, clutch size typically ranges from four to six eggs. Clutch size within species of North American woodpeckers is greater in more northerly populations and also appears to be affected by food availability. Migratory species tend to have larger clutches, while species with greater sexual dimorphism in bill length have smaller clutches, as do species that depend on wood-boring beetle larvae.

The Ivory-billed Woodpecker *(Campephilus principalis)*, which is probably extinct, had the smallest clutch—two or three eggs—of all North American woodpeckers. The Northern Flicker has the most variable clutch size, ranging from three to 12 eggs. To determine a flicker's egg-laying potential, a researcher once removed eggs from a flicker nest, one egg per day, always keeping at least two eggs in the nest; the female laid more than 70 eggs during the season.

All woodpeckers lay white eggs, presumably because there is no benefit to camouflaging colors within a cavity nest. Despite this family's wide range of body sizes, incubation periods among species vary little; most range from 11 to 14 days. Hatching tends to be synchronous.

Young woodpeckers are altricial, and fledging time varies from 21 to 30 days. Time to fledging does not appear to correlate to body size: Small Downy Woodpeckers fledge in about 25 days, while much larger Pileated Woodpeckers take about 27 days.

Ivory-billed Woodpecker. The majestic Ivory-billed Woodpecker was last reliably reported in the United States in the mid-1950s and in Cuba in 1987. A breeding pair must have required a huge area of mature woods with many standing dead trees to provide food; they peeled back sheets of bark to expose beetle larvae. This bird, now probably extinct, was presumably the victim of wholesale logging.

Movements

Most woodpeckers are nonmigratory, although some species exhibit gradations of migration or seasonal movements. Yellow-bellied and Red-naped Sapsuckers are migratory throughout most of their ranges, but many birds spend the winter within the United States. Red-breasted and Williamson's Sapsuckers, Northern Flickers, and Red-bellied, Red-headed, and Lewis's Woodpeckers are partial migrants; that is, birds in northern populations of these species migrate, while others are year-round residents.

Montane species, such as Williamson's Sapsucker, make elevational migrations, moving down from higher elevations during winter. Others engage in less predictable seasonal movements, referred to as "wandering," in which they travel in search of food or future breeding sites. White-headed, Lewis's, and some Pileated Woodpeckers sometimes wander hundreds of miles during the nonbreeding season. Acorn Woodpeckers will wander if their granaries run out of food.

Conservation

Woodpeckers tend to be habitat specialists; as such, they are to some extent at risk of extinction when their habitat is threatened. Most woodpecker species are too poorly studied for scientists to know if their populations are increasing or decreasing.

Based on Breeding Bird Survey data, however, Red-headed and Lewis's Woodpeckers and Northern Flickers are declining, while Hairy, Red-bellied, and Pileated Woodpeckers are known to be increasing. Currently the only endangered woodpecker species in North America is the Red-cockaded, but the Red-headed and Lewis's Woodpeckers are on the WatchList. Also on the WatchList are the Gilded Flicker and the White-headed, Nuttall's, and Arizona Woodpeckers; these species are vulnerable primarily because of their small ranges.

Red-cockaded Woodpeckers live in old pine savannas, park-like habitats with widely spaced trees and tall grass. These areas are sustained by regular fires, so the birds nest only in living trees (fires burn the dead trees). This species normally nests in trees that are at least 60 years old, as these older trees have a large heartwood diameter—necessary if the bird is to excavate a cavity that does not fill with sap.

Historically, this woodpecker's nesting tree of choice was the Longleaf Pine *(Pinus palustris)*, which is resistant both to fire and wood-boring beetles. Longleaf Pines decreased dramatically in numbers through the 1800s and well into the 1900s as a result of timber harvesting, agricultural clearing, and sap harvesting for turpentine production; regional declines continue today. Ironically, trees damaged for turpentine production were avoided in later timber harvests, and in some areas they are the only trees old enough for Red-cockaded Woodpeckers to use for nesting.

In many areas, Longleaf Pines have been replaced in managed pine forests by Loblolly Pines *(Pinus taeda)*, which are thought to be faster-growing. Loblollies are less well adapted to fire and bark beetles, however, and fire suppression has allowed a deciduous understory to grow, making the habitat inhospitable to Red-cockaded Woodpeckers.

Saving this species requires preserving and expanding its habitat. Research has shown that burning the habitat every three to six years is important. Regular burning serves multiple functions, the most important of which is keeping scrub oak out of the forests. Regularly burned forests take on park-like qualities, with few tall understory shrubs. In addition, reduced understory improves recruitment of Longleaf Pine saplings, and encourages the native grasses.

A secondary effect of burning is that animal predators and competitors associated with non-pine communities are reduced. If rotation harvest rates and intensities allow enough old trees to remain, territories eventually accumulate cavity trees so that when competitors take over a cavity, Red-cockadeds have another cavity to use.

As an additional aid, metal restrictors fitted around a cavity can prevent larger woodpecker species from expanding the entrance and taking over the cavity. Finally, it is possible to create new cavities with drills and chain saws. Red-cockaded Woodpeckers will quickly colonize newly created cavities in appropriate habitat.

The Ivory-billed Woodpecker historically occurred only in the southeastern United States and in Cuba but is probably now extinct; the last confirmed sightings were from Louisiana in the mid-1950s and from Cuba in 1987. This species was always considered rare, and most of the reported decline was in the late 1800s and early 1900s. The primary cause of decline was loss of mature, bottomland hardwood swamp forest. During the final phase of the species' decline, collection for museums and by private collectors caused a significant reduction in numbers. Despite rumors, there has not been a confirmed sighting of this species within the United States in decades. A major expedition in Louisiana in 2002 was unable to find any evidence that the species persists. However, because large areas of suitable habitat in the southeastern United States have not been adequately surveyed, some ornithologists are hopeful that this bird may still exist.

Accidental Species

Eurasian Wrynecks *(Jynx torquilla)* generally occur throughout the Palearctic, wintering in Africa and Asia; one has been seen on the Seward Peninsula, Alaska, in fall. A winter specimen from southern Indiana was apparently transported there in a shipping crate. Great Spotted Woodpeckers *(Dendrocopos major)* are resident from western Europe to Japan and have on a few occasions been recorded on Attu Island in the western Aleutians.

J. Michael Reed

Tyrant Flycatchers

Family Tyrannidae
Order Passeriformes

Tyrant flycatchers are very small to medium-size perching birds, with large heads, broad and flattened bills, short legs, pointed wings, and, in most species, rictal bristles around the base of the bill. Their tails are usually of medium length, except for two species with extremely long tails. Upperpart colors are commonly grays, browns, and greens; the underparts are lighter colors. A few species are more boldly marked, and several have bright yellow underparts. The sexes are usually alike, but they differ dramatically in the Vermilion Flycatcher *(Pyrocephalus rubinus)* and the Rose-throated Becard *(Pachyramphus aglaiae)*. Tyrant flycatcher habitats include grasslands, farmlands, savannas, streams, river edges, marshes, brushy areas, and open woodlands of varied ages. Many species frequent edges where one habitat meets another, such as openings within a forest or where woodlands border fields.

Taxonomy

The Passeriformes (songbirds) is the world's largest order of birds; taxonomists divide it into two groups: the suboscines and the oscines. The suboscines are a predominantly New World group found mainly in Central and South America. Tyrannidae is the only family that extends north into North America. Other suboscine families are the ovenbirds (Furnariidae), woodcreepers (Dendrocolaptidae), antbirds (Thamnophilidae), antthrushes and antpittas (Formicariidae), tapaculos (Rhinocryptidae), cotingas (Cotingidae), manakins (Pipridae), planteaters (Phytotomidae), and the Sharpbill (a unique species in its own family, Oxyruncidae).

The suboscines differ from oscines in four ways: Suboscines have a simple syrinx (the sound-producing structure in the respiratory tract). The small bone that transmits sound through the middle chamber of the ear has a distinctive shape. Their mitochondrial DNA is organized in a unique way. And suboscines, so far as is known, do not learn their songs, unlike oscines, which do.

Worldwide Family Features

- 3½–11" (9–28 cm) perching birds of grasslands, wetlands, brushy areas, woodlands. (Length excludes tail-streamers.)
- About 420 species in about 104 genera worldwide; occur throughout the Americas. 37 species in 10 genera found throughout North America; plus 8 or 9 accidental species.
- Eat insects while breeding; many also eat fruit in other seasons. Catch flying insects in midair; often return to perch with prey.
- Territorial in breeding season. Most species seen singly or in family groups; a few aggregate at roosts, at stopover sites on migration, and on wintering grounds. Monogamous for 1 breeding season; extra-pair copulations in some species. Temperate zone species migratory.
- Breed first at 1 year old.
- Open-cup nest most common; also nest in tree cavities or build ball-shaped

arboreal nests with inner chamber. Nests placed from ground level to more than 50' (15 m) high in tree. Female builds nest. Some species reuse nests.
- 2–8 (usually 3–5) short to long subelliptical eggs; white or creamy background, variably marked with brown or gray spots, or streaking in some species. Female incubates, for 13–17 days. Hatching asynchronous over 1–3 days. 1 or 2 broods per year.
- Altricial young hatch with sparse light gray, buffy white, or dusky down, mostly on crown and back. Cavity nesters naked at hatching but soon develop light down. Fledge at 12–23 days, earlier if disturbed. Female broods; both sexes feed young.
- Adult annual survival 30–75%. Among oldest on record: 13 years, 11 months (Great Crested Flycatcher).

384

Subfamilies

Tyrannids are divided into four currently recognized subfamilies, based on characteristics of the skull and syrinx. However, these subfamilies are not clearly defined, and future changes in classification are possible.

The subfamily Elaeniinae (tyrannulets and elaenias) includes more than 180 species, but only one, the Northern Beardless-Tyrannulet *(Camptostoma imberbe)*, breeds in North America. A second tyrannid subfamily, Platyrinchinae (todyflycatchers and flatbills), is unrecorded in North America. The subfamily Fluvicolinae (fluvicoline flycatchers) contains several genera of North American breeders, including four species of pewees (genus *Contopus*), 11 of *Empidonax*, three of phoebes *(Sayornis)*, and the Vermilion Flycatcher.

The fourth subfamily, Tyranninae (tyrannine flycatchers), includes as North American breeders four species in the genus *Myiarchus*, the Great Kiskadee *(Pitangus sulphuratus)*, the Sulphurbellied Flycatcher *(Myiodynastes luteiventris)*, and eight species of kingbirds (genus *Tyrannus*).

Evidence from syringeal structure, the skull, and DNA–DNA hybridization studies indicates that the becards (genus *Pachyramphus*) and tityras (genus *Tityra*) are tyrannids rather than members of the family Cotingidae, as formerly believed. The placement of these genera within subfamilies remains to be determined.

Cryptic Species

Numerous tyrannid species are not easily distinguishable by sight, even with birds in the hand. However, species in several genera that differ little or not at all in appearance have evolved different vocalizations and other behaviors. The genera *Elaenia, Contopus, Empidonax, Myiarchus,* and *Tyrannus* contain cryptic species that look similar to one another but sound different and do not interbreed where they occur together.

Since 1955 new evidence has led to the recognition of several cryptic species among the North American Tyrannidae. The former "Traill's Flycatcher" has been split into the Alder Flycatcher *(Empidonax alnorum)* and the Willow Flycatcher *(E. traillii),* which differ most prominently in their vocalizations and nest structure. The "Western Flycatcher" is now separated into the Pacific-slope Flycatcher *(E. difficilis)* and the Cordilleran Flycatcher *(E. occidentalis)* on the basis of protein differences and different call notes in breeding males. A dull-colored population *(E. d. insulicola)* of the Pacific-slope Flycatcher breeding in the Channel Islands off southern California is possibly a third cryptic species within the "Western Flycatcher" complex, but further study is needed.

The former "Tropical Kingbird" has been divided into the Tropical Kingbird *(Tyrannus melancholicus)* and Couch's Kingbird *(T. couchii);* vocalizations are the most conspicuous differences between the two. Other species that look alike but have different songs or calls are the Eastern Wood-Pewee *(Contopus virens)* and the Western Wood-Pewee *(C. sordidulus),* and the Dusky Flycatcher *(Empidonax oberholseri)* and Hammond's Flycatcher *(E. hammondii).*

Tyrant flycatchers often respond to the broadcasting of recorded vocalizations of their own species, but frequently not to those of other species. Experimental playback of vocalizations has been important in defining species limits in the species pairs of Alder and Willow Flycatchers and Tropical and Couch's Kingbirds. However, individual birds are best identified from their own vocalizations rather than their responses to broadcast recordings.

There are remarkably few hybrids known among tyrant flycatcher species. A *Contopus* × *Empidonax* hybrid has been found, and there are several records of hybrids between the Western Kingbird *(Tyrannus verticalis)* and the Scissor-tailed Flycatcher *(T. forficatus).* Perhaps hybrid tyrant flycatchers occur more frequently but are not recognized because the parental species are so similar.

Prominent Genera

Many of the genera of tyrant flycatchers have recognizable morphological, behavioral, and ecological traits. It is frequently easiest to identify an unfamiliar flycatcher by first deciding to what genus it belongs, then sorting through the possible members of that genus. This process may be most familiar to western birders, as many genera in the West have multiple representatives. In the East, most tyrant flycatcher genera have only one regular species, except for the genus *Empidonax,* which has several confusing eastern members.

Pewees (Genus* Contopus*) The four North American species are specialized for aerial hawking, with their relatively broad and long bills and long wings. All lack a conspicuous eye-ring. They often sit on exposed perches and return to the same position after flying out in pursuit of prey. In this genus, comparisons of body and bill size, the presence or absence of wing-bars, and the patterning of light and dark on the underparts help separate North American species, but vocalizations are often a better guide. The two wood-pewees are generally indistinguishable except by their vocalizations or by measurements of birds in the hand.

***Genus* Empidonax** The 11 North American species of *Empidonax* (sometimes called "empids") look remarkably alike. Most have a light-colored eye-ring, relatively short wings, and prominent wing-bars. Vocalizations, breeding habitat, and nest structure provide some of the most reliable features for recognizing species in this genus. With birds in the hand, banders often use the relative lengths of the outer primaries, also known as the wing formula, for identification. Non-vocalizing migrants are especially difficult to identify but can be common in many habitats. Empids often flick their wings or tail while perched. Of these body movements, the most diagnostic is a downward, phoebe-like tail wag given by the Gray Flycatcher *(E. wrightii).*

***Phoebes (Genus* Sayornis*) and* Pyrocephalus** The three species of phoebes are larger than most wood-pewees or *Empidonax* flycatchers and lack eye-rings and prominent wing-bars. Phoebes typically forage near the ground; when they perch, they flip their tails extensively. Members of this genus choose nest sites with a solid overhang above the nest, and often nest on buildings, bridges, or other human structures. Phoebes are

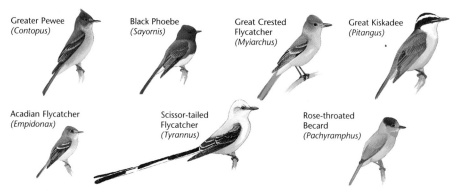

Greater Pewee
(Contopus)

Black Phoebe
(Sayornis)

Great Crested Flycatcher
(Myiarchus)

Great Kiskadee
(Pitangus)

Acadian Flycatcher
(Empidonax)

Scissor-tailed Flycatcher
(Tyrannus)

Rose-throated Becard
(Pachyramphus)

Tyrannid diversity. *North American tyrant flycatchers mostly fall into five distinct genera:* Contopus *(pewees),* Empidonax *flycatchers,* Sayornis *(phoebes),* Myiarchus *flycatchers, and* Tyrannus *(kingbirds). While the southern border specialties, such as the Great Kiskadee (genus* Pitangus*), are diverse and unrelated, for convenience they can be considered a sixth group. The Rose-throated Becard is considered a tyrant flycatcher based on current research, but it is unclear how its genus (*Pachyramphus*) is related to the others.*

Tyrannid tail-flicking. The tail movements of many tyrant flycatcher species can provide clues to their identification. One of the more distinctive motions is the deliberate dipping or wagging motion of the phoebes, which may even show subtle differences between species. The reason for these motions, and the selection pressures that have allowed species-specific motions to develop, are unknown. The Black Phoebe (top) and Eastern Phoebe (bottom) are shown.

As is true with several of the previous groups, the single member of this genus that is widespread in the East, the Eastern Kingbird *(T. tyrannus)*, is easy to identify. A greater challenge is presented in the West, where up to four species, including the Thick-billed Kingbird *(T. crassirostris)*, can be found breeding in southern Arizona.

Two long-tailed species, the Scissor-tailed Flycatcher and the rare Fork-tailed Flycatcher *(Tyrannus savana)*, were formerly classified as a separate genus *(Muscivora)*; however, apart from the very long tail feathers, they strongly resemble the other kingbirds in structure and behavior. The distinctive Scissor-tailed frequents open country such as grasslands in Texas and Oklahoma, where it is a favored sight along highways.

therefore more likely to be found near human dwellings than are wood-pewees or empids. A very similar species ecologically is the brilliantly colored Vermilion Flycatcher. The only member of the genus *Pyrocephalus,* the Vermilion Flycatcher inhabits open country near water and conspicuously flips its tail when perching.

Genus **Myiarchus** The four members of this genus that breed in North America are mostly larger than phoebes and have yellow on the belly. All nest in tree cavities or nest boxes. Brown-crested Flycatchers *(M. tyrannulus)* regularly nest in desert riparian habitats, while Ash-throated Flycatchers *(M. cinerascens)* and Great Crested Flycatchers *(M. crinitus)* often take over bluebird nest boxes. These species are noted for placing snake skins in their nests. One nonbreeding species, La Sagra's Flycatcher *(M. sagrae),* is a casual visitor to Florida.

Kingbirds (Genus **Tyrannus***)* These large, conspicuous tyrant flycatchers commonly occur in open country or on woodland edges, and are specialized with long, pointed wings for aerial hawking. Eight species breed in North America, while a ninth species is a rare but regular visitor.

Southern Border Specialties (Genera **Pachyramphus, Camptostoma, Pitangus,** *and* **Myiodynastes***)* Members of several genera widespread in the neotropics barely enter the United States along its southern border. A number of these species appear distinctive to North American birders, unlike the cryptic species in many of the genera listed above. This impression is misleading, as the "southern border specialties" are often members of confusing sets of species in areas south of our range. Thus both the Great Kiskadee and the Sulphur-bellied Flycatcher look very similar to close relatives found from Mexico to South America. Only a "limited" North American perspective makes these species seem less cryptic than members of *Myiarchus* or *Tyrannus*.

Two other species that barely cross the U.S.–Mexico border are the Rose-throated Becard and the Northern Beardless-Tyrannulet. The becard is a sluggish, stocky, and inconspicuous bird of limited distribution in southeastern Arizona and the Rio Grande Valley of southern Texas. In both areas, it is highly sought after by visiting birders. The Northern Beardless-Tyrannulet is a tiny bird that has a wider range in southern Arizona than the becard but can be just as difficult for birders to find. This is due in part to the tyrannulet's active foraging behavior. Its flitting and hopping, performed to glean insects from leaves, is more similar to the foraging of kinglets (genus *Regulus*) or a Verdin *(Auriparus flaviceps)* than a typical tyrant flycatcher.

Variation

Tyrant flycatchers are quite varied in the extent and timing of their molts. Depending on the species, mature individuals have a complete or incomplete prebasic molt that occurs either in the breeding range, in the wintering area, or partly in both.

Differences in the timing of the molt can sometimes aid in identification. For example, Hammond's and Dusky Flycatchers, which look very similar, can be separated in early fall by plumage differences related to molt. Hammond's molts before migrating, in contrast to the Dusky, which molts on the wintering grounds. Thus in fall, migrating adult Hammonds are darker, in fresh plumage, while adult Duskys are worn and pale.

Some species show seasonal changes. In fresh plumage during fall or early winter, for example, adults of many species show more yellow on their underparts.

In most species, appearance changes little with age, but adults of a few species are distinctly more colorful than immatures;

Tyrannid variation. Most flycatchers look the same regardless of age or sex. One notable exception is the Vermilion Flycatcher, in which first-year males (shown here) only gradually acquire the solid red underparts and forehead of older males. Male Vermilion Flycatchers also can be easily distinguished from females.

examples include the Vermilion Flycatcher, the Scissor-tailed Flycatcher, and the male Rose-throated Becard. The sexes differ conspicuously in only a few species, including the Vermilion Flycatcher and the Rose-throated Becard. Most species have little or no geographic variation.

Habitats

Tyrant flycatchers occur in an enormous range of habitats but are usually absent from the coldest environments, including Arctic and alpine tundra. Populations that breed in frigid regions migrate and winter to the south, avoiding severe conditions. Most tyrannids that capture flying insects or pluck insects from vegetation require open spaces in which they can maneuver. These open spaces can be above low canopies, such as in shrub-dominated habitats, or under or within higher canopies, as in the open woodlands used by the Acadian Flycatcher *(Empidonax virescens)*.

Birds show considerable specificity of habitat in the breeding season, when closely related species in the same region often occupy different habitats. Breeding habitat can thus be a useful clue in identifying tyrant flycatchers.

Environmental factors that appear relevant to habitat use by tyrant flycatchers include the wetness of a site, height and density of vegetation, and whether deciduous, coniferous, or mixed vegetation dominates. For example, in early summer in western North America, a small *Empidonax* flycatcher in tall, mature old-growth coniferous woodlands is likely to be Hammond's Flycatcher, rather than the very similar-looking Dusky Flycatcher, which forages lower to the ground in open woodlands and mountain chaparral.

Across North America, the Willow Flycatcher is often found in dense growths of willows, as its name suggests. However, even in the breeding season, habitat should be used cautiously in identification. For example, Alder Flycatchers, which are extremely similar in appearance

Tyrannid hawking behavior. All tyrant flycatchers forage mainly by flying out from a perch and capturing insects in midair. Empidonax flycatchers (below) generally choose an inconspicuous perch and fly out rather weakly, often returning to a different perch. In contrast, the pewees (above) and kingbirds choose a prominent perch and fly out strongly, usually returning to the same perch.

to Willow Flycatchers, also occur in willows in some localities.

During migration and while wintering, tyrant flycatcher species tend to frequent habitats similar to those they use for breeding. But they can also occur in highly dissimilar settings, so again caution is necessary in applying habitat as an aid in identification.

Food and Foraging

Tyrannids are mainly insectivorous, especially when breeding, but at times virtually all species eat small fruits. Some species, such as the Eastern Kingbird and the Sulphur-bellied Flycatcher, consume large quantities of fruit on the wintering grounds.

While tyrant flycatchers eat insects of all the major taxonomic groups, true flies (dipterans) are a dietary staple. Bees, wasps, ants, grasshoppers, beetles, and true bugs are well represented in tyrannid diets. The percentage of each group in the diet varies with seasonal and regional availability, as well as the size of the flycatcher species and its foraging techniques.

Although Eastern Kingbirds have often been blamed for consuming honeybees, kingbirds have a relatively minor impact on honeybee populations compared with other factors, such as mites that attack the bees.

Tyrant flycatchers are sit-and-wait predators. They remain on a perch until they sight an insect, then fly out to grab it in the air—a maneuver termed "sallying" or "hawking." Flycatchers seize their food directly in the bill, but they apparently do not use the bill to move vegetation or litter to uncover hidden prey. Small tyrannids, such as many of the *Empidonax* flycatchers, often hawk beneath a cover of shrubs or trees, gleaning insects or spiders from leaves or branches.

Some tyrant flycatchers—for example, phoebes—commonly fly down from a perch to take insects or spiders on the ground, a behavior known as "ground-sallying" that they share with bluebirds. Although any tyrant flycatcher may fly to the ground for food, they do not ordinarily move along the ground but instead fly from one place to another. Their infrequent terrestrial locomotion usually involves one or a few hops covering only a short distance.

Larger tyrant flycatchers often hold a freshly caught large prey item in the bill and beat it against their perch. There are reports of some *Empidonax* flycatchers holding prey down with one foot while perching and dismembering it with the bill. *Myiarchus* flycatchers have been recorded catching prey as large as dragonflies, hummingbirds, and small lizards.

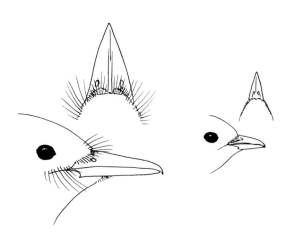

Rictal bristles. *Most tyrant flycatchers, such as the Tropical Kingbird (left), have developed an array of stiff bristles (modified feathers) around the mouth. The Northern Beardless-Tyrannulet (right), which forages mainly by gleaning rather than catching insects in midair, has no rictal bristles.*

Adaptations to Lifestyle

The broad, flattened bill of many tyrant flycatchers represents their most conspicuous difference from other passerines. Kingbirds and other species that regularly hawk prey in the air have a large, broad bill that maximizes their chances of seizing at least some part of an airborne insect when they snap the bill shut. Certain Old World flycatchers in the family Muscicapidae also hawk in the air and have the same bill shape, but this has evolved independently, as the two families are not closely related.

Tyrannids that regularly glean insects off foliage have a narrower, more pointed, forceps-like bill—such as the Northern Beardless-Tyrannulet, which has a vireo-like bill shape.

Well-developed rictal bristles around the base of the beak are characteristic of most tyrant flycatchers, but the bristles' relative size differs considerably from genus to genus. Aerial hawkers such as *Empidonax* flycatchers and kingbirds have conspicuous bristles, but the Northern Beardless-Tyrannulet has none, hence the name "beardless."

Bristles were once thought to act as a funnel directing insects into the mouths of aerial hawkers. However, in the laboratory, tyrant flycatchers with bristles taped down or clipped off are not impaired when catching flying insects. Thus bristles do not appear to be an insect-capturing device. Other explanations are that the bristles protect the eyes from high-speed collisions with insects or that movement of the bristles somehow informs the bird about the position or movement of prey held in the bill.

Species that regularly hawk insects in the air and migrate long distances—for example, wood-pewees and the Eastern Kingbird—have longer wings than other tyrannids. Longer wings are aerodynamically more efficient for sustained flight at high speed, in contrast to shorter, more rounded wings, which are better at generating lift for takeoff and low-speed flight.

Tyrannid heads and bills. *The bill shape of tyrant flycatchers is relatively consistent: broad and flat, with a small hook at the tip. The relative size of the bill, however, varies widely between species and relates to the size of prey that is pursued. The short, petite bill of the Least Flycatcher (top) is used for capturing gnats and midges, and the long, sturdy bill of the Gray Kingbird (bottom) for capturing large flying insects such as dragonflies, bees, and beetles.*

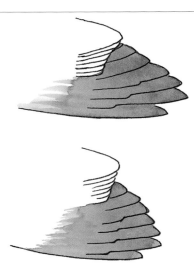

Tyrannid wing shape. In the Tyrannidae, *species are so similar in appearance that subtle structural clues become important for identification. Researchers studying birds in the hand use the relative lengths of the primaries, which determine the shape of the wingtip, to identify some very similar species. Here the long, pointed wingtip of an Eastern Wood-Pewee (above) is compared to the relatively short, rounded wingtip of a Least Flycatcher (below). These differences are readily apparent in the field. More subtle differences exist between even the most closely related species of* Empidonax *flycatchers.*

Tyrant flycatcher species often differ in the relative lengths of their primaries, presumably reflecting specializations for differences in flight. These differences can be measured by the primary extension, which is the distance that the longest primaries extend beyond the secondaries and tertials when the wing is folded alongside the body, or by the wing formula (the relative lengths of the outer primaries). Differences in primary extension can sometimes be seen in birds at close range, while wing formulae are measured by banders on birds in the hand.

Among *Empidonax* flycatchers, primary extension is relatively long in the Acadian, Alder, and Hammond's Flycatchers but comparatively short in the Dusky, Gray, Least *(E. minimus),* and Buff-breasted *(E. fulvifrons)* Flycatchers.

The strikingly long tails of the Scissor-tailed and Fork-tailed Flycatchers are longer in males than females and notably contribute to the showiness of displaying birds.

Breeding

New World flycatchers usually appear to be monogamous within a breeding season. However, occasionally a male pairs with two females; examples include the

Eastern Kingbirds attacking Red-tailed Hawk. Kingbirds *are named for their aggressive nature. A kingbird will defend its territory and nest against all predators, even to the point of "riding" the back of a flying hawk or crow, all the time pecking the back of the head.*

Buff-breasted and Least Flycatchers and the Eastern Phoebe *(Sayornis phoebe)*. In Eastern Kingbirds, paternity studies using genetic information have revealed that eggs are regularly fertilized by a male other than the mate. In some tyrannids, such as the Great Crested Flycatcher, the male closely guards the female during her fertile period to reduce opportunities for extra-pair copulations.

DNA studies have shown that second broods of the Eastern Phoebe are more likely than first broods to include young sired by males other than the mate. One inference is that caring for post-fledging young from the first brood distracts the male from guarding his mate during the second nesting and increases the chances of her mating with another male. It would not be surprising if occasional non-monogamous relationships were found in other species.

Males defend territories against others of the same species. In closely studied species, such as the Eastern Kingbird, the home range of breeding birds decreases in size after a pair completes nest-building and incubation. In some species, such as the Least Flycatcher, territories appear to be clumped, as though constituting a colony.

Territorial disputes between tyrant flycatcher species occur in a few cases where ranges overlap and habitats abut. Such adversarial pairings include the Alder and Willow Flycatchers and the Dusky and Gray Flycatchers.

Tyrant flycatchers are often aggressive toward other insectivorous birds. For example, in New Hampshire woodlands, breeding Least Flycatchers frequently chase American Redstarts *(Setophaga ruticilla)*, and redstart population densities are lower where nesting Least Flycatchers are numerous.

Breeding kingbirds are exceptionally aggressive toward potential predators. Both their generic and family names *(Tyrannus* and Tyrannidae) refer to their tyrannical attacks, which commonly include the mobbing of perched or flying hawks and crows. Like other passerines, a

Vermilion Flycatcher aerial courtship display. A few species of tyrant flycatchers engage in dramatic aerial courtship displays. The Vermilion Flycatcher is one of the most striking. The male flies up above the treetops with slow, exaggerated wingbeats and with the brilliant red breast and crown expanded. At the top of the climb he gives a series of sharp, twittering notes before parachuting back to his perch.

mobbing kingbird usually attacks from above and to the rear of the bird being mobbed. Eastern Kingbirds sometimes even "ride" on the backs of flying hawks and crows while pounding them with their bills. Mobbing by a pair appears to be very effective in driving predators out of kingbirds' territories.

Vocalizations and Displays

Tyrant flycatchers typically sing during the breeding season, but they give call notes to a varying extent throughout the year. They vocalize least during fall migration. The bill-snapping of foraging tyrant flycatchers is often audible in the field year-round.

As suboscines, tyrant flycatchers have vocalizations that tend to lack the musical qualities birders appreciate in many oscine songs. Vocalizations are among the best clues for identifying tyrannids, and experienced birders can often identify vocalizing tyrant flycatchers, including difficult species such as the two wood-pewees, the Tropical/Couch's kingbird complex, and many *Empidonax* and *Myiarchus* flycatchers, especially outside a species' usual range.

Although tyrannids lack the rich vocal repertoire of many oscines, tyrannid species produce a variety of sounds. For example, the Great Crested Flycatcher produces at least 12 distinct vocalizations. Some tyrannids, such as the Eastern Wood-Pewee, have an elaborate song given early and late in the day during the breeding season, sometimes referred to as a dawn song or twilight song.

Some tyrannids have elaborate displays. For example, the Western Kingbird male performs a courtship display in which he flies up to 50 feet (15 m) in the air and then tumbles down wildly. Spectacular aerial courtship displays also occur in other tyrannids, including the Vermilion Flycatcher, Cassin's Kingbird *(Tyrannus vociferans),* and the Scissor-tailed Flycatcher.

Experiments with Alder and Willow Flycatchers and the Eastern Phoebe reveal that their vocalizations are innate—that is, that they develop without learning. Flycatchers seem unable to learn the vocalizations of another species even if reared by foster parents of that species or frequently exposed to recorded vocalizations. Neuroanatomical studies show that the Eastern Phoebe lacks critical cell groups in the forebrain that are used for song-learning by oscines.

Furthermore, the songs of tyrannids do not vary among geographic areas in the way that the songs of oscines frequently do. Sometimes individual birds have unusual vocalizations, but whether or not these are inherited is unknown. Presumably genetic changes affecting vocalization occur at least occasionally.

In general, closely related tyrannid species differ in both their call notes and their songs. However, the highly similar Pacific-slope and Cordilleran Flycatchers differ only slightly.

Nests, Eggs, and Young

Nest locations vary greatly within the tyrannid family. At one extreme, Yellow-bellied Flycatchers *(Empidonax flaviventris)* place their nests on or only slightly off the ground in the side of a mound or in the upturned roots of a tree, often hiding them in moss. In contrast, other species have arboreal nests far off the ground, with many species occasionally nesting more than 30 feet (9 m) high.

The most common nest shape for tyrant flycatchers is a cup. Cup-shaped nests are used by pewees, *Empidonax* flycatchers, phoebes, and kingbirds. *Myiarchus* flycatchers and the Sulphur-bellied Flycatcher nest in tree cavities. The Northern Beardless-Tyrannulet, Great Kiskadee, and Rose-throated Becard each build an enclosed domed nest with a side entrance.

The cup-nesting phoebes commonly have a solid overhang above the nest to protect it, while some 90 percent of Buff-breasted Flycatcher nests have an overhead canopy of vegetation. An overhang may shield the nest from rain or prevent convective heat loss on cold nights.

Human structures such as bridges and buildings have greatly increased the number of suitable nest sites for the phoebes, which previously were limited to natural sites such as rock or mud cliffs, or perhaps large trees that provided a suitable overhang. Eastern Phoebe nests can either rest on top of a supporting surface or be attached by mud to a vertical surface.

Compared with the open-cup design, cavity nests provide better protection for eggs and nestlings from the weather and predators. However, the number of hole-nesting birds often exceeds the number of cavities available in an area. Furthermore, migratory tyrannids such as the Dusky-capped Flycatcher *(Myiarchus tuberculifer)* can be outcompeted for nests in areas where hole-nesting species of other families are permanent residents. Nevertheless, these migrants do find sites, in part because they can modify holes that other species cannot use. For example, *Myiarchus* species fill large cavities with nest material to form a smaller nest chamber. In an exceptional case, a pair of Ash-throated Flycatchers attempted to nest in a pair of overalls hung on a clothesline to dry. The nesting material they carried into a hole in one leg fell out the bottom of the leg until the

Tyrannid nests. Most tyrant flycatchers build a simple cup nest (for example, that of the Western Wood-Pewee, left), but the placement and exact structure of the nest varies significantly among species. Exceptions include the Sulphur-bellied Flycatcher and the Myiarchus flycatchers (such as the Ash-throated Flycatcher, below on this page), which nest in cavities, and three tropical species: The Northern Beardless-Tyrannulet and Great Kiskadee both build a globular ball of sticks, and the Rose-throated Becard (opposite page) builds a long, hanging basket.

owner of the pants tied it closed. The birds eventually filled up the leg with nesting material and successfully reared a brood.

The Great Kiskadee ordinarily builds a woven domed nest, but in Brazil it occasionally nests in cavities. Observers have suggested that the capacity to build a woven domed nest, which provides much of the protection of a cavity nest, evolved in response to limited availability of true cavity nest sites.

Studies with marked birds indicate that the female alone builds the nest. Nest construction takes as few as four days in the Western Kingbird and up to two weeks in the Eastern Phoebe.

Many *Empidonax* flycatchers use a nest only once. In contrast, phoebes frequently reuse old nests, either in a single season or in a subsequent year. Considerable time and energy can be saved by reusing a nest rather than building a new one; renovation of a phoebe nest may require as little as four days. Nest reuse also occurs fairly often in the Western Kingbird. The advantages of reusing nests are sometimes offset by a damaging buildup of residual nest parasites, such as mites.

Most male tyrant flycatchers lack the bare incubation patches on the belly that females use to heat the eggs and brood the young. Exceptional cases of males with incubation patches have been recorded—for example, in the Black Phoebe *(Sayornis nigricans)* and the Great Crested Flycatcher—but it is unknown whether such males ever incubate the eggs or brood young.

The altricial young hatch asynchronously over one to three days and remain as nestlings for 12 to 23 days. After fledging, the young are cared for out of the nest for an additional two to three weeks. Both parents feed the young. Parents regularly swallow fecal sacs produced by the nestlings for the first four or five days after hatching but subsequently carry off the sacs and drop them away from the nest.

Some species (for example, the Eastern Phoebe) regularly produce two broods in a season. Acadian Flycatchers apparently have two broods in southern areas but only one to the north. Other species only occasionally have more than one brood per season (for example, the Least Flycatcher). Many species of tyrant flycatchers probably renest following nest failure; the Buff-breasted Flycatcher may start as many as five nests in a season if a series of failures occur.

Predation by snakes, mammals, or birds such as jays is a leading cause of nest losses. Sometimes severe spring weather contributes to adult mortality. Violent summer storms can also adversely affect species nesting in exposed sites. One June storm in Oklahoma destroyed 25 out of 40 Scissor-tailed Flycatcher nests, mainly through loss of supporting limbs or the toppling of entire trees.

Tyrannids defend themselves against brood parasitism by cowbirds with varying degrees of success. Breeding Willow and Buff-breasted Flycatchers frequently chase away cowbirds, and Least Flycatchers are aggressive even toward models of Brown-headed Cowbirds (*Molothrus ater*) placed near their nests. Eastern Kingbirds and Scissor-tailed Flycatchers regularly remove cowbird eggs placed in their nests. Brood parasitism is unreported for the Black Phoebe.

In the Bahamas, researchers placed artificial Shiny Cowbird *(Molothrus bonariensis)* eggs in the nests of Gray Kingbirds *(Tyrannus dominicensis)* to examine the kingbirds' response. They found that the kingbirds removed most of the foreign eggs within 48 hours.

Migration

Most North American tyrant flycatchers migrate southward for the nonbreeding season. Some species, such as the Eastern Kingbird, travel thousands of miles. Tyrannids are generally considered to be nocturnal migrants, but the Western Kingbird, Eastern Kingbird, and Scissor-tailed Flycatcher are at times diurnal migrants.

When unfavorable weather prevents overwater crossings, large flocks of Eastern Kingbirds sometimes gather along coastlines. Flocks of dozens to hundreds have been seen during the fall migration at Cape May Point, New Jersey, and other coastal sites; a flock of an estimated half million birds was reported from Florida in late August 1964.

About two-thirds of the tyrannid species breeding in North America normally move far enough south that they leave their breeding range entirely. Southern Mexico is the wintering ground for the greatest number of species that breed in North America. Long-distance migrants breeding in western North America tend to winter in Central America. Winter ranges are poorly known for certain members of cryptic species, such as the Western and Eastern Wood-Pewees or the Pacific-slope and Cordilleran Flycatchers, because these birds are almost impossible to distinguish from each other in the winter, when they are not very vocal.

In contrast, many eastern North American species migrate into South America. The Sulphur-bellied Flycatcher leaves its breeding range (from southern Arizona south to Costa Rica) to migrate south to winter entirely in South America (from eastern Ecuador to northern Bolivia); it is

Scissor-tailed Flycatcher migration. The Scissor-tailed Flycatcher is one of the few species of tyrant flycatchers that actively migrate during the day. In some places, large numbers can be seen migrating low overhead during spring and fall.

exceptional among birds breeding in the northern tropics in having such a long migration.

Many of the southern border specialties, as well as the Black Phoebe and the Vermilion Flycatcher, are largely nonmigratory, but even these species show some southward movement, particularly from the northern parts of their breeding ranges. Tyrant flycatchers with populations regularly wintering in limited parts of the southern United States include the Black Phoebe, Eastern Phoebe, Say's Phoebe *(Sayornis saya)*, Vermilion Flycatcher, Great Crested Flycatcher, Great Kiskadee, Western Kingbird, and Scissor-tailed Flycatcher.

Among North American tyrannids, so far as is known, ecologically similar species tend not to winter in the same region. For example, the very similar Alder and Willow Flycatchers exhibit a "leapfrog" migration pattern in which the Alder, which breeds to the north of the Willow in North America, migrates farther south, into South America. The Willow moves south only into Central America and perhaps extreme northwestern Colombia.

Tyrant flycatchers show strong site fidelity for their breeding grounds. In 1804 John James Audubon marked Eastern Phoebes with a silver thread around the leg and observed the same individuals returning to the area to breed the

next year. The same pair of Eastern Kingbirds sometimes mates in successive years in the same vicinity. This probably reflects the site fidelity of both birds because, as for most other passerines, there is no evidence that the male and female migrate or winter together between the breeding seasons.

Exceptional movements are also sometimes made. For example, the Fork-tailed Flycatcher, which breeds in Central and South America, has been found many times in the central and eastern United States and in southern Canada. Most well-documented North American records involve the southern South American subspecies *(Tyrannus savana savana)* that migrates northward from March to May before the austral winter, rather than the resident subspecies found in Central America. Spring appearances of the Fork-tailed Flycatcher in North America are examples of migratory overshooting, an exceptional but not infrequent phenomenon in which migrating birds fly in the proper direction but go too far. The more numerous fall records represent birds migrating in the wrong direction and ending up in the northern autumn rather than the southern spring. Strays of the Fork-tailed—and the Variegated Flycatcher *(Empidonomus varius)*; see Accidental Species, below—have appeared more than 1,000 miles (1,600 km) north of their usual ranges.

Conservation

Within the last 150 years, several tyrannid species have undergone major shifts in their breeding range. For example, the Western Kingbird greatly extended its range eastward across the Great Plains during the 20th century, thanks to the spread of human settlements, with their planted trees and structures such as utility poles, towers, and buildings. Such features offered potential nest sites where none had previously existed.

On the other hand, the numbers and range of the Buff-breasted Flycatcher in Arizona appear to have been greatly reduced in the 20th century by fire suppression, which has deprived the species of the openness it needs in much of its pine woodland habitat.

In eastern North America, the Willow Flycatcher has apparently expanded its breeding range northward, while the southern boundary of the Alder Flycatcher's breeding range has retreated northward. Some have suggested that the Willow has been outcompeting the Alder, but the changing ranges of the two species might alternatively be explained by climatic warming or by the natural regrowth of woodlands, which would exclude the Alder Flycatcher from areas formerly opened for agriculture or lumbering, whereas the floodplain habitat for Willows might persist because of the effects of flooding.

None of the tyrant flycatcher species breeding in North America is currently considered to be at risk of imminent extinction. However, the southwestern subspecies of the Willow Flycatcher *(Empidonax traillii extimus)*, with a breeding range centered in southern California, Arizona, and New Mexico, has a population estimated at only a few hundred individuals and has been included on the U.S. Endangered Species List.

Breeding Bird Surveys report declines for the Least Flycatcher, Eastern Kingbird, and perhaps Vermilion Flycatcher. Larger declines have been detected for the Olive-sided Flycatcher *(Contopus cooperi)* and both wood-pewees. The WatchList of species potentially at risk includes the Greater Pewee *(Contopus pertinax)*.

Concern exists for several species for which there is no strong evidence of a significant decline. Biologists are monitoring Hammond's Flycatcher because of its close association with mature old-growth coniferous woodlands, which have been extensively cut in recent decades. Destruction of riparian vegetation in the Alder Flycatcher's South American wintering habitats might adversely affect that species.

The Buff-breasted Flycatcher has one of the most restricted breeding ranges among bird species nesting in North America. Individual birds in that limited breeding range in southeastern Arizona are potentially subject to daily disturbance by birders and other people. The species is common in Mexico and probably not at risk globally.

Reasons for Declines

The lack of pertinent data makes the ideas presented here conjectural, and probably no one factor is responsible for all tyrannid declines.

The southern edge of the breeding range of the Olive-sided Flycatcher has apparently been moving northward in eastern North America since the 19th century, but the cause is unknown. Recent population declines in both this species and the Western Wood-Pewee may be due to major losses of wintering habitat in the South American Andes, the result of human activity. The Greater Pewee is of concern because of its relatively limited breeding range within the United States, although loss of its wintering habitat in Central America is also a potential threat.

Experimental field studies have shown that breeding Eastern Wood-Pewees are adversely affected by the heavy browsing of vegetation by White-tailed Deer. Great increases in deer populations in recent decades may have changed the forest canopy structure over much of the eastern North American breeding range of the Eastern Wood-Pewee.

Willow Flycatcher. The southwestern subspecies of the Willow Flycatcher, which nests in riparian habitat in that region, has recently been listed as endangered because of population declines resulting from habitat loss and other factors.

Accidental Species

Several tyrant flycatchers have been recorded as accidentals in North America. Most of these species have been found close to the Mexican border and have typical ranges that extend from Mexico south into Central or South America. For example, Nutting's Flycatcher *(Myiarchus nuttingi)*, which closely resembles the Ash-throated Flycatcher, has been found in Arizona and California during winter. The Piratic Flycatcher *(Legatus leucophaius)*, which gets its common name from aggressively taking over nests of other species, has occurred in Texas and New Mexico, with records from spring and fall. Also in Texas, a Greenish Elaenia *(Myiopagis viridicata)* has been found once in May, a Masked Tityra *(Tityra semifasciata)* once in February, and the Tufted Flycatcher *(Mitrephanes phaeocercus)* in both winter and spring.

A second group of accidental species includes those that are usually found in the Caribbean. Both the Cuban Pewee *(Contopus caribaeus)* and Caribbean Elaenia *(Elaenia martinica)* have been reported from Florida in spring.

There are widely dispersed records of a South American species, the Variegated Flycatcher. These sightings come from as far afield as Maine, Ontario, Florida, Tennessee, and New Mexico, with birds found in both spring and fall, mirroring the pattern of vagrancy found among Fork-tailed Flycatchers, which also originate in South America.

The Loggerhead Kingbird *(Tyrannus caudifasciatus)* has been reported in Florida, but all six reports have been questioned, and there is apparently no confirmed record in North America.

George A. Clark, Jr.

For Least Flycatchers and Eastern Kingbirds, forest maturation in eastern North America might be eliminating suitable breeding habitat. Both species use open or young woodland habitats. Eastern Kingbirds reach their highest population densities in the Great Plains, but even there, modification of habitats for agriculture, as well as pesticide use, may have contributed to declines.

The southwestern subspecies of the Willow Flycatcher breeds in dense vegetation alongside rivers and streams, and has been placed at risk through destruction of this habitat by cutting, fires, and overgrazing by cattle; an important risk is also posed by increased brood parasitism of cowbirds associated with cattle grazing in the region. Management efforts have been directed at saving riparian vegetation and placing cattle in other areas, as cattle degrade riparian vegetation. Degradation of riparian habitats is also considered to be a factor in the decline of the Vermilion Flycatcher.

Shrikes

Predatory songbirds with hooked bills, shrikes are roughly robin-size black, gray, and white birds found in open habitats from Arctic tundra to desert grasslands. Both North American species inhabit semi-open countryside with plentiful hunting perches, such as isolated trees and scrub, fence posts, wires, hay bales, and even rooftops. In winter, Loggerhead Shrikes *(Lanius ludovicianus)* sometimes occur in areas that lack trees but have utility wires or fence posts. Both species often cache their food on barbed wire or thorn trees.

Taxonomy

There has been much disagreement about the close affiliations of this family. Shrikes have been traditionally linked to two primarily African groups of birds with similar hooked bills—the bushshrikes and the helmetshrikes. Sometimes these groups are included in the family Laniidae, expanding the family to more than 100 species. Based on DNA–DNA hybridization studies, however, the shrikes are currently not considered close relatives of either African family, but instead are placed with the corvids and vireos as part of a large group of families that evolved in Australia (see the Crows and Jays chapter for more details).

Each of the two North American shrike species has substantial geographic variation, reflected in a number of described subspecies. The Loggerhead Shrike has eight subspecies and is restricted to the Americas, while the Northern Shrike *(Lanius excubitor)* has nine subspecies, but only two of these are found in North

Laniid diversity. The two North American shrikes are very similar and are both considered true shrikes, a predominantly Old World group of about 29 species. The Loggerhead Shrike is shown.

Worldwide Family Features

- 6–13" (15–32 cm) open-country songbirds.
- About 29 species in 3 genera worldwide, in Eurasia, Africa, and North America. 2 species in 1 genus breed throughout North America; plus 1 accidental species.
- Carnivorous; eat large insects, small rodents, reptiles, small songbirds. Usually search for prey from perch; pounce on prey items from above. Store excess captured prey impaled on spines.
- Most species territorial. A few African species are cooperative breeders, found in flocks year-round. Most species monogamous for season; polygyny noted in some species. Solitary outside breeding season. Tropical species resident; temperate and subarctic species migratory.
- Breed first at 1 year old.

- Cup nest has foundation of twigs and rootlets lined with feathers and hair; built by both parents; placed in bushes and trees 3–50' (1–15 m) high; occasionally use old crow or raptor nests; nests placed on ground in 1 species. Rarely reuse nests for 2nd brood within a season.
- 1–9 subelliptical eggs; ground color variable, including whitish, yellow, greenish, reddish, with brownish blotches. Female incubates. Hatching asynchronous, at 13–17 days. 1 or 2 broods per year, rarely 3.
- Altricial young hatch with sparse down; initially brooded by female, later fed by both adults. Fledge at 13–21 days; thereafter, in some species each adult cares for part of brood for up to a month.
- Adult annual survival about 50%. Among oldest on record: 12 years, 6 months (Loggerhead Shrike).

Shrike head and bill. Shrikes use their strong hooked bill to kill and dismember prey. The Northern Shrike is shown.

America. The Northern Shrike is also found in Eurasia and Africa. The southern Old World populations of this species, which the Europeans call the Great Grey Shrike, are sometimes split off as a separate species.

Habitats

The Northern Shrike nests largely in open and scattered spruce woods and in alder and willow scrub on the periphery of the tundra. It often uses burned areas for hunting. In the winter months, most birds move southward into southern Canada and the northern United States, where they can be found on roadsides, around farm fields, and even at bird feeding stations. During years in which vole (especially *Microtus* species) populations "crash" in the northern parts of its range, the Northern Shrike stages invasions similar to those of the Rough-legged Hawk *(Buteo lagopus)* and the northern owls—such as the Snowy Owl *(Nyctea scandiaca)*—sometimes reaching as far south as Bermuda and Florida.

The more southerly Loggerhead Shrike is a permanent resident over much of its range. Populations in the northern Great Plains and northeastern states withdraw to the south in winter. This species' breeding habitat is typically open country or pastureland with a scattering of suitable small trees (often thorn-bearing trees) providing nesting sites and hunting perches. Its winter habitat requirements are much the same as for the Northern Shrike; in the southern tier states, palmetto and cacti provide hunting perches.

Food and Foraging

When these fierce songbirds are hunting, they can remind an observer of small raptors more than passerines. Like kestrels, both North American shrikes perch-hunt. Loggerhead and Northern Shrikes take similar prey: Small mammals and large insects form the bulk of their diet, but they also take birds, reptiles, and some amphibians. Shrikes can kill and cache birds as large as Northern Mockingbirds *(Mimus polyglottos)*, and one Loggerhead Shrike was observed taking a Mourning Dove *(Zenaida macroura)*. Shrikes require open hunting areas, ideally where short herbaceous growth is interspersed with patches of bare earth.

When a shrike sights prey, it leaves its hunting perch in swift, direct pursuit, seizing most prey items on the ground and dispatching them immediately. A shrike kills vertebrate prey by pounding its bill into the base or back of the skull and then using its hooked bill to sever the spinal cord between the prey's neck vertebrae, as falcons do.

Shrikes also consume small insects on the ground where captured. Using its feet or bill, a shrike carries larger species—such as grasshoppers, crickets, beetles, and all vertebrate prey—to a storage site called a larder. The prey is impaled on a thorn, fence barb, or broken twig, or wedged into a branch fork. This habit of impaling prey is the source of another name for a shrike—"Butcher Bird."

Storing prey helps the birds survive long periods of inclement weather, especially periods of heavy snowfall. Birders can locate favored shrike perches even in a bird's absence by looking for cached food. Regurgitated pellets of fur, feathers, bone, and chitinous material can often be found on the ground below these sites.

Breeding

At the start of the breeding season, male shrikes build up a cache site to increase their chances of attracting a mate. Males whose larders have been experimentally

Loggerhead Shrike at larder. Shrikes often impale their prey on sharp twigs, thorns, or barbed wire, or wedge it into forked twigs, for later consumption. The quality of a male's larder indicates the male's hunting prowess as well as the quality of his territory and may influence a female's choice of a mate.

removed by researchers have less success in finding a mate.

Pairs engage in bonding displays that include head-bowing and spreading the wings and tail. However, Northern Shrikes frequently take "tours" of their territories in order to police them before beginning nest construction. Territorial invasions and border disputes are rarely settled by fighting; instead shrikes use stereotyped posturing and rapid, repeated calling to resolve conflicts.

Both North American shrike species sing and use brief contact calls in maintaining territories and pair bonds. Males often engage in courtship feeding, especially during incubation. Their wings quivering, females solicit food by uttering calls that are reminiscent of fledglings begging for food. Males guard their mates intensely, as neighboring males may attempt extra-pair copulations.

The female probably selects the nest site. Both sexes build the nest, although the male provides most of the materials. Loggerhead Shrikes occasionally attempt a second brood during favorable weather and at lower elevations and latitudes. Second broods are extremely rare for Northern Shrikes.

Conservation

In the 1800s, when settlers cleared land for pasture, the Loggerhead Shrike may have expanded its breeding range into New York, Vermont, Pennsylvania, Ontario, Quebec, and other areas, including many southern states. Since then, land-use practices have changed drastically. Open pasturelands and orchards have been replaced by cultivated fields or young forest, both of which are unsuitable habitat for shrikes.

Within the last 70 years, the Loggerhead Shrike has declined precipitously in Canada and the northeastern United States, and around the Great Lakes. In addition to habitat loss, Loggerhead Shrikes may be hurt by excessive pesticide use.

The "San Clemente" Loggerhead Shrike *(Lanius ludovicianus mearnsi)* is found only on California's San Clemente Island, where about 40 birds remain. Their habitat has been severely affected by the grazing of feral goats and sheep. The San Diego Zoo has initiated captive breeding and reintroduction efforts. Meanwhile, the subspecies is on the U.S. Endangered Species list.

There is little information on Northern Shrike population dynamics.

Accidental Species

There are several North American records of the Brown Shrike *(Lanius cristatus),* which normally breeds in eastern Asia. North American records are mostly from Alaska, with a few from California and one from Nova Scotia. Two of the Alaska records are from the month of June; all others are from September to early December. One bird overwintered in California from November to late April.

Alec Humann

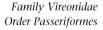

Vireos

 Vireos are small, foliage-gleaning passerines with cylindrical, slightly hooked bills that have two tooth-like notches near the tip of the upper bill. They are generally plain green above, and whitish, washed yellow, or olive below. Vireos can have wing-bars, modest to distinct eye-rings, eye-lines, and/or superciliary lines. They can be confused with wood-warblers, but vireos are bigger-headed, thicker-billed, and more deliberate in their movements than wood-warblers. Vireos inhabit thicket and forest habitats, generally favoring deciduous plant communities. Vireos range broadly in temperate and tropical North and South America, with the greatest number of species in Mexico and the southwestern United States.

Taxonomy

The taxonomic status of vireos has long been debated. There is superficial similarity of form within the genus *Vireo*, but there is also enough genetic variation for some researchers to propose that certain species be split into several species, and that a single genus should not encompass them all. The recent split of the "Solitary Vireo" into three species was driven by this proposal.

Many earlier assessments placed the shrike-vireos (*Vireolanius* species) and the peppershrikes (*Cyclarhis* species), both found in Mexico and Central America, in separate, single-genus families. Both groups are currently included in the single family Vireonidae.

The vireos formerly were linked with the nine-primaried oscines because of superficial similarities, including the vestigial 10th primary feather of some vireonids. More recently vireos have been

Vireonid diversity. *All North American members of the family are included in a single genus, and there is only minor variation among species. All are characterized by a somewhat stout head, a slightly hooked bill, and a simple plumage pattern. The White-eyed Vireo is shown.*

Worldwide Family Features

- 4–7" (10–18 cm) perching birds of thicket and forest habitats.
- About 51 species in 4 genera worldwide; all in Western Hemisphere, predominantly Central America. 15 species in 1 genus occur regularly in North America; found throughout continent north to central Canada; plus 1 accidental species.
- Eat insects and other invertebrates, fruit, some seeds.
- Territorial. Seasonally monogamous or sequentially polygynous. In winter, some species join mixed-species flocks; others territorial. Highly migratory to sedentary, depending on species.
- Breed first at 1 year old.

- Well-formed, pendulous, open-cup nest made of coarse and fine grasses, leaf and bark fibers, and spider silk; suspended from fork of small branch. Female builds entirely or mostly. Do not reuse nests.
- 3 or 4 (occasionally 2–5) subelliptical to oval eggs, usually white with modest to light speckling. Usually both parents incubate, for 12–16 days. Hatching typically over 1–2 days. 1 or 2 broods per year.
- Altricial young hatch naked or with natal down. Fledge at 10–12 days. Both parents feed young.
- Adult annual survival 55–75%. Mean longevity 2–4 years from hatching. Among oldest on record: 13 years, 6 months (Warbling Vireo).

aligned with the crows and jays and the shrikes based on similarities in DNA–DNA hybridization.

For identification purposes, vireos are sometimes split into two groups: those with both wing-bars and eye-rings (spectacles), such as the White-eyed Vireo *(Vireo griseus);* and eye-lined species without wing-bars, such as the Warbling *(V. gilvus)* and Red-eyed Vireos *(V. olivaceus).* Each group can be further subdivided; for example, the "Solitary Vireo" complex—the Blue-headed *(V. solitarius),* Plumbeous *(V. plumbeus),* and Cassin's *(V. cassinii)* Vireos—forms a distinct subset within the eye-ringed group. The Black-capped *(V. atricapillus),* Warbling, and Hutton's *(V. huttoni)* Vireos are distinctive, and each is probably most closely related to respective sister species in Mexico and Central America.

The "Eastern" and "Western" subspecies of the Warbling Vireo in North America—*Vireo gilvus gilvus* and *V. g. swainsoni,* respectively—are different in plumage, size, vocalizations, genetics, and ecology. They may be split into different species in the future, but this decision is complicated by the presence of a western intermediate, *V. g. brewsteri,* whose affinities are unclear. Geographically separate subspecies of Hutton's Vireo in California

and Arizona may also warrant full species status, although movement of individuals between groups (and therefore gene flow) may still occur.

Genetic studies have not shown the spectacled Gray *(Vireo vicinior)* and Yellow-throated *(V. flavifrons)* Vireos to be related to the similarly spectacled "Solitary Vireo" complex. Bell's Vireo *(V. bellii)* is likewise difficult to place but is probably related to the White-eyed Vireo. Other relatives of the White-eyed Vireo found across the Caribbean are an example of adaptive radiation, like the more famous Darwin's finches of the Galápagos Islands. One of these island species is the Thick-billed Vireo *(V. crassirostris),* which is widespread on the smaller islands of the Greater Antilles and has been observed on a few occasions in southeastern Florida.

Variation

With the exception of the Black-capped Vireo, the sexes are similar in plumage. The Black-capped is also unique among vireos in having delayed plumage maturation; yearling males in their first potential breeding season generally have gray napes, a plumage more like that of females. A few other songbird groups, such as the cardinals, also show delayed plumage maturation.

Habitats

Most North American vireos prefer habitats with broad-leafed foliage for foraging and nest-building. Vireos are sometimes split into groups based on whether they occupy thickets or forests. Examples of thicket types include the White-eyed, Bell's, and Black-capped Vireos, while the woodland species include the "Solitary" group and the Red-eyed and Yellow-throated Vireos.

Because most vireos forage in basically the same way, they coexist by exploiting particular habitat niches. In one area of the Edwards Plateau of central Texas, up to six species—the White-eyed, Bell's,

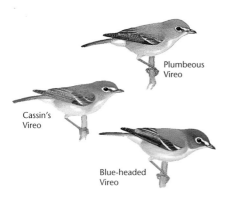

Plumbeous Vireo

Cassin's Vireo

Blue-headed Vireo

"Solitary Vireo" complex. These three closely related species were formerly considered a single species, the "Solitary Vireo." The three differ in subtleties of plumage and song, but they do not differ appreciably in shape, habits, or call notes.

Black-capped, Gray, Yellow-throated, and Red-eyed—might exist in close proximity, each in a slightly different habitat.

Where niches overlap, potentially competing species can avoid one another by foraging on different substrates, as do Red-eyed and Blue-headed Vireos, prone to deciduous and coniferous trees, respectively. Red-eyed and Philadelphia *(Vireo philadelphicus)* Vireos maintain separate territories but can overlap in taller forests, where the Philadelphias are usually in the higher stratum of vegetation.

Vireos can be solitary but during non-breeding periods will loosely associate with mixed-species foraging flocks that can provide the twin benefits of group vigilance for predators and information about food sources. For example, Blue-headed Vireos appear with flocks built around chickadees and titmice; Hutton's Vireos regularly occur with western mixed-species flocks. Vireos may accompany chickadees and titmice in mobbing owls or other potential predators. However, species such as the Yellow-throated, Black-capped, and Bell's Vireos (and probably others) may be among the last to appear in a mobbing flock in response to screech-owl or pygmy-owl calls.

Food and Foraging

The diet of vireos generally consists of insects (often butterfly and moth caterpillars), other arboreal invertebrates, and fruit. Adults frequently bring softer-bodied insects to the young. Many vireos in more arid habitats are able to meet their water

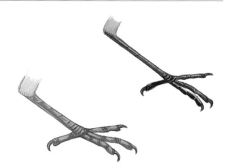

Vireo foot. The legs and feet of vireos are relatively thick and strong-looking compared to the legs and feet of wood-warblers. Here a White-eyed Vireo foot (left) is compared with that of an Orange-crowned Warbler (Vermivora celata, right).

needs from their solid diet. During winter and at other times when weather conditions leave them no other choice, vireos eat more berries and supplement their diet with seeds. The Red-eyed Vireo eats only fruit during winter.

The Gray Vireo establishes territories in its desert wintering range to defend the fruit of the Elephant-tree *(Bursera microphylla),* a species that may in turn depend on the vireo for seed dispersal. The almost complete overlap of Elephant-tree distribution and Gray Vireo winter range suggests a genuine codependency.

Vireos are generally foliage gleaners, and most feed very deliberately. They hop or fly between perches, then pause, turning or twisting their heads, and poking or probing among and under leaves and smaller branches before capturing a resting insect or moving to the next perch. This can make them easier to find through binoculars than the more active wood-warblers and kinglets. However, a number of thicket species, such as the White-eyed, Bell's, and Black-capped Vireos, are more active and can be difficult to locate in vegetation.

Vocalizations

Most vireos have songs made up of alternating short and melodious phrases and can be persistent singers. The seemingly monotonous song pattern of the wide-

Vireo head and bill. Vireos all have a rather stout, cylindrical bill with a slightly hooked tip and one or two tiny notches near the tip of the upper portion of the bill. The Red-eyed Vireo is shown.

Vireo female–female aggression. Female vireos may show intense aggression toward other females intruding on their territory, perhaps in order to minimize extra-pair copulations, although other explanations are possible. This behavior is probably common among territorial songbirds with monogamous mating systems. Black-capped Vireo females are shown.

spread Red-eyed Vireo should be familiar to most birders in eastern and central North America. Its song patterns are similar to those of other eastern species, such as the Yellow-throated, Blue-headed, and Philadelphia Vireos. On close inspection, however, the songs are more complex than just two different phrases repeated over and over again. Most vireo phrases are constructed of two to five syllables drawn from a repertoire of about 20 to 40 notes.

The Black-capped Vireo draws from a repertoire that is an order of magnitude greater than that of other vireo species. The function of this complexity is uncertain, but it may be linked to several other unique features of Black-cappeds, including the delayed plumage maturation noted in males. Other species with longer and more complex phrasing include the Warbling and Bell's Vireos; Bell's also has a more rapid song.

In vireos, patterns of cadence and repetition of phrases can tell a listener where a bird is relative to its nest. For example, a male Black-capped Vireo will repeat or truncate specific phrases when approaching its nest, and will be much less vocal when traveling with a female. The phrases in alternating sets will change from time to time, but each set usually includes one or two phrases from the previous set. Individual birds can sometimes be distinguished through a unique

note or two within a phrase, or through unique phrases of their own.

Some vireo species that occur together on the breeding grounds will sometimes sing songs that sound similar. If songs are an effective defense for maintaining one's territory from intruding males of the same species, then singing a song similar to a competing species may keep out those competing males as well. For example, Philadelphia Vireos are believed to mimic songs of Red-eyeds. These species generally do not have overlapping territories, except in tall forests, and similar songs may help them in defending these spaces. In contrast, Blue-headed Vireos that overlap in range with Red-eyeds use different notes, tone quality, and speed of delivery; the Blue-headed's songs—higher and "sweeter" than the Red-eyed's—are readily identified by even modestly attuned field observers.

While song probably advertises territory during the breeding season, it is also used in conjunction with courtship flight displays. Song development probably begins within 30 days of fledging, while the young males are still on their parents' territory, although the young birds' first songs can be quite rudimentary. Song can develop rapidly, however, and some young are closely replicating adult songs within two months of fledging.

Other telltale vocalizations can reveal the presence of vireos. Many species give short, light, but raspy *zhree, chee, rheee,* or *eeh* notes in short series or singly; these usually indicate alarm or agitation (as when a birder approaches). These notes are common to most species of North American vireos. However, the single note varies enough from species to species that experienced birders may be able to identify vireos just from call notes alone.

Breeding

Vireo pairs generally maintain seasonally monogamous or sequentially polygynous pair bonds. Males guard their mates to reduce the risk of extra-pair copulations during critical nest-building and egg-laying periods. However, opportunities for extra-pair copulations can be frequent—for example, during the brief periods when males are incubating, which begin with the penultimate or pre-penultimate eggs. Moreover, males appear to show strong interest in any females entering their territories, and resident females sometimes direct intense aggression at trespassing females.

Nests

Vireos build an intricately woven, pendulous, open-cup nest made mostly of papery leaves, fibrous bark, and coarse grasses. The nest is lined with fine grass and abundant spider silk. The lips of the nest are attached to small, subterminal branch forks with grass strands strengthened with spider silk; they hang into more open areas of a tree or shrub. This placement helps avoid damage from collisions with other branches or twigs should the nest sway. The Gray Vireo uses a different approach, building on sturdier, more internal branches, frequently with some underlying support.

Some species, such as Bell's and Black-capped Vireos, place their nests about 3 feet (1 m) high, while the nests of more arboreal species, such as the Warbling Vireo, may be considerably higher.

Males of some vireo species sometimes build the crude beginnings of a nest platform. One or more of these "bachelor pads" may be present in the territories of unmated males; however, males are inept in nest construction beyond this point. Females select one of these pads, or another site, and perform most of the nest construction, while the male follows along, probably guarding his mate. The pair's single-minded focus on nest construction makes them easy for cowbirds (*Molothrus* species) to detect, and they frequently become hosts for these brood parasites.

Eggs and Young

Most vireos lay three to four eggs (occasionally five) per clutch; three is typical for clutches laid later in the season. Tropical species lay two or three eggs. The eggs are usually whitish and lightly speckled to pure white (the latter occurs in Black-capped Vireos).

Both males and females incubate. Some male vireos have a rudimentary brood patch. Incubation normally begins in earnest with the penultimate egg, making a runt in the brood a possibility. Incubation times vary from 12 to 16 days. Most nestlings fledge within 10 to 12 days after hatching.

Vireos can raise more than one brood per year, but they are also commonly parasitized by cowbirds. Vireos' incubation times are generally longer than those of cowbirds. If they hatch at all, the later-hatching vireo young cannot compete for food with their larger cowbird nestmates, and soon die. Some vireos abandon parasitized nests and renest. However, time in the breeding season is still lost and can limit vireos to single broods, if that.

Vireos provide extensive post-fledging care, normally up to 40 days, sometimes more than 50, after the young leave the nest. However, parents often split duties, with the male attending fledged young while the female cares for a second nest. The male and female can also split care of the brood. Females sometimes move on to another mate, with or without part of the first brood.

Vireo at nest. All vireos build a neat, open-cup nest suspended in the fork of a branch and lined with fine grasses and spider silk. Here a Hutton's Vireo has just finished its nest.

Movements

Thirteen of the 14 vireo species that breed in North America are migratory; Hutton's Vireo is generally, though not entirely, sedentary. While most vireos winter (or are resident) in Central America, the closely related Red-eyed, Black-whiskered *(Vireo altiloquus),* and Yellow-green *(V. flavoviridis)* Vireos winter almost entirely in South America.

The Red-eyed Vireo's breeding range encompasses the north–south gamut of the whole vireo family—from the southwestern part of the District of Mackenzie in Canada to central Argentina—but with a gap in Central America. In this gap is found its close relative, the Yellow-green Vireo. North American subspecies of the Red-eyed Vireo are the longest-distance migrants in the genus, with Canadian breeders possibly wintering in Peru. Some of the South American subspecies of the Red-eyed Vireo (referred to as the *chivi* group of subspecies) are unique among vireos for migrating north from breeding areas in Argentina to winter in the Amazon Basin. Thus some Red-eyeds that breed in Canada may winter farther south than their counterparts that breed in Argentina.

Conservation

The Black-capped Vireo and the "Least" Bell's Vireo *(Vireo bellii pusilla)* are on the U.S. Endangered Species List. Both have limited ranges and are threatened by cowbird parasitism; their plight is often exacerbated locally by habitat degradation. Some habitat loss can occur from fire suppression, which allows wooded areas to mature beyond what is suitable for these thicket species. Moreover, agricultural practices have destroyed much of the habitat available for the "Least" Bell's Vireo in the Central Valley of California. Where cowbird control programs have been maintained, vireo populations have rebounded.

There is also concern for Caribbean species probably suffering from habitat loss. Some, such as the Puerto Rican Vireo *(Vireo latimeri)* and the Black-whiskered Vireo, may also have poor reproductive success due to parasitism by recently invading Shiny Cowbirds *(Molothrus bonariensis).* Some ornithologists worry that Black-whiskered Vireo populations in southern Florida may decline as the Shiny Cowbird continues to invade Florida.

Breeding Bird Survey data depict extensive areas of decline for other subspecies of Bell's Vireo, while White-eyed and Red-eyed Vireos are increasing in some places, declining in others. The Gray and Yellow-throated Vireos generally show increases.

According to Breeding Bird Survey data, Cassin's, Plumbeous, and Blue-headed Vireos are all increasing, but researchers studying the "Appalachian" race of the Blue-headed Vireo *(Vireo solitarius alticola)* believe that this subspecies is declining.

Accidental Species

The Yucatan Vireo *(Vireo magister)* of the Yucatán Peninsula and adjacent islands has been recorded once (April to May) at High Island in Texas.

Joseph A. Grzybowski

Crows and Jays

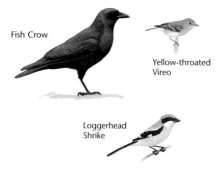

Corvids are medium-size to large perching birds with rounded wings and tails. North American members of the genus *Corvus* have wingspans that range from 29 inches to 4 feet 5 inches (90–135 cm). Corvids have strong bills and feet. Their legs are scaled in front but smooth behind, and nearly all species have stiff, bristle-like feathers covering the nostrils. Many have predominantly black or blue plumages, although some species are boldly patterned or brightly colored. Corvids are generally bold, noisy, and gregarious, and most terrestrial North American habitats—including some of the bleakest areas, such as deserts and the high Arctic—are home to at least one species.

Taxonomy

The crows and jays are part of a large radiation of crow-like birds that, according to recent biochemical evidence, probably originated in Australia. From a common crow-like ancestor evolved families of birds that superficially resemble wrens, titmice, nuthatches, swallows, warblers, flycatchers, and robins, as well as the Corvidae. Other families in this radiation—such as the birds-of-paradise (family Paradisaeidae) of New Guinea, lyrebirds (Menuridae) of Australia, and the more widespread drongos (Dicruridae) found from Africa through Asia to Australia—are unique in their appearance and behavior. Besides the Corvidae,

Fish Crow

Yellow-throated Vireo

Loggerhead Shrike

***Crow-like assemblage.** Recent DNA–DNA hybridization studies suggest that corvids arose from an Australian ancestor, which also gave rise to many of the distinctive Australian families, including wren-like, warbler-like, flycatcher-like, and other groups. North American shrikes and vireos are thought to be early offshoots of the same line.*

the only other families of this large assemblage that are found in North America are the vireos and the shrikes.

The predominantly blue New World jays represent a large radiation within the Corvidae that is confined to the Americas. The Old World corvids are often dominated by gray, brown, or iridescent plumages, and in the Americas are represented by only a few species, such as magpies, nutcrackers, and the Gray Jay *(Perisoreus canadensis)*. The mostly black crows and ravens are found worldwide except for the neotropics, barely occurring south of Mexico. The long-tailed magpies and treepies are most numerous in the tropics of Southeast Asia.

The mostly bluish jays, together with the Brown Jay *(Cyanocorax morio)*, represent an assemblage of corvids unique to the Americas. They are found in most forest and scrub habitats south of the Canadian boreal forest. The *Cyanocitta* jays—the Blue Jay *(C. cristata)* and Steller's Jay *(C. stelleri)*—have prominent crests. The crestless *Aphelocoma* jays—the Mexican Jay *(A. ultramarina)* and the scrub-jays—have long tails and few markings except for contrasting upper backs, some hint of a necklace below a pale throat, and an eye-line in the scrub-jays. The tropical *Cyanocorax* jays—the Green Jay *(C. yncas)* and the Brown Jay—have prominent bushy feathers between the bill and the eyes. Members of this genus can be quite boldly patterned; the Brown Jay, sometimes placed in its own genus, is unusual in being very dully attired.

The three scrub-jays have only recently been recognized as separate species; previously they were classified as a single species, the "Scrub Jay." The Florida Scrub-Jay *(Aphelocoma coerulescens)* differs markedly in both morphology and behavior from the Western Scrub-Jay *(A. californica)*, which is widespread in the western United States. The Island Scrub-Jay *(A. insularis)* is larger and darker, and is restricted to a single island off the coast of California.

The short-tailed Pinyon Jay *(Gymnorhinus cyanocephalus)* is unique in many ways. Although it has the blue plumage characteristic of the American jays, it lacks the feathers covering the nostrils of nearly all other family members; this is reflected in its genus name, which means "naked nose." Unlike other jays, the Pinyon Jay does not hop when on the ground but walks like crows and nutcrackers.

Although considered a jay, the Gray Jay belongs to a different group within the Corvidae than the other New World jays. It is the sole American representative of the Old World jays. These jays have large, round heads and small bills, making them appear rather like huge

Corvid diversity. *The corvids vary in size and color, but all have strong legs and feet and stout, straight bills. They range from the all-black crows and ravens in the genus* Corvus *(Common Raven, top) to the smaller, brilliantly colored New World jays (Green Jay, bottom left). Other distinctive North American corvids include the Gray Jay, Clark's Nutcracker, and the magpies (Yellow-billed Magpie, bottom right); each is related to different groups of Old World corvids.*

chickadees. Bold and tame, Gray Jays are frequent campground visitors in far-northern regions of North America and the mountainous West.

The magpies are large, very long-tailed birds, boldly patterned in black and white. They are found in open areas. Two

Worldwide Family Features

- 7½–28" (19–70 cm) perching songbirds found in wide range of habitats, from forests to deserts.
- About 118 species in 24 genera worldwide, found on all continents except Antarctica; largest number of genera in Southeast Asia. 20 species in 8 genera occur throughout North America.
- Omnivorous. Jays are insect and mast specialists; crows and ravens are opportunistic scavengers. Typically glean food from plants and ground surfaces, but can learn to get food from many unique situations.
- Monogamous; may pair for life. Some species have frequent extra-pair copulations, others none. Several species have cooperative breeding and helpers at nest. Some maintain permanent territories, others do not; a few colonial. Some form large roosts and feeding flocks outside breeding season. Most species nonmigratory or partially migratory.

- Breed first at 3–5 (rarely 1 or 2) years old.
- Both sexes build basket nest of sticks, with woven lining, usually in a tree; some use mud; magpie nests are covered. Female usually does more work; helpers may join in. Larger species may reuse nests; most species build new ones.
- 3–8 short to long subelliptical eggs; lightly bluish-green, with brown markings of varying intensity. Female incubates, beginning with penultimate egg. Hatching slightly asynchronous after 17–20 days. 1 brood per year (2 in a few species).
- Young altricial; some have down; hatchling jays are naked. Fledge at 18–40 days. Both sexes care for young; feed them for several weeks or even months after fledging.
- Adult annual survival averages 75–90%. Among oldest on record: 17 years, 7 months (Mexican Jay).

species occur in North America: the Black-billed Magpie *(Pica hudsonia)*, which is found throughout much of the West, and the Yellow-billed Magpie *(P. nuttalli)*, which is largely confined to central California. Until 2000 the Black-billed Magpie was considered to be a subspecies of the similar Eurasian Magpie *(P. pica)* of the Old World. These two species were split, however, on the basis of behavioral, morphological, and genetic differences. Moreover, vocalizations and behavior suggest that the Black-billed Magpie may be more closely related to the Yellow-billed Magpie than to its former conspecific.

An unusual member of the family, Clark's Nutcracker *(Nucifraga columbiana)* of western coniferous forests, has a chisel-like bill and gray, black, and white plumage. Its pointed bill is adapted for opening pinecones to extract the seeds.

Crows and ravens, all in the genus *Corvus,* make up nearly half of the family Corvidae worldwide. They are easily recognized by their large size, stout build, and dark appearance. Although some *Corvus* species in other parts of the world have extensive white or gray markings, all the species in North America are completely black. All have relatively broad rounded tails, broad slotted wings (see Adaptations to Lifestyle, below), and thick black beaks. While recognizing members of *Corvus* is easy, distinguishing between crow and raven species can be difficult. Voice is often the best clue to species identity. One or two species of *Corvus* are found in most habitats throughout North America.

Corvid foot. *The legs and feet of corvids are sturdy, with very strong, grasping toes. The tarsus is scaled in front but smooth in back. The Common Raven is shown.*

Variation

In the family Corvidae, the sexes are not distinguishable by plumage. In most species the females are slightly smaller than the males, but such differences are not obvious in the field.

Juvenal plumage is distinguishable from adult plumage, but sometimes only by degree. In the Gray Jay and the scrub-jays, juveniles have head feathers of a different color than adults and are markedly different in appearance. In all other corvid species, the juveniles are only subtly duller than adults. Young Mexican and Brown Jays have pale bills that gradually darken as the birds age. Often, paler skin around the bill or eye also reveals the immaturity of young corvids, as does a pale mouth lining.

Young jays molt their juvenal body feathers several months after fledging but retain their original flight feathers; these can become very worn by the next summer and sometimes help observers identify young birds. In crows, the juvenal wing feathers often weather into a dull brown, contrasting with the young birds' black backs and distinguishing them from adults. The juvenal tail feathers of all corvid species are more pointed than the blunt-tipped tail feathers of adults; these differences can sometimes be distinguished at close quarters or in birds in the hand.

Most species of the family Corvidae in North America are represented by a single subspecies. The Common Raven *(Corvus*

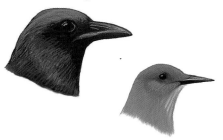

Corvid heads and bills. *Most corvids have the strong, slightly curved bill shape and dense nasal bristles shown by the American Crow (left). The bill of the Pinyon Jay (right) differs markedly; it is straight and pointed, and lacks nasal bristles.*

corax), the American Crow *(C. brachy-rhynchos)*, and the Blue Jay are among those that have more than one subspecies, but these differ little in appearance and are difficult to distinguish in the field. Geographically separated forms of the Gray Jay and especially Steller's Jay, however, are quite different and are readily identified.

Food and Foraging

Although truly omnivorous, jays predominantly eat insects and mast (nuts and large seeds that accumulate on the forest floor). In addition, they will eat a variety of seeds and fruit, and any animals they can subdue. Magpies, crows, and ravens eat more carrion than jays, but they too depend primarily on invertebrates and vegetable foods. Many species, especially the crows, have become adept at exploiting food made available by people as waste or crops.

Clark's Nutcracker and the Pinyon Jay are highly dependent upon the seeds of pine trees and will fly miles to find and gather them, but they will supplement this diet with anything any other corvid would eat. Corvids can also be significant predators at bird nests, eating the eggs and nestlings of other birds.

As opportunists, corvids, especially the crows and ravens, will take advantage of any available food source. Urban crows frequent dumpsters, compost piles, and other sources of waste food, and many have become adept at opening plastic trash bags. In North America, the Tamaulipas Crow *(Corvus imparatus)* of eastern Mexico can be seen most easily at the Brownsville, Texas, landfill. Despite their large bills, crows and ravens cannot open large carcasses and depend on other animals or cars to make carrion available.

All corvids store extra food, most burying it in the ground or hiding it in trees. The Gray Jay has special glands that produce sticky saliva, which it uses to fasten food items to tree branches, far above any possible snow cover. Many jays, especially Clark's Nutcrackers, store huge quantities of seeds and nuts. They store most of these items singly, caching thousands each year. The birds frequently dig up and rebury cached food, perhaps to check the condition of their stores, but probably also to refamiliarize themselves with the location of the items.

As specialized caching birds, corvids are able to remember thousands of individual locations. Those species that rely most on caches, such as nutcrackers and Pinyon Jays, have the best memories. Forgotten or unused seeds have been responsible for the regeneration of forests; many corvids are important seed dispersers for various tree species, especially pines and oaks.

Corvids often hold food items under their feet to peck them, and can open large nuts, such as acorns, in this way. When pecking, the birds hit the item with only their lower bill. The New World jays have a special flange on the lower jaw that braces it against the skull and makes it a more effective chisel.

Gray Jay plumage variation. *Male and female crows and jays of all ages show little variation in plumage. One notable exception is the Gray Jay, in which juveniles (left) are much darker and have a dark gray head, quite unlike the adult plumage (right).*

Intelligence

Corvids, especially the crows and ravens, are purportedly among the most intelligent of all birds. In some psychological tests crows have performed as well as monkeys. Ravens and magpies have a nonverbal ability to "count" up to seven—they recognize groups of different sizes up to seven. In fact, they can accomplish this task about as well as people who make the assessment without using words to count.

Although corvids are undoubtedly intelligent, as birds go, some of the reports of their intelligence may be overstated. A recent study investigating whether American Crows use passing cars to open nuts for them found no evidence of such an apparently intelligent act. Crows, unable to open large nuts on their own, do drop nuts onto roads. They are then able to harvest the nuts after cars run over them and open them up. However, the study found that crows were not more likely to drop nuts onto pavement if cars were approaching than if no cars were around; the crows may be just dropping nuts onto a hard surface to break them. Northwestern Crows *(Corvus caurinus)* drop shellfish such as clams onto hard surfaces to break them.

Experiments with Common Ravens, on the other hand, have demonstrated that they can show true insight when solving problems, without prior trial-and-error learning. Ravens faced with a novel task, such as getting food that is dangling on the end of a string, were able to assess the problem and then use their feet to hold the string and pull the food up. They performed this action without missteps the first time they attempted it.

Similarly, the New Caledonian Crow *(Corvus moneduloides)* of the South Pacific reportedly makes complicated hooked tools out of leaves and twigs to probe in holes for food and even stores the tools for later use. The wariness of crows and ravens, the ability of jays, ravens, and crows to learn and take advantage of new situations, and especially the corvid ability to exploit human activity for their own benefit certainly give the impression that these birds are intelligent animals.

Adaptations to Lifestyle

As birds "specialized to be generalists," corvids typically have a medium build, although some are large. Most species have somewhat stout, medium-length bills; the long, pointed bills of Clark's Nutcracker and the Pinyon Jay are specialized for opening pinecones. Corvid legs are rather long for songbirds, reflecting the amount of foraging they do on the ground, but the legs are still short compared to those of birds in general. Tails in this family are of medium length; only the magpies have truly long tails.

The wings are rather short in jays to moderately long in crows and ravens; all are moderately rounded. The larger species show pronounced slotting—gaps between the primaries on an extended wing that provide extra lift, which is important to large birds. Ravens have especially pronounced slotting in their wingtips and, like vultures, which are also wing-slotted, carrion-feeding specialists, soar often and may travel long distances to find carrion.

Members of the family Corvidae are typically social birds. Some, such as Mexican Jays and Florida Scrub-Jays, live in extended family groups year-round. Pinyon Jays maintain large social flocks

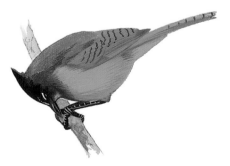

Steller's Jay pounding on nut. Corvids can hold a difficult food item such as a nut in their feet while pounding with the tip of the lower bill to open it.

American Crows mobbing Great Horned Owl. All corvids are rather noisy and bold. Traveling in small groups, they mob predators with belligerent calls and cautiously aggressive actions. This behavior serves the purpose of alerting other animals to the presence of a predator and in many cases is sufficient to drive the predator away.

even during the breeding season. Other species, like the Fish Crow *(Corvus ossifragus)*, are found predominantly in solitary pairs while breeding but congregate in large groups in the nonbreeding season.

When in groups, especially family groups, many corvids guard one another. Some birds forego foraging to spend time on guard. Such sentinels are often conspicuous, sitting up on exposed perches. Unlike flycatchers, shrikes, or other birds that forage from such perches, corvid sentinels rarely sally after flying prey or drop down on terrestrial prey. When the sentinel spots predators, it gives alarm calls; the other group members then hide, fly away, or come and mob the predator, depending on the call given.

Winter aggregations of crows, ravens, and magpies can be truly impressive. These birds may congregate at abundant sources of food during the day or come together at night to roost in large numbers. The largest known American Crow roosts in the 20th century, found in the central plains of Oklahoma and Nebraska, numbered more than 1 million birds. Why these birds gather from miles around to spend the night together has not been completely explained. Some evidence indicates that information about profitable foraging areas may be passed on at roosts; hungry birds can follow well-fed ones to better feeding sites the

next day. Another explanation is that the birds gather near reliable feeding areas, where they can be sure to get something to eat first thing in the morning and again at the end of the day.

Large roosts may also offer protection from predators and the comfort of converging at warm, sheltered spots. Many crow roosts are shifting from rural woodlots into urban areas, where they incur the wrath of people intolerant of the noise and mess. It may be that the streetlights at urban roosts allow the crows to watch for Great Horned Owls *(Bubo virginianus),* one of their most dangerous predators.

Vocalizations

Although included in the songbird order, no members of the family Corvidae have pretty songs. All, however, are noisy and easily distinguished by their vocalizations. Many species have very large vocal repertoires, including loud and harsh territorial calls and predator alarms, and softer, often more musical notes used in close quarters for communication with a mate or family member. Many species on occasion make rattling noises or even clear, bell-like notes.

Corvids are very active in mobbing of predators. They often serve as a woodland alarm system that alerts other animals to the presence of potential danger. Owls seem to be prime objects of corvid verbal abuse. The calls of an American Crow mobbing a Great Horned Owl attract all other crows within earshot. An owl can quickly be surrounded by more than 100 angry crows. Although the crows rarely make physical contact with the owl, the constant harassment can make the predator leave the area.

Most corvids are excellent mimics. Blue Jays frequently mimic the calls of hawks, and their renditions can be quite convincing. Other species often include extensive mimicry in the soft warbling songs they use in intimate situations. Unfortunately, these pretty vocalizations carry only short distances to nearby birds and rarely are heard by birders. Crows and ravens can mimic human speech, although they rarely do so in the wild.

Western Scrub-Jay at nest. All corvids build a loose, bulky cup of sticks, typically in a tree or bush; ravens often build on a ledge or man-made structure.

Breeding

Many species of corvids have complicated life stories. In Florida Scrub-Jays, Mexican Jays, and some populations of American Crows, the young remain with their parents for several years and assist them in raising subsequent broods; family groups of American Crows can include 15 individuals.

Mexican Jays have perhaps the most complicated family lives, in which several pairs may have active nests concurrently in a single group territory; individual Mexican Jays may feed young in several nests within their flock's territory at once. Once the young fledge from their nests, they are fed by all the adults in the group. Tests on the DNA of these groups indicate that a great deal of mixed parentage exists in each nest. The apparent parents may not in fact be the real parents; instead, the eggs in one nest may be from several different adults.

In contrast, the closely related Florida Scrub-Jay also has many individuals attending a single nest, but all the young are the offspring of a single breeding pair.

Raising young corvids is a time-consuming process, perhaps because of their large size. In most species the young are dependent on the adults long after they leave the nest. Hatchling jays are born naked, hence the phrase "naked as a jaybird." Other species are born with some down.

Adults bring food to the young many times a day, sometimes tearing larger items into chunks and carrying them in their extensible throats. They may keep feeding the young for weeks or even months after fledging.

Movements

Many corvid species are permanent residents. Some Florida Scrub-Jays may spend their entire lives within little more than a half-mile (1 km) of their hatching sites. Other species are migratory, although in some populations only certain individuals, often nonbreeders, migrate, while others in the same population are permanent residents. Species that migrate travel during the day. Large flights of migrating Blue Jays and American Crows can be seen at well-known migration observatories, such as Point Pelee, Ontario, and Cape May, New Jersey.

Some of the western jays, as well as Clark's Nutcracker, have periodic irruptions. Perhaps stimulated by localized mast failures, these species frequently turn up in large numbers far outside their normal range and habitat.

Black-billed Magpie nest. *The magpies surround their bulky cup nest with sticks arranged in a loose framework up to 3 feet (1 m) in diameter. Appearing as a large mass of sticks in a tree, the nest may have more than one entrance hole.*

One of the smallest members of the genus *Corvus*, the Eurasian Jackdaw *(C. monedula)*, occurs throughout the Palearctic and was found at scattered locations in northeastern North America during the 1980s. Although these birds may have ridden ships across the Atlantic, the fall migration of jackdaws in Europe has a strong westerly component, with many from the mainland wintering in Britain and Ireland. This tendency to migrate to the west could lead to more North American records in the future.

Conservation

The U.S. Fish and Wildlife Service classifies one North American corvid species, the Florida Scrub-Jay, as threatened. This species is an extreme habitat specialist, restricted to the relict, highly fragmented, fire-maintained Florida scrub. The birds are extremely sedentary and rarely disperse far enough to colonize distant islands of scrub. As its habitat gets turned into shopping malls, houses, and citrus groves, the Florida Scrub-Jay faces growing threats to its existence.

The closely related Island Scrub-Jay is restricted to a single Channel Island off the coast of southern California. Although the species is common on Santa Cruz Island, such a small population is vulnerable to catastrophic events such as epidemics and is on the WatchList.

Other corvid species are in no danger of extinction and in fact are expanding their populations in North America. Because they like both trees and open spaces, American Crows probably occurred with far less frequency before settlers opened up the eastern forests and planted trees across the prairies. Now adapting to urban environments, American Crows are continuing a slow but significant increase in their numbers.

Also probably following humans, their ornamental plants, and their bird feeders is the Blue Jay, which has become increasingly common west of its traditional range east of the Great Plains. Fish Crows also have expanded their range and are now common farther inland than ever before. They have spread inland up large river systems as far as the Ohio River in Indiana.

Common Ravens were probably more common in eastern North America when the forests were intact, but they became much more numerous in eastern North America in the 1990s than at any other time in the 20th century. Scientists cannot say whether the birds are simply taking advantage of increasing forest cover or are making a behavioral shift toward greater tolerance of humans. In western North America, ravens take advantage of expanding human settlement to colonize arid environments they have avoided in the past. The presence of large flocks of Chihuahuan Ravens *(Corvus cryptoleucus)* in the deserts of Texas and Arizona is presumably aided by the sustenance they obtain from garbage outside of towns.

Because many jays and crows are birds of the forest edge, the fragmentation of forests through development and logging (and the resultant increase in forest-edge habitat) may result in higher nest predation pressure on small birds by these corvids. Species thought to be significant nest predators include the Blue and Steller's Jays and the American Crow.

Kevin J. McGowan

Larks

 A very successful Old World group adapted to open-country conditions, larks are small to medium-size songbirds. The Horned Lark *(Eremophila alpestris)*, the only lark species native to the New World, has either a white or a yellow face, a black face mask, "horns," and a breastband. Body color varies from light tan to reddish and often matches the local soil color. The introduced Sky Lark *(Alauda arvensis)* is more nondescript and sparrow-like in appearance. Larks have slender, sharp bills strong enough for husking small seeds. These birds, which walk rather than hop, live in countryside with short grass, in habitats that range from desert to alpine.

Taxonomy

Larks are a distinct family with characteristics of the syrinx and legs that are unlike all other oscines. The syrinx of larks lacks the bony pessulus (a structure that helps create sound) that is present in all other oscine passerines. The leg characteristics, such as scales on both the front and back of the tarsi, were generally considered primitive among oscine families, and therefore larks were traditionally classified next to the swallows, another passerine family thought to have early origins. However, larks and swallows are not particularly closely related to each other.

Physically and in terms of behavior, larks resemble pipits and wagtails as well as certain New World sparrows such as the longspurs (for example, all walk in bare soil and form social flocks), but larks differ in the musculature of the syrinx. None of these other families, however, appears to be particularly closely related to the larks, and the larks' closest relatives remain uncertain.

There are 26 subspecies of Horned Lark in the New World, each subtly different in color and size. Subspecies from desert locations tend to be smaller and to have paler backs; those from the Arctic are larger and have longer wings; and those from moist habitats have darker backs. Subspecies from areas with red soil, such as Oaxaca, Mexico, and the Central Valley of California, have reddish backs. Many of these races intergrade with neighboring ones, presumably reflecting gene flow between populations.

The Horned Lark is widespread from the Arctic to Mexico, with an isolated South American population in Colombia. The same species is also found in Eurasia, where it is called the Shore Lark. In Europe, the Horned Lark breeds on rocky ridges in northern areas or on alpine tundra in the south, and winters on open beaches. In North America, where there are no competing lark species, Horned Larks are more widely distributed in open habitats.

Pacific Northwest

southeast Arizona

south Texas

Alaudid diversity. Although the family Alaudidae is represented in North America by only one native species, the Horned Lark, that species is widespread, with a variety of different subspecies, each colored to match the local habitat. Horned Larks from different regions are shown.

Food and Foraging

Larks take seeds from the ground or from plant stems, jumping up and pulling them off, if necessary. They take insects off the ground, sometimes after a chase. They generally feed on bare ground, but to reach food under snow they scratch with their feet and throw snow aside with their bills. When feeding, Horned Larks move at a faster rate than Snow Buntings or longspurs, with which they gather in large flocks during migration and in winter.

Lark head and bill. Larks have a stout but pointed bill well adapted to a varied diet of small seeds and insects picked from the ground or from grasses. The Horned Lark is shown.

Adaptations to Lifestyle

In addition to the matching of their back colors to that of the background, the adaptations of larks include flexible foraging and social behaviors, and distinctive flight and aerial displays.

In the open, poorly vegetated habitats in which they are found, larks run rather than hop, and crouch in depressions to escape inclement weather or detection by predators. Their wings are long and pointed, suitable for flight in windy

Lark foot. The feet of larks are characterized by an elongated hind claw, which is longer in species inhabiting areas with soft soil. Certain pipits and longspurs have similar long hind claws. The Horned Lark is shown.

conditions. These birds use their sharp, strong bills for digging in the soil. Their hind toes have a long nail, which is longer in species that live where soils are soft. Larks use both the bill and the feet to make a roost or nest depression.

During the nonbreeding season, larks form large nomadic flocks that tend to be concentrated in a small space and thus are difficult for predators to locate. Flocking in open country allows the birds to spot predators from a great distance.

Northern and high-elevation subspecies of Horned Larks are migratory, whereas southern ones are permanent residents. Intermediate races are partial migrants, with some individuals migrating, others not. Winter flocks of larks may contain several subspecies, which can be detected by differences in the color of the throat, supercilium, and back.

Worldwide Family Features

- 4–9" (10–23 cm) open-country songbirds.
- 91 species in 19 genera worldwide, primarily in Africa and Eurasia. 1 species breeds in North America, in open habitats throughout continent except southeastern U.S.; plus 1 introduced species.
- Eat small seeds and insects gleaned aboveground or dug from bare soil.
- Most species territorial and presumed seasonally monogamous; polygyny rare. Some resident species defend territories throughout year; may pair for life. Many species nonmigratory, but northern breeders migrate. In migration and winter, often form large flocks.
- Breed first at 1 year old.

- Female usually builds cup-like nest of grasses, lined with fine grasses, often hair; on ground, often against clump of grass or behind rock in open, sparsely vegetated area. Probably do not reuse nests.
- 2–9 subelliptical eggs, pale with blotches of black or brown. Female incubates, for 10–16 days. Hatching synchronous. 1–3 broods per year.
- Altricial young hatch covered with sparse, light-colored down on head and back. Fledge at 10–20 days; fly by 12–18 days. Both sexes care for young.
- Adult annual survival poorly studied, but known to be 65% in Sky Lark. Among oldest on record: 8 years, 5 months (Sky Lark); 7 years, 11 months (Horned Lark).

Breeding

In breeding environments that range from alpine tundra to overgrazed pasture, many larks adjust their behavior to fit their resources in several ways. They breed in certain areas only in some years or only after a fire because they prefer either sparse vegetation or no growth at all around their nest. Their territory size can depend on the abundance of food resources, and their diets can change opportunistically. Finally, they exhibit interspecific territoriality, driving off potentially competitive species.

In other ways, breeding by larks is typical of many passerine species. For instance, they appear to be monogamous during the breeding season; the females build the nest and do most of the incubating; and both parents feed the young. Larks breed two or three times a year at low elevations and latitudes, once a year at high elevations and latitudes.

Introduced Species

Because of the appeal of the Sky Lark, which has inspired literary works such as Shelley's poem "To a Skylark," there have been many attempts to introduce the species to the New World, but the bird, native to Eurasia, has survived in only a few places.

In the early 20th century, 150 Sky Larks were released on Vancouver Island, British Columbia, and by 1962 there were at least 1,000 birds in this population. Because of the development of housing and the loss of agricultural habitats, this population is now limited to a few small relic areas at the north end of the Saanich Peninsula; by 1995 only about 100 birds were left. A few Sky Larks have colonized San Juan Island, Washington, 11 miles (18 km) to the east.

The Asian subspecies of the Sky Lark *(Alauda arvensis pekinensis)* has occurred naturally in Alaska, and one individual was present for seven years in California. The subspecies has recently tried to breed in the Pribilof Islands, off Alaska.

Horned Lark aerial display. *Larks are justly famous for their flight songs, delivered from high in the air during a floating display flight. The habit of singing in flight presumably arose as a means of broadcasting song in open habitat with no raised perches. The display is primarily territorial but may also be used to attract a mate.*

Conservation

According to Christmas Bird Count and Breeding Bird Survey data, Horned Larks have declined in the northern Midwest (North Dakota, Iowa, and Illinois) and in California. For such a versatile bird and one that likes overgrazed pastures, this seems surprising. Pesticide poisoning has been implicated in some losses. An organophosphorus insecticide, Fenthion, has killed larks when sprayed on crops. Another pesticide, Carbofuran, has killed many birds, including Horned Larks. Whatever the causes, Horned Lark decline is a serious problem that bears close scrutiny. However, populations of the species overall, especially those in most western areas, are stable.

Charles H. Trost

Swallows and Martins

Family Hirundinidae
Order Passeriformes

Swallows are small to medium-size songbirds with long, pointed wings; long, forked or square tails; short, wide bills; and inconspicuous legs and feet. Their plumage is brown, gray, or iridescent blue or green, with contrasting patches of reddish brown or white in some species. They forage for aerial insects in wide, swooping flight, often returning repeatedly to sweep through clouds of swarming insects. Swallows are most often found near water, and they need open areas (away from or above the forest canopy) to catch food. Beyond these basics, their habitats are largely defined by their opportunistic foraging habits.

Taxonomy

Relationships among most swallows are well known, particularly in the case of the North American species, which are some of the best-studied wild birds in the world. Recent comparisons of DNA have provided an exceptionally good understanding of the group's genealogy. This knowledge, combined with copious information on life histories, has facilitated the study and interpretation of swallow evolution. Despite these advances, the assignment of species to genera is still in flux, largely because taxonomists have changed their view of what constitutes a genus. The number of genera worldwide has ranged from 10 to 35, and now is considered to be about 15.

The Barn, Cliff, and Cave Swallows (*Hirundo rustica, Petrochelidon pyrrhonota,* and *P. fulva,* respectively) are members of a single taxonomic group with worldwide representation. The Barn Swallow is

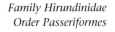

Hirundinid diversity. *The swallows are all aerial insectivores with similar morphology and habits, but they can be divided into cavity nesters, represented here by the Violet-green Swallow (left), and mud nesters, represented by the Barn Swallow (right).*

Worldwide Family Features

- 4–8" (10–20 cm) aerial songbirds of open areas, often near water.
- About 89 species in 15 genera worldwide; on all continents except Antarctica, with greatest diversity in Africa and South America. 9 species in 6 genera occur in North America; found throughout continent; plus 5 accidental species.
- Feed almost exclusively on aerial insects taken by hawking. At least 1 species eats berries in winter.
- Some species establish dispersed territories; others, aggregated nesting groups; still others, colonies. Monogamous; seasonal in most species. All North American species migratory; some forming extremely large flocks during migration.
- Breed first at 1 year old.

- Nest sites range from tunnels excavated in sandbanks; to artificial or natural holes or crevices in trees, banks, or cliffs; to cups or gourd-shaped enclosures, both built from mud. Many species nest near humans. Nest built by male and female or by female alone. Often reuse nests.
- 4–7 eggs in temperate species, 2 or 3 in tropical species; subelliptical or oval and usually white, spotted and freckled in some species. Incubation 11–20 days, by female in most species. Hatching usually synchronous. 1 or 2 broods per year.
- Altricial young naked with eyes closed at hatching. Fledge at 17–30 days. Both parents provide care.
- Adult annual survival 50–60%. Among oldest on record: 13 years, 9 months (Purple Martin).

found throughout the Northern Hemisphere. The Cliff and Cave Swallows, which occur in North and Central America and the Caribbean, are closely related to each other and to similar species in the Old World. All of these species construct their nests from mud.

The Tree Swallow *(Tachycineta bicolor)*, Violet-green Swallow *(T. thalassina)*, Purple Martin *(Progne subis)*, and Northern Rough-winged Swallow *(Stelgidopteryx serripennis)* are North American representatives of a large New World assemblage that reaches its greatest diversity in the neotropics. These New World endemics are distinguished by a common nesting characteristic—all species build their nests in the holes and crevices of trees, cliffs, or banks. Another member of this group, the Bahama Swallow *(T. cyaneoviridis)* of the Bahamas, occurs rarely in Florida.

The Northern Rough-winged Swallow is replaced in Central and South America by the closely related Southern Rough-winged Swallow *(Stelgidopteryx ruficollis)*. At times these two forms have been considered one species.

The final North American breeding species is the Bank Swallow *(Riparia riparia)*, which occurs throughout the Northern Hemisphere and has three close relatives in Africa and Asia. The Bank Swallow is allied with the New World hole-nesting species, but instead of adopting nest holes, the *Riparia* species excavate nest tunnels in sandbanks (hence the British name "Sand Martin" for the Bank Swallow).

Swallow head and bill. *All swallows have a relatively broad, rounded head and small bill; they have a broad and expansive mouth well adapted to catching small insects in flight. The Purple Martin is shown.*

"Rough" wings. *The rough-winged swallows get their name from the recurved, "rough" barbs on the leading edge of the outer primary of adult males. A similar structure has evolved independently in an unrelated genus of swallows in Africa. Ornithologists have been unable to ascertain the function of these "rough" feathers.*

Scientists have not yet determined the closest relatives of the swallows. Comparisons of DNA sequences and DNA–DNA hybrids indicate only that swallows loosely belong to a large conglomeration of passerine birds, including Old World warblers, babblers, titmice, and many other small insectivores.

Variation

In most species of swallows, males and females have similar plumages. The Purple Martin is the only North American breeding swallow species in which the sexes look dramatically different as adults.

The Tree Swallow has one of the most interesting plumage sequences of all North American birds. It is one of the very few species whose females have a distinctive subadult plumage (subadult male plumages are much more common). A female's plumage in her first breeding year is dominated above by brown, with a small number of iridescent green feathers (sometimes these are absent altogether). In the second breeding year, females gain a much darker and iridescent green-to-blue plumage, but only in their third breeding season do they acquire plumage that begins to rival the iridescent blue-green of males. In general, juvenile swallows, including male Tree Swallows, molt into adult-like plumage in the winter after they fledge; until then most of them simply look like dull versions of their elders.

The distinctive long, forked tail of the Barn Swallow makes it the easiest of North American swallows to identify, although in level flight the feathers are often swept back and resemble a single long point behind the bird. The Barn Swallow's tail gives the bird remarkable maneuverability, and it helps males to attract mates. However, these advantages are offset by the cost of an unusually long tail, including the extra energy required for flight and the bird's increased vulnerability to predators. European researchers have measured the costs and benefits of long tails by artificially lengthening or reducing tail length in males.

Cliff Swallow drinking on the wing. Like some other aerial species such as swifts and flycatchers, swallows drink and bathe from the air, simply flying over the water and dipping the bill to drink, or splashing into the water momentarily to bathe.

Two groups of swallows—the rough-wingeds and the unrelated sawwings of Africa (genus *Psalidoprocne*)—get their "rough wings" from recurved barbs on the outer webs of their primaries. In both groups, the roughened feathers are found only on adult males. The purpose of these feather modifications has been the subject of speculation for decades. Despite recent attempts to test the advantages of these feathers, their function remains elusive.

Food and Foraging

Many swallow species employ an opportunistic feeding strategy, foraging far and wide in search of ephemeral food sources. The birds may feed in large fields or small forest openings; they may forage mainly above the forest canopy or low over water.

All swallows feed on aerial insects, but they often use different hunting strategies. The Violet-green Swallow, Cliff Swallow, and Purple Martin tend to feed over land and at a greater altitude than other species. Observers often liken these high-flying swallows, which eat swarming airborne insects, to such tubenosed seabirds as storm-petrels, which feed on masses of zooplankton. Both types of birds are strong fliers and exploit large swarms of free-floating prey.

During the breeding season, Barn and Northern Rough-winged Swallows usually feed at a low altitude, generally over fields and water, respectively, and, together with the Tree Swallow, tend to be more solitary while feeding than other North American swallows. Gregariousness, or the lack of it, while feeding is partly related to nesting behavior. For example, Bank and Cliff Swallows, which nest in colonies, appear to be the most social of swallows in regard to their foraging habits.

Outside the breeding season, the foraging patterns of swallows may change dramatically. While migrating and on their wintering grounds, Barn Swallows and Tree Swallows often forage alone all day, yet may congregate in huge flocks that roost together.

The Tree Swallow is one of the few birds capable of digesting the wax in bayberries (*Myrica* species), an important food source for Tree Swallows wintering in the southern United States, especially during cold snaps. A large flock of Tree Swallows alighting to feed on bayberry bushes while emitting a chorus of buzzing calls is a spectacle few observers are likely to forget.

Breeding

Swallows are monogamous breeders. In species such as the Bank and Barn Swallows, both parents build the nest, but in the Purple Martin and Tree Swallow, among others, the female does most of the work with only a little help from the male. Females do all the incubation in many species, but both parents incubate in the Bank, Barn, Cliff, and probably Cave Swallows. Males help to feed the young in all species.

Tree Swallow at nest box. Tree Swallows nest in cavities near water, such as old woodpecker holes. The draining of swamps and cutting of dead trees has reduced the number of natural nest sites, and more and more often these swallows are using nest boxes, including those placed for other species such as bluebirds.

Nests

The swallows' habit of feeding in the open, away from forests and in clear view of predators, has placed a premium on protected nest sites near feeding areas. In the course of their evolution, swallows have developed three alternative strategies to facilitate this nesting need. One of the strategies is to excavate tunnels, as Bank Swallows do. In many New World species, the strategy is to nest in naturally occurring holes and crevices. Perhaps the most interesting strategy is to construct protected nest sites out of mud. By constructing their own nest sites, swallows free themselves from the constraint imposed by a limited number of nest holes in trees, banks, or cliffs, a freedom that has allowed them to invade food-rich habitats that previously would have been inhospitable.

Mud-based nests vary from the simple cup of the Barn Swallow or the high-walled cup of the Cave Swallow to the enclosed, gourd-shaped structure with a spout-like entrance tunnel built by the Cliff Swallow. Mud nesting reaches a pinnacle in Cliff Swallows, which pack dozens to thousands of gourd-shaped nests together in colonies on cliffs and bridge walls. Most mud nesters mix mud with dried vegetation. Species that build more complicated nests, however, usually collect mud by the mouthful, without any vegetation.

Barn Swallow at nest. Barn Swallows used to build their mud and grass nests on cliff ledges and even in small trees, but they have shifted almost entirely to nesting in buildings and under bridges. In these prime nesting sites they form loosely aggregated nesting groups.

Cliff Swallow nests in colony. *Cliff Swallows are intensely colonial, packing dozens to thousands of their gourd-shaped mud nests into a small area under eaves, bridges, or cliff ledges. Requirements for a nesting site are a vertical surface protected by an overhang, nearby open areas for foraging, and a good supply of mud for building nests.*

Many swallow species use man-made structures for breeding. In North America, the Tree Swallow and the eastern subspecies of the Purple Martin originally nested in riparian snags and woodpecker holes; now these species mainly inhabit nest boxes. Barn, Cliff, and Cave Swallows once nested in caves or overhanging cliffs; now they nest mainly on buildings, under bridges, and in culverts. The Northern Rough-winged Swallow often nests in pipes and man-made holes, while a few species—notably western Purple Martins and Violet-green Swallows—still rely mainly on natural nest sites.

Breeding Sociality

Although morphologically similar, swallow species vary dramatically in their sociality when breeding. Some, such as the Northern Rough-winged Swallow, are dispersed breeders; that is, they do not cluster their nests. Others, such as the Barn Swallow and the Purple Martin, are fundamentally territorial when breeding, but often nest in aggregations—under bridges or in "hotel-type" nest boxes, respectively. Still other species, such as the Cliff and Bank Swallows, are obligate colonial nesters, meaning that they are always found in groups; these species live in colonies consisting of a few to thousands of nests.

A classic question in ornithology is why obligate coloniality evolved. It occurs in species, such as Cliff Swallows, that group together and display such correlated behaviors as the ability to recognize their fledged young in a large crowd. Some scientists have suggested that colonial swallows nest together primarily to share information about the location of food. Facilitated communication would be

Bank Swallow colony. Bank Swallows excavate their own tunnels for nesting in steep sandbanks, where large numbers of birds may nest colonially. Such sandbanks, often shared with a pair of Belted Kingfishers (Ceryle alcyon), have become scarcer as land is developed and streams are channelized.

particularly important to species that rely on patchily distributed, ephemeral food sources.

On the other hand, colonial nesting has distinct disadvantages. Colonies attract predators and invertebrate parasites, and they increase the opportunities for promiscuity, forced extra-pair copulation, and egg-dumping (brood parasitism). A snake can simply climb from nest to nest and devastate a colony, because swallows are not powerful enough, even in large groups, to deter such a predator. Lice and other parasites can move easily through a colony or remain in nests that are reused from year to year. Close living with other pairs also may interfere with monogamy; for example, females may solicit copulations from males nesting nearby, or they may "dump" their eggs in adjacent nests to be cared for by unwitting foster parents.

Swallows that nest colonially are more likely to build enclosed nests with entrance spouts. These gourd-shaped nests may act as barriers that alleviate the problems of invertebrate parasitism, brood parasitism, and extra-pair copulation.

Conservation

Swallows present an interesting paradox for conservationists. Human activity has increased or stabilized the numbers of Barn Swallows, Cliff Swallows, Cave Swallows, Tree Swallows, and some subspecies of Purple Martins by creating nesting sites. However, development has simultaneously and dramatically shrunk some of their native habitat, notably the swamps and wetlands that are home to Purple Martins and Tree Swallows. Researchers have no idea what effect defor-estation, agriculture, and pollution have on swallows, although presumably they reduce the numbers of nest sites and prey.

Worldwide, there are a few threatened swallow species, and each has an extremely limited range. For example, the White-eyed River Martin (Pseudochelidon sirintarae) is known only from specimens taken prior to 1980 at a single lake in northern Thailand. In the New World, the Golden Swallow (Tachycineta euchrysea) has been extirpated from Jamaica and is limited to highland forests in Hispaniola. The nature of the evolutionary forces that produced such limited ranges in birds with such strong flight remains one of the most intriguing problems in swallow biology.

Accidental Species

Three swallows have not been recorded in North America in more than 100 years. The Cuban Martin (Progne cryptoleuca) was found in the Florida Keys in May 1895. The Gray-breasted Martin (P. chalybea), native to central and tropical South America, was recorded in Texas in April 1880 and May 1889. The Southern Martin (P. elegans) of South America was found in Key West, Florida, in August 1890.

More recently, the Brown-chested Martin (Progne tapera) of tropical South America was identified from a specimen at Monomoy, Massachusetts, and has been sighted in Florida and New Jersey in mid- to late fall. The Common House-Martin (Delichon urbica) breeds in Eurasia and northern Africa and winters in Africa and southern Asia; it is accidental in Alaska in summer and on Saint Pierre and Miquelon Islands, south of Newfoundland, in May.

Frederick H. Sheldon
and David W. Winkler

Chickadees and Titmice

 Chickadees and titmice are small, sociable, energetic songbirds with short, conical, pointed bills. They often have black or brown caps and throat patches or small crests. In North America, the species without crests are called chickadees, while those with crests are titmice. (In Europe, parids are called tits.) Within this family, males and females look alike, as do immatures and adults. Chickadees and titmice are found in a wide range of wooded and suburban habitats. Parids, like nuthatches and corvids, are well known for their behavior of hiding seeds in storage sites that they return to at a later time. Except during the breeding season, parids often lead flocks composed of many different species through woodlands, searching for food.

Taxonomy

In the past, the Paridae has been thought to include members of both the Remizidae (the penduline tits) and the Aegithalidae (the long-tailed tits). These three families are currently classified as close relatives, but this view has been questioned. It appears that the Bushtit *(Psaltriparus minimus)* and other long-tailed tits might be more closely related to the Old World warblers and gnatcatchers than to the parids. That the penduline tits of Eurasia and Africa are closely allied with the Paridae is less controversial.

Almost all chickadees and titmice were at one time considered to belong to a single genus, *Parus.* However, DNA–DNA hybridization studies have resulted in the separation of the *Parus* species into six distinct genera. All North American chickadees are now members of the genus *Poecile,* while all North American titmice belong to the genus *Baeolophus.*

Parid diversity. *The family Paridae is represented in North America by two genera that are similar in most respects. All have strong legs and short, stout bills. The chickadees (such as the Boreal Chickadee, left) all have a dark cap and bib; the titmice (Bridled Titmouse, right) all have a short crest.*

The new, restricted definition of the genus *Parus* includes only Old World species, such as the Great Tit *(Parus major).*

Within North American species in the genus *Poecile,* several are widely recognized as closely related: The Gray-headed Chickadee *(P. cincta,* formerly called the "Siberian Tit"), Boreal Chickadee *(P. hudsonica),* and Chestnut-backed Chickadee *(P. rufescens)* form a superspecies.

The Black-capped Chickadee *(Poecile atricapilla)* and the Carolina Chickadee *(P. carolinensis)* occasionally hybridize and have been viewed as belonging to one species, but Black-cappeds are now thought to be more closely related to the Mountain Chickadee *(P. gambeli),* with which they also occasionally hybridize. Studies of the mitochondrial DNA of Carolina Chickadees in the southern United States have found that eastern and western populations have some genetic differences, although no known morphological or voice characteristics separate these two groups.

The relationships of the titmice are also complex. The former "Plain Titmouse" is now divided into two species: the Oak Titmouse *(Baeolophus inornatus)* and the Juniper Titmouse *(B. ridgwayi).* The Tufted Titmouse *(B. bicolor)* has a distinct group of subspecies in Oklahoma and Texas, the "Black-crested" Titmice (collectively called the *atricapillus* group). This group was once considered a separate species; given the recent amount of change in parid taxonomy, it may be raised to the species level again in the future.

Carolina and Black-capped Chickadees hybridize across a very narrow region that extends from New Jersey west to Kansas; along parts of the narrow border between the species' ranges, there are narrow gaps (30–60 miles/50–100 km wide) where no chickadees are found. "Black-crested" and other Tufted Titmice intergrade along a north–south line in east-central Texas. In both situations, the hybrid zone has remained stationary throughout the 20th century.

Parid heads and bills. All parids have a sturdy, short, and stout bill used for picking up small prey as well as for pounding on seeds and nuts. On the left is the Black-capped Chickadee; on the right, the Tufted Titmouse.

Habitats

Members of the family Paridae are residents in wooded areas throughout North America, from the Mexican border north to the treeline of the taiga zone. The high-latitude and high-elevation species favor more widespread coniferous habitats over deciduous stands.

Many chickadees and titmice are common visitors to urban and suburban feeding stations. In both urban settings and many natural habitats, the scarcity of suitable nesting sites may limit the size of local breeding populations.

During periods of unfavorable weather or food shortage, all parid species will temporarily move to habitats that offer relatively better weather or more food resources. Even the Mountain Chickadee, a species generally limited to montane coniferous forests, has been found in sagebrush plains during such times.

Food and Foraging

Chickadees and titmice eat mainly caterpillars, spiders, and insects, including their eggs and larvae, but they also eat seeds, especially sunflower seeds, and berries. The Gray-headed Chickadee has even been known to feed at animal carcasses during the winter. Individuals that come to feeders carefully choose the plumpest seeds, fly to cover, and either store or consume them. They anchor larger food items with the feet and hammer them open with the bill. These "confiding" birds can even be induced to take seeds from a human hand.

Worldwide Family Features

- 4–6" (10–15 cm) woodland songbirds.
- About 53 species in 8–12 genera worldwide; found mostly in Northern Hemisphere, but also in southern Africa and Indonesia. 11 species in 2 genera breed in North America; occur over most of continent.
- Omnivorous. Eat mainly insects, especially insect and spider eggs and larvae; also seeds, especially sunflower, in winter.
- Territorial. Monogamous; most species pair for life. Outside breeding season, forage in flocks with other songbirds. Most species sedentary; some relocate seasonally a short distance from breeding territory.
- Breed first at 1 year old.
- Cup-shaped nest built in cavity; usually built by female, although both sexes may excavate hole if necessary; foundation of coarse plant matter is lined with finer, softer fibers. Reuse of nests rare in most species.
- 2–19 (typically 5–10) short sub-elliptical, white eggs, often with reddish-brown spotting. As female incubates, male feeds her. Hatching synchronous after 11–18 days. 1 or 2 broods per year.
- Altricial young born with sparse down. Female broods young; both parents feed, especially late in nesting period. Young fledge at 13–24 days.
- Adult annual survival 50–76% in the few species studied. Among oldest on record: 15 years (Blue Tit, *Cyanistes caeruleus*, of Eurasia); 13 years, 3 months (Tufted Titmouse).

Members of the Paridae share several diagnostic feeding behaviors. Specialized leg muscles enable these birds to feed acrobatically (they often feed while hanging upside down), making them particularly adept at exploiting resources in difficult locations, such as buds at the ends of twigs. Parids also store food in temporary storage sites called caches. The food may be placed in a cache and retrieved almost immediately, as when a chickadee moves many sunflower seeds from a feeder and stuffs them in nearby tree bark. In this case the caches merely help the bird get most of the food for itself. At other times, the caches may be more long-term, such as when chickadees store seeds collected in the fall for use later in the winter. This strategy, which involves significant spatial memory, is crucial for overwintering in harsh environments.

Parid foraging. The strong legs and feet and stout bill of parids are put to good use in feeding behaviors such as hanging upside down at the tip of a branch and holding a seed with the feet while pounding it open. The Black-capped Chickadee is shown.

An often-cited example of "cultural learning" in birds was the habit among some populations of European parids of raiding milk bottles. Beginning in Great Britain in the 1920s, tits would appear after the bottles were delivered to doorsteps and tear through the bottles' cardboard or foil covers to drink the cream at the top.

Outside the nesting season, parids form the nucleus of roving flocks as they search for food. The parids help to keep the group together by vocalizing frequently.

In response to their limited ability to gather food during the short winter days, parids at high elevations and latitudes are able to go into a state of regulated hypothermia, lowering their body temperature from a diurnal 107.6° F (42° C) to a nocturnal 86° F (30° C). This ability allows the birds to conserve vital energy reserves. While in this torpid state, they are able to fly, although feebly, to escape predation.

Most parids spend the nonbreeding season in flocks composed of one- or two-family groups of the parid species found in a region (often both a chickadee and a titmouse species) plus individuals or pairs of nuthatches, woodpeckers, kinglets, and other wintering insectivorous birds. Exceptions to this flocking habit are the Oak Titmouse, which remains territorial all year, and the Juniper Titmouse and the Gray-headed Chickadee, for which the flocks may be restricted to family groups.

Black-capped Chickadee at nest. All parids nest in cavities, within which they build a cup-shaped nest. Here a bird carries nesting material into a cavity.

Breeding

In late winter, parid pairs part from mixed-species flocks and begin to defend territories for the breeding season.

Courtship displays in this family are not complex; they include visits to possible nest sites and ritual feeding of the female by the male. Most North American parid species are believed to mate for life.

Parids build a cup-shaped nest in a cavity. Common nest sites include tree cavities, old woodpecker cavities, and nest boxes; more unusual sites include pipes and holes in wooden fence posts. There are reports of Mountain Chickadees using abandoned mammal burrows and Carolina Chickadees using old nests built by Cliff Swallows *(Petrochelidon pyrrhonota)*. The highest reported nest sites (100'/30 m above the ground) are those of Tufted Titmice.

The pair either cleans out the pre-existing cavity of an old site or excavates a new one; the female usually chooses the nest site. When an existing cavity is chosen, some parids may excavate the hole further to make it more suitable.

Some species, such as Boreal and Black-capped Chickadees, regularly excavate, while other species, including the Mountain Chickadee and Bridled Titmouse

Mobbing

Mobbing is a poorly understood phenomenon in which one or more members of a species, or even several species in concert, chase, dive-bomb, or surround a predator or klepto-parasite, often vocalizing vigorously. The intent of such attacks is largely to encourage the "enemy" to move on to another area.

Mobbing is most common among swallows, gulls and terns, crows, blackbirds and orioles, tyrant flycatchers, and parids. It occurs mostly during the nesting season, although birds also mob during winter. In some cases, it is thought that the purpose of the mobbing is to distract predators away from the nest sites. Collective mobbing by several species probably serves both to keep control of potential threats in the area and to teach younger birds how to recognize predators.

When a chickadee or titmouse locates a threat, it commences mobbing, often only scolding the predator from a nearby perch, but sometimes actually striking the enemy from behind. In addition to the mobbing species noted above, other birds often participate or fly in to investigate the scene; these may include wood-warblers, kinglets, tanagers, and even nonpasserines like goatsuckers, woodpeckers, and cuckoos. Some birds, such as thrushes, may take a more passive role, flying in to join a mobbing flock but rarely leading the charge.

Mobbing involves some risk to the mobbers, a factor that is difficult to study and quantify. Since predators are the focus of attention in a mobbing event, they lose the element of surprise that often facilitates their attacks. Predators sometimes depart in response to mobbing and sometimes do not, and the success of a particular act of mobbing can be difficult to gauge.

The birder who listens carefully for the scolding calls of parids is often rewarded with the sight of a predator—a small perched owl, or a squirrel, snake, raccoon, or domestic cat. Many birders find that whistling like a small owl can attract numbers of birds, even at midday. Imitating mobbing calls can have similar results and provide close views of inquisitive birds.

Boreal Chickadees mobbing a Boreal Owl. *Parids are social, bold, and inquisitive, traits that endear them to humans but make them among the most tenacious and aggressive songbirds when mobbing owls or other predators. Chickadees and titmice usually take the lead in announcing the presence of a small owl.*

Mountain Chickadees at a feeder. Chickadees and titmice are among the most loyal and frequent visitors to bird feeders, carefully selecting a seed and flying back to the woods to consume it. Given how many calories the birds consume in sunflower seeds when these are available, one wonders how they survive the winter in northern climates without feeders, eating spider and insect eggs.

(Baeolophus wollweberi), do not. In species that excavate, both sexes cooperate in the work. Cavity excavation can take up to two weeks.

Construction of the nest is predominantly by the female and lasts an average of five days (up to 11 days in the Tufted Titmouse). The female stuffs the cavity with a foundation of coarse plant material, such as leaves, bark strips, and mosses. She then lines the egg cup with finer materials, like feathers, animal hair, and plant down; Tufted Titmice often use snake skins. The Mexican Chickadee *(Poecile sclateri)* is unique among parids in placing crushed beetles around the cavity entrance, probably to deter predators. Parids are not significantly parasitized by cowbirds, thanks to the small dimensions of their nest entrances.

As most species produce one brood per season, the adults continue to care for their young after fledging; occasionally adults and young remain together into the winter months. Those species that have a second brood, such as Mexican Chickadees and Tufted Titmice, have been known to employ fledged young from earlier broods as food providers during the second nesting.

Movements

Most members of this family are basically sedentary, but many species engage in seasonal movements a short distance away from the nesting territory. Montane species may move to lower elevations during periods of food shortages.

Some species, such as the Boreal and Black-capped Chickadees, stage irregular irruptive movements in which they travel many miles south of their typical winter ranges. These irruptions are especially noted in the Black-capped Chickadee. In some winters, thousands of Black-cappeds may move into the northeastern United States. Sometimes called invasions, these movements are in response to food shortages. These diurnal movements involve individuals usually flying at low altitudes, except when they attempt water crossings.

Conservation

The practice of maintaining bird-feeding stations across North America has benefited many parids, and some species appear to have maintained or even increased their populations in recent decades. However, the Boreal, Mountain, and Carolina Chickadees have undergone long-term declines. Both Bridled and Oak Titmice are included on the WatchList.

The Mexican Chickadee, Gray-headed Chickadee, and Bridled Titmouse, which have limited ranges in North America, are potentially threatened by local habitat destruction or degradation.

As with all cavity-nesting species, local parid populations may decline with the removal of dead and dying trees, a common practice in areas where people live. Snag retention, a forestry practice that keeps or even creates standing dead trees in commercial forest stands, should help maintain populations.

Alec Humann

Penduline Tits (Verdin)

Family Remizidae
Order Passeriformes

The Verdin *(Auriparus flaviceps)* is a very small songbird with a short, conical, pointed bill. Adults are gray with a yellow head, and males and females look nearly alike. Immatures have distinct plumages that lack the chestnut coverts and yellow head of adults. Verdins, permanent residents throughout the U.S. desert Southwest and most common in the Sonoran Desert, favor low-elevation areas with thorny scrub that border washes and waterways; they can be locally common in suburban areas landscaped with desert plants. Verdins also occasionally occupy waterside growths of willows, poplars, and other riparian vegetation. Their high-pitched calls are a familiar sound in lowland desert washes.

Taxonomy

The Verdin, once included with chickadees and titmice in the family Paridae, is now placed in a separate family along with the penduline tits of Eurasia and Africa; the sole species in its genus, it is the only North American member of the family. The penduline tits are still considered to be closely related to the parids, because members of the two groups have similar behaviors. Both engage in active, acrobatic foraging in vegetation and hang upside down while feeding.

Verdin. Verdins are small and superficially chickadee-like, but with different calls and habits and more sharply pointed bills.

In the past, the Verdin has been grouped with the Bananaquit *(Coereba flaveola)* and the gnatcatchers *(Polioptila* species) rather than with the penduline tits. Initial DNA–DNA hybridization studies supported a close relationship with the gnatcatchers, but later studies suggest the current taxonomy is correct.

Food and Foraging

Verdins work dexterously through thorny desert vegetation in pursuit of their insect prey. In addition, they probe for nectar at flowers and hummingbird feeders, and consume fruits and berries. They rarely take water directly, deriving it instead through food items.

Verdins glean insects mostly from plant surfaces. They can hang upside down while foraging and sometimes use their feet to pull the tips of branches closer for inspection. They may hold larger items, such as large spiders or their cocoons, tightly underfoot while tearing them apart with the bill.

Verdins are "nectar-robbers" rather than true pollinators. They slit the corollas of long tubular flowers to access the nectar, thus bypassing the flower structures designed to deposit pollen on insects and birds. These cuts at the flower bases are often seen on plants such as the Tree Tobacco within a Verdin's territory. Nectivorous insects make use of the slits cut by Verdins to rob nectar.

During the heat of the day, Verdins slow their activity and seek out shaded areas. They sometimes join mixed-species foraging flocks.

Breeding

The male and female construct the breeding nest over the course of about a week; the male sometimes builds nests at several sites before the female chooses a suitable one. Verdins sometimes appropriate materials from other Verdin nests that are under construction or left over from previous seasons. The nest is situated in the outer branches of a thorny bush, usually a few feet off the ground.

Verdin nests are spherical, with an exterior fashioned from thorny twigs, points facing outward, and held tight with spider webs, lichen, leaves, and fur. The interior consists of less formidable twigs, with a central chamber lined with feathers, hair, or fur. There is one side entrance concealed by an overhang. Nests built early in the season have entrances situated opposite the prevailing winds to avoid the cool spring air; later nests have entrances facing the wind to take advantage of evaporative cooling.

The female feeds the young for the first five days or so; after that, both parents feed. After the young are fledged, the male assumes full care while the female begins a second clutch.

Verdins are unusual in their habit of building roosting nests. Roost sites can be old nests used for rearing young or new nests that are constructed specifically for

Verdin nest. Verdins build a spherical nest out of thorny twigs. The side entrance is concealed by overhanging twigs. These features presumably deter would-be predators.

roosting. They typically serve individuals, although sometimes newly fledged young roost together. Roosting nests are located in branch forks rather than out among the branch ends and thus afford protection from cold desert nights.

Conservation

Verdins are sparsely distributed within their range but fairly common where appropriate habitat exists. They increased in Arizona over the late 19th century as mesquite brushlands spread but have been declining in the late 20th century.

Alec Humann

Verdin head and bill. The Verdin's short, stout bill is similar to a chickadee's but more sharply pointed; it is well suited to the bird's normal diet of small insects and seeds.

Worldwide Family Features

- 3–4½" (7.5–11 cm) songbirds of forests and brushlands.
- 13 species in 5 genera worldwide; occur predominantly in Eurasia and Africa. 1 species breeds in North America, in arid regions of U.S. Southwest.
- Eat mostly insects; also plant matter, such as berries, nectar. Glean insects from plant surfaces; slit flower corollas for nectar.
- Most species territorial. Form pairs or small family groups during breeding season and later; occasionally seen singly in nonbreeding season. Some species monogamous; others polygynous or even cooperative breeders. Short pair bonds, sometimes more than 1 per

season. Temperate species migratory; most African species resident.
- Breed first at 1 year old.
- Large oval or cocoon-shaped nest with small side opening, placed in bush, reed, or low tree. Both parents build nest, which is sometimes reused.
- 3–10 subelliptical, greenish-blue eggs with reddish-brown spotting. Female incubates, for 13–17 days. Hatching synchronous. 1 or 2 broods per year.
- Altricial young naked at hatching. Fledge at 17–26 days. Both adults feed young.
- Adult annual survival 60%. Among oldest on record: 5 years, 7 months (Verdin).

Long-tailed Tits (Bushtit)

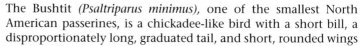

Family Aegithalidae
Order Passeriformes

The Bushtit *(Psaltriparus minimus)*, one of the smallest North American passerines, is a chickadee-like bird with a short bill, a disproportionately long, graduated tail, and short, rounded wings that make its flight weak and laborious. Mostly gray with brown highlights, males and females are nearly alike. Bushtits are found in a variety of open forest and shrubland habitats.

Taxonomy

The Bushtit is a member of an Old World group known as the long-tailed tits. Ornithologists once grouped these birds with the chickadees and titmice in the family Paridae. Later, differences in nest structure and genetic composition between the groups led researchers to place the long-tailed tits in a separate family.

The Bushtit was formerly split into two species, the "Common Bushtit" and the "Black-eared Bushtit," based on plumage characteristics that are distinctive but variable. The "Common Bushtit" forms have gray auriculars, or "ear" patches. Subsequently researchers have shown that the "Black-eared Bushtit" is the result of polymorphism within the species. Nonetheless, taxonomists recognize a number of Bushtit subspecies, which are separated into three groups. One group is found along the Pacific coast, a second in the interior United States south to Mexico, and a third primarily in Mexico and Guatemala. Black-eared birds are most

Bushtit. *Only one species of the small family Aegithalidae occurs in the New World. Members of this family were once combined with the chickadees and titmice in a single family.*

Bushtit head and bill. *The Bushtit head and bill are superficially chickadee-like, but note the slightly decurved and very small bill.*

Worldwide Family Features

- 3–6½" (8–16 cm) songbirds of open woods and shrublands.
- 8 species in 3 genera worldwide; found mostly in Eurasia, especially in Himalayas and China. 1 species breeds in North America, from Pacific coast to mountainous regions of the interior West.
- Eat mostly insects gleaned from leaves and other plant surfaces; occasionally berries, seeds.
- Somewhat territorial when nesting; outside nesting season, can travel in large mixed-species flocks. Monogamous for 1 breeding season, rarely longer; some species have helpers at nest. Nonmigratory, or partial migrants.
- Breed first at 1 year old.

- Large, pendulous nest has entrance near top; suspended from several branches or twigs in tree or bush. Made from spider webs and a wide array of plant materials, lined with feathers and animal hair. Both sexes construct nest, which is not reused; materials may be recycled for later nests.
- 2–15 (normally 5–12) white, subelliptical eggs. Both parents incubate for 12–18 days. Hatching synchronous. 1 or 2 broods per year.
- Altricial young naked at hatching. Fledge at 14–19 days. Both adults feed young, even after fledging.
- Adult annual survival poorly known. Among oldest on record: 8 years, 5 months (Bushtit).

common south of the United States but can be found in the mountains of western Texas and southern New Mexico. Many birds intermediate between the black-eared and gray-eared forms occur in populations along the U.S.–Mexico border.

Food and Foraging

Bushtits are very active foragers. Outside the nesting season, they form large flocks comprising several family groups and led by a single bird or perhaps a set of leaders. Such flocks often stay together over a period of several years, driving off outsiders. When two Bushtit flocks meet, the males engage in territorial displays that include agitated calling, brief tail-chasing, and occasional fighting. Bushtit flocks sometimes join mixed-species foraging flocks that pass through their winter territory.

Bushtit nest. The nest of the Bushtit is a large, pendulous sack with an entrance near the top. Despite their small size, Bushtits aggressively defend the vicinity of the nest from predators.

Bushtits pick insects and spiders from leaf and twig surfaces, sometimes hanging upside down to reach prey items. When moving on to the next bush or tree, individuals fly out more or less singly, each bird following the one ahead of it. Flock members maintain contact with light, high-pitched call notes.

On winter nights, foraging flocks roost communally in dense cover, often huddling shoulder to shoulder during cold spells. At the onset of a new breeding season, flocks begin to break up as pairs seek out territories. However, pairs rejoin their roosting flocks at night until nest construction is completed.

Breeding

Bushtit courtship is brief and includes posturing and calling; no song is known. Pairs sometimes remain together over several seasons.

Bushtit nests are pendulous and sometimes reach 12 inches (30 cm) in length, with an entrance near the top. When the outer shell of the nest is completed, the pair spends the night roosting inside it.

A nest can take from two weeks to almost two months to complete, but adults will abandon a nest they are building if disturbed. Bushtits recycle previously gathered materials to use at a new site.

Both parents incubate and share the brooding and feeding of the young. Breeding pairs sometimes have the help of other Bushtits in feeding their young. These helpers are usually unmated males or breeders whose own nests have failed. Unlike other cooperatively breeding species, Bushtit helpers are rarely young from a previous brood.

Some nests contain huge clutches of eggs thought to result from communal nesting, in which several females place eggs in one nest and all adults care for the young. The Bushtit's complex social system is not yet fully understood.

Conservation

Bushtits are fairly common across their range, and have recently expanded into the Pacific Northwest. The species' wide, variable habitat choices keep its population safe, on the whole.

Alec Humann

Nuthatches

Nuthatches are small forest songbirds that superficially resemble small, stocky woodpeckers. Like woodpeckers, they climb on tree trunks and glean food from bark crevices or by excavating small holes. Nuthatches are not closely related to woodpeckers, however, and can be distinguished by their small size, square tail, different climbing methods, and the upturned underside to the bill. Most species are predominantly gray and white or gray and reddish, often with a brown head or eyestripe. Nuthatches are found primarily in mature, open forests, where they frequently move both up and down tree trunks, unlike creepers and woodpeckers, which typically move only up. Nuthatches also forage on stems, branch tips, and pinecones, and sometimes come to feeders in winter.

Taxonomy

Of the 25 Sittidae species worldwide, 24 belong to the genus *Sitta,* the true nuthatches. The remaining species, the Wallcreeper *(Tichodroma muraria)* of Eurasia, is generally placed in a separate subfamily within the family Sittidae, but some authorities place it in its own family (Tichodromidae). The family's greatest diversity is in southern Asia, which has 15 species.

Relationships among the nuthatches are debated, particularly for species living in China and the former Soviet Union. Among North American species, the Brown-headed Nuthatch *(Sitta pusilla)*

and the Pygmy Nuthatch *(S. pygmaea)* have been considered to belong to one species in the past, but plumages, morphology, and calls differ.

Sittid diversity. *Nuthatches vary little, and all North American species are in a single genus; in fact, 24 of the 25 species in the family worldwide are in the genus* Sitta. *The only exception is the very different Wallcreeper of Eurasia, which is placed in its own subfamily. The Red-breasted Nuthatch is shown.*

Worldwide Family Features

- 4–7½" (10–19 cm) woodland songbirds.
- 25 species in 2 genera, found throughout Northern Hemisphere. 4 species in 1 genus breed in North America; occur from subarctic south into Mexico.
- Eat mainly invertebrates and nuts; in fall and winter, store seeds and sometimes invertebrates in small caches.
- Generally territorial year-round; may feed in small flocks. Monogamous for season. Some species have additional adults associated with mating pair and breed cooperatively. Often join mixed-species foraging flocks in nonbreeding season. Most species resident; some show irruptive movements in nonbreeding season.
- Breed first at 1 year old.
- In most species, both sexes excavate cavities in trees for nesting. Some

species use natural cavities that they line with vegetation, sometimes fur and feathers. Occasionally use nest boxes. Nest reuse from year to year unusual.
- 2–13 (usually 5–9) subelliptical to short subelliptical eggs; white with markings that vary from peppered spots to blotches of brown, red, purple, gray. Incubation usually 11–20 days; in some species, shared by parents; in others, only female incubates. Hatching synchronous. Usually 1 brood per year, rarely 2.
- Altricial young naked except for some dark gray down; fledging time 18–30 days. Both sexes care for young.
- Adult annual survival little known; estimated at 50%. Among oldest on record: 9 years, 10 months (White-breasted Nuthatch).

The Red-breasted Nuthatch *(Sitta canadensis)* is one of five species worldwide that once were viewed as a single species. Recent phylogenetic work supports the close relationship of these species—based on morphological, genetic, and behavioral characteristics—but does not suggest that they are a single species.

Geographic variation exists within several species, but there is disagreement over the number of subspecies. Among North American species, variation is most extreme in the widespread White-breasted Nuthatch *(Sitta carolinensis)*, which exhibits distinct vocal differences among birds from the East, the Rocky Mountains, and the West. This variation results in from six to 11 subspecies. Another widespread species, the Red-breasted Nuthatch, lacks geographic variation altogether.

Brown-headed Nuthatch using a tool. *The Brown-headed Nuthatch is one of the few species of North American birds known to use tools. This species has been observed using a small piece of bark to pry off other bits of bark to expose invertebrate prey hidden beneath.*

Food and Foraging

Nuthatches eat invertebrates, seeds, and nuts. White-breasted and Red-breasted Nuthatches are well known for their foraging style—in addition to foraging while moving up trunks, facing up, they commonly forage while walking down tree trunks, facing down—although Red-breasteds also spend much time foraging in the canopy. Brown-headed and Pygmy Nuthatches feed in clusters of pine needles at the tips of branches, often hanging upside down while foraging.

White-breasted Nuthatch "hatching" a nut. *Nuthatches are named for their habit of wedging a hard food item such as a nut into a bark crevice and hammering or hacking ("hatching") it with the bill to open it.*

Nuthatches will often take a seed, fly to a tree branch, jam the seed into a crevice in the bark, and hack open the seed by pounding on it with the bill. The word "nuthatch" originated in Europe and refers to this foraging technique; "hatch" is thought to be a corruption of the Old English word "hack."

Nuthatches take invertebrates from bark and crevices, locating them by sight; they also excavate them from wood, nuts, and even crops such as corn. Brown-headed Nuthatches are among the few bird species known to use a tool. Some individuals hold a piece of bark in the bill and use it to flake off another piece of bark, uncovering invertebrates.

During the nonbreeding season, nuthatches often join mixed-species feeding flocks that include chickadees, creepers, and kinglets. Brown-headed Nuthatches often form single-species flocks containing more than 20 birds.

In fall and winter, nuthatches store nuts and invertebrates in caches for future consumption. These storage sites, which are dispersed and often hold only one seed per cache, are located in bark crevices and under branches, and are often covered with bark, lichens, moss, and snow. White-breasted Nuthatch males store food on tree trunks, while females create caches in more varied sites.

Adaptations to Lifestyle

Nuthatches are found mainly in mature forests. Pygmy and Brown-headed Nuthatches are pine specialists, Red-breasteds are spruce and fir specialists, and White-breasteds live in mature deciduous forests. The last two overlap in mixed coniferous and deciduous forests.

Like woodpeckers, nuthatches are adapted to an arboreal lifestyle. The nuthatch body tends to be stocky; body sizes range from the 4¼-inch (11 cm) Pygmy Nuthatch of North America to the Giant Nuthatch *(Sitta magna)* of Southeast Asia, which can be as large as 7½ inches (19 cm) from bill tip to tail tip. The largest North American species is the White-breasted Nuthatch, which is almost 6 inches (15 cm) long.

The legs of nuthatches are short and sturdy, and their long claws help them grip onto trees. When foraging on vertical surfaces, birds grasp the substrate with one leg and use the other leg as a prop. This climbing method is unlike that of woodpeckers and creepers and enables nuthatches to move down trees as easily as up. The reasons nuthatches forage by climbing down trees are not fully known; it may be that they can spot prey hidden from creepers, woodpeckers, and other upward-facing feeders.

Research on the energetics of locomotion suggests that it is more efficient for

Nuthatch head and bill. *Nuthatches have a strong, straight bill, with the underside angled up toward the tip, that they use for tapping and prying bark to expose food. The Brown-headed Nuthatch is shown.*

birds to forage as woodpeckers or creepers do—flying down to a low point on a trunk and feeding while moving up the tree. Birds moving up the tree can use gravity and stiff tail feathers to prop themselves against the trunk, and both woodpeckers and creepers are noted for having stiff rectrices. However, if a woodpecker or creeper were inverted on a tree trunk, its tail would not provide support and the bird would fall.

Like certain other species, nuthatches will roost together for warmth during the nonbreeding season. More than 100 Pygmy Nuthatches have been recorded in a single cavity.

Breeding

Nuthatches are monogamous. However, up to 30 percent of Pygmy Nuthatch pairs and up to 20 percent of Brown-headed Nuthatch pairs are cooperative breeders; up to three additional (helper) adults assist Pygmy Nuthatch parents, while Brown-headed Nuthatches usually have only one helper. These extra adults, usually first-year males, help throughout the breeding cycle, from nest building to feeding the young. The frequency of helping probably depends on habitat availability, with more birds helping when a lack of open territories prevents the helpers from breeding.

All nuthatches nest in cavities. White-breasted Nuthatches nest in existing cavities, while other species normally excavate their own. Cavity excavation takes from one to eight weeks. Cavities are

Nuthatch foot. *The legs and feet of nuthatches are strong, with long toes and long, sharp claws for gripping bark. The White-breasted Nuthatch is shown.*

lined with a combination of vegetation, fur, and feathers. Some nuthatches modify their cavities in unusual ways: Red-breasted Nuthatches smear sap around the entrances to their nests, and White-breasted Nuthatches sweep around their nest holes with noxious-smelling insects. Some Old World species use mud to decrease the size of their nest cavity entrances. Each of these behaviors probably helps keep predators from entering the nests.

Cavity-nesting birds generally produce pure white eggs, but nuthatches are an exception to this pattern. Their eggs are white but have markings varying from peppered spots to heavy blotches. Biologists suggest that the eggs of cavity-nesting birds are white because cavity nesters have no need for the camouflage pigment provides. If camouflage is the only function of pigmentation in eggs, it might follow that cavity nesting evolved relatively recently in nuthatches and there has not been enough time for egg color to change. The reasons for egg patterning, however, may be more complex.

White-breasted Nuthatch climbing. *Nuthatches climb using only their feet, unlike woodpeckers and creepers, which use the tail as a prop. The smaller species often hang upside down from pinecones.*

ical winter range to survive. At these times, the birds move south in what is called an irruption, and they can be common in areas where they usually are rare. Red-breasted Nuthatch irruptions occur quite frequently and have resulted in records of individuals as far south as southern Texas.

Movements

For the most part, nuthatches are not migratory, although some populations of White-breasted Nuthatches do migrate. In poor food years, many Red-breasted Nuthatches are forced to leave their typ-

White-breasted Nuthatch egg. *The eggs of nuthatches are spotted and streaked with brown. Most other cavity-nesting species have plain white eggs. Why nuthatches lay patterned eggs rather than plain is unknown.*

Conservation

Because nuthatches are habitat specialists, they are at risk of local extinction when their habitat is at risk. Red-breasted and White-breasted Nuthatches, however, have enormous ranges, which should protect them from the effects of local habitat losses.

According to Breeding Bird Survey data, Brown-headed Nuthatches are declining, while Red-breasted Nuthatches are increasing. Pygmy Nuthatch populations are too poorly sampled to discern changes in size. Breeding Bird Survey and Christmas Bird Count data indicate that the White-breasted Nuthatch is increasing; however, breeding populations along the southeastern coastal plains of Georgia and the Carolinas have declined drastically. The Brown-headed Nuthatch is on the WatchList because of the species' small range and apparent population declines.

J. Michael Reed

Creepers

Creepers are small arboreal birds characterized by a light build; long, curved claws; short legs; a fairly long tail with stiffened, pointed tips; and a thin, decurved bill. Males and females look alike. The predominantly brown upperparts are speckled with white, buff, and black, providing excellent camouflage when the birds inch up a tree trunk or along a branch; the underparts are much paler. Creepers live primarily in mature coniferous or mixed coniferous-deciduous forests; they prefer shaded and wet areas.

Taxonomy

Relationships within the Certhiidae are not well understood. The AOU and most researchers consider the family to include seven species worldwide—six tree-creepers in the genus *Certhia* and the Spotted Creeper *(Salpornis spilonotus)* of Africa, which is in a different subfamily. Other analyses, based on DNA–DNA hybridization, group the tree-creepers with wrens, gnatcatchers, and gnatwrens in a large family that includes about 100 species in 23 genera.

While some classification systems have considered the Brown Creeper *(Certhia americana)* of North America to be con-specific with the Eurasian Tree-Creeper *(C. familiaris)* in the past, the most recent evidence supports their separation based on differences in vocalizations. The 12 recognized subspecies of the Brown Creeper vary in only minor ways. Clinal variation in body size occurs from north

Brown Creeper. The single North American representative of the family Certhiidae is nearly identical to five other species of the genus Certhia, *found in Europe and Asia. The greatest diversity occurs in the Himalayas.*

Creeper head and bill. Creepers have a very thin and decurved bill adapted for probing into tiny bark crevices to extract insects and spiders. The Brown Creeper is shown.

Worldwide Family Features

- 5–7" (12–18 cm) woodland songbirds.
- 7 species in 2 genera worldwide; found throughout much of temperate Northern Hemisphere, south to Central America. 1 species occurs throughout much of North America.
- Eat invertebrates by gleaning and probing bark; also nuts and seeds in winter.
- Territorial during breeding season. Seasonally monogamous. Generally solitary during nonbreeding season, but may join mixed-species foraging flocks. Northern populations at least partially migratory; southern populations resident.
- Breed first at 1 year old.
- Nest is "hammock" of twigs, bark fibers, mosses, and spider cocoons, lined with

feathers; placed against tree trunk, in protected site (under branch, bark) off ground. Female builds nest. Do not reuse nests.
- 3–9 (usually 5 or 6) white, subelliptical eggs, lightly spotted with brown. Female incubates for 13–15 days. Hatching synchronous. 1 or 2 broods per year.
- Altricial young naked at hatch except for long, grayish down, especially on head. Fledge at 13–18 days. Both sexes care for young.
- Little data on survival. Among oldest on record: 7 years, 8 months (Eurasian Tree-Creeper); 4 years, 6 months (Brown Creeper).

to south, with larger subspecies in the north; northern subspecies are much larger than those in Mexico.

Although Brown Creepers have physical features convergent with those of woodpeckers, they are not closely related, and in the field the two groups are readily distinguishable. Birders in Central America can mistake woodcreepers (family Dendrocolaptidae) for Brown Creepers, but woodcreepers are tropical suboscine birds more closely related to the tyrant flycatchers than to any other North American species.

Brown Creeper "hammock." The nest of a creeper is a hammock-shaped mass of spider cocoons, fine bark strips, mosses, and feathers, placed behind a loose sheet of bark.

Food and Foraging

Creepers eat invertebrates, adding seeds and nuts to their diet during winter. They forage primarily on tree trunks and the undersides of limbs, gleaning spiders, insects, and other small invertebrates from the surface or removing them from cracks and crevices with a tweezer-like bill. This foraging behavior is similar to that of many woodpeckers. In winter, they sometimes join mixed-species foraging flocks.

The Brown Creeper's foraging behavior is also more like that of a woodpecker than other passerines in that it uses its tail for support when climbing a tree. The Brown Creeper is the only songbird that molts its tail as woodpeckers do, retaining the important central feathers while the other tail feathers molt and regrow. (See Nuthatches for a comparison of foraging techniques.)

A Brown Creeper's coloring keeps it well camouflaged while it forages on trees. It often freezes in the presence of a perceived threat.

It is challenging for creepers to glean enough food to survive during cold winter days, when using energy efficiently is important. Like some other small birds, Brown Creepers sometimes roost in groups in the nonbreeding season. Huddling together in a crevice is thought to help the birds stay warm. More than 10 birds in a roost is uncommon.

Breeding

The Brown Creeper builds its nest against a tree trunk, usually concealing it under loose bark or a limb, or inside a cavity. The nest, crescent-shaped and partly suspended, is made of twigs, bark strips, mosses, and spider cocoons, and is lined with the feathers of other birds. The female builds the nest, which can take between six and 30 days to complete.

Brown Creeper foot. Brown Creepers' legs are short, but the toes, especially the hind toe, are long, with long, curved claws. This foot structure, similar to that of nuthatches, helps birds cling to the bark of trees.

Conservation

Breeding Bird Survey data indicate that Brown Creeper populations are stable throughout much of their North American range, but with local declines.

J. Michael Reed

Wrens

Wrens are small to medium-size brownish songbirds that are typically active and vocal. They have thin, curved bills and short, rounded wings. Many carry their tails in an upright, "cocked" posture. They are generally brown above and pale below; some have bars or spotting on the underparts, and many have barring on the tail. Male and female wrens look alike. Wrens do not have distinctive breeding colors, although the Marsh and Sedge Wrens (*Cistothorus palustris* and *C. platensis,* respectively) molt their body feathers twice each year without changing appearance. Wrens occupy scrubby habitat and undergrowth, from forest interiors to deserts. Most species adapt well to the presence of humans, and several use nest boxes.

Taxonomy

As a family, wrens have been placed near the dippers and mockingbirds in traditional linear classifications. North American birders are used to seeing the wrens placed near the chickadees, nuthatches, and creepers, with which the wrens often associate ecologically. However, DNA–DNA hybridization studies indicate that the wrens are most closely related to the gnatcatchers and gnatwrens, which are currently placed in the Old World warbler family, and more

Troglodytid diversity. *Wrens are all relatively short-tailed and thin-billed brownish birds that glean food from bark, rocks, and soil. They range in size from the tiny Winter Wren (left) to the much larger Cactus Wren (right).*

Worldwide Family Features

- 3½–9" (9–22 cm) songbirds of scrub and undergrowth.
- About 76 species in 17 genera worldwide; found throughout New World, with 1 species also in Eurasia. 9 species in 7 genera occur in North America; found from southern Alaska and central Canada south to Mexican border.
- Primarily insectivorous; eat plant material rarely. Glean food from ground, plant surfaces, cracks and crevices of rocks and trees.
- Most species monogamous, defending all-purpose territories. Several species polygynous, with some males defending territories containing multiple females; others monogamous, with varying levels of extra-pair paternity. Usually pair for life; some migrating species pair for single season only. Northern species migratory; most other species nonmigratory. Some species join mixed-species flocks in winter.

- Breed first at 1 year old, later in some tropical species that breed cooperatively.
- Nests made of grasses, plant fibers, feathers. May nest in rock crevices, cup nests in cavities, or woven globular nests attached low in vegetation. Male generally helps build nest; female completes nest lining. Some species build nests for roosting. Will reuse cavities but not other nests.
- Typically 2–7 (up to 10) subelliptical to oval eggs that are white, cream, or pink with brownish mottling. Female incubates. Hatching, typically asynchronous, after 12–20 days. 2 broods common in most species, occasionally 3.
- Altricial young born with trace of down. Both parents care for young; fledge after 10–23 days.
- Adult annual survival 25–45%. Among oldest on record: 9 years (House Wren); tropical species may live longer.

Wren head and bill. The wrens have slender and relatively long bills. Many species, such as this Bewick's Wren, are marked with long, pale "eyebrow" stripes.

distantly to the creepers. Some taxonomists have suggested combining these groups into a single family, but this proposal has yet to receive widespread acceptance.

Many species have multiple subspecies. The House Wren *(Troglodytes aedon)* in particular has posed taxonomic problems. This species occurs from Canada to Tierra del Fuego. Across this broad range, subtle variations can be sorted into three subspecies groups, each of which has been considered a separate species in the past: the *aedon* group of North America; the *brunneicollis* group, found in montane regions of northern Central America and Mexico, with some populations in the United States near the Mexican border; and the *musculus* group, found in Central and South America. Genetic studies indicate that the three groups probably represent separate species.

Habitats

Wrens live in a wide variety of habitats, from the canyonlands of the western and southwestern United States (the Canyon and Rock Wrens, *Catherpes mexicanus* and *Salpinctes obsoletus*, respectively) to the understory of Pacific Northwest old-growth forests (the Winter Wren, *Troglodytes troglodytes*) to cactus-covered regions of the Chihuahuan Desert (the Cactus Wren, *Campylorhynchus brunneicapillus*). Wrens seem to prefer low, shrubby habitat, often in the transition zones between ecosystems, such as forest edges or lake margins.

Food and Foraging

All wrens are primarily insect eaters, although Carolina *(Thryothorus ludovicianus)* and Bewick's *(Thryomanes bewickii)* Wrens consume some berries and plant seeds in winter. Otherwise, wrens are active foragers, gleaning insects and other arthropods and invertebrates from nooks, crannies, and crevices with their slender bills.

The Canyon Wren is highly specialized in crevice gleaning. It has a strongly flattened skull that is joined to the spinal column toward the rear of the skull rather than directly underneath it. It also has a very thin, elongated bill. These features combine to allow this bird to reach deep into narrow rock fissures in pursuit of small arthropod prey. Bird enthusiasts in some parts of the desert Southwest place mealworms in special feeders attached to the walls of their homes, in order to watch Canyon Wrens crawl along the walls in their search for food.

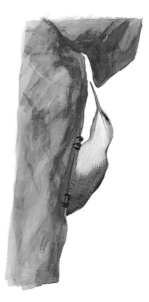

Crevice gleaning. The Canyon Wren (shown here) forages almost exclusively among the crevices of vertical rock cliffs. All wrens have a flattened head, although this characteristic is most pronounced in the Canyon Wren, allowing it to insert its long bill farther into narrow crevices.

Vocalizations

Wrens sing loudly and frequently, and some species sing throughout the year. Their songs are extremely variable. Some species, such as the Cactus Wren, produce very gruff, atonal songs. Others, such as the House Wren and the Carolina Wren, have highly musical, rollicking songs.

Carolina Wren singing. Wrens are renowned for their songs. All species have remarkably loud and complex songs for such small birds. One of the loudest songs is given by the Carolina Wren.

Wrens have song repertoires that vary in size from three songs for the Canyon Wren to as many as 219 songs recorded in a western Marsh Wren. This wide variation in repertoire size may be related to sexual selection, as species thought to be monogamous, such as the Canyon and Cactus Wrens, have smaller repertoires than those known to be polygynous, such as the House and Marsh Wrens.

Repertoire sizes can also vary across the range of a single species. For instance, eastern populations of the Marsh Wren have much smaller repertoires than western populations and appear to have much less polygynous mating. The Winter Wren exhibits a similar pattern, with western populations having longer, more varied songs.

Scientists have intensively studied the use of song repertoires by male Marsh and Carolina Wrens. Male Marsh Wrens do not randomly pick songs from their very large repertoires (which average about 50 songs per male in the East, about 150 in the West) but tend to follow a few specific patterns. Thus a male will cycle from one song to the next, moving through his repertoire in a fairly predictable fashion. Neighboring males often will engage in matched counter-singing. The two males will follow the same song series, one of them offering the song just given by his rival. The function of matched counter-singing among Marsh Wrens is unknown, but observers have suggested that it may "normalize" relationships between territorial neighbors, possibly reducing active aggression and the injuries that result from it.

Averaging about 32 songs per male, Carolina Wrens typically have much smaller repertoires than Marsh Wrens and use them differently. Male Carolina Wrens sing an individual song over and over, in bouts of anywhere from five to 250 repetitions, before switching to another. However, in close encounters with territorial neighbors, they switch songs more often, usually engaging in matched counter-singing like the Marsh Wren. Researchers hypothesize that matched counter-singing in the Carolina Wren calibrates the distance between two rival males. Since both males know how each song should sound, they can determine how far away their rival is by how degraded (by trees, brush, and incidental noise) his song sounds. Thus if a male gives a song known by his neighbor, he very clearly announces his presence and location on his territory, possibly preventing territorial incursions.

Male wrens do not take sole responsibility for territorial defense. Female Carolina Wrens, for example, also advertise their presence vocally by singing with their mates. A pair typically gives this display when the male begins an aggressive territorial song in response to a neighboring male. His mate will then approach and give a chattering call that overlaps the male's song, making for a rather unmusical "duet."

Breeding

All wrens are territorial, defending nesting territories through the breeding season, and nonmigratory species defend all-purpose territories year-round. Vocalization is the wren's primary defense strategy, followed up if necessary by often intense physical confrontation.

A number of wrens—including the Cactus, House, Marsh, Sedge, and Bewick's Wrens—regularly destroy the eggs of members of their own and other species. In cavity nesters such as the House and Bewick's Wrens, egg destruction probably results from competition for limited nesting sites. An experimental study of Cactus Wrens has suggested that egg destruction might reduce competition for food (which could improve nesting success), and that fewer active nests near the wrens' own nests can reduce predation by making the area a less conspicuous and fruitful hunting ground.

Nests

The nests of wrens vary in complexity. Some species weave tight, well-made structures; others simply stuff grass and feathers into an available hole. Both males and females participate in nest construction. The male often builds a foundation, which the female finishes or lines with feathers or other fine material.

House and Bewick's Wrens usually construct nests by lining natural or artificial cavities. Winter and Carolina Wrens are perhaps the most catholic of wrens in their nesting preferences, placing their cup nests in crevices, low vegetation, or even on the ground. Rock and Canyon Wrens are similarly undiscriminating, constructing their cup nests in rock fissures, cavities, and tunnels. Cactus, Marsh, and Sedge Wrens always construct globular, woven nests above the ground in vegetation.

Several species of wrens are interesting because they make nests for uses other than breeding. The nonmigratory Cactus Wren builds individual roosting nests, which it uses year-round. Male Winter, Marsh, and Sedge Wrens make a number of nests (sometimes more than 20 in one breeding season for the Sedge Wren). Marsh and Sedge Wrens may use one of these nests for roosting, but in general the extras probably act as decoys for predators. Studies of the Winter Wren in Europe show that females prefer males with the most nests on their territory, possibly because nest-building ability is a sign of a male's quality.

Eggs and Young

Wrens found in North America produce between three and 10 small eggs, an inch or less (15–24 mm) in length. The largest species, the Cactus Wren, produces fewer eggs (typically three) than the other species' usual four to six. The eggs vary in background color from white to cream, tan, or pink, often with brownish

Marsh Wren at nest. Many wrens build their nests in natural or artificial cavities, but some species always build a nest out in the open. The Marsh Wren builds an oval nest with a side entrance, strapped to reeds. A male sometimes builds several nests within his territory, only one of which is used for breeding. "Dummy" nests may help to distract predators or may provide information to female wrens about a suitor's abilities.

mottling that ranges from faint to very strong. The female incubates the eggs for 12 to 15 days in the smaller species, up to an average of 16 days in the Cactus Wren.

The altricial young have natal down when they hatch, primarily on the head and back. They are usually fed by both parents until fledging, which occurs at 10 to 17 days in the small-bodied species, and at an average of 21 days in Cactus Wrens. Both parents continue to feed the young for about two weeks after fledging, unless the female begins another clutch, in which case the male often takes sole responsibility for the brood. In a number of species, the young return to the breeding nest to roost for some time after fledging.

Wrens do not have a very distinctive juvenal plumage, though juveniles generally exhibit some differences from adults, including mottling of their underparts or indistinct patterning.

Marsh and Sedge Wrens are unusual among wrens in that they have a spring molt. Wrens, like most songbirds, have a complete autumn molt, but Marsh and Sedge Wrens also have a virtually complete molt in spring, when most songbirds replace feathers in only a few areas, and other wrens do not molt at all. It is thought that the abrasive nature of marsh vegetation may cause excessive feather wear in these species, making more frequent feather replacement necessary.

In temperate species, young birds breed as yearlings. However, in some tropical species, especially relatives of the Cactus Wren, the young may stay with their parents for a number of years and help to raise their siblings, a behavior called cooperative breeding.

Migration

Most members of the wren family are nonmigratory. However, many of the migratory species occur in North America. Winter, House, Marsh, and Sedge Wrens are highly migratory, abandoning most of their breeding range in winter. Of the remaining wren species, only Bewick's and Rock Wrens exhibit a tendency to withdraw from the northern (and for Bewick's, the eastern) portions of their ranges for the winter.

Wrens appear to be nocturnal migrants, though species with short migrations may migrate during the day. Migrations for wrens are generally not as long as for most neotropical migrants; all species winter in the southern United States and Mexico.

Conservation

No species of North American wren is considered threatened or endangered. However, the "Appalachian" Bewick's Wren *(Thryomanes bewickii altus)* is of great concern for conservationists. This subspecies has declined severely, possibly due to expansion of House Wren populations as a result of changing habitats. This has apparently brought the two species into conflict, to the detriment of Bewick's Wren. The provision of nest boxes does not work as a management strategy since it only provides more territory for the two species to fight over. House and Bewick's Wrens do not seem to compete strongly in the far western part of their range, where Bewick's Wren populations are more stable.

Carolina, Winter, and House Wrens show significant, widespread increases, according to Breeding Bird Survey data, while Rock and Cactus Wrens may be declining. Carolina Wren populations can fluctuate in size, as the species tends to expand northward after mild winters, and these northern birds can be devastated by cold winter weather. However, populations in the core range of the species appear stable.

Finally, although widespread negative population trends have not been detected for Marsh and Sedge Wrens, these species deserve special attention because both their breeding and wintering habitats are particularly vulnerable to urban and agricultural development.

F. Keith Barker

Dippers

Dippers are stocky, medium-size, slate-gray songbirds with short, stubby tails and wings. They are found exclusively along bodies of water. Dippers require stretches of swiftly flowing river, stream, or creek a quarter mile to 2½ miles (400 m–4 km) long, with rocks and sand on the bottom to provide habitat for their invertebrate prey. Ideally such streams are scattered liberally with boulders for perching. These birds are the most aquatic of songbirds and are especially well known for their ability to walk and feed underwater.

Taxonomy

Historically dippers have been thought to be closely related to the wrens and the thrushes, and they are usually placed near both families in traditional taxonomies. Several lines of evidence, however, point to a closer relationship with the thrushes, including studies of egg-white proteins, DNA–DNA hybridization, and juvenal plumages.

American Dipper. The family Cinclidae is unique but apparently closely related to thrushes. The sole representative in North America is very similar in structure and habits to the four other species in the family worldwide.

Worldwide the five dipper species are found in Europe, northern Africa, Asia, and the Americas. Two species are found in South America. One species, the American Dipper *(Cinclus mexicanus)*, breeds in North America. All dippers are extremely alike morphologically and behaviorally, and all are placed in one genus.

Food and Foraging

American Dippers are usually seen either foraging or preening. They typically feed on aquatic insects and their larvae but will also capture other invertebrates, small fish, and fish eggs. Dippers commonly forage using three different methods. Usually they wade through shallow water, frequently submerging their heads to look for prey and diving in to capture items. In water too deep for wading, dippers use the same technique but paddle with their feet instead of walking. The

Worldwide Family Features

- 5½–8" (14–20 cm) streamside songbirds.
- 5 species in 1 genus worldwide, in Europe, northern Africa, Asia, and Americas. 1 species breeds in North America, in western mountain systems from Alaska to Panama.
- Eat mainly aquatic insects; also other small aquatic animals. Glean prey from sand and surface of rocks under water.
- Highly territorial during breeding season; much less so in winter, but still quite aggressive. Usually monogamous; occasionally polygynous; form pair bonds for life. Elevational and short-distance migrations found in some populations.

- Breed first at 1 year old.
- Female, often with male's help, builds spherical, covered nest made of grasses and leaves, often coated with moss. Nest situated in inaccessible locations above streams. Often reuse nests.
- 2–5 (usually 4 or 5) oval to subelliptical, white eggs; female incubates for 14–17 days. Hatching typically synchronous. 1 or 2 broods per year.
- Altricial young naked at hatch; fledge at 20–26 days; both sexes care for young.
- Adult annual survival 35–55%. Among oldest on record: 7 years, 10 months (White-throated Dipper of Eurasia); 7 years, 2 months (American Dipper).

Dipper head and bill. Dippers are unusual among birds in that they have feathering on their eyelids. The tiny white feathers are flashed whenever the bird blinks, which can be as often as 50 times a minute; these conspicuous white flashes are thought to be a signal to other dippers.

birds will also occasionally dive from a perch jutting out of the water and forage underwater on the stream bottom, usually for less than 15 seconds.

While not foraging, dippers preen frequently and for prolonged periods of up to 10 minutes. Extended bouts of preening are thought to be necessary to maintain the waterproofing and insulating qualities of the plumage under the harsh conditions of rushing water to which dippers are exposed.

After the breeding season in some areas, aquatic invertebrate populations at lower elevations have been depleted by the demands of the nesting effort, leading many birds to migrate upstream temporarily to higher elevations. They will often stay on their territories through the winter if the water remains ice-free; otherwise, starting in late fall they move to lower elevations to search for open water near which they can spend the winter. Dippers rarely stray far from foothills, however.

Adaptations to Lifestyle

Dippers get their name from their habit of moving the entire body up and down, twitching or stretching the wings, and often bobbing the tail. In addition, if they are disturbed the birds blink their white-feathered eyelids conspicuously, often while dipping. Experts have proposed several explanations for dipping. One hypothesis is that dipping is a way for the birds to deter attacks by demonstrating their physical fitness to potential preda-

tors, which would explain why human observers see so much of this behavior.

Dipping may also be a technique for more accurately locating prey or a way to communicate with conspecifics in a noisy environment. These hypotheses may also explain the bobbing behavior of Spotted Sandpipers *(Actitis macularia)* and wagtails, which often occur in similar habitats.

Dippers possess a unique suite of adaptations that allow them to exploit fast-flowing streams. Their stubby wings are well adapted both for flight and for use as flippers while swimming in turbulent creeks. Their strong legs and toes, along with their wings, allow them to forage efficiently in currents powerful enough to knock over a human. Dippers have a thick coat of down and up to twice as many contour feathers as nonaquatic passerines of comparable size, traits that provide insulation from cold waters.

The oxygen capacity of the blood of dippers is also much higher than that

American Dipper foraging underwater. Dippers forage mostly by walking into shallow running water and reaching to the bottom with the bill. In slightly deeper water they swim by paddling their feet, duck-like. Dippers occasionally dive completely underwater for a few seconds, using their short, powerful wings to move about in currents often strong enough to knock down an adult human.

of nonaquatic songbirds, allowing them to remain submerged for up to 30 seconds while foraging. Their vision is facilitated by the iris sphincter muscles, which are more developed in dippers than in most birds, allowing the curvature of the lens to adapt to seeing both above and below water.

Vocalizations

The typical call of the dipper, often heard as the bird flies, is harsh and rattle-like, reminiscent of a high-pitched Belted Kingfisher *(Ceryle alcyon)* call. The song consists of a large number of distinct phrases strung together, with most re-peated two to four times before the next phrase begins. Songs vary tremendously in length, but most last less than one minute. Both sexes sing all year long, with a peak early in the breeding season. The song is used to establish breeding territo-ries (in spring) and winter territories (in fall and winter), as well as to attract mates and during foraging. Unlike many song-birds, dippers rarely sing to advertise their territory once it is established, presum-ably because their noisy environment limits the effectiveness of singing.

Breeding

For dippers, the main criterion for selec-tion of breeding territories is the presence of adequate nest sites. Nests are built on horizontal outcrops of cliff edges above a creek, underneath bridges, behind water-falls, or, less often, on boulders in a creek. Fast-flowing water under or over a nest site makes it more desirable.

During courtship, the male may feed the female after she begs from a crouched position with quivering wings, following which the male often sings with neck and bill stretched upward. The pair may then conduct a flight chase, in which each bird closely follows the other's com-plex aerial maneuvers, often leaving the stream area and singing in flight. The flight chase can easily be distinguished

American Dipper at nest. *The American Dipper's nest appears from the outside to be a ball of mosses. The nest is typically placed on an inaccessible ledge near a deep and fast-running section of a stream—for example, on a small cliff alongside a waterfall. The birds have taken advantage of human encroachment and find many suitable nest sites under bridges.*

from territorial birds chasing off intrud-ers; in the latter, intruders and pursuing birds make a beeline for the territorial boundary before landing to face off, and no acrobatics are involved.

Conservation

Pollution and silt accumulation on stream beds can destroy invertebrate popula-tions, causing dippers to abandon a waterway. In Europe, White-throated Dippers *(Cinclus cinclus)* living near pol-luted streams have experienced problems with reproduction and the development of young.

Because of the specialized habitat of dippers and the large size of their territo-ries, the major annual avian censuses probably do not reflect American Dipper population trends well. However, the birds will probably continue to fare well in areas where water quality and stream substrate are maintained. They adapt easily to living in urban areas that meet their habitat requirements, and may have high population densities in towns thanks to the added nest sites that bridges supply.

Thomas Knight

Bulbuls

Family Pycnonotidae
Order Passeriformes

Bulbuls are small to medium-size songbirds. The sexes are similar in size and appearance in most species, though males are larger in some. Bulbuls are commonly gray, brown, or olive-green, with yellow, red, or black markings. Relative to other songbirds of similar size, their plumage is long and soft, especially on the rump, and they often have hair-like feathers on the nape. Bulbuls' bodies are moderately slender; their bills are relatively slender and slightly decurved. The birds have well-developed rictal bristles. Many species have striking head patterns and brightly colored undertail coverts. Some, including the Red-whiskered Bulbul *(Pycnonotus jocosus)*, the only species in North America, have a prominent crest. In India, the Red-whiskered Bulbul is found in hills up to 8,200 feet (2,500 m) in elevation; in Florida, it lives in suburban areas dominated by exotic, fruit-bearing trees.

Taxonomy

Members of the clearly defined bulbul family resemble the predominantly Old World babbler family, but some anatomical studies suggest a closer relationship to the cuckooshrikes (Campephagidae), which occur from Africa to the Pacific Islands. DNA–DNA hybridization studies support a close relationship with the Old World warblers, kinglets, and swallows. The superficially similar silky-flycatchers and waxwings are only distantly related to bulbuls.

Worldwide there are between 120 and 138 species in 14 to 21 genera, found in the western Palearctic, Africa, Madagascar, and southern Asia, east to the Philippines and Indonesia. The genus *Pycnonotus,* found in Africa and especially southern Asia, contains about 50 species.

Red-whiskered Bulbul. The Red-whiskered Bulbul has been introduced in Florida and is the only North American representative of this large Old World family.

Food and Foraging

Bulbuls eat a mixture of fruits and other plant material, as well as insects and other animal food. They take mostly smaller

---

Worldwide Family Features

- 5½–11" (14–28 cm) forest and garden songbirds.
- Up to 138 species in 21 genera worldwide; widespread in Africa and Asia. 1 species introduced in southern Florida.
- Eat mostly berries, fruit, insects; also seeds, buds, nectar. Mainly glean food from vegetation.
- Territorial. Probably monogamous, but little data on mating systems. Outside breeding season occur in pairs or small flocks; some species gregarious year-round when food is available. Most species do not migrate.
- Breed first probably at 1 year old.
- Usually build open, cup-shaped nest of twigs, grasses, rootlets; often poorly

concealed, in fork of small tree or bush; usually close to ground, but sometimes to 45' (14 m) high. Built primarily by female, with some help from male. Do not reuse nests.
- Usually 2–5 subelliptical to oval eggs; smooth and glossy; pink, cream, or white, with speckles or blotches. Female does most incubation, usually for 10–14 days. Hatching synchronous. Up to 3 broods per year.
- Altricial young naked at hatching; fledge at 9–16 days. Both parents provide care after fledging.
- No data on annual survival. Among oldest on record: 11 years, 1 month (Red-whiskered Bulbul in Australia).

fruits, which they can easily manipulate in their bills, but will eat fruits up to 1½ inches (4 cm) in diameter by probing into mushy areas. In captivity, they eat sliced oranges, apples, bananas, and avocados, but wild birds do not damage intact fruit in orchards. They flycatch, and at roosts they hawk flying insects from trees, shrubs, or wires. Red-whiskered Bulbuls also eat seedlings, flower parts, and nectar, and glean a variety of larval and adult insects from vegetation.

Bulbuls typically roost in groups, often in fig trees, mangos, exotic palms, pines, or Australian-pines (genus *Casuarina*). Members of this active, noisy family appear to be weak fliers. Most bulbul species, including the Red-whiskered, are nonmigratory.

Breeding

Pairs are often accompanied by a third adult bird (the sexes of most bulbuls cannot be differentiated in the field) whose role is not known. Pairs stay in close proximity to one another, often feeding together; one bird may feed the other.

Bulbuls are among the first birds to start singing in the morning; they may also sing on moonlit nights. Their songs are generally "cheerful," lively, and loud; because of this, many species are prized as cage birds. The song of the Red-whiskered Bulbul consists of melodic whistles and *churp* notes.

Most bulbuls are not aggressive, even around their nest sites, although some species are pugnacious. During courtship,

Bulbul nest. The Red-whiskered Bulbul's nest is a cup of fine twigs and grasses placed low in a bush or small tree. Incorporated into the structure are larger materials, such as sheets of tree bark or strips of plastic.

the male bows his head and spreads his tail while quivering his drooping wings. The male also gives quiet croaks and may feed the female.

In Florida, the Red-whiskered Bulbul builds a cup-shaped nest of fine twigs, grasses, and rootlets, embellishing it with strips of plastic, bark, paper, dried leaves, or snakeskin. It places the nest 2 to 8 feet (0.6–2.4 m) up in a small tree or bush. In India, this species commonly builds its nest in thatch walls or roofs of inhabited huts.

Conservation

The Red-whiskered Bulbul was introduced to Florida in 1960, when five to ten birds from eastern India escaped from captivity. They first nested in 1961, and by 1970 their descendants numbered about 250. The Florida population lives in an area of some 25 square miles (65 sq km) in the southern part of the greater Miami area. Such a small population is in constant danger of extirpation.

James D. Rising

Bulbul head and bill. The Red-whiskered Bulbul, shown here, has a short bill and a perky crest. The small, red "whisker" patch can be difficult to see.

Kinglets

Kinglets are tiny, highly active songbirds that are so small it would take three to five birds to total an ounce. Among North American birds, only certain hummingbirds are smaller. Kinglets' greenish plumage remains unchanged year-round. The Ruby-crowned Kinglet *(Regulus calendula)* has a pale eye-ring and, on males, an erectile red crown patch that is usually concealed. The Golden-crowned Kinglet *(R. satrapa)* has a white "eyebrow" stripe, yellow crown, and on males an erectile orange patch within the yellow crown that also is rarely visible. Kinglets are known for their excited fidgeting and wing-flicking while feeding. These primarily coniferous forest birds nest extensively throughout boreal spruce-fir forests. During migration, they can occur in a variety of other habitats, from broadleaf woodlands to open fields to patches of weeds on barrier beaches.

Taxonomy

All six species of kinglets worldwide strongly resemble each other, both anatomically and behaviorally, although the Ruby-crowned Kinglet differs in many respects and probably deserves its own genus.

Regulid diversity. All six of the world's kinglets, including the two North American species, are in a single genus. They are tiny, structurally similar, insect-gleaning birds that constantly flick their wings. The Golden-crowned Kinglet is shown.

Until recently, the kinglets were classified with the Old World warblers in a large group that also included the thrushes and Old World flycatchers. Based on recent DNA–DNA hybridization studies, the AOU has now assigned the kinglets to full family status. These studies also raise questions about which birds are the closest relatives of the kinglets. Currently the family is retained in a traditional position, next to the Old World warblers, in most taxonomies.

John James Audubon described a third species of North American kinglet, "Cuvier's Kinglet" *(Regulus cuvieri)*, from a specimen collected in Pennsylvania. He included a plate illustration of this form in his 1829 edition of *Birds of America* but did not save the specimen. No other example of Cuvier's Kinglet has been found,

---

Worldwide Family Features

- 3–4½" (8–11 cm) woodland songbirds.
- 6 species in 1 genus worldwide; found in North and Central America, Eurasia, the Mediterranean, and southern Asia. In North America, 2 species breed regularly; distributed over much of continent.
- Eat arthropods and their eggs, gleaned from foliage; also occasionally fruit, sap.
- Territorial; join mixed-species flocks during winter and migration. Presumably monogamous. Northern breeders generally migratory; more southerly birds often resident year-round.
- Breed first at 1 year old.

- Deep, cup-shaped nest, placed in conifers. Female builds, using mosses, lichens, grasses, conifer needles, paper strips, bark.
- 3–12 short elliptical to subelliptical eggs, dull white to cream-colored, faintly spotted. Female incubates for 14–17 days. Hatching presumably synchronous. 1 or 2 broods per year.
- Altricial young naked at hatching. Fledge at 16–22 days. Both sexes care for young.
- Adult annual survival poorly known. Among oldest on record: 7 years (Goldcrest, in Europe); 5 years, 7 months (Ruby-crowned Kinglet).

450

Hover-glean foraging. Both North American kinglets, but especially the Ruby-crowned (shown), often forage by hovering briefly to reach the otherwise inaccessible ends or undersides of branches where insects may be hiding.

and the bird is now suspected to have been an aberrant plumage of the Golden-crowned Kinglet.

Food and Foraging

Kinglets are active foragers, gleaning arthropods and various insect and spider eggs from the leaves and branches of coniferous and broadleaf trees and shrubs. They forage anywhere from treetops to the ground and often catch active prey by briefly hovering or flycatching. While the two North American species have similar foraging habits, the Ruby-crowned is more prone to hovering and flycatching. Kinglets frequently flick their wings while foraging, in contrast to warblers and vireos.

Kinglets will join mixed-species foraging flocks during migration and in winter. Golden-crowned Kinglets often join flocks dominated by chickadees. Ruby-crowned Kinglets are found during migration with mixed flocks of wood-warblers as well as with chickadees and titmice.

The Golden-crowned Kinglet and the closely related Goldcrest *(Regulus regulus)* of Eurasia are the smallest birds able to routinely endure freezing temperatures while maintaining a normal body temperature (103–107° F/39–41° C). They apparently do not enter a state of torpor during cold nights, but survive instead by huddling together in protected areas. Nevertheless, Golden-crowned Kinglet populations are often reduced during severe winters, particularly when ice storms make foraging difficult.

Breeding

Male kinglets are territorial during the breeding season, defending their territories mostly with vigorous singing. Males raise and lower their colorful crown patch feathers (red in Ruby-crowneds, orange in Golden-crowneds) in aggressive encounters with other males. While the male Golden-crowned Kinglet's yellow crown stripe is usually visible, its central orange patch, like the red crown feathers of the Ruby-crowned male, is often covered by other head feathers. Occasionally, however, when other males are present or when responding to a birder "pishing," males will vigorously raise and lower their crowns. Flocks of migrating male Ruby-crowneds also often show their crown feathers when they forage in close proximity to one another.

Kinglet crown patch. Male kinglets, such as these Ruby-crowneds, have a concealed crown patch of intense color that can be raised in aggressive encounters with other kinglets.

Kinglet head and bill. Kinglets have a small, weak, and slender bill well suited for gleaning tiny insects from vegetation. The Ruby-crowned Kinglet is shown.

Once pairing occurs, the male defends the territory while the female builds the nest, at a site of her choice. Kinglets construct hanging, deep, cup-like nests. They place their nests in conifers, usually spruces, anywhere from near ground level to high in the tree canopy. Outer nest materials typically include lichens, mosses, spider webs, small twigs, and bark strips; the inner lining consists of soft materials such as feathers, rootlets, hair, spider webs, and insect cocoons.

Both species have large clutch sizes, sometimes up to 11 eggs in the Golden-crowned Kinglet and 12 eggs in the Ruby-crowned, although usually fewer. They are noted for large clutch sizes in relation to body size; the mass of a clutch can be up to 78 percent of the female's body mass. The sexes generally share parental duties. Ruby-crowned Kinglets have one brood per year, but Golden-crowneds may have two broods. When there is a second clutch, the male Golden-crowned feeds the first brood of fledglings while the female incubates the new eggs.

Vocalizations

Kinglets sing vigorously throughout the breeding season. They also sing in winter and during migration, although much less frequently. The male Ruby-crowned has a particularly complex, rich warbling song; the Golden-crowned's song is much higher pitched and shorter.

Kinglets also call frequently throughout the year, with call notes that are quite different: a thin, repeated whistle for the Golden-crowned, a staccato chatter for the Ruby-crowned.

Migration

Both North American species are migratory throughout much of their ranges, wintering extensively throughout the central and southern United States. The winter range of the Ruby-crowned Kinglet is in general more southerly than that of the Golden-crowned, extending into central and southern Mexico, and appears to be determined primarily by the bird's sensitivity to cold temperatures. Both species are permanent residents in parts of the continent's western mountain region. The Golden-crowned Kinglet is a permanent resident in much of northern New England and adjacent eastern Canada, and the species also has a small permanent population in Mexico and Central America.

During migration the Ruby-crowned Kinglet forages in a wide variety of habitats, including shrublands, while the Golden-crowned remains more oriented to forests, usually coniferous ones. Ruby-crowneds will join mixed flocks of wood-warblers, even in old fields and along barrier beaches.

Conservation

Neither North American species is considered to be at risk. Christmas Bird Count analyses suggest modest population increases in both species. Breeding Bird Survey results indicate that the Ruby-crowned Kinglet has declined in the eastern United States and in parts of Canada. The Golden-crowned Kinglet has increased in recent decades, perhaps due to reforestation of spruce trees throughout the Northeast, though Breeding Bird Survey data suggest some decline in the western parts of its range.

John Kricher

Old World Warblers and Gnatcatchers

Family Sylviidae
Order Passeriformes

The sylviid warblers are small to medium-size, insectivorous song-birds with slender legs and bills. North American representatives of this family belong to two very different subfamilies. One includes the gnatcatchers, small birds with a slender, pointed bill surrounded by rictal bristles. Gnatcatchers have drab plumage—grays, white, and black—with season-ally changing head patterns that differ with sex and species. They seem to be in constant motion—flashing their wings and bobbing, cocking, or switching the tail back and forth. They generally live in woodlands, riparian areas, desert scrub, and sagebrush. The other subfamily is the sylviine warblers, small, active birds that are often brownish, greenish brown, or dull green, with subtle facial markings and a narrow, pointed bill; the sexes are similar in plumage, with little seasonal variation. The only species of sylviine warbler to breed in North America, the Arctic Warbler *(Phylloscopus borealis)*, lives in dense willow thickets in Alaska.

Taxonomy

Sylviidae was formerly a subfamily in the very large family Muscicapidae, which included the Old World flycatchers, thrushes, babblers, Old World warblers, and many other groups. In the late 1990s the AOU elevated each of these groups to family status based on DNA–DNA hybridization studies.

The family Sylviidae includes two distinct groups currently classified as subfamilies: the Sylviinae (Old World warblers) and the Polioptilinae (the gnatcatchers and gnatwrens; gnatwrens are found only in Central and South America). These two groups, however, may not be each other's closest relatives and might be placed in separate families in

Sylviid diversity. This very large and diverse Old World family is represented in North America by the gnatcatchers (California Gnatcatcher shown on left), an exclusively New World subfamily, and by two species of sylviid warblers that barely enter western North America from Asia (Arctic Warbler, right).

the future. DNA–DNA hybridization analyses suggest that Old World warblers are closely related to babblers and bulbuls and that gnatcatchers and gnatwrens are allied to the wrens. These relationships remain to be verified using additional techniques.

One genus from each subfamily occurs regularly in North America. Four gnat-catchers in the genus *Polioptila* and the Arctic Warbler in *Phylloscopus* all breed in North America, while the Dusky War-bler *(Phylloscopus fuscatus)* is a rare visitor to the West Coast. The family as a whole includes nearly 300 species worldwide.

Members of Sylviidae are similar to some wood-warblers and vireos but are smaller, more delicate, and more active. In appearance, gnatcatchers resemble tiny Northern Mockingbirds *(Mimus polyglottos)*. Like the mockingbird, gnat-catchers have a variable, warbling song that sometimes includes notes of other species. The kinglets, formerly included with the sylviids but now in their own family, are also tiny, insectivorous, busy birds, but they are easily distinguished from gnatcatchers by their yellowish-green plumage, rounder body, shorter tail and bill, and colorful crown spot, which can be red, orange, or yellow.

Some sylviine warblers are similar in appearance to certain North American wood-warblers, especially the Tennessee

Warbler *(Vermivora peregrina)*. Taxonomically, however, these groups are quite distinct; for example, the sylviine warblers have 10 functional primary feathers instead of the nine found in the American wood-warblers.

Habitats

Of all the North American gnatcatcher species, the Blue-gray Gnatcatcher *(Polioptila caerulea)* has the widest and most northerly distribution, occurring throughout most of eastern North America. Its habitats include open scrub, woodland edges, scattered trees, and forest openings. The other three species prefer more

Sylviid heads and bills. Gnatcatchers (Blue-gray Gnatcatcher shown on left) have slender, pointed bills with prominent rictal bristles. Sylviid warblers (Arctic Warbler, right) have slightly thicker, pointed bills. Both groups forage by gleaning small insects from vegetation.

arid to semiarid habitat along desert washes or in areas with scattered shrubs. The California Gnatcatcher *(P. californica)* has the most limited habitat and distribution; it is found only in the coastal scrub, or chaparral, of southwestern California and Baja California.

Generally, breeding distributions of the four North American gnatcatchers do not overlap, but in winter migrant Blue-gray Gnatcatchers move into the desert scrub habitat used by Black-tailed Gnatcatchers *(Polioptila melanura)*. Three species can occur together in the dry desert canyons of southeastern Arizona where the Black-capped Gnatcatcher *(P. nigriceps)* is sometimes present.

The Arctic Warbler breeds in western Alaska in willow scrub and open coniferous or mixed coniferous-deciduous forests.

Food and Foraging

The diet of sylviids consists primarily of small insects and spiders, which they glean from the tips of branches. Their tiny, long, and slender bills enable them to also probe into small crevices on woody substrates.

Worldwide Family Features

- 3½–8" (9–20 cm) songbirds found in a wide range of habitats.
- About 284 species in 50 genera worldwide, with most species in Eurasia, Africa, and Australia. 6 species in 2 genera occur in North America; found mostly in continental U.S., with greatest number of species in Southwest; plus 3 or 4 accidental species.
- Primarily insectivorous; glean prey items from shrubs, capture them in flight, or hover-glean.
- Mostly monogamous, although some species are polygynous. Nonmigratory species use large winter home range that includes breeding territory. Migratory species territorial in breeding season; can join mixed-species feeding flocks in winter.
- Breed first at 1 year old.
- Nest structure variable among species. Gnatcatcher nest is tiny, tightly woven, compact cup, saddled on a branch; made of plant fibers, bark, spider webs,

covered with lichens. *Phylloscopus* nest is dome-shaped with side entrance, made of mosses, grasses, vines; built on ground or low vegetation. Both sexes build nest. Do not reuse old nests, but can recycle material.
- 2–7 subelliptical eggs; whitish, bluish, pink, buff, or greenish ground color, variably speckled with brownish dots that occasionally form wreath around larger end; occasionally heavily mottled. Both sexes incubate 9–17 days; hatching presumed synchronous. 1 or 2 broods (rarely 3) per year.
- Altricial young naked at birth with little down; fed tiny insects by both parents. Fledge at 10–16 days; remain with adults for several weeks.
- Adult annual survival 45–60%. Among oldest on record: 12 years (Reed Warbler, *Acrocephalus scirpaceus*, and Barred Warbler, *Sylvia nisoria;* both in Europe); 4 years, 2 months (Blue-gray Gnatcatcher).

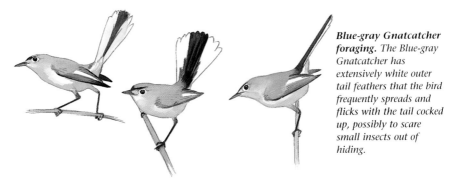

Blue-gray Gnatcatcher foraging. *The Blue-gray Gnatcatcher has extensively white outer tail feathers that the bird frequently spreads and flicks with the tail cocked up, possibly to scare small insects out of hiding.*

Arctic and Dusky Warblers hover-glean mosquitoes from the upper canopy and in shrub layers. They also feed in low ground cover and on the ground. Gnatcatchers constantly move through foliage, searching for prey with quick movements of the head and flicking motions of the wings and cocked tail. Besides surface gleaning, gnatcatchers glean prey from bushes while hovering; when the prey is flushed, they quickly sally out to catch it in midair.

Breeding

Gnatcatchers form monogamous pair bonds, but whether these bonds last more than one season is unknown. The pair forages together in a territory defended primarily by the male, though females will attack intruding females. Mates maintain close contact, either visually or vocally, but are separated during the incubation and nesting periods, when the females spend more time at the nest. Arctic Warblers are territorial and may cluster into loose "neighborhoods"; occasionally a male simultaneously mates with two females.

During the breeding season, male sylviids sing advertising songs, primarily while establishing territories and nesting. They sing from elevated perches, while foraging with a female, or frequently while in motion.

In gnatcatchers, both sexes build a tiny, tightly compact, cup-shaped nest of plant fibers and bark strips; it looks like a large hummingbird nest. The outside walls are stuccoed with crustose lichens when available; these probably help conceal the nest. The nest is anchored to a supporting branch with spider webs or caterpillar silk.

The bird perches on the nest site as it builds up the sides of the nest, forming it by pushing the material upward with its bill and forcing it outward by rotating its body and pushing against the sides. Additional spider webbing is used to more firmly attach the sides to the supportive branch and nearby twigs.

Gnatcatchers frequently have two broods a year but do not use the same nest for both broods. First nests require about two weeks to build. Second nests, usually built solely by the male, take less than a week to make. Gnatcatchers are model recyclers. Nest material from a previous nest is often used to build the nest for a second brood, although first nests infested with parasites such as mites or fleas are not recycled. It is fascinating to watch a gnatcatcher as he flies back and forth, destroying and constructing a nest at the same time.

Gnatcatchers lay from two to six (usually four) eggs, one each morning, after the nest lining is finished. Only the female has an incubation patch, yet both sexes incubate. Incubation lasts 11 to 15 days. The altricial young are fed by both parents; they leave the nest about 10 to 15 days after hatching. The young continue to be fed by both parents for three more weeks, unless the pair has another brood, in which case feeding ceases after about 18 days.

The Arctic Warbler builds its dome-shaped nest on the ground near the base of a shrub, so it is hidden in vegetation with just the side entrance hole exposed. The nest, lined with fine grasses, is made of mosses, grasses, and dead vines. The bird lays from three to seven eggs (usually five or six). Only the female incubates; incubation lasts 11 to 13 days. Both sexes feed nestlings and young.

Gnatcatchers frequently are hosts to parasitic Brown-headed and Bronzed Cowbirds (*Molothrus ater* and *M. aeneus,* respectively). As a pair of gnatcatchers frantically feeds a young cowbird, taking turns placing insects in the cowbird's comparatively huge, gaping mouth, they look as though they could almost be devoured themselves.

Gnatcatcher nest. Gnatcatchers build a tiny cup nest out of plant fibers bound together with spider webs, fastened to the top of a large branch and covered with lichens or other small items, very much like the nests of hummingbirds. The California Gnatcatcher is shown.

Migration

All gnatcatchers except Blue-grays are permanent residents throughout their ranges. The northern populations of Blue-gray Gnatcatchers migrate long distances to the southern United States and Central America. Florida breeding populations of Blue-grays are apparently completely replaced in winter by birds that bred farther north. The sexes migrate at the same time, possibly in pairs.

The Arctic Warbler arrives in Alaska from Siberia in June. At the end of the breeding season, between late August and early November, the bird migrates from Alaska back to Siberia and eastern Asia, then moves southward to its wintering grounds in tropical southeastern Asia. Dusky Warbler records in Alaska are mostly from spring sightings, while the California and Mexico records are from autumn.

Conservation

Breeding Bird Surveys indicate that Black-tailed Gnatcatcher populations are stable and that Blue-gray Gnatcatcher populations may be increasing. California Gnatcatcher populations are declining based on censuses conducted in their specialized habitat.

The U.S. Fish and Wildlife Service estimated in 1992 that there were about 2,562 pairs of California Gnatcatchers in southwestern California, and about 2,800 pairs in Mexico. Distributed much more widely in the past, this species is declining in number due to extensive loss and fragmentation of its coastal chaparral habitat as a result of development. The bird has threatened status on the U.S. Endangered Species List.

Accidental Species

Four vagrant species from Asia have been recorded in North America. Middendorff's Grasshopper-Warbler *(Locustella ochotensis)* and the Wood Warbler *(Phylloscopus sibilatrix)* have been recorded on islands west of the Alaskan mainland in the period June to October. The Lanceolated Warbler *(L. lanceolata)* has been recorded in California in September and in the western Aleutians during June and July. A Yellow-browed Warbler *(P. inornatus)* was photographed on St. Lawrence Island, Alaska, in September 1999.

Kathleen Groschupf

Old World Flycatchers

Family Muscicapidae
Order Passeriformes

The Old World flycatchers are a diverse group of songbirds, and the relationship between this family and other groups has been long debated. At times, membership in the "primitive insect eaters," as the Muscicapidae has been called, included well over 1,500 species in 258 genera, including all of the thrushes, Old World warblers, gnatcatchers, and babblers, as well as many other Old World groups. Currently the family is limited to a set of mostly African and Eurasian species with wide bills, long tails, and an active foraging mode. Many species in this group hawk or sally after flying insects, and are prominent in woodland habitats.

The Old World flycatchers are not at all closely related to the tyrant flycatchers of the New World, despite the two families' similar names, comparable behavioral traits, and related morphology (such as prominent rictal bristles).

Six Old World flycatchers have been recorded as accidentals in Alaska, mostly on the Aleutian Islands and at other sites around the Bering Sea. There have been multiple records of the Red-breasted Flycatcher *(Ficedula parva)* and the Gray-spotted Flycatcher *(Muscicapa griseisticta),* while the Narcissus Flycatcher *(F. narcissina),* the Mugimaki Flycatcher *(F. mugimaki),* the Siberian Flycatcher *(M. sibirica),* and the Asian Brown Flycatcher *(M. daurica)* are much rarer. All of these species breed in Siberia and winter in southeast Asia or India. Most of the North American appearances have been in spring, suggesting that these birds were migrants that overshot their intended destinations or were blown off course by storms.

John B. Dunning, Jr.

Muscicapid diversity. *The Muscicapidae is a diverse Old World family whose members reach North America only as rare wanderers. They share many convergent features with the tyrant flycatchers of the New World but are unrelated. Many species are drab, like most tyrant flycatchers, but species in the genus* Ficedula *(such as the Red-breasted Flycatcher, shown here) are relatively brightly colored.*

Worldwide Family Features

- 4½–6" (11–15 cm) woodland songbirds.
- At least 117 species in 18 genera throughout the Old World, especially Africa, Eurasia, and Indonesia. 6 species in 2 genera accidental in Alaska.
- Eat flying insects, fruit. Insects captured in air or plucked from vegetation; fruit gleaned from plants.
- Territorial. Most species are probably monogamous for season; a few species polygynous. Temperate zone species migratory.
- Breed first at 1 year old.
- Nest is open cup placed in tree or shrub, on embankment, or in cavity. Made from mosses, dry grasses, and leaves, lined with finer materials. Built by female in some species, both parents in others. Do not reuse nests, but may reuse sites, especially cavities.
- 2–8 smooth, subelliptical eggs; greenish, blue, or white with spotting. Female incubates in some species, both parents in others. Incubation lasts 12–15 days. Hatching usually synchronous. 1 or 2 broods per year.
- Altricial young hatch sparsely covered with down. Fledge at about 12–17 days. Both parents feed young.
- Little information on adult annual survival for most species; where known, ranges from 40% to 70%. Among oldest on record: 15 years (Pied Flycatcher, *(Ficedula hypoleuca,* in Europe).

Thrushes

Thrushes are generally alert, compact, small to medium-size songbirds with an upright posture. They often hop along the ground when foraging. Their bills are usually straight and relatively thin, but not sharply pointed. Some thrush plumages are muted browns with various degrees of spotting on the breast, while others are brightly colored. Juveniles of most species, even those that are not spotted as adults, have prominently spotted underparts. Sexual dimorphism is obvious in many species, with males generally brighter than females. While many turdids inhabit woodlands, some occur in open areas. Many members of this family are well known for their rich, melodious songs.

Taxonomy

The Turdidae is a large family of birds that is thought to be most closely related to the Old World flycatchers. In the past, and in some current taxonomies, these two groups have been combined into a single family (Muscicapidae), along with a number of other groups that are now considered to warrant family status of their own.

Some taxonomies also distinguish between two groups of thrushes. The true thrushes include the bluebirds (in the genus *Sialia*), Townsend's Solitaire *(Myadestes townsendi)*, the spotted thrushes *(Hylocichla* and *Catharus*, sometimes called "brown thrushes"), the robins *(Turdus)*, and two robin-like species (the Varied Thrush, *Ixoreus naevius*, and the Aztec Thrush, *Ridgwayia pinicola)*. The chat-thrushes are a predominantly Old World group, but two species—the Bluethroat *(Luscinia svecica)* and the Northern Wheatear *(Oenanthe oenanthe)*—are found in Arctic North America.

According to the classification most consistent with the AOU's, the family Turdidae worldwide includes 21 to 25 genera and 173 to 176 species of true thrushes (formerly in the subfamily Turdinae), and 30 genera and 155 species of chat-thrushes, a group that includes the chats, Old World robins, redstarts, and wheatears. This latter group contains many European species that were familiar birds to early immigrants to America. The colonists often named birds in their new homeland after familiar European birds that the new birds resembled. Thus the North American avifauna includes redstarts and a chat, but these are wood-warblers and not thrushes. Even the American Robin *(Turdus migratorius)*, a true thrush, is not closely related to the European Robin *(Erithacus rubecula)*, which is in the chat-thrush group.

In 1998, the AOU gave full species status to Bicknell's Thrush *(Catharus bicknelli)*, once classified as a subspecies of the more widespread Gray-cheeked Thrush *(C. minimus)*. The separation was based largely on differences in protein types and mitochondrial DNA patterns, as well as slight differences in plumage, song, and both breeding and wintering ranges.

Some spotted thrushes in the genus *Catharus*, particularly the Hermit Thrush

Turdid diversity. *Thrushes can be subdivided into two main groups. The true thrushes include most species found in the Americas, including the bluebirds, solitaires, robins, and spotted thrushes (such as Bicknell's Thrush, left). The chat-thrushes are a predominantly Old World group (Northern Wheatear, right). All are relatively long-winged and long-legged songbirds that forage mostly on the ground.*

Turdid head and bill. All thrushes (such as this American Robin) have a relatively slender, but not sharply pointed bill adapted for eating soft foods, such as insects, worms, and berries, but not seeds.

(C. guttatus), have distinctive subspecies. The Hermit Thrush is the most widely distributed of the spotted thrushes and the only one that routinely winters throughout much of the southern United States. It has eight subspecies divided into three geographic groups: the Pacific coastal group and the western interior mountains group, with three subspecies each; and the eastern group, with two subspecies.

The Veery *(Catharus fuscescens)* has six subspecies, with western populations darker above and more spotted than eastern populations. Swainson's Thrush *(C. ustulatus)* has four subspecies; western populations are brighter above and have buffier breasts.

Habitats

North American thrushes nest and winter in a wide variety of terrestrial habitats.

Nesting Habitats

Catharus thrushes are basically woodland birds, occupying broadleaf, mixed, or coniferous forests, depending on the species. The Wood Thrush *(Hylocichla mustelina)* breeds in mature eastern broadleaf forests and sometimes in suburban woodlots near closed-canopy forests. The American Robin has extraordinarily broad habitat preferences and may rank as one of the most adaptable American birds; it occurs throughout North America in virtually all forest types, as well as in open areas such as lawns and parklands. The Varied Thrush nests in coniferous forests throughout the Pacific Northwest, from low elevations to the treeline. Townsend's Solitaire is essentially a montane species, nesting in coniferous western forests.

Bluebirds live in woodlands adjacent to open areas. The Eastern Bluebird *(Sialia sialis)* and the Western Bluebird *(S. mexicana)* are both found in open woodlands, meadows, orchards, and farmland edges. The Mountain Bluebird *(S. currucoides)* occurs, as its name implies, at relatively high

---

Worldwide Family Features

- 5–13" (12–33 cm) woodland songbirds.
- About 330 species in about 54 genera worldwide, on all continents and many oceanic islands. North America has 18 breeding species or regular visitors in 9 genera; found throughout continent; plus at least 10 accidental species.
- Eat mostly arthropods and worms while breeding, fruit during migration and winter. Glean food from soil surface or pluck it from vegetation.
- Highly territorial during breeding season; sometimes individuals (not mated pairs) defend winter territories. Some species form flocks during migration and winter. Generally monogamous for season; extra-pair copulations in some species. Most temperate-zone species migratory.
- Breed first at 1 year old.

- Nest typically an open cup lined with grassy material and sticks, sometimes reinforced with mud. Usually placed in tree or other object 6½–50' (2–15 m) off ground; some species nest on ground or in tree cavity. Built almost entirely by female. Same nest used for 2nd broods.
- 2–10 (usually 4 or 5) subelliptical to oval, pale blue eggs, some flecked with brown. Typically only female incubates, for 10–17 days; hatching synchronous. Most species have 2 broods per year; some can raise 3.
- Altricial young sparsely covered with gray or drab down at hatching. Fledge at 8–19 days. Both sexes feed young.
- Adult annual survival 30–75%. Among oldest on record: 20 years, 3 months (Eurasian Blackbird); 13 years, 11 months (American Robin).

Bluebird foraging. *Bluebirds engage in some unusual (for thrushes) foraging methods. They hover to catch insects or to pluck berries from branches and use a technique known as ground-sallying: flying from a perch and settling briefly on the ground to capture an insect before returning to a perch. The Western Bluebird is shown.*

elevations throughout the western mountains, often in recently burned areas.

The chat-thrushes that breed in North America nest only in high Arctic regions, the Bluethroat in patches of scrubby willows on open tundra and the Northern Wheatear in rocky areas, often along the coast.

Winter Habitats

Spotted thrushes tend to winter in a range of forest types, from mature to young second-growth. Color-banding studies have shown that they do not form pairs until they return to the breeding areas, but individuals of some species, particularly the Wood Thrush, defend their winter territories with direct aggression (chases, physical contact, displacement of one bird by another), as well as a series of call notes.

The Wood Thrush has a high level of winter site fidelity, returning to exactly the same territory year after year. Not all Wood Thrushes succeed in obtaining a winter territory; "floaters" are subordinate birds that are presumably prevented from establishing a territory by more dominant birds. Floater birds appear to have lower survivorship rates than those that maintain winter territories.

Wintering American Robins occupy mainly the same habitat types as they do in the breeding season: closed-canopy forests, swamps, woodlots, woodland edges, and open areas; if the ground is not frozen, they forage for worms. Unlike spotted thrushes, American Robins are often gregarious on their wintering grounds, moving in flocks as they seek out fruit-laden plants.

During winter, Varied Thrushes sometimes forage on lawns and in parklands, although they are generally more wary than American Robins. Eastern and Western Bluebirds typically winter in the same habitats they use for breeding, while Mountain Bluebirds are found in open, arid grasslands. Solitaires are particularly attracted to juniper-dominated shrublands.

Food and Foraging

Thrushes are foraging generalists; they consume a wide variety of animals, including worms and arthropods, and virtually all species also consume fruit when available. They often flock to fruiting trees, although not all species are gregarious; the American Robin often feeds in large flocks, while bluebirds routinely forage in small flocks.

Long-distance migrants such as Swainson's Thrush and the Veery prefer woodland fruits (Spicebush, Sassafras, Black Tupelo, Flowering Dogwood) that are rich in lipids, which is the most efficient fuel for their long flights. These species migrate in late summer and early fall, when such fruits are most plentiful. When traveling south, they generally ignore fruits low in lipids; those that remain on the plants throughout the winter may serve as food for the birds as they return north in spring.

Thrushes feed in a variety of ways, depending upon the species. Many, particularly the spotted thrushes, the robins, and the Varied Thrush, are ground-feeders for much of the year. These birds move

American Robin foraging.
American Robins and other
thrushes often forage on the
ground, standing upright with
head cocked to watch for prey,
then hopping forward when
they see it. These actions are
very similar to those of other
visual foragers, such as plovers.

methodically over the ground, typically hopping a few yards, then pausing and sometimes tossing leaves with their bills. Robins routinely cock their heads from side to side; research has demonstrated that this behavior is a form of visual hunting—in other words, the birds are looking for prey (usually worms), not listening for it.

Bluebirds feed by gleaning insects from foliage, and they also occasionally hover and flycatch. They frequently capture insects on the ground, briefly alighting from a perch as they snatch the prey item, a foraging behavior called ground-sallying; the Mountain Bluebird, in particular, hunts in this manner. Townsend's Solitaire exhibits much the same kind of foraging behavior as the bluebirds and often occupies similar habitats, including recently burned areas. Solitaires often flycatch and may also hover briefly while plucking fruits.

Some thrush species serve an important ecological role by dispersing the seeds of certain plants. The American Robin and the Eastern Bluebird feed heavily on Eastern Redcedars and are long-distance seed dispersers for this species. Townsend's Solitaire, among the most important of western avian seed dispersers, concentrates on several species of junipers and also consumes the fruits of various mountain-ashes, serviceberries, Texas Madrone, and numerous other plants. Spotted thrushes are important long-distance seed dispersers of such woodland plants as Virginia Creeper, various dogwoods, Black Tupelo, and Spicebush.

Breeding

Male thrushes return early to the nesting area to establish breeding territories. They sing vigorously to advertise their presence on a territory and will aggressively attempt to drive away rival males. When confronting other members of the species, thrushes employ body posturing, which includes raising their crown feathers, wing-flicking, and tail-flicking. Other reported behaviors presumed to be agonistic include bill-snapping and gaping (opening the bill wide).

Direct physical combat also occurs, although less frequently. Male American Robins and Townsend's Solitaires directly grapple with one another when contesting territorial boundaries. Bouts between birds include aggressive chasing, grappling, and supplanting, in which one bird flies directly at another, forcing it to relinquish its perch.

While thrushes are usually considered monogamous, recent investigations provide evidence that extra-pair copulation occurs among some species. Polygynous behavior has been reported in the Wood Thrush, but at a relatively low level. In another study, Townsend's Solitaire has been shown to both seek extra-pair copulations and to lay eggs in the nests of other birds of the same species.

Following the establishment of territories, thrushes form strong pair bonds that last throughout the breeding season, usually for two broods. Males tend to stay close to females throughout nest-building. Bluebird males have been shown to guard their mates to reduce the potential for copulation with other males. Both sexes will act aggressively if the nest is threatened.

Territory size varies, presumably in relation to quality: The higher a territory's quality, the smaller its size, because there is little value in a bird defending more space than it needs. Territories range from a couple of acres (less than a hectare) to 5 or 6 acres (2–2.5 ha) or more. The territory serves as the principal foraging area, though in some species there is evidence that both the male and female sometimes forage beyond their territorial boundaries.

Thrushes place their nests toward the center of the territory. Most species construct an open-cup nest from twigs, grasses, mosses, bark strips, pine needles, and weeds. The American Robin and occasionally some other species, such as the Wood Thrush, use a foundation of mud. The female usually builds the nest, but in some species, including the American Robin and the bluebirds, males may assist. Birds typically reuse a nest for a second brood.

Most spotted thrushes nest high on the horizontal branches of trees or shrubs, but the Veery and eastern populations of the Hermit Thrush build ground nests. The American Robin nests in a wide variety of locations and trees, often very near houses. The Varied Thrush nests in conifers. Bluebirds nest in old tree cavities (either natural or excavated by woodpeckers) and also use bird boxes. Townsend's Solitaires usually

nest in depressions on the ground or along embankments.

As is true for most open-cup nesters, thrushes are exposed to a wide variety of nest predators, including weasels, Red Squirrels, skunks, raccoons, jays and crows, various snakes, and even Black Bears. The Wood Thrush, Veery, and Hermit Thrush experience intense levels of nest parasitism by the Brown-headed Cowbird (Molothrus ater), while thrushes that breed in cavities (bluebirds) or in the far north, as well as larger species (the American Robin), are not commonly parasitized.

Vocalizations

Thrushes are perhaps best known for their remarkable range of songs. Sonogram analyses of several species' songs reveal complex patterns and considerable variability among individuals.

The Common Nightingale (Luscinia megarhynchos), an Old World chat-thrush species, is considered one of the world's finest avian singers. Solitaires (genus Myadestes), most species of which are found in mountainous regions of Central and South America, are also outstanding singers. The song of the Wood Thrush is characteristic of eastern broadleaf forests, while that of the Varied Thrush haunts Redwood and Douglas-fir forests in the Pacific Northwest.

In North America, the thrushes are among the most melodious of birds. The American Robin sings a repetitive, tuneful

Turdid nests. Most thrushes build a cup nest in a tree, often incorporating mud into the structure. Some species (such as the Hermit Thrush, shown here) build on the ground. A few thrushes (the bluebirds) nest in cavities, such as old woodpecker holes or birdhouses.

warble similar to such non-thrush species as the Rose-breasted Grosbeak *(Pheucticus ludovicianus)* and the Scarlet Tanager *(Piranga olivacea)*. Bluebirds sing a soft warbled song, while Townsend's Solitaire sings a complex warbled song that is audible at a long distance. The Varied Thrush has perhaps the most distinctive song of any North American thrush: an eerie, prolonged whistle in a minor chord.

The spotted thrushes have flute-like songs that rise or fall in pitch. Their song patterns are similar but usually easy to distinguish in the field. The songs of Gray-cheeked and Bicknell's Thrushes are especially similar, but researchers have conducted tape-playback experiments to demonstrate that these two species ignore each other's songs.

During the breeding season males sing, usually from an exposed perch or the tree canopy, to signal territorial possession to prospective mates as well as rival males. Evidence suggests that thrush songs contain both innate and learned components. For example, studies of Wood Thrushes have concluded that of the three parts of the male's song, the central part is learned from members of the same species, while the first and third parts may be either innate or invented.

Townsend's Solitaire has an elaborate song that varies from one male to another. Solitaires are unusual among thrushes in that they sing throughout the year, with two annual peaks (April to May and September to November) that correlate with the establishment of breeding and wintering territories.

Call notes also serve essential signaling functions during the breeding season and on the wintering territory. Many different call notes have been described for various thrush species, and their exact functions are not at all clear. Some calls appear to signal danger or hostility, some to communicate with a mate, some to defend winter territories. Thrushes routinely emit species-specific call notes during nocturnal migrations. Birders can take advantage of these flight calls to identify high-flying migrants.

Movements

The spotted thrushes are long-distance migrants, with all but the Hermit Thrush wintering in the neotropics. Much variation exists among species. The Wood Thrush, for example, winters primarily in Central America, although some reach northern South America. Swainson's Thrush has a wider wintering range, extending from central Mexico as far south as northern Argentina and Paraguay. The Veery winters mostly in Central America and northern South America but can extend into central Brazil and Amazonia.

The Gray-cheeked Thrush migrates to South America to winter in the vast rain forest of Amazonia, while Bicknell's Thrush seems to be confined in winter to the Caribbean islands, which means that the winter ranges of these two similar species do not overlap. The Hermit Thrush winters extensively in the southern United States and Mexico, although some far-western populations seem to be permanent residents.

Spotted thrushes migrate at night, typically flying along with many other species, including wood-warblers, orioles, tanagers, and other thrushes. Nocturnal migrants, particularly the spotted thrushes, tend to fly at low altitudes and may fall victim to collisions with various towers or buildings. In Indiana, for instance, Swainson's Thrushes are among the most common migrants killed in collisions with windows and buildings. In the East, long-distance migrants crossing the Gulf of Mexico time their flights to take advantage of major weather fronts. Typically, thrush spring migration accompanies warm fronts with southerly winds, and fall migration follows on the heels of cold fronts with northwesterly winds.

American Robins often migrate by day in single-species flocks and winter largely in the southern United States, although some range as far south as Guatemala.

The Varied Thrush has a somewhat irregular migration pattern. This species migrates south from the Pacific Northwest to California, with some continuing as far as northern Baja California; it also routinely occurs as a winter rarity as far east and south as Virginia and rarely to Florida. Populations can vary dramatically throughout much of its wintering range. It is unclear why this species shows these irregular fluctuations in abundance or why some end up in far eastern North America.

Townsend's Solitaires are somewhat nomadic wanderers, seeking out concentrations of fruit. They normally winter in the West and in central Mexico but, like the Varied Thrush, may also occur as a winter rarity in the East, where they are associated with plants that are abundant in berries.

The three bluebird species are only partially migratory. Those nesting farthest north do migrate, but only as far as the southern United States and Mexico. Both Eastern and Western Bluebirds are permanent residents over much of the southern parts of their ranges.

The Bluethroat, which nests in the far northwestern parts of Alaska and more commonly in Eurasia from Scandinavia to Siberia, migrates west across the Bering Sea and winters in southeastern Asia and the Near East. Similarly, the Northern Wheatear is a predominantly Old World species that migrates from its restricted North American breeding grounds in Alaska and Canada to winter in Africa. Off-course wheatears are found throughout North America in small numbers, especially during migration periods, and they have been found as far south as Puerto Rico and the Bahamas.

Other rare thrushes in North America occur largely due to movements during the nonbreeding season. Fieldfares *(Turdus pilaris)*, long-distance migrants from Eurasia, occasionally wander to North America rather than to their traditional wintering grounds. Three other species— the Clay-colored Robin *(T. grayi)*, Rufous-backed Robin *(T. rufopalliatus)*, and Aztec Thrush—are all Central American species that sometimes wander north from Mexico into the southern United States during the nonbreeding

Spotted juveniles. Many adult thrushes have a spotted pattern on the breast, and even the species that are not spotted as adults have a spotted breast when in juvenal plumage. The Western Bluebird (left) and the American Robin (right) are shown.

season. Clay-colored Robins sometimes also breed in the Rio Grande Valley of Texas.

Conservation

The populations of several thrush species are increasing, while others are undergoing serious declines. The Eastern Bluebird, for many years a declining species, is now experiencing a strong population resurgence throughout much of its range, probably due in part to aggressive conservation programs that have erected bluebird nest boxes in suitable habitat. The Mountain Bluebird, also benefiting from the increased availability of nest boxes, has increased in many parts of its range. Unfortunately, the Western Bluebird has not fared as well and is experiencing declines throughout parts of its range, particularly California foothills and coastal forests.

Breeding Bird Survey results indicate that populations of the Hermit Thrush have increased over extensive parts of its range. It has been suggested that the Hermit Thrush, the only spotted thrush that does not winter in the neotropics, is not negatively affected by the widespread deforestation occurring throughout much of Central America. The American Robin is also increasing in much of its range, perhaps because it is not adversely affected by forest fragmentation; indeed, increasing suburban habitats resulting from this fragmentation may have benefited the species.

Major population declines for the Wood Thrush and the Veery have been documented using data from the Breeding Bird Survey. Because these species winter in Central America and nest in areas subject to much recent forest fragmentation, they may be subject to population stress on both their wintering and breeding grounds. They also may suffer from collisions with buildings and towers, as well as the loss of stopover habitats, during migration.

Careful studies have shown that in areas of highly fragmented small forest plots Wood Thrushes sometimes actually fledge more Brown-headed Cowbirds than Wood Thrush young. The species is also subject to predation from American Crows *(Corvus brachyrhynchos),* Common Grackles *(Quiscalus quiscula),* and Blue Jays *(Cyanocitta cristata),* all species that benefit from the increased edge habitats that result from forest fragmentation. It is difficult to measure accurately the reproductive success of the Wood Thrush. Some populations that appear to have remained stable have paradoxically reared almost no young. The apparent stability is likely due to influxes of birds that were hatched elsewhere, so-called "source" populations that augment what would otherwise be declining "sink" populations.

There is little information on population trends in the Gray-cheeked and Bicknell's Thrushes, though Bicknell's has declined somewhat within its small breeding range in New England. Bicknell's Thrush is potentially at risk from fragmentation of its breeding grounds, loss of breeding habitat from the development of ski resorts, negative effects of acid rain, and loss of wintering habitat in the Greater Antilles. Both the Wood Thrush and Bicknell's Thrush have been placed on the WatchList.

Accidental Species

Several species of Asian thrushes wander very rarely to western North America. The Eyebrowed Thrush *(Turdus obscurus)* sometimes occurs during spring migration on the western Aleutian Islands, the Pribilof Islands, and mainland Alaska, and the Dusky Thrush *(T. naumanni)* has occurred in Alaska and western Canada in spring and fall.

The Siberian Rubythroat *(Luscinia calliope)* has been found, mostly during spring migration, in the western Aleutians, on St. Lawrence Island and the Pribilofs in the Bering Sea, and even in southern Ontario during winter. The Siberian Blue Robin *(L. cyane)* has been seen in the Aleutian Islands (Attu) in late May. A third chat-thrush, the Red-flanked Bluetail *(Tarsiger cyanurus),* also occurs mainly in spring in the western Aleutians (Attu) and the Pribilofs, but has been found in California (Farallon Islands) in November. Finally, a chat-thrush thought to be a Rufous-tailed Robin *(Luscinia sibilans)* was seen on Attu in June 1999 but has yet to be formally accepted by the AOU.

The Stonechat *(Saxicola torquata)* breeds widely from Europe and Africa through northern and central Asia, and has been seen during both spring and fall in Alaska. A Stonechat from Siberia has also been found in New Brunswick in fall. Two more Eurasian species, the Redwing *(Turdus iliacus)* and the Eurasian Blackbird *(T. merula),* have both been found in eastern Canada and New England, with most records from winter.

The White-throated Robin *(Turdus assimilis),* which is found from Mexico to Colombia and Ecuador, is accidental in winter in southern Texas. The Orange-billed Nightingale-Thrush *(Catharus aurantiirostris),* of Mexico and Central America, has been recorded once, in April, in extreme southern Texas.

John Kricher

Babblers (Wrentit)

Family Timaliidae
Order Passeriformes

The large babbler family is represented in the Americas by a single species, the Wrentit *(Chamaea fasciata)*, a small songbird with a short, brown bill and a long, rounded tail that is often cocked. Males and females look alike, as do adults and juveniles, with olive-brown or dark brown plumage above and paler or pinkish-brown underparts. The Wrentit typically occupies coastal sage scrub and chaparral habitats but can occur anywhere there is adequate shrub cover, including valley oak woodlands, old-growth conifer forests, suburban yards, and urban parks. It often skulks in dense scrub, hopping about in the underbrush much like a wren, and making short flights; it appears averse to crossing open spaces.

Taxonomy

Scientists have questioned the taxonomic status of the Wrentit since its discovery in 1846. Initially they considered it to be a species intermediate between the wrens and the chickadees and titmice—hence its name (formerly "Wren-tit")—and assigned it to its own family. In the 1980s, DNA–DNA hybridization studies revealed that the Wrentit is genetically similar to both the Old World warblers and the Old World babblers. Because the Wrentit is closest behaviorally and morphologically to Old World babblers, taxonomists now place the bird in that family.

Food and Foraging

The Wrentit forages in shrubs and trees, actively gleaning insects and spiders from bark and, less frequently, from leaves or stems. It rarely forages on the ground. Fruit, such as elderberries and blackberries, is also an important part of the Wrentit's diet, as are seeds in winter. Parents often feed nestlings butterfly and moth larvae, such as inchworm moths.

Vocalizations

Birders often identify the Wrentit by its distinctive, loud song, which has been likened to the sound of a Ping–Pong ball bouncing on a table. Males and females sing year-round, both to advertise their territories and to communicate with their mates. Females usually sing only in response to a male, and their song lacks the male's trill at the end. Studies of Wrentits and wrens, which may nest in close proximity to one another, showed that Wrentits tend not to sing concurrently with wrens, but rather delay their song by a few minutes, thereby avoiding acoustic interference.

Breeding

Wrentits form long-term monogamous pair bonds, with the male and female maintaining close contact throughout the year, preening each other and foraging and roosting together. Both males and females sing, build the nest, incubate the eggs, care for the young, and defend the territory.

Wrentit. *The Wrentit is the only North American representative of the Old World family of babblers.*

Wrentit head and bill. *The short, stout bill of the Wrentit is chickadee-like but slightly larger and decurved, adapted for a diet of berries, seeds, and insects.*

Wrentit nest. *Wrentits build an open-cup nest of tightly woven grasses and bark shreds bound together with spider webs. This species often reuses nest materials; here a bird pulls material from an old nest to use in a new one.*

The Wrentit is extremely sedentary. Its breeding territory ranges in size from 1 to 5 acres (0.4–2 ha), and once a pair establishes its territory, it remains there year-round and rarely leaves. Before acquiring a territory, Wrentits often move several miles, although one-year-olds may settle on or near their natal territory.

Males and females build a tight, open-cup nest, placing it low to the ground, usually in the crook of a shrub. They often breed in coastal sage or coyote brush, fashioning their nests from the bark of these shrubs, bound together with cob-webs. If the pair renests, either because the first brood fails or to rear a second, they often recycle nest materials.

Nest failure due to predators such as jays and snakes is common, and Wrentits frequently attempt to renest. A pair generally rears one brood but can sometimes rear a second one. The clutch is usually four eggs, but can be three or (rarely) five.

Compared to other open-cup-nesting songbirds, the Wrentit's incubation and nestling periods are long—15 to 16 days each. Even more unusual is the long period of parental care, which generally continues for 30 days after fledging.

Conservation

The Wrentit appears to be quite adaptable, using riparian scrub and suburban habitat in addition to its more typical coastal sage scrub and chaparral. Breeding Bird Survey data show no evidence of a general population decline since 1966. In eastern California and central Oregon, the Wrentit's range appears to have expanded, possibly due to increased scrub habitat resulting from deforestation. Even so, the sedentary nature of the Wrentit makes it vulnerable to habitat isolation that can promote the extirpation of small local populations.

Nadav Nur and Geoffrey R. Geupel

Worldwide Family Features

• 3½–16" (9–41 cm) songbirds of scrublands, woodlands, and reed beds.
• About 270 species in 50 genera worldwide; most species found in tropical Asia, fewer in Africa and northern Eurasia. 1 species occurs in North America, in California and Oregon.
• Eat insects and spiders gleaned from bark or from ground; also fruit and seeds.
• Most species maintain group territories, often year-round, and nest communally or as dispersed pairs throughout group territories. Some species monogamous. Nonmigratory, largely sedentary.
• Breed first at 1 or 2 years old.
• Open-cup or domed nest made of bark, coarse grass, sometimes framed by twigs; placed in shrub low to ground. Both sexes build nest. Do not reuse nest but sometimes recycle materials.
• 2–7 (up to 11 when multiple females lay in 1 nest) subelliptical, whitish, blue, or green eggs, with markings ranging from unmarked to heavily spotted. Both sexes incubate, for 13–25 days. Hatching usually synchronous. 1 or 2 broods a year.
• Altricial young naked or downy at hatching. Fledge at 12–22 days. Both parents perform parental care, with help from nonparents in at least 2 species.
• Adult annual survival 60–88%. Among oldest on record: 15 years (Arabian Babbler, *Turdoides squamiceps*); 12 years, 7 months (Wrentit).

Mockingbirds and Thrashers

Mimids are medium-size songbirds well known for their vocal repertoires and mimicking abilities. Most species are various shades of brown and gray, and some have streaking on their pale underparts. They generally have short, rounded wings, long legs and tail, and a long, often decurved bill. Mimids live in a wide variety of habitats, from wet, dense thickets to arid deserts, chaparral, and sagebrush steppes.

Taxonomy

Most field guides place the family Mimidae after the thrushes because of the superficial similarity between *Catharus* thrushes and the thrashers. DNA–DNA hybridization data suggest, however, that mimids are most closely related to the starlings.

The family Mimidae includes thrashers, mockingbirds, catbirds, and tremblers, all of which are 10-primaried oscines generally linked by their size and appearance. The 10 species that breed in North America fall into three groups: the thrashers (genera *Toxostoma* and *Oreoscoptes*), the Northern Mockingbird *(Mimus polyglottos)*, and the Gray Catbird *(Dumetella carolinensis)*.

Mimids are fairly distinctive in appearance and behavior among North American birds. Traditionally they were considered close relatives of the wrens, some of which have similarly shaped bills and, like mimids, are often found on or near the ground—for example, the Rock Wren *(Salpinctes obsoletus)* and the Canyon Wren *(Catherpes mexicanus)*. However, mimids are significantly larger and lack the barred tail of the wrens. The Cactus Wren *(Campylorhynchus brunneicapillus)* is particularly thrasher-like in appearance, with its relatively large size, brown plumage, spotted underparts, and long, slightly decurved bill.

The Northern Mockingbird, the only widespread North American member of the distinctive genus *Mimus*, is known

Worldwide Family Features

- 7½–12" (19–30 cm) songbirds of desert, shrub, and other habitats.
- About 34 species in 11 genera worldwide; found exclusively in Americas, outside of boreal habitats. North America has 10 breeding species in 4 genera and 1 regular visitor; found throughout U.S. and southern Canada, with greatest number of species in Southwest; plus 2 accidental species.
- Eat insects and small fruit gleaned from ground and low vegetation; dig in leaf litter with bill to uncover prey items.
- Males vigorously defend breeding territories; in winter, some species territorial. Monogamous; pairs last several years in some species. Most species resident; a few are facultative migrants; Gray Catbird is long-distance neotropical migrant. Some species form small flocks during migration or when feeding at fruiting trees.
- Breed first at 1 year old.

- Cup-shaped nest of coarse twigs, lined with finer grasses and fibers; usually placed in dense vegetation, cactus, or yucca, sometimes within mass of sticks forming a platform. Both sexes usually build nest. Nests sometimes reused in same season, rarely in subsequent years.
- 2–6 subelliptical eggs; often bluish to bluish-green with reddish to brown spotting, mottling, or blotches. Both sexes incubate in most species (only female in some), for 11–15 days. Hatching synchronous or asynchronous. 2 or 3 broods per year.
- Altricial young hatch covered with sparse down. Fledge at 12–15 days, sometimes slightly longer. Both sexes care for young for up to 3 weeks after fledging.
- Adult annual survival 56–80%, but few studies. Among oldest on record: 14 years, 10 months (Northern Mockingbird).

Mimid diversity. *The family Mimidae is represented in North America by four genera, three of which have only one North American breeding species (shown here from left to right): the short-billed and secretive Gray Catbird in* Dumetella; *the long-tailed and conspicuous Northern Mockingbird in* Mimus; *and the short-billed Sage Thrasher, which is usually found in sagebrush, in* Oreoscoptes. *The seven North American species in the genus* Toxostoma *(represented here by Le Conte's Thrasher, far right) are mostly secretive ground-dwellers with long bills and tails.*

for its astonishing ability to mimic other species' songs. Similar in shape to some thrashers, especially Bendire's *(Toxostoma bendirei)*, it is distinguished by its conspicuous white wing-patch. Birders sometimes confuse the Northern Mockingbird with the Loggerhead Shrike *(Lanius ludovicianus)*, which also has a white wing-patch. The Gray Catbird is more thrush-like in shape but, like other mimids, has a complex, versatile song.

There is no geographic variation in the Northern Mockingbird, the Sage Thrasher *(Oreoscoptes montanus)*, and Bendire's Thrasher. Clinal variation in the Gray Catbird and the Brown *(Toxostoma rufum)*, California *(T. redivivum)*, and Crissal *(T. crissale)* Thrashers is weak; each has two or three subspecies that intergrade where their ranges approach one another. The Long-billed *(T. longirostre)*, Le Conte's *(T. lecontei)*, and Curve-billed *(T. curvirostre)* Thrashers have a moderate to strong degree of geographic variation, with well-defined ranges for the subspecies.

Subspecies of the Curve-billed Thrasher form two distinct groups. Two (or three) subspecies (the *curvirostre* group) are found in the eastern part of the species' range and share a white breast with distinct spotting, a white throat, distinct white wing-bars, and broad white tips on the tail feathers. Three western subspecies (the *palmeri* group) have a grayer throat, a grayer breast with less distinct spotting, less distinct wing-bars, and reduced white rectrix tips. Recent genetic studies have

proposed full species status for these two subspecies groups. A similar pattern of genetic variation within Le Conte's Thrasher suggests that this species may also be split in the future.

In addition to the 10 species that regularly breed in North America, the Bahama Mockingbird *(Mimus gundlachii)*, normally found in the Bahamas and West Indies, has occurred in southern Florida at least 30 times between 1973 and 2000. The vast majority of these records occurred during April and May.

Variation

All mimids undergo a prebasic molt after the breeding cycle is completed. Hatching-year birds undergo only a partial prebasic molt, replacing some wing coverts, some tertials, and occasionally some rectrices. There is a very limited prealternate molt, if any.

Bill size and shape vary greatly among adult mimid species. For example, the

Mimid bill shape. *The bills of mimids vary from the short, straight, thrush-like shape of the Gray Catbird bill (left) to the elongated, curved bill of the Crissal Thrasher (right).*

Curve-billed and Crissal Thrashers have long, decurved bills, whereas the Gray Catbird and Northern Mockingbird have relatively short, straight bills. Juveniles of most species have shorter, straighter bills, as compared to adults. This sometimes poses identification problems; in particular, Curve-billed Thrasher young often have bills that more closely resemble those of the sympatric Bendire's Thrasher.

Habitats

As a family, mimids occur in a wide range of habitats, from dense second-growth vegetation, preferred by the Gray Catbird and the Brown Thrasher, to the open, sparsely vegetated deserts inhabited by some southwestern thrashers. Some species, such as the Northern Mockingbird, are habitat generalists, occurring in cultivated and suburban habitats as well as more natural environments. Other species are highly specialized, including the chaparral-dwelling California Thrasher and the Sage Thrasher, which breeds almost exclusively in the sage-dominated Great Basin Desert.

Four southwestern thrasher species that have overlapping ranges—the Curve-billed, Bendire's, Crissal, and Le Conte's—occur in different habitats. Le Conte's Thrasher has the most restricted range, preferring sparsely vegetated sandy desert with saltbush. Similar in shape but darker, the Crissal Thrasher prefers more vegetated desert washes and dense thickets of mesquite, and the species ranges into higher-elevation pinyon pine and juniper shrublands.

The Curve-billed and Bendire's Thrashers live in a broader range of habitats and are more likely to occur near ranches or towns; each species, however, has its particular preferences. Bendire's Thrasher has a decidedly local distribution in Arizona; it frequents deserts dominated by cholla cacti, slightly higher-elevation grassland-desert habitats with yucca, and more northerly areas within its range dominated by sagebrush and juniper.

The Curve-billed Thrasher lives in a variety of desert habitats, but most frequently in cactus-rich deserts intermixed with mesquite.

Food and Foraging

Mimids feed on insects and fruit, the composition of their diet varying with season and location. North American species feed extensively on small fruit, especially during the nonbreeding season. Berries make up as much as 50 percent of some species' diets, including the Gray Catbird and the Northern Mockingbird. The Gray Catbird gleans insects or small fruit while foraging in small shrubs and also sometimes hovers or flycatches; one account reported these birds feeding extensively on emerging dragonflies in a marsh.

The Northern Mockingbird feeds mainly on the ground, running or hopping short distances and then lunging after prey items. While on the ground, the bird raises and lowers its wings in a conspicuous jerky movement that exposes its white wing-patches; this wing-flashing behavior is perhaps a means of startling insects.

Thrashers probably get their name from their well-known behavior of "thrashing" the ground for insects (although

Northern Mockingbird wing-flashing display.
When foraging actively, the Northern Mockingbird often raises one or both wings jerkily above its back, exposing the white wing-patches. This behavior may serve to scare insects out of hiding and is analogous to the tail-flashing of gnatcatchers, the American Redstart (Setophaga ruticilla), and other species. The same action may be used in territorial displays.

Crissal Thrasher digging.
The longer-billed thrashers sweep their bills briskly back and forth to move debris or to dig in the ground, uncovering crickets and other prey. The loud thrashing noises made during this activity can lead observers to the bird.

one account suggests the name came from a bird "thrashing" a nest intruder). The bills of several thrasher species are highly modified for sweeping back and forth in the leaf litter under dense vegetation. Thrashers often pick up leaves and twigs and toss them out of the way. Le Conte's Thrasher has been known to flip items as heavy as one and a half times its body weight.

Thrashers commonly search for food by digging holes in the ground with the bill. The Curve-billed Thrasher digs holes as deep as 2 inches (5 cm), and Le Conte's Thrasher may dig more than 3 inches (8 cm). Thrashers sometimes throw dirt and sand vigorously away from the pit they are digging. The noisy spectacle often provides a good opportunity for birders to locate these secretive species. Bendire's Thrasher, which has a shorter, straighter bill, is not known to dig holes.

While most species tend to be nondiscriminating in their prey selection, some thrashers appear to favor larger insects; for example, the California Thrasher seeks out Jerusalem crickets. Bendire's Thrasher often feeds on ants, termites, and large insects. Many species are omnivorous; examinations of Le Conte's Thrashers' stomachs have revealed small snakes, lizards, and scorpions. Brown Thrashers have been known to feed on lizards, salamanders, and small frogs.

Mimids also appear to be nondiscriminating in their selection of edible berries, taking advantage of whatever is locally available. Most species climb up into shrubs to glean berries. Even shy species such as the California Thrasher forage in the open for fruit. Sage Thrashers gather in small flocks to feed in the open on berries.

Some species also feed on other vegetative matter. The Curve-billed Thrasher eats agave flowers and a variety of cactus seeds, including those of Saguaros. The California Thrasher feeds on domestic fruit, such as grapes and fallen oranges, and also frequents feeders, as do Curve-billed and Crissal Thrashers. Those species that are partially migratory (such as Bendire's and Sage Thrashers) are most likely facultative migrants, traveling different distances depending upon where good fruit crops occur in a particular year.

The desert thrashers are well adapted to their harsh environment. Their sandy brown color matches their environment, protecting them from predators, and their long, curved bills are well suited for digging in hard, dry soil. Most of these species get water from the food they consume. The Curve-billed Thrasher feeds occasionally on Saguaro fruit during the heat of the day, when it is most likely to get both food and water with little expenditure of energy. Le Conte's Thrasher, which pants when heat-stressed, often spends the heat of the day resting in well-shaded areas.

Breeding

All North American mimids are essentially monogamous; the few reports of polygyny are mainly limited to the Northern Mockingbird. Pair-bonding usually occurs at the onset of the breeding season, especially in migrant species such as the Gray Catbird, but can occur at any season in some of the resident thrashers. In some species, particularly Le Conte's and Curve-billed Thrashers, pairs can bond for several years.

Most species engage in courtship displays at the onset of bonding. The Northern Mockingbird has several different displays, one of which is an elaborate flight display in which the male jumps off a perch in mid-song, flaps a couple of times as it rises in the air, then "parachutes" with open wings back to its perch. The birds also use wing-flashing in their territorial displays. The Gray Catbird raises its head up or down while fluffing out its body feathers. Displays in several of the resident thrashers involve elaborate songs but otherwise have been described as subdued or brief, perhaps because they can form pair bonds at any time of the year.

Nest-building varies among species. The male Northern Mockingbird constructs the nest, usually building several before a female selects one; the female then usually finishes the lining. The female Gray Catbird does most of the nest construction, although the male usually contributes some material. In thrashers, both sexes share the responsibility of nest-building, although in some species (such as Le Conte's) the participation of individual males varies considerably.

Mimids typically conceal their nests in dense vegetation. Desert species that nest in more open habitats place them in relatively shady locations. The Curve-billed

Brown Thrasher nest. *All mimids build a simple cup nest in a bush or low tree, usually with a rough exterior of sticks and twigs.*

Thrasher has the greatest nesting success when it builds its nest in yucca or cholla cactus, presumably because the sharp thorns and leaf points of these plants discourage predators.

Some mimids (Bendire's, Le Conte's, and California Thrashers) have been known to reuse nests in a single season, particularly if the first brood is successful. Nest reuse typically involves major renovation of the original nest. In general, none of these species will reuse a nest in a subsequent breeding season.

Vocalizations

One of the defining traits of a mimid is its propensity for complex songs and calls. As in other songbirds, the main function of the male's song is most likely a combination of territorial defense, mate attraction, and in some cases possibly mate guarding.

The Mimidae is one of the few families whose species incorporate a high degree of mimicry into their vocalizations. Little is known about the development of their songs. The primary song appears to be mostly learned, particularly in those species that engage in a significant amount of mimicry, such as the Northern Mockingbird, the Gray Catbird, and a few of the thrashers.

Le Conte's Thrasher begins mimicking the sounds of surrounding birds and mammals about six to nine months after fledging. The Curve-billed Thrasher has an innate component to its call; chicks only a few days old are able to give calls similar to adult *wit-WEET-wit* calls.

Once a mimid "learns" a phrase, it generally retains it throughout the year; for example, the California Thrasher's winter song can mimic calls and songs of species that are only summer residents of its habitat. Northern Mockingbirds mimic parts of songs they must have learned on their wintering grounds; they have been heard repeating vocalizations of the Buff-collared Nightjar *(Caprimulgus ridgwayi)* and the Thick-billed Kingbird *(Tyrannus crassirostris)* in portions of Arizona where

Mimid vocalizations. All mimid species sing, from a conspicuous perch, a long series of complex phrases strung together, often repeating a phrase one or more times and often including mimicry of other species. The Brown Thrasher (shown here) improvises as it sings, changing phrases slightly so that its total repertoire cannot be quantified easily. Songs of the Northern Mockingbird differ fundamentally from those of the Brown Thrasher (and perhaps others) in that the phrases are stereotyped, each individual using a repertoire of 150 to 300 phrases and repeating them the same way every time.

neither species occurs. In New Jersey, a Gray Catbird was heard mimicking a Brown-crested Flycatcher *(Myiarchus tyrannulus)*, whose song the catbird must have learned in Central America.

The songs of some species are more structured than others. Brown, Long-billed, and Bendire's Thrashers rarely, if ever, mimic, and their songs consist of distinct paired or sometimes tripled phrases. The Northern Mockingbird, Gray Catbird, and most of the other thrashers have long, complex songs of warbles, squeaks, guttural notes, and melodious phrases that sometimes continue unabated for as long as 10 to 20 minutes. Analysis of the Le Conte's Thrasher's song revealed hundreds of distinct phrases, many of which were not regularly repeated. One four-and-a-half-minute Gray Catbird song included 170 distinct phrases.

Males do most of the singing, but some females, including California Thrashers, will also sing vigorously and occasionally counter-sing with the males.

Singing typically peaks at the onset of the breeding season. In the desert Southwest, some thrashers, particularly the Crissal and Le Conte's, begin singing by mid-January. Some species, the Northern Mockingbird in particular, sing well into the evening and begin again about an hour before dawn. The songs can carry long distances. Le Conte's Thrashers have been heard nearly a half mile (750 m) away.

Although song appears to be most important during pair-bonding and territorial defense, many species sing, albeit infrequently, throughout the year. Many species have "whisper" songs, given most frequently near the nest or when an intruder is present. All species have various species-specific calls that serve different functions, such as intruder alert, communication between mates, and general alarm.

For one pair of species, songs and (especially) calls can help in identification: The *wit-WEET-wit* calls of the Curve-billed Thrasher and the *chuk* call of the Bendire's Thrasher are perhaps more reliable cues than morphological field marks for separating the two species.

Movements

Several mimids—such as the California, Crissal, and Le Conte's Thrashers—are permanent residents within their range. Other species—in particular the Brown, Bendire's, and Sage Thrashers—are partial migrants; northern populations of these species migrate south, but southern populations most likely remain in place year-round. Brown Thrashers are most likely nocturnal migrants, as is evident from radio tower kills, and large flocks of Sage Thrashers migrate diurnally in northern Arizona. The northern portion of the Sage Thrasher population migrates away from its breeding grounds and winters in a variety of desert habitats where other species, such as the Crissal and Bendire's Thrashers, already occur. Sage Thrashers also move to juniper-laden foothills in years when fruit is abundant.

Bendire's Thrashers have been reported at migrant stopover habitat on the Colorado River and at oases in the Mojave Desert. They are most likely northern birds moving south, but they may also be dispersing immatures. The latter phenomenon is responsible for extralimital records of the normally sedentary Curve-billed Thrasher, which has made it to the upper Midwest.

The Gray Catbird, the only neotropical migrant in the family Mimidae, vacates most of its summer range in North America to winter mainly in Mexico, Central America, and the Caribbean. Small numbers also winter in the southeastern United States. This bird is mainly a nocturnal migrant across the Gulf of Mexico. During its migration, it visits shrubby second-growth habitats similar to its breeding areas. Under proper weather conditions in spring, however, vast numbers of Gray Catbirds can swarm over all kinds of coastal habitats along the Gulf coast from Texas to southern Florida, a phenomenon known as a migratory "fallout."

Conservation

Ornithologists generally believe that populations of many of the mimids, including such common species as the Gray Catbird, Brown Thrasher, and Northern Mockingbird, have declined during the past two decades. Breeding Bird Surveys document declines in these species as well as the Curve-billed and California Thrashers. Catbirds are declin-

ing the most in Canada, according to Breeding Bird Survey data. More study is needed to determine the causes for such reductions, but reforestation in eastern North America tends to eliminate the early successional shrub habitat used by mimids.

In the Southwest, conversion of desert to agricultural lands and expanding development in metropolitan areas such as Phoenix and Tucson, Arizona, are major causes of habitat loss for most of the desert thrashers, including the Crissal, Curve-billed, Bendire's, and Le Conte's. The California Thrasher in the chaparral habitats of coastal California and the Long-billed Thrasher in southern Texas are suffering similar fates as development encroaches into their habitats.

Several species are on the WatchList (Le Conte's, Bendire's, Curve-billed, California, and Long-billed Thrashers), while Le Conte's Thrasher is of special concern in California. Currently no mimids are considered endangered species by any state, provincial, or federal government agency.

Accidental Species

The Blue Mockingbird (*Melanotis caerulescens*), previously thought to be a Mexican endemic, has occurred very rarely in Arizona, New Mexico, and Texas during fall and winter. These records are thought to represent naturally dispersing individuals, as this species is known to disperse in fall and winter from higher elevations into riparian habitats in northern Mexico. However, the species is kept as a cage bird in Mexico, so some records, including a recent California sighting, may be escapees.

There is one old record of the Black Catbird (*Melanoptila glabrirostris*) from extreme southern Texas; this species is from Mexico's Yucatán Peninsula. The origin of the specimen has been questioned, but the record is included in the AOU Check-list.

Gary H. Rosenberg

Starlings and Mynas

Starlings and mynas are medium-size songbirds with strong legs and feet; they are often seen foraging on the ground. Males are generally slightly larger than females. Their silky plumage is commonly dark, with metallic purples, greens, blues, or black, and sometimes includes white, rufous, pink, or crimson. The wings are short and triangular or rounded. The tail is usually short and square, but some species have long tails. Most Sturnidae species are highly gregarious, especially when feeding and roosting in winter, and many are colonial breeders. Four species have been introduced in North America: The European Starling *(Sturnus vulgaris)* is widespread across the continent; the three myna species have very limited distributions.

Taxonomy

The Sturnidae is a homogeneous Old World family whose relationships are debated. Traditionally it was placed close to the crows, although some experts have suggested a closer relationship with such Old World groups as the weavers (Ploceidae), drongos (Dicruridae), or Old World orioles (Oriolidae), or with the New World blackbirds. Egg-white protein studies in the 1970s suggested a relationship to the wood-swallows (Artamidae) of Australasia, as well as to the weavers and drongos. DNA–DNA hybridization data indicate that the starlings' closest relatives are the mockingbirds, and indeed that the starlings could be placed in the same family as the mockingbirds.

In currently accepted taxonomies, the family has 110 to 114 species in 24 to 27 genera worldwide. Some species have been introduced widely around the world.

The European Starling is a member of the typical starlings (genus *Sturnus*), which contains 16 species. The Crested Myna *(Acridotheres cristatellus)* and the Common Myna *(A. tristis)* belong to the typical mynas genus, which includes seven species found in southern Asia and western Indonesia. The Hill Myna *(Gracula religiosa)* is found from India to the East Indies and Philippines; the nominate form ("Eastern" Hill Myna) has been introduced in North America.

Habitats

Members of this family commonly occur in open areas, such as farms, savannas, and steppes, but also live in woodlands and forests. Many species, including the four introduced in North America, are closely associated with human habitations. The European Starling is common in urban centers but also successful in woodland edge habitats. The Hill and Crested Mynas are found along city streets, and in parks, gardens, and rural areas. The Common Myna is often found near large shopping centers. All myna species roost in small flocks on buildings, bridges, and wires, and in trees.

Sturnid diversity. *This exclusively Old World family has been introduced in North America, where four species in two groups are found. The European Starling (left) is a highly gregarious, temperate-zone species with a straight, slender bill. The mynas (Common Myna shown, right) are less gregarious, generally tropical and subtropical species.*

Food and Foraging

Sturnids eat a variety of animal and plant food, mainly insects and other invertebrates, but also fruit, nectar, grain, and the eggs of other birds. They often forage on the ground, probing with the bill.

Starlings have specially developed muscles that allow them to pry open their bills while probing in the soil, and thereby capture prey unavailable to other foragers. This feeding behavior, called gaping, is also found in blackbirds and has been suggested as a reason why European Starlings can winter in temperate areas where other insectivores cannot.

Mynas forage on the ground, picking fallen fruit. The diet of Crested Mynas is 60 percent fruit and berries when these are available; most of their remaining food is insects and earthworms, which they feed as staples to their young. Hill Mynas are also largely frugivores but eat nectar, insects, and small reptiles.

Young European Starlings form large independent feeding flocks in late summer and autumn; young mynas do not.

Sturnid head and bill. *Starlings have a straight, tapered bill, which they force into soil or vegetation and open with powerful muscles, thus creating a hole and exposing prey. (The European Starling is shown.) Mynas have thicker bills and often bare skin around the face.*

Breeding

Most Sturnidae species are monogamous. European Starlings are generally monogamous, but in many populations males may change mates between broods. The males' second mates receive little help with the young.

The songs in this family are usually varied, containing melodious whistles and warbles. Many species are good mimics. European Starlings, especially the males, are vocal all year, except when molting. Their song is rich and varied, and often incorporates elements from the songs of Killdeers *(Charadrius vociferus)*, meadowlarks (genus *Sturnella*), and other species. Sturnids also mimic sirens, police whistles, and human speech.

European Starlings nest in a variety of cavities, including woodpecker holes, birdhouses, and crevices in buildings. They compete for nest sites with secondary cavity nesters such as bluebirds (genus *Sialia*) and even some primary cavity excavators such as the Red-headed Woodpecker *(Melanerpes erythrocephalus)*, sometimes evicting the woodpecker. They defend only the immediate nest and a small area around it, and will nest semicolonially if there are suitable nesting sites clustered together. The male selects the nest site and initiates the nest-building;

Worldwide Family Features

- 6–17" (15–43 cm) terrestrial songbirds.
- About 113 species in up to 27 genera worldwide, in Africa, Eurasia, many Pacific Islands. 4 species in 3 genera introduced to North America; 1 species continent-wide, 3 with limited ranges.
- Eat mainly insects, also other invertebrates, fruit, nectar, grain, bird eggs. Often forage on ground, probing with bill.
- Many species colonial. Most highly gregarious, especially when feeding and roosting. Most species probably monogamous, though duration of pair bond varies. Most species resident; European Starling partly migratory.
- Breed first probably at 1 year old.
- 2 types of nest: pile of plant fragments

in tree cavity, other cavity, or rock crevice; and domed or cup-shaped nest in a bush or on ground. Male selects site and starts nest, then female helps. Cavity nesters reuse cavities, some materials.
- 2–10 eggs (usually 3–5): elliptical to subelliptical; spotted or immaculate; pale bluish or greenish-white. Both sexes incubate, for 10–24 days. Hatching synchronous. Usually 2 broods per year.
- Altricial young nearly naked at hatch. Fledge at 15–35 days. Both parents care for young.
- Adult annual survival 47–55% (European Starling in Europe). Among oldest on record: 20 years, 1 month (European Starling).

the female selects the male. The Hill and Crested Mynas nest in crevices or cavities in buildings, poles, and trees, in nest boxes, or behind vines on trees. The North American breeding biology of the Common Myna has not been studied.

Both parents brood the young, but the males are probably inefficient at brooding as they do not have fully developed incubation patches. In the European Starling, the female incubates 60 percent of the time during the day, and 100 percent of the time at night. If his mate dies, the male European Starling may feed the young alone.

Starling wing-wave display. Male European Starlings often hold their wings loosely spread and slowly wave them when singing.

Movements

Most sturnids are resident, although they may wander widely when conditions are poor. The European Starling is partly migratory: Some individuals migrate in some years but not in others; most or all birds withdraw from northern or high-elevation sites. Starlings roost in huge numbers within their winter range.

European Starling evicting Red-headed Woodpecker from nesting cavity. Cavity-nesting species that rely on existing cavities, such as the European Starling, are often limited by the availability of nest sites. Starlings overcome this by accepting all manner of cavities, often aggressively evicting other species, including those that excavate their own cavities, such as the Red-headed Woodpecker. Declines of native cavity-nesting species such as bluebirds have been blamed on starlings.

Conservation

The three introduced species of mynas in North America all have small populations with limited distributions and may not persist for long. The Crested Myna was introduced into the Vancouver, British Columbia, area around 1897. After reaching a peak in the 1920s and 1930s, the population started declining. By the mid-1990s, there were fewer than 100 birds in North America, all in the greater Vancouver area. The Common Myna became established in southern Florida in 1983, and has been increasing there. Hill Mynas are found in Florida and California but do not seem to be established.

After 100 European Starlings were introduced into Central Park, in New York City, in 1890 and 1891, they rapidly spread across the continent, reaching the West Coast by the 1950s. Although their numbers have declined recently, especially in Canada, this species is one of the most abundant birds in North America, with a population estimated at 200 million individuals. Starlings are a threat to some cavity-nesting native bird populations and are considered pests by some farmers and city managers.

As with all introduced species, conservation concerns focus on the potential impacts of these species on native birds, rather than on protecting the introduced species.

James D. Rising

Accentors

Accentors are small songbirds that look somewhat like sparrows. Most species have brown and gray plumages; some have streaking or strong head markings. Many accentors breed in stunted conifer forests at high latitudes, while others are found in open habitats, including high mountain slopes and river edges. The Hedge Accentor (*Prunella modularis*, formerly called the "Dunnock" or "Hedge Sparrow") is common in European gardens and suburbs; its common name refers to its habit of nesting in the wide hedges that separate sections of English gardens.

Relationships between the accentors and other passerine families are obscure, but Prunellidae has been linked at various times to the finches, Old World warblers, pipits, *Passer* sparrows, the estrildid finches (Estrildidae) of Africa, southern Asia, and Australia, and the weavers (Ploceidae) of Africa and Asia. The morphological feature that distinguishes this family is a uniquely shaped bill—wide at the base and sharp-pointed, but with a laterally swollen appearance, so that the culmen is rounded in cross section. An accentor uses its bill to flick over leaves and debris while foraging.

Most accentor species are poorly known, but the Hedge Accentor is very well studied. It has one of the most plastic mating systems of all birds. Within a small population, one can find different birds engaging in monogamy, polygyny, polyandry, and even more unusual associations such as polygynandry, in which either sex may mate with more than one member of the opposite sex.

One species, the Siberian Accentor (*Prunella montanella*), is a rare migrant in the Aleutian Islands and western Alaska, and is accidental in other parts of northwestern North America. Records are mainly from the period October through January. It usually breeds in boreal and subarctic forests of Siberia.

John B. Dunning, Jr.

Siberian Accentor. *The Siberian Accentor, with its superficially sparrow-like appearance and sharply pointed bill, is typical of the world's 13 accentors. All are in the genus* Prunella.

Worldwide Family Features

- 6–7" (15–18 cm) terrestrial songbirds.
- 13 species in 1 genus worldwide; occur throughout Eurasia, with greatest number of species in China and central Asia. 1 species accidental in North America.
- Eat insects in summer, seeds and fruit in winter; glean from ground, boulders, or low scrub.
- Territorial in summer; territories often clumped. At least 2 species have non-monogamous pairings; most others not well studied. Some species migratory.
- Breed first probably at 1 year old.

- Nest a compact cup of twigs, plant stems, and moss; placed in shrub or low tree; built by female. Occasionally reuse old nests of other songbirds.
- 4–6 subelliptical, smooth, glossy, blue or blue-green eggs. Female incubates, for 10–13 days. Hatching probably synchronous. 2 broods per year, occasionally 3.
- Altricial young with scanty but long, dull black down at hatching. Fledge at 10–12 days. Both parents feed young.
- Little information on adult annual survival, but about 50% in Hedge Accentor, which can live at least 9 years.

Wagtails and Pipits

Wagtails and pipits are small to medium-size passerines. Wagtails have bright and contrasting pied or yellow plumage, and most pipits have streaked and cryptically colored brown plumage. All wagtails have long tails that they often wag up and down, and strongly undulating flight. Adult wagtails are sexually dimorphic in plumage and wing size, with males more colorful and somewhat larger. The American Pipit *(Anthus rubescens)* bobs its tail frequently, the Red-throated Pipit *(A. cervinus)* only occasionally, and Sprague's Pipit *(A. spragueii)* rarely or not at all. Male and female pipits look alike, with males slightly larger. Motacillids are found in a variety of open habitats. In North America, wagtails are largely restricted to remote parts of Alaska and northwestern Canada, where they occur mostly along seacoasts and riverbanks, in coastal villages, and in open, shrubby areas along roads. Pipits are more widespread; they inhabit rocky alpine and Arctic tundras and shortgrass prairies during the breeding season, and open fields during winter.

Taxonomy

The family Motacillidae is currently considered to be closely related to the Old World sparrows, accentors, estrildid finches (Estrildidae), and weavers (Ploceidae), based on morphology and DNA–DNA hybridization studies. Other molecular data, however, suggest a different story and imply a close relationship among the motacillids, the Old World warblers, and the Old World flycatchers.

The family is subdivided into two distinct groups, the brightly colored wagtails and the drab pipits. Despite these

Motacillid diversity. The motacillids are all small, ground-dwelling songbirds with relatively long legs and tails. North American species are in two genera that differ in color and habits. The wagtails (Motacilla) *are brightly colored, very long-tailed species; the Yellow Wagtail is shown (left). The pipits* (Anthus) *are drab-colored, shorter-tailed species; Sprague's Pipit is shown (right).*

plumage differences, members of the two groups are quite similar in both structure and behavior. Although the taxonomy of North American species appears fairly straightforward, four of the six species are part of predominantly Old World species complexes, each of which has a complicated taxonomic history.

The White Wagtail *(Motacilla alba)* is a widespread species that breeds throughout much of Eurasia, as well as in western Alaska. The species is subdivided into several distinct forms within its Old World range and is closely related to several other black and white wagtails. One of these other species, the Black-backed Wagtail *(M. lugens)*, also breeds rarely in western Alaska and in the past has been combined with the White Wagtail because of limited hybridization between the two taxa. The third North American wagtail, the Yellow Wagtail *(M. flava)*, also has a complex taxonomy when the species is considered throughout its entire range. In Eurasia the species shows considerable morphological variation, especially in male head coloration, and up to a dozen subspecies are recognized. The taxonomic status of these different forms is unclear, but it is possible that the Yellow Wagtail may be split into more than one species.

The most widespread North American species, the American Pipit, was formerly lumped with the Water Pipit *(Anthus spinoletta)* of Eurasia. However, there are substantial differences in mitochondrial DNA between these species, and no evidence of interbreeding where their distributions overlap.

As this survey suggests, most North American motacillids have close ties to Old World species. But based on genetic data and vocal characteristics, Sprague's Pipit is apparently much more closely related to South American pipits than to either the Old World pipits or the other species found in North America.

Motacillid head and bill. All motacillids, such as this Red-throated Pipit, have a slender, pointed, warbler-like bill used for gleaning insects and small seeds from vegetation and from the ground.

Habitats

In North America, White and Black-backed Wagtails live near sea cliffs, where they commonly associate with seabird colonies; along seacoasts and sand and gravel riverbanks; on grassy terraces with overhanging vegetation; and in coastal villages. The Yellow Wagtail occurs mostly in open shrubby areas, including dwarf-shrub meadows; moist areas with tussocks and hummocks; along creeks, roadsides, and ditches; and near mining operations. Wagtails occur in North America only during the breeding season.

Pipits are found in open country with low vegetation. In western Alaska, the Red-throated Pipit prefers rocky tundra sites where stony ground and dwarf-shrub meadows are juxtaposed; during the nonbreeding season, it inhabits damp, grassy areas and riverbanks. The American Pipit breeds in Arctic and alpine tundra meadows, on stony ground, and sometimes in high subalpine meadows; it spends the nonbreeding season on open shores and in fields. Sprague's Pipit occupies shortgrass prairies in the northern

Worldwide Family Features

- 5½–8½" (14–21 cm) songbirds of waterside and open habitats.
- About 65 species in 5 genera worldwide; pipits occur on all continents except Antarctica (but found on subantarctic island of South Georgia); wagtails mostly in Old World. 6 species in 2 genera occur throughout North America; plus 5 accidental species.
- Eat terrestrial and aquatic invertebrates gleaned from ground and edges of ponds and streams.
- Strongly territorial during breeding season; wagtails also have winter and migratory stopover territories. Monogamous, probably for season; pairs form during migration and on arrival at breeding grounds. Engage in elaborate courtship and threat displays. Some species flock during nonbreeding periods; others solitary. Many species migratory.
- Breed first at 1 year old.
- Open-cup nest, domed in some pipits; built of dry leaves and grass stems, lined

with fine grasses, leaves, hair, feathers. Placed on ground under overhanging vegetation, also in burrows, buildings, and cavities and crevices of cliffs. Built by both sexes in most species, by female in some.
- 2–9 (usually 4–6) subelliptical eggs; white or light green to dark olive, covered with dense gray or brown spotting, often with fine dark streaks. Both sexes (sometimes female only) incubate, for 11–15 days. Hatching generally synchronous. 1 or 2 (rarely 3) broods per year; renest if 1st nest lost.
- Altricial young have sparse down on back and head at hatch. Female broods nestlings for up to 6 days; both parents feed. Fledge at 10–16 days; both parents feed for 14–18 days after fledging.
- In Palearctic species, adult annual survival 34–65%; no data for North America. Among oldest on record: 9 years, 11 months (White Wagtail).

Great Plains during breeding, grasslands and fields when not breeding.

Foraging Habitats

In their prenesting period, wagtails forage mostly near human settlements, dumps, and farms; they often follow agricultural machinery. They also often forage on driftwood along seacoasts, on the muddy banks of rivers and lakes, or on dry moss-lichen tundra. In the nesting season, wagtails forage mostly along gravelly sections of rivers, in shallow-water areas along seacoasts, and in towns. They occasionally forage on floating leaves and plant debris and near seabird colonies, picking insect pupae from fallen nests.

Wagtail "wagging." The wagtails are named for their habit of vigorously wagging or pumping their long tail up and down. The purpose of this action is unknown, but it is common in other open-country birds, such as phoebes, the Palm Warbler (Dendroica palmarum), some shorebirds, and others. The White Wagtail is shown.

During the nesting season, the Red-throated and American Pipits and the Yellow Wagtail often forage on the muddy edges of ponds, marshes, wet meadows, and agricultural fields, as well as in stony terrain, boulder fields, and snow patches. During migration and in winter, these three species look for food on mudflats, grasslands, shorelines, coastal beaches and flats, and in agricultural fields. Sprague's Pipit mostly forages in short-grass areas that are sometimes only sparsely vegetated.

Food and Foraging

Motacillids have broad diets that include many terrestrial and aquatic invertebrates, such as small crustaceans, mollusks, earthworms, and especially arthropods (spiders, insects, millipedes). Sprague's Pipit includes more grasshoppers and crickets in its diet.

Wagtails mostly forage on the ground, by picking insects off the surface of the ground and running after more mobile prey. They may also snatch insects off walls and buildings while flying, or flycatch above the water or ground. The Yellow Wagtail flycatches less frequently than other wagtails and is the only North American wagtail that routinely digs through debris in search of food. Wagtails often associate with moving groups of cattle, sheep, and horses, as well as with wild ungulates. Association with grazing animals greatly increases the foraging success of wagtails.

For the most part, pipits feed alone during the breeding season, and in loose, noncooperative flocks during migration and winter. Like wagtails, pipits forage on the ground, gleaning prey from vegetation or the ground while walking or running, and frequently changing direction. Infrequently, pipits make short flights from the ground or boulders to pursue aerial prey. The American Pipit sometimes wades in shallow water to forage on aquatic insect larvae.

Vocalizations and Displays

The presence of wagtails and pipits is often revealed by their frequent use of short call notes, given both while the birds are on the ground and especially when they are in flight. Call notes are often single syllables, such as the *zit* contact call of the Black-backed and White Wagtails or the *squeet* of Sprague's Pipit, or two- to three-syllable calls, such as the sharp *tsewee* of the Yellow Wagtail (which is continuously given in flight and is also an alarm call) and the *jijik* of the Black-backed and White Wagtails.

Perhaps most familiar to North American birders is the American Pipit's *slip-ip*, given on the ground or in the air.

Breeding songs of wagtails and pipits are often given in flight displays, while the birds are feeding or near the nest, or when aerial predators are in sight. The American Pipit's song is a continuously repeated *tseewl* or *pleetrr*, given in flight or from the ground. American Pipit flight displays last up to 30 seconds, during which the male may climb up to 130 feet (40 m) above the ground. The display flight of the male Sprague's Pipit is much longer, lasting from 15 to 41 minutes. The male may fly from 150 feet (45 m) to more than 300 feet (90 m) above the ground, while flying into the wind. The song begins with a few reedy, twittering *shirl* notes that continue for 2 to 3 seconds before descending into a series of similar notes and ending with a final double note.

Wagtails often give their more complex courtship songs from the tops of tussocks or bushes, as well as in flight along the perimeter of the breeding territory. Good examples are the courtship song of the Black-backed Wagtail—a *chichit chichit chuy chuy chuku chuku chi chi chi*, 5 to 15 seconds in duration—and the territorial song of the Yellow Wagtail, described as a repeated, high-pitched *tzeeu tzeeu tzeek, tzeeu tzeeu tzeek*.

Breeding

North American motacillids are socially monogamous, but extra-pair copulations are occasionally observed in some wagtails. Pairs can form on wintering grounds or during migration, but most pairing occurs just after the birds arrive on their breeding grounds. Most pairs remain together throughout a breeding season, occasionally re-pairing in subsequent seasons. Nothing is known about courtship feeding behavior, but the male brings food to the female while she incubates and broods their nestlings.

Motacillids are territorial during the breeding season. The breeding territories of wagtails are sometimes placed close together, even in habitats in which they could be spaced farther apart. The territories vary in size from 2 to 5 acres

Pipit song flights. The open habitats used by pipits lack trees or bushes from which birds can broadcast their songs. Both common North American species sing during flight displays, but the flight paths are quite different. The American Pipit (left) flies up to 130 feet (40 m) high on a relatively short path, singing once or several times during a 30-second flight. Sprague's Pipit (right) climbs to several hundred feet and, barely visible from the ground, sings dozens of songs for up to 40 minutes or more before dropping back to the ground.

(0.75–2 ha). Birds in coastal villages may nest as close as 100 feet (30 m) to each other. Pipit breeding territories vary in size from ½ to 5 acres (0.20–2 ha). In dense populations in Wyoming, American Pipit territories can be as small as less than half an acre (0.16 ha), in which case the birds often feed outside the defended space around their nests. In all species, both sexes defend the breeding territory, advertising their presence by display flights along the boundaries or by calling from song perches.

Nests and Eggs

Wagtails and pipits build their nests on the ground, usually placing them in a slight hollow protected by overhanging vegetation, sod, or rock.

The White Wagtail nests in cavities and crevices in rock cliffs or abandoned buildings and in ditches along roads. The Black-backed Wagtail builds its nests on coastal rock cliffs up to 100 feet (30 m) high, on beaches under washed-up logs, under railroad ties, in burrows, and in buildings and other man-made structures. It also nests in the open, on the ground next to a tussock. The Yellow Wagtail nests on the ground, in moss or sedge, or it may excavate a shallow cavity in the ground. It often places its nest under mats of overhanging vegetation in dirt banks.

The American Pipit sometimes nests in stony terrain but more often in meadows, dwarf-willow thickets, tussocks, or eroded banks. The Red-throated Pipit may nest in similar sites, but more often it nests along stream banks (less often on level, grassy tundra). Sprague's Pipit nests in dense, grassy, and relatively tall vegetation with little bare ground.

Wagtails and pipits build their nests from dry, thick grass stems and dwarf willows, as well as bark shreds, lichens and mosses, sedge leaves, and twigs. The nests are lined with rootlets and grasses, deer and dog hair, ptarmigan feathers, and sometimes the hair of ground squirrels. Occasionally a dry-grass nest is held together with mud. Wagtail nests are often large, loose structures. Sprague's Pipit nests may be domed.

Clutch size in North American wagtails varies from four to seven eggs, the most common number being five. North American pipits lay from three to seven eggs. North American wagtails and pipits produce a single brood each year, although the evidence for Sprague's Pipit is limited. The birds may renest if their first nests are destroyed.

During egg-laying wagtails and pipits incubate infrequently; full incubation begins after the last egg is laid or on the day before, and lasts 11 to 15 days. In wagtails, both parents incubate, but females incubate for significantly longer periods of time. The female incubates mostly in the morning and evening and at night; either sex incubates during the middle of the day. The female sometimes covers the eggs with lining material when she leaves the nest. In pipits, only the female incubates.

Male pipits and some male wagtails feed their mates during incubation—Red-throated Pipits at or near the nest, American Pipits generally at some distance from the nest.

Young

After hatching, the female either eats the broken eggshells or carries them out of the nest and drops them in flight. The nestlings are altricial and nidicolous.

Only the female broods the nestlings, most often in the mornings and evenings, continuing until they are five or six days old. Both parents participate equally in delivering food to the nestlings. These food deliveries (there can be as many as 275 each day) are most frequent in the early morning and late afternoon. Both parents either eat or carry away the fecal sacs of the young; older nestlings often defecate over the rim of the nest.

In most North American motacillids, the young leave the nest when they are 12 to 15 days old, but they can leave earlier, at 9 days old, if the nest is disturbed. Sprague's Pipit nestlings leave the nest when they are 10 or 11 days old. In all species, both parents usually continue to feed the fledglings for 14 to 18 days after they depart the nest.

Migration

North American White and Black-backed Wagtails migrate to and from wintering grounds in southeastern Asia. Yellow Wagtails and Red-throated Pipits return to their wintering grounds by crossing the Chukchi and Bering Seas, then following the Asian coastline to southern Asia and the East Indies. American and Sprague's Pipits migrate to wintering grounds in the southern United States and northern Mexico, and American Pipits also move as far south as Guatemala and El Salvador.

In both spring and fall, North American wagtails migrate singly or in small groups of three to 10 birds, often of the same sex. Wagtails migrate mostly by day, along coastlines of oceans and large lakes. Pipits migrate in flocks of up to a few hundred individuals. Migrating American Pipits often follow coasts and river corridors, whereas Sprague's Pipits tend to move broadly through the eastern Great Plains.

Conservation

The growing number of human settlements, roads, bridges, and industrial works along northwestern coastlines has increased suitable breeding and foraging habitats for all three wagtails. The White Wagtail is easily attracted to nest boxes, especially those under bridges near human settlements.

Currently there appears to be little cause for conservation concern for American and Red-throated Pipits, as the birds' remote Arctic and alpine breeding grounds are relatively secure from significant human disturbance. American Pipits have also recently colonized the Sierra Nevada in California and the White Mountains in New Hampshire.

Based on Breeding Bird Survey data, Sprague's Pipit appears to be experiencing a rangewide decline. The loss of native prairie, as well as such agricultural activities as cattle grazing, burning, and haying, may have a negative effect on the bird's breeding populations. Partners in Flight ranks Sprague's Pipit as a high-priority species. Sprague's Pipit has also been placed on the WatchList because of threats to its breeding habitats and recently was listed as threatened in Canada.

What happens on the wintering grounds of all the North American motacillid species is largely unknown and needs study, since it may also affect the birds' population dynamics. Christmas Bird Count data suggest a possible decline in American Pipits, but this trend may in fact be a result of shifts of wintering populations to areas where less land has been converted from agricultural to urban use.

Global warming models project treeline advances and reduced future breeding habitat in Arctic and alpine regions for tundra-breeding species. Farther south, agricultural practices, especially use of chemical contaminants, are known to adversely affect migratory American and Red-throated Pipits.

Accidental Species

Five Eurasian species of motacillids have occurred as accidentals in North America, with the bulk of the records coming from the western Alaskan islands.

The Gray Wagtail (*Motacilla cinerea*), Olive-backed Pipit (*Anthus hodgsoni*), and Pechora Pipit (*A. gustavi*) are all very rare but regular migrants on some of these islands. The Tree Pipit (*A. trivialis*) has also been found in western Alaska in spring. Farther south, there are single records of the Gray Wagtail and Olive-backed Pipit in California in fall, and of the latter species in Nevada in spring. Finally, the Citrine Wagtail (*M. citreola*) has been documented in Mississippi during winter.

Alex Badyaev and Paul Hendricks

Waxwings

Medium-size, berry-eating songbirds of open woods, hedgerows, and orchards, waxwings have sleek gray and brown plumage and an erectile head crest. Their bodies are plump and their wings pointed. They have small legs and feet, and a small, wide, notched bill. The medium-length, square tail has a terminal yellow band. Both North American species have high, thin calls. Waxwings form cohesive flocks. Their flight is strong, and flocks may turn abruptly in unison.

Taxonomy

Waxwings are most closely related to the silky-flycatchers of the New World and the Palmchat *(Dulus dominicus)* of Hispaniola, sometimes considered subfamilies within the Bombycillidae. DNA–DNA hybridization studies suggest that these three families are close relatives of the dippers, Old World flycatchers, thrushes, and starlings.

None of the other flocking passerines, such as the blackbirds and starlings, shows the stately, upright posture of waxwings, nor the head crest, plump body

Bombycillid diversity. *The world's three species of bombycillids are very similar, differing mainly in size and plumage details. The Bohemian Waxwing, shown here, is the largest species.*

with soft, sleek, gray and brown plumage, and small legs and feet.

Food and Foraging

Waxwings feed predominantly on sugary fruits, relying almost completely on them for seven months of the year, from fall to early spring. During this period, both North American waxwing species occur virtually anywhere within their range where they can find fruit crops, including ornamental plants in cities. Waxwings migrate southward in winter, seeking fruit in itinerant flocks of up to hundreds or even thousands of birds. Occasionally large flocks of Bohemian Waxwings *(Bombycilla garrulus)* invade the northern United States, presumably because of fruit shortages in more northerly regions (for example, the cedar and mountain-ash fruits that often persist into winter in Canada).

Worldwide Family Features

- 6–8½" (15–21 cm) woodland songbirds.
- 3 species in 1 genus worldwide, all in northern temperate zone. 2 species breed in North America; widespread across continent.
- Eat sugary fruit, plucked from branches; in summer, sally or glean for insects, often near water.
- Gregarious and nonterritorial; form large nonbreeding flocks that search out fruit crops. Monogamous. Migratory; nomadic and irruptive, especially Bohemian Waxwing.
- Most breed first at 1 year old.
- Woven cup nest made of twigs and grasses, lined with finer material; placed in high tree fork in open woods or edge habitat. Built mostly by female; also reports of both mates building. May reuse materials from old nests.
- 2–6 (typically 4–6) subelliptical to oval eggs; pale blue or blue-gray, sparsely spotted with black and gray blotches. Female incubates, for 12–15 days. Hatching asynchronous over 2–3 days. 1 or 2 broods per year.
- Altricial young hatch naked and blind. Fledge at 14–17 days. Both parents feed nestlings.
- Adult annual survival estimated at 45–55%. Among oldest on record: 12 years, 7 months (Bohemian Waxwing).

Waxwing head and bill. The waxwings have a relatively short, broad bill with a slight hook, adapted for gripping and swallowing large berries. They also have long crests and smooth, silky plumage, as shown on this Cedar Waxwing.

Important fruits for waxwings during fall and winter include those of viburnums, dogwoods, pokeweed, grape, mountain-ash, apples, hawthorns, and junipers. In eastern North America the most common juniper is the Eastern Redcedar *(Juniperus virginiana)*; their fondness for this food source gave Cedar Waxwings *(Bombycilla cedrorum)* their name. Winter flocks of waxwings may be very docile as they loiter at fruit crops. In spring, waxwings feed on remnant fruit crops, as well as buds, sap drips, and the flowers of apple, cherry, aspen, cottonwood, maple, and oak trees.

In summer, insects become important in the waxwing diet, although fruit still dominates. Waxwings often feed on insect outbreaks. Fruits they eat in summer include strawberry, serviceberry, mulberry, cherry, blueberry, blackberry, and honeysuckle. Even when breeding, local family groups may aggregate at fruit crops.

The flocking behavior of waxwings has probably evolved at least in part in response to the nature of their diet. Both the fruit and the animal foods they eat are very patchy in their distribution, and flocking is a more effective means of searching for clumped food resources than individual foraging.

Waxwings typically pluck the whole fruit while perched on a branch, deftly stretching to reach the food; they may also pluck fruit while hovering briefly. They typically sally for aerial insect prey, especially emerging aquatic forms, often from an exposed perch. They also glean insects from vegetation.

Wing and Tail Coloration

Waxwings are named for the red waxy "droplets" on the ends of the secondary flight feathers of adults. Most information on these droplets, which are unique to this family, has been learned through studies of the Cedar Waxwing. The color of the droplets comes from carotenoid pigments that are found in the birds' diet of fruit and that cannot be synthesized by the birds directly. The same pigments also produce red or yellow coloration in the feathers of other birds, such as House Finches *(Carpodacus mexicanus)*, but no other bird sequesters the pigments in droplets such as those seen in the waxwings. In the bombycillids, deposits of a bright red carotenoid (astaxanthin) are concentrated in flat, expanded extensions of the rachis that project beyond the feather vanes. Immature waxwings have few or no droplets, but the number and size of droplets gradually increases with each basic molt, at least over the first few years.

In the tail, yellow carotenoids are normally incorporated into the vanes at the tips of the feathers, producing a yellow band across the tip of the tail that is not waxy like the wingtips.

Further evidence of the link between the waxwings' diet and the carotenoid pigmentation in their feathers can be

Waxy "droplets" on wings. Waxwings are named for the modified tips of their secondaries, in which the flattened extension of the rachis beyond the vane contains a dense concentration of red pigment. It may appear waxy, hence the name, but the texture is more like plastic. The Cedar Waxwing is shown.

Tail bands. The appearance of Cedar Waxwings with orange tail tips in recent years is a fascinating story of the unanticipated effects of human actions. The fruit of an introduced honeysuckle provides a different pigment than is contained in the fruits of native shrubs and trees, and waxwings that consume those fruits during the critical weeks of tail feather growth develop orange rather than the typical yellow tail tips.

seen in a recent shift in the tail tip coloration of some waxwings. In some areas of eastern North America, Cedar Waxwings with orange tail bands have become increasingly common since the early 1960s, when exotic shrub honeysuckles (*Lonicera* species) became widely established in landscaping practices. When waxwings eat the fruits of these honeysuckles while molting their tail feathers, an unusual red carotenoid pigment (rhodoxanthin) in the fruit is deposited in the tail band, along with yellow carotenoids. The result is an orangish tail band; the exact color depends on how much exotic honeysuckle fruit the bird ate during feather growth. Most affected waxwings are first-year birds that are fed these fruits while growing their first tail feathers as nestlings during the summer.

Breeding

The breeding season of waxwings is among the latest of North American passerines and is apparently cued to the midsummer ripening of fruit. The birds lay eggs from early June through early August; active nests have been reported as late as October. They breed in open woods, often near streams or still waters that provide aquatic insects, as well as in woodland edge habitat that provides fruiting plants.

Cedar Waxwings select mates of similar age, as can be seen by comparing the waxy tips of mated pairs. Cedar Waxwing pairs often nest twice in a summer; Bohemian Waxwings nest once.

The cup-shaped waxwing nest is made of twigs and grasses, and lined with finer materials, such as rootlets, grasses, animal hair, pine needles, spider webs, or moss. Waxwings will use their own or other species' old nests as sources of building materials, or even renovate previously used nests. Breeding sites may change each year, depending upon the local availability of fruit. Active nests sometimes occur in local "clumps," presumably near fruit supplies. Both Cedar Waxwing mates may gather nesting material, but the female does most of the nest construction. Both mates of the Bohemian Waxwing build the nest.

Conservation

Cedar Waxwing populations have increased across the continent, according to data from Breeding Bird Surveys. Increases in population sizes of both North American waxwings in the eastern part of the continent since the late 1970s can be explained by at least two environmental changes. First, early successional habitats containing fruiting shrubs and trees have increased in abundance with the regrowth of eastern forests on lands previously cleared for agriculture.

Perhaps more important, waxwings appear to have rebounded sharply because of the elimination of DDT from agriculture. For both species, sharp population increases occurred in the mid-1970s, immediately following the banning of DDT. Waxwings would be especially vulnerable to DDT poisoning because of their tendency to feed on insect outbreaks. Dense aggregations of insects would have been the targets of DDT applications, and the incapacitated insects would have been especially vulnerable to avian predators.

Mark Witmer

Silky-flycatchers

Family Ptilogonatidae
Order Passeriformes

Silky-flycatchers are medium-size, fruit- and insect-eating songbirds. They typically have short broad bills, soft silky plumage, long slender tails, and conspicuous rictal bristles. Their plumages are black, gray, or brown; some species have touches of yellow or white. Three of the four species are crested, which gives them a distinctive silhouette when perched. The Phainopepla *(Phainopepla nitens)* is the only Ptilogonatidae species to be found regularly in North America or to display evident sexual differences: Males are black, females gray. Phainopeplas are found in the arid southwestern United States in various scrubland and open woodland habitats; they have a particularly strong association with mistletoe, which they feed on, and mesquite.

Taxonomy

Silky-flycatchers are more closely related to the waxwings than to either the tyrant flycatchers or the Old World flycatchers; they sometimes are classified as a subfamily of the Bombycillidae.

Food and Foraging

Silky-flycatchers feed diurnally on a wide variety of seasonal small fruits and berries; they also eat beetles, true bugs, moths, flies, and caterpillars. They obtain berries by plucking them from the tree or by hover-gleaning—grabbing berries during short sallying flights. They also often take insects on the wing.

The Phainopepla is closely tied to the availability of the berries of mistletoes *(Phoradendron* species), parasitic plants that grow on the trunk and branches of mesquite *(Prosopis* species) and other desert trees. The Phainopepla consumes the berries, then quickly digests and voids them, its sticky excrement attaching the seeds to the tree in which the bird is perched. The seeds sprout and become established on new trees and continue their parasitic life cycle. The Phainopepla also eats the berries of buckthorns, elders, junipers, and ornamental pepper trees.

Phainopepla. This strictly New World family includes only four species of medium-size, long-tailed birds. Only the Phainopepla regularly occurs in North America.

Worldwide Family Features

- 6½–9½" (16–24 cm) tropical and subtropical songbirds.
- 4 species in 3 genera worldwide, from southwestern U.S. south to western Panama. 1 species breeds in North America; plus 1 accidental species.
- Eat mainly berries, other fruit, and insects, often caught on the wing.
- Somewhat social; nest in loose colonies. Territory size varies with food abundance. Probably monogamous. Form small flocks in nonbreeding season; will move to areas of high fruit density.
- Breed first at 1 year old.

- Cup-shaped nest of plant matter, spider webs, hair; placed in central fork of tree or shrub 4–50' (1.2–15 m) high. Built by male or by both sexes in some species.
- 2 or 3 (rarely 4) subelliptical eggs; grayish or bluish, with heavy mottling. Both parents incubate, for 14–16 days. Hatching believed to be synchronous. 2 or 3 broods per year.
- Altricial young hatch naked and helpless. Fed by both parents. Fledge at 18–25 days.
- Little information on survival or longevity.

Breeding

Phainopeplas are monogamous, and breeding pairs often form loose colonies in high-quality habitat. Where berries, fruit, and insects are concentrated, Phainopeplas have large feeding and nesting territories. Where food resources are scattered, birds defend only the nest tree and forage over a large, undefended area.

During courtship, the male displays by flying as high as 300 feet (90 m) over his territory, making circles and erratic zigzag patterns, and often chasing the female. The male also feeds the perched female. Phainopepla nests, built exclusively by the male, are typically situated in the center of a tree, often in a mistletoe clump. Shaped like small, shallow cups, the nests appear small for adult birds. The nests consist of twigs, leaves, weeds, plant fibers, and spider webs bound together and lined with animal hair and plant materials.

Both parents incubate, but the male does most of the work during daylight hours. Both parents feed the chicks crushed berries and insects. Fledging occurs within 18 to 25 days, an unusually long time for open-cup-nesting songbirds.

Movements

Ornithologists believe Phainopeplas breed first in lowland deserts, and then move to higher, moister habitats; birds from the deserts of Arizona and California are thought to move to oak and chaparral habitats in coastal California and southeastern Arizona in April and May. Evidence indicates that the birds

Mistletoe/mesquite habitat. The Phainopepla typically builds a neat cup nest in a mesquite tree, often near mistletoe berries. In the southwestern deserts, nesting coincides with the peak of mistletoe berry abundance and the beginning of spring insect populations. Later, with nesting complete and the berries depleted, the birds move to higher, moister habitats, where many may nest a second time, feeding on different berries and insects.

may nest a second time following these movements. Some Phainopeplas remain as permanent residents in the lowland mesquite habitats along the Colorado River. Large wintering populations along the lower Colorado River typically depart by May and return in late September.

Conservation

The Breeding Bird Survey has shown that the Phainopepla population trend has been stable since the 1960s. Nonetheless, the Phainopepla's reliance on mistletoe berries and mesquite makes this species vulnerable to habitat loss, berry crop failure, and severe cold (which kills the mistletoe). Although mesquite is spreading because of the degradation of grassland habitats in parts of the Southwest, mature mesquite forests continue to be destroyed, removing important habitat for this species.

Accidental Species

The Gray Silky-flycatcher *(Ptilogonys cinereus),* a resident of subtropical forests of Mexico and Central America, has been documented twice in Texas. Sight records also exist for southern Arizona and southern California. The California bird may have been an escapee.

David J. Krueper

Phainopepla head and bill. *This species has a short, broad bill with conspicuous rictal bristles. The bill is used both for eating berries and catching flying insects.*

Olive Warbler

The Olive Warbler *(Peucedramus taeniatus)* is a small passerine that is currently placed in its own family. Males have a distinctive orange-brown head and breast with a black mask around the eye, dark upperparts with two bold white wing-bars, and pale underparts. Females have a yellow face and breast, and a less prominent mask. North American birders are most likely to spot the Olive Warbler in the Arizona mountains that border Mexico; the species also occurs in southwestern New Mexico and the highlands of Central America. Throughout much of their range, Olive Warblers are permanent residents in montane forests, where they are closely associated with conifers, especially pines and firs.

Taxonomy

Traditionally taxonomists placed the Olive Warbler with the American wood-warblers, as the species shares many features with parulids, including nine functional primaries, similar plumage patterns (especially with *Dendroica* warblers),

Olive Warbler. *The unsettled taxonomic history of the Olive Warbler has included time in the Old World warbler and wood-warbler families. New DNA and other evidence suggests that the species is an early offshoot of the New World nine-primaried oscine group and consequently deserves its own family.*

and an active arboreal foraging style. Other features, however, suggest that Olive Warbler is quite different from the wood-warblers; these include skeletal and muscular details, egg color, and call notes.

In addition, unlike wood-warblers, Olive Warbler nestlings defecate along the edges of their nest, giving it a distinctive "fouled" appearance; this behavioral trait is unusual among songbirds but is also found in members of the family Fringillidae, which may be closely related to the Peucedramidae.

Genetic studies, using both DNA–DNA hybridization and mitochondrial DNA, suggest that the Olive Warbler is not closely related either to the parulids or to any other North American group, although it is clearly part of the nine-primaried oscine assemblage. Currently the AOU places the species in its own family to recognize its uncertain affiliations.

Worldwide Family Features

- 5–5½" (13–14 cm) songbird of high-mountain coniferous forests.
- 1 species worldwide; occurs from southwestern U.S. to Nicaragua.
- Eats insects gleaned from leaves, needles, twigs, bark.
- Territorial on breeding grounds; apparently monogamous. Frequently joins mixed-species flocks. Generally nonmigratory, but most leave northern part of range in winter; some migrate downslope.
- Breeds first usually at 1 year old.
- Nest is open cup of rootlets, plant stalks, other plant fibers, lichens, moss; placed high in conifer, away from trunk. Female builds nest. Does not reuse nest.
- 3 or 4 subelliptical eggs; grayish- or bluish-white, with heavy speckling. Female incubates; incubation period and hatching unknown. 1 brood per year.
- Altricial young naked at hatching. Both adults feed; only female broods. Nestling and fledging periods unknown; may associate with parents for several months after fledging.
- No information on adult annual survival or longevity.

Variation

Plumage variation in Olive Warblers extends beyond the sexual differences described above. Young males in the northern part of the range do not obtain their adult breeding colors until their second breeding season, a phenomenon called delayed plumage maturation. During their first summer as full-grown birds, these males have orange-yellow heads and look more like adult females than the much brighter adult males. In Mexico, young Olive Warbler males apparently do not show delayed plumage maturation.

Food and Foraging

Olive Warblers glean insects and other arthropods from the needles, branches, and twigs of pines and occasionally oaks; in southern Arizona, they concentrate their feeding activities in Ponderosa Pines. While they tend to forage fairly high in the trees, Olive Warblers will sometimes descend to within a few feet of the ground. Their foraging style is a slow hopping or creeping among needles and twigs, as the birds search for prey in the conifers.

Breeding

Because Olive Warblers place their nests high in tall pine trees, well away from the trunk, researchers know very little about their breeding habits. Olive Warblers build their nests with rootlets and plant stalks, and line them with fine rootlets and plant down. They sometimes

Olive Warbler nest. The Olive Warbler builds a neat cup nest in the outer branches of a tall conifer. Unlike most other passerines, the adults do not carry fecal sacs away from the nest; by the time the young fledge, the outside of the nest is completely covered with a layer of fecal material.

cover the nest with lichens or mosses, in a manner similar to that of Blue-gray Gnatcatchers *(Polioptila caerulea)*. Females apparently do all nest construction, although the males stay close by.

The female typically lays a clutch of three or four eggs, so darkly colored and heavily speckled that one researcher proposed the species be called the "Black-egged Warbler." It is not known how long the female incubates the eggs or how long the chicks remain in the nest after hatching. Both sexes feed the chicks, although the female seems to do all of the brooding. After fledging, the young may stay with their parents through the next fall and winter.

Conservation

The Olive Warbler is placed on the Watch-List because of its relatively restricted breeding and wintering ranges, but it is reasonably common in the highlands of Mexico and Central America. Increased logging of pine forests south of the United States could have a negative effect on this species; however, it is not considered a threatened species anywhere in its range.

John B. Dunning, Jr.

Olive Warbler head and bill. The Olive Warbler's bill is slightly thinner and less pointed than that of the wood-warblers; instead it more closely resembles the bill of the Old World warblers.

Wood-Warblers

Wood-warblers are small to medium-size songbirds, active and often brightly colored. Their plumage is usually dominated by yellows and olives, but many also have black, gray, blue, white, brown, orange, or red hues. Like most insectivorous birds, wood-warblers have thin bills (although some, notably chats, have heavier bills). Partial to wooded habitats, breeding wood-warblers are most diverse in the northern boreal regions and in the forests of eastern North America. The greatest number of species occur from the Great Lakes east to New England and the Canadian Maritime Provinces and southward into the Appalachian Mountains. Fewer species breed in western North America; these occur mainly in montane and coastal regions. In the neotropics, wood-warblers are most diverse in foothill and lower montane habitats.

Taxonomy

Wood-warblers are part of the large assemblage of "nine-primaried" songbirds, which are more diverse in the Americas than anywhere else. Wood-warblers differ from Old World warblers and other groups of small, predominantly insectivorous songbirds in that they lack a functional 10th primary. They are further defined by different anatomical features, such as the configuration of certain muscles.

Taxonomists have long found it hard to draw firm lines between the various nine-primaried songbirds and so at times have merged such groups as the wood-warblers, tanagers, cardinals, grosbeaks, New World buntings, blackbirds, orioles, and New World sparrows into a single

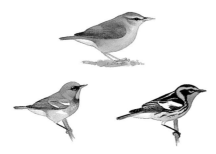

Parulid diversity. *The wood-warblers are a group of small and often brightly colored birds with relatively short and thin bills. Shown here are the stocky, large-billed Swainson's Warbler (top), the slight, small-billed Northern Parula (below left), and the brightly colored Blackburnian Warbler (below right).*

large family, the Emberizidae. However, the AOU now recognizes separate families within the group and has placed the wood-warblers in their own family, the Parulidae.

The name "warbler" also applies to other groups of small songbirds, particularly the Old World warblers (or sylviids) of Eurasia, Africa, and the Indo-Malayan region. Some Old World warblers, such as the Arctic Warbler *(Phylloscopus borealis)*, are similar in shape and behavior to many wood-warblers, but the sylviids are generally more subtly colored—in olive, buff, gray, and brown—and have only a marginal breeding distribution in North America. The sylviid group that is most widespread in North America is the gnatcatchers, which are very different from the wood-warblers in shape, behavior, and habitat (see Old World Warblers and Gnatcatchers).

Scientists have differed as to which birds are the wood-warblers' closest relatives, variously naming the tanagers (some small, insectivorous tanagers, such as those in the South American genus *Hemispingus*, are remarkably warbler-like in appearance); the neotropical honeycreepers (various small, nectar-feeding birds, most of which are now considered tanagers); and even the blackbirds and orioles. The Olive Warbler *(Peucedramus taeniatus)* was often believed to be a wood-warbler but now is considered distantly related enough to be in its own family (Peucedramidae).

Parulid heads and bills. *Wood-warblers have relatively slender and pointed bills, but there is considerable subtle variation within the family. The Cerulean Warbler (left), typical of the genus* Dendroica, *has a rather stout and blunt-tipped bill. Among the subtle variations in bill shape are the rather broad and flat bills (with well-developed rictal bristles) of the flycatching species, such as the American Redstart (second from left); the slender and very pointed bill of flower-probing species, like the Tennessee Warbler (third from left); and the stout bill of insect- and berry-eating species, such as the Yellow-rumped Warbler (right).*

The plumages of some wood-warblers and vireos are confusingly similar. For example, the male Pine Warbler *(Dendroica pinus)* looks very similar to the Yellow-throated Vireo *(Vireo flavifrons)*, and some plumages of the Tennessee Warbler *(Vermivora peregrina)* are much like those of the Philadelphia Vireo *(Vireo philadelphicus)*. However, wood-warblers are readily distinguished from the unrelated vireos by their bills, which in warblers are thinner and have no hook at the tip; most warblers also have thinner legs and are generally more active.

Kinglets resemble wood-warblers, but they are smaller in overall size and smaller-billed than even the smallest warbler. Although similar in ecology, kinglets have never been considered closely related to the parulids, as they show more overall similarity to the Old World warblers.

Most North American wood-warblers are closely related to one another; in fact, the boundaries of many genera are disputed—*Vermivora, Parula,* and *Dendroica* seem particularly close. A relatively large number of hybrids are known between

Worldwide Family Features

- 4–7½" (9.5–19 cm) forest, shrubland, or marsh songbirds.
- About 116 species in 26 genera worldwide; occur in temperate, tropical, and subtropical regions of Americas, from western Alaska east to Newfoundland and south to northern Argentina. 53 species in 16 genera occur in North America; plus 3 accidental species and 1 presumably extinct species.
- Mainly insectivorous, feeding on insects gleaned from leaves, twigs, bark; many species feed on nectar and small fruits in winter and during migration.
- Generally territorial on breeding grounds; may gather in mixed-species flocks in migration and on wintering grounds. Generally monogamous. Pair bonds seasonal in temperate species, multi-year in some. Most North American species migratory, while most tropical species sedentary.

- Breed first usually at 1 year old.
- Nest usually an open cup of grasses, leaves, bark, other plant fibers; built in shrub or tree, or on ground hidden by grasses or roots; a few species build domed nests or are cavity nesters. Female builds nest. Do not reuse old nests.
- 1–7 (usually 4 or 5) subelliptical eggs; whitish, creamy, light blue, or pale olive; speckled or stippled with reddish-brown in nearly all species. Both parents incubate, for 9–15 days. Hatching synchronous. 1 or 2 broods per year.
- Altricial young naked at hatching; develop juvenal plumage without downy stage. Fledge after 8–12 days; may be dependent on parents for several weeks after fledging. Fed by both adults.
- Adult annual survival 36–67%. Maximum longevities usually 6–8 (rarely 10) years. Among oldest on record: 11 years, 6 months (Common Yellowthroat).

wood-warblers of different genera (for instance, Kentucky × Blue-winged Warbler, a hybrid of *Oporornis formosus* and *V. pinus*), which is evidence that the genera are closely related.

The largely neotropical genera are more distantly related to other North American wood-warblers; these include such species as the Painted Redstart *(Myioborus pictus)* and its relatives, as well as members of the genus *Basileuterus,* such as the Rufous-capped *(B. rufifrons)* and Golden-crowned Warblers *(B. culicivorus).* The most extreme in terms of appearance among North American wood-warblers is the Yellow-breasted Chat *(Icteria virens),* but based on DNA–DNA hybridization studies, even this outsized and odd-sounding wood-warbler is clearly a parulid.

Wood-warblers of the genus *Vermivora* are characterized by their sharply pointed bills. Most *Vermivora* species are like the Orange-crowned Warbler *(V. celata)* in having relatively plain plumage, although the Blue-winged Warbler and the Golden-winged Warbler *(V. chrysoptera)* are more boldly marked. The Northern *(Parula americana)* and Tropical Parulas *(P. pitiayumi)* are small wood-warblers with bold wing-bars, short tails, and bicolored bills.

For the most part, the diverse genus *Dendroica* includes species with wing-bars

Wood-warbler foot. *The legs and feet of wood-warblers are relatively thin and weak-looking. All passerines have a similar toe arrangement, with three toes forward and one back. The families differ in subtleties of scaling patterns and leg and toe proportions, and in many cases it is not possible to assign a bird to a family based on leg and foot structure alone. The Orange-crowned Warbler is shown.*

and tail spots, and many can also be prominently spotted or striped on the upperparts, sides, and flanks. Within this genus, several sets of species seem to form related groups. For instance, the Black-throated Green Warbler *(D. virens),* which is common in the East, is very closely related to the Townsend's *(D. townsendi)* and Hermit Warblers *(D. occidentalis)* of the West and the Golden-cheeked Warbler *(D. chrysoparia)* of Texas.

Two single-species genera—*Mniotilta* and *Setophaga*—are related to *Dendroica* but have distinctive shapes and forms associated with specialized foraging habits. The Black-and-white Warbler *(M. varia),* with its long decurved bill and strong legs and claws, forages by trunk-creeping, while the American Redstart *(S. ruticilla),* with its flattened bill, rictal bristles, and wide wings, is suited to flycatching. In contrast, members of *Dendroica,* such as the Blackburnian Warbler *(D. fusca),* forage mainly by gleaning prey off the surfaces of leaves and twigs.

Three other North American wood-warblers that are placed in their own genera are the Prothonotary *(Protonotaria citrea),* Worm-eating *(Helmitheros vermivorus),* and Swainson's Warblers *(Limnothlypis swainsonii),* but their relationships to other genera are uncertain.

Yellow-breasted Chat. *The Yellow-breasted Chat is the most "unwarbler-like" warbler. It is larger than any other species, with a stout, tanager-like bill and very unusual song and calls. Despite constant speculation about its taxonomic relationships, all evidence points to it being simply a large and unusual wood-warbler.*

Hybrid warbler. *The Blue-winged and Golden-winged Warblers hybridize occasionally wherever their ranges meet, and the hybridization has been studied for more than 100 years. The hybrids are distinctive enough that they were first described as new species—"Brewster's Warbler" (shown here) and "Lawrence's Warbler"—and they still cause excitement among birders when they are found. The hybrid zone of the two species has shifted northward gradually over time, as both species have shifted their range to the north.*

The Ovenbird *(Seiurus aurocapillus)* and the closely related waterthrushes are brownish, terrestrial wood-warblers that walk on the ground. The yellowthroats (genus *Geothlypis*) are marsh- and scrub-dwellers thought to be closely related to *Oporornis*, a genus whose members (for example, the Kentucky Warbler) occupy thickets and forest understory. The very active wood-warblers of the genus *Wilsonia*, such as the Canada Warbler *(W. canadensis)*, often sally for insects and flip or flick their tails expressively.

The redstarts (sometimes called "white-starts") of the genus *Myioborus* are found mainly in montane regions of the neotropics; only the Painted Redstart is normally found as far north as the United States. The *Myioborus* redstarts are not considered particularly close relatives of the American Redstart. The neotropical genus *Basileuterus* has more species than most parulid genera but is rarely seen in North America; both the Rufous-capped and Golden-crowned Warblers are occasionally seen along the U.S.–Mexico border.

The genus *Cardellina* contains only the distinctive Red-faced Warbler *(C. rubrifrons)* and is probably most closely related to warblers of the southern Mexican mountains. The rest of the wood-warblers found in the neotropics belong to a handful of small genera, including the chats of the genus *Granatellus*, which are not closely related to the Yellow-breasted Chat in spite of their names, and five monotypic genera found only in the West Indies.

Wood-warbler species occasionally hybridize. Where hybrids are common, they provide important evidence about species limits. After extensive study of hybridization between the former "Myrtle Warbler" and "Audubon's Warbler," scientists lumped the two taxa into a single species, the Yellow-rumped Warbler *(Dendroica coronata)*.

Blue-winged and Golden-winged Warblers also hybridize occasionally where their ranges meet, as do Hermit and Townsend's Warblers, but taxonomists still classify these as separate species. Scientists' interpretations of these situations continually change as more data are amassed and species concepts evolve.

Variation

Although the plumages of most adult wood-warblers exhibit only slight or moderate seasonal change, a few species, notably the male Blackpoll Warbler *(Dendroica striata)* and the Bay-breasted Warbler *(D. castanea)*, have strikingly different alternate and basic plumages. What makes it hard to identify wood-warblers during the fall, rather than dull basic plumages, is the predominance of birds in their hatching year. Immatures in their first fall often are considerably duller than their adult counterparts. Separating all these dull, similar-looking immatures—a real birding challenge—prompted Roger Tory Peterson to label these plumages the "confusing fall warblers" in his classic field guide.

In many species, birds in their first year can be distinguished in the field from adults by subtle plumage characteristics, and they can almost always be distinguished in the hand by such features as rectrix shape, flight feather color, and molt patterns.

Among North American species, the American Redstart is distinctive in that males in their first year molt into a female-like plumage that the males keep throughout their first breeding attempts. Young males in this female-like plumage can attract mates and raise young but are generally less successful than older males. They are also subordinate to older males in territorial disputes, so they often end up in poorer territories.

The juvenal plumage that wood-warblers acquire in the nest is often more conspicuously spotted and streaked than later plumages. The juvenal body plumage is rapidly replaced by their first basic plumage during the first several weeks after the young leave the nest. In most species, birds in juvenal plumage rarely venture away from the area immediately around the nest.

In their first winter and spring young wood-warblers retain most or all of their juvenal tail feathers, primaries, and secondaries, which helps observers in distinguishing them from older birds. In some species, such as the American Redstart, the first prebasic molt, which replaces juvenal plumage, may be well underway even before fledging.

In late winter and spring most wood-warblers undergo a partial prealternate

Hooded Warbler head pattern variation in adult females. *The head pattern of adult female Hooded Warblers varies from plain olive and yellow in first-year females (top) to black and yellow, almost like the adult male (bottom).*

molt. In some species—for example, the Bay-breasted, Blackpoll, and Yellow-rumped Warblers—this molt involves much of the body feathers and coverts. In most species, however, the prealternate molt involves only some head and body feathers. In addition, a few species, such as the Yellow-breasted Chat, have no prealternate molt.

Sexual dimorphism in wood-warblers varies from slight to strong. The sexes of the Magnolia Warbler *(Dendroica magnolia)* can readily be told apart, for instance, while those of the Northern Waterthrush *(Seiurus noveboracensis)* cannot.

Most North American wood-warblers show little variation from one part of their range to another, but a few species have multiple subspecies. The Yellow Warbler *(Dendroica petechia)* and the Common Yellowthroat *(Geothlypis trichas),* two widespread species, show the most geographical variation. Ten or more subspecies of each occur north of Mexico. The validity and boundaries of subspecies are not always agreed upon, but the patterns of geographical variation remain of great interest.

When identifying wood-warblers, observers should pay special attention to

"Confusing fall warbler." *Some wood-warblers, mostly species in the genus* Dendroica, *acquire a drab basic plumage before fall migration. This change, combined with the large numbers of poorly marked immature birds, such as this first-winter female Blackpoll Warbler, makes the identification of fall wood-warblers particularly challenging.*

general shape (especially relative tail length), plumage colors and patterns (such as the presence of wing-bars, tail spots, body streaking, and face patterns), behavior (including tail movements and locomotion), and voice (including call notes, flight notes, and songs). It is also helpful to learn the characteristics of the various genera; for example, the sharply pointed bill of *Vermivora,* the furtive habits of *Oporornis,* and the thin, buzzy, and often very high-pitched songs of many *Dendroica* species.

Birders commonly see migrant wood-warblers in flight and with practice can identify them by their shape, size, plumage pattern, and flight call. Flight calls can be clear and sweet (as, for example, in the Black-throated Green Warbler and its relatives) or more buzzy (as in the Cape May Warbler, *Dendroica tigrina).*

Black-throated Green Warbler in juvenal plumage. *The juvenal plumage of wood-warblers is worn very briefly as the young birds leave the nest and follow the parents begging for food. By the time young birds are independent, most individuals have molted into their first basic plumage. This is convenient for birders, as many juvenile wood-warblers have a plumage quite unlike the adult and are very tricky to identify; an example is this juvenile Black-throated Green Warbler.*

Habitats

Wood-warblers generally live in well-wooded habitats, with the greatest mix of species occurring in regions that have both coniferous and hardwood (deciduous) forests. Some species, such as Grace's Warbler *(Dendroica graciae)* and the Pine Warbler, are partial to conifers in the breeding season; other species,

Wood-warbler tail feathers as a guide to age. *In the hand the age of most wood-warblers can be determined by the shape and color of the tail feathers. The juvenal feathers (left) that are grown as the young bird fledges and worn through the first breeding season are narrower and more pointed than on adults (right), as well as being browner and more susceptible to wear.*

such as the Cerulean Warbler *(D. cerulea),* prefer deciduous trees while breeding. The Yellow-throated Warbler *(D. dominica)* varies geographically in its habitat preferences, with some populations choosing sycamore groves and others opting for pine woodlands.

In the West, some wood-warblers also associate during the breeding season with habitats dominated by certain trees. Black-throated Gray Warblers *(Dendroica nigrescens)* are often found in forests dominated by oaks, pinyon pines, or junipers. Wilson's Warbler *(Wilsonia pusilla)* is commonly seen in patches of broadleaf trees and shrubs such as alder and willow thickets, while the Orange-crowned Warbler uses both deciduous and coniferous habitats.

Timber practices, such as the removal of deciduous shrubs, can influence which species are found in a given area. MacGillivray's Warbler *(Oporornis tolmiei)* has benefited from widespread logging in western coniferous forests, as it breeds in dense stands of young trees that appear several years after clear-cutting. Recently, however, timber companies in the West have changed their forest regeneration practices by planting pines

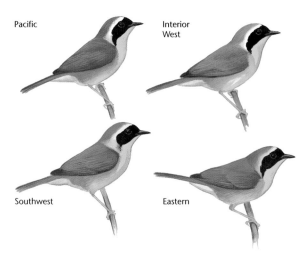

Pacific   Interior West   Southwest   Eastern

Common Yellowthroat variation. *One of the most numerous and widespread wood-warblers is also one of the most variable and has up to 14 subspecies named. Much of the variation is subtle and clinal, involving overall color, extent of yellow on the underparts, color of the pale forehead band, and size. Adult males are shown.*

instead of spruce on harvested lands. The resulting pine stands are not used by MacGillivray's Warbler, so this practice could render large areas of western managed forests unsuitable for this species.

Many parulids, including several members of the genus *Vermivora*, breed in brushy forest margins or clearings. The Common Yellowthroat is often abundant in extensive stands of marsh vegetation such as cattails or tules, and also occurs in other damp, weedy, or brushy habitats. Its close Mexican relative, the Gray-crowned Yellowthroat *(Geothlypis poliocephala)*, is found in grassy or damp brushy habitat and rarely occurs as far north as the Rio Grande. In the arid zones of the Southwest, Lucy's Warbler *(Vermivora luciae)* and other breeding species, such as the Yellow Warbler and the Yellow-breasted Chat, are restricted to riparian woodlands along desert watercourses.

A few wood-warblers are extreme habitat specialists. Kirtland's Warbler *(Dendroica kirtlandii)*, for example, nests almost exclusively in early successional Jack Pine *(Pinus banksiana)* woodlands of lower Michigan. The Golden-cheeked Warbler uses oak-juniper highlands on or near the Edwards Plateau region in Texas. While several wood-warblers are associated with swamps and riparian habitats, the Louisiana Waterthrush *(Seiurus motacilla)* is unique among North American wood-warblers in its preference for areas around fast-flowing streams. The Painted Redstart occupies streamside canyons in the Southwest, but these areas do not necessarily have flowing water year-round.

Winter Habitats

During winter, many wood-warblers occupy a variety of relatively open, often disturbed, areas. Flocks of Yellow-rumped Warblers and Palm Warblers *(Dendroica palmarum)*, for example, are often seen in weedy fields as long as some cover is nearby. Northern Waterthrushes and Prothonotary Warblers, among others, live in mangrove swamps during the winter. Hooded Warblers *(Wilsonia citrina)* segregate by sex into different habitats during winter; most male Hoodeds occupy semi-evergreen forests, while females are more common in shrublands and brushy fields. This type of habitat segregation in winter is also found in the Black-throated Blue Warbler *(Dendroica caerulescens)*, Magnolia Warbler, American Redstart, and Northern Parula.

Food and Foraging

Wood-warblers are mainly insectivorous, gleaning their invertebrate prey from twigs, leaves (both dead and alive), buds, and catkins. They eat mainly moth and butterfly larvae, but they also take a variety of other arthropods.

Foraging Black-and-white Warbler in "creeping" posture. Among the many diverse foraging techniques of the wood-warblers is the creeping motion of the Black-and-white Warbler. It creeps along the bark of tree trunks and large branches, gleaning insects just as nuthatches do.

In a series of classic studies, Robert MacArthur in the 1950s and 1960s and Douglass Morse in the 1970s studied wood-warbler foraging in the spruce woods of New England. They showed that wood-warblers sharing the same habitat are able to reduce competitive overlap and coexist by exploiting different portions of the trees. For example, where Black-throated Green and Yellow-rumped Warblers overlap, the Black-throated Greens feed mostly at mid-levels of the conifers, while the Yellow-rumpeds forage higher up. Where the Black-throated Greens are absent, however, the Yellow-rumpeds feed lower down. Both Black-throated Greens and Yellow-rumpeds, in turn, seem to restrict Northern Parulas to the outermost branches in the mid- and upper canopy. In their absence, parulas expand their foraging niche.

Some species specialize for much of the year. The Worm-eating Warbler, for example, probes clusters of dead leaves for its prey. Waterthrushes and Swainson's Warbler obtain their food mostly on the ground from dead leaves and fallen branches; streamside-dwelling waterthrushes will even occasionally take small fish. The Black-and-white Warbler creeps along trunks and branches in a style reminiscent of nuthatches.

Although wood-warblers generally have rather small, slender bills, subtle variations in bill shape adapt different species to slightly different diets. The relatively broad bills and well-developed rictal bristles of the American Redstart and Wilson's Warbler are suited to their aerial flycatching habits. The Yellow-throated Warbler's relatively long bill allows it to probe into crevices in trunks, branches, and pinecones. The fine, sharply pointed bills of many *Vermivora* species appear to be related in part to the birds' habit of feeding on nectar during the nonbreeding season.

Fruit, mainly small berries, is an important part of many wood-warblers' diets, especially in fall and winter. In the East, Yellow-rumped Warblers fatten up on bayberries and other rich fruits in fall and early winter. The ability of Yellow-rumpeds to use this fruit as a food source

Worm-eating Warbler probing dead leaves. An interesting foraging specialization is that of the Worm-eating Warbler, which spends a great deal of time probing clusters of hanging dead leaves for insects.

Yellow-rumped Warbler eating bayberries. In most parts of North America the Yellow-rumped Warbler is the only wood-warbler that is regularly seen in winter. The species manages to survive where other wood-warblers cannot partly because of its ability to digest the hard waxy coating on bayberries. By taking advantage of this food source these warblers can survive the winter months when no insects are active.

when no insects are available enables them to winter farther north than those warblers that are strictly dependent on insects. Nectar is another important source of energy for wood-warblers, particularly in winter, and many species are often seen at flowers and are even known to visit hummingbird feeders. The Tennessee Warbler, for example, commonly frequents flowering trees on its wintering grounds.

Although wood-warblers are not especially social birds, they often occur in flocks outside of the breeding season. These flocks may consist of a single species or, more often, several species of wood-warblers and non-warblers alike. Yellow-rumped and Pine Warblers, for example, often forage in fields at the edges of woodlands alongside Chipping Sparrows *(Spizella passerina)*, bluebirds, and other species. In winter, many wood-warblers such as the Nashville Warbler *(Vermivora ruficapilla)* travel with large flocks of tanagers, vireos, orioles, grosbeaks, and other species, both residents and migrants. Some species, in contrast, are territorial during the winter and thus spread out thinly through their chosen habitat; the Louisiana Waterthrush and the Hooded Warbler are examples.

Breeding

Wood-warblers are generally monogamous, territorial birds, and their territories are widely spaced and not particularly clumped in their nesting habitat. Regular polygyny has rarely been documented in wood-warblers, although DNA fingerprinting techniques have revealed frequent extra-pair matings in species such as the Hooded Warbler.

In spring, males usually arrive on the breeding grounds about a week before females. They proclaim their territories by incessant singing; once the females arrive, courtship, mating, and nest-building follow quickly. Wood-warblers often breed when they are one year old, but at this age they are generally less successful in raising a brood than older birds.

Vocalizations

Among North American parulids, usually only the males sing, although female song has been documented in a few well-studied species, such as the Yellow Warbler. Wood-warbler songs are usually rather high-pitched and often include a series of notes or trills. The songs of many species contain emphatic inflections, often at the end, while other species give monotonous trills.

Many wood-warblers that inhabit the woodland understory (for example, Swainson's and Hooded Warblers) or streamsides (the Louisiana Waterthrush) have rich, loud, ringing songs. Conversely, species that spend much of their time in the upper levels of forests usually have higher, thinner songs, such as those of the Black-throated Blue Warbler. The Yellow-breasted Chat, with its harsh notes and rich whistles, is atypical among North American wood-warbler songsters. It is found in dense thickets, where the loud and varied notes and sounds that make up chat songs may be necessary to carry for any distance.

Wood-warbler song perches are often higher and more open than their normal foraging beats. Skulkers like the Connecticut Warbler *(Oporornis agilis)* and the Mourning Warbler *(O. philadelphia)* will sit high in a spruce and sing for minutes on end. A few wood-warblers, notably the waterthrushes, the Ovenbird, and the Yellow-breasted Chat, give extended flight songs.

Parulid songs serve mainly to proclaim territory and attract mates. Many wood-warblers give somewhat different songs depending on the stage of the breeding cycle, the time of day, and the occasion. Scientists have studied wood-warblers' songs extensively, although different authors vary in the terminology they use for different song types.

David Spector reviewed what was known about parulid song in 1992, especially with regard to the functions of various song types. He found that members of *Dendroica, Vermivora, Parula,* and the American Redstart and Black-and-white Warbler share a common song system. In these species, males have two distinct groups of songs. The first grouping of songs, sometimes called accented-ending or first-category songs, are sung during the day, are relatively simple, and are often sung near females. These songs appear to function primarily in mate attraction. Males that lose their mates will rapidly increase the number of first-category songs that they sing.

Connecticut Warbler singing. *The Connecticut Warbler is known among birders for being very difficult to see, but singing males choose a song perch high in a spruce tree and can then be tracked down and admired for minutes on end.*

The second type of song is sometimes called an unaccented-ending or second-category song. These songs are typically delivered rapidly at dawn and are used in male-to-male interactions. Second-category songs are often more complex than first-category songs, but this tendency needs more study.

The Chestnut-sided Warbler *(Dendroica pensylvanica)* provides a good example of this song system. Male Chestnut-sideds have one to four different versions of first-category songs, all of which appear to be shared among males in a population. Each male also has two to ten versions of second-category songs, which are not shared among males. The first-category songs are typically given in the presence of females and from the interior of the male's territories. The use of these songs declines when a male Chestnut-sided is mated. Second-category songs are usually given at dawn along the edges of the territory during disputes with other males.

Another group of wood-warblers has a different song system. This group includes the Prothonotary, Worm-eating, and Swainson's Warblers, as well as the yellowthroats and members of the genera *Seiurus* and *Oporornis*. These species have one primary song type per male, and a

***Chestnut-sided Warbler
singing.*** *The singing behavior
of the Chestnut-sided Warbler
has been well studied. Males
use two different song types for
different purposes: a strongly
accented simple song directed
mostly at females, and a more
complex unaccented song
directed mostly at other males.*

second, more complex song called the extended song. The latter is often given as part of a flight display. Less research has been done on the functions of these songs than in the *Dendroica-Vermivora* system. Spector suggests that primary songs act as all-purpose long-distance signals, while extended songs are used in intense close encounters with either sex. The flight song of the Yellow-breasted Chat may function as an alarm call or distraction display as well as territory advertisement.

Songs of the three species in the genus *Wilsonia* are poorly described, but those of the Hooded Warbler resemble the first song system of *Dendroica* and *Vermivora*.

Female wood-warblers are known to sing rarely in at least 10 North American species as well as in some tropical warblers. Female song may function in conflicts among females or in strengthening the pair bond between newly mated individuals.

One striking feature that Spector points out is that the dawn songs of Ovenbirds, Yellow Warblers, American Redstarts, and other warblers are more elaborate than songs given at other times of the day. The same pattern of complex songs at dawn is found in tyrant flycatchers, swallows, and chickadees, among other species, but the relative complexity of dawn and daylight songs has not been well studied.

Like most songbirds, wood-warblers show some individual and geographical variation in their songs. Among Northern Parulas, for example, more westerly populations consistently sing a different song, with a slightly upslurred ending, than do populations east of the Appalachian Mountains and along the southeastern coast.

Wood-warblers also give a variety of simple call notes. Those that birders hear most commonly year-round are the simple location or contact calls, often referred to as chip notes. Because these vary among species, they are excellent aids to field identification—distinctive chip calls, for example, are perhaps the best way to distinguish immature Mourning *(pwich)* and MacGillivray's *(chik)* Warblers in the field. However, the chip calls of closely related species (for example, Hermit and Black-throated Green Warblers) can be quite similar. The quality of the chip note and the speed with which a series of chips is delivered depends on how agitated the calling bird is—chip notes may get louder and more frequent, for example, in response to a birder's pishing sounds.

The flight note is another common call of wood-warblers, given in flight to indicate the position of the caller or to alert flock mates that the caller is leaving. This call is usually higher-pitched

Lucy's Warbler at nest. *Only two species of North American wood-warblers nest in cavities, Lucy's Warbler and the Prothonotary Warbler. All other species build a cup nest either on the ground or in a shrub or tree.*

than the chip note and may be clear or buzzy, piercing or soft, depending on the species. Wood-warblers also give various other calls when alarmed or when they are interacting, but most of these have not been well studied.

Nests and Young

Wood-warblers' nests are usually small, open cups made from coarse plant fibers such as grass stems, leaves, and bark strips. The nests are lined with softer materials, including plant downs and fibers. Some species, such as the Northern Parula and the Cape May Warbler, use considerable amounts of moss in their nests. A few species, such as the Ovenbird, construct a dome of grass stems and leaves over the nest.

Many species build their nests on the ground, concealing them under clumps of annuals or small shrubs; these ground-nesters even include species such as the Red-faced Warbler and the Black-and-white Warbler that habitually forage high up in shrubs and trees. Nests of Virginia's Warbler *(Vermivora virginiae)* can also be found on the ground, near or under low shrubs. Other wood-warblers build at various heights in shrubs or trees, sometimes as high as 65 feet (20 m) or more. Two species, the Prothonotary and Lucy's Warblers, nest in tree cavities.

In most cases, only the female builds the nest and performs the incubation duties. While she is incubating, the male often feeds her. A female wood-warbler usually lays four or five eggs. The eggs are pale—the ground color varying from light blue or pale olive to creamy or whitish—and marked with small, dark spots that are generally concentrated around the large end. Incubation generally lasts 9 to 15 days.

Wood-warbler chicks are altricial, hatching naked, blind, and unable to regulate their body temperature. Both parents feed them, and they remain in the nest for 8 to 12 days. Upon leaving the nest, the young are barely able to fly, and the parents continue to feed them for as long as four to five weeks after fledging. During this time, part of the brood is cared for by the male, the other part by the female. The begging calls of the young are quite conspicuous during this period.

Bay-breasted Warblers at nest. *All wood-warblers are generally monogamous, with the female doing most of the work of nest-building and incubation. The male often brings food to the female as she incubates, as shown here.*

American Redstart exhausted on beach. The migration of many species of wood-warblers involves water crossings, and a poorly prepared bird or one that meets adverse weather conditions may perish at sea or be so exhausted on reaching land that it will drop down at the water's edge, where it is vulnerable to predators while it recovers. Famous warbler-watching locales such as Point Pelee, Ontario, and coastal Texas depend partly on this phenomenon, as spring cold fronts can ground massive numbers of tired birds.

Adults become agitated when humans approach either the nest or young fledglings, giving excited chip calls and often running on the ground or hopping through low vegetation with wings and tail partially spread.

Movements

One of the most captivating things about wood-warblers, to birders and scientists alike, is the magnitude and intricate nature of their annual migrations. Nearly all populations of North American wood-warblers are migratory. There are only a few sedentary populations, mainly in the South, such as the Pine Warbler, the Common Yellowthroat, and the Florida subspecies of the Prairie Warbler *(Dendroica discolor paludicola)*.

Departing from breeding areas in the continent's northern, eastern, and montane western regions, most North American wood-warblers head south to winter in the southernmost United States (especially the coastal regions), Mexico, Central America, the Caribbean, and northern South America. The scope and patterns of wood-warbler migration have been studied for decades. Each generation of researchers has benefited from increasingly sophisticated radar to visually track bird movements at night, as well as a growing network of banding stations, which provide information on the migratory pathways of individual birds.

Migration is critical in the annual cycle of a bird. Because of the energetic demands of migration, birds need to load up with fuel for their journey in the form of stored body fat. Also, migration must be timed correctly; it cannot coincide with other energetically demanding phases of the annual cycle, such as molt and breeding.

Wood-warbler migration strategies vary with the species, and even among populations within a species, but there are two constants in the daily cycle of any migrating parulid: long flights, generally undertaken at night, and rest and refueling during the day. A migrating wood-warbler usually takes flight shortly after dusk and continues flying until dawn, or as soon after dawn as it can find good stopover habitat where the migrant can find food to replenish its fat stores and safety from predators.

Depending on weather conditions and a number of other circumstances, migrating wood-warblers may continue their journey through part of the day. For instance, birds migrating across the Gulf of Mexico will start at night and must continue until they reach land, regardless of when daybreak is. When exhausted and hungry birds make landfall after crossing large bodies of water, they may feed for a short period in whatever habitat they find themselves, then fly a bit farther to get to better habitat in which to spend the day. This can lead to short diurnal flights as birds sort themselves out among habitats.

Increasingly, studies have shown the importance of stopover habitats in which migrants can rest and feed. To northbound wood-warblers in spring, such habitats are especially critical along the Gulf coast or in desert riparian corridors of the Southwest, where arriving migrants have just flown long distances over water or inhospitable terrain.

Migrating Northern Waterthrushes are unusual among wood-warblers in that they will defend edges of ponds and streams, aggressively driving off competitors. Most other wood-warbler species may act aggressively toward flock mates on occasion but are not territorial.

Spring Migration

In eastern North America, wood-warblers use a few major routes during spring migration. Many species wintering in the West Indies and northeastern South America pass through the Caribbean islands, then Florida and the southern Atlantic coastal states, on their way to more northerly breeding grounds; such species include the Black-throated Blue and Connecticut Warblers.

Species that winter in Central America and northwestern South America are more likely to migrate northward, passing through the Yucatán Peninsula and across the Gulf of Mexico, seeking the coastline from central Texas to western Florida (but mainly eastern Texas and

Louisiana) as landfall after their flight across the Gulf. After resting and refueling, these birds move north toward their breeding grounds. Species taking this route include the Bay-breasted and Blue-winged Warblers. Their overwater flight may take as little as 12 hours or more than twice that long, depending on the prevailing winds.

Migrants over the Gulf encountering headwinds may land on offshore oil rigs or ships, but many perish in the sea. Those that make it across the Gulf can be exhausted, sometimes landing in spectacular "fallouts" (the stressed migrants sometimes encountering throngs of birders hoping for just such an event).

Other Mexican and Central American winterers, such as the Nashville Warbler, migrate around the western end of the Gulf of Mexico, following a land route through eastern Mexico and Texas. Different species vary in their faithfulness to narrow migration routes. Typically, the most widespread breeding species, such as the Yellow Warbler and the Northern Waterthrush, migrate along a broad front.

Most wood-warblers that breed in the West south of the boreal regions winter in Mexico and northern Central America. They migrate northward in spring through the southwestern deserts, then farther north along mountain ranges and valleys that are oriented north–south; this pattern is typical of Townsend's and MacGillivray's Warblers.

Wood-warblers in flight.
Nearly all wood-warblers are migratory, flying mainly at night and communicating with high lisping or buzzy flight calls. During spring and fall the migratory restlessness of these birds can often be seen in the morning and evening, when even secretive species such as the Ovenbird might climb to the treetops and take off on long flights. Shown here are a Cape May Warbler (left) and an American Redstart (right).

Fall Migration

When they migrate south in the fall, most wood-warblers do not simply retrace their spring routes. In much of North America, the birds' fall migration involves an easterly shift in their migration routes; for example, many wood-warblers that migrate north in spring through the Midwest may migrate south closer to the Atlantic coast.

Many Blackpoll Warblers apparently migrate from their breeding territories in Alaska and Canada to the northern Atlantic coast. From there they launch southeastward over the Atlantic Ocean on headings that would take them to western Africa (if they had sufficient fat reserves to get that far). When the birds reach the latitude of Bermuda, however, they encounter the trade winds, which consistently blow southwesterly. The migrants either change direction to follow the trade winds or are simply blown southwestward until they reach the West Indies. Blackpoll Warblers use this route to reach their wintering grounds in northern South America.

In the West, migrants tend to move southward through the mountains. Fewer wood-warblers move through the western lowlands in fall than in spring; thus, while large numbers of Hermit Warblers move through southern California's deserts and foothill oak woodlands in spring, most of the birds' fall migration is through high-elevation coniferous forests.

Vagrancy

The ability of tiny (mainly 0.2–0.7 oz/ 6–20 gm) wood-warblers to migrate long distances is astonishing. But distance, inclement weather, physical obstacles, and other factors take their toll, causing high mortality among the migrants. Nor do all individuals unerringly migrate along the "right" routes to the "right" destination. Vagrancy is a fact of life for wood-warblers, and vigilant birders have expanded the wood-warbler lists of most states and provinces to 30 and even 40 species. Scientists are actively studying vagrancy patterns in parulids and how those patterns relate to weather, population trends, breeding success, and other factors.

Vagrancy in wood-warblers is undoubtedly due, in part, to migrants simply losing their bearings, and to storms and unusual wind patterns. One common form of vagrancy in spring is "overshooting," in which the birds arrive for short periods well to the north of their normal breeding range. Hooded Warblers, to give one example, frequently overshoot breeding sites in the eastern United States and land in late spring anywhere from Massachusetts to the Maritime Provinces of Canada.

Scientists have hypothesized that many fall vagrants arrive far out of their normal wintering range because of "mirror-image" orientation, a tendency for the birds to swap east and west orientations during their journeys. A bird intending to fly southeast in fall would instead head southwest. This may explain the relatively frequent occurrence of many eastern boreal wood-warblers on the coast of California in fall. For example, Black-throated Blue Warblers breed mainly from the Great Lakes and southeastern Canada south to the Appalachians and winter in the West Indies; yet this species has appeared in California some 700 times probably due to mirror-image migration at some point in its travels.

Bachman's Warbler. *Bachman's Warbler is almost certainly extinct, with no confirmed records since 1962. The species was always enigmatic, found only in scattered southern swamps and apparently never common.*

Golden-cheeked Warbler. Kirtland's Warbler has a smaller total population, but the steep decline in numbers of the Golden-cheeked Warbler is cause for grave concern. This species nests only in oak-juniper woodlands in central Texas, and as more and more of that habitat is cleared for ranchland and development, the survival of the species is uncertain.

Testimony to the vagrancy of wood-warblers may be seen in records from both Florida and northern California of the Golden-cheeked Warbler, whose breeding range is restricted to a small area in Texas.

Conservation

Populations of many wood-warblers have clearly declined in the last few decades. The causes of such declines are less clear, and probably involve many factors that affect breeding and wintering habitats and migration routes.

Three wood-warbler species merit special concern, although for the Bachman's Warbler (*Vermivora bachmanii*) that concern may have come too late, as it is now probably extinct. The other two—Kirtland's Warbler and the Golden-cheeked Warbler—are listed as endangered by the U.S. Fish and Wildlife Service.

Bachman's Warbler apparently was a habitat specialist, found in dense stands of natural cane in both its summer and winter habitats. It once bred in deep swamp forests of the southeastern United States and wintered in Cuba. The forests in which it bred were largely cut for timber and the land converted to agriculture, while its winter habitat was cleared for sugarcane plantations. The last confirmed record of this species in the wild was from South Carolina in 1962, although scattered sightings were reported through the 1980s.

Kirtland's Warbler is the most celebrated endangered species in the midwestern United States. It breeds in numbers only in the lower peninsula of Michigan, where Jack Pine grows in dense stands on sandy soils. Kirtland's Warbler winters in the Bahamas. The species has probably always been rare because it is dependent on young stands of Jack Pine that arise after large forest fires on its breeding grounds. Older pine stands lack the vegetation structure that Kirtland's apparently prefers.

During most of the 20th century, land managers vigorously suppressed natural fires (the "Smokey the Bear" policy), eliminating the generation of new, suitable habitat for this wood-warbler. In addition, the spread of the Brown-headed Cowbird (*Molothrus ater*) into Michigan dramatically lowered Kirtland's breeding success, as the cowbirds parasitized nearly all its nests. Cowbird control and a liberalized fire policy have allowed Kirtland's Warbler to increase from a low of only 167 pairs in 1974 and 1987 to more than 700 pairs in the late 1990s.

The Golden-cheeked Warbler breeds only in central Texas, especially in the Edwards Plateau area, and winters in Central America. It is another habitat specialist, using old stands of juniper and oak woodlands for breeding. The primary threat to this species comes from the clearing of its breeding habitat for housing developments and agriculture. The Golden-cheeked was listed as endangered in 1990, and a National Wildlife Refuge was created specifically to protect some of its habitat. The decision to list the species as endangered affected many land developers in and around Austin, Texas, and remains very controversial.

Although not listed as endangered, the Colima Warbler (*Vermivora crissalis*) has one of the smallest breeding ranges of any North American bird, limited in the United States to the Chisos Mountains in Big Bend National Park, Texas. Since it is found in a national park, the species is well protected there, and its population is stable. The Colima Warbler is also found in adjacent Mexico, but the areas in which it breeds are very remote. Because of its limited range, it is a difficult bird to study. Even though the range of the Colima Warbler in the United States is well protected, conservation biologists are usually concerned about any species with such a limited distribution, and for that reason the Colima Warbler is on the WatchList.

Conservationists have serious concerns about many other North American wood-warblers. Some species are placed at risk by their own ecological specialization. For example, several wood-warbler species, including the Cape May and the Bay-breasted Warblers, rely heavily during the breeding season on larvae of the Spruce Budworm *(Choristoneura fumiferana)*, populations of which fluctuate dramatically. The diverse wood-warbler communities that exploit Spruce Budworms in northeastern North America are probably affected by large-scale control measures aimed at this forest "pest."

Wood-warblers can also be impacted by limited habitats, as mentioned above for the Kirtland's and Colima Warblers, and special needs for nest sites such as the cavities required by Prothonotary and Lucy's Warblers.

Even a factor such as nest materials can be limiting; the bark of the Ashe Juniper *(Juniperus ashei)*, for example, is very important to the Golden-cheeked Warbler. Declines in both Northern and Tropical Parulas are related in part to declines in epiphytic plants and lichens, which the birds use for nesting. The epiphytes are very sensitive to air pollution and acid rain. Loss of nesting material has been associated with range contraction of Northern Parulas in Massachusetts, New York, and New Jersey, and of Tropical Parulas locally in southern Texas.

Many wood-warbler populations are threatened by the loss or modification of

Ovenbird. Much recent research has focused on the effects of forest fragmentation on the breeding success of songbirds such as the Ovenbird. Even though these species use a relatively small breeding territory, researchers have found that the birds have much better breeding success in large, continuous stands of forest than in smaller forest patches.

their breeding habitat. Habitats do not have to be cleared or destroyed for the birds to feel the negative effects. Even more subtle changes resulting from habitat fragmentation, the invasion of exotic plants, growing populations of browsers such as deer, or a rise in feral predators can devastate wood-warbler populations.

The fragmentation of habitat increases the ratio of habitat edge to interior, providing more avenues for invasion by predators such as feral cats, dogs, foxes, and crows and jays. They also make wood-warblers more vulnerable to brood parasites such as the Brown-headed Cowbird. In addition to its role in Kirtland's Warbler conservation, cowbird trapping has reversed the declines of some populations of Yellow Warblers and other species in the Southwest.

The ongoing destruction of forests throughout Central America and northern South America is certainly affecting populations of many species that breed in North America. Species that require primary forests for their winter habitat (for example, Kentucky and Hooded Warblers) are likely to be most strongly affected by deforestation in the neotropics. Species that prefer edge habitat on their wintering grounds, including Common Yellowthroats and Ovenbirds, are probably less affected. The continuing loss of forests in the northern neotropics virtually ensures that wintering populations of many North American wood-warblers will be increasingly at risk.

Migration means high mortality for wood-warblers, even under natural conditions. However, landscape changes made by humans may have increased migration mortality to levels that could threaten wood-warbler populations. Direct mortality from collisions with lighted communications towers, plate glass windows, and other structures is an obvious risk, although the significance of this mortality to entire populations is unknown.

It is even more difficult to quantify mortality or loss of physical conditioning from the alteration of critical migration stopover habitats. Coastal woodlands along the Gulf coast, for example, are important refueling stops for species that migrate across the Gulf of Mexico. Increased urbanization and habitat alteration along these coastlines has surely affected many migrant wood-warblers, but it is hard to know how much it has contributed to population trends.

The decline of many wood-warbler species has resulted in their listing by many states, provinces, and regions as species of conservation concern. Thirteen species are included on the WatchList, recognizing population declines, limited distributions, or threats to breeding or wintering habitats. Four species—Prairie, Prothonotary, Cerulean, and Golden-winged Warblers—show population declines throughout their ranges, in addition to habitat losses in the breeding and wintering ranges. Scientists are monitoring and mapping the Cerulean and Golden-winged Warblers intensively.

The Lucy's, Colima, Hermit, and Red-faced Warblers are included on the WatchList because of their limited breeding distribution or perceived threats to their breeding habitat. Particular attention has been paid to the loss of old-growth conifer forests in the Pacific Northwest, where Hermit Warblers breed, and the southwestern riparian forests used by the Lucy's Warbler. Finally, five wood-warbler species are on the WatchList due to threats to their wintering habitats. This reflects concern about the loss of tropical forests and woodlands in western Mexico (Virginia's Warbler), the Caribbean (Swainson's, Worm-eating, and Black-throated Blue Warblers), and Central America (Swainson's, Worm-eating, and Kentucky Warblers).

The long-term conservation of wood-warblers in North America will require a combination of monitoring, habitat preservation and restoration, cowbird control, reduction in human-caused migration mortality, and partnerships and incentives to promote habitat preservation in neotropical wintering areas.

Accidental Species

Three additional species of wood-warblers that are native to Mexico have occasionally been recorded in the United States. The Crescent-chested Warbler (*Parula superciliosa*) breeds in western Mexico south through the mountains of Central America. It has been recorded several times in Arizona and once in Big Bend National Park, Texas.

The Slate-throated Redstart (*Myioborus miniatus*) is a darker relative of the Painted Redstart found from northern Mexico to South America. It has been recorded in Arizona, New Mexico, and western Texas. The Fan-tailed Warbler (*Euthlypis lachrymosa*) has an active foraging style somewhat like that of an American Redstart. Normally found from Mexico to northern Central America, it has been recorded in the desert canyons of southeastern Arizona.

Kimball L. Garrett
and John B. Dunning, Jr.

Bananaquit

One of the most common and widespread birds of the Caribbean, the Bananaquit *(Coereba flaveola)* is small and warbler-like, with a strong, downcurved bill and brightly colored plumage boldly patterned in black, white, and yellow. In the West Indies, the word "quit" refers to any small bird, including the grassquits (genus *Tiaris* of the family Emberizidae) and the Orangequit *(Euneornis campestris),* a Jamaican tanager. The Bananaquit occurs in almost all wooded habitats in its range and also frequents gardens, parks, and other areas with many flowers. It feeds on nectar and is known for its nectar-robbing: "stealing" its food without pollinating the flowers.

Taxonomy

Researchers have sometimes linked the Bananaquit to the neotropical honeycreepers, a group of small, nectivorous tanagers, and occasionally to the wood-warblers. Currently the bird has its own family, Coerebidae, separated from typical tanagers and wood-warblers by subtle but distinct morphological features and by its globe-shaped nest. The relationships among the tanagers, sparrows, wood-warblers, and related groups, including the Bananaquit, are not well understood. A recent study of mitochondrial DNA suggests that the closest relatives of the Bananaquit may be the grassquits, which are usually placed with the New World sparrows.

Variation

The Bananaquit varies considerably in appearance throughout its range. Most forms have a distinct white superciliary stripe, and many also have yellow on their underparts. In the southern part of the species' range in South America, birds are rather gray above, while northern South American birds are darker.

Bananaquits on some Caribbean islands are almost all black, except for a yellowish wash on the breast. Birds that have shown up in Florida all appear to be of the Bahama race *(Coereba flaveola bahamensis),* with a white throat and superciliary stripe, yellow underparts, and blackish upperparts.

Food and Foraging

The Bananaquit feeds primarily on nectar, which it sips from large flowers, often tubular flowers also visited by hummingbirds. Records in southern Florida are usually of birds visiting gardens with exotic flowers. Like hummingbirds, the Bananaquit usually enters the flower from the front, in the process picking up pollen that it can then transfer to other plants. Thus, like hummingbirds, the Bananaquit can be an important pollinator of some tropical flowers.

When feeding on larger flowers, however, the Bananaquit often pierces a small hole in the side of the flower's corolla near its base and drinks the nectar through the hole. This behavior is called "nectar-robbing," since the bird gathers the nectar reward without doing the work of pollination. Wintering wood-warblers, tropical hummingbirds, and other species make use of these slits to rob nectar when the Bananaquit is not in the immediate vicinity and able to defend the flowers.

Bananaquit. *Currently considered the sole member of the family Coerebidae, the Bananaquit is a taxonomic enigma. The combination of its nesting habits, decurved and pointed bill, and high, thin voice makes it unlike any other species.*

510

The Bananaquit sips nectar from the flowers of many plants, including at least 50 different species in Trinidad. It will also visit sugar bowls on tables in open cafes and bowls of syrup put out by merchants in outdoor markets to attract the birds to their stands. In addition to nectar, the Bananaquit eats small insects and many kinds of fruit, and will also feed at the sap holes created by wintering Yellow-bellied Sapsuckers *(Sphyrapicus varius)*.

Breeding

The Bananaquit builds its nest in a tree or shrub about 5 to 30 feet (1.5–9 m) above the ground, usually near the end of a branch. The nest is a messy domed globe of leaves and grasses, with an entrance hole either on the side or underneath. It is similar to the stick nest of a Verdin *(Auriparus flaviceps)*, but messier. Both sexes appear to help with nest-building.

Although the Bananaquit can breed throughout the year, most active nests are found from February to June. A clutch consists of two or three heavily spotted eggs. When not breeding, a bird may use its nest for nighttime roosting; it may also take over the domed nests of other species for this purpose.

On many Caribbean islands, the Bananaquit's song—a wheezy, buzzy series of notes—is a familiar sound. Males from different islands sing different songs; on some islands the song is reduced to a simple trill. Males can sing incessantly during

Bananaquit "nectar-robbing." A special skill of the Bananaquit is nectar-robbing: cutting a small slit at the base of a tubular flower to drink nectar, but without contacting the flower's pollen, thus providing no benefit to the flower. Verdins are also nectar-robbers.

the breeding season. They may begin singing while still in juvenal plumage, and in some cases will breed when less than one year old.

Conservation

The Bananaquit can be the most abundant bird in many Caribbean island habitats, especially in second-growth scrubby areas, around towns, and near human dwellings. Many fruit farmers consider the bird to be a pest because of its fruit-eating habits. However, the Bananaquit is also beneficial to farmers, as it eats many insects that damage crops, such as weevils and caterpillars. Overall this bird coexists with humans quite easily.

John B. Dunning, Jr.

Worldwide Family Features

- 4–5" (10–13 cm) nectar-eating songbird.
- 1 species worldwide; occurs on Caribbean islands (except Cuba), Mexico, Central America, and northern South America; rare visitor to southern Florida.
- Eats nectar, small insects, fruit. Probes flowers; gleans insects and fruit from vegetation.
- Territorial; probably monogamous. Nonmigratory, but can make long-distance movements, perhaps in response to availability of flowers.

- Breeds first usually at 1 year old, sometimes younger.
- Nest a loose, messy, thick-walled globe of grasses and plant fibers, with bottom or side entry hole; placed near tip of tree branch. Both sexes build.
- 2–6 oval eggs, white with brown flecks. Female incubates, for 12–13 days. Hatching synchrony not reported. 2 or more broods per year.
- Altricial young. Fledge within 15–18 days. Both parents feed young.
- Adult annual survival about 65%. Among oldest on record: 6 years, 7 months.

Tanagers

Family Thraupidae
Order Passeriformes

Worldwide, tanagers are a diverse group that is difficult to characterize. However, North American tanagers are medium-size songbirds with rather stout bills. They are dramatically sexually dimorphic; adult males are some of North America's most intensely colored birds, while females and immatures are drab, varying from dull yellow to olive. Tanagers are forest-dwellers, occurring in North America at elevations up to 10,000 feet (3,000 m). Their habitats range from large Ponderosa Pine tracts to dense mixed forests to lower-elevation cottonwoods along streams. Scarlet Tanagers *(Piranga olivacea)* may also reside in suburban areas. Tanagers can be secretive, and despite the male's brightly colored plumage, they are more often heard than seen.

Taxonomy

Tanagers belong to the New World nine-primaried oscines, a large assemblage traditionally considered to be composed of a number of families or subfamilies, including the tanagers, wood-warblers, New World sparrows, cardinals, blackbirds and orioles, and others. Some recent classifications lumped all of these groups into a single family—the Emberizidae. With the 1998 publication of the seventh edition of the AOU Check-list of North American Birds, the tanagers have been placed in a separate family, the Thraupidae.

The tanagers show a close affiliation with the other nine-primaried oscines and are often linked to the Bananaquit *(Coereba flaveola)* and the wood-warblers. A recent analysis of mitochondrial DNA,

however, suggests that the group is not well defined, and its closest relations are unclear.

All North American tanagers belong to a single genus, *Piranga,* with the exception of the Western Spindalis *(Spindalis zena),* a West Indian species that is a sporadic visitor to heavily landscaped gardens and dense shrublands in southern Florida. The Western Spindalis is one of several species that were collectively treated as a single species, the "Stripe-headed Tanager." In 2000, the AOU Check-list committee split the "Stripe-headed Tanager" into four species and reverted to the original common name for the group—spindalis.

Recent genetic studies indicate that three genera currently placed within the tanagers (including *Piranga*) in fact belong in the cardinal family, and that two genera previously believed to be cardinalids probably are tanagers. (See the Taxonomy section in the Cardinals and Allies chapter.)

Variation

Beginning at the end of July or early August, the male Scarlet Tanager molts from his bright red and black alternate plumage to a drab, female-like basic plumage. Individuals show varying degrees of red splotches until molting is complete. Male Western Tanagers *(Piranga ludoviciana)* also lose some color in winter (most notably their red heads) but otherwise retain the same overall color pattern as

Thraupid diversity. *The North American tanagers all belong to the genus* Piranga *(represented here by the Western Tanager, left), except for the Western Spindalis (right), a rare visitor. All are characterized by a stout bill and, in adult males, bright colors. Although members of* Piranga *resemble some tropical tanagers, recent genetic evidence suggests that they should be moved to the family Cardinalidae.*

they have in summer. Adult males begin to regain their summer colors in March and April. The other North American tanagers do not change plumage seasonally.

There is some geographic variation in the Summer *(Piranga rubra)* and Hepatic *(P. flava)* Tanagers. Western populations of Summer Tanagers are slightly larger and paler compared to eastern birds; western females typically appear grayer above, while some eastern females may show an overall reddish wash. Taxonomists have at times recognized five or more subspecies of Hepatic Tanagers, based on differences in size and intensity of coloration; only two of these subspecies occur in North America.

Food and Foraging

North American tanagers are largely insectivorous. They eat a wide variety of insects but seem to prefer wasps, bees, caterpillars, moths, and beetles (adults and larvae). Tanagers pick their prey from leaves and branches as they move slowly about in trees and shrubs; females tend to forage higher up. They will also capture insects through aerial sorties. Summer and Hepatic Tanagers frequently capture flying bees and wasps, bringing them back to a perch to break off the stingers before eating them.

Fruit, including berries, wild grapes, and cherries, is also an important component

Immature male Summer Tanager molting. *The partial prealternate molt of the Summer Tanager creates a patchy red and yellow appearance in first-spring males.*

Thraupid head and bill. *Tanagers have a stout, somewhat pointed bill adapted for eating large insects and fruit. Most North American species (but not the Summer Tanager, shown here) have a small "tooth" along the edge of the upper bill.*

Worldwide Family Features

- 4–12" (10–30 cm) woodland songbirds.
- More than 254 species in 65 genera worldwide; only in Western Hemisphere, with greatest variety in tropical forests. 6 species in 2 genera found in North America; occur from southern Yukon and Northwest Territories and southern Quebec and Ontario south through much of continent; 1 introduced species no longer present.
- Eat insects; also fruit, especially in late summer. Most food plucked from vegetation with bill; sometimes flycatch.
- Some species territorial. Typically solitary during nonbreeding season; occasionally occur in small groups, particularly during spring migration. Most species presumed monogamous. In North American species, pair bonds seasonal. North American species migratory; most tropical species either permanent residents or elevational migrants.
- Breed first at 1 year old.

- Nest an open cup or saucer, loosely constructed from coarse material such as stems, twigs, grasses, bark; lined with softer matter, including fine grasses, blossoms, hair, plant down. Located 4–75' (1–25 m) high in tree, usually near end of horizontal branch. In species studied, only female builds nest. Nests not known to be reused.
- 2–5 (usually 3 or 4) pale blue or pale green, subelliptical to short subelliptical eggs, minutely speckled to boldly blotched with gray or brown. Female incubates, for 11–14 days. Hatching synchronous. Usually 1 brood per year, occasionally 2.
- Altricial young covered with fine down at hatching. Both parents feed. Fledge at 9–15 days.
- Adult annual survival about 75%. Among oldest on record: 10 years, 1 month (Scarlet Tanager).

Western Tanager at nest.
This female Western Tanager is building a nest typical of the family—a rather shaggy cup of twigs and grasses placed high in a tree on a horizontal branch.

of a tanager's diet, particularly in late summer. The birds usually swallow berries whole, sometimes using the bill to husk the skins. Tanagers occasionally visit feeders, where they have been known to accept pieces of orange, banana, bread, doughnut, and cake, as well as cornmeal and peanut butter mixtures.

Breeding

North American tanagers are highly territorial. They sing loudly and frequently to defend their territories and to attract mates. A male Scarlet or Summer Tanager may react aggressively if one hears the other's song, often counter-singing in response. Some male tanagers will chase off intruding males and have also been known to chase females, perhaps as part of courtship. Males may also chase females back to the nest during incubation.

All North American breeding species appear to be monogamous, but no long-term studies or genetic analysis of parentage have been done. Our knowledge of the mating systems of these relatively common birds is surprisingly poor.

The Flame-colored Tanager *(Piranga bidentata)*, which occurs regularly in the pine-oak forests of western Mexico, is a rare summer visitor to the mountains of southeastern Arizona. It has been known to nest there paired with Western Tanagers, raising both hybrid tanagers and cowbirds *(Molothrus* species).

Vocalizations and Displays

Males often sing from a high perch when establishing breeding territories, then shift to mid-heights. Tropical tanagers are generally considered to be weak singers. However, North American *Piranga* species are well known for their loud, rich songs. The songs may be more rapid or interspersed with aggressive call notes during territorial disputes.

The female Scarlet Tanager also sings, particularly while foraging or gathering nest materials. Her song is typically softer and shorter than the male's. The reason for the female's singing is unclear. Researchers speculate that it serves as a way for mated birds to communicate when they are separated.

Both sexes use a variety of calls, depending on the circumstance; for example, they use different calls when there is a disturbance, when they are distressed, and during courtship. Females also call when the young have hatched, perhaps to indicate that the male should bring food. Males may call or sing to coax chicks to accept food.

There are no apparent regional dialects in the advertising songs of Scarlet Tanagers. However, Summer Tanager songs do vary geographically; eastern birds sing at a faster tempo and at lower maximum and minimum frequencies than those in western populations.

Tanagers use a variety of displays. A female Scarlet crouches, raises the bill, and flutters half-open wings close to the body as a way to initiate copulation or when receiving food. Tanagers use various other displays that involve wing and tail movements; these are given as mating behavior or aggressive posturing, depending on the context. In one Scarlet Tanager courtship display, the male spreads his wings and displays his back from a perch below the female.

Nests and Young
Tanagers build their nests near the ends of horizontal branches of either coniferous or deciduous trees, depending upon the species. Some tanager nests are so loosely constructed that the eggs are visible from below or through the sides. Only females build the nest, typically completing the nest-building in two to seven days, although Scarlet Tanagers have been known to complete the task in a single day.

Both parents feed the young, and males will sometimes feed incubating females. Most tanagers are thought to produce only a single brood each year, although Western and Summer Tanagers will lay a second clutch if the first is destroyed, and Summer Tanagers will sometimes try to raise two broods in a year. There have been several cases of interspecific helping, in which male Scarlet Tanagers fed young Chipping Sparrows *(Spizella passerina)*, at least until their own offspring hatched.

Migration

The four common North American breeding species—the Hepatic, Summer, Western, and Scarlet Tanagers—are neotropical migrants, spending the winter in tropical forests of Central and South America. Tanagers begin arriving back in North America in April, and breeding takes place in May and June. By late July, the birds begin their migration south, and all have left by late October or early November. Tanagers migrate primarily at night, as evidenced by birds found dead below communication towers.

Conservation

Breeding Bird Survey data from 1966 to 1999 show a statistically significant decline in Scarlet Tanagers in the northeastern United States and Ontario that has become more pronounced since the 1980s. Summer Tanager populations appear to be stable or only slightly decreasing. Western Tanagers show a statistically significant increase from 1980 to 1999, while Hepatic Tanagers are not reported enough on Breeding Bird Survey routes for trends to be assessed accurately.

In response to some regional studies showing that tanager species reacted negatively to forest fragmentation, the Cornell Laboratory of Ornithology initiated Project Tanager to study fragmentation effects on breeding tanagers in the United States and Canada. This study showed that while increasing fragmentation reduced the suitability of specific breeding sites, the degree to which this happened differed among tanager species and geographic regions. For example, in Scarlet Tanagers, there was a strong negative fragmentation effect in the largely deforested Midwest and Mid-Atlantic coast regions but only a weak one in the largely forested Northeast. In Western Tanagers, elevation was as important as fragmentation in determining habitat suitability.

During periods of unseasonably cold, wet spring weather, there are occasional large die-offs of tanagers upon their arrival in northern latitudes.

In the 1960s and 1970s, an introduced species, the Blue-gray Tanager *(Thraupis episcopus)*, was established in southern Florida. Common residents throughout Central America and northern South America, Blue-grays were popular cage birds. Escaped birds were sighted in Hollywood, Florida, in 1960, and breeding was confirmed there by 1961. The population slowly increased in the Miami area for a decade, then decreased. The last Blue-gray Tanager was reported during a southern Florida Christmas Bird Count in the mid-1970s.

Allison Childs Wells and Jeffrey V. Wells

New World Sparrows

Family Emberizidae
Order Passeriformes

The New World sparrows are small to medium-size songbirds that often have a brown, streaked appearance and rounded wings. Emberizids use their conical bills for husking seeds in winter. The habitats preferred by members of this family are often dominated by shrubs or grasses but can range from desert to grassland to mature pine forest. Some species adapt well to human-altered ecosystems and are familiar yard birds.

Taxonomy

Worldwide there are about 319 to 321 emberizid species in 72 genera; members of the family are found on all continents except Australia and Antarctica. Emberizidae is primarily a Western Hemisphere family, although the "Old World buntings" (genus *Emberiza*) occur mainly in the Old World. About 146 species are often considered part of the tanager family or the cardinal family.

Emberizids are generally dressed in brown or gray, often with streaks on the breast or back. Males and females are often indistinguishable. If the sexes have different plumages, the differences are usually subtle; the few exceptions to this rule include the Eastern Towhee *(Pipilo erythrophthalmus)*, the Lark Bunting *(Calamospiza melanocorys)*, the longspurs, and the grassquits, among other species.

All species have conical bills, but otherwise bill shape can vary from relatively long and slender (for example, the Seaside Sparrow, *Ammodramus maritimus*) to more short and deep (for example, the Lark Bunting). No emberizids have bills quite as massive as the cardinals and grosbeaks or many of the finches.

The emberizids are part of the New World nine-primaried oscines, which also includes the wood-warblers, tanagers, blackbirds and orioles, cardinals, and various smaller groups. From 1983 to 1997, most members of this grouping were considered to be in a single family called the Emberizidae. In the 1998 edition of the AOU Check-list, each of these groups was restored to the status of a separate family, the typical treatment before 1983.

Their drab brown plumages and conical bill separate the emberizids from most other members of the New World nine-primaried oscines. The tanagers and wood-warblers are generally brightly colored and can be sexually dimorphic in plumage. The blackbirds and orioles are strongly dimorphic in plumage, size, or both, and are generally larger than most emberizids.

Within the New World nine-primaried oscines, the group closest in shape, size, and appearance to the emberizids is the Cardinalidae—the cardinals, grosbeaks, and buntings. These species also have conical bills, but most are strongly sexually dimorphic in plumage. No emberizid has a bill to match the seed-crushing jaws of the Northern Cardinal *(Cardinalis cardinalis)* or Blue Grosbeak *(Guiraca caerulea)*. Similarly, the gaudy male breeding plumage of the Painted Bunting

Emberizid heads and bills.
All of the New World sparrows have conical bills, but bill size and shape vary from relatively short and deep (Lark Bunting, left) to long and slender (Seaside Sparrow, center) to short and petite (Brewer's Sparrow, right).

(Passerina ciris) makes even the most colorful sparrows seem pretty dull.

Two odd species in the New World nine-primaried oscines—the Bobolink *(Dolichonyx oryzivorus)* in the blackbird family and the Dickcissel *(Spiza americana)* in the cardinal family—are very sparrow-like in appearance (especially the females) and can be confusing to birders.

Most emberizid species are called "sparrows"; however, some are given the name "bunting," including the Snow Bunting *(Plectrophenax nivalis)*, the Lark Bunting, and the Eurasian members of the genus *Emberiza*, such as the Rustic Bunting *(E. rustica)*. None of these species is closely related to the buntings of the Cardinalidae.

In Europe, the members of the Emberizidae are routinely called buntings, in part because "sparrow" is used by Europeans to refer to the unrelated Old World genus *Passer*, which includes the House Sparrow *(Passer domesticus)*. Older literature sometimes follows the European tradition and calls most members of the sparrow family "buntings." Since the Emberizidae family was at one point

Emberizid diversity. *The majority of New World sparrows are brown-patterned, ground-dwelling birds with short, conical bills; all are closely related. They vary from the small and intricately patterned Le Conte's Sparrow (left) to the large and plain California Towhee (right).*

lumped with the Fringillidae (the true finches), some authors use the term "finches" to refer to the sparrows. Thus care must be taken when searching for information on the sparrow family.

Recent Splits

The introduction of molecular genetic techniques has revolutionized the study of species limits by providing a different way to measure how similar populations are to one another. These studies, along with new field research, have resulted in new species being split from old, variable

Worldwide Family Features

- 4–9½" (10–24 cm) ground-dwelling songbirds.
- About 319 species in 72 genera; found mostly in Americas, but also in Eurasia and Africa. 50 species in 18 genera regularly occur in North America; breed from Arctic treeline to Mexican border, with relatively few species in Florida peninsula; plus 10 accidental species and at least 1 regular escapee.
- Most species eat insects in breeding season, seeds at other times. Glean most food from surface of ground or low vegetation. Feed insects to young.
- Most species territorial in breeding season and seasonally monogamous; a few polygynous. In winter, many species form flocks that can be large. Many species have strong dominance hierarchies. Most species migrate short distances or are permanent residents.
- Breed first at 1 year old.

- Nest is open cup made of grasses and forbs, placed in vegetation or on ground; built by female. Rarely reuse old nests.
- 2–9 (usually 3–5) subelliptical eggs, often white or bluish with dark markings, but can be plain; in different species, markings range from light mottling on wide end to dense, dark pattern covering egg. Female incubates, for 11–14 days. Hatching synchronous. 1 or 2 broods per year, sometimes more.
- Altricial young fledge at 5–19 days, earlier if nest disturbed. Both sexes care for young; male may assume care for independent young as female begins 2nd clutch.
- Adult annual survival 35–91%, most less than 60%. Among oldest on record: 13 years, 4 months (White-crowned Sparrow).

ones. Thus the "Brown Towhee" has been split into the Canyon Towhee *(Pipilo fuscus)* and the California Towhee *(P. crissalis)*, and the "Rufous-sided Towhee" has been split into the Eastern Towhee and the Spotted Towhee *(P. maculatus)*.

The "Sharp-tailed Sparrow" has been split into two species, with inland populations now referred to as Nelson's Sharp-tailed Sparrow *(Ammodramus nelsoni)* and most of the Atlantic coast populations referred to as the Saltmarsh Sharp-tailed Sparrow *(A. caudacutus).*

The primary authority for North American bird names is the Check-list committee of the AOU. The committee usually waits until substantial evidence has been published in the ornithological literature before voting to make proposed changes official. Thus several other splits have been proposed but have not yet been adopted by the committee. These include suggestions to split the Sage Sparrow *(Amphispiza belli)* and Brewer's Sparrow *(Spizella breweri)* into two species apiece, and to split the Fox Sparrow *(Passerella iliaca)* into three or four species. The taxonomy of the Savannah Sparrow *(Passerculus sandwichensis)* is also complex, and this species could be split in the future.

Prominent Genera

Based on the illustrations in many field guides, beginning birders often start to identify sparrows by looking at the breast, for it seems that the sparrows can be divided into those that have breast streaks and those that do not. This can be a distracting way to begin, however, because most juvenile sparrows have streaks (even when adults of the same species do not), and a few species can have some streaks at some ages but not at others. For instance, the normally clear-breasted White-throated Sparrow *(Zonotrichia albicollis)* has breast streaks in its first winter.

It is far more productive to look at the overall shape, size, and coloration of a sparrow and to classify it as to genus first, then work out which species it is. This is particularly true of winter flocks, in which sparrows of several species may occur together. The following sections describe the most prominent North American emberizid genera.

Genus* Pipilo *(Towhees) Towhees are the largest emberizids. They have stout bills, long tails, and somewhat rounded wings. Several species, such as the Green-tailed Towhee *(P. chlorurus)*, have

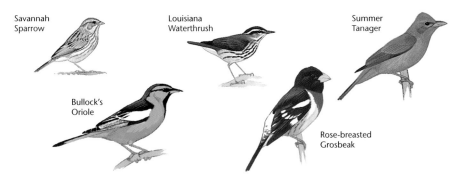

New World nine-primaried oscine families. Some authorities combine all of these birds into a single family, but the current AOU Check-list separates them into five main families, based on differences in voice, habits, and morphology. Bill shape and size help to separate these groups, although there is overlap in these traits between some of the families. In general, though, New World sparrows (Savannah Sparrow shown) have short, conical bills; icterids (Bullock's Oriole, Icterus bullockii) have long, tapered, pointed bills; wood-warblers (Louisiana Waterthrush, Seiurus motacilla) have smaller, slender, pointed bills; cardinals (Rose-breasted Grosbeak, Pheucticus ludovicianus) have very stout, conical bills; and North American tanagers (Summer Tanager, Piranga rubra) have fairly heavy, less pointed bills. Still, there are certain genera (for example, seedeaters) that seem to fall between families.

Woodland and shrubland species. Most members of Pipilo *(such as the Spotted Towhee, left) and* Aimophila *(Rufous-crowned Sparrow, right) stay close to the cover of trees or shrubs and rarely join large flocks. Some* Aimophila *species, such as Cassin's and Botteri's Sparrows, are grassland specialists, but they too do not form large flocks.*

distinctive plumages and are not likely to be confused with most other sparrows. The "brown towhees," such as Abert's Towhee *(P. aberti),* are plainer. Towhees are often found in edge or shrubby habitat, where they dig in leaf litter with a distinctive "double-scratch" motion that is also used by some other sparrows (see Food and Foraging, below). They are relatively solitary, joining mixed-species flocks only as the flocks move through the towhee's territory.

Genus Aimophila This genus contains several medium-size, long-billed sparrows mostly restricted to Mexico. Five species range northward into the southwestern United States, while Bachman's Sparrow *(A. aestivalis)* is found exclusively in the Southeast. The North American *Aimophila* species are mostly brown or gray-brown, with relatively long bills and rounded tails that are long for their body size, which helps to separate them from other sparrows found in the same habitats. Some Mexican *Aimophila* species are much more strikingly plumaged—for example, the colorful Five-striped Sparrow *(A. quinquestriata),* which barely crosses the border into Arizona.

Several species of *Aimophila*—Cassin's *(A. cassinii),* Botteri's *(A. botterii),* and Bachman's Sparrows—have distinctive songs that are a greater aid in identification than plumage characteristics. These species are almost invisible in their dense

shrub- and grass-dominated habitats until the males begin singing their songs in flight or from conspicuous perches. In the Southwest, these displays are timed to begin with the summer monsoon rains.

Genus Spizella This group of small sparrows is distributed throughout North America. Members of the genus breed from the Arctic tundra (American Tree Sparrow, *S. arborea*) to the desert scrublands of the Mexican border region (Black-chinned Sparrow, *S. atrogularis*). *Spizella* sparrows have short, sharp-pointed bills and long, notched tails. Some species are well adapted to human-associated habitats—for example, the Chipping Sparrow *(S. passerina)*—and are familiar suburban birds. In winter, most *Spizella* sparrows form sizable single-species flocks that roam over large areas of fields or dry grasslands.

The northernmost breeding populations of Brewer's Sparrow are sometimes considered a separate species, the "Timberline Sparrow" *(S. "taverneri")*.

Genus Amphispiza This group of arid-habitat sparrows has two, three, or four species, depending on which taxonomy one uses (the AOU lists two). They have long tails, medium-size bills, and distinctive gray tones in their plumage. Some authorities advocate splitting the Sage Sparrow into two species: the "Sage Sparrow" *(A. "nevadensis"),* which breeds in the Great Basin Desert; and the darker,

"Timberline Sparrow." Spizella *sparrows typically form single-species flocks in winter. Some researchers consider the northern breeding populations of the Brewer's Sparrow to be a separate species, the "Timberline Sparrow." Its wintering range and habits are unknown.*

Desert, grassland, and woodland edge species. Amphispiza *sparrows (such as the Black-throated Sparrow, upper left) breed in deserts and arid shrublands, while* Ammodramus *sparrows (Nelson's Sharp-tailed Sparrow, upper right) are found in grasslands and saltmarshes. The* Melospiza *(Song Sparrow, below) and* Passerella *sparrows are more habitat generalists, although they are often found in woodland or wetland edges.*

more heavily marked "Bell's Sparrow" *(A. "bellii")* of southern California.

The Five-striped Sparrow has sometimes been included in *Amphispiza* because of its gray plumage, but it is better placed in the genus *Aimophila* because of its body shape and long bill.

Genera* Ammodramus *and* Passerculus *(Grassland Sparrows) The genus *Ammodramus* consists of seven short-tailed, flat-headed sparrows with rounded wings and large bills. These species and the Savannah Sparrow, the sole member of the genus *Passerculus,* are often found in the same open grassland habitats.

The basic shape of the *Ammodramus* sparrows separates them from most other sparrows, when one can get a good look at the birds. Unfortunately, all species in this group are skulkers, difficult to flush and difficult to follow, so getting a good look can be a problem. Many vocalizations in this group are insect-like.

The Savannah Sparrow is widespread and has many subspecies that reflect a good deal of geographic variation. It has a short tail but longer wings than most *Ammodramus.* One feature that helps separate the Savannah Sparrow from the other grassland sparrows, especially on the wintering grounds, is flushing behavior. Most *Ammodramus* sparrows wait to flush until a birder has almost stepped on them. They then fly a long distance and settle back down into the grass. Savannah Sparrows flush when an observer is farther away and are likely to settle in

shrubs or trees, or on fences, if available.

Several distinctive subspecies of the Savannah Sparrow can be found in coastal southern California, and at least one—the "Large-billed" Sparrow *(Passerculus sandwichensis rostratus)*—has been proposed as a separate species. The pale "Ipswich" Sparrow *(P. s. princeps)* of the northern Atlantic coastline was considered a separate species until the 1970s.

***Genera* Melospiza *and* Passerella** These two genera contain a small number of medium-size, long-tailed sparrows often found among shrubs or along forest or wetland edges. The Song Sparrow *(M. melodia),* one of the most familiar songbirds across much of North America, has been well studied by ecologists in many parts of its range. Beginning birders can improve their sparrow identification by becoming intimately familiar with the shape, behavior, songs, and calls of their local Song Sparrows. However, there is considerable geographic variation in size and plumage, with up to 31 described subspecies, providing the potential for confusion among traveling birders.

Lincoln's Sparrows *(M. lincolnii)* like to hide in dense brush piles, while Swamp Sparrows *(M. georgiana)* often winter in dense marsh vegetation, making both species hard to see. A peculiar blackish subspecies of the Swamp Sparrow *(M. g. nigricans)* breeds in the marshes of Delaware Bay and associated rivers. The winter range of this subspecies has not been found.

"Thick-billed"   "Slate-colored"

"Sooty"   "Red"

Fox Sparrow regional variation.
Ornithologists have long recognized the regional variation of Fox Sparrows and have subdivided the species into four main groups. Recent research on DNA and voice, alongside careful review of plumage and size data, has reinforced these distinctions, leading some ornithologists to suggest splitting the Fox Sparrow into four species, as shown. Still, these groups are very closely related, and more research is needed to clarify the situation.

The Fox Sparrow is currently placed in a separate genus *(Passerella)*, but it has been lumped into *Melospiza* at times. Some ornithologists propose splitting the Fox Sparrow into as many as four separate species: the "Slate-colored Fox-Sparrow" *(P. "schistacea")*, which lives in the mountains of western Canada and the United States; the "Red Fox-Sparrow" *(P. "iliaca")*, which breeds in eastern and northern Canada; the "Sooty Fox-Sparrow" *(P. "unalaschcensis")*, found in southeastern Alaska and coastal British Columbia; and the "Thick-billed Fox-Sparrow" *(P. "megarhyncha")*, which ranges from central California to northern Mexico and Arizona.

Genus Zonotrichia These four sparrows are found around shrubs and woodland edges, and are some of the largest emberizid species found in woodland habitats. White-throated Sparrows are among the most common migrant and wintering sparrows in eastern North America, while White-crowned Sparrows *(Z. leucophrys)* are among the most common migrants in the West. The Golden-crowned Sparrow *(Z. atricapilla)* and the Harris's Sparrow *(Z. querula)* have more limited distributions; both are considered exciting rarities when they are spotted in the East. *Zonotrichia* sparrows often join mixed-species flocks in the winter. They can be attracted to outdoor feeding stations but usually prefer to feed close to cover (within about 10'/3 m) and rarely use elevated feeders.

Genus **Junco** Juncos are grayish, medium-size sparrows with white outer tail feathers and often with white bellies. In the past there were up to six described species of juncos in North America. In the 1970s, however, all the junco populations with dark eyes were lumped into one species (the Dark-eyed Junco, *J. hyemalis*), leaving only the Yellow-eyed Junco *(J. phaeonotus)* of Arizona and Mexico as a separate species.

Juncos are familiar winter residents over much of northern North America. Many people call Dark-eyed Juncos "snowbirds," as the birds arrive with the start of winter in many areas. The Yellow-eyed Junco, found in the mountains of southeastern Arizona, can be so tame in winter that a bird looking for food may walk over a person's feet.

Genera **Calcarius** *and* **Plectrophenax** Most birders know the longspurs and the Snow Bunting only as birds that occupy open countryside during winter. These species are found in large flocks sweeping over agricultural fields, open rangeland, and other poorly vegetated habitats. They have long wings, short tails with distinctive color patterns, and pudgy bodies.

The four longspurs in the genus *Calcarius* often winter in flocks that can number in the hundreds of individuals and usually flush while observers are still far away. The flocks then sweep over large areas, repeatedly climbing into the sky and dropping low over the ground again. Eventually the flock will settle, sometimes close to its initial flushing point. Snow Buntings and McKay's Buntings *(Plectrophenax hyperboreus)* hybridize occasionally and are sometimes considered to be a single species.

Variation

Most emberizids undergo a typical songbird molt and plumage sequence. They change all their feathers during a prebasic molt in late summer and early fall, and most species molt some feather tracts in a prealternate molt in spring. This prealternate molt is not extensive enough to change the appearance of most species for the upcoming breeding season. Only a few sparrow species (for example, the longspurs and the Lark Bunting) change their appearance dramatically in the spring through a prealternate molt. At least nine species do not undergo a prealternate molt at all.

Overall there is little sexual dimorphism or age-related variation in most sparrows. Juveniles are often streaked, even in species whose adults do not have prominent breast streaking, and a few species have a distinctive first basic plumage (for example, the White-crowned Sparrow).

One species has a unique degree of morphological variation (at least among sparrows). The White-throated Sparrow has a plumage polymorphism—two forms (morphs) that interbreed and are found throughout the species' range. The "tan-

Arctic nesters. Some members of Calcarius *(such as the Lapland Longspur, left) and* Plectrophenax *(Snow Bunting, right) breed in high-Arctic tundra, while others breed in prairies. In winter, most of the Arctic-breeding species visit wide open countrysides farther south in North America.*

striped" morph is duller overall, with alternating tan and brown stripes on the crown, and dull yellow lores. The "white-striped" morph is brighter, with alternating white and black crown stripes and bright yellow lores. The variation is neither age- nor sex-related; instead, a simple genetic combination codes a bird's plumage into one of the two morphs. Breeding and genetic studies have shown that individuals tend to select mates of the other morph type, thus maintaining each plumage in the species.

Habitats

Emberizids are widespread, found in habitats as divergent as deserts, suburban backyards, and openings in conifer forests. They are often associated with habitats dominated by grass or shrubs. Few species are found in mature, closed-canopy forests. In fact, emberizids associated with forests are likely to be found in early successional woodlands or disturbed forest edges, rather than the interiors of mature forest patches.

Bachman's Sparrows, however, occupy old-growth forests of Longleaf Pine *(Pinus palustris)* in the southeastern United States. This is the classic case of the exception proving the rule: Old-growth Longleaf Pine forest has a diverse grass and forb community kept quite open (with few dense shrubs) by natural fires. Thus this forest has structural characteristics similar to those of edge or old-field habitats used by other sparrows.

White-throated Sparrow morphs. The brightly colored, "white-striped" morph of the White-throated Sparrow (left) is usually dominant over duller, "tan-striped" individuals (right) in winter flocks. This plumage variation is not related to age or sex.

For most emberizid species, habitat quality depends on three things: foraging resources, refuge from predators, and breeding locations. Foraging resources for most sparrows consist of insects in the soil, leaf litter, and low vegetation during summer, and seeds during winter, though a few species in the southwestern or southern United States, such as Abert's Towhee, feed on insects all year long.

Refuge from predators (mainly bird-hunting hawks and mammals) is provided by shrubs or deep grasses, to which sparrows flee when threatened. Cassin's, Bachman's, and Black-throated *(Amphispiza bilineata)* Sparrows have been observed fleeing predators by running into rodent burrows or other underground openings.

Breeding sites are usually small shrubs or the ground at the base of a shrub or grass clump. Some species show marked preferences in selecting their nest substrate. For example, Canyon Towhees in Arizona often place their nests in cholla cacti. In South Carolina, Bachman's Sparrows frequently place their nests at the base of a grass clump, often Broomsedge. No sparrow species uses a single type of nest site exclusively, however.

Food and Foraging

Emberizids eat insects and other invertebrates during the breeding season and seeds during the nonbreeding season. Different species found in the same area during the breeding season will have similar diets, as each species feeds on whatever insects are most common and easy to catch. During the winter, however, different species of emberizids specialize in particular seed types. Birds with small bills can pick up and husk small seeds most efficiently, while large-billed species can open larger seeds. Studies of the ecology of wintering sparrows have focused on how species divide the available seed resources so that different types of sparrows can coexist.

Both sparrow parents feed insects to their nestlings, unlike some of the finches, which feed seeds to their young. Nestlings and fledglings especially favor soft-bodied prey such as caterpillars. Large insects such as grasshoppers are often "prepared" by the parents, which remove difficult parts like legs before feeding the insects to their young. As young birds grow, they are given larger prey.

In winter, seeds are the predominant food for most emberizids. In selecting seeds, sparrows are limited by their ability to crack and remove a seed's outer husk. Small birds with small, pointed bills can rapidly husk small seeds with thin husks but are stymied by larger seeds, which large sparrows can use their heavier bills to crack open. A bird feeder filled with large sunflower seeds will therefore be used less by sparrows and more by larger birds, such as Northern Cardinals, or by birds with heavier bills, such as House Finches *(Carpodacus mexicanus)*. Millet is a preferred food in bird feeders because many sparrow species can husk this small, thin-coated seed.

The same holds true in more natural habitats. Areas dominated by plants that produce large seeds will support wintering large-billed emberizids. Habitats that contain only small-seeded plants will be used by species with smaller bills. A knowledge of local plants and the annual variation in wild food supply will help birders predict what emberizids might be found in a given area each winter.

Most species glean food items from the ground or pluck them from vegetation. They search for food in several ways. The most stereotyped of their techniques is the "double-scratch," in which the birds simultaneously rake the claws of both feet across the ground, pushing leaf litter to the side and digging into the upper surface of the soil. In deep litter, a series of kicks may be required to expose new material.

A scratching bird maneuvers to position its head directly over the area being scratched, so that the bird is ready to pounce on or pick up any food item

"Double-scratch" foraging.
The "double-scratch" method, demonstrated here by a male Eastern Towhee, is practiced by many of the larger sparrows. In one abrupt sequence, while the body remains relatively stationary, a slight hop allows the feet to reach far forward, then sweep backward, kicking debris out from underneath the bird to reveal food items, and just as quickly return forward to a normal standing position.

exposed at the end of each series of scratches. This foraging technique is distinctive, comparable to the bill-thrashing of many thrashers and the one-foot scratch employed by many quail species. With experience, birders can identify the rhythmic sound of a double-scratching emberizid by ear.

The double-scratching technique is often used by foraging towhees, Song Sparrows, and members of the genus *Zonotrichia*. Other species that are known to double-scratch at least occasionally include the Olive Sparrow *(Arremonops rufivirgatus)*, Vesper Sparrow *(Pooecetes gramineus)*, Seaside Sparrow, Savannah Sparrow, and American Tree Sparrow.

Not surprisingly for such a large family, emberizids use many other foraging techniques as well, and most species use several. Species that don't double-scratch will search in leaf litter with less rhythmic or stereotyped behaviors. Some sparrows, such as juncos, will climb into low vegetation and pluck food items from branches. Field Sparrows *(Spizella pusilla)*, juncos, and other small sparrows will fly up onto a tall grass stem, ride the stem down to the ground as it bends under the bird's weight, and then pluck seeds from the seed head as it sits on the ground.

The tiny White-collared Seedeater *(Sporophila torqueola)* climbs weed and grass stems and plucks seeds directly from the seed head. American Tree Sparrows and Snow Buntings have been recorded jumping against weed stems or beating them with their wings in flight,

then feeding on the seeds that have dropped to the ground below.

Breeding sparrows use some of the same techniques to find and capture soil invertebrates. Most species search the soil, leaf litter, and low vegetation for insects. The Savannah Sparrow and Lincoln's Sparrow forage for insects from the tips of shrub and tree branches, much like warblers. Lincoln's Sparrows have also been observed flycatching for moths, while Five-striped Sparrows will pick insects out of spider webs. Longspurs chase flushed insects across the ground, flying erratically on long flights low to the ground.

Anatomical and Physiological Adaptations

Small variations in bill and foot morphology are thought to be related to foraging adaptations of different sparrows. For instance, the Swamp Sparrow has a smaller bill but longer legs than the closely related Song Sparrow. The small bill is thought to be related to the Swamp Sparrow's greater dependence on insects in its diet, while the Song Sparrow's heavier bill is needed to husk seeds. The Swamp Sparrow's relatively long legs allow the bird to wade in shallow water.

Another example is the Seaside Sparrow, with its relatively long, slender bill and large feet for its body size. The long bill is useful for probing in damp mud, a foraging specialty of this species, while their large feet allow Seaside Sparrows to cross wet mud without sinking.

Dark-eyed Junco "riding" a grass stem. *An interesting foraging method practiced by some smaller sparrows is to fly up to a seed cluster atop a slender grass stem and "ride" it to the ground, where the weight of the bird holds the stem down while the bird picks off the seeds at leisure.*

Because sparrows shift their diet seasonally, their morphology must be generalized enough to handle both seeds and insects. While relatively few changes in overall morphology occur on a seasonal basis in sparrows, the anatomy of the digestive tract does change. The intestines of towhees studied in California lengthen in the nonbreeding season. Longer intestines mean that the birds retain food for a long time, an advantage when dealing with relatively hard-to-digest plant material, such as seeds.

One other seasonal morphological change is that the bills of some species, such as the Spotted Towhee, get shorter in winter than in summer. It is thought that the seed diet of towhees in winter requires that they eat more grit, and the combination of grit and hard seeds grinds down the bill to a shorter average length than found in the same birds in summer.

Seaside Sparrow adaptations. *Compared to other members of the genus* Ammodramus, *the Seaside Sparrow has large feet and a relatively long bill, traits that allow it to forage effectively in the mud of its saltmarsh habitat.*

While some sparrows routinely drink water, desert-dwelling species such as the Black-throated Sparrow can obtain the water they need from their diet. Insects are especially rich in water, but even dry-looking seeds contain enough water to support many birds. When additional water is needed, sparrows will drink dew or water from puddles, streams, and pond edges.

Behaviorial Adaptations: Flocking and Cover

Two major behavioral adaptations that vary among emberizids have evolved in response to the patchy and unpredictable distribution of food resources. If food is distributed unpredictably, a bird must spend most of its time searching for it. While searching, a bird is vulnerable to predation, especially by predators that rely on surprise (for example, *Accipiter* hawks).

One behavior emberizids use to solve the twin problems of finding food and avoiding predation involves looking for food close to "refuge cover," physical structures such as sheltering vegetation that provide protection from predators. In the second behavior, sparrows in winter often forage in flocks and use the combined vigilance of their flockmates to help spot predators.

The morphology of the bird, its typical habitat, and the distribution of food resources all combine to determine how much a given species uses either of these behaviors. Large emberizids with rounded wings, such as towhees, are not very agile fliers. Towhees therefore stay close to cover, rarely venturing far from a refuge. Towhees do not need to join large flocks, as they are usually in a protected area. They will forage with small numbers of other sparrows, though, when a flock moves into the towhees' foraging area.

Species such as White-throated, Song, and Swamp Sparrows are more agile than towhees. These species readily form small flocks, which allows them to search for food farther from cover than individual birds might risk. At least one member of a flock should see a predator from far enough away that the flock members are able to fly back to a refuge without being caught. This idea, the "many eyes" hypothesis, is often given to explain the evolutionary advantage of flocking.

Still other species have longer wings, a more powerful takeoff, and other morphological adaptations to increase agility that allow the birds to forage safely far from cover. Savannah Sparrows form flocks that feed in areas distant from any refuge. The longspurs and the Snow Bunting, perhaps the most extreme members of this behavioral group, form large flocks that stay in open areas far from cover.

Not all species find the same solutions to a given situation. A few, such as Grasshopper Sparrows *(Ammodramus savannarum)* and other *Ammodramus* sparrows, forage far from cover with Savannah Sparrows but are not as agile in escaping predation. They do not flock together but instead try to avoid capture by freezing on the ground, fleeing only if a predator comes very close.

Birders who understand the different strategies of flocking and foraging can use this information as an identification tool. Birds that flush to cover from the edge of a field are likely to be different species than birds that flush from the middle of the field.

As a birder moves across the middle of a large field, wintering Savannah Sparrows might flush in large numbers. A single bird that flushes differently, especially one that flushes unusually close by, might be a Le Conte's Sparrow *(Ammodramus leconteii)* or Baird's Sparrow *(A. bairdii)*. If a large number of sparrows flush at the same time, a practiced birder will scan the ground from which the flock left. A bird remaining while others flush might be using different escape rules, perhaps indicating it is a different species.

The refuge cover chosen by a fleeing bird can also be a good identification tip. Song and White-throated Sparrows typically dive into low shrubs at the edge of an open area. Vesper and Savannah Sparrows are more likely to perch high in their chosen refuge. In the southeastern United States, wintering Vesper Sparrows often flee to the highest available treetops and can be separated from Savannah Sparrows almost by that trait alone.

Some grassland sparrows avoid shrubby refuges and instead will dive back into grass patches when flushed. The first hint that you have found an *Ammodramus* sparrow can be when a bird flushes almost at your feet, flies for 300 feet (90 m) or so, and drops back down into the grass.

In the West, sparrows can also be separated in part based on their flocking and flushing behavior, and their use of cover. In Arizona, for instance, Canyon Towhees and Rufous-crowned Sparrows *(Aimophila ruficeps)* do not flock extensively and rarely move far from dense cover in arid grassland and desert edges. In the same habitats, White-crowned Sparrows form flocks and move farther from cover, although still staying reasonably close to shrubs. Where the two species overlap, Harris's Sparrows normally forage twice as far from cover as White-crowned Sparrows, but both species tend to stay within 25 feet (8 m) of cover.

Flocking sparrows often show strong dominance hierarchies. This is true both within and among species. Within single-species flocks, older males can often dominate younger males and females. Older females may dominate younger females. In the White-throated Sparrow,

Chipping Sparrow at nest.
Most sparrows build open-cup
nests, often placed in a shrub
or tree. The cup is neatly woven
from nonwoody vegetation and
is usually lined with finer
materials such as animal hair.

brightly colored white-striped individuals dominate tan-striped birds. In flocks composed of several species, dominance is often related to body size. Thus Eastern Towhees dominate White-throated and Song Sparrows, but both of the latter dominate Field Sparrows.

Studies with juncos show that dominant birds are able to gain access to resources whenever they want, while subordinate birds get supplanted by dominants and have their access to food limited. To gain adequate resources, subordinates must sometimes take greater risks—for instance, by returning first to an exposed feeding site after the flock has been flushed by a predator. In extreme cases, dominant birds drive subordinates from a flock, reducing flock size.

Birders can use a knowledge of dominance hierarchies. When a foraging flock is flushed, the first birds to return are often subordinates, and it is worth waiting to see what other species might appear. Dominant birds such as towhees, Fox Sparrows, and Golden-crowned Sparrows are often present in small numbers in the original flock and are usually slow to reappear.

Breeding

Most sparrows follow the stereotyped "typical songbird" pattern of breeding. Pairs appear monogamous and defend summer territories, in which they both forage and raise their young. Most territorial defense is done by the males, and song plays an important role in this defense. Females defend their territory from intruding females.

Females do the nest-building and typically all of the incubation, but both sexes feed the young. Females in some species, especially *Ammodramus* and *Aimophila* sparrows, do not flush from their nests until a predator (or birder) is extremely close. Broods of fledged young are sometimes split between a pair, with the male taking primary responsibility for some fledglings while the female cares for others. In some cases, males feed older fledglings while the female prepares to nest again.

Many sparrows in the southern United States have two or more broods per year. In most species, many nests are lost to predators, and pairs will nest repeatedly until they rear at least one brood to independence.

There are exceptions to all these generalizations, although strikingly different social systems such as cooperative breeding are unknown within the New World sparrows. Clay-colored Sparrows *(Spizella pallida)* defend normal territories at the start of the breeding season, but after the establishment of territory boundaries, pairs spend a lot of time foraging far from their territories. No overt acts of aggression occur when male Clay-colored Sparrows encounter each other away from breeding sites.

Some sparrows are polygynous, including Savannah and Saltmarsh Sharp-tailed Sparrows, Lark Buntings, and, on rare occasions, Lapland Longspurs (Calcarius lapponicus). A few males in populations of Swamp, Bachman's, and some other sparrows may be bigamous (the male is mated with two females at the same time). Generally the percentage of bigamous males in these species is less than 5 percent of a given population. Smith's Longspurs (Calcarius pictus) are polygynandrous (members of both sexes may have more than one mate).

One of the most unusual breeding systems among emberizids is found in the Saltmarsh Sharp-tailed Sparrow. In southern populations, males do not form pair bonds with females or defend classic territories. Instead males move throughout their home range, surveying the area from exposed perches and attempting to mate with any females they find. Several males may attempt to mate with a female at once, and a female may copulate with several males during a short period. Many matings are forced. This breeding strategy, which has been described as "scramble competition polygyny," is commonly found in nonterritorial animals such as frogs, but it is rare in birds. Scrambling for matings puts a premium on a male's ability to produce sperm, and male Saltmarsh Sharp-tailed Sparrows have enormous testes for their size.

Nelson's Sharp-tailed Sparrow, and perhaps northern populations of the Saltmarsh Sharp-tailed Sparrow, appear to have a more conventional polygynous breeding system, but breeding biology in these populations is not well known.

Even in species that appear to be strictly socially monogamous (that is, one male and one female defend a territory and cooperate to raise broods), genetic evidence is accumulating that many birds mate with more than one individual. In most cases, the evidence consists of offspring in the nest whose genetic composition indicates that the male defending the territory is not their father. This paternity evidence suggests that extra-pair copulations, in which the female mates with a male other than her mate, sometimes produce young.

Only a few genetic studies have investigated paternity patterns in sparrows. In the two largest studies, about a third of White-crowned Sparrow offspring and a fifth of Chestnut-collared Longspur (Calcarius ornatus) offspring were the result of extra-pair copulations. About 15 percent of male Field Sparrows in Pennsylvania were found to be attending offspring they had not sired. Most of these studies had small samples and were done in a limited area. This is a very active field of research, and many more studies will be published in the near future.

Vocalizations and Displays

Territorial males sing persistently from the beginning of the breeding season through various stages of nesting. Females of most species sing rarely, if ever. Sparrows use song both to deter intruding males from remaining in their territory and to attract females. Songs are produced at a much-reduced frequency in the nonbreeding season, although all Zonotrichia species, as well as Song, Fox, American Tree, and other sparrows will sing on bright sunny days in winter far from their breeding ranges.

The songs of the various races of the White-crowned Sparrow are particularly well studied, and much of what we know about song development, learning, and the physiology of song production comes from research on this species.

Some of the most spectacular songs are given by territorial males of several grassland species. Lacking tall perches to sing from, these males sing while in flight. McCown's Longspur (Calcarius mccownii) gives its flight song while floating down through the air on stiffly held wings, having climbed high to perform this display. The Chestnut-collared Longspur also sings while descending during a flight display but flaps its wings while floating down.

Many Aimophila and most Ammodramus species live in structurally simple habitats and can give their territorial songs while in flight. Grasshopper, Le Conte's, Seaside, and both Nelson's and

Saltmarsh Sharp-tailed Sparrows give flight songs while flying low (3–20'/1–6 m) over the ground. Cassin's and Botteri's Sparrows sing while flying between song perches in desert grasslands. Bachman's Sparrow often gives its typical territorial song from a perch but performs a more complex "excited song" while flying up to a high song perch. This second song type, more bubbly and longer than the typical song, is often given by agitated males.

Some emberizids give a relatively simple song, such as the string of chip notes produced by the Chipping Sparrow or the "hiccup" of Henslow's Sparrow *(Ammodramus henslowii)*. More complicated songs are produced by species such as Yellow-eyed Juncos, Song Sparrows, and Black-throated Sparrows, all of which sing relatively variable songs.

In addition, repertoire size (the number of different songs sung by each male) varies substantially among species. White-crowned Sparrows have several different song types, but each male sings only one or, rarely, two songs. Male Five-striped Sparrows have fairly simple songs, but each male has a very large repertoire; individuals have produced hundreds of different songs within a single observation period.

Most species also have an array of non-song vocalizations. Members of a pair will usually have a call note that helps each member of the pair locate the other or contact their young; for example, female Bachman's Sparrows give a rich, sweet call as they leave the nest.

Emberizids also have alarm calls that are more piercing and ventriloquial (presumably so that other sparrows are

Song Learning and Development

The normal development of song in male sparrows is fairly well known, based on intensive field and laboratory studies of White-crowned Sparrows. Juvenile males in this species learn songs not just from their fathers but also from other male White-crowned Sparrows in the general vicinity of the nest (the "aural environment").

The development of song passes through stages. At first, a general song model is memorized by a young male, who then practices singing it as he matures until he can copy the model. During this practice, he may add and later discard novel song elements. Several songs may emerge during this period of "plastic song," but eventually each male White-crowned Sparrow ends up with just one or, rarely, two songs in his repertoire. This song usually matches that sung by other males in the neighborhood.

The White-crowned Sparrow has dialects, specific songs shared by neighboring groups of territorial males. Incoming males learn an area's dialect by copying adjacent singing males. In this way, a dialect becomes a cultural trait that is passed down through generations of males in a given area. A male

whose territory straddles a border between dialects may become "bilingual," capable of singing a song type of both dialects.

Male White-crowned Sparrows use song to distinguish neighbors from strangers, and to distinguish different dialects, subspecies, and species. Dialects are also known in the Spotted Towhee (but not the Eastern Towhee), the Swamp and American Tree Sparrows, and the Snow Bunting.

White-crowned Sparrow singing

alerted without attracting potential predators to the call giver). This ventriloquial aspect is common in the alarm calls of many other species. Different species that flock together often give similar alarm calls.

One distinctive vocalization is the "squeal-duet" performed by members of the "brown towhee" complex (Canyon, Abert's, and California Towhees). The squeal-duet is a musical jumble of notes sung by members of a pair simultaneously. It helps to maintain the pair bond and informs a bird of its mate's location. Towhees that have been separated for any period of time will often perform the squeal-duet upon encountering each other anew. In desert washes in Arizona, squeal-duets by Canyon Towhees may be one of the most common vocalizations heard after the morning chorus is over.

Many of the typical (or "primary") songs given by male emberizids are used to defend the territory from other males. Males are strongly aroused by hearing an unfamiliar song and may approach the singer (or tape recorder) closely and display irritation at the intrusion. Another response is counter-singing, in which a territory holder flies to an exposed perch and matches the songs of a stranger phrase by phrase. Counter-singing is thought to send an "I'm here and I know you're there" message, which helps establish territory ownership and territorial boundaries without physical confrontation. Savannah and Bachman's Sparrows, among others, counter-sing as their primary response to unfamiliar song and therefore may not react aggressively to tape recordings.

Nests

Emberizids typically place their nests either on the ground at the base of a shrub or clump of grass, or in a shrub or short tree within 3 or 4 feet (about 1 m) of the ground. A few species, such as Abert's Towhee, will place a nest as high as 15 to 20 feet (5–6 m) above the ground. Most sparrows build open-cup nests made of grasses, weed stems, and other coarse,

nonwoody vegetation. The nests are lined with finer roots, grasses, and animal hair.

In a few species, the nests are domed over with grasses, creating an entrance hole on one side. In Bachman's Sparrow, the grasses of the dome are woven together with overhanging grasses, pine needles, or other living or dead vegetation, making the nest extremely hard to find.

Sparrows may take anywhere from two to 12 days to construct a nest (three or four days is common). Field Sparrows take five to eight days to build nests early in the summer, but only two or three days later in the breeding season. Nests are usually not reused, even by pairs attempting to raise more than one brood in a single summer.

Eggs

Sparrows usually lay clutches of three to five eggs, occasionally six or more. Clutches as large as nine eggs are known for Snow Buntings. The coloration of the eggs is variable. White, bluish, or tan are the usual background colors, and the eggs can be lightly or heavily blotched.

Eggs range in size from $\frac{2}{3} \times \frac{1}{2}$ inches (17×13 mm) for the White-collared Seedeater to $1 \times \frac{3}{4}$ inches (25×19 mm) for the California Towhee, and are subelliptical in shape. Females do all the incubation; they are fed or assisted by males in a few species. Incubation periods range from 11 to 14 days, although the incubation periods of the Rufous-crowned Sparrow and McKay's Bunting are not documented.

Young

New World sparrow chicks are altricial. Both adults feed and care for the young; most brooding is done by females. Fledging often occurs after nine to 12 days in undisturbed nests. The young will leave the nest at much earlier ages (for example, six days after hatching in the Lark Sparrow, *Chondestes grammacus*) if the nest is disturbed by a predator or a curious birder. This ability to leave the nest early is especially well developed in

Bachman's Sparrow nest. *Many sparrows nest on the ground, and several ground nesters weave a partial canopy of grasses and weeds over the nest to help conceal their offspring.*

Movements

Most sparrows are short-distance migrants or permanent residents. The migratory species tend to winter within the southern United States; thus few sparrows are true neotropical migrants.

Sparrows that breed in the far north, such as the American Tree and Harris's Sparrows and the Snow Bunting, migrate south to the northern United States. Species that breed in southern Canada or the northern United States often winter along the Gulf or Atlantic coasts of the southeastern United States (Henslow's Sparrow, for example) or in the arid Southwest (Brewer's and White-crowned Sparrows).

Birds that breed in the southwestern United States are often residents (for example, Black-throated Sparrows and Canyon Towhees). Montane species, such as the Yellow-eyed Junco, show elevational migration, moving downslope in the winter and returning to high elevations to breed.

In some species, breeding populations in the northern United States move south in the winter but are replaced by birds of the same species that bred farther north. Thus it may seem that a given species is resident throughout the year, but careful study of banded birds shows a turnover of individuals from season to season.

In western populations of the Chipping Sparrow and some other species, a form of facultative migration has been described. Sparrows that winter in the Southwest can be very common some years and absent in others. Migrating birds appear to move into southern Arizona and New Mexico and search for areas with a suitable food supply where they can settle for the winter. In years of good food production, large numbers of Chipping, Brewer's, Savannah, and Lark Sparrows and Dark-eyed Juncos will winter in a local area. In poorer years, these sparrow flocks continue south, eventually reaching reliable food supplies in northern Mexico. Because seed production is closely tied to

ground-nesting species, whose nests are attacked by a wide range of predators.

Because the young may have to make an early departure, the legs of ground-nesting species often develop faster than the wings, so that by nine days of age, the chick's legs have grown to adult size while its total body size, bill characteristics, and feathers are much less developed.

Immature Stages

Immature sparrows may depend on adults for up to 21 to 35 days after fledging. In small species, the period of dependence may be shorter (14 days), although few studies of fledgling biology have been conducted.

Studies of Yellow-eyed Juncos have shown that the young are most vulnerable at two stages after fledging. Many die in the first few days after leaving the nest, in part because they do not discriminate among approaching objects, even predators, when begging for food. The second period of vulnerability occurs in the first days after the adults stop feeding the young. At this time, the inexperienced birds die mostly from starvation. In some species, the young flock together for extended periods after attaining independence from their parents. First flight occurs at age eight to 14 days, often five days or more after fledging.

summer rainfall, the numbers of wintering migrant sparrows in Arizona can be predicted by the amount of rain during the previous summer's monsoons.

Banding studies have also shown that birds of different ages and sex may winter in different portions of their species' range. This phenomenon is best studied in the Dark-eyed Junco. Males winter farther north than females, and younger males winter farther north than older individuals. These patterns may result from the birds' need to strike a balance between surviving the winter and getting back to the breeding grounds in the spring. Birds wintering in the south are subjected to less stressful weather, but birds wintering farther north can return more quickly to the breeding grounds and may get the best territories.

Thus Dark-eyed Junco males need to risk the harsh winters in order to be closer to the breeding grounds and so winter farther north than females, who do not compete for territories and can take their time in returning. Young males winter the farthest north, perhaps because they have the most to gain from early arrival on the breeding grounds. Older, established males will almost always reclaim their old territories. Younger males, on the other hand, must work hard to claim a breeding spot. Early return gives these younger males an advantage over later arrivals.

Conservation

Many emberizids are of conservation concern, primarily because of habitat loss, especially grasslands and old fields.

Highly Specialized and Threatened Species

No emberizids are currently on the U.S. Endangered Species List throughout their entire range. Henslow's Sparrow is considered endangered in Canada.

Two subspecies are listed as endangered under the U.S. Endangered Species Act: the "Florida" Grasshopper Sparrow *(Ammodramus savannarum floridanus)* and the

Dark-eyed Junco flock dynamics. Male Dark-eyed Juncos of the eastern "slate-colored" race are dominant over females in winter flocks. Since subordinate birds have less access to food, females do not fare well in flocks composed of many males. Females therefore tend to winter farther south, away from most of the males, who stay farther north.

"Cape Sable" Seaside Sparrow *(A. maritimus mirabilis)*, both found in Florida. Two other subspecies are listed as threatened: the "San Clemente" Sage Sparrow *(Amphispiza belli clementeae)* and the "Inyo" California Towhee *(Pipilo crissalis inyoensis)*, both of California. Another subspecies, the "Dusky" Seaside Sparrow *(Ammodramus maritimus nigrescens)* of northern Florida, went extinct in the 1980s.

Three species—Henslow's, Baird's, and Bachman's Sparrows—have declined precipitously over much of their ranges and are listed as threatened or endangered by various state or regional authorities. These species are often considered "species of management concern" by land-management agencies.

Nineteen emberizid species are on the WatchList, including Abert's Towhee, McCown's and Smith's Longspurs, Bachman's, Rufous-winged *(Aimophila carpalis)*, and Henslow's Sparrows, and both Nelson's and Saltmarsh Sharp-tailed Sparrows. The number of emberizids on the WatchList indicates that extensive concern exists for North American sparrows, even though few populations are threatened enough to be placed on the U.S. Endangered Species List. Sparrows make up 18 percent of all species included on the WatchList, despite the fact that the family Emberizidae includes only about 7 percent of North American birds.

Recent Trends in Populations

Analysis of population trends in Breeding Bird Survey data confirms that emberizids in general are declining. Thirty-three species were recorded on enough Breeding Bird Survey routes from 1967 to 1999 for their population dynamics to be analyzed. Of these, 17 species show significant declines throughout their North American ranges, and an additional six species show regional declines. Only two of the 33 species—Lincoln's and Swamp Sparrows—increased significantly.

The strongest decline is shown by Henslow's Sparrow (7.7 percent population decline per year from 1967 to 1999). Species declining more than 3 percent per year include Bachman's, Brewer's, Field, Grasshopper, Black-throated, and Lark Sparrows. Many species show complex patterns of population change. Song Sparrows, for instance, increased significantly in eight states and provinces, decreased in 13, and remained stable in 17 others.

Several of the 8 species that show no strong pattern of population change during the Breeding Bird Survey analysis period are on the WatchList because of threats to their habitats rather than population declines. These include Abert's Towhee, McCown's Longspur, and Baird's, Sage, and Nelson's Sharp-tailed Sparrows.

Henslow's Sparrow. As much as 30 percent of the known world population of Henslow's Sparrows may now be found in southern Indiana, in restored grasslands covering abandoned surface coal mines and former military bases.

Reasons for Changes

As is true of most declining species in North America, the primary cause of emberizid population decline is habitat loss. The grassland species, in particular, have suffered from the widespread conversion of their habitats to agriculture and to housing developments. Grassland specialists such as Cassin's and Grasshopper Sparrows are declining, as are species that use shrub grasslands, such as the Lark and Brewer's Sparrows.

Bachman's Sparrow was associated with old-growth Longleaf Pine forests across the southern United States. The harvest of more than 90 percent of this habitat has greatly reduced this species.

On the other hand, cutting of older forests has created habitat for various early-succession species in forest lands. Green-tailed Towhees and Dark-eyed Juncos are often cited as beneficiaries of timber cutting in the West.

Many common emberizids in the East are associated with early successional habitat stages, such as old fields or young forests. Although still reasonably common, many of these species are declining as their habitats mature. Modern agriculture has eliminated tree lines and fence rows from much of the agricultural Midwest, while urbanization has paved over pockets of unused land near towns and cities.

In much of the northeastern and southern United States, a wave of farm abandonment in the early 1900s created early successional habitat suitable for some species of birds. These lands have now passed on into later successional stages. Both conversion of habitat to other uses and forest succession have been suggested as reasons for declines in such sparrow species as the Field Sparrow and the Eastern Towhee. The latter species was recently identified as having one of the sharpest population declines of any eastern bird.

In western North America, numerous factors affect native bird habitats. One of the most important is grazing policy. Overgrazing of public rangelands results in decreased breeding success in many grassland species, including emberizids. Trampling of riparian vegetation by cattle further reduces habitat quality for shrubland species. Grazing has been strongly associated with the population decline of McCown's Longspur, among other species, and could be a threat to Abert's Towhee, a riparian specialist.

Sparrows are less affected by habitat destruction in the neotropics, as relatively few species migrate to areas south of the United States. However, land use in the Mexican border states has the potential to impact sparrows that breed or winter in that region. The rare White-collared Seedeater has declined strongly in Texas since the 1930s, probably due to both land conversion for agriculture in Texas and population decreases farther south, in the heart of its range.

Many emberizids accept the eggs of both Brown-headed *(Molothrus ater)* and Bronzed *(M. aeneus)* Cowbirds, and some local populations are heavily parasitized. For instance, the Olive Sparrow has one of the highest rates of parasitism by Bronzed Cowbirds recorded for any host species in southern Texas. Song and Chipping Sparrows are also commonly parasitized. This has not been cited as a major factor in population declines, however.

Larger species such as towhees accept eggs but are poor hosts because their large young can outcompete the smaller cowbird nestlings. Smaller hosts are more likely to raise cowbird young to fledging. Field and Clay-colored Sparrows often desert parasitized nests. Parasitism rates are low in *Aimophila* and *Ammodramus* sparrows, perhaps because of the birds' cryptic nest placement.

Possible Actions to Reverse Declines

Merritt Island National Wildlife Refuge in Florida was created to protect the "Dusky" Seaside Sparrow, but this action proved insufficient. Management of water levels within the refuge to reduce mosquito numbers drowned the sparrows' nests for several breeding seasons

in a row. By the time this problem was discovered, only six male "Dusky" Seaside Sparrows remained. The last confirmed record of this subspecies in the wild was from Florida in 1980.

Federal government properties within the range of the "Florida" Grasshopper Sparrow that include grassland habitat are managed in part to protect this endangered subspecies. These properties include military bases, where habitat is maintained in good condition by regular burning around firing ranges.

The "Cape Sable" Seaside Sparrow is found in two regions of the Everglades near Shark River Slough. This subspecies has declined by more than 50 percent since 1992. Reproduction by "Cape Sable" Seaside Sparrows is limited by the onset of the summer rains, which raise water levels and flood nests. Long-term changes in water levels and the frequency of fires within Everglades National Park also affect the population's dynamics, but these influences are poorly understood. Management policies of Everglades National Park, especially manipulations of water depth in sparrow habitat, are designed in part to accommodate this endangered subspecies. Additional land purchases in the East Everglades area are being pursued to help protect the bird.

"Dusky" Seaside Sparrow. This very distinctive subspecies, at times considered a full species, disappeared with very little warning after its Atlantic coast marsh habitat was altered by mosquito control efforts.

A recovery plan for the "San Clemente" Sage Sparrow, restricted to San Clemente Island, California, was begun in 1984. The plan emphasizes the removal of feral pigs, goats, and other grazing animals from the island, as well as control of the erosion and the exotic plants associated with overgrazing. With these actions, which are continuing, Sage Sparrow numbers on the island have stabilized.

Other sparrows are the subject of regional management action. Breeding populations of Henslow's Sparrow are often protected in the Midwest and Northeast. Research on how Bachman's Sparrows are affected by timber management in the southeastern United States is a priority of the U.S. Forest Service. Typically little management is done to protect habitat on the wintering range of most species, although loss of early successional or grassland habitat on their wintering grounds may be acutely disruptive for many species.

Accidental Species

Two species of grassquits have been recorded in North America. The Yellow-faced Grassquit *(Tiaris olivacea)* is a variable species found from Mexico to northern South America, and in the Caribbean. It has been recorded in Florida in April and July (presumably the West Indian subspecies) and in southeastern Texas in January (presumably the Mexican subspecies). The Black-faced Grassquit *(T. bicolor)* of the West Indies has been found in Florida, mainly from December to mid-April.

Both grassquit species, the White-collared Seedeater, and related species are routinely kept in captivity in Latin America, and some captive individuals may be imported illegally into North America.

Occurrences of these species in North America must be assessed skeptically if the birds are found at locations or during seasons that are inconsistent with the species' natural range. Several Florida records of the Cuban Grassquit *(Tiaris canora)* may be of escapees, or they may be of natural wanderers from Cuba or from the Bahamas, where this species has been introduced.

There is one old record of Worthen's Sparrow *(Spizella wortheni)* from New Mexico in 1884. Worthen's Sparrow, a gray version of the Field Sparrow, is rarely seen even within its range in arid northeastern Mexico and seems an unlikely candidate for additional visits north of the border.

In addition to the Rustic Bunting, seven species of the Old World genus *Emberiza* have been found in North America, primarily in the Aleutian Islands and western Alaska. Most of these species are very rare in the New World, with fewer than ten records apiece.

Accidentals recorded in Alaska include the Pine Bunting *(Emberiza leucocephalos)*, Little Bunting *(E. pusilla)*, Yellow-breasted Bunting *(E. aureola)*, Gray Bunting *(E. variabilis)*, Pallas's Bunting *(E. pallasi)*, Yellow-throated Bunting *(E. elegans)*, and Reed Bunting *(E. schoeniclus)*. The Little Bunting has also been recorded once in California. All of these species breed in eastern Asia, and most winter in southeast Asia or India. Most have appeared in spring (May to June), presumably as migrants that overshot their normal breeding grounds or were blown off course by spring storms.

The Red-crested Cardinal *(Paroaria coronata)* is native to South America and has escaped from captivity in California and southern Florida. It is not considered fully established in either area.

John B. Dunning, Jr.

Cardinals and Allies

Family Cardinalidae
Order Passeriformes

Members of the family Cardinalidae are medium-size to large song-birds of open habitats and woodland edges. Males and females are often strikingly different; the males of certain species exhibit some of the most beautiful and colorful plumages found among North American birds. Females are more cryptic. The bills of cardinalids are robust and conical for eating seeds in the nonbreeding season. Cardinalids typically inhabit early successional scrub and forest edges; some species also occur in deserts and agricultural areas.

Taxonomy

The most closely related families to car-dinalids are tanagers and New World sparrows; less closely related are the wood-warblers and the blackbirds and orioles. These families all belong to the New World nine-primaried oscines group.

The Cardinalidae includes several groups that are most easily distinguished by their bill sizes. Two large-billed groups are the cardinals (genus *Cardinalis*) and the grosbeaks (genus *Pheucticus*). The most common small-billed group within the family is the buntings (genus *Passerina*). One species that upsets this simple pattern is the Blue Grosbeak *(Guiraca caerulea)*, which is most closely related to the buntings but has a relatively large bill. Birders should also be aware that birds in other families have similar-sounding names, such as the Evening Grosbeak *(Coccothraustes vespertinus)*, which is a finch, and the Lark Bunting *(Calamospiza melanocorys)*, a New World sparrow.

The most divergent species within the family is the sparrow-like Dickcissel *(Spiza americana)*. Some taxonomies placed the Dickcissel with the blackbirds, but genetic studies confirm that it is a cardinalid, closely related to the *Passerina* buntings and their relatives.

Genetic studies completed in the late 1990s show that the taxonomy of the Cardinalidae is far from simple. This research suggests that three genera—*Chlorothraupis*, *Habia*, and *Piranga*—that are currently placed within the tanagers in fact belong to the Cardinalidae. The first two genera are South American tan-agers that are relatively poorly known. *Piranga*, however, includes the familiar tanagers that breed in North America, such as the Scarlet Tanager *(P. olivacea)*. These species are similar in morphology and ecology to the rest of the tanager family. If the genetic evidence is correct and *Piranga* tanagers are more properly linked to the cardinalids, then their similarity to tanagers must be due to convergence.

Cardinalid diversity. *The North American cardinalids can be subdivided into three main groups: the cardinals, in the genus* Cardinalis, *which are large-billed, long-tailed, and crested (represented here by the Pyrrhuloxia, left); the grosbeaks, in the genus* Pheucticus, *which are large-billed and short-tailed (Rose-breasted Grosbeak, second from left), and the buntings, in the genus* Passerina, *which are small-billed and short-tailed (Lazuli Bunting, third from left). The Dickcissel (right) is an aberrant species whose placement has long been debated, but all recent evidence points to a close relationship to the other cardinalids.*

Similarly, some Latin American genera currently placed with the cardinalids probably do not belong in that family, such as *Saltator* and *Porphyrospiza*, which are found from Mexico to South America and in the Lesser Antilles. The same genetic studies indicate that these genera probably belong with the tanagers, again suggesting that their morphological similarity to the cardinals and buntings is a result of convergence. As this guide follows the seventh edition of the AOU classification, which was published prior to the genetic studies referred to above, readers should consult the Tanagers chapter for information on the North American tanagers. However, the placement of these species could move in the future as the new research is assessed.

Cardinals and tanagers. Ornithologists have always acknowledged a close relationship among all nine-primaried oscines (mainly the wood-warblers, tanagers, cardinals, New World sparrows, and blackbirds and orioles) and are sometimes forced into some rather arbitrary decisions about familial relationships. Recent evidence shows that certain tanagers, including those in the genus Piranga *(for example, the Hepatic Tanager,* Piranga flava, *left), are more closely related to cardinalids, such as the Varied Bunting (right), than to other tanagers; this genus may be shifted to the family Cardinalidae in the future.*

Subspecies
Some cardinalid species vary considerably in size and plumage color both within and among populations, while others do not. The Northern Cardinal *(Cardinalis cardinalis)*, the Blue Grosbeak, and the Yellow Grosbeak *(Pheucticus chrysopeplus)* of Central and South America are each classified into as many as 17 subspecies, with extensive intraspecific variation in morphology and plumage color.

Worldwide Family Features

- 4½–11" (11–28 cm) songbirds of scrub, woodland, open areas.
- About 43 species in 12 genera; occur only in New World. 13 species in 7 genera occur in North America; found across continent from central Canada south to Mexico.
- Eat seeds, grains, fruit, insects, flower buds, blossoms. Glean food from ground, low shrubs and trees.
- Territorial during breeding season. Mainly monogamous; pair bonds seasonal in migratory species, may be year-round in permanent residents. In some species, some males are simultaneously or sequentially polygynous. Extra-pair copulations noted in some species. All North American species migratory, except Northern Cardinal and Pyrrhuloxia; most tropical species nonmigratory.
- Breed first at 1 year old; males in species with delayed plumage maturation attempt to breed at 1 year old, but are usually less successful than older males.

- Open-cup nest, usually 1½–20' (50 cm–6 m), with most 3–10' (1–3 m), above ground. Made mainly of grasses, stems, leaves; lined with finer grasses, animal hair. Some species use twigs, coarse grasses, bark in outer cup. Female builds nest; in some species, male may help. Do not reuse nests.
- Usually 3 or 4 (rarely 2) subelliptical to oval eggs; pale bluish- to greenish-white, sometimes with brownish or reddish spots. Usually female incubates (sometimes both sexes), for 11–14 days. Hatching usually synchronous but may take up to 48 hours. Most North American species have 1 or 2 broods, rarely 3.
- Altricial young hatch naked except for down that varies from white to shades of gray. Fledge at 9–13 days. Both sexes feed young; in a few species, male feeds young after fledging.
- Adult annual survival about 50–75%. Among oldest on record: 15 years, 9 months (Northern Cardinal).

In addition, during the breeding season two cardinalid species are each distributed into two separate breeding populations. Painted Buntings *(Passerina ciris)* are divided into an eastern population that breeds along the Atlantic coast from southern North Carolina to north-central Florida and a western population that breeds from southwestern Louisiana west through Texas and northern Tamaulipas, Mexico, and north through central Kansas. Varied Buntings *(P. versicolor)* breed in southwestern Texas and southern Arizona through much of Mexico to northern Guatemala, and they also have a separate breeding population on the southern tip of Baja California.

Both of these species show significant variation between their disjunct breeding populations, especially the Varied Bunting, which differs dramatically in size and plumage color. Indeed, there are arguments for splitting each of these two species into two separate species. There are no molecular genetic data that compare these populations yet. Rather, the separation is suggested by differences in morphology, as well as differences in behavior, such as the timing and location of migration in Painted Buntings (see Movements, below).

Variation

Like many tanagers and wood-warblers, all North American cardinalids are strongly sexually dimorphic in adult plumage color during the breeding season; females typically are much duller and more cryptically colored. Many male cardinalids change plumage color seasonally, becoming more cryptic and female-like in color in the nonbreeding season. Cardinalids are also somewhat sexually dimorphic in body size. The polygynous Dickcissel is the champion in this regard; males are 30 percent heavier than females.

Cardinalids are unusual among birds in that males of all North American species except the Northern Cardinal and Pyrrhuloxia *(Cardinalis sinuatus)* exhibit delayed plumage maturation: They do not acquire their full adult plumage by their first potential breeding season (at about 10 to 12 months of age). In these species, most one-year-old males wear plumages that can range from completely female-like—for example, the Painted and Varied Buntings—to intermediate between male and female, as in the Indigo Bunting *(Passerina cyanea)* and the Black-headed Grosbeak *(Pheucticus melano-*

Complex Molt Cycle

The Indigo Bunting and some other species of cardinalids undergo a complex molt cycle involving four separate generations of body feathers in the first year. Birds fledge wearing juvenal plumage, which is quickly replaced by a similar supplemental plumage. This is replaced again during the fall by the first basic plumage, and again the following spring by the first alternate plumage. Adults undergo a more normal two-molt cycle, with a complete molt to basic plumage in late summer, and a partial molt to alternate plumage in spring. These illustrations show a young male Indigo Bunting before (left) and after (right) the first prebasic molt in the first fall. In this molt birds acquire new body feathers similar to those of adult males, and

new inner secondaries and outer primaries with blue edges. Another body molt in spring (first prealternate molt) gives rise to the first alternate plumage, which typically is intermediate between that of adult females and males except for the retained brown inner primaries.

Delayed plumage maturation. Many male cardinalids exhibit delayed plumage maturation; that is, males in their first breeding season do not acquire the bright colors they will show in subsequent years. The male Painted Bunting is essentially female-like in its first breeding season, as shown here.

cephalus). These males are often capable of breeding but are less successful at attracting mates than older males, presumably because females prefer older males.

Another distinctive characteristic of most cardinalids (exceptions include the Dickcissel and *Pheucticus* species) is that young birds undergo two molts during their first summer and fall after fledging instead of the more usual single molt. During the first, the presupplemental molt, which typically begins a few days after fledging, they replace most or all of their body plumage but do not change plumage color very significantly.

Food and Foraging

Cardinalids eat insects, seeds and grains, fruit, and, to a minor extent, flower buds and blossoms. Temperate species eat mainly seeds and grains during the non-breeding season and insects and fruit during the breeding season, while sub-tropical and tropical species generally eat more insects and fruit. All species feed their young only insects.

Cardinalids usually forage alone, on or within a few yards of the ground. They may, however, occasionally forage at considerable heights on tree buds, blossoms, and fruit; migrating Rose-breasted *(Pheucticus ludovicianus)* and Black-headed Grosbeaks will forage high in flowering

trees to feed on buds in the spring. During the nonbreeding season, many species forage in flocks ranging from a few individuals to hundreds, or even thousands in the case of the Dickcissel.

Many species also visit feeders—for example, Painted and Indigo Buntings in southern Florida during the winter, the Rose-breasted Grosbeak during spring migration, and the Black-headed Grosbeak during the breeding season.

Breeding

Except for the polygynous Dickcissel, cardinalids are primarily monogamous. This is notable because many other passerines with delayed plumage maturation employ other breeding strategies. For example, various blackbirds are polygynous and often breed colonially.

Besides the Dickcissel, the only other exceptions to strict monogamy in cardinalids are the Indigo, Lazuli *(Passerina amoena),* and Painted Buntings. In these species, polygyny has been reported for 5 to 35 percent of males. DNA fingerprinting indicates that in Indigo Buntings, 35 percent of clutches contain at least one hatchling produced through extra-pair copulation; this amounts to about 13 percent of all offspring. Extra-pair copulations have been observed in other

Cardinalid head and bill. The cardinalids are all seed-eating birds, and a few species (such as the Northern Cardinal, shown here) have evolved very stout, conical bills with strong jaw muscles capable of cracking the hardest seeds.

Passerina buntings as well, but paternity has not been verified through genetic studies.

Vocalizations and Displays

The vocal behavior of cardinalids is unusual in at least two respects. First, in the huge majority of passerines, only males sing. However, females of at least three cardinalid species—the Northern Cardinal, Pyrrhuloxia, and Black-headed Grosbeak—sing regularly, although typically less frequently than males and at a lower volume.

Second, Indigo and Lazuli Buntings, and possibly other cardinalids, exhibit "song-matching," which means they do not learn their songs in the nest. Instead, when one-year-old males return to the breeding grounds to attempt breeding for the first time, they learn their songs from older males occupying neighboring territories. Most males retain these songs, which bear no resemblance to those of their fathers, for life.

Eggs

Cardinalid eggs vary in color and pattern from unmarked to spotted. The Varied Bunting is unique among cardinalids in that its eggs are dimorphic in color: Eggs verified to be from Arizona are lightly spotted (contrary to what is written in field guides), while eggs verified from western Texas are unspotted and indistinguishable from the eggs of Lazuli and Indigo Buntings. However, museum collections contain both spotted and unspotted Varied Bunting eggs from throughout the species' range, including Texas and Arizona, indicating either that some museum specimens are mislabeled or that some Texas populations have spotted eggs while some Arizona populations have unspotted eggs.

Movements

While a few species are nonmigratory (for example, those in the genus *Cardinalis*), most cardinalids are neotropical migrants.

A few cardinalids undergo so-called molt-migration. They do not molt their flight feathers on the breeding ground or wintering ground; instead, they stop at an area along their migratory route for a month or so in order to molt these feathers, then continue to the wintering area. For example, the western population of Painted Buntings undergoes its annual flight-feather molt at stopover sites, mainly in southern Arizona and northwestern Mexico. In contrast, the eastern population molts on its breeding ground before migration. The reason for this difference in migration strategies is not well understood, but it probably has to do with differences in food availability on the western versus the eastern breeding grounds at the time of molt.

Movements of a different kind have brought some rare species into the southern United States. The Blue Bunting (*Cyanocompsa parellina*) is a casual winter visitor to the lower Rio Grande Valley of Texas, and there is one record from

Movements. *The two disjunct populations of Painted Bunting differ dramatically in their migration. In the map above breeding grounds are shown in orange, migration areas are yellow, and wintering grounds are blue. Eastern birds winter in southern Florida, the Caribbean, and southern Central America. Western birds, in contrast, migrate to northwestern Mexico in late summer where they undergo a molt to basic plumage, then migrate south in the fall to wintering grounds in southern Mexico. A similar molt-migration to spend the late summer in northwestern Mexico has been documented in Bullock's Oriole (Icterus bullockii) and other species; the region must provide abundant food and a benign climate at a time of year when these species are molting.*

Louisiana. Its visits have become more frequent in recent years, perhaps in response to large-scale habitat losses in northeastern Mexico. The Crimson-collared Grosbeak *(Rhodothraupis celaeno)* is also a casual visitor to southern Texas from northern Mexico. Both these species may wander north in response to poor habitat conditions in their normal ranges.

Some cardinalids move in irruptions when their habitat is under stress. In drought years, and presumably in years when food is scarce, Dickcissels wander widely outside their breeding range. In the summer of 1988, for example, many congregated on the coastal plain of South Carolina and Georgia, presumably in search of food.

Conservation

Most cardinalids have stable populations, while some are experiencing noticeable changes in either population trends or ranges. Interestingly, several species are both declining in much of their traditional range and expanding in other areas. Two species, the Dickcissel and the Painted Bunting, are included on the WatchList.

In the 1800s Dickcissels were common breeders along the East Coast of North America from the Carolinas to Massachusetts, but for unknown reasons they disappeared almost entirely from this region after 1900. During the 1900s they greatly extended their range in the Midwest, perhaps because of beneficial changes caused by human development and agriculture. They are still common in the core of their range from Texas north through the Great Plains but are declining in many areas within this core range. Breeding Bird Survey data show significant declines in many states and in the central United States as a whole. Dickcissels are on the WatchList because of these declines and because they are persecuted as an agricultural pest on their wintering grounds in South America, where huge flocks of Dickcissels can strip fields bare of grain.

The Painted Bunting is the other cardinalid on the WatchList. Data from Breeding Bird Surveys indicate that both breeding populations of this species are declining significantly. The entire breeding range of the eastern population is relatively small and confined to coastal and riparian areas that are under extreme pressure from human development. In addition, the parasitic Brown-headed Cowbird *(Molothrus ater)* has expanded its range into the southeastern scrub habitat that is preferred by Painted Buntings. Eastern Painted Buntings have no adaptations to recognize or respond to cowbird parasitism. Western birds have coexisted with cowbirds for thousands of years. Thus it is not surprising that eastern Painted Buntings suffer brood parasitism rates as high as 80 percent, while western buntings are parasitized less.

In the 1990s, Shiny Cowbirds *(Molothrus bonariensis)* also expanded their range from South America and the Caribbean into the southeastern United States. To date, there are no records of the Shiny Cowbird parasitizing Painted Buntings, but it may pose a threat in the future if this species becomes fully established in North America.

Other cardinalid species also show complex patterns of population change but are not in as precarious a position as the Dickcissel and the Painted Bunting. Blue Grosbeaks are increasing slightly throughout most of their range, and they have expanded recently in New Jersey, Ohio, and North Dakota. Indigo Buntings are declining continent-wide according to Breeding Bird Surveys and show especially strong declines in Florida, South Carolina, and parts of the Midwest and New England. On the other hand, Indigo Buntings have increased their breeding range in Arizona and New Mexico. Where they now overlap in range, Indigos hybridize with Lazuli Buntings in the Great Plains, California, Colorado, and other areas.

Christopher W. Thompson

Blackbirds, Orioles, and Allies

Family Icteridae
Order Passeriformes

Icterids are medium-size to large songbirds. Many species are entirely black with noticeable iridescence; some have bright red or yellow markings. A distinct subgroup, the orioles, is composed of species that are largely yellow or orange with black and white markings. Perhaps the most distinctive trait of icterids is their strong, straight, pointed bill. Members of the family live in open habitats, ranging from grasslands and marshes to urban parks and agricultural fields. A few species are associated with open forests or forest edges, and sometimes with deep forest, especially if swamps are present. Perhaps more than any other family of North American birds, this group has adapted very well to human-altered habitats.

Taxonomy

The icterids belong to the New World nine-primaried oscines, a group of songbirds thought to be of relatively recent origin and found mainly in the Americas. Other families in this group include the cardinals, tanagers, New World sparrows, and wood-warblers. As the name of the group implies, these birds have only nine functional primaries, not 10, like most other songbirds. Until recently, these families were classed as subfamilies of the family Emberizidae, but their status as separate families has been reinstated. The relationships between the families are not clearly understood.

Within the icterids there are five major divisions, based on DNA-sequence data. North American icterids fall into three of these five groups: the orioles; the meadowlarks and their allies, including the Bobolink *(Dolichonyx oryzivorus)* and the Yellow-headed Blackbird *(Xanthocephalus xanthocephalus)*; and the grackles, blackbirds, and their allies, including the cowbirds.

The orioles, the most colorful group within the Icteridae, have extensive orange, yellow, and black markings. Female North American orioles tend to be much duller than males, but this is not true in the tropics. In North American orioles that are mostly tropical in range—such as the established exotic Spot-breasted Oriole *(Icterus pectoralis)* and the native Altamira Oriole *(I. gularis)* and Audubon's Oriole *(I. graduacauda)*—the female is largely indistinguishable from the male in plumage. Female Baltimore Orioles *(I. galbula)* are exceedingly variable, and some are almost as brightly colored as males. In general, immature male orioles look very similar to adult females but

Icterid diversity. North American icterids fall into three main groups. Orioles (represented here by Scott's Oriole, left) are boldly marked with black and orange or yellow plumage and have a sharply pointed bill. The meadowlarks (Eastern Meadowlark, center) are cryptically colored with a mixture of browns, tan, black, and yellow, and have a long, straight bill and a short tail; recent genetic studies suggest that the distinctive Bobolink and Yellow-headed Blackbird should be placed in this group. The remaining species are predominantly black or dark brown, are gregarious, and have straight, pointed bills (Red-winged Blackbird, right).

they usually have more black on the face, head, and back than females.

The meadowlarks are yellow below with a bold black V on the breast but have streaks and intricate patterns on their upperparts for camouflage. Breeding male Bobolinks are striking black, white, and gray birds, while females are small, brown, and streaked much like a sparrow. Bobolink males lose their bright plumage in the nonbreeding season and develop a female-like plumage. The scientific name of the Western Meadowlark, *Sturnella neglecta,* stems from the bird being originally overlooked as a separate species due to its similarity to the Eastern Meadowlark *(S. magna).* The Arizona subspecies of Eastern Meadowlark has been proposed as a separate species—"Lilian's Meadowlark." This subspecies differs from the eastern subspecies in plumage and habitat but not in vocalizations.

The Baltimore and Bullock's Orioles *(Icterus bullockii)* were considered a single species, the "Northern Oriole," based on hybridization between the two forms where their ranges met in the Great Plains. Further analysis of the species'

Great Plains populations determined that the extent of the hybridization was not increasing over time and thus was not evidence that the two forms were merging. Recent genetic studies have suggested that Bullock's and Baltimore Orioles are not even each other's closest relatives.

Variation

Most North American male icterids are largely black, with a few species showing bright red or yellow "flash colors" on the wings (called "epaulets") or the head. In many cases black icterids sport beautiful iridescence, which can be appreciated only at close quarters and in good light. Most females of these black icterid species are brownish or brownish-black and are sometimes streaked like a sparrow.

In general, icterid molts are similar to those of most other songbirds. After breeding, the feathers are replaced in a prebasic molt. Most icterids do not have a prealternate molt in the late winter or spring that brings them into a "breeding" plumage. Instead, changes between winter and breeding appearances occur

Worldwide Family Features

- 6–18" (15–45 cm) open-country, marsh, and open-forest songbirds.
- About 103 species in 24 genera worldwide, found only in Americas. 23 species in 8 genera regularly recorded in North America, including 1 established exotic; found throughout North America except for alpine and Arctic tundra; plus 2 accidental species.
- Eat mostly insects when breeding, fruit and grains when not. Some species entirely insectivorous; others also consume nectar.
- May be strongly territorial; some species colonial; many flock in nonbreeding and sometimes breeding season. Very diverse mating systems: Many polygynous species; extra-pair fertilizations well documented; some species monogamous. Northern species migratory.
- In most species, females breed first at 1 year old, males at 2 years old or later.
- Bulky cup nests made of soft vegetative material, placed on ground, in aquatic

vegetation, or in trees. Orioles weave pendant, basket-shaped nests. Female usually builds nest; in some species, male may help. Do not reuse nests. Brood-parasitic cowbirds do not make nests.
- Usually 4 or 5 eggs, but cowbirds may lay more than 40. Shape variable, ranges from long elliptical to short oval. Coloring ranges from white to blue; usually strongly spotted or speckled; typically have bold dark scrawls, often on wide end. Female incubates, for 10–16 days. Hatching synchronous or asynchronous. Usually 1 or 2 (sometimes 3) broods per year.
- Altricial young have sparse buffy or gray down at hatch; fledge at 8–17 days. Parental care by one or both sexes, depending on mating system and nesting stage.
- Adult annual survival 34–86%. Among oldest on record: 20 years, 11 months (Common Grackle).

Icterid feather wear. Most icterids molt their feathers only once a year, and seasonal changes in appearance are accomplished through wear. The feathers of the male Red-winged Blackbird have broad rufous or buffy edges when fresh in fall (left), but the pale edges are weaker than the heavily pigmented black base of the feather; as the pale tips wear off through the winter, the plumage is transformed to uniform black without any molt.

through the wear of the feather tips. Thus Rusty Blackbirds *(Euphagus carolinus)* do not molt out of their rusty winter colors into a black breeding plumage; instead, their rusty feather tips wear off, revealing the black feather bases.

The Red-winged Blackbird *(Agelaius phoeniceus)*, the Tricolored Blackbird *(A. tricolor)*, the meadowlarks, and some orioles also change their appearance through the wear of feather tips by early summer, revealing the underlying color. Thus a male Red-winged Blackbird observed in the fall with bold buffy edging on the upper- and underparts is not necessarily an immature; the bird could be a freshly molted adult male.

The most peculiar characteristic of icterid molts is that non-oriole icterids molt their tails quite unlike most other passerines. The typical songbird pattern is for the central tail feathers to be molted first and the outer feathers last (centrifugal tail molt). Most icterids have the reverse pattern (centripetal tail molt), starting with the outer rectrices and ending with the central pair. Orioles, on the other hand, molt like most passerines. In addition, some icterids shed all of their rectrices nearly simultaneously, rendering them tail-less for two to three weeks.

Habitats

Most icterids are common birds that have adapted well to human-created habitats. While orioles do most of their foraging in trees, the rest of the icterids forage on the ground in a variety of habitats, including grasslands, agricultural fields, lawns, golf courses, marshes, swamps, and beaches. Many species breed in one habitat and forage in another. Red-winged Blackbirds, for example, often breed in cattail marshes, but once breeding ends the birds leave the marshes and forage in nearby fields.

Brown-headed Cowbirds *(Molothrus ater)* also forage in fields, particularly where livestock are found, but they search for nests of host species in more wooded habitats and so tend to use forest edges for breeding. A peculiar trait of this species is that its breeding activities take place in the early part of the day, while foraging takes place later in the day. Thus habitat choice varies depending on the time of day.

The Rusty Blackbird, one of the more specialized icterids, is particularly fond of foraging in forest ponds and wooded swamps. Orioles breed and forage in forests, but they tend to inhabit open woodlands and riparian forests more than mature upland forests. The Hooded Oriole *(Icterus cucullatus)* has a specific fondness for palms; in California it almost entirely depends on the availability of *Washingtonia* fan palms for nesting. The planting of this palm as an ornamental has allowed the Hooded Oriole to expand its range northward significantly.

Food and Foraging

Orioles are insectivores throughout the year. Baltimore Orioles have a noted appetite for caterpillars, even some of the hairier species that most other birds avoid. Orioles, particularly those that winter in Central and South America, will also sip nectar from flowers. In the recent past, Hooded, Bullock's, Baltimore, and Scott's Orioles *(Icterus parisorum)* have learned to use hummingbird feeders as a food source. The Altamira Oriole sports a thick bill and a hard, bony palate, which it uses to crack small

Icterid heads and bills. Icterid bills vary in length and thickness, but all have relatively straight and pointed bills. Shown here are the Eastern Meadowlark (left), which has a relatively slender and long bill, and the Brown-headed Cowbird (right), with a relatively short and stout bill.

branches and twigs in order to expose larvae and other food inside.

The rest of the blackbirds eat mainly insects while breeding and feed on fruits and grains when not breeding. This is true for species such as Red-winged Blackbirds, grackles, and cowbirds. Red-winged Blackbirds, Common Grackles *(Quiscalus quiscula),* and Brown-headed Cowbirds, along with other icterids, are sometimes considered pest species due to the large amounts of valuable grain they consume. The Bobolink used to be known as the "ricebird" due to its habit of raiding southern rice fields for food during its migration. Bobolinks are still thought of as pests in South America, where they forage in rice paddies.

The icterids are endowed with strong bills, which are usually very straight and have a sharp tip. A few species have a thicker, shorter bill that resembles that of finches and sparrows, but with a very straight culmen and a noticeable bend along the cutting edge, near the gape.

The musculature controlling the opening and closing of the bill is modified in the icterids, allowing them to open their bills with great strength. They use this adaptation to their advantage in a behavior known as "gaping," in which the birds insert the bill into a substrate (soil, vegetation, mud, bark) and forcibly open it, creating a hole that allows the birds to reach food otherwise hidden and inaccessible to other passerines. Members of this family gape into the ground, bark, crevices, plant stalks, flowers, and many other substrates. Many experts consider gaping the main reason why icterids have been so successful. The primarily Old World starlings also use this feeding technique.

Species that use gaping as a major foraging technique tend to have strong, longish bills with straight and sometimes flattened culmens. The best examples are the meadowlarks. Both North American species spend a great deal of time gaping for food in the grasslands they inhabit. The long, thin, somewhat decurved bill of the Hooded Oriole is surely an adaptation for foraging on nectar.

Icterids are generalists when foraging, often ingeniously exploiting newly available food sources. In the West, Brewer's Blackbird *(Euphagus cyanocephalus)* is a common parking lot species. This bird has learned that car grilles are wonderful places from which to pick off nutritious insects. Within minutes of a car being parked, a Brewer's Blackbird may begin to investigate the grille and clean it of anything edible. Species of grackles living near water have been seen fishing,

Western Meadowlark "gaping." Icterids have complex bill musculature that allows them to force the bill open with considerable strength. This enables the bill to be inserted into the ground or among grass stems, then opened, prying apart the substrate. While this happens the eyes rotate slightly forward and the birds can see directly between their jaws into the hole they have created. Starlings use a similar technique.

Icterid nests. *Nests of icterids are diverse. Blackbirds and grackles build simple cup nests. Cowbirds build no nests. Meadowlarks (Western shown, left) build a domed cup on the ground. Orioles (Baltimore shown, right) build a pendant basket, in some species up to 2 feet (60 cm) long.*

either by hovering over the water and picking small fish from the surface or by wading in shallow water and grabbing the fish as they swim by.

Even more surprising are many records of icterids catching, killing, and eating other birds. This behavior is well known in Common Grackles. One Common Grackle in downtown Toronto would use buildings to its advantage to corner small passerines and then dispatch them with its large beak. In unseasonal snowstorms, when food becomes difficult to find, Rusty Blackbirds have also been known to kill and eat birds. However, normally the Rusty Blackbird is one of the more specialized blackbirds in terms of food choices, feeding largely on aquatic invertebrates it finds by flipping leaves at the water's edge and gaping into the mud.

In addition to their bill and muscle adaptations for gaping, ground-foraging icterids have strong, thick legs for walking on the ground. Orioles also have relatively strong legs for gripping branches, as they are acrobatic foragers, sometimes even hanging from a branch in order to reach a distant prey item.

Breeding

Some of the icterids (orioles, for example) follow the common breeding strategy of most North American passerines. Pairs are seasonally monogamous, and both sexes help raise the young, although the female does most of the work. Territoriality in these monogamous icterids varies depending on the quality of the habitat. In very good habitats where there is plenty of food, territoriality may break down to the point where breeding assemblages are almost colonial in nature. This occurs in several North American orioles, as well as in Common Grackles and Rusty Blackbirds.

In other icterids, such as Red-winged and Yellow-headed Blackbirds, the male defends a territory where multiple females will nest, while the male mates with all of them in a polygynous mating system. Recent DNA fingerprinting work has revealed that while the territorial male in most species fathers the majority of the young in his territory, the females do sneak off and copulate with neighboring males; these copulations sometimes produce offspring. In polygynous situations females do not defend the territory against other males, but they will chase off foreign females from the vicinity of their nest site.

The extent to which males help at the nest in polygynous breeders varies. Males are much more likely to help at the fledgling stage and later in the breeding season, when there are fewer chances for them to mate with females or when the

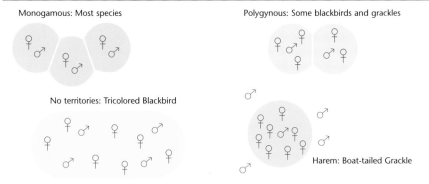

Monogamous: Most species

Polygynous: Some blackbirds and grackles

No territories: Tricolored Blackbird

Harem: Boat-tailed Grackle

Icterid mating systems. Mating systems of the icterids are diverse. Most species are monogamous and territorial, but some blackbirds and grackles are polygynous. In the Tricolored Blackbird, each male mates with one to several females in a colony without forming individual territories. The Boat-tailed Grackle also nests colonially, but the highest-ranking male defends a group of females (a harem) against copulations by other males.

need to defend their territory is less pressing. They also tend to help the first female that settles in the territory (the "primary female") to a greater extent than later-arriving females. Thus a primary female on a poor territory may sometimes do as well as the second or third female on a good territory.

Tricolored Blackbirds may look similar to Red-winged Blackbirds, but their breeding strategy is quite different. Tricolored Blackbirds tend to be polygynous but are not territorial. Their nesting takes place in colonies, which can contain huge numbers of nests. Within colonies, nesting is extremely synchronized, which probably decreases the risk of nest predation for individual females. If a female's nest is surrounded by thousands of others, all at the same stage in the nesting cycle, the chance that any individual nest will be lost to a predator is greatly reduced.

Another breeding strategy used by some icterids is harem-defense polygyny. The Boat-tailed Grackle *(Quiscalus major)* is noted for this and is the only known harem-defending bird in North America, although Great-tailed Grackles *(Q. mexicanus)* probably also have this mating system. In this system, the male defends a group of females against other males from the breeding colony and does not allow lower-ranking males to mate. The

highest-ranking male (the "alpha male"), who tends to be the oldest and heaviest, performs the majority of the copulations in the colony. Nevertheless, the alpha male sires only 25 percent of the young, even though he may perform up to 87 percent of the observed copulations; it is likely that females copulate with lower-ranking males when foraging elsewhere. This type of mating system is exactly that of Northern Elephant Seals and many other mammals, but in birds it is found only in the icterids.

In harem-defense polygyny, the males establish an extremely competitive dominance hierarchy, which over time presumably selects for the evolution of larger males. Not surprisingly, icterids that practice this system of breeding (such as some oropendolas and caciques of the neotropics) show some of the most pronounced sexual size dimorphism in the avian world; males of these species are much larger than females.

In general, the more the males of a species have to compete for access to mates, the greater the sexual size dimorphism in that species, with males usually larger than females. In polygynous systems, males are under heavy competition for access to mates, and many will not obtain a mate at all. In monogamous systems, most males breed, and they have to compete less to secure a mate.

A look at the difference in size between the sexes, from the most monogamous icterids to the most polygynous, is instructive. Males of the Orchard Oriole *(Icterus spurius)*, a monogamous species, are 6 percent larger than females. In Red-winged Blackbirds and Yellow-headed Blackbirds (which defend polygynous breeding territories), the males are 18 and 19 percent larger, respectively. In Boat-tailed Grackles (polygynists that defend harems), the males are 22 percent larger.

Brood Parasitism

Perhaps the most exceptional icterid breeding strategy is that of the cowbirds, which are brood parasites. They do not make a nest and care for their own eggs and young, but instead lay their eggs in the nests of other species, forcing the host birds to do the work of caring for the cowbird eggs and young.

North American cowbird species do not parasitize a single host species but instead use a variety of hosts. This lack of dependence on any one host means that cowbirds can cause population declines in host species without significantly affecting their own ability to find more host nests. This is not the case for brood parasites that have an exclusive dependence on one host species, as do many Old World cuckoos.

When cowbirds are raised in nests of species that are larger than cowbirds, the cowbird young have little effect on the nesting success of the host. In these cases, the major cost for the host is that female cowbirds frequently peck or remove a host egg when laying their own. However, when the host species is smaller than the cowbird, the large and aggressive cowbird young can outcompete the host young, often causing them to starve and fail to fledge. Cowbirds have thus been blamed for declines in many songbird species.

Biologists think that the Brown-headed Cowbird was once restricted to the Great Plains, where it followed wandering American Bison herds that churned open the thick prairie sod, giving cowbirds

Brown-headed Cowbird young being fed by Kirtland's Warbler. Brood parasitic cowbirds lay eggs in other birds' nests and leave the rearing of the young to the host species. The rapidly growing cowbird chick makes it nearly impossible for smaller host species to raise their own young. As cowbird populations have increased, their parasitism has been blamed for declines of many of their host species. Recovery of the Kirtland's Warbler population has been attributed, at least in part, to human control of the Brown-headed Cowbird population in the warbler's breeding areas.

access to disturbed soil for feeding. Some hypothesize that cowbirds evolved their brood-parasitic breeding strategy so that cowbird adults could move with the bison. However, the cowbird group appears to have originated in South America, away from bison. It seems more plausible that the Brown-headed Cowbird was "pre-adapted" to follow bison due to its peculiar breeding strategy.

The common view is that human manipulation of habitat has allowed the Brown-headed Cowbird to colonize North America from coast to coast, causing problems for host species throughout. However, recent evidence suggests that this may not be true. For example, the Brown-headed Cowbird population in the interior of British Columbia is significantly differentiated from California and Great Plains populations, implying that cowbirds from those populations did not spread into British Columbia but rather that this population has existed for a long time. What may have changed is the abundance of Brown-headed Cowbirds, but not their range.

It is also clear that brood parasitism is only one factor affecting populations of songbirds, and in most cases it is not the most important one. Habitat loss and predation may be more significant.

Cowbirds have their greatest impact on rare and restricted-range host species such as Kirtland's Warbler *(Dendroica kirtlandii)* and the Black-capped Vireo *(Vireo atricapillus)*. Kirtland's Warblers breed only in the lower peninsula of Michigan. Human control of cowbird populations there, begun in 1972, reduced brood parasitism to negligible levels. The warbler population did not increase, however, until an accidental wildfire near the breeding grounds greatly increased suitable habitat starting in 1991. Kirtland's Warblers require young, dense Jack Pine *(Pinus banksiana)* stands that regenerate following intense fires. Thus cowbird control alone was not sufficient to restore the warbler population; lack of suitable habitat was also a critical problem.

Vocalizations and Displays

The icterids have some very obvious and stereotyped displays. A prominent one is the bill-up display, a sign of aggression in which the bird sleeks down its plumage and points its bill up while facing another bird. Often the recipient of the display will return a bill-up display to the first bird. This warning display is often given in foraging situations when one bird comes too close to another.

Most ground-foraging icterids use the song-spread display (also called the ruff-out display) as their major territorial or mate-attraction display. Perhaps the best known such display is that of the male Red-winged Blackbird, in which the bird spreads its wings and partially spreads its tail while flaring its bright red epaulets and giving its *kon-ka-reeeee* song.

In their versions of the song-spread, the Common Grackle and Brewer's Blackbird spread their tails, droop their wings, and ruffle up their plumage as they spit out their soft, unmusical songs. Brown-headed Cowbirds cock their tails, fluff up their plumage, droop their wings, and sometimes hop as they give their bubbling gurgle of a song. The displays of the Bronzed Cowbird *(Molothrus aeneus)* are even more dramatic; the males keep the wings spread and forward as they hop, making it appear as if they were holding a cape Dracula-style in front of them as they sing. Orioles do not song-spread but give melodious songs or chatters while on their territory.

The orioles are surely the most accomplished singers of the icterid group, but the songs of other blackbirds are notable for their sheer oddity. The Yellow-headed Blackbird's song, for example, sounds like a rusty gate turning on its hinges. Great-tailed Grackles make sounds reminiscent of breaking sticks or ripping cloth. Brown-headed Cowbirds emit a liquid gurgle. The meadowlarks sing melodious territorial songs, often from a fence post adjoining their field or grassland, but at times they may take to the air to give a bubbling flight song. This latter style is used almost exclusively by Bobolinks, which are renowned for their flight song.

Individual male Bobolinks have a repertoire of two song types, which do not appear to have different "meanings" and are given in random order during a singing bout. More interesting is that different colonies have their own dialects, which are most similar when colonies are close to each other and most divergent when colonies are far apart.

In many icterids, including Red-winged Blackbirds, Brewer's Blackbirds, and Baltimore Orioles, the females sometimes sing. In Brewer's Blackbird, the females sing often, and female songs are not unlike male songs. Red-winged Blackbird females sing commonly, but their song is very different from that of the male; it is also often accompanied by a female version of the song-spread

Boat-tailed Grackle displays. *Many display behaviors are shared, albeit in slightly modified forms, by all the grackles, cowbirds, and blackbirds. Here a male Boat-tailed Grackle is shown performing a bill-up display (left), two variants of the song-spread display (center), and a flight display (right).*

display. In orioles, the songs of females are similar to those of males but are simpler in structure. Cowbird vocalizations tend to be sex-specific; the gurgle song and the flight whistle are given only by the male, while the typical cowbird rattle is almost always given by the female.

Migration

Most icterids are short-distance migrants or year-round residents. In general, northern populations are the most migratory. For example, Common Grackles breeding in Canada are migratory, largely vacating their Canadian range in the winter, while those breeding along the coast of the Gulf of Mexico are resident. In general, migratory eastern populations of the Common Grackle move between north and south without much east–west movement. However, westernmost breeding grackles move southeastward in the fall, exhibiting a noticeable east–west bearing in their migration. To some extent, this is also true for Brewer's Blackbird and the Western Meadowlark; both have a winter range that extends east of the breeding range.

Topographic features apparently act as barriers to the migration of some species. For example, migratory Common Grackles tend not to cross the Appalachian Mountains. Most of the North American icterids, except the orioles and the Bobolink, are strictly diurnal migrants.

Only a few North American icterids (the Orchard Oriole, Bullock's Oriole, Baltimore Oriole, Yellow-headed Blackbird, and Bobolink) can be considered neotropical migrants. The Bobolink is the champion migrant in this family and is among the most migratory of North American passerines, making an annual 12,500-mile (20,000-km) round-trip journey. After breeding, Bobolinks migrate to marshes, particularly along coasts, where they molt before continuing south. Molt-migration is also known in Bullock's Oriole, which vacates its breeding areas early in the summer and moves to the desert Southwest for its molt, before continuing south.

Southbound migrant Bobolinks travel to Florida and over the Caribbean, stopping on Caribbean islands before making landfall in northern South America. Bobolinks have been sighted flying over Bermuda, suggesting that many leave the United States well north of Florida and make long nonstop flights to Caribbean islands or all the way to South America. Where they make landfall is not known. Northbound migration routes tend to lie west of the southbound routes; many northbound spring migrants crossing the Gulf of Mexico are detected in Louisiana. Laboratory work has shown that Bobolinks use Earth's magnetic field as their primary guide to navigation, but they also use the stars as navigational aids.

Conservation

No icterids are listed as endangered species in the United States or Canada. In fact, population expansions are more common than decreases, thanks mainly to the family's ability to adapt to human-influenced environments. The Great-tailed Grackle, one of North America's fastest-expanding species, now breeds nearly to the Canadian border; early in the 20th century this species was hardly found north of the U.S.–Mexico border.

Brown-headed Cowbird populations also expanded greatly during the 20th century, but in general the cowbird has shown a population decline since the 1980s, based on Breeding Bird Survey data. The Bronzed Cowbird is spreading and now breeds in Louisiana, where it was previously unknown.

One of the most recent immigrants to the North American continent is the Shiny Cowbird *(Molothrus bonariensis)*, which used Caribbean islands as stepping-stones for crossing from northern South America to Florida. Flocks of this species, first recorded in the United States in 1985, have been seen not only in Florida but elsewhere in the southern part of the country. The bird is now presumed to breed in the United States, but difficulties in distinguishing Shiny Cowbird eggs and young from those of Brown-headed Cowbirds have made it hard to confirm this. Vagrant Shiny Cowbirds have been observed as far north as Maine and New Brunswick and west to Texas and Oklahoma.

Other range expansions that are not as well known include the eastern spread of Brewer's Blackbird into the Great Lakes region; the spread of Red-winged Blackbirds and Brown-headed Cowbirds to Alaska; and the western spread of Common Grackles, which now breed west of the Continental Divide in Idaho. The Streak-backed Oriole *(Icterus pustulatus)* is now best considered a very rare breeder as opposed to a vagrant; in recent years this western Mexican species has bred in Arizona, and it is a rare but regular wanderer to California, Arizona, and once to both Oregon and Wisconsin.

Tricolored Blackbird populations have generally declined in the recent past, and the bird is considered a species of management concern in California. However, its breeding range has spread north recently; colonies are now regularly found in northern Oregon, and a new one has been located in southern Washington.

Grassland birds in general are declining in North America, and icterids that breed in this habitat are no exception. Both meadowlark species and the Bobolink have declined since the 1960s, based on Breeding Bird Survey data. More intensive human use of hayfields, especially hay cutting early in the summer, has devastated some Bobolink populations, as the early haying destroys nests with eggs or young.

The most widespread orioles are also showing significant declines, according to the Breeding Bird Survey. Orchard and Bullock's Orioles have been reduced in numbers since the 1960s, while the Baltimore Oriole shows more recent losses. Hooded and Scott's Orioles, on the other hand, have increased throughout their ranges.

Perhaps the most troubling decline shown by a North American icterid is that of the Rusty Blackbird. Its numbers dropped by 90 percent between the mid-1960s and the late 1990s, based on Breeding Bird Survey and Chistmas Bird Count data. The reasons for this decline are unclear, but Rusty Blackbirds specialize in foraging at the shores of wooded ponds and forested swamps, habitats that are threatened throughout the continent. Acid rain, and its effects on aquatic invertebrates, may be another factor.

Accidental Species

Two species are considered accidental in North America, the Tawny-shouldered Blackbird *(Agelaius humeralis)*, normally found in Cuba and Hispaniola, and the Black-vented Oriole *(Icterus wagleri)*, which normally occurs from northern Mexico south to northern Central America. Two Tawny-shouldered Blackbirds were collected at Key West in the 1930s, one in February and one in May; more recent sightings have not been substantiated. Prior to 2000, there were three records for the Black-vented Oriole, two in Texas (April–October) and one in southeastern Arizona (April).

Alvaro Jaramillo

Finches and Allies

Fringillids are small to medium-size songbirds, most with conical bills and forked and relatively short tails. Males and females have differently colored plumages. North American finches fly fast and undulate in the air; they give high-pitched calls in flight, and their songs tend to be longer and more complex than those of other families of finch-like North American birds. Most fringillids are arboreal, preferring open forests or forest canopies, shrublands, and forest edges, but some species that occur in desert and tundra habitats are terrestrial.

Taxonomy

The relationships among various families of finches and finch-like birds are controversial. Historically, scientists have placed fringillids closest to, or within, the New World nine-primaried oscine complex, which includes the New World sparrows, wood-warblers, tanagers, cardinals, and blackbirds and orioles. Like members of this complex, all fringillids are nine-primaried; their 10th (outer) wing primary has been reduced to a tiny pin hidden under the outer coverts. DNA–DNA hybridization studies support an alliance between fringillids and the New World nine-primaried oscines. The fringillids are primarily Old World in their distribution and presumably evolved separately from the New World groups.

Fringillid diversity. *The Fringillidae is represented in North America by two subfamilies, the Fringillinae (of which only the Brambling, shown at top left, strays regularly to North America) and the Carduelinae, whose members range in size and color from the Lesser Goldfinch (center right) to the Pine Grosbeak (bottom).*

Analyses of mitochondrial DNA suggest that two additional families comprised entirely of nine-primaried species, namely, the wagtails and pipits and the Old World sparrows, are also closely related to the Fringillidae.

More distantly related to fringillids are two Old World families of finch-like birds, the estrildid finches (Estrildidae) and the weavers (Ploceidae), both of which contain some nine-primaried species. The fringillids differ from other groups of finch-like birds in their behavior, their biochemistry, and in subtle skull characteristics, including the structure of the interorbital septum and bony palate.

Worldwide, Fringillidae is divided into three subfamilies. Fringillinae contains one genus, *Fringilla,* and includes the chaffinches and the Brambling *(F. montifringilla).* Carduelinae, the cardueline finches, contains about 18 to 20 living genera of finches, grosbeaks, canaries, and their allies. Drepanidinae, the Hawaiian honeycreepers, contains about 12 living and five extinct genera.

Some ornithologists once placed Hawaiian honeycreepers closest to certain nectar-feeding tanagers, but most experts now agree that the tanagers are only distant relatives of honeycreepers, which are now placed close to the Carduelinae. The precise phylogenetic position of the Hawaiian honeycreepers among fringillids remains controversial. While both mitochondrial DNA sequences and morphological evidence suggest that the honeycreepers are cardueline finches, DNA–DNA hybridization data support their classification as a separate subfamily. Both molecular evidence and morphology suggest that cardueline finches and Hawaiian honeycreepers are closer to each other than either group is to the Fringillinae.

The cardueline finches pose other taxonomic problems. For example, some scientists doubt that certain genera, including *Carpodacus* (rosefinches) and *Carduelis* (goldfinches, siskins, greenfinches, and allies), contain members of only one evolutionary lineage. These genera therefore may be split into several genera in the future.

Six genera of fringillids, all cardueline finches, breed in North America, and all of these genera also occur in the Palearctic. The Brambling, an abundant Palearctic fringilline species, is a regular migrant in western Alaska. Several North American species of cardueline finches—the Pine Grosbeak *(Pinicola enucleator),* both redpolls, and both crossbills—also occur widely throughout the Old World.

Similarly, some Old World species are closely allied to North American forms. For example, the Eurasian Siskin *(Carduelis spinus)* is very close to the Pine Siskin

Fringillid head and bill. *Members of the Fringillidae are seed-eaters, and all have short, conical bills adapted for cracking seeds. The Evening Grosbeak, shown here, has the largest bill among the North American species in the family.*

Fringillid wing structure. *Finches have nine primary feathers (shaded area), a characteristic that suggests this family may be closely related to the large assemblage of New World nine-primaried oscines. Finches also possess a vestigial 10th primary, reduced to a tiny, pin-like feather hidden beneath the outermost coverts.*

Worldwide Family Features

- 4–10" (10–25 cm) primarily arboreal songbirds.
- About 150 species in 32 genera worldwide; found globally, except Australia, Antarctica, Madagascar, and southern Indian subcontinent; largely Holarctic, with greatest diversity in central Asia and Hawaiian Islands. 17 species in 7 genera occur in North America; plus 6 accidental species.
- Eat mainly seeds and buds plucked from trees and shrubs; some Hawaiian honeycreepers probe flowers for nectar; insectivorous to varying degrees.
- Loosely colonial while nesting; male defends female and very small territory around nest. Monogamous. Often flock in nonbreeding season. Strong seasonal movements in many species, but often irregular in timing and extent. Crossbills nomadic; Hawaiian honeycreepers nonmigratory.

- Breed first usually at 1 year old or less.
- Compact open-cup nest made of twigs, grasses, mosses; located in trees, bushes, rock crevices, grass tussocks. Male rarely helps build nest. Most species do not reuse nests.
- 2–6 subelliptical, oval, or pyriform eggs; usually off-white to greenish, unmarked or with brown streaks and spots. Female incubates, for 10–16 days; male feeds incubating female (except *Fringilla* species). Hatching synchronous. 1–3 broods per year.
- Altricial young naked at hatching or with sparse grayish down on head and back. Fledge after 9–25 days; one or both parents feed for 15–30 days after fledging.
- Adult annual survival usually 55–75%. Among oldest on record: 17 years, 6 months (Eurasian Bullfinch), 15 years, 3 months (Evening Grosbeak).

(C. pinus). The evolutionary lineages of cardueline finches are most diverse in Asia, particularly in the Himalayan region, which supports the idea that the Old World is the center of origin for these finches.

The Common Redpoll *(Carduelis flammea)* and Hoary Redpoll *(C. hornemanni)* have traditionally been considered separate species, although recent studies show no genetic differences between them. Moreover, their plumage color grades along a continuous spectrum in areas where both forms breed. Still, there are arguments against merging the two forms into a single species: They have measurable differences in vocalizations and bill shape (shorter in the Hoary Redpoll), and they apparently do not hybridize readily.

Variation in morphology and plumage among many cardueline finches poses problems for taxonomists in classifying species. The rosy-finches of the genus *Leucosticte* differ greatly in plumage color and size across the range of the group. The Black Rosy-Finch *(L. atrata),* Gray-crowned Rosy-Finch *(L. tephrocotis),* and Brown-capped Rosy-Finch *(L. australis)* have in the past been lumped together as races of a single species, which is sometimes also combined with the Asian Rosy-Finch *(L. arctoa).*

Although the White-winged Crossbill *(Loxia leucoptera)* shows no geographic variation, the Red Crossbill *(L. curvirostra)* is highly variable, occurring as about nine different forms that are distinctive in vocalization and morphology (see the box on Red Crossbill forms, below). These various forms are apparently sympatric breeders where their ranges overlap. Like the redpolls, the forms of Red Crossbill show no genetic differences, and they grade into one another in both morphology and plumage color.

The Pine Grosbeak contains several distinctively marked geographic forms that differ in size, bill shape, and vocalizations. Western subspecies of the Pine Grosbeak have musical, song-like calls that modulate greatly in pitch, while eastern forms have simpler, whistled calls.

Western populations of the House Finch *(Carpodacus mexicanus)* also show great geographic variation. The Lesser Goldfinch *(Carduelis psaltria)* has green-backed (western) and black-backed (Texas) forms. The American Goldfinch *(Carduelis tristis),* Evening Grosbeak *(Coccothraustes vespertinus),* and Purple Finch *(Carpodacus purpureus)* also show moderate degrees of geographic variation.

Variation

Worldwide, fringillids exhibit great variation in bill shape, body size, and plumage. North American species express only part of this range of variation.

Bills

One of the most spectacular hallmarks of fringillids is the tremendous diversity of their bill structure, which is generally related to the principal foods of the different species. Hawaiian honeycreepers show the most variation in the size and shape of the bill, but even the relatively few North American species exhibit a wide range of bill types, from thin and pointed (Pine Siskin) to conical (goldfinches, Brambling, and rosy-finches) to stubby and slightly hooked (Pine Grosbeak). The crossbills are the only birds in the world with truly crossed bills, a characteristic that allows them to bite and pry between the scales of conifer cones.

Plumage

All fringillids that breed in North America have sexually dimorphic plumage: Males are variously ornamented with yellow, orange, red, and pink, while females are more drab. (On average, females are 3 to 5 percent smaller than males in bill size and body size.) Neither sex changes appearance seasonally, with the exception of the male American Goldfinch, which loses its bright summer colors in winter.

The genus *Carduelis* includes the smallest cardueline finches. They range in color from yellow and black (goldfinches) to streaky brown (siskins) to

Variation in rosy-finches. *The five distinctive populations of rosy-finches in North America are currently grouped into three species, but they have also been considered to be a single variable species. The birds differ in plumage and size, but habits and voice are apparently similar in all, and the resolution of their taxonomic status awaits more research. The Gray-crowned Rosy-Finch has three populations: from the Bering Sea (top left), Pacific coast (top center), and interior West (top right). The Brown-capped Rosy-Finch is shown on the lower left, the Black Rosy-Finch on the lower right.*

those ornamented with red (redpolls). Female *Carduelis* are the least distinctive members of the Fringillidae, resembling certain sparrows and wood-warblers.

The crossbills and the Pine Grosbeak resemble each other in that their adult plumage is solid and unstreaked (juvenile crossbills are heavily streaked); the males are orangish to pink and red, while the females are greenish. The Pine Grosbeak, however, is much larger than a crossbill and has a relatively longer tail.

Color variation within species is especially strong in crossbills and the House Finch; males of these species range from yellow to red, depending on age, geographic origin, and diet. For example, most male House Finches in Hawaii (where they have been introduced) are orange or yellow; their hue is mostly related to the quantity and chemical makeup of the carotenoid pigment in their food. House Finches in eastern North America, where they are also introduced, and in the West, where they are native, sometimes show the same orange or yellow tones.

Contrary to many published accounts, a male cardueline finch's color is not a reliable indicator of age, although younger males may more often show yellowish to orange plumage. There are many records of young birds with both streaked juvenal plumage and numerous red adult feathers. Old males may take on yellowish plumage if they do not eat enough of certain foods (possibly insects) just before the autumn molt. Captive males of normally red species molt into yellow plumage unless their diet is supplemented with carotenoid pigments such as bottled rhodaxanthin.

In some cardueline genera, including *Carpodacus, Pinicola, Coccothraustes,* and

House Finch color variation. *The red pigment of this species, as in all other red birds, is acquired from the diet. House Finches in the Southwest (and even more so in Hawaii) apparently have difficulty obtaining or assimilating enough pigment, and many individuals end up yellowish instead of red. The same deficiency occurs very rarely in Purple and Cassin's Finches.*

certain species of *Carduelis,* the plumage of juveniles somewhat resembles that of adult females. In *Loxia,* however, the streaked juveniles are unlike either adult.

Molt

Molt occurs in late summer to early autumn for cardueline finches of all ages. Adults (one year old and up) replace their entire plumage. Juveniles replace mainly their body feathers, retaining their first set of wing and tail feathers, but they also replace some upperwing coverts and, rarely, some tertials. After the pre-basic molt, first-year birds of most species resemble adults. In the Brambling, Pine Grosbeak, the Great Basin race of the House Finch, and several Old World species, however, males do not molt into full adult plumage for another year. All first-year cardueline finches can be distinguished from adults by such features

---

Nine North American Forms of Red Crossbill

At least nine forms of Red Crossbill occur in North America. These forms differ from one another in their average bill size and structure, body size, and the structures of their flight calls and alarm calls; the different forms are generally referred to as call types. These call types have different, though broadly overlapping, geographic ranges and habitats, despite the fact that all wander widely in search of food.

Differences in bill size and structure among the various call types reflect their preferences for the cones of different conifer species. In general, the larger- and stouter-billed types forage most efficiently on larger and harder cones (pines); the smaller-billed types forage most efficiently on smaller and softer cones (spruces, firs, hemlocks). Two types prefer Lodgepole Pine; another prefers Western Hemlock; and yet another is partial to Eastern and Western Hemlock, White Pine, Red Spruce, White Spruce, and Sitka Spruce.

Ornithologists agree on the existence of these types, but there is no consensus yet on whether the forms should be considered separate species, nor do the call types correspond well to subspecies that were named by earlier researchers. These forms do not freely interbreed when they inhabit the same forests. This, combined with diagnosable differences in their vocalizations, leads some researchers to suggest that all are separate species. On the other hand, the differences between forms are very slight, diagnostic flight calls are learned, and some mixed pairs have been documented.

Preliminary evidence from Red Crossbills in Europe suggests that a similar system, with numerous previously unrecognized but vocally and morphologically distinctive call types, also exists in the Old World. Shown below are the head of a call type 2 bird with Ponderosa Pine cone (top left), type 5 with Lodgepole Pine cone (bottom left), type 4 with Douglas-fir cone (top right), and type 3 with Western Hemlock cone (bottom right).

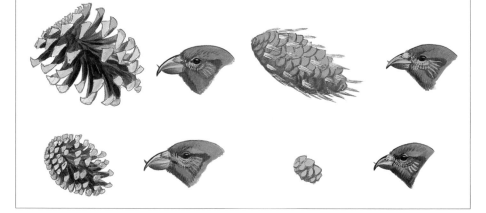

as buffy edges on their flight feathers and wing coverts, but these come into view only at very close range.

In spring, the American Goldfinch undergoes an additional molt into its brighter yellow breeding colors, and males of the black-backed form of the Lesser Goldfinch also lose their female-like winter appearance. Even without a spring prealternate molt, however, cardueline finches in summer often appear brighter and glossier than those in fresh fall plumage. This is particularly true for males of the red species and comes about as the more heavily pigmented feather barbs become exposed after several months of wear and abrasion of the less pigmented outer barbules.

Males of reddish species such as cross-bills, the Pine Grosbeak, and the *Carpodacus* finches may show blotches of yellow or orange within their otherwise red plumage, often around the head. These blotches usually contain newer feathers that have replaced plumage lost in sticky sap or through injuries.

Habitats

Most cardueline finches prefer open forests, in which the trees are rather widely spaced, to dense forests or thick undergrowth. Few members of this group occupy the forest interior, and most prefer forest edges. Unlike many kinds of New World sparrows, none takes refuge in deep grass to escape predation, preferring to flee to trees and shrubs.

The Pine Siskin and the crossbills often occur in dense forest, where they spend most of their time in the forest canopy, making occasional forays to the ground in open areas for water, grit, and nesting material. The Pine Grosbeak is a denizen of boreal spruce and fir forests, where it inhabits forest openings and bogs. The goldfinches are birds of open shrublands with scattered trees. Redpolls prefer open country and nest in the taiga zone near the treeline. The three species of rosy-finches are found in treeless areas, such as tundra and rocky outcrops.

Food and Foraging

More than any other group of finch-like birds, the cardueline finches depend on a vegetarian diet. They eat mostly seeds and buds even during the breeding season and feed regurgitated seeds to the young; this distinguishes them from other seed-eaters, such as sparrows, which become highly insectivorous while breeding.

Cardueline finches feed primarily on the seeds of trees, wildflowers (especially composites), and shrubs. A few species, including redpolls and goldfinches, consume some grass seeds. For the most part, cardueline finches consume seeds and buds still attached to trees and bushes. Sparrows and buntings, in contrast, feed mostly on seeds that have fallen to the ground.

Lawrence's Goldfinches foraging on thistle seeds. All cardueline finches have short, strong legs. The smaller species and the crossbills use their legs to clamber around seed heads and cones, even hanging upside down in the search for food. Goldfinches are so partial to thistle seed that special thistle-seed feeders have been designed to attract them.

However, cardueline finches are not exclusively vegetarian. They take animal matter, especially arthropods and their larvae, mostly on an opportunistic basis during the warmer months.

Cardueline finches are highly gregarious in all seasons, and their feeding flocks are based on hierarchies of social dominance. For most of the year, males dominate females, but with the onset of the breeding season, females begin to dominate males.

Breeding

During courtship, females solicit food from their prospective mates by crouching, fluttering their wings, and giving begging calls. Males respond with either mock feeding or by actually regurgitating food into the female's mouth. Some male cardueline finches, including goldfinches, siskins, and crossbills, give loud songs while flying in circles around a treetop in which the female may be perched.

As in many other songbirds, cardueline finches are monogamous. A major behavioral difference between cardueline finches and other songbirds, however, is that rather than defend an all-purpose territory surrounding the nest, a male defends a female.

While nesting, males become aggressive toward other males of their species that show interest in their mates or venture too near the nest. Otherwise, mated males are relatively tolerant of others near the nesting area. In fact, during the nesting season and while females are incubating or brooding the young, males often form small feeding flocks that may travel long distances away from the nests.

During courtship and before nest construction, males may show interest in potential nest sites and even carry sticks or other nesting material in their bills. Despite this initial enthusiasm by the male, the female selects the nest site and constructs the nest. While she gathers nesting material, the male typically accompanies her closely and may perch and sing while she builds.

Among the cardueline finches, the female incubates the eggs and broods the newly hatched young. There are anecdotal accounts of males sitting on nests, but such instances are rare. Only females develop incubation patches. The female rarely leaves the nest during the incubation period; meanwhile, the male does virtually all of the foraging for the pair, returning to the nest every one or two hours to regurgitate food into the mouth of the incubating female. For several days after hatching, the young are fed mostly by the female; the diet of the chicks consists almost entirely of regurgitated seeds brought to the female by the male.

Males and females both eat the fecal sacs of their young in the first days after hatching. Soon, however, they stop eating the sacs, and fecal material then begins to accumulate on the rim of the nest, which becomes increasingly littered with feces along its edges as the young get older. This "messy" condition can be a key to identifying abandoned cardueline nests, since other species that use open-cup nests usually remove all fecal sacs. Hawaiian honeycreepers and, oddly, the Olive Warbler (*Peucedramus taeniatus*) also let the fecal matter of their young accumulate on the edges of their nests.

After the young are four or five days old, the male feeds both the female and the young in the nest. At this time the nestlings begin to maintain their own body temperatures, allowing the female to leave the nest for longer periods as long as the air is not too cool.

After the young fledge, both male and female continue feeding them for 15 to 30 days. During this period, a female may find a new mate and raise another brood, leaving the begging young in the care of the father alone. House Finches have been known to produce more than two broods in a season.

Most cardueline finches breed in their first year; Red Crossbills may even breed when less than four months old and still in their streaked juvenile plumage.

Vocalizations and Displays

Vocalizations are very important to fringillids at all times of the year. All cardueline finches give species-specific flight calls, sometimes termed contact calls or location calls, that are the same for both males and females. Highly mobile birds, cardueline finches spend a great deal of time flying high above the treetops from one food patch to another. Fortunately for birders, finches usually call in flight, making it possible to identify species without seeing the birds.

Besides their flight calls, fringillids have a diverse repertoire of other sounds, including songs, alarm calls, and soft contact notes among foraging flocks or pairs. Juveniles give species-specific begging calls, which change as the young birds develop. Females occasionally sing, but in most cases only around the time of nest-building. Because the songs of females are not as loud and robust as those given by males, they are often referred to as "whisper songs."

Males sing while perched or in flight. Their songs are generally long and contain many separate elements and trills; it is not unusual for a male to sing a rich and varied song for a full minute or more. This contrasts with songs given by males in other finch-like families such as the New World sparrows, whose songs are shorter (often less than two seconds), less variable, and more stereotyped. Many cardueline finches, notably Cassin's Finch *(Carpodacus cassinii)* and the Lesser Goldfinch, imitate vocalizations of other species as part of their own songs.

The flight calls of cardueline finches not only assist in species recognition and flock cohesion, but they may also serve as a means for individuals to recognize each other. In species studied to date, the flight call of a particular individual is nearly invariant and different from those of conspecifics. The subtle differences among individual flight calls are almost indiscernible to humans, but presumably the birds use them for individual recognition.

Call-matching, in which the male and female of a pair duplicate each other's flight call precisely, has been observed in American Goldfinches, Cassin's Finches, and Red Crossbills. Presumably this helps a pair maintain their bond and allows mates to find each other among conspecifics. Further study is needed to determine whether all cardueline finches exhibit call-matching between mates.

Many of the distinctive calls in these species are learned. Indeed, cardueline finches are well known for their vocal learning ability. The domestic Common Canary *(Serinus canaria)*, a cardueline finch of the Azores and Canary Islands off western Africa, is perhaps the most thoroughly studied bird in terms of the interaction between genetics and environment and the effects of both on the neurological and behavioral development of vocalizations.

Movements

Cardueline finches are well known for their strong tendency to roam. Most species do not have regular migration patterns and cycles; their patterns of movement and their numbers vary greatly from year to year.

Fluctuations in food supply exert the strongest influence on the movement of finches, which may travel great distances to find suitable foraging areas. A Common Redpoll banded in Fairbanks, Alaska, one winter was recaptured 3,000 miles (5,000 km) to the east near Montreal, Quebec, the next winter. Most of these kinds of movements occur in winter, when finches may "irrupt," becoming abundant in areas where they have been uncommon or rare for several years. Common and Hoary Redpolls and Purple Finches have relatively regularly occurring patterns of irruption, with invasions occurring about every two years.

The dispersive lifestyle of finches is best exemplified by crossbills, which are highly nomadic and irregular, with no predictable cycles of movement. Evidently the availability of conifer cones plays a large role in where these birds winter and where they breed. In fact, crossbills will breed in almost any month, but less commonly in autumn, when they molt. Even in species that have fairly regular spring and fall migrations, such as the American Goldfinch and the Purple Finch, the number of birds moving over different areas varies annually.

Conservation

Cardueline finches also vary in number because of population cycles and range expansions and contractions. The matter awaits detailed study, but there is evidence that the Evening Grosbeak has expanded its range eastward over the past century from its point of discovery (the Lake Superior region) to Newfoundland. Similarly, the White-winged Crossbill may be expanding its range southward in the Rocky Mountain region; there are reports of the bird breeding as far south as New Mexico and Colorado.

In less than 50 years, the eastern population of the House Finch has blossomed from a small founding population on Long Island, New York, to one that covers a breeding area almost as large as that of the Wood Thrush *(Hylocichla mustelina)*—southern Canada south to Florida and west to the edge of the Great Plains—and undoubtedly contains more individuals.

Population declines and range contractions have also occurred. The Newfoundland population of the Red Crossbill began to decline at the same time that the Red Squirrel *(Tamiasciurus hudsonicus)*, a competitor for conifer cones, was introduced to the island in the 1940s. Logging of the conifer forests in the Northeast and the Great Lakes region in the 1800s decimated local populations of the Red Crossbill, which depends on mature cone-bearing trees,

such as Eastern White Pine *(Pinus strobus)* and Eastern Hemlock *(Tsuga canadensis)*, for its survival. Eastern populations are now increasing significantly.

Since the 1960s, according to the Breeding Bird Survey, Purple Finches have experienced significant declines throughout their range in both the East and the West, but the reasons for these declines are unclear.

Competition with similar species may cause population declines in some finches; the waning of the Purple Finch in the East coincides with the arrival there of the House Finch. Disease can also affect finch populations. For example, the House Finch has recently experienced a slight downward population trend, most likely because of widespread infection with a bacterial disease that affects the eye and leads to blindness. The disease has now begun to affect the American Goldfinch as well.

Despite declines in numbers for some cardueline finches, most species are not threatened. The only fringillid on the WatchList is Lawrence's Goldfinch *(Carduelis lawrencei)*, which, although not declining, is considered vulnerable because of its small range.

Accidental Species

Accidentals include a number of species common in Europe or Asia. The Common Chaffinch *(Fringilla coelebs)* is found in western Europe and has been recorded once in Newfoundland in May. Eurasian species that have wandered mainly in spring to Alaska include the Common Rosefinch *(Carpodacus erythrinus)*, the Eurasian Siskin, the Oriental Greenfinch *(Carduelis sinica)*, the Eurasian Bullfinch *(Pyrrhula pyrrhula)*, and the Hawfinch *(Coccothraustes coccothraustes)*. Scattered records of these species in other parts of North America generally are considered to be escapees from captivity.

Jeff Groth

Exotic "Finches"

Each year hundreds of thousands of birds are imported into North America as part of the pet trade. Most people think this trade is largely comprised of parrots and parakeets (see discussion in the Parrots and Allies chapter), but in fact a majority of imported birds are various kinds of finches or related seed-eating birds.

These "finches" belong to several bird families, all of which have a conical, seed-crunching bill. These families include the finches and their allies, as well as the estrildid finches (Estrildidae), the weavers (Ploceidae), and the Old World sparrows. The latter two families are closely related and have been lumped together in a single family in the past.

Finches have many advantages as pets. They typically are small, requiring only a little space, and are often excellent singers. The popularity of cage birds such as the Common Canary *(Serinus canaria)* of western Africa and the Zebra Finch *(Taeniopygia guttata)* of Australia is a testament to the ease with which these birds can be kept in captivity. As with parrots, the large trade in these species means that escaped birds can create feral populations in the milder parts of North America. For example, three fringillid finches—the European Goldfinch *(Carduelis carduelis)* of Eurasia, Yellow-fronted Canary *(S. mozambicus)* of sub-Saharan Africa, and Common Canary—are all occasionally seen in the wild in North America.

The estrildid finches include about 158 species in 30 genera found in Africa, Asia, and Australia. They are small to medium-size (many species are the size of an American Goldfinch, *Carduelis tristis,* or smaller), brightly colored finches with small, conical bills. Common in aviaries, estrildid finches seem to be prone to escape and have become established as exotics in many parts of the world. By the early 1980s some 35 species of estrildids had been released or escaped in areas outside their native range, with 21 species established as self-sustaining populations.

Exotic "finches." *Small seed-eating songbirds are often kept in captivity in North America and occasionally escape into the wild. Among these are members of two families not native to the continent: the Estrildidae (represented here by the Nutmeg Mannikin, left) and the Ploceidae (Orange Bishop, right).*

In North America, the most common estrildid finches to escape captivity have been the Java Sparrow *(Padda oryzivora)* and the Nutmeg Mannikin *(Lonchura punctulata).* Native to Indonesia, the Java Sparrow has been present at various times in southern Florida, southern California, Hawaii, and Puerto Rico. The Nutmeg Mannikin, also called the Spotted Munia or Spice Finch, is also established in California and southeastern Florida. This bird is native to southern Asia and the Philippines.

The weavers, comprising about 118 species in 17 genera, have small to medium-size bodies with larger conical bills than estrildid finches. Weavers are renowned for their ability to weave elaborate nests out of grasses. Originally found in Africa, about 16 species have been introduced throughout the world, especially to various island nations. They feed largely on seeds and can become agricultural pests, descending in flocks on fields of ripening grain. One member of this group, the Orange Bishop *(Euplectes franciscanus)* of sub-Saharan Africa, has escaped in large numbers in southern California and is established there.

John B. Dunning, Jr.

Old World Sparrows

Old World sparrows are short-legged, stoutly built seed-eaters whose short, strong bill has a decurved culmen. The birds resemble New World sparrows but have heftier bodies and stouter bills. Most species lack bright colors; shades of brown, buff, or gray dominate, with black or white markings. Old World sparrows can be readily distinguished from other "little brown jobs" by their simple song, in which they repeat single elements with no particular rhythm or beginning and end; they vocalize all day and year-round. These birds are found near human habitation and cultivated areas.

Taxonomy

The Old World sparrows are sometimes confused with New World sparrows because of similarities in size, shape, coloration, foraging behavior, and flocking habits. Despite these similarities, however, the two families are not particularly closely related. While some New World sparrows can be found in some urban habitats as well as more natural locations, the Old World sparrows in North America are found exclusively near buildings and farms.

The Passeridae formerly was classified as a subfamily (Passerinae) allied with two other Old World groups, the Ploceinae (typical weavers) and Bubalornithinae (buffalo-weavers) in the family Ploceidae (weavers). The groups are similar in their shared manner of weaving nests, but each has now been elevated to family status. Passerids are also thought to be closely related to the pipits, accentors, and perhaps the finches, based on DNA–DNA hybridization and other genetic studies.

The family Passeridae is represented in North America by two introduced species:
the House Sparrow *(Passer domesticus)* and the Eurasian Tree Sparrow *(P. montanus)*. Both were released in the mid-1800s to control insect pests or to provide new Americans with a reminder of a homeland left behind. The House Sparrow is now considered the most ubiquitous avian species in the world.

Variation

During the breeding season, male House Sparrows have brighter colors and a more prominent black bib than during winter. This change, however, is acquired through feather wear, rather than molt. With the prebasic molt in the fall, the black feathers of the bib and breast patch are tipped with white, but with abrasion of the feathers the bib becomes larger and is uniformly black by the breeding season. A recent study found that males actively preen breast feathers in late winter to increase wear and expose the black bib. The male's bill, horn-colored during the nonbreeding season, turns black during the breeding season. Adult females and juveniles are plainer than males. Male House Sparrows are larger than females.

Passerid diversity. The two species of this family introduced to North America are both in the genus Passer. *They are superficially similar to emberizid sparrows but stockier, with a stouter bill and different calls. The House Sparrow is shown.*

Passerid head and bill. The stout, strong bill of Passer *sparrows has a decurved culmen and a relatively blunt tip, as seen in this House Sparrow.*

The spread of House Sparrows in North America has proven to be a case study of evolutionary change. In about 120 years, North American populations have become more variable than the English and German populations from which the introduced birds originated. Within North America, larger birds have evolved in the north and in areas of cold winter temperatures.

Male and female Eurasian Tree Sparrows are alike in plumage, which is unique for the "black-bibbed" sparrows of the genus *Passer*. Both sexes have a black bill during the breeding season that becomes horn-colored during the nonbreeding season. Also unlike all other members of the genus, male and female sit side by side at the nest hole and engage in mutual preening.

Habitats and Foraging

Both North American species live close to human habitation, particularly where buildings are located near cultivated areas. House Sparrows will even live inside man-made structures such as airport terminals, grain elevators, cafeterias, hardware stores—practically anyplace with easy access to nest sites and food.

Where the species overlap, the more aggressive House Sparrow dominates, and the Eurasian Tree Sparrow moves out to suburbs, parks, and farmlands, where it nests in tree cavities. Both species often displace other hole-nesting birds. At harvest time these birds will congregate in farm fields to forage but return to buildings to roost.

Most foraging occurs on the ground in tight flocks, with dominant individuals supplanting subordinates; at feeders, females supplant males. Adults feed primarily on cereal grains, grass and weed seeds, and seed sprouts, switching to insects and spiders when feeding nestlings. They readily eat scraps of food and birdseed provided by humans.

Passer sparrows forage primarily during the day but will gather insects attracted to lights at night. They can catch flying insects and often peck at insects smashed against automobile radiators. At the end of the breeding season, independent young, joined later by adults, form large flocks near abundant food, usually in a field of ripening grain or, in urban areas, on reseeded winter lawns. Smaller flocks are found closer to protective cover, such as a hedgerow or building, than are larger flocks.

Worldwide Family Features

- 5–7" (12–18 cm) songbirds of arid, rocky areas; some live near humans and cultivation.
- 36 species in 4 genera worldwide; native mostly to Palearctic, with greatest diversity in northern Africa and Europe. North America has 2 introduced species in 1 genus; 1 species found throughout North America south of Alaska, 1 limited to Illinois and Missouri.
- Primarily eat grains, but also insects, especially when feeding young. Sometimes eat berries, buds. Feed on ground or in vegetation; also scavenge.
- Gregarious; nests and roosting sites often clumped together; some species territorial. Usually monogamous, but polygyny and extra-pair copulations seen in some species; pair bond lasts year-round and for life. Foraging birds flock; in winter, large flocks form near grainfields and other abundant food. Nonmigratory.
- Breed first at 6 months to 1 year old.
- Nest is globular, messy mass of vegetative matter in branches of tree or bush, rock crevice, tree hole, or cavity in man-made structure. North American species often use nest boxes. Male chooses site; both sexes build nest. Reuse nests.
- 1–8 (usually 4–5) eggs. Subelliptical; whitish with wreath of dark dots or spots on larger end. Usually both sexes incubate, for 9–16 days. Hatching synchronous. Up to 4 (usually 2 or 3) broods per year.
- Altricial young. Fledge at 10–21 days, earlier if nest is disturbed. Both sexes care for nestlings.
- Adult annual survival 45–65%. Among oldest on record: 13 years, 4 months (House Sparrow).

Breeding

During the breeding season, males advertise with chip, cheep, or chirrup notes. Females that have lost their mate will cheep to attract another.

Pairs are monogamous, usually for life, although extra-pair copulations can be frequent. Lost mates are quickly replaced during the breeding season. Pairs most often gather in small colonies. Nest boxes are prime nest sites, but the birds build nests almost anyplace high on a building where they can tuck in nest material.

The outside of the nest is made of coarse vegetative matter, formed into a globular shape that fits in the enclosed space or cavity; the inside is lined with finer material. When built in a nest box, the nest material may be in the shape of a small cup, or the material may fill up the box. The birds may weave feathers, string, or paper into the nest. Occasionally they build, in a tree or bush, a large, dome-shaped nest with a side entrance.

Old World sparrows frequently reuse their nests, both for successive broods within a breeding season and in subsequent years. Nests are also used for roosting in winter and may become filthy and harbor fleas and mites.

Both parents feed the nestlings tiny insects and spiders, and larger prey as the nestlings grow. House Sparrow young fledge at 10 to 14 days, Eurasian Tree Sparrows at 15 to 20 days. The fledglings are attended primarily by the male for several days, then join other juveniles in foraging and roosting flocks.

Both North American species are sedentary, usually moving no farther than a mile or so (1.5–2 km) from their birthplace. Juveniles (especially females) may disperse in flocks to found new colonies.

Conservation

Following their introduction to North America from 1850 to 1867, House Sparrows rapidly increased, and soon the birds were considered pests because of

Eurasian Tree Sparrow at nest. Both this species and the House Sparrow usually nest in a crevice or cavity. Both species are typically found near human habitation, and they often use buildings and other man-made structures, such as the insides of streetlights or even the cone of a traffic light. The nest itself is a small cup inside a globular mass of sticks, grass, and feathers.

their messy nesting habits and aggressive foraging style. They also take over nest sites used by bluebirds and martins. Various methods employed to limit their numbers failed. However, recent changes in farming practices, such as the switch to monoculture crops and the heavy use of pesticides, have resulted in a widespread decline of the House Sparrow across North America. In spite of this decline, the species is still one of the most common birds on the continent.

Eurasian Tree Sparrows were initially introduced to St. Louis, Missouri, in 1870, and have spread only into east-central Missouri and central Illinois. Soon after the species' introduction, House Sparrows moved into the same area and took over nest boxes put out for Eurasian Tree Sparrows. Nonetheless, the species persisted and remains locally common within its American range. Eurasian Tree Sparrow populations in Illinois show a gradual increase in numbers since the 1960s. The species' spread out of the St. Louis area is probably slowed by the presence of the more aggressive House Sparrow.

Kathleen Groschupf

Glossary

ABA. American Birding Association. A major North American organization for amateur birders, the ABA publishes the journal *Birding*.

Accidental. Not regularly occurring in a region. In this book, typically used to mean a species recorded fewer than 10 times in the past 25 years in continental North America, but with a few exceptions. *See also* pages 10–11.

After-shaft. A well-developed second feather emanating from the shaft of a body feather; typically soft and often downy, and probably important in maintaining warmth; may be perceived as a "double feather." Most developed in grouse, quail, and allies. Also called an after-feather or hypoptile.

Agonistic. Opposing; especially used to describe behaviors involved in conflicts between individuals.

Aigrette. Long, loose breeding feathers used in courtship displays by herons and egrets. Also called plumes.

Airfoil. A structure around which air flows, creating lift; for example, a bird's wing.

Air sac. A part of the respiratory system unique to birds; a thin-walled structure through which air flows during respiration. With the lungs, the air sacs allow air to flow along a one-way route so that newly inhaled air does not mix with older air in the system, unlike the dead-end respiration system of mammals.

Allopatric. Occurring in different geographic areas. *See* Sympatric.

Allopreen. To perform maintenance of feathers on another individual; often solidifies the pair bond or other strong relationship between individuals.

Alternate plumage. In birds that have two molts per year, typically the generation of feathers grown during the less complete of the two molts; usually occurs in late winter and spring, prior to breeding. Unless the prealternate molt is a complete molt, the plumage worn during the breeding season is a combination of alternate plumage and unmolted (retained) basic plumage.

Altricial. Helpless at hatching. An altricial hatchling is naked or sparsely downy, unable to leave the nest, and its eyes are closed. *See* Precocial.

Alula. A group of small feathers on the forward edge of the wing near the base of the primaries. Raising the alula feathers into the air flowing over the wing generates additional lift.

Anaerobic. Occurring in the absence of oxygen.

Anisodactyly. Arrangement of the toes in which three toes are directed forward, one backward; the typical avian pattern.

AOU. American Ornithologists' Union. One of three major ornithological professional societies in North America; publishes the journal *The Auk* and *The Check-list of North American Birds,* the standard authority for avian names and systematics in North America.

Area-sensitive species. An organism whose distribution is restricted to relatively large patches of habitat. Such species tend to be missing from highly fragmented landscapes.

Arthropod. Insects, crustaceans, spiders, and other members of the phylum Arthropoda.

Aspect ratio. A measure of wing shape, expressed as the wing's length divided by its width; used in the study of flight performance.

Assortative mating. The tendency of individuals to select mates similar to themselves. Where two populations overlap, assortative mating is evidence that the two populations are reproductively isolated and thus may be separate species.

Asynchronous hatching. Hatching that takes place over a period of several days. *See* Synchronous hatching.

Auriculars. Feathers covering the side of the head, including the ear openings. Also called ear coverts.

Banding. Marking individual birds by placing metal or plastic rings (bands) on the legs, making the birds individually identifiable when recaptured.

Barbicels. Tiny hooks on barbules that connect with adjoining barbules to form the interlocked, rigid structure of a feather vane.

Barbs. Projections off the shaft of a feather that form the broad vanes.

Barbules. Projections from the barbs of a feather that overlap and interlock with a system of hooks and ridges.

Basic plumage. The set of feathers worn throughout the year in birds that have only one annual molt (the prebasic molt). In species that have two molts per year, the basic plumage usually is the one attained through a complete molt and worn during the nonbreeding season.

Benthic. Associated with the floor of oceans or other bodies of water.

Bigamy. Breeding relationship in which one male is mated to two females.

Biological Species Concept. Definition of "species" that emphasizes the reproductive isolation between groups of organisms. *See* Phylogenetic Species Concept.

Bolus. A lump of food, often composed of small items, carried as a unit in the throat. Swallows, for example, deliver a bolus of tiny insects to their nestlings.

Boreal. Associated with the northern coniferous forests of Canada and Alaska.

Breeding Bird Survey. An annual monitoring program conducted by volunteers and coordinated by the U.S. Geological Survey and the Canadian Wildlife Service. Operated since 1966, the BBS provides continent-wide population trends for species whose populations can be sampled from roadsides.

Bristles. Long, stiff feathers with mostly naked shafts, often found near the mouth and eyes. *See* Rictal bristles.

Brooding. A behavior in which parents warm nestlings or young that cannot maintain their own body temperatures. While young are still in the nest, a brooding adult may appear to be incubating eggs.

Brood parasitism. Reproduction by laying eggs in the nests of other birds, leaving the nest owners to provide parental care. May be interspecific (eggs laid in the nests of other species) or intraspecific (eggs laid in nests of the same species). Also called nest parasitism. *See* Host.

Brood patch. A defeathered area on the lower abdomen in which the skin has thickened and become rich with blood vessels. Feathers on the belly are often dropped as the brood patch develops prior to incubation.

Brood reduction. A reproductive strategy in which a female produces more eggs than she will normally be able to raise; often seen in boobies, herons, eagles, and other large birds. If there is not enough food for all young, late-hatching offspring, weak and small compared to their nest mates, will be killed through starvation or direct attacks by siblings. *See* Siblicide.

Caching. Storage of food items for later retrieval and use.

Calamus. The largely hollow, proximal portion of the feather shaft that attaches to the skin.

Call-matching. Vocalization in which the male and female of a pair duplicate each other's flight call precisely. Found in members of the finch family.

Caruncle. A fleshy, brightly colored growth on the skin of the face or neck, prominent on turkeys and other gallinaceous birds.

Casual. Not regular in occurrence in a region but seen occasionally. Implies more frequent occurrence than "accidental," but not likely to be seen each year.

Centrifugal tail molt. Replacement of the tail feathers starting with the innermost pair and proceeding outward, with the shedding and growth of one pair of feathers at a time. This pattern is shown by most passerines.

Centripetal tail molt. Replacement of the tail feathers starting with the outermost pair of rectrices and proceeding inward, with the shedding and growth of one pair of feathers at a time. This pattern is shown by members of the blackbird family, except the orioles.

Cere. A raised, fleshy area at the base of the maxilla (upper mandible), especially on raptors.

Cetacean. Member of the mammalian order that includes whales and dolphins.

Chaparral. A dense, brushy habitat consisting of woody shrubs with small, thick, evergreen leaves.

Chitin. Horny material that forms part of the hard outer integument of insects, arachnids, and crustaceans.

Christmas Bird Count. An annual monitoring program conducted by volunteers and coordinated by the National Audubon Society. Conducted in late December and early January, CBCs provide long-term population trends for wintering species in North America.

Circumpolar. In the Northern Hemisphere, refers to species found in tundra or boreal habitats that stretch across North America and Eurasia.

Clappering. Nonvocal communication created by slapping the upper and lower parts of the bill together; especially associated with storks.

Clinal. Relating to gradual morphological or physiological change in a group of related organisms, usually along a line of environmental or geographic transition.

Clutch. A set of eggs.

Co-evolution. An evolutionary process in which two or more species change dramatically over time in response to one another. Examples include predators and prey, and brood parasites and their hosts.

Colony. A spatially discrete cluster of breeding territories, usually tightly packed together.

Communal nesting. Breeding system in which several females place eggs in the same nest and all adults care for the young. *See* Cooperative breeding.

Complete molt. The replacement of feathers in all tracts of the body within a short time. *See* Partial molt.

Conspecific. Belonging to the same species.

Continental shelf. Shallow area, often tens of miles wide, that lies between a continent and the deep ocean.

Continental slope. Point at the edge of the continental shelf at which the ocean bottom drops off, extending down to the deep ocean floor.

Contour feathers. The outer coat of feathers of the body, wings, and tail that gives a bird its appearance. Contour feathers have two vanes along their shaft, with the barbs of the vanes interlinked as smoothly connected units. Other body feathers, such as down and semiplumes, lack the interlocking system that shapes the vanes. Often the term contour feathers is used to refer to just the outer body feathers, excluding the flight feathers.

Convergent evolution. The development of similar features in unrelated species exposed to similar environmental factors. Example: the talons and hooked bill of owls and hawks.

Cooperative breeding. Breeding system in which nonparental adults help a breeding pair raise young. The nonparental adults, called extra-pair helpers, auxiliaries, or supernumeraries, usually do not breed. *See* Communal nesting.

Cosmopolitan. Found widely throughout a region; often used to refer to species with a worldwide distribution.

Countershading. A plumage pattern of light underparts and dark upperparts that serves to disguise the outline of a bird and contributes to concealment.

Counter-singing. Behavior in which a territory holder matches the songs of a neighbor or stranger phrase by phrase. Counter-singing is thought to send an "I'm here and I know you're there" message; it helps establish territory ownership and territorial boundaries without physical confrontations.

Coverts. Small contour feathers that cover the base of the flight feathers on both the upper and lower surfaces of the tail and wing.

Crèche. A flock of unrelated young brought together for protection, often guarded by a single parent bird, while other adult birds feed or rest. Often seen in waterbirds that breed along beaches or on islands.

Crepuscular. Active at dawn and dusk.

Crop. An expandable pouch in the esophagus; serves as a temporary storage area for food. Not found in all birds.

Cryptic. Serving to conceal, as in cryptic plumage or cryptic placement of nests. Cryptic species look alike but do not interbreed where they occur together.

Culmen. The central ridge of the maxilla, running from forehead to bill tip.

Dabble. To reach with the bill into shallow water to obtain food, without diving or leaving the surface of a body of water.

DDT. Dichlorodiphenyltrichloroethane; an organic pesticide banned in the United States in the early 1970s, in part due to its toxic effect on birds. Still used in other parts of the world, especially in South America, where it can contaminate neotropical migrants.

Decurved. Curved downward; most often used to describe a bill shape.

Definitive plumage. Any "mature" plumage (basic, alternate, or supplemental) that is attained after all immature plumages and that does not change further with age, being renewed each subsequent year by an essentially identical plumage. Attainment of definitive plumages is not necessarily related to sexual maturity.

Delayed plumage maturation. A phenomenon that occurs when a bird reaches sexual maturity before developing its definitive plumages. Frequently, delayed plumage maturation occurs only in the males of a species, but it may also occur only in females or in both sexes.

Dichromatism (*adjective:* dichromatic). Variation in plumage color in which individuals have one of two distinct plumage types. *See* Dimorphism.

Dimorphism. Occurring in two forms that may differ in size, shape, color, or other characteristics. Often used to refer to differences between the sexes within a species. *See* Polymorphism.

Dispersal. Movement of individuals to new living areas. Includes both the initial movement from the place of birth to the first site at which the bird will attempt to breed (natal dispersal) and subsequent movement from one breeding location to another (adult dispersal). Also, wandering by individuals away from the breeding range and habitats in late summer, especially in herons and related species (postbreeding dispersal).

Display. A ritualized signal intended to convey a specific message.

Distal. Farther away from the central portion of the body.

Distribution. The area or range over which a species is found.

DNA–DNA hybridization study. A method of examining the genetic similarity of two kinds of birds by creating hybrid

DNA strands and measuring how much energy is required to break the strands. Used to estimate the relatedness of taxa.

DNA fingerprinting. Use of genetic markers (specific strands of DNA) to resolve the identity of unique individuals within a population. Used in studies of parentage and estimates of reproductive success.

Dorsal. Referring to the back or upperparts.

Drag. A force that opposes movement. In avian flight, drag reduces the lift produced by air moving over the wing.

Dummy nest. A nest built to make a territory attractive to females, to distract predators or nest-parasitizing birds from the actual egg nest, as an alternate nest to which the parent can move eggs or chicks if the first nest is disturbed, or as an additional roosting or nursery area.

Echolocation. A process of navigation through the use of reflected sound; most often associated with bats but also practiced by some swifts, nightjar relatives, and a few other birds.

Eclipse plumage. A drab, female-like plumage worn by some male ducks in fall, while they simultaneously molt all their flight feathers and thus cannot fly.

Ecotone. A habitat created by the juxtaposition of different habitats merging into each other; may support distinctive "edge" species.

Edge effect. The physical and biotic changes in a community due to the presence of sharp edges between adjacent habitats, especially where open habitats are created in large, previously undisturbed habitat blocks. Also, the increased diversity and abundance of organisms found at habitat junctions.

Egg-dumping. The practice of placing eggs in a nest built by another bird.

Elliptical. Egg shape equally rounded at both ends and broadest in the middle.

Emergent vegetation. Vegetation that is rooted underwater but has foliage extending above the water's surface.

Endangered species. An organism in imminent danger of extinction throughout all or a significant portion of its range. See Threatened species.

Exotic. Non-native; often used to refer to an introduced species.

Extinction. The death of all individuals of a population (local extinction) or a species (global extinction).

Extirpation. The loss of all individuals from an island, local population, or region; generally implies that the species still exists in other areas.

Extra-pair copulation. Behavior in which a socially monogamous individual mates with an individual other than the one with which it has an established pair bond.

Extra-pair fertilization. The successful production of a fertilized egg that results from a copulation with an individual other than the mate.

Extra-pair helpers. Individuals that help breeding individuals raise offspring. Also called auxiliaries or supernumeraries. See Cooperative breeding.

Eyeshine. Reflection from the tapetum, the vascular membrane of the retina within the eye of goatsuckers, owls, kiwis, and other nightbirds.

Facial shield. A hard plate on the forehead of some birds, especially coots, used as a breeding ornament or for species identification.

Facultative. Optional; used especially for traits that may be exhibited by only some members of a population or by individuals in some years or situations but not others. Example: Facultative migration in the fall occurs when a bird population moves different distances in different years, depending on the availability of food in various parts of the wintering ground. See Obligate.

Fallout. Migratory phenomenon in which birds are forced down by inclement weather or winds into any habitat they can find. During such events birders can see large numbers of birds and a variety of migrants within a small area.

Family. A taxon that is a subset of an order and that contains one or more genera. Names of avian families end in "–idae". See Taxonomic classification.

Feather tracts. Regions of the skin to which feathers are attached. Also called pterylae.

Fecal sac. The mucous membrane in which feces of nestlings are wrapped.

Filoplume. A specialized feather found on the body under the contour feathers, with very few barbs that are mostly concentrated toward the tip of the shaft. The function of filoplumes is poorly known; they may help a bird sense the position of individual feathers within its coat.

Fledging. The development in young birds of the feathers necessary for flight. More generally, developing enough independence to leave the nest and move in the general nest area, while still dependent on parental care.

Fledgling. A young bird that has left the nest but is not yet completely independent of parental care.

Flight feathers. Collective name for the long feathers of the wings and tail.

Forbs. Nonwoody, nongrassy plant species found in the understory and ground layer; includes many wildflowers.

Forest. A habitat dominated by trees. True forests have a closed canopy at least 30 feet (10 m) high, while open forests or woodlands have smaller or more widely spaced trees. *See* Woodland.

Form. A taxon or unit of classification; a morphologically distinguishable group of organisms. *See* Taxon.

Gape. The opening created when the mouth is opened wide; it is noticeably large in species that forage on aerial insects (swallows, swifts, nightjars). Also called the rictus. Used by some birders to refer to the area or the angle at which the maxilla and mandible meet. In nestlings, often used to refer to the brightly colored areas in the corners of the open mouth, also called the rictal flanges. In the last context, brightly colored gapes may be retained by young birds after they leave the nest and thus can be used to determine the age of immature birds.

Gaping. A foraging technique in which a bird thrusts its bill into the soil and forcibly opens the bill, creating an opening. Found mainly in starlings and members of the blackbird family.

Genetic monogamy. Pairing of a single male and single female to produce young, all of which are the genetic offspring of the pair. *See* Social monogamy.

Genotype. The genetic characteristics of an individual. Unlike phenotypic traits, the genotype of an individual does not vary with circumstances. *See* Phenotype.

Genus (*plural:* genera). A taxon that is a subset of a family and that contains one or more species. *See* Taxonomic classification.

Gizzard. Muscular organ that is part of the avian digestive system. Food in the gizzard is ground up by the combined action of muscular contraction and the hard stones (grit) retained in the gizzard.

Gorget. Iridescent throat patch on hummingbirds.

Guano. Large deposits of bird feces that accumulate in sites that birds regularly use, such as breeding colonies.

Gular fluttering. A cooling behavior in which birds rapidly flap membranes in the throat to increase evaporation; particularly obvious in cormorants, pelicans, and their relatives.

Gular pouch. A bare throat pouch that can be expanded to accommodate large prey; found in pelicans and their relatives.

Hacking. A conservation and rehabilitation practice in which birds released into the wild are provisioned with food while they gradually become independent. The location at which the bird is released is called the hack site.

Hallux. Hind toe.

Helpers at the nest. *See* Extra-pair helpers.

Heterodactyly. Arrangement of the toes in which the inner front toe is turned backward such that two toes point forward and two backward. Found in trogons.

Holarctic. Relating to the biogeographic region that includes the northern parts of the Old and New Worlds, and that comprises the Nearctic and Palearctic regions.

Home range. The area that an animal uses in the course of its daily activities. Not necessarily defended. *See* Territory.

Host. Bird whose nest receives eggs laid by brood parasites. The hosts then provide parental care to the unrelated young that hatch from the parasitic egg, often to the detriment of their own young.

Hyoid apparatus. A collective term for the bones of the tongue and associated connective tissues, found in the upper throat. Small in most species, the apparatus is greatly expanded in the woodpeckers and hummingbirds, with two long, thin "horns" supporting a long, extendable tongue.

Immature. A young bird no longer under parental care but not yet old enough to breed; a bird that is not yet fully adult.

Incubation patch. *See* Brood patch.

Intergrading. The merging of characteristics of two populations where their ranges come into contact. The intergrading of morphological traits is often interpreted as evidence that two forms are not reproductively isolated and should be treated as a single species.

Internal compass. The hypothesized mechanism that allows organisms to orient themselves so as to proceed in the proper direction during long-distance movements such as migration. In birds, several internal compass systems have been proposed, but none are well investigated.

Intertidal zone. Shallow coastal area of marine habitats exposed at low tide and covered by seawater at high tide.

Introduced species. *See* Exotic.

Invasion. *See* Irruption.

Irruption. A sudden large movement of individuals into an area where they are generally uncommon, often on an unpredictable basis. Also called invasion.

Juvenal (*adjective*). Refers to the first plumage attained after a bird loses its down feathers.

Juvenile. A bird wearing its juvenal body feathers. In most songbirds juvenal feathers are molted within a few weeks of leaving the nest; thus songbirds are generally considered to be juveniles for only a short period. Some species such as hawks and tubenoses retain juvenal body plumage for a full year.

Kleptoparasitism. Strategy of stealing items, such as food or nest materials, from other individuals. Seen especially in frigatebirds and jaegers.

Lamellae (*singular:* lamella). A comb-like structure at the edge of the bill; used to filter tiny food items from water.

Lanceolate. A long, slender shape, like a thin leaf.

Laterally compressed. Thinner in width than is typical for similar birds. Used to describe body shape in rails and bill shape in puffins and anis.

Lek. Associated with an extreme form of polygyny (lekking) in which males gather in tiny territories to display to visiting females, who select males for copulation. Can refer to either the group of males or the piece of ground where the territories are located.

Lift. An aerodynamic force that moves a bird off the ground and keeps it in the air; produced by air moving around and past the airfoil formed by the wings. *See* Airfoil.

Littoral. A shallow-water habitat found immediately along the coasts or edges of lakes and oceans.

Loafing platform. A nest-like structure built by coots and waterfowl where young can rest out of the water.

Lores. The area between the eyes and the base of the bill.

Mandible. The lower portion of the bill; often referred to as the lower mandible.

Mantle. The group of feathers in the center of the back. Also used to refer to the back and inner portion of the folded wings of a bird at rest, especially when this region is a single color.

Mast. Nuts and other large fruits that accumulate on the forest floor.

Maxilla. The upper portion of the bill; often referred to as the upper mandible.

Microhabitat. The particular parts of a habitat an individual uses in the course of its daily activities; usually refers to a subset of conditions within a broad habitat type. Example: Louisiana Waterthrushes forage along the edges of streams (a microhabitat) within deciduous forests (a habitat).

Migration. Annual movements between breeding and wintering sites, usually between areas of different latitude. Also can be an elevational movement between breeding sites in mountains and adjacent lowland areas.

Migratory overshooting. An exceptional but not infrequent phenomenon in which migrating birds fly in the proper direction but beyond the normal distance.

Mirror-image orientation. Phenomenon in which migrating individuals apparently reverse the east–west orientation of their migration and move to areas outside their normal range. Thought to be the reason why numbers of eastern species arrive on the California coast in autumn.

Mitochondrial DNA study. Research on the origins and relationships among species and other taxa, using similarities and differences in the genetic composition of the DNA found in the cellular mitochondria, the organelles within a cell that produce energy for cellular functions.

Mobbing. Harassment by a group of birds, directed at a predator or other intruder with the aim of forcing the target to move out of the vicinity.

Molt-migration. An annual migration pattern that includes a movement from the breeding ground to a temporary location where molt occurs, followed by a later migration to the wintering range. Found in ducks and some passerines.

Monogamy. Relationship in which a single male and female establish an exclusive pair bond during one reproductive cycle.

Morph. One or more distinctive plumages seen in certain species; represents a plumage variation that is retained throughout life by an individual and is not related to the age or sex of the individual. Also called a phase.

Morphology. Physical attributes of an individual.

Muskeg. A large region of poorly drained wetlands with scattered trees, common in the northern boreal forest.

Naricorns. Raised, horny tubes (nostril sheaths) on top of the bill that encase the nostrils of members of the order Procellariiformes, the tubenoses; may help direct the salt drops excreted from the salt glands away from the eyes.

Nearctic. Relating to the biogeographic subregion that includes Greenland and North America north of tropical Mexico.

Nectivorous. Nectar-eating.

Neotropics. The biogeographic region that includes southern Mexico and Central America, the Caribbean, and South America.

Neritic. Relating to the portion of the ocean composed of the shallow waters over the continental shelf.

Nest parasitism. *See* Brood parasitism.

New World. The Western Hemisphere, including North and South America.

Nidicolous. Reared for a time in a nest. Altricial young are always nidicolous. Some precocial young may be nidicolous too; that is, they are capable of locomotion but do not actually leave the nest.

Nidifugous. Leaving the nest soon after hatching. Nidifugous young are always precocial.

Nine-primaried oscines. A subgroup of the oscines within the order Passeriformes. Unlike other passerines that have 10 full, functional primary feathers on each wing, the nine-primaried oscines have a 10th primary so reduced that it does not function in flight. The New World nine-primaried oscines include the wood-warblers, tanagers, New World sparrows, cardinals and buntings, and blackbirds and orioles, and are generally thought to be closely related; from 1983 to 1998, the AOU considered all these groups to be members of one family.

Nomadism (*adjective:* nomadic). Movement in which a population shifts from site to site between seasons in a relatively unpredictable manner. Differs from migration in that individuals do not move each year to defined breeding and wintering ranges, and may not even move every year.

Nuclear DNA study. Research on the origins and relationships among species and other taxa, using similarities and differences in the genetic composition of the DNA found in the nucleus of cells.

Obligate. Required; also, exhibited by all members of a species without exception. *See* Facultative.

Old World. The Eastern Hemisphere, including Africa, Eurasia, and Australia.

Orbital ring. A fleshy ring around the eye; contrastingly colored in some species.

Order. A taxon that is a subset of a class and that contains one or more families. Scientific names of avian orders end in "–formes". *See* Taxonomic classification.

Oscines. One of two major subdivisions of the order Passeriformes. Oscines have a more complex syrinx and distinctive DNA patterns and middle ear bone shapes, and they generally must learn their most complex vocalizations. Includes virtually all North American passerines except the tyrant flycatchers. *See* Suboscines.

Oval. Egg shape that is rounded at the largest end and tapered at the other end. Often used to describe the typical egg shape.

Palearctic. The biogeographic region that includes Eurasia, northern Arabia, and Africa north of the Sahara.

Pantropical. Occurring throughout the tropical regions of the world.

Parasitism. *See* Brood parasitism.

Partial molt. The replacement of feathers in only some of the body's feather tracts. *See* Complete molt.

Partners in Flight. A collaborative conservation project combining the efforts of state and federal land-management agencies and nongovernmental conservation groups. Initially Partners in Flight brought attention to the conservation of neotropical migrant birds; currently the project has broadened its scope to native North American birds in general.

Passerine. A member of the order Passeriformes, often referred to as a songbird.

PCBs. Polychlorinated biphenyls, a class of chemicals used as lubricants and insulation materials and in printing ink. Long-lived in the environment, PCBs are difficult to clean up and have toxic effects on birds and their reproduction.

Pectinate. Having tooth-like projections similar to the teeth of a comb. Found on the toes of grouse and the middle claw of some species, such as the Barn Owl.

Peep. General name for several small sandpiper species in the genus *Calidris*.

Pelagic. Associated with deep waters of the open ocean.

Pellet. A mass of indigestible material including fur, feathers, and bones regurgitated by hawks, owls, herons, and other predatory birds. When found in numbers below a regular roost or nest site, pellets can be analyzed to determine the diet of birds.

Permafrost. A permanently frozen layer of earth beneath the surface.

Phase. *See* Morph.

Phenotype. The observable physical characteristics of an organism, which may change within an individual in response to environmental factors. *See* Genotype.

Philopatry. The tendency of individual birds to breed near the site where they were hatched and raised.

Phylogenetic Species Concept. A definition of "species" as the smallest aggregate of organisms that share a unique evolutionary history. *See* Biological Species Concept.

Phylogeny. The pattern of evolutionary history shown by a group of organisms.

Phytoplankton. Microscopic plants that form the base of many aquatic food chains.

Pied. Of two or more colors in blotches.

Pinfeathers. New growing feathers encased in a horny sheath during the early stages of molt.

Pishing. A sound birders make to attract curious birds; may sound like the calls of mobbing or distressed birds.

Polyandry. A breeding relationship in which one female is mated to two or more males. May be either simultaneous (female bonds with multiple males at the same time) or sequential (female bonds with different males at different times within the same season).

Polygamy. A general term for mating systems in which members of one sex attempt to form pair bonds with several members of the other sex. Polyandry and polygyny are both types of polygamous mating systems.

Polygynandry. A rare breeding system in which members of both sexes have more than one partner.

Polygyny. A breeding relationship in which one male is mated to two or more females. May be either simultaneous (male bonds with multiple females at the same time) or sequential (male bonds with different females at different times within the same season).

Polymorphism. The quality of existing in two or more forms. Used in context of plumage patterns, genetic compositions, or other patterns. *See* Dimorphism.

Polynya. A productive, open-water habitat within an area of sea ice, created by persistent upwellings, where seabirds can forage year-round despite the high latitude.

Powder down. A feather type that has special barbs that disintegrate into a fine powder used in preening and waterproofing the feather coat. Especially prominent in herons and bitterns.

Prealternate molt. The molt that results in the production of the alternate plumage.

Prebasic molt. The molt that results in the production of the basic plumage.

Precocial. Capable of a high degree of independent activity from birth. A precocial hatchling has heavy down, is soon mobile, and often requires little direct parental care. *See* Altricial.

Preen gland. The source of the oil that a preening bird rubs on its feathers to maintain them in good condition; located on the lower back near the rump. Also called the uropygial gland.

Primary. One of the long, outermost flight feathers of the wing, attached to the manus or "hand" bones of the forelimb.

Primary extension. The distance that the longest primaries extend beyond the secondaries and tertials when the wing is folded alongside the body. Also called primary projection.

Proximal. Nearer to the central portion of the body.

Pyriform. Egg shape with the larger end distinctly blunt and rounded, and the opposite end narrowing to a distinct point; "pear-shaped."

Race. Subspecies. *See* Taxonomic classification.

Rachis. The portion of the central shaft of a feather to which the vanes are attached.

Radiation. The evolution of several closely related species from a single ancestor, especially when the species evolve morphological differences that allow the coexistence or spread of the species to occupy many different habitats or ecological roles. Also called adaptive radiation.

Range. The geographic area or spatial distribution in which a species is normally found.

Rare. Present in a given location but unlikely to be seen without considerable effort, usually because the species is found in small numbers or because (for nonresident species) it is present in only some years. Usually implies a more regular occurrence than "accidental." Globally, can refer to a species that is locally common within a very restricted range.

Rectrices (*singular:* rectrix). The long flight feathers of the tail.

Recurved. Curved upward or backward.

Regular species. In this book, generally a species that has been recorded 10 or more times in the last 25 years in continental North America, but with some exceptions. *See also* pages 10–11.

Remiges (*singular:* remex). The long flight feathers of the wings.

Resident. A nonmigratory species that completes its annual cycle within a fixed area. *See* Sedentary.

Reverse migration. A phenomenon in which migrating individuals orient in the direction opposite the normal one for the species at that season. Example: for Northern Hemisphere migrants, flying north in the fall instead of south.

Rictal bristles. Stiff, hair-like modified contour feathers that occur in a row and project from each side of the corners of the mouth (rictus); each feather (bristle) is equipped with a muscle that moves it. May funnel food into the mouth, protect the bird's eyes from insect legs and wings, or have a tactile function similar to the whiskers of some mammals.

Riparian. Associated with rivers and streams.

Rounded. The shortest version of an elliptical egg shape; spherical.

Salt flats. Barren areas with highly saline and alkaline soils, formed through the concentration of mineral residues in salt water. Many salt flats occur in deserts or sinks, where surface water drains into low basins and quickly evaporates.

Scrape nest. A rudimentary ground nest site, usually with no lining, that a bird forms by creating a shallow depression in the ground.

Secondary. One of the shorter flight feathers of the wing, attached along the ulna in the "inner wing."

Sedentary. Nonmigratory; generally used for birds that do not move long distances in dispersal or other movements. *See* Resident.

Sedges. Grass-like plants, many in the genus *Carex,* that are often found in wetlands.

Semiplumes. Feathers that lie beneath the contour feathers and that, like down, lack interlocking barbules and barbicels; fluffy in appearance, they probably add insulation.

Semi-precocial. Describes young that have characteristics of precocial young at hatch (open eyes, down, capacity to leave the nest) but that remain at the nest and are cared for by parents until close to adult size. *See* Precocial.

Sexual selection. A type of natural selection affecting traits that influence an individual's ability to attain or choose a mate, rather than traits that influence an individual's ability to survive. Thought to be responsible for the evolution of many elaborate morphological features, such as long plumes, bright colors, and complex display behaviors.

Shaft. A feather's stiff central structure, to which the vanes are attached.

Shorebirds. Sandpipers, plovers, and their close relatives of similar size and ecology, often associated with coastal and inland wetlands. Does not include the long-legged wading birds and gulls, terns, and their relatives. *See* Waders.

Siblicide. The death of young caused by fighting with siblings. Often occurs in larger birds (eagles, herons) in years when there is not enough food to feed all chicks. *See* Brood reduction.

Sink population. A breeding group that does not produce enough offspring to maintain itself in coming years without immigrants from other populations.

Social monogamy. The monogamous association between a male and a female that cooperate in producing a clutch of eggs and (often) raising the resulting young. Does not imply that the male and female in the pair are the genetic parents of all the young. *See* Genetic monogamy.

Songbird. The common name for members of the order Passeriformes, also called the passerines.

Song repertoire The number of different individual songs produced by a single bird. Also called vocal repertoire.

Source population. A breeding group that produces enough offspring to be self-sustaining and that often produces excess young that must disperse to other areas.

Southern Ocean. The continuous expanse of ocean between Antarctica and the southern tips of the other continents.

Species. A taxon that is a subset of a genus and that may contain one or more subspecies (races). *See* Taxonomic classification.

Stereotyped. Behaviors that are distinctive and consistently used in a particular situation. Generally used to refer to behaviors, such as courtship displays, that are considered to be innate.

Stoop. To dive in the air; used especially for falcons in courtship or when attacking prey.

Stray. An individual bird found in a region outside of its regular range. *See* Vagrant.

Subelliptical. Egg shape rounded at both ends but elongated and tapering toward the rounded ends, with the broadest point nearer one end than the other.

Subfamily. A taxon that is a subset of a family and that contains one or more genera. *See* Taxonomic classification.

Suboscine. One of two subdivisions of the order Passeriformes. Suboscines have a relatively simple syrinx, a distinctly shaped columella (the small bone of the middle ear), a unique arrangement of mitochondrial DNA, and innate songs that do not require learning. Predominantly a South and Central American group; the only major suboscine family in North America is the tyrant flycatchers. *See* Oscine.

Subspecies. A geographical subset of a species, showing discrete differences in morphology or coloration compared to other members of the species. Subspecies may also differ in their habitat, voice, and other behavior, but they can interbreed. Often the lowest taxonomic level within a classification system. Also called a race. *See* Taxonomic classification.

Substrate. Surface.

Subtropical. Habitats and climates that are tropical in nature but found north or south of the tropics.

Succession (*adjective:* successional). The sequence of plant communities that occur following disturbance and that culminate in a region's dominant habitat type.

Supercilium (*adjective:* superciliary). Eyebrow.

Superspecies. A group of species that seem to have had a relatively recent common ancestor. *See* Taxonomic classification.

Supplemental plumage. A generation of feathers, additional to the basic and alternate plumages, found in a few birds that have more than two molts per year.

Suspended molt. A molt that is halted for a short period—for example, during migration or due to a food shortage—and then resumed at a later date.

Sympatric. Occurring in the same geographic area. *See* Allopatric.

Synchronous hatching. Hatching in which all chicks hatch within a 24-hour period. Also called simultaneous hatching. *See* Asynchronous hatching.

Syndactyly. Arrangement of the toes in which the outer and middle front toes are partially joined; found in kingfishers, hoopoes, and their relatives.

Syrinx. The structure through which most avian vocalizations are produced; found at the base of the trachea where the bronchial tubes are attached. Variation in the complexity of the syrinx is used as a taxonomic characteristic for defining different groups.

Taiga. Ecological zone south of the tundra and north of the temperate zone, dominated by conifer trees and harsh winters. Also called northern boreal forest.

Tarsus (*plural:* tarsi). The lower leg. The major bone in this region of the leg is the tarsometatarsus, which is a fusion of structures called ankle and foot bones in mammals. The avian equivalent of the mammalian lower leg bones (the tibia and fibula) is found in the "drumstick," or what appears to be the upper leg in most birds.

Taxon (*plural:* taxa). A unit used in grouping and naming living organisms; a general term that can refer to any level of a taxonomic classification. Family, genus, and species are all taxa. The term taxa is also often used to refer to the number of distinct forms within a family, or other taxonomic grouping, when there is ambiguity as to whether some of those forms are species or subspecies. In this context also called a form.

Taxonomic classification. Hierarchical system for grouping and naming types of living organisms. The highest-level taxon is the kingdom, which is typically broken down into subgroups called divisions (for plants) and phyla (for animals). Phyla are divided into classes (birds are in the class Aves) and then into orders. Orders are subdivided into families. Within families, birds are grouped at other taxonomic levels, given here in sequence from larger groupings to smaller: subfamily, tribe, genus, superspecies, species, and subspecies (race).

Territory. A defended area in which an animal resides. *See* Home range.

Tertials. The flight feathers of the wing closest to the body; the three innermost secondaries.

Thermal. A rising body of warm air. Used by some soaring birds to gain height without flapping.

Threatened species. An organism likely to become endangered within the foreseeable future throughout all or a significant portion of its range. *See* Endangered species.

Torpor. A period of reduced activity and metabolism in which organisms can save energy; not as deep a reduction in metabolic activity as hibernation. Birds in torpor can be roused to normal activity relatively quickly. Small birds such as hummingbirds routinely go into torpor during cool evenings or colder seasons.

Totipalmate feet. A condition in swimming birds of the order Pelecaniformes in which webbing is extended to connect all four toes.

Tract. *See* Feather tracts.

Trap-lining. Conducting daily rounds of food sources. Example: hummingbirds visiting patches of flowers and artificial feeders in a predictable sequence.

Treeline. Elevation or latitude above which trees cannot grow.

Triangulation. A technique for finding a position, often of prey, by means of taking bearings from two or more fixed points. Some species (some owls, harriers) have asymmetrical ear openings that improve triangulation using sound.

Tribe. A taxon that is a subset of a subfamily and that contains one or more genera. *See* Taxonomic classification.

Tubenoses. Colloquial name for members of the order Procellariiformes, which includes the albatrosses, the shearwaters and petrels, and the storm-petrels; reflects the presence of tubular sheaths (naricorns) that encase the nasal openings on the top of the bill. *See* Naricorns.

Tundra. Habitats beyond the treeline at high altitudes or elevations that lack a permanent ice or snow cover; usually dominated by low-lying vegetation, including mosses, lichens, small shrubs, and forbs.

Upland. Pertaining to areas away from coastlines and the floodplains of rivers, streams, and other bodies of water.

Upwelling. Oceanic areas where deep waters rich in nutrients rise to the surface because of the shape of the ocean bottom, the presence of continental land masses, or contact between water currents.

Urohydrosis. The habit of releasing feces onto the scaly portions of the leg as a cooling mechanism, using evaporative cooling of the fluids. Found in storks and New World vultures.

Uropygial gland. *See* Preen gland.

Vagrant. An individual bird that appears in an area well outside the known range for that species. *See* Stray.

Vane. The flat portion of the feather extending off the rachis of the shaft; the feather "webbing."

Ventral. Referring to the belly or underparts.

Waders. Long-legged, long-necked birds found in wetlands and coastal habitats; includes herons and their relatives, ibises and spoonbills, storks, and flamingos. Among North American birders, does not refer to shorebirds, as it does elsewhere in the world. *See* Shorebirds.

WatchList. A conservation program identifying species that are declining or have limited ranges but are not yet threatened or endangered. The WatchList is a cooperative project of the National Audubon Society and Partners in Flight.

Wattle. An unfeathered flap or growth of skin on the face or neck that hangs down below the head; often brightly colored or wrinkled. Found especially on turkeys, jacanas, and some plovers.

Wing-bar. A light-colored bar on a wing, formed by pale tips on the covert feathers or pale bases of the flight feathers.

Wing-flicking. A rapid movement of the wings of a bird otherwise at rest; seen, for example, in some kinglets and *Empidonax* flycatchers. Such movements, along with pumping of the tail, are sometimes described as "nervous" habits.

Wing formula. The relative lengths of the primaries, used as a measurement of wingtip shape. Cryptic species such as those in the tyrant flycatcher genus *Empidonax* can be identified in the hand using their species-specific formula.

Wing-loading. Total body weight per unit of wing area. Used in the analysis of flight performance.

Woodland. A habitat dominated by trees, but with less overhead canopy and tree density than found in true forests. In woodlands trees are often small, and the ground is commonly covered with grass or forbs. *See* Forest.

Zooplankton. The tiny animals, including protozoans, crustaceans, mollusks, and larval fish, that feed on phytoplankton and are eaten by vertebrate predators. Both zoo- and phytoplankton lack the ability to move independently and depend on water currents for movement.

Zygodactyly. Arrangement of the toes in which the outer front toe is turned backward, such that two toes point forward and two backward. Found in woodpeckers, cuckoos, parrots, and some other groups.

Author Biographies

DAVID ALLEN SIBLEY (Artist and technical consultant; *Habitats and Distributions; Storks; Thick-knees; Jacanas; Coursers and Pratincoles*), son of the well-known ornithologist Fred Sibley, began seriously watching and drawing birds in 1969, at age seven. He has written and illustrated articles on bird identification for many regional and national publications, as well as several books. Since 1980 he has traveled throughout the North American continent in search of birds, both on his own and as a leader of bird-watching tours. This intensive travel and bird study culminated in the publication of his comprehensive guide to bird identification, *The Sibley Guide to Birds*, in the fall of 2000. You can see more of David's artwork at *www.sibleyart.com*.

CHRIS ELPHICK (Technical consultant; *Flight, Form, and Function; Behavior; Habitats and Distributions; Populations and Conservation; Jacanas*) grew up in England and was introduced to birding by his father, Dennis, an avid amateur birder and bird bander. He earned his Ph.D. from the University of Nevada, Reno, for his work on the conservation implications of different methods of managing rice fields in California. His research focuses primarily on the conservation of waterbirds, especially shorebirds, and on large-scale conservation planning. He coauthored the *Birds of North America* accounts on the Greater Yellowlegs and Hudsonian Godwit and is a scientific advisor for the Great Basin Bird Observatory and the forthcoming *Nevada Breeding Bird Atlas*. Currently he is a Research Scientist at the University of Connecticut, Storrs.

JOHN B. DUNNING, JR. (Technical consultant; *Flight, Form, and Function; Behavior; Habitats and Distributions; Parrots and Allies; Hoopoe; Old World Flycatchers; Accentors; Olive Warbler; Wood-Warblers; Bananaquit; New World Sparrows; Exotic "Finches"*) is an Associate Professor of Wildlife Ecology at Purdue University. He received a Ph.D. in Ecology from the University of Arizona for his work on foraging ecology and community structure in towhees. His research currently focuses on conservation biology and on the response of bird populations to large-scale changes in habitat distribution. He has published over 50 papers and two books, most notably a compilation of body masses for over 6,300 species of birds worldwide. He authored or coauthored the *Birds of North America* accounts on the Buff-breasted Flycatcher, Buff-collared Nightjar, Cassin's Sparrow, and Bachman's Sparrow.

GEORGE L. ARMISTEAD (*Rails, Gallinules, and Coots; Limpkin*) is currently pursuing an M.S. in Environmental Studies at the University of Pennsylvania. Since 1994 he has worked at Visual Resources for Ornithology (VIREO), a collection of bird photographs managed by the Academy of Natural Sciences of Philadelphia. He has assisted in ornithological projects in the United States and Central America. His writing has appeared in *The American Bird-Watcher, Birding*, and *North American Birds*.

ALEX BADYAEV (*Wagtails and Pipits*) became interested in wagtails while researching avian biology throughout the eastern Palearctic and Alaska. He earned his Ph.D. from the University of Montana for work on the evolution of avian sexual dimorphism. He is currently a visiting faculty member at Auburn University, Alabama. He has published more than 50 professional papers and coauthored the *Birds of North America* accounts on the White, Black-backed, and Yellow Wagtails.

F. KEITH BARKER (*Wrens*) received a Ph.D. in Evolutionary Biology from the University of Chicago. He is currently a Frank M. Chapman Postdoctoral Fellow at the American Museum of Natural History. His work focuses on historical patterns of behavioral diversification in birds, and their ecological correlates. His dissertation focused on the evolution of cooperative breeding and duetting behavior in wrens. He is the author of four peer-reviewed papers.

ROBERT A. BEHRSTOCK (*Barn Owls; Typical Owls; Nighthawks and Nightjars*) has worked as a museum curator, university instructor, fisheries biologist, and birding tour leader. Now primarily a writer, photographer, and environmental consultant, he develops a variety of ecotourism-related projects for Fermata, Inc., in Texas. He has authored more than 30 papers in both popular and scientific formats, and has published hundreds of photos in such venues as *BBC Wildlife, Handbook of Birds of the World*, and various books and birding magazines.

EDWARD S. BRINKLEY (*Loons; Grebes; Albatrosses; Shearwaters and Petrels; Storm-Petrels; Tropicbirds; Boobies and Gannets; Pelicans; Cormorants; Darters [Anhinga]; Frigatebirds;*

Gulls, Terns, and Allies), formerly Professor of European Literature and Film at the University of Virginia, now runs the Sterling House Bed and Breakfast in Cape Charles, Virginia, and guides birding tours in the Americas and Iceland. He has served as editor of *North American Birds,* authored 40 articles on birds and marine life, contributed sections to *The Breeding Birds of Virginia, Bull's Birds of New York,* and the forthcoming *Wings over Virginia,* and coauthored pocket field guides to waterbirds. He is currently working on books on Atlantic seabirds and the avifauna of the Virginia coast.

RICK CECH *(Flight, Form, and Function; Origins, Evolution, and Classification; Behavior; Habitats and Distributions)* is a field naturalist, writer, and nature photographer specializing in birds, butterflies, and habitat ecology. He coauthored the *National Audubon Society Field Guide to Florida* and was a consultant for the *National Audubon Society Interactive CD-ROM Guide to North American Birds.* A past president of the Linnaean Society of New York, he is currently working on a natural history of East Coast butterflies.

GEORGE A. CLARK, JR. *(Tyrant Flycatchers)* is Professor Emeritus at the University of Connecticut, Storrs, and former State Ornithologist of Connecticut. He received his Ph.D. from Yale University. His work has focused on the distribution, behavior, structure, and evolution of birds. He was coeditor for *Perspectives in Ornithology/Essays Presented for the Centennial of the American Ornithologists' Union,* and author or coauthor of book chapters in *The Atlas of Breeding Birds of Connecticut, Handbook of Avian Anatomy,* and *The Waterfowl of the World, Volume 4,* and of more than 60 research papers in journals.

CHARLES T. COLLINS *(Swifts)* completed his M.S. at the University of Michigan and his Ph.D. at the University of Florida. His primary research interest is the breeding biology and foraging ecology of swifts. Other research interests include growth, demography, and natal pterylosis. Currently he is a Professor of Biological Sciences at California State University, Long Beach, where he has been studying nesting terns and skimmers in southern California and the demography of the endemic Island Scrub-Jay on Santa Cruz Island.

WILLIAM E. DAVIS, JR. *(Herons, Egrets, and Bitterns)* is Professor of Science at Boston University. He is past president of the Association of Field Ornithologists and the Nuttall Ornithological Club and is currently

president of the Wilson Ornithological Society. He is the author or editor of seven books, including *Dean of the Birdwatchers: A Biography of Ludlow Griscom.* He has published more than 300 reviews and 200 professional and popular papers and notes.

DAVID J. DELEHANTY *(Chachalacas and Allies; Grouse, Turkeys, and Allies; New World Quail)* is Assistant Professor of Avian Biology at Idaho State University. He completed his degrees at the Universities of North Dakota (M.S.) and Nevada (Ph.D.). His research examines the relationship between consumption of carotenoid pigments and annual fecundity in galliform birds and other animals. His publications include coauthorship of the *Birds of North America* Mountain Quail account, as well as several papers on the Mountain Quail.

KIMBALL L. GARRETT *(Parrots and Allies; Wood-Warblers)* has been the Ornithology Collections Manager at the Natural History Museum of Los Angeles County since 1982. He is past president of the Western Field Ornithologists. Coauthor of *Birds of Southern California: Status and Distribution* and *A Field Guide to Warblers of North America,* he has also published some 30 peer-reviewed papers and many popular articles. His current research centers on the status and ecology of naturalized non-native species of birds in California's urban areas.

GEOFFREY R. GEUPEL *(Babblers [Wrentit])* is currently Director of Terrestrial Research at the Point Reyes Bird Observatory in California. He received a B.S. in Biology from Lewis and Clark College and has studied the population ecology of the Wrentit and other coastal scrub birds for 20 years. He is also chair of California Partners in Flight.

KATHLEEN GROSCHUPF *(Old World Warblers and Gnatcatchers; Old World Sparrows)* earned an M.S. from Stephen F. Austin State University in Texas and a Ph.D. from Virginia Polytechnic Institute and State University. Her research focused on the songs and singing behavior of *Aimophila* sparrows. Her publications include the *Birds of North America* accounts on the Five-striped Sparrow, Varied Bunting, and Rufous-winged Sparrow. Her current work is on bioacoustical analyses of avian vocalizations and the natural history of birds in Arizona.

JEFF GROTH *(Finches and Allies)* is a Research Biologist at the American Museum of Natural History in New York City, where he is working on the molecular genetics of birds including finches, galliforms, and

Spotted Owls. He earned an M.S. at Virginia Polytechnic Institute and a Ph.D. in Zoology from the University of California, Berkeley, for his work on the behavior, morphology, and population genetics of North American crossbills.

JOSEPH A. GRZYBOWSKI *(Vireos)* is Professor of Anatomy at the University of Central Oklahoma, Edmond, and Research Associate with the Oklahoma Museum of Natural History, in Norman. He also serves as Southern Great Plains Regional Editor for *North American Birds*. His recent focus has been the demography and ecology of Black-capped Vireos and the community dynamics of cowbird/songbird host systems. He has published numerous technical and popular articles and authored the *Birds of North America* Black-capped Vireo account.

PAUL HENDRICKS *(Wagtails and Pipits)* is a Zoologist at the Montana Natural Heritage Program. He earned his Ph.D. from Washington State University for studies of the breeding ecology of the American Pipit. His interests include Arctic and alpine ecology and avian life history strategies and adaptations to harsh climates. He has authored or coauthored more than 50 papers, including the *Birds of North America* accounts on the American Pipit, Golden-crowned Sparrow, and Brown-capped Rosy-Finch.

ALEC HUMANN *(Loons; Grebes; Albatrosses; Shearwaters and Petrels; Storm-Petrels; Tropicbirds; Boobies and Gannets; Pelicans; Cormorants; Darters [Anhinga]; Frigatebirds; Gulls, Terns, and Allies; Shrikes; Chickadees and Titmice; Penduline Tits [Verdin]; Long-tailed Tits [Bushtit])* is a naturalist in the Buffalo, New York, region. He has worked as a raptor biologist at Cape May Bird Observatory, lectured on bird identification and conservation, conducted seasonal bird surveys, and led birding tours in the United States and Canada. He is currently working on a full revision of Beardslee and Mitchell's *Birds of the Niagara Frontier Region*.

ALVARO JARAMILLO *(Blackbirds, Orioles, and Allies)* is a Biologist at the San Francisco Bay Bird Observatory, California, where he specializes in bird responses to riparian habitat restoration. He also leads professional birding tours throughout the Americas for Field Guides, Inc. His past research has focused on Argentine cowbirds. In addition to *New World Blackbirds: The Icterids*, he has published many articles on the identification and distribution of North and South American birds. He is currently working on a field guide to the birds of his native Chile.

IAN L. JONES *(Auks)* is Associate Chair of the Atlantic Cooperative Wildlife Ecology Research Network at the Memorial University of Newfoundland. He earned his M.S. at the University of Toronto, where he studied parent-offspring vocal communication in Ancient Murrelets. His Ph.D. at Queen's University focused on the behavioral ecology of the Least Auklet, and subsequent research included the evolution of ornaments and social behavior of *Aethia* auklets. He has published 30 research papers concerning auk biology and coauthored *The Auks*.

THOMAS KNIGHT *(Dippers)* is completing his Ph.D. at Princeton University with work on the cultural transmission of song in Hawaiian honeycreepers. He also has studied physiological adaptations in embryos of the Willow and White-tailed Ptarmigan, habituation in the Black-billed Magpie, and song in the American Dipper. Before beginning his bachelor's degree he spent 10 years as a zookeeper at four zoos.

JOHN KRICHER *(Kinglets; Thrushes)* is a Professor of Biology at Wheaton College, in Massachusetts. He earned his Ph.D. from Rutgers University. His books include *A Neotropical Companion* and three ecology field guides. He has authored or coauthored the *Birds of North America* accounts on the Black-and-white Warbler and Glossy Ibis, in addition to more than 80 articles. He has served as president of the Wilson Ornithological Society, the Association of Field Ornithologists, and the Nuttall Ornithological Club. He is currently on the board of directors of the American Birding Association.

DAVID J. KRUEPER *(Kingfishers; Silky-flycatchers)* is Avian Senior Technical Specialist for the Bureau of Land Management at the San Pedro Riparian National Conservation Area. He has researched and monitored avian migratory use of desert riparian habitats in the Sonoran Desert and worked on riparian habitat management issues in Alaska, California, Arizona, New Mexico, and Sonora, Mexico. He has authored or coauthored numerous professional and nonprofessional articles on avian ecology.

STEPHEN A. LAYMON *(Cuckoos, Roadrunners, and Anis)* is a wildlife researcher and consultant, Adjunct Professor at San Francisco State University, and Instructor at Cerro Coso Community College. He has a Ph.D. in Wildlife Ecology from the University of California, Berkeley. His work focuses on declining bird species, including the Spotted Owl and Yellow-billed Cuckoo. He has authored over 60 publications and reports.

KEVIN J. MCGOWAN *(Crows and Jays)* is an ornithologist and Curator of the Bird and Mammal Collections at Cornell University. He received his Ph.D. from the University of South Florida for work on the social development of young Florida Scrub-Jays. His main research concerns the behavioral ecology of birds, especially the American and Fish Crows. He has published over 25 professional articles and is a member of the New York State Avian Records Committee.

NADAV NUR *(Babblers [Wrentit])* is Director of Population Ecology at the Point Reyes Bird Observatory, California. He received an M.S. in Biostatistics from the University of Washington and a Ph.D. in Zoology from Duke University. His research has included the development and application of novel statistical methods for understanding avian population dynamics. He is the author or coauthor of over 45 peer-reviewed scientific publications, including *A Statistical Guide to Data Analysis of Avian Monitoring Programs.*

WAYNE R. PETERSEN *(Plovers and Lapwings; Oystercatchers; Stilts and Avocets)* is Field Ornithologist at the Massachusetts Audubon Society and Vice President of the American Birding Association. He is a New England Regional Editor for *North American Birds* and *American Birds* and has presented workshops for the ABA's Institute for Field Ornithology. He authored or coauthored *Birds of Massachusetts, The National Audubon Society Pocket Guide to Songbirds and Familiar Backyard Birds (East),* and over 40 articles.

J. MICHAEL REED *(Populations and Conservation; Woodpeckers and Allies; Nuthatches; Creepers)* is an Assistant Professor of Biology at Tufts University. He received his M.S. from the University of Montana and his Ph.D. from North Carolina State University, where he worked on Red-cockaded Woodpecker population biology and conservation. Primarily interested in population biology, behavior, and species conservation, he has done work on the Spotted Sandpiper, Hawaiian Stilt, Black-throated Blue Warbler, and Red-naped Sapsucker. He has published over 50 scientific papers, and coedited a symposium on shorebird ecology.

JAMES D. RISING *(Bulbuls; Starlings and Mynas)* is a Professor of Zoology at the University of Toronto, where he specializes in the evolution and systematics of birds. He received his Ph.D. from the University of Kansas and has done field work in Mexico, Costa Rica, the United States, and Canada. He is the author of *A Guide to the Identification and Natural History of the Sparrows of the*

United States and Canada, as well as more than 60 technical papers.

GARY H. ROSENBERG *(Mockingbirds and Thrashers)* is a tour leader for Wings, Inc., secretary of the Arizona Bird Committee, and a co-regional editor for *North American Birds.* He received his M.S. in Zoology from Louisiana State University. He has authored or coauthored nearly 20 articles and research papers for professional and popular birding journals.

MARGARET RUBEGA *(Flight, Form, and Function; Origins, Evolution, and Classification)* is an Assistant Professor of Ecology and Evolutionary Biology at the University of Connecticut, Storrs, where her research focuses on the ecology, evolution, and mechanics of feeding in birds. She is also the Connecticut State Ornithologist. She received a Ph.D. in Biology from the University of California, Irvine, for work on the functional morphology and ecology of feeding in Red-necked Phalaropes.

ROBERT and **MARTHA SARGENT** *(Hummingbirds)* are field ornithologists specializing in hummingbird research. They founded The Hummer/Bird Study Group, Inc., dedicated to the study of hummingbirds and other neotropical migrants. They operate a seasonal bird banding station on the Alabama Gulf coast and are licensed to band hummingbirds in most of the eastern United States. The Sargents coauthored the *Birds of North America* account on the Ruby-throated Hummingbird and published a book on that species. They have authored or coauthored numerous papers and are past president and treasurer, respectively, of the Alabama Ornithological Society.

WILLIAM J. SENG *(Ibises and Spoonbills; Flamingos; Cranes)* is an independent field biologist with a B.S. in Marine Resource Management. He has been involved in research projects for the Cape May Bird Observatory, including spring and fall migratory hawk counts and field work for the *Breeding Bird Atlas of New Jersey,* and has served several seasons as principal observer at the Avalon Seawatch, an annual migratory seabird survey.

FREDERICK H. SHELDON *(Swallows and Martins)* is a Curator at the Louisiana State University Museum of Natural Science. His current research concerns the evolution of swallows. He has also studied the population genetics and biogeography of swallows and martins. He has coauthored papers on the phylogeny and classification of swallows and on swallow nesting behavior. He is the author of more than 50 scientific papers.

HELEN SNYDER *(New World Vultures; Hawks and Allies; Falcons and Caracaras)* is a wildlife biologist who has done research on endangered birds for many years. Her studies have included Puerto Rican Parrots, the California Condor, and the Northern Goshawk. She has authored or coauthored a dozen papers and, with husband Noel Snyder, is coauthor of *The California Condor: A Saga of Natural History and Conservation* and *Raptors: North American Birds of Prey*. She is now retired and lives in Arizona.

CHRISTOPHER W. THOMPSON *(Cardinals and Allies)* is Research Scientist for the Washington State Department of Fish and Wildlife and visiting scholar in the Zoology Division of the Burke Museum at the University of Washington, Seattle. His research has focused on the evolution of color patterns in birds and the adaptive significance of their molting strategies. He is currently working on the management and conservation of seabirds. He has published more than 50 peer-reviewed academic papers.

CHARLES H. TROST *(Larks)* studied the physiology and behavior of the Horned Lark for his Ph.D. at the University of California, Los Angeles. His research examined the evolution of adaptations to harsh environments. Since 1968 he has worked as an ornithologist at Idaho State University, Pocatello, where he is now Professor Emeritus. He has researched the behavior and ecology of the Black-billed Magpie and wrote the *Birds of North America* account on that species. He has authored or coauthored over 50 publications.

NILS and SARAH WARNOCK *(Sandpipers, Phalaropes, and Allies)* have studied shorebirds for the past 15 years. Nils Warnock is Codirector of the Wetlands Program at the Point Reyes Bird Observatory, California. He earned his Ph.D. for work on the winter ecology of Dunlins. Sarah Warnock teaches science in primary, elementary, and high school. She earned her M.S. with work on the winter ecology of Western Sandpipers. Together they have published over 40 papers and book chapters on shorebirds.

MILTON W. WELLER *(Ducks, Geese, and Swans)* is Professor Emeritus in Wildlife and Fisheries Sciences at Texas A&M University. He has worked worldwide with waterfowl and other waterbirds, with special emphasis on wetland conservation and management. He has authored, coauthored, or edited more than 100 scientific papers, in addition to *The Waterfowl of the World, Volume 4; The Island Waterfowl; Waterfowl in Winter; Freshwater Marshes;* and *Wetland Birds: Habitat Resources and Conservation Implications.* Among his honors are the Gulf Conservation Award, the Lifetime Achievement Award of the Society of Wetland Scientists, and the Aldo Leopold Award Medal of the Wildlife Society.

ALLISON CHILDS WELLS and JEFFREY V. WELLS *(Pigeons and Doves; Tanagers).* Allison Childs Wells is Communications and Outreach Director at the Cornell Laboratory of Ornithology. She has written on natural history subjects for magazines and other publications, including *Bull's Birds of New York State.* She received her M.F.A. from Cornell University. Jeffrey V. Wells is National Bird Conservation Director for the National Audubon Society. He received his M.S. and Ph.D. from Cornell University. His research includes the breeding ecology of grassland birds, biogeographic patterns in North American birds, and conservation assessments. He is the author of *Important Bird Areas of New York State* and has published dozens of scientific and popular articles.

SHERI L. WILLIAMSON *(Trogons)* is founder and director of the Southeastern Arizona Bird Observatory. Her field work on trogons includes an article on the first nesting of Eared Trogons in the United States. She is the author of the *Birds of North America* account on the Blue-throated Hummingbird and a guide to attracting and feeding hummingbirds. She is currently writing a field guide to hummingbirds of the United States and Canada.

DAVID W. WINKLER *(Swallows and Martins)* is Associate Professor and Curator of Birds in the Department of Ecology and Evolutionary Biology at Cornell University. He studies the evolution of the life histories of birds with a combination of conceptual models, experimental tests, and phylogenetic comparisons. He is the author of about 45 peer-reviewed papers on birds and avian ecology and evolution.

MARK WITMER *(Waxwings)* is Professor of Biology at Bryn Mawr College, Pennsylvania. His research focuses on nutritional adaptations and how nutritional needs shape the ecology and behavior of animals. In addition, he has been involved in conservation work, including projects with Philippine Eagles and captive-bred Peregrine Falcons. He has authored and coauthored at least 14 peer-reviewed papers.

Species Checklist

This checklist includes all of the bird species discussed in this book that have been reported in the United States (excluding Hawaii) and Canada. This is not an "official" checklist for this region as the list includes many introduced species that are not considered established, as well as several species that have been reported in North America recently but are not yet accepted by the appropriate checklist committees. Check boxes are placed against those species that are included in the main AOU Check-list for the region; introduced species are given check boxes if they are considered to be established by the AOU; species that have not been officially accepted are denoted by italic type. The AOU Check-list is continually being revised as new species are reported and reviewed, as the status of introduced species changes, and as taxonomic changes are evaluated.

In the checklist that follows we give the scientific and common names of each order and family of birds, followed by the common names of each species in the family (scientific names for species can be found by consulting the index and family chapters). Accidental species as defined in this book (see Introduction) are identified by an (A) after the species name, introduced or escaped species by an (I), and extinct species by a †.   *March 2001*

GAVIIFORMES
Loons

Gaviidae
Loons
- [ ] Red-throated Loon
- [ ] Arctic Loon
- [ ] Pacific Loon
- [ ] Common Loon
- [ ] Yellow-billed Loon

PODICIPEDIFORMES
Grebes

Podicipedidae
Grebes
- [ ] Least Grebe
- [ ] Pied-billed Grebe
- [ ] Horned Grebe
- [ ] Red-necked Grebe
- [ ] Eared Grebe
- [ ] Western Grebe
- [ ] Clark's Grebe

PROCELLARIIFORMES
Tubenoses

Diomedeidae
Albatrosses
- [ ] Yellow-nosed Albatross (A)
- [ ] Shy Albatross (A)
- [ ] Black-browed Albatross (A)
- [ ] Light-mantled Albatross (A)
- [ ] Wandering Albatross (A)
- [ ] Laysan Albatross
- [ ] Black-footed Albatross
- [ ] Short-tailed Albatross

Procellariidae
Shearwaters and Petrels
- [ ] Northern Fulmar
- [ ] Herald Petrel
- [ ] Murphy's Petrel
- *Great-winged Petrel* (A)
- [ ] Mottled Petrel

- [ ] Bermuda Petrel (A)
- *Fea's Petrel*
- [ ] Black-capped Petrel
- [ ] Dark-rumped Petrel (A)
- [ ] Cook's Petrel
- [ ] Stejneger's Petrel (A)
- *Bulwer's Petrel* (A)
- *White-chinned Petrel* (A)
- *Parkinson's Petrel* (A)
- [ ] Streaked Shearwater (A)
- [ ] Cory's Shearwater
- [ ] Pink-footed Shearwater
- [ ] Flesh-footed Shearwater
- [ ] Greater Shearwater
- [ ] Wedge-tailed Shearwater (A)
- [ ] Buller's Shearwater
- [ ] Sooty Shearwater
- [ ] Short-tailed Shearwater
- [ ] Manx Shearwater
- [ ] Black-vented Shearwater
- [ ] Audubon's Shearwater
- [ ] Little Shearwater (A)

Hydrobatidae
Storm-Petrels
- [ ] Wilson's Storm-Petrel
- [ ] White-faced Storm-Petrel
- [ ] European Storm-Petrel (A)
- [ ] Fork-tailed Storm-Petrel
- [ ] Leach's Storm-Petrel
- *Swinhoe's Storm-Petrel* (A)
- [ ] Ashy Storm-Petrel
- [ ] Band-rumped Storm-Petrel
- [ ] Wedge-rumped Storm-Petrel (A)
- [ ] Black Storm-Petrel
- *Markham's Storm-Petrel* (A)
- [ ] Least Storm-Petrel

PELECANIFORMES
Totipalmate Birds

Phaethontidae
Tropicbirds
- [ ] White-tailed Tropicbird

- [ ] Red-billed Tropicbird
- [ ] Red-tailed Tropicbird (A)

Sulidae
Boobies and Gannets
- [ ] Masked Booby
- [ ] Blue-footed Booby
- [ ] Brown Booby
- [ ] Red-footed Booby
- [ ] Northern Gannet

Pelecanidae
Pelicans
- [ ] American White Pelican
- [ ] Brown Pelican

Phalacrocoracidae
Cormorants
- [ ] Brandt's Cormorant
- [ ] Neotropic Cormorant
- [ ] Double-crested Cormorant
- [ ] Great Cormorant
- [ ] Red-faced Cormorant
- [ ] Pelagic Cormorant

Anhingidae
Darters (Anhinga)
- [ ] Anhinga

Fregatidae
Frigatebirds
- [ ] Magnificent Frigatebird
- [ ] Great Frigatebird (A)
- [ ] Lesser Frigatebird (A)

CICONIIFORMES
Herons, Ibises, Storks, New World Vultures, and Allies

Ardeidae
Herons, Egrets, and Bitterns
- [ ] American Bittern
- [ ] Yellow Bittern (A)
- [ ] Least Bittern
- [ ] Great Blue Heron

- ☐ Great Egret
- ☐ Chinese Egret (A)
- ☐ Little Egret
- ☐ Western Reef-Heron (A)
- ☐ Snowy Egret
- ☐ Little Blue Heron
- ☐ Tricolored Heron
- ☐ Reddish Egret
- ☐ Cattle Egret
- ☐ Chinese Pond-Heron (A)
- ☐ Green Heron
- ☐ Black-crowned Night-Heron
- ☐ Yellow-crowned Night-Heron

Threskiornithidae
Ibises and Spoonbills
- ☐ White Ibis
- ☐ Scarlet Ibis
- ☐ Glossy Ibis
- ☐ White-faced Ibis
- ☐ Roseate Spoonbill

Ciconiidae
Storks
- ☐ Jabiru (A)
- ☐ Wood Stork

Cathartidae
New World Vultures
- ☐ Black Vulture
- ☐ Turkey Vulture
- ☐ California Condor

PHOENICOPTERIFORMES
Flamingos

Phoenicopteridae
Flamingos
- ☐ Greater Flamingo

ANSERIFORMES
Ducks, Geese, and Swans

Anatidae
Ducks, Geese, and Swans
- ☐ Black-bellied Whistling-Duck
  - *West Indian Whistling-Duck* (I)
- ☐ Fulvous Whistling-Duck
- ☐ Bean Goose (A)
- ☐ Pink-footed Goose (A)
- ☐ Greater White-fronted Goose
- ☐ Lesser White-fronted Goose (A)
- ☐ Emperor Goose
- ☐ Snow Goose
- ☐ Ross's Goose
- ☐ Canada Goose
  - *Red-breasted Goose* (I)
- ☐ Brant
- ☐ Barnacle Goose
  - *Ruddy Shelduck* (I)
  - *Common Shelduck* (I)
- ☐ Mute Swan (I)

- ☐ Trumpeter Swan
- ☐ Tundra Swan
- ☐ Whooper Swan
- ☐ Muscovy Duck
- ☐ Wood Duck
  - *Mandarin Duck* (I)
- ☐ Gadwall
- ☐ Falcated Duck (A)
- ☐ Eurasian Wigeon
- ☐ American Wigeon
- ☐ American Black Duck
- ☐ Mallard
- ☐ Mottled Duck
- ☐ Spot-billed Duck (A)
- ☐ Blue-winged Teal
- ☐ Cinnamon Teal
- ☐ Northern Shoveler
- ☐ White-cheeked Pintail (A)
- ☐ Northern Pintail
- ☐ Garganey
- ☐ Baikal Teal (A)
- ☐ Green-winged Teal
- ☐ Canvasback
- ☐ Redhead
- ☐ Common Pochard (A)
- ☐ Ring-necked Duck
- ☐ Tufted Duck
- ☐ Greater Scaup
- ☐ Lesser Scaup
- ☐ Steller's Eider
- ☐ Spectacled Eider
- ☐ King Eider
- ☐ Common Eider
- ☐ Harlequin Duck
  - Labrador Duck †
- ☐ Surf Scoter
- ☐ White-winged Scoter
- ☐ Black Scoter
- ☐ Long-tailed Duck
- ☐ Bufflehead
- ☐ Common Goldeneye
- ☐ Barrow's Goldeneye
- ☐ Smew (A)
- ☐ Hooded Merganser
- ☐ Common Merganser
- ☐ Red-breasted Merganser
- ☐ Masked Duck
- ☐ Ruddy Duck

FALCONIFORMES
Diurnal Birds of Prey

Accipitridae
Hawks and Allies
- ☐ Osprey
- ☐ Hook-billed Kite
- ☐ Swallow-tailed Kite
- ☐ White-tailed Kite
- ☐ Snail Kite
- ☐ Mississippi Kite
- ☐ Bald Eagle
- ☐ White-tailed Eagle (A)
- ☐ Steller's Sea-Eagle (A)
- ☐ Northern Harrier
- ☐ Sharp-shinned Hawk
- ☐ Cooper's Hawk
- ☐ Northern Goshawk

- ☐ Crane Hawk (A)
- ☐ Gray Hawk
- ☐ Common Black-Hawk
- ☐ Harris's Hawk
- ☐ Roadside Hawk (A)
- ☐ Red-shouldered Hawk
- ☐ Broad-winged Hawk
- ☐ Short-tailed Hawk
- ☐ Swainson's Hawk
- ☐ White-tailed Hawk
- ☐ Zone-tailed Hawk
- ☐ Red-tailed Hawk
- ☐ Ferruginous Hawk
- ☐ Rough-legged Hawk
- ☐ Golden Eagle

Falconidae
Falcons and Caracaras
- ☐ Collared Forest-Falcon (A)
- ☐ Crested Caracara
- ☐ Eurasian Kestrel (A)
- ☐ American Kestrel
- ☐ Merlin
- ☐ Eurasian Hobby (A)
- ☐ Aplomado Falcon
- ☐ Gyrfalcon
- ☐ Peregrine Falcon
- ☐ Prairie Falcon

GALLIFORMES
Gallinaceous Birds

Cracidae
Chachalacas and Allies
- ☐ Plain Chachalaca

Phasianidae
Grouse, Turkeys, and Allies
- ☐ Chukar (I)
  - *Red-legged Partridge* (I)
  - *Black Francolin* (I)
- ☐ Himalayan Snowcock (I)
- ☐ Gray Partridge (I)
- ☐ Ring-necked Pheasant (I)
  - *Common Peafowl* (I)
- ☐ Ruffed Grouse
- ☐ Greater Sage-Grouse
- ☐ Gunnison Sage-Grouse
- ☐ Spruce Grouse
- ☐ Willow Ptarmigan
- ☐ Rock Ptarmigan
- ☐ White-tailed Ptarmigan
- ☐ Blue Grouse
- ☐ Sharp-tailed Grouse
- ☐ Greater Prairie-Chicken
- ☐ Lesser Prairie-Chicken
- ☐ Wild Turkey
  - *Helmeted Guineafowl* (I)

Odontophoridae
New World Quail
- ☐ Mountain Quail
- ☐ Scaled Quail
- ☐ California Quail
- ☐ Gambel's Quail
- ☐ Northern Bobwhite
- ☐ Montezuma Quail

GRUIFORMES
Rails, Cranes, and Allies

Rallidae
**Rails, Gallinules, and
Coots**
- [ ] Yellow Rail
- [ ] Black Rail
- [ ] Corn Crake (A)
- [ ] Clapper Rail
- [ ] King Rail
- [ ] Virginia Rail
- *Baillon's Crake* (A)
- [ ] Sora
- [ ] Paint-billed Crake (A)
- [ ] Spotted Rail (A)
- *Purple Swamphen* (I)
- [ ] Purple Gallinule
- [ ] Azure Gallinule (A)
- [ ] Common Moorhen
- [ ] Eurasian Coot (A)
- [ ] American Coot

Aramidae
Limpkin
- [ ] Limpkin

Gruidae
Cranes
- [ ] Sandhill Crane
- [ ] Common Crane (A)
- [ ] Whooping Crane

CHARADRIIFORMES
Shorebirds, Gulls, Auks, and Allies

Burhinidae
Thick-knees
- [ ] Double-striped Thick-knee (A)

Charadriidae
Plovers and Lapwings
- [ ] Northern Lapwing
- [ ] Black-bellied Plover
- [ ] European Golden-Plover
- [ ] American Golden-Plover
- [ ] Pacific Golden-Plover
- [ ] Mongolian Plover
- [ ] Collared Plover (A)
- [ ] Snowy Plover
- [ ] Wilson's Plover
- [ ] Common Ringed Plover
- [ ] Semipalmated Plover
- [ ] Piping Plover
- [ ] Little Ringed Plover (A)
- [ ] Killdeer
- [ ] Mountain Plover
- [ ] Eurasian Dotterel

Haematopodidae
Oystercatchers
- [ ] Eurasian Oystercatcher (A)
- [ ] American Oystercatcher
- [ ] Black Oystercatcher

Recurvirostridae
Stilts and Avocets
- [ ] Black-winged Stilt (A)
- [ ] Black-necked Stilt
- [ ] American Avocet

Jacanidae
Jacanas
- [ ] Northern Jacana

Scolopacidae
Sandpipers, Phalaropes, and Allies
- [ ] Common Greenshank (A)
- [ ] Greater Yellowlegs
- [ ] Lesser Yellowlegs
- [ ] Marsh Sandpiper (A)
- [ ] Common Redshank (A)
- [ ] Spotted Redshank
- [ ] Wood Sandpiper (A)
- [ ] Green Sandpiper (A)
- [ ] Solitary Sandpiper
- [ ] Willet
- [ ] Wandering Tattler
- [ ] Gray-tailed Tattler (A)
- [ ] Common Sandpiper (A)
- [ ] Spotted Sandpiper
- [ ] Terek Sandpiper (A)
- [ ] Upland Sandpiper
- [ ] Little Curlew (A)
- [ ] Eskimo Curlew †?
- [ ] Whimbrel
- [ ] Bristle-thighed Curlew
- [ ] Far Eastern Curlew (A)
- [ ] Slender-billed Curlew (A)
- [ ] Eurasian Curlew (A)
- [ ] Long-billed Curlew
- [ ] Black-tailed Godwit
- [ ] Hudsonian Godwit
- [ ] Bar-tailed Godwit
- [ ] Marbled Godwit
- [ ] Ruddy Turnstone
- [ ] Black Turnstone
- [ ] Surfbird
- [ ] Great Knot (A)
- [ ] Red Knot
- [ ] Sanderling
- [ ] Semipalmated Sandpiper
- [ ] Western Sandpiper
- [ ] Red-necked Stint
- [ ] Little Stint
- [ ] Temminck's Stint (A)
- [ ] Long-toed Stint (A)
- [ ] Least Sandpiper
- [ ] White-rumped Sandpiper
- [ ] Baird's Sandpiper
- [ ] Pectoral Sandpiper
- [ ] Sharp-tailed Sandpiper
- [ ] Purple Sandpiper
- [ ] Rock Sandpiper
- [ ] Dunlin
- [ ] Curlew Sandpiper
- [ ] Stilt Sandpiper
- [ ] Spoonbill Sandpiper (A)
- [ ] Broad-billed Sandpiper (A)
- [ ] Buff-breasted Sandpiper
- [ ] Ruff

- [ ] Short-billed Dowitcher
- [ ] Long-billed Dowitcher
- [ ] Jack Snipe (A)
- [ ] Common Snipe
- [ ] Pin-tailed Snipe (A)
- [ ] Eurasian Woodcock (A)
- [ ] American Woodcock
- [ ] Wilson's Phalarope
- [ ] Red-necked Phalarope
- [ ] Red Phalarope

Glareolidae
Coursers and Pratincoles
- [ ] Oriental Pratincole (A)

Laridae
Gulls, Terns, and Allies
- [ ] Great Skua
- [ ] South Polar Skua
- [ ] Pomarine Jaeger
- [ ] Parasitic Jaeger
- [ ] Long-tailed Jaeger
- [ ] Laughing Gull
- [ ] Franklin's Gull
- [ ] Little Gull
- [ ] Black-headed Gull
- [ ] Bonaparte's Gull
- *Gray-hooded Gull* (A)
- [ ] Heermann's Gull
- [ ] Gray Gull (A)
- [ ] Band-tailed Gull (A)
- [ ] Black-tailed Gull
- [ ] Mew Gull
- [ ] Ring-billed Gull
- *Kelp Gull*
- [ ] California Gull
- [ ] Herring Gull
- [ ] Yellow-legged Gull
- [ ] Thayer's Gull
- [ ] Iceland Gull
- [ ] Lesser Black-backed Gull
- [ ] Slaty-backed Gull
- [ ] Yellow-footed Gull
- [ ] Western Gull
- [ ] Glaucous-winged Gull
- [ ] Glaucous Gull
- [ ] Great Black-backed Gull
- [ ] Sabine's Gull
- *Swallow-tailed Gull* (A)
- [ ] Black-legged Kittiwake
- [ ] Red-legged Kittiwake
- [ ] Ross's Gull
- [ ] Ivory Gull
- [ ] Gull-billed Tern
- [ ] Caspian Tern
- [ ] Royal Tern
- [ ] Elegant Tern
- [ ] Sandwich Tern
- [ ] Roseate Tern
- [ ] Common Tern
- [ ] Arctic Tern
- [ ] Forster's Tern
- [ ] Least Tern
- [ ] Aleutian Tern
- [ ] Bridled Tern
- [ ] Sooty Tern
- [ ] Large-billed Tern (A)

☐ White-winged Tern
☐ Whiskered Tern (A)
☐ Black Tern
☐ Brown Noddy
☐ Black Noddy
☐ Black Skimmer

Alcidae
Auks
☐ Dovekie
☐ Common Murre
☐ Thick-billed Murre
☐ Razorbill
   Great Auk †
☐ Black Guillemot
☐ Pigeon Guillemot
☐ Long-billed Murrelet
☐ Marbled Murrelet
☐ Kittlitz's Murrelet
☐ Xantus's Murrelet
☐ Craveri's Murrelet
☐ Ancient Murrelet
☐ Cassin's Auklet
☐ Parakeet Auklet
☐ Least Auklet
☐ Whiskered Auklet
☐ Crested Auklet
☐ Rhinoceros Auklet
☐ Atlantic Puffin
☐ Horned Puffin
☐ Tufted Puffin

COLUMBIFORMES
Pigeons and Doves

Columbidae
Pigeons and Doves
☐ Rock Dove (I)
☐ Scaly-naped Pigeon (A)
☐ White-crowned Pigeon
☐ Red-billed Pigeon
☐ Band-tailed Pigeon
☐ Oriental Turtle-Dove (A)
☐ Ringed Turtle-Dove (I)
☐ European Turtle-Dove (A)
☐ Eurasian Collared-Dove (I)
☐ Spotted Dove (I)
☐ White-winged Dove
☐ Zenaida Dove (A)
☐ Mourning Dove
   Passenger Pigeon †
☐ Inca Dove
☐ Common Ground-Dove
☐ Ruddy Ground-Dove
☐ White-tipped Dove
☐ Key West Quail-Dove
☐ Ruddy Quail-Dove (A)

PSITTACIFORMES
Parrots

Psittacidae
Parrots and Allies
   Sulphur-crested Cockatoo (I)
   Cockatiel (I)
☐ *Budgerigar* (I)
   Peach-faced Lovebird (I)

☐ Rose-ringed Parakeet (I)
☐ Monk Parakeet (I)
   Carolina Parakeet †
   Blue-crowned Parakeet (I)
☐ Green Parakeet (I)
   Mitred Parakeet (I)
   Red-masked Parakeet (I)
   Dusky-headed Parakeet (I)
   Black-hooded Parakeet (I)
   Chestnut-fronted Macaw (I)
☐ Thick-billed Parrot
☐ White-winged Parakeet (I)
   Yellow-chevroned Parakeet (I)
   White-fronted Parrot (I)
   Yellow-lored Parrot (I)
   Hispaniolan Parrot (I)
☐ Red-crowned Parrot (I)
   Lilac-crowned Parrot (I)
   Red-lored Parrot (I)
   Blue-fronted Parrot (I)
   Mealy Parrot (I)
   Yellow-headed Parrot (I)
   Yellow-naped Parrot (I)
   Yellow-crowned Parrot (I)
   Orange-winged Parrot (I)

CUCULIFORMES
Cuckoos and Allies

Cuculidae
Cuckoos, Roadrunners, and Anis
☐ Common Cuckoo (A)
☐ Oriental Cuckoo (A)
☐ Black-billed Cuckoo
☐ Yellow-billed Cuckoo
☐ Mangrove Cuckoo
   Dark-billed Cuckoo (A)
☐ Greater Roadrunner
☐ Smooth-billed Ani
☐ Groove-billed Ani

STRIGIFORMES
Owls

Tytonidae
Barn Owls
☐ Barn Owl

Strigidae
Typical Owls
☐ Flammulated Owl
☐ Oriental Scops-Owl (A)
☐ Western Screech-Owl
☐ Eastern Screech-Owl
☐ Whiskered Screech-Owl
☐ Great Horned Owl
☐ Snowy Owl
☐ Northern Hawk Owl
☐ Northern Pygmy-Owl
☐ Ferruginous Pygmy-Owl
☐ Elf Owl
☐ Burrowing Owl
☐ Mottled Owl (A)
☐ Spotted Owl
☐ Barred Owl
☐ Great Gray Owl

☐ Long-eared Owl
☐ Stygian Owl (A)
☐ Short-eared Owl
☐ Boreal Owl
☐ Northern Saw-whet Owl

CAPRIMULGIFORMES
Goatsuckers and Allies

Caprimulgidae
Nighthawks and Nightjars
☐ Lesser Nighthawk
☐ Common Nighthawk
☐ Antillean Nighthawk
☐ Common Pauraque
☐ Common Poorwill
☐ Chuck-will's-widow
☐ Buff-collared Nightjar
☐ Whip-poor-will
☐ Jungle Nightjar (A)

APODIFORMES
Swifts and Hummingbirds

Apodidae
Swifts
☐ Black Swift
☐ White-collared Swift (A)
☐ Chimney Swift
☐ Vaux's Swift
☐ White-throated
   Needletail (A)
☐ Common Swift (A)
☐ Fork-tailed Swift (A)
☐ White-throated Swift
☐ Antillean Palm-Swift (A)

Trochilidae
Hummingbirds
☐ Green Violet-ear
☐ Green-breasted Mango (A)
☐ Broad-billed Hummingbird
☐ White-eared Hummingbird
☐ Xantus's Hummingbird (A)
☐ Berylline Hummingbird
☐ Buff-bellied Hummingbird
☐ Cinnamon Hummingbird (A)
☐ Violet-crowned Humming-
   bird
☐ Blue-throated Humming-
   bird
☐ Magnificent Hummingbird
☐ Plain-capped Starthroat
☐ Bahama Woodstar (A)
☐ Lucifer Hummingbird
☐ Ruby-throated Humming-
   bird
☐ Black-chinned Humming-
   bird
☐ Anna's Hummingbird
☐ Costa's Hummingbird
☐ Calliope Hummingbird
☐ Bumblebee Humming-
   bird (A)
☐ Broad-tailed Hummingbird
☐ Rufous Hummingbird
☐ Allen's Hummingbird

TROGONIFORMES
Trogons

Trogonidae
Trogons
- [ ] Elegant Trogon
- [ ] Eared Trogon

UPUPIFORMES
Hoopoes and Allies

Upupidae
Hoopoe
- [ ] Eurasian Hoopoe (A)

CORACIIFORMES
Kingfishers and Allies

Alcedinidae
Kingfishers
- [ ] Ringed Kingfisher
- [ ] Belted Kingfisher
- [ ] Green Kingfisher

PICIFORMES
Woodpeckers and Allies

Picidae
Woodpeckers and Allies
- [ ] Eurasian Wryneck (A)
- [ ] Lewis's Woodpecker
- [ ] Red-headed Woodpecker
- [ ] Acorn Woodpecker
- [ ] Gila Woodpecker
- [ ] Golden-fronted Woodpecker
- [ ] Red-bellied Woodpecker
- [ ] Williamson's Sapsucker
- [ ] Yellow-bellied Sapsucker
- [ ] Red-naped Sapsucker
- [ ] Red-breasted Sapsucker
- [ ] Great Spotted Woodpecker (A)
- [ ] Ladder-backed Woodpecker
- [ ] Nuttall's Woodpecker
- [ ] Downy Woodpecker
- [ ] Hairy Woodpecker
- [ ] Arizona Woodpecker
- [ ] Red-cockaded Woodpecker
- [ ] White-headed Woodpecker
- [ ] Three-toed Woodpecker
- [ ] Black-backed Woodpecker
- [ ] Northern Flicker
- [ ] Gilded Flicker
- [ ] Pileated Woodpecker
- [ ] Ivory-billed Woodpecker †?

PASSERIFORMES
Passerine Birds

Tyrannidae
Tyrant Flycatchers
- [ ] Northern Beardless-Tyrannulet
- [ ] Greenish Elaenia (A)
- [ ] Caribbean Elaenia (A)
- [ ] Tufted Flycatcher (A)
- [ ] Olive-sided Flycatcher
- [ ] Greater Pewee
- [ ] Western Wood-Pewee
- [ ] Eastern Wood-Pewee
- [ ] Cuban Pewee (A)
- [ ] Yellow-bellied Flycatcher
- [ ] Acadian Flycatcher
- [ ] Alder Flycatcher
- [ ] Willow Flycatcher
- [ ] Least Flycatcher
- [ ] Hammond's Flycatcher
- [ ] Gray Flycatcher
- [ ] Dusky Flycatcher
- [ ] Pacific-slope Flycatcher
- [ ] Cordilleran Flycatcher
- [ ] Buff-breasted Flycatcher
- [ ] Black Phoebe
- [ ] Eastern Phoebe
- [ ] Say's Phoebe
- [ ] Vermilion Flycatcher
- [ ] Dusky-capped Flycatcher
- [ ] Ash-throated Flycatcher
- [ ] Nutting's Flycatcher (A)
- [ ] Great Crested Flycatcher
- [ ] Brown-crested Flycatcher
- [ ] La Sagra's Flycatcher
- [ ] Great Kiskadee
- [ ] Sulphur-bellied Flycatcher
- [ ] Piratic Flycatcher (A)
- [ ] Variegated Flycatcher (A)
- [ ] Tropical Kingbird
- [ ] Couch's Kingbird
- [ ] Cassin's Kingbird
- [ ] Thick-billed Kingbird
- [ ] Western Kingbird
- [ ] Eastern Kingbird
- [ ] Gray Kingbird
- [ ] Loggerhead Kingbird (A)
- [ ] Scissor-tailed Flycatcher
- [ ] Fork-tailed Flycatcher
- [ ] Rose-throated Becard
- [ ] Masked Tityra (A)

Laniidae
Shrikes
- [ ] Brown Shrike (A)
- [ ] Loggerhead Shrike
- [ ] Northern Shrike

Vireonidae
Vireos
- [ ] White-eyed Vireo
- [ ] Thick-billed Vireo
- [ ] Bell's Vireo
- [ ] Black-capped Vireo
- [ ] Gray Vireo
- [ ] Yellow-throated Vireo
- [ ] Plumbeous Vireo
- [ ] Cassin's Vireo
- [ ] Blue-headed Vireo
- [ ] Hutton's Vireo
- [ ] Warbling Vireo
- [ ] Philadelphia Vireo
- [ ] Red-eyed Vireo
- [ ] Yellow-green Vireo
- [ ] Black-whiskered Vireo
- [ ] Yucatan Vireo (A)

Corvidae
Crows and Jays
- [ ] Gray Jay
- [ ] Steller's Jay
- [ ] Blue Jay
- [ ] Green Jay
- [ ] Brown Jay
- [ ] Florida Scrub-Jay
- [ ] Island Scrub-Jay
- [ ] Western Scrub-Jay
- [ ] Mexican Jay
- [ ] Pinyon Jay
- [ ] Clark's Nutcracker
- [ ] Black-billed Magpie
- [ ] Yellow-billed Magpie
- [ ] Eurasian Jackdaw
- [ ] American Crow
- [ ] Northwestern Crow
- [ ] Tamaulipas Crow
- [ ] Fish Crow
- [ ] Chihuahuan Raven
- [ ] Common Raven

Alaudidae
Larks
- [ ] Sky Lark (I)
- [ ] Horned Lark

Hirundinidae
Swallows and Martins
- [ ] Purple Martin
- [ ] Cuban Martin (A)
- [ ] Gray-breasted Martin (A)
- [ ] Southern Martin (A)
- [ ] Brown-chested Martin (A)
- [ ] Tree Swallow
- [ ] Violet-green Swallow
- [ ] Bahama Swallow
- [ ] Northern Rough-winged Swallow
- [ ] Bank Swallow
- [ ] Cliff Swallow
- [ ] Cave Swallow
- [ ] Barn Swallow
- [ ] Common House-Martin (A)

Paridae
Chickadees and Titmice
- [ ] Carolina Chickadee
- [ ] Black-capped Chickadee
- [ ] Mountain Chickadee
- [ ] Mexican Chickadee
- [ ] Chestnut-backed Chickadee
- [ ] Boreal Chickadee
- [ ] Gray-headed Chickadee
- [ ] Bridled Titmouse
- [ ] Oak Titmouse
- [ ] Juniper Titmouse
- [ ] Tufted Titmouse

Remizidae
Penduline Tits (Verdin)
- [ ] Verdin

Aegithalidae
Long-tailed Tits (Bushtit)
- [ ] Bushtit

Sittidae
Nuthatches
☐ Red-breasted Nuthatch
☐ White-breasted Nuthatch
☐ Pygmy Nuthatch
☐ Brown-headed Nuthatch

Certhiidae
Creepers
☐ Brown Creeper

Troglodytidae
Wrens
☐ Cactus Wren
☐ Rock Wren
☐ Canyon Wren
☐ Carolina Wren
☐ Bewick's Wren
☐ House Wren
☐ Winter Wren
☐ Sedge Wren
☐ Marsh Wren

Cinclidae
Dippers
☐ American Dipper

Pycnonotidae
Bulbuls
☐ Red-whiskered Bulbul (I)

Regulidae
Kinglets
☐ Golden-crowned Kinglet
☐ Ruby-crowned Kinglet

Sylviidae
Old World Warblers and Gnat-catchers
☐ Middendorff's Grasshopper-Warbler (A)
☐ Lanceolated Warbler (A)
☐ Wood Warbler (A)
☐ Dusky Warbler (A)
Yellow-browed Warbler (A)
☐ Arctic Warbler
☐ Blue-gray Gnatcatcher
☐ California Gnatcatcher
☐ Black-tailed Gnatcatcher
☐ Black-capped Gnatcatcher

Muscicapidae
Old World Flycatchers
☐ Narcissus Flycatcher (A)
☐ Mugimaki Flycatcher (A)
☐ Red-breasted Flycatcher (A)
☐ Siberian Flycatcher (A)
☐ Gray-spotted Flycatcher (A)
☐ Asian Brown Flycatcher (A)

Turdidae
Thrushes
☐ Siberian Rubythroat (A)
☐ Bluethroat
☐ Siberian Blue Robin (A)
Rufous-tailed Robin (A)
☐ Red-flanked Bluetail (A)

☐ Northern Wheatear
☐ Stonechat (A)
☐ Eastern Bluebird
☐ Western Bluebird
☐ Mountain Bluebird
☐ Townsend's Solitaire
☐ Orange-billed Nightingale-Thrush (A)
☐ Veery
☐ Gray-cheeked Thrush
☐ Bicknell's Thrush
☐ Swainson's Thrush
☐ Hermit Thrush
☐ Wood Thrush
☐ Eurasian Blackbird (A)
☐ Eyebrowed Thrush (A)
☐ Dusky Thrush (A)
☐ Fieldfare
☐ Redwing (A)
☐ Clay-colored Robin
☐ White-throated Robin (A)
☐ Rufous-backed Robin
☐ American Robin
☐ Varied Thrush
☐ Aztec Thrush

Timaliidae
Babblers (Wrentit)
☐ Wrentit

Mimidae
Mockingbirds and Thrashers
☐ Gray Catbird
☐ Black Catbird (A)
☐ Northern Mockingbird
☐ Bahama Mockingbird
☐ Sage Thrasher
☐ Brown Thrasher
☐ Long-billed Thrasher
☐ Bendire's Thrasher
☐ Curve-billed Thrasher
☐ California Thrasher
☐ Crissal Thrasher
☐ Le Conte's Thrasher
☐ Blue Mockingbird (A)

Sturnidae
Starlings and Mynas
☐ European Starling (I)
☐ Common Myna (I)
☐ Crested Myna (I)
Hill Myna (I)

Prunellidae
Accentors
☐ Siberian Accentor (A)

Motacillidae
Wagtails and Pipits
☐ Yellow Wagtail
☐ Citrine Wagtail (A)
☐ Gray Wagtail (A)
☐ White Wagtail
☐ Black-backed Wagtail
☐ Tree Pipit (A)
☐ Olive-backed Pipit (A)
☐ Pechora Pipit (A)

☐ Red-throated Pipit
☐ American Pipit
☐ Sprague's Pipit

Bombycillidae
Waxwings
☐ Bohemian Waxwing
☐ Cedar Waxwing

Ptilogonatidae
Silky-flycatchers
☐ Gray Silky-flycatcher (A)
☐ Phainopepla

Peucedramidae
Olive Warbler
☐ Olive Warbler

Parulidae
Wood-Warblers
Bachman's Warbler †
☐ Blue-winged Warbler
☐ Golden-winged Warbler
☐ Tennessee Warbler
☐ Orange-crowned Warbler
☐ Nashville Warbler
☐ Virginia's Warbler
☐ Colima Warbler
☐ Lucy's Warbler
☐ Crescent-chested Warbler (A)
☐ Northern Parula
☐ Tropical Parula
☐ Yellow Warbler
☐ Chestnut-sided Warbler
☐ Magnolia Warbler
☐ Cape May Warbler
☐ Black-throated Blue Warbler
☐ Yellow-rumped Warbler
☐ Black-throated Gray Warbler
☐ Golden-cheeked Warbler
☐ Black-throated Green Warbler
☐ Townsend's Warbler
☐ Hermit Warbler
☐ Blackburnian Warbler
☐ Yellow-throated Warbler
☐ Grace's Warbler
☐ Pine Warbler
☐ Kirtland's Warbler
☐ Prairie Warbler
☐ Palm Warbler
☐ Bay-breasted Warbler
☐ Blackpoll Warbler
☐ Cerulean Warbler
☐ Black-and-white Warbler
☐ American Redstart
☐ Prothonotary Warbler
☐ Worm-eating Warbler
☐ Swainson's Warbler
☐ Ovenbird
☐ Northern Waterthrush
☐ Louisiana Waterthrush
☐ Kentucky Warbler
☐ Connecticut Warbler
☐ Mourning Warbler

☐ MacGillivray's Warbler
☐ Common Yellowthroat
☐ Gray-crowned Yellowthroat
☐ Hooded Warbler
☐ Wilson's Warbler
☐ Canada Warbler
☐ Red-faced Warbler
☐ Painted Redstart
☐ Slate-throated Redstart (A)
☐ Fan-tailed Warbler (A)
☐ Golden-crowned Warbler
☐ Rufous-capped Warbler
☐ Yellow-breasted Chat

Coerebidae
Bananaquit
☐ Bananaquit

Thraupidae
Tanagers
☐ Hepatic Tanager
☐ Summer Tanager
☐ Scarlet Tanager
☐ Western Tanager
☐ Flame-colored Tanager
☐ Western Spindalis

Emberizidae
New World Sparrows
☐ White-collared Seedeater
    Cuban Grassquit (I)
☐ Yellow-faced Grassquit (A)
☐ Black-faced Grassquit (A)
    Red-crested Cardinal (I)
☐ Olive Sparrow
☐ Green-tailed Towhee
☐ Spotted Towhee
☐ Eastern Towhee
☐ Canyon Towhee
☐ California Towhee
☐ Abert's Towhee
☐ Rufous-winged Sparrow
☐ Cassin's Sparrow
☐ Bachman's Sparrow
☐ Botteri's Sparrow
☐ Rufous-crowned Sparrow
☐ Five-striped Sparrow
☐ American Tree Sparrow
☐ Chipping Sparrow
☐ Clay-colored Sparrow
☐ Brewer's Sparrow
☐ Field Sparrow
☐ Worthen's Sparrow (A)
☐ Black-chinned Sparrow
☐ Vesper Sparrow
☐ Lark Sparrow
☐ Black-throated Sparrow
☐ Sage Sparrow
☐ Lark Bunting
☐ Savannah Sparrow
☐ Grasshopper Sparrow

☐ Baird's Sparrow
☐ Henslow's Sparrow
☐ Le Conte's Sparrow
☐ Nelson's Sharp-tailed
    Sparrow
☐ Saltmarsh Sharp-tailed
    Sparrow
☐ Seaside Sparrow
☐ Fox Sparrow
☐ Song Sparrow
☐ Lincoln's Sparrow
☐ Swamp Sparrow
☐ White-throated Sparrow
☐ Harris's Sparrow
☐ White-crowned Sparrow
☐ Golden-crowned Sparrow
☐ Dark-eyed Junco
☐ Yellow-eyed Junco
☐ McCown's Longspur
☐ Lapland Longspur
☐ Smith's Longspur
☐ Chestnut-collared Longspur
☐ Pine Bunting (A)
☐ Little Bunting (A)
☐ Rustic Bunting
☐ Yellow-throated
    Bunting (A)
☐ Yellow-breasted
    Bunting (A)
☐ Gray Bunting (A)
☐ Pallas's Bunting (A)
☐ Reed Bunting (A)
☐ Snow Bunting
☐ McKay's Bunting

Cardinalidae
Cardinals and Allies
☐ Crimson-collared Grosbeak
☐ Northern Cardinal
☐ Pyrrhuloxia
☐ Yellow Grosbeak
☐ Rose-breasted Grosbeak
☐ Black-headed Grosbeak
☐ Blue Bunting
☐ Blue Grosbeak
☐ Lazuli Bunting
☐ Indigo Bunting
☐ Varied Bunting
☐ Painted Bunting
☐ Dickcissel

Icteridae
Blackbirds, Orioles, and Allies
☐ Bobolink
☐ Red-winged Blackbird
☐ Tricolored Blackbird
☐ Tawny-shouldered
    Blackbird (A)
☐ Eastern Meadowlark
☐ Western Meadowlark
☐ Yellow-headed Blackbird

☐ Rusty Blackbird
☐ Brewer's Blackbird
☐ Common Grackle
☐ Boat-tailed Grackle
☐ Great-tailed Grackle
☐ Shiny Cowbird
☐ Bronzed Cowbird
☐ Brown-headed Cowbird
☐ Black-vented Oriole (A)
☐ Orchard Oriole
☐ Hooded Oriole
☐ Streak-backed Oriole
☐ Bullock's Oriole
☐ Spot-breasted Oriole (I)
☐ Altamira Oriole
☐ Audubon's Oriole
☐ Baltimore Oriole
☐ Scott's Oriole

Fringillidae
Finches and Allies
☐ Common Chaffinch (A)
☐ Brambling
☐ Gray-crowned Rosy-Finch
☐ Black Rosy-Finch
☐ Brown-capped Rosy-Finch
☐ Pine Grosbeak
☐ Common Rosefinch (A)
☐ Purple Finch
☐ Cassin's Finch
☐ House Finch
☐ Red Crossbill
☐ White-winged Crossbill
☐ Common Redpoll
☐ Hoary Redpoll
☐ Eurasian Siskin (A)
☐ Pine Siskin
☐ Lesser Goldfinch
☐ Lawrence's Goldfinch
☐ American Goldfinch
    European Goldfinch (I)
☐ Oriental Greenfinch (A)
    Yellow-fronted Canary (I)
    Common Canary (I)
☐ Eurasian Bullfinch (A)
☐ Evening Grosbeak
☐ Hawfinch (A)

Passeridae
Old World Sparrows
☐ House Sparrow (I)
☐ Eurasian Tree Sparrow (I)

Ploceidae
Weavers
☐ Orange Bishop (I)

Estrildidae
Estrildid Finches
    Nutmeg Mannikin (I)
    Java Sparrow (I)

Index

Page numbers in italics refer to illustrations. Page ranges after group or family names refer to the entire chapter in which that group is discussed.

DATE			

ARCTIC OCEAN

QUEE

Prince
Patrick
Island

M'Clure Stra

Saint
Lawrence
Island

Seward
Peninsula

Brooks Range

Beaufort
Sea

Banks
Island

Amundsen Gulf

Nunivak
Island

PRIBILOF
ISLANDS

Bering
Sea

Yukon   River

ALASKA
(U.S.)

Victo
Islan

ALEUTIAN ISLANDS

Alaska Range

YUKON
TERRITORY

Mackenzie River

Great
Bear Lake

Kodiak
Island

Gulf of
Alaska

Wrangell Mts.

Yukon River

Mackenzie Mts.

NORTHWEST
TERRITORIES

Great
Slave La

Coast Mountains

Lake
Athabasca

Peace R.

A

QUEEN
CHARLOTTE
ISLANDS

BRITISH
COLUMBIA

ALBERTA

G

R

E

Saskatchewan R.

Vancouver
Island

ROCKY

SASKATCH
EWAN

PACIFIC OCEAN

WASHINGTON

Coast Range

Columbia R.

Missouri River

MONTANA

OREGON

Coast Ranges

IDAHO

M

WYOMING

Sierra Nevada

CENTRAL VALLEY

NEVADA

Great
Salt Lake

O

U

N

UNI

CALIFORNIA

GREAT
BASIN

UTAH

Colorado River

COLO
RAD

Coast Ranges

MOJAVE
DESERT

GRAND
CANYON

COLORADO
PLATEAU

T

A

NEW
MEXIC

CHANNEL
ISLANDS

ARIZONA

SONORAN
DESERT

I

N

CHIHUAHUA
DESERT

S

M E X I